HANDBOOK OF LITERACY AND TECHNOLOGY

Transformations in a Post-Typographic World

HANDBOOK OF LITERACY AND TECHNOLOGY

Transformations in a Post-Typographic World

Edited by

David Reinking
The University of Georgia

Michael C. McKenna
Georgia Southern University

Linda D. Labbo
The University of Georgia

Ronald D. Kieffer
The University of Georgia

LEA LAWRENCE ERLBAUM ASSOCIATES, PUBLISHERS
1998   Mahwah, New Jersey   London

Lawrence Erlbaum Associates, Inc., Publishers
10 Industrial Avenue
Mahwah, New Jersey 07430

Cover designed by Kathryn Houghtaling Lacey

Library of Congress Cataloging-in-Publication Data

Handbook of literacy and technology : transformations in a post-typographic world / edited by David Reinking . . . [et al.].
    p.   cm.
  Edited papers presented at a conference held in Atlanta in Oct. 1996.
  Includes bibliographical references and index.
  ISBN 0-8058-2642-4 (cloth : alk. paper).
  1. Reading—Computer-assisted instruction—Congresses. 2. English language—Composition and exercises—Computer-assisted instruction—Congresses. 3. Educational technology—Congresses. 4. Literacy—Congresses. I. Reinking, David.
LB1050.37.H36 1998
371.33—dc21   97-42351
                                                 CIP

Books published by Lawrence Erlbaum Associates are printed on acid-free paper, and their bindings are chosen for strength and durability.

Printed in the United States of America
10 9 8 7 6 5 4 3 2

*This volume is dedicated to the memory of
Dr. Alan Purves*

Contents

Introduction:
Synthesizing Technological
Transformations of Literacy
in a Post-Typographic World

David Reinking
The University of Georgia

There is something ironic, maybe even perverse, about reading this printed page, given that this edited volume is about how electronic forms of reading and writing may be transforming conceptions of literacy as the world moves into the 21st century. It might even be argued that, as a book, this volume undermines a major premise justifying its existence. As implied by its title, the rationale for this volume is founded to some extent on the belief that we are heading toward a post-typographic world; that is, one in which printed texts are no longer dominant. Or, as Negroponte (1995) put it, again ironically in a printed book entitled *Being Digital*, a world that is moving from atoms to bits. Creating a conventional printed document aimed at exploring that premise might in itself seem to be a strong counterargument against its major thesis.

However, there is another view that must be considered. The conventional printed pages between two covers here mask the strong undercurrent of change that was much more evident in the preparation of this volume than is evident in its final form as a printed document. For example, taken as a whole, the many e-mail exchanges among the authors and editors working to prepare this book would rival the length of the book itself. Likewise, much of the work in writing manuscripts and preparing them for publication in this volume was done electronically. There was also an extended discussion between the editors of the book and representatives of the publisher about conditions under which portions of this book might be made available electronically on the World Wide Web. Thus, electronic forms of reading and writing have affected the development and final form of this work in subtle but important ways.

From this perspective, a printed book about electronic reading and writing is not a contradiction, but more a testimony to the fact that we are in the midst of a transformation that is not yet fully consummated. Even more, that view points to the importance of reflecting on and analyzing the transformations that are occurring now before their effects are fully realized. Understanding how literacy may be affected by a shift from printed to digital forms is more than an academic exercise. The cumulative force of the perspectives put forth by the contributors of this book advance a convincing argument that the transformations of literacy that are beginning to become evident are major threads running through the fabric of daily life. The effects of transformations brought about by a move from a literacy based on printed pages to one based on digital displays on computer screens are likely to be felt across the sociocultural spectrum in areas such as medicine (might our physical lives be texts embodied in ongoing digital records of bodily functions?), law (how is intellectual property to be viewed in a digital world?), government and international relations (can totalitarian regimes or even independent nations survive when all citizens have uninhibited access to information digitally?), economics (how must marketing and advertising change as people increasingly move away from newspapers and magazines to the World Wide Web?), and communication (how will peoples' lives and the communication business be affected if a single interactive device brings news, information, and entertainment into the typical home?).

To varying degrees, the chapters and parts of this book all acknowledge these broad societal effects, but they are all rooted in a concern for the educational implications of transforming literacy in a post-typographic world. This emphasis is understandable for several reasons. First, all of the contributors have strong ties to and investment in education, although they have unique perspectives and interests. Second, the background of this volume, discussed in more detail momentarily, is that it is a component of a larger project funded by the National Reading Research Center (NRRC) through the Office of Educational Research and Improvement of the U.S. Department of Education. The NRRC's mission has included, most prominently, conducting research that will improve literacy in elementary and secondary schools. Finally, speculating about how the transformation of literacy is effecting broad societal change must eventually lead to the question of how we can best prepare the next generation of adults to live in a literate world that may be much different from the one of our youth. Similarly, there is a strong belief that digital forms of reading and writing represent a powerful stimulus for transforming traditional educational structures and practices. In this sense, all questions about literacy are also questions about education.

To engage in the analysis and speculation that this book encourages is no small task and even entails some risk for the editors, the contributors, and thereby for readers, too. They must walk a fine line between exercising rigorous scholarship, extrapolating conclusions from what is sometimes an extremely limited base of theory and research (see Kamil & Lane, chap. 19, this volume), drawing on rich personal experience, and speculating about the future, simultaneously resisting the temptation to offer or seek prophetic oracles. The danger of giving into unmitigated pronouncements especially about the effects of technology is highlighted by a feature in *Newsweek* magazine ("Cloudy Days in Tomorrowland," 1997), which published some of this century's most off-target predictions. For example, Horace Rackham, Henry Ford's lawyer predicted that, "The horse is here to stay, but the automobile is only a novelty—a fad" (p. 86). Or, Daryl Zanuck, the movie mogul, claimed in 1946 that "[television] won't be able to hold on to any market it captures after the first six months. People will soon get tired of staring at a plywood box every night" (p. 86). Or, even more recently, in 1977, Kenneth Olson, president and founder of Digital Equipment Corporation, stated that "There is no reason for any individual to have a computer in their home" (p. 86).

I believe my fellow editors and the contributors who have collaborated on this project have admirably met the challenges posed by the topic of this book, tempering raw speculation with informed perspectives from diverse fields of scholarship and from relevant practical experience. I am confident that their efforts will be viewed in the years to come as a milestone in defining the issues and agendas that increasingly merit the attention of scholars and educators interested in literacy.

In the remainder of this Introduction I, too, face a formidable challenge in making a personal contribution to this project, for I attempt to synthesize major issues and conclusions that cut across chapters and across the book's six major parts. In an effort to avoid what I see as a limitation of many chapters introducing edited volumes, I focus on a synthesis of the book's content as opposed to summarizing the individual chapters and parts. Readers interested in brief summaries of the individual parts should note that a summary has been included at the beginning of each part. However, before synthesizing important ideas in this book, I believe it may be useful to contextualize the book by providing a brief explanation of its background and organization, and by deconstructing the key words in its title.

BACKGROUND AND OVERVIEW OF THIS BOOK

Like many edited books, the birth of this volume is linked to a scholarly conference. However, unlike other edited books that are often proceedings or selected papers assembled after a conference, the chapters in this volume, from the beginning, were the focal point for planning and holding the conference to which they are related. The integral connection between the conference and the book is explained by the fact that they were proposed jointly as a synthesis and dissemination project in the final year of the NRRC's 5-year funding by the Office of Educational Research and Improvement of the U.S. Department of Education. This fifth-year project, which was funded from March 1996 through February 1997, proposed bringing together a group of leading scholars and educators to explore the relation between technology and literacy and the extent, if any, to which that relation was transforming literacy. Each individual invited to participate in the project agreed to author or coauthor a chapter related to one of the "transformation" themes that comprise the parts of this book. Authors submitted preliminary drafts of their chapters 1 month prior to the conference, and these drafts were then circulated to each of the other authors in their respective parts of the book.

The conference held in Atlanta in early October 1996 was divided into two distinct but overlapping sets of meetings. The meetings on the first day were limited to the invited lead authors, each of whom brought an invited guest, typically a coauthor or colleague interested in the book's themes. During the day, authors and their invited guests met in small groups corresponding again to the six themes that comprise the parts of this book. In the small group discussions, the authors reacted to each others' chapters and synthesized issues, questions, and research most central to their respective areas of transformation. A graduate student acted as a recorder for each group. The extensive small group sessions were followed by a large group discussion in which each small group summarized the major points of its deliberations. Meetings on the second and third days of the conference were open to researchers and educators who had responded to a nationally disseminated announcement inviting participation in the second open phase of the conference. Approximately 180 researchers and educators attended these meetings, many of whom presented papers and symposia that they had submitted for review in the call for conference papers. Interspersed among the paper sessions, symposia, two keynote addresses, and technology demonstrations that comprised the second and third days of the conference were conference theme sessions in which the authors in the respective sections of the book summarized and discussed their chapters and the small group discussions that had occurred during the first day of the conference.

The rich discussions and interactions that occurred during these planned conference activities were supplemented substantially and substantively by many opportunities for informal meetings and discussions during breaks, luncheons, and spontaneously planned dinner meetings among authors and conference participants. After the conference sessions, there were opportunities for continued discussions, for example through a listserv that conference participants were invited to join.

After the conference, authors were asked to revise the preliminary drafts of their chapters, taking into account the discussions that occurred at the conference. Original or revised drafts were reviewed carefully by the editorial team, who read several chapters in editorial meetings held weekly until each chapter had been read and discussed. Based on that editorial review process, an editor assigned to each author's part of the volume would communicate the editorial teams' feedback and suggestions for revisions to the respective authors. Thus, the complete process of formulating this book required a measure of dedication, patience, perseverance, and professionalism that I believe exceeds that involved in the compilation of many edited volumes. The contributors to this volume and my fellow editors have again performed admirably in that regard, and I am confident that the reader of this volume will reap the rewards of their dedicated efforts and the rich and varied interactions that shaped each of the chapters.

DECONSTRUCTING THE TITLE OF THIS VOLUME

The title of this book contains several key words that merit some discursive explanation beyond the intuitive meanings that might be derived by simply examining the book's content. Particularly the words *literacy, technological, transformations*, and *post-typographic* portend meanings that intertwine, not only to define the book's focus and content, but that also reflect subtle historical and intellectual forces creating the context, within which exist the real and potential changes addressed by the contributors to this book. Moreover, deconstructing these terms quickly reveals controversy, debate, and unexamined assumptions just below the surface of their literal, everyday meanings. Thus, in this section I briefly discuss these key words to provide a glimpse into the historical and intellectual context of the book's six transformation themes examined more closely in a subsequent section of this Introduction.

Literacy

What exactly it is that should be included within the conceptual domain of literacy has become increasingly fuzzy, especially among those educators and researchers whose professional interests emanate from that term. Among those professionals, an ambivalence about the disciplinary boundaries of literacy has been the consequence of several converging trends during the previous 15 years. Literacy as a topic of interest and study has become decidedly cross-disciplinary and to a lesser extent interdisciplinary as the result of these trends. For example, in the instructional arena, the concept of emergent literacy has highlighted the integration of language processes in young children's development of literacy (see Labbo & Kuhn, chap. 5, this volume), a shift in perspective that has effectively eliminated the previous separation of reading and writing instruction in the minds of leading educators and researchers, if not entirely, in classrooms and schools. Researchers who not that long ago saw themselves conducting complementary but disjoint research agendas focused on either reading or writing now more frequently refer to their work as focusing on literacy.

At the same time, researchers have adopted broader theoretical frameworks for considering how people become literate in a way that helps them function in society and similarly how social factors impinge on literacy development. The almost exclusive focus on the cognitive dimensions of reading and writing still prevalent through the late 1980s has given way to a deepening interest in the social dimensions of literacy expressed in orientations that range from the theoretical such as situated cognition (Newman, Griffin, & Cole, 1989) and socially mediated learning (Vygotsky, 1978) to the ideological, such as critical pedagogy (Freire, 1983) and feminism (Commeyras & Alvermann, 1996). Supporting and reinforcing this emphasis on the social dimensions of literacy has been a turn toward qualitative research methods, which have moved increasingly into the mainstream of literacy research, thus widening further the lens through which literacy is viewed and consequently how it is defined.

Today, the relatively narrow view expressed by Venezky (1995) in his definition of literacy as "minimal ability to read and write in a designated language, as well as a mindset or way of thinking about the use of reading and writing in everyday life" (p. 142) is being supplanted by much broader views such those reflected by Olson (1994), who defined literacy as "the competence to exploit a particular set of cultural resources . . . [it] is not just learning the abc's; it is learning to use the resources of writing for a culturally defined set of tasks and procedures" (p. 43). This broader view grounded in the sociocultural aspects of literacy has also encouraged literacy researchers to seek out other new perspectives from diverse disciplines in framing their work. For example, Labbo (1996; Labbo & Kuhn, chap. 5, this volume) and Lemke (chap. 17, this volume) draw on the field of semiotics to analyze how electronic forms of reading and writing might be understood in classrooms, schools, and society. Likewise, I (Reinking, 1995) have argued that literary theory provides a perspective that can help us compare important differences in printed and digital texts. For example, Bolter (1991; see also chap. 1, this volume) argued that disputes about whether deconstructionism is a valid way to view texts become moot when reading hypertexts because hypertexts literally operationalize the abstract concepts that deconstructionism applies to printed texts. Literacy has also come to include an increased emphasis on critical reading from a social constructivist (see Myers, Hammett, & McKillop, chap. 4, this volume). Philosophical viewpoints, especially those pertaining to epistemology, have also captured the attention of literacy researchers (e.g., see Cunningham & Fitzgerald, 1996).

The increasing prevalence of and interest in electronic forms of reading and writing advances concretely the trend toward broader definitions of literacy (Reinking, 1994). Digital forms of expression are increasingly replacing printed forms and there is a widespread consensus, at least intuitively, that this shift has consequences for the way we communicate and disseminate information, how we approach the task of reading and writing, and how we think about helping people to become literate. In fact, within the literacy research community, there have been explicit calls for broadening conceptions of literacy to include electronic forms of reading and writing (e.g., Reinking, 1994, 1995). Because digital texts are more likely to employ multimedia, thus shifting the balance of textual information away from alphabetic prose toward pictorial representations (see Bolter, chap. 1, this volume), several writers have called for expanding definitions of literacy to include multiple symbol systems. Flood and Lapp (1995), for example, argued that today's children need to acquire visual literacy, and similarly, The Cognition and Technology Group at Vanderbilt University (1994) introduced the term *representational literacy*, which encompasses the ability to use multimedia effectively in communicating meaning. Interestingly, the awareness of how new technologies may be changing literacy has also led to a resurgence of interest in historical analyses of literacy (e.g., Bolter, 1991; Moore, Monaghan, & Hartman, 1997; Purves, chap. 14, this volume).

Thus, the content of this book reflects the expanding boundaries of literacy on two parallel yet interacting levels. On one level, the increasing prevalence of electronic forms of communication promises to transform the acts of reading and writing by virtue of the unique characteristics of digital texts. Those characteristics, although perhaps not immediately recognized by those heavily invested in print (Reinking, 1992, 1995), suggest adding new literacy skills and awareness such as composing an e-mail message or developing strategies for composing and reading hypertexts or locating information on the World Wide Web. On another level, the more general interest in how diverse perspectives and fields of study enrich understandings of literacy is applied here to considering what the larger effects of a technological transformation may be. For example, how might a semiotic or a social constructivist perspective help us better understand digital texts and their potential effects on literacy. Readers of this book will quickly discern that both levels of the trend toward expanding the boundaries of literacy are to varying degrees present within and across the chapters and parts that follow.

Technological

Prior to the mid-1980s, it would have been rare to find the word *literacy* and any form of the word *technology* in the same sentence, let alone combined to form the title of a book. That it is not unusual for these words to appear together today in referring to how computers are affecting literacy highlights a developing awareness underlying the content of this book. That awareness began in the mid-1980s when computers were gaining a strong foothold among people who were not computer scientists or hobbyists. As computer use became popularized due to the development of microcomputers and advanced especially by the development of computerized spreadsheets and word processing, people began to view the computer as a useful tool for everyday work, and beyond work, as a device for recreation, amusement, and education. It was not long before educators interested in literacy began to think about how computers might affect reading and writing, although it is important to note that there had been some prominent work connecting computers to reading instruction that predated by more than a decade the advent of the microcomputer (Atkinson & Hansen, 1966). A strong interest in technology and literacy emerged among at least a small core of educators whose interests were driven primarily by the power of word processing as a new tool for writing and by the new instructional options computers offered for teaching conventional reading and writing skills (Reinking & Bridwell-Bowles, 1991). Researchers also began attending to these developments, looking simultaneously at how computer-based instructional activities and writing compared to more conventional print-based activities. They also began to see the advantages of using computers to gather and analyze data (Kamil & Lane, chap. 19, this volume). A few even began to contemplate how computers might be used to alter the presentation of texts or to analyze and adapt textual content to enhance literacy (e.g., Frase, 1987; L'Allier, 1980; McConkie & Zola, 1987; Reinking & Schreiner, 1985).

However, educators and researchers considered to be in the mainstream of the field of literacy have just begun to acknowledge and understand that technology is not just a clearly circumscribed topical subinterest such as vocabulary instruction, reading difficulties, or assessment. Instead, it is a much more fundamental component of written communication deeply embedded within historical understandings of literacy (e.g., Eisenstein, 1983; Kaufer & Carley, 1993; Olson, 1994). Thus, it would be a mistake to contextualize the chapters in this book as representing only the latest response to the relatively recent appearance of computers as a singularly new technology for written communication. The tendency in the previous 15 years to view the topic of technology and literacy as synonymous with computers is explained partially by the fact that during the lifetimes of most people living at the turn of the millennium, printed materials will still have been the dominant technology for writing and reading. Figuratively speaking, it is as difficult for those who have become fully literate within a world dominated by print to see how their own literacy has been shaped—indeed limited—by the technology used to produce and disseminate printed materials as it is for a fish to think about the water in which it swims. Or, as Alfred North Whitehead observed, to understand a period of history, historians must consider what topics received no attention in the discourse of that period because these ignored topics represent the unquestioned assumptions of the time.

Thus, the fact that technology for at least three centuries prior to 1980 was rarely discussed in the context of literacy does not mean that technology had no bearing on literacy; it only means that its influence was subliminal. Why consider the relation of technology to literacy when only a single technology is predominant, when that technology is so firmly entrenched that it is inconceivable to imagine any other technology replacing it, and when the defining artifact of that technology (a book) has become a sociocultural icon anchoring some of the most fundamental values and perspectives inculcated in the Western world? (Lanham, 1989, 1993; Reinking, 1997). These rhetorical questions are not meant to discount the fact that technological improvements have had effects over the previous three centuries and that occasionally these effects have been noted. For example, many technological improvements have increased the efficiency of producing and disseminating printed materials since the development of the printing press, and some of these improvements have influenced literacy in profound ways. There is no doubt that the increased dissemination of printed materials has affected literacy; nonetheless, the basic process of applying ink to paper has remained unchanged. Although there has been a strong tendency to interpret new digital technologies as merely extensions of print technologies (e.g., word processors attached to printers [Bolter, 1991] and fax machines [Negroponte, 1995]), the inherently unique characteristics of reading and writing with computers are beginning undeniably to exert their influence. It is becoming more obvious that electronic texts represent a substantively new technology that does not readily mesh with the assumptions that have arisen from the technology of print.

So, the critical question we now face as we move into the 21st century is not simply how digital technologies will affect conceptions of literacy and how it is achieved, but also a larger, more self-reflective, question: How does any technology of reading and writing interact with literacy? It is not easy to seek an answer to the latter question, but as mainstream literacy educators and researchers are beginning to discover, there is a literature relevant to addressing it. For example, historical and cross-cultural analyses of reading and writing, many of which are focused on comparing oral and literate cultures, must eventually address the technological dimensions of literacy (cf. Bolter, 1991; Kaufer & Carley, 1993; McLuhan, 1962; Olson, 1994; Ong, 1982; Purves, chap. 14, this volume; Scribner & Cole, 1978; Tierney & Damerin, chap. 15, this volume). Also relevant to the question is the literature analyzing how the technological attributes associated with various media affect cognitive processing (Salomon, 1979). These different but related literatures reveal the complexity of trying to understand fully the relation between technology and literacy and they identify controversial and opposing views that have yet to be resolved. For example, does technology play a strong or weak role in shaping literacy? Some writers argue against the strong position of "technological determinism" (see Bruce & Hogan, chap. 16, this volume). Or, is the link between technology and literacy so intimate that writing must most fundamentally be defined as a technology? (Ong, 1982). To what extent, if any, do alternative technologies for writing affect thinking (cf. Olson, 1994), even to the extent of defining a worldview? (e.g., linear, compartmentalized vs. hypertextual views of our own lives; see Bolter, 1991). Can reading and writing in electronic environments be thought of as defining a communication medium distinctly separate from print? (e.g., Daniel & Reinking, 1987; Reinking, 1987). What are the most relevant attributes and features separating alternative symbolic media (Salomon, 1979) and do these differences affect learning? (Clark, 1983). Readers of this book will find such questions explicitly or implicitly underlying many of the chapters that follow.

Transformations

As the titles of the six parts that follow suggest, *transformation* is the operative word unifying the content of this book. The respective sections that follow examine how digital technologies may be transforming the most basic components of literacy (texts, readers, and writers), the teaching and learning of becoming literate (instruction, classrooms, and schools), and the broader dimensions of literacy and how it might be studied (society and literacy research).

Unlike related words such as *reformation* or simply *change,* the word *transformation* reinforces a point made at the outset of this chapter: This book appears at a time during which the potential effects of the digital age on literacy have not yet been fully realized or recognized. The fact that thoughts about such potentialities appear here as a conventional book is an indication that we are in a period of transformation. In a morphological sense, transformation suggests a connection between an earlier form and an emerging form, connoting a degree of tentativeness; those meanings apply aptly to the position in which those interested in literacy find themselves today. It is becoming clearer that digital technologies cannot be easily assimilated into the practical and conceptual dimensions of literacy derived from print. Likewise, their increasing prevalence suggests that they cannot simply be ignored. However, it is still uncertain if they will lead us to a revolutionary new era where many of the fundamental assumptions of print-based literacy are substantially revised or even replaced.

Uncertainty, then, is a quality inherent to any transformation. However, accepting that inevitable uncertainty should not make us so complacent that we feel no compulsion to consider systematically the consequences of an incomplete transformation or how we might build bridges between the known and the unknown. To allow events to unravel ad hoc with no systematic analysis of the alternatives and their consequences will ensure that we have no control over the ultimate results of the transformation we are experiencing. Realizing the risks of complacency in the face of change, for example, has driven the more militant members of what Rheingold (1993) called "virtual communities" to defend rigorously freedom of expression on the Internet. Perhaps understandably given their conservative propensities, educational institutions have been more sanguine and less proactive about advancing their own relative interests in a digital era. As a case in point, educators have mounted little systematic resistance to attempts at extending print-based interpretations of copyright law into the digital domain, a development that promises to restrict substantially educational opportunities (Okerson, 1991; Reinking, 1996). Thus, the transformation themes discussed in this book may contribute not only to contemplating what type of literacy will emerge from the chrysalis of our current uncertainty but how we might still intervene to shape positively that transformation.

Also worth noting is that underlying the various transformations discussed by the contributors of this book is a paradox. From a historical perspective we are riding a juggernaut of change fueled sometimes daily by new examples of how conventional printed and other analog forms such as videotape and photographic film are giving way to digital forms. It is remarkable to contemplate how little time has passed since the typewriter, the phonograph or audiotape player, the card catalog, and the microfiche reader were all considered part of the latest technologies supporting the operation of the "modern" library (or media center, as they have come to be known), which, filled with books, has been society's sanctioned institution for preserving information and cultural knowledge (see Purves, chap. 14, this volume). Although the technologies found in libraries 15 years ago have not been fully replaced, digital technologies continue to erode the importance and relevance of those that remain, including, most poignantly, books themselves. For those who surf the Internet today or who increasingly rely on e-mail and electronic journals for the latest developments in their field, the conventional library, so revered a few years ago, may already be viewed as a nostalgic anachronism. For such changes to occur in less than two decades—let alone within a single lifetime—is but a nanosecond in the course of recorded history.

However, despite rapid technological developments affecting the entire spectrum of daily literacy, indeed in part because of them, fundamental transformations on a conceptual and cultural level occur much more slowly. Individuals as well as institutions adapt slowly and even overtly resist technological possibilities that threaten the status quo. Instead of replacing outdated technologies, we unnecessarily retain them in combination with new technologies to create anomalous hybrids. For example, in many libraries today there are computer terminals connected to the Internet, which makes many of the libraries' physical resources less convenient if not obsolete. Or, alphabetic listings of topics can still be found in some multimedia encyclopedias where Boolean keyword searches obviate the need for such listings.

These relatively subtle examples point to more consequential manifestations of how transformations on a purely technological level have outpaced our collective ability to embrace them. There is no better example than the public school where reading and writing are explicitly taught, but more importantly where literacy is institutionalized and inculcated in the broadest sense. Many writers have lamented the failure of technology to transform schools, often placing the blame squarely on schools for their unenlightened views (e.g., Papert, 1993). Other writers have been more dispassionate, examining a range of factors that work against technology being integrated meaningfully into classroom instruction (e.g., Means, 1994; Means et al., 1993). For example, Bruce and Rubin (1993) found that progressive ideas about process writing and reading for meaningful purposes that provided the rationale for some comprehensive computer-based activities, collectively labeled QUILL, were benignly undermined by the teachers who used QUILL because the teachers were driven by the need to accomplish more conventional goals for reading and writing by engaging students in standard practices and processes associated with those goals. Likewise, as Neilsen (chap. 8, this volume) documents, allowing students to experience the greater freedom afforded by technological alternatives to reading and writing can wreak havoc on the established distribution of power in schools.

Nonetheless, there is ample evidence in the following chapters that transformations in literacy-related instruction can happen and perhaps are beginning to take root. Kieffer,

Hale, and Templeton (chap. 9, this volume) describe how one teacher's involvement with technology led her to employ new forms of literacy assessment and to expand her own professional horizons. Likewise, Garner and Gillingham (chap. 13, this volume) document the positive transformations that can occur when elementary and secondary school teachers fully integrate e-mail and Internet access into their teaching and the life of their respective classrooms. However, it is still difficult to determine if these relatively local transformations are guideposts for the future or only anomalies that inspire admiration and perhaps emulation. The end results of technological transformations are perhaps especially difficult to predict not only because of late they have occurred so rapidly, but because throughout history their ultimate influence is sometimes hidden by seemingly larger social and historical forces and by the interaction among sometimes seemingly disjoint technological advances (Burke, 1978). Thus, it would not be fair to expect the chapters that follow to predict with fine precision what the literacy landscape of the 21st century will be. However, they do offer insight into relevant developments and perspectives that help us to become more attuned to the changes in reading and writing that seem increasingly ineluctable.

Post-Typographic

It may not be possible from our present vantage point to predict the precise results of a technological transformation of literacy, but the final substantive word in this book's title implies a strong general prediction. That is, we are moving to a post-typographic world in which the technologies of print will no longer be the dominant form of written communication (Reinking, 1995). Even more implicitly, moving from printed to electronic forms of writing means fundamental and broad-ranging consequences for a literate culture (Lanham, 1989, 1993; Tuman, 1992a, 1992b).

Before discussing the basis for this prediction and some of its implications, however, the derivation of the word *post-typographic* needs to be addressed. The prefix *post-*, although perhaps somewhat overworked in the current academic vernacular, has the usual meaning of "subsequent to" or "later than." *Typographic*, however, is more problematic. Although its original meaning is derived from creating images through the process of using molded metal forms (i.e., type) to imprint ink on paper, it has come to have a more inclusive, generic meaning. For some scholars (e.g., Tufte, 1983) typography or typographic can refer more generally to the visual appearance of any written text, particularly as to how various visual elements might be arranged to create a written document and how that arrangement might influence readers' perceptions, attitudes, and understandings. Given this broader view of typographic, the relevant issues transcend a particular medium; that is, there is a typographical dimension to all texts whether they are displayed on printed pages or on computer screens, whether they are static printed images or animated video displays. In either case there are empirical and aesthetic issues regarding the arrangement, appearance, and proportion of prose and graphics. In this sense, *post-typographic* is an illogical term because written texts by definition must have some visual form.

Thus, the word *post-typographic* in the title alludes to the narrower, more literal definition related to the technologies of print such as paper, ink, presses, and typewriters. However, this narrower definition also includes newer technologies such as the laser printer or fax machine that "artificially" produce or simulate printed documents. In short, as used in the title of this book any text displayed on a sheet of paper or other static, material surface is considered to be typographic. Texts in digital form displayed electronically on dynamically alterable surfaces such as a computer screen are considered to be post-typographic.

This material distinction seems to ground the thinking of several writers who have employed the term *post-typographic* to highlight broad conceptual changes directly related to literacy. McLuhan (1962) was perhaps the first to introduce the term and certainly the first to popularize it as a peg for the broad cultural implications of a shift from what he called the "hot" electronic media away from the "cold" medium of print. Others (Bolter, 1991; Landow, 1992; Moulthrop, 1991; Moulthrop & Kaplan, 1994; Murphy, 1988) have used it to describe the influence of electronic media in operationalizing postmodern views of meaning or to suggest that writing in electronic media is more rhetorical compared to printed media, where writing is more philosophical (Lanham, 1989, 1993). Ong (1982), although he was writing before the computer had any notable effect on transforming written communication, presaged those effects by predicting that they would add to an emerging post-typographic world that he described as a "second orality." In each of these cases the term *post-typographic* is used to mark an intellectual or cultural watershed created by a transformation precipitated by technologies that are no longer bound by typographic communication.

Although the accuracy of these writers' predictions about the sociocultural and cognitive consequences of a post-typographic world cannot yet be fully verified, the evidence that the world is becoming post-typographic in at least a literal sense continues to mount. We are far from ruling out printed materials in any definition of literacy, but almost daily there are examples of printed documents giving way to electronic ones; thus, the idea of an almost paperless world no longer seems far-fetched. Electronic submission of income tax returns, considered a novelty a few years ago, is becoming increasingly routine. Today we can sign for deliveries using a stylus on an electromagnetic tablet. Nurses record patients' vital signs and medications digitally, sometimes relaying the information through wireless connections to hospital databases that can be accessed remotely by physicians. More electronic encyclopedias are sold than printed ones. Students at most major universities peruse course offerings and register in front of computer terminals and their professors frequently engage them in e-mail and submission of work electronically. Newspapers and magazines increasingly join other commercial enterprises in jumping to the World Wide Web to augment or replace conventional avenues for disseminating information and advertising through printed materials. For example, Lynch (1997) reported that while the number of websites increased from 130 in June 1993 to more than 650,00 in January 1997, the percentage of commercial sites (i.e., site addresses ending in .com) over the same period increased from 2% to 63%.

These trends fuel and are fueled by the increasing costs of producing printed materials, which has created a budgetary crisis for many research libraries (Okerson, 1991). In fact, it is within the normally conservative academic sector that some of the strongest evidence for a shift toward a post-typographic world can be found. For example, even the powerful edifice of tenure based on publication in scholarly journals is beginning to crack. Increasingly, top researchers, especially in esoteric areas of the hard sciences, are circumventing the protracted process of disseminating their work through conventional publication in printed journals; instead they correspond via e-mail, listservs, and bulletin boards with geographically and sometimes methodologically diverse colleagues sharing findings and getting feedback on a daily basis (Stix, 1994). As Burbules and Bruce (1995) observed:

> The capacities of electronic networks . . . are altering the way scholars produce writings and their intellectual relations to one another . . . [These networks] may create an entirely

new niche of collaborative publishing, in which the distribution, revision, and continuous co-construction of knowledge can no longer be attributed to individual authors. (pp. 12, 16)

Likewise, many mainstream professional organizations such as the International Reading Association are instigating new online journals, often struggling through the process of merging or replacing established protocols for submission, review, and publication in printed journals with the exigencies of launching an electronic journal (M. Dillner, personal communication, December 3, 1996). The likelihood that this trend toward electronic journals will continue escalating is supported by Okerson (1991), who documented the declining number of printed journal subscriptions affordable to libraries. Similarly, Stix (1994) cited an Association of Research Libraries' report that electronic journals increased from approximately 100 to 400 from 1991 to 1994. Such developments threaten to undermine some widely held assumptions about the relation between academic scholarship and publication, many of which date back to the late middle ages (Eisenstein, 1983; Kaufer & Carley, 1993)

Among the key words in this book's title, post-typographic may be the most discomforting, not only to some scholars who see electronic texts as unwelcome intrusions into their established rituals, but also to any reader heavily invested in a typographic world. That may include almost all contemporary readers to some extent. Beyond the obvious economic risks that create discomfort among publishers and authors who are rightly nervous about how a post-typographic world may affect their livelihood, there is a more pervasive and subtle discomfort that pervades collectively the public psyche. The prospect of a post-typographic world reveals the deep-seated attachment most contemporary readers and writers have to printed materials, especially books. Books are not just artifacts of a particular technology for reading and writing, they are cultural icons that anchor the experience of being literate (Reinking, 1995, 1997). The changes implied by the term *post-typographic* ultimately threaten to remove that anchor, which may explain some of the milder forms of resistance to the idea that the book may one day evoke the same nostalgia that those of us past 30 have for the phonograph. It certainly explains more strident, sometimes even maudlin, defenses of books as inherently superior to electronic media (e.g., Birkerts, 1994). For, as Lanham (1993) stated:

> Efforts to defend the codex book as the bastion of Western culture [is as if] defending the wrapper would protect what is in the box . . . these efforts to galvanize the codex book in the face of encroaching electronic expression miss the two basic points that should underlie such a campaign. . . . Before we fix on the book as the center of humanistic culture, shouldn't we have a better idea of **what books do to us and for us?** [bold in original]. . . . Having decided what we want to protect, how do we make sure it survives the movement from book to screen? (p. 99)

As Lanham's view suggests, if there is something worth defending about preserving the book and by extension all printed materials, that defense must go beyond temporary technological inconveniences or preferences for the comfortable and familiar. It may be more convenient for the time being to read a book in bed or at the beach, but there is little technological justification for preferring a book to a computer for leisurely reading on an airplane, especially when a computer could contain the texts of an entire library. If there is some special quality about making meaning in print, is it inconceivable to duplicate that quality in electronic form? The chapters of this book spring from the belief that at the threshold of the 21st century we are also on the threshold of a post-typographic era in which printed materials, if not on their way to obsolescence, will never again completely dominate literate activity.

SYNTHESIZING THEMES, QUESTIONS, ISSUES, AND TENTATIVE CONCLUSIONS

The six parts of this book are intended to provide a comprehensive framework for considering how literacy might be transformed by new digital technologies. In writing their chapters, authors were asked to consider the following general questions intended to integrate the themes that might be addressed in their respective sections:

- *Transforming texts:* What are the differences between printed and electronic texts, and what are the implications of new textual forms for defining literacy, especially in regard to teaching and learning in schools?
- *Transforming readers and writers:* How do electronic reading and writing change conceptualizations of literacy development from childhood through adulthood?
- *Transforming schools and classrooms:* What are the effects of introducing new reading and writing technologies into schools and classrooms?
- *Transforming instruction:* How can instruction be adapted in response to the changing literacy landscape, and how can teachers and students exploit forms of reading and writing to enhance teaching and learning?
- *Transforming society:* What are the broad societal implications of the increasing prevalence of electronic forms of reading and writing?
- *Transforming literacy research:* What are the questions that must be addressed as digital reading and writing become more common, and what approaches to research will be most useful in addressing those questions?

Given the breadth of these questions and the level of speculation they imply, it would be presumptuous to assert that a single edited volume could fully address any one of them. For example, despite our best efforts, we were unable to obtain a commitment to participate in the conference or book from qualified individuals to address the important issue of equitable access to technology and its implications for literacy among nonmainstream populations. Nonetheless, the chapters that follow discuss this issue and other areas that might have been covered in more depth. Despite inevitable limitations in coverage, my fellow editors and I are confident that the following chapters will precipitate additional dialogue about these transformation themes and the issues raised by the guiding questions. We hope that the transformation framework and guiding questions will give focus to the dialogue about technology and literacy in the future, as indeed it did among authors and participants who attended the NRRC Conference where small and large group sessions aimed at synthesizing dominant issues in relation to the six transformation themes. In this section, I summarize briefly a few of the dominant issues and conclusions that cut across several if not all of the parts of this book and that I believe are especially poignant. To me these conclusions are poignant because they increase my confidence that at least among those interested in digital forms of reading and writing—and hopefully among all literacy educators and researchers—we have reached a higher plane of awareness about the relation between technology and literacy. In highlighting these few conclusions, I draw not only on the content of the chapters, but also on my participation in the formal discussions at the conference and the informal discussions with authors and my fellow editors at various stages of this project.

I take comfort in knowing that any limitations in my discussion here might be addressed through further dialogue not only among the participants in this project but by readers as well. In the first instance, the small profit from the conference and the royalties from this book have been earmarked to underwrite future opportunities for the contributors to meet for face-to-face discussions of technology and literacy. Readers who wish to make a comment directly to me or to one of the other contributors may do so using the e-mail addresses listed at the end of the volume.

Electronic and Printed Texts Are Qualitatively Different

This conclusion is supported explicitly by the authors of the chapters in the Transforming Texts section that immediately follows this chapter, but it is at least implicitly assumed by authors in other parts as well. Furthermore, taken together, the chapters in this volume indicate that we have moved beyond an earlier perspective that treated printed texts as the standard to which newer electronic forms of reading and writing must be compared (cf. Reinking, 1992; Reinking & Bridwell-Bowles, 1991). For example, questions about whether students using word processing write as well or better than those using conventional materials have given way to questions about how students might adapt to and employ effectively electronic forms of reading and writing (cf. Beach & Lundell, chap. 6; Myers et al., chap 4; Garner & Gillingham, chap. 13, all this volume). Electronic texts are presented unquestionably as common and viable alternatives to printed texts, and they are discussed on their own terms, not in comparison to or in competition with printed texts. It is inconceivable today that anyone would expect to find theory or research invalidating the use of word processing or suggesting that people should return to writing conventional letters instead of using e-mail, although impassioned arguments in support of books over electronic media suggest that there are still vestiges of this perspective operating. Today, we are more interested in defining precisely what the unique characteristics of electronic texts are (e.g., Bolter, chap. 1, this volume), how those characteristics might broadly affect literacy (e.g., Tierney & Damarin, chap. 15, this volume), and how we might use those characteristics to effect improvements in literacy (e.g., the following chapters: Anderson-Inman & Horney, chap. 2; Kamil & Lane, chap. 19; Labbo & Kuhn, chap. 5; Lemke, chap. 17; McKenna, chap. 3; Myers et al., chap. 4, all this volume).

In addition, it is evident in this volume and in much of the recent literature that hypertext has become perhaps the quintessential example of how printed and electronic texts differ. The concept of hypertext makes marginal sense at best if it is divorced from digital media, and so it intuitively encapsulates the potential uniqueness of electronic texts. Hypertexts help us to become consciously aware of the intimate relation between literacy and technology because they remind us that conventional texts are linear and hierarchical to some extent because of the technology used to produce them (Bolter, 1991). The new genre of textual organization that hypertexts represent suggests an entirely new way to think about the process of reading and writing, which has societal and cultural implications as argued by Purves (chap. 14, this volume; see also Tierney & Damarin, chap. 15, this volume). Likewise, hyptertexts and the companion term *hypermedia* are powerful examples of how electronic texts shift reading and writing away from the alphabetic code and toward a wider range of symbolic elements (e.g., Bolter, chap. 1; Lemke, chap. 17; Leu et al., chap. 12, all this volume)

What is considered to be a text, what elements comprise a text, and how texts are appropriately structured are central issues in establishing any conception of literacy.

Acknowledging that electronic and printed texts differ substantially in these fundamental respects, as I think many of the chapters strongly indicate we must, is an important development in our evolving understanding of technological transformations of literacy in a post-typographic world.

There Is an Important Sociocultural and Historical Dimension to Considering the Relation Between Technology and Literacy

One could not read many chapters in this book without realizing that thinking about technology in the context of literacy does not mean focusing exclusively on hardware and software (see especially Bruce, in press; Bruce & Hogan, chap. 16, this volume). Instead, to a remarkable extent, the chapters that follow highlight how technology and literacy cannot be divorced from each other or from the sociocultural and historical landscape in which they exist. This perspective is in sharp contrast to most earlier books about technology and literacy.

The interaction between technology and social, cultural, and historical trends is not a new idea. For example, Burke (1978) in *Connections*, his popular television series and book, cleverly highlighted how technological developments interact with seemingly unrelated events. A personal favorite is his story of how the crusaders returned from the Near East with the knowledge of producing cheap muslin cloth, which increased the wearing of underwear, which created rags when the underwear wore out (collected conveniently by those who already were collecting bones for fertilizer), which led to the development of a cheap writing material (paper), which made viable the printing press only because paper was relatively cheap compared to other writing surfaces. What is new is that those of us interested in literacy are beginning to see not only the sociocultural dimensions of literacy, an awareness that has been steadily increasing during the previous 10 years, but that we are beginning to see that technology is an essential component of that awareness (Tierney & Damarin, chap. 15, this volume).

This conclusion is most explicitly drawn from the chapters in the subsequent part of this volume entitled "Transforming Society." There, the chapters range from exploring broad historical perspectives (e.g., Purves, chap. 14) to an analysis of economic forces in the workplace that connect to trends toward a global workforce (Mikulecky & Kirkley, chap. 18). However, clear traces of this perspective can be seen across many of the chapters in other sections as well. For example, Neilsen (chap. 8) reports how introducing students to e-mail can redistribute power in the microcosm of a single school, and Garner and Gillingham (chap. 13) describe its potential for expanding the multicultural awareness of students whose classroom experiences are no longer cut off from participating with students from other cultures in the macrocosm of all schools. As these chapters clearly suggest, understanding how technologies may contribute to a transformation of literacy can only be considered fundamentally as a sociocultural and historical phenomenon.

The New Technologies of Electronic Reading and Writing Are Slowly but Steadily Transforming Classrooms, Schools, and Instruction

Papert (1993) has argued that schools treat technology as the body's white blood cells treat an invading virus. Many educational institutions at all levels often enthusiastically obtain hardware and software, but through benign neglect, passive implementation, or even active resistance fail to exploit the potential of new technologies to transform positively teaching and learning. Overall, the tenor of the literature addressing the transformation potential of technology in schools is decidedly pessimistic (e.g., Means, 1994; Means et al., 1993).

As I have argued elsewhere (Reinking, 1997) innovative uses of computer-based technologies in classrooms typically have no established instructional niches, requiring that innovation be implemented from the ground up. The chapters in this book document the obstacles that must be faced by those who wish to implement more than perfunctory uses of technology in schools. Educators committed to exploring the potential of new technologies must sometimes marshall heroic energy to overcome a variety of problems that I have categorized as logistical (e.g., How can I allow my students adequate time to explore the World Wide Web when I have only one computer in my classroom or I can get in the lab only once a week?), technological (e.g., How could a network be set up so that my students could easily share their online journals?), financial (e.g., My students could join the chat room discussion with that children's author if my school could afford to buy me a fast modem.), pedagogical (e.g., What would be a good way to introduce my students to word processing?), curricular (e.g., How do I integrate word processing into the curriculum and what existing topical area might be eliminated to make room for it?), and interpersonal or public relations issues (e.g., How can I convince my principal, students' parents, and colleagues that having my students use a spell checker may not turn them into poor spellers?).

Despite this pervasive pessimism, the chapters that follow portray several examples of how positive transformations of classrooms, schools, and instruction are possible and feasible. Fittingly, because literacy remains at the core of virtually all educational endeavors, the transformations emanate from but extend beyond reading and writing activities. Again, the most explicit examples come from the two sections focusing specifically on transformations in the domain of education where it is easy to see the diverse points at which technology and literacy intersect with the curricular goals of schools. For example, Kieffer et al. (chap. 9) describe how portfolio assessment might be transformed when it is computerized and how involvement with constructing such portfolios can affect pervasively a teacher's orientation to teaching and evaluation both of her students and herself. Leu et al. (chap. 12) describe the possibilities for involving teachers in developing computer software customized to their specific needs and circumstances. Askov and Bixler (chap. 10) describe the transformation possibilities of using technology in improving literacy among adults, and Kinzer and Risko (chap. 11) describe how technology can bring preservice teachers into closer contact with the realities of becoming a successful teacher of literacy. Fawcett and Snyder (chap. 7) describe how literacy broadly conceived as all teaching and learning in schools can be systematically transformed with a focus on technology at the level of an entire school district. Technological transformations possible in educational environments are also firmly embedded in other parts of the volume (see Anderson-Inman & Horney's discussion in chap. 2 of how electronic texts can enhance studying and learning among students who experience reading difficulties; Myers et al.'s discussion in chap. 4 of how multimedia can develop a critical stance toward written materials; Labbo & Kuhn's discussion in chap. 5 of how computer-based writing activities contribute to literacy development among young children; and Lemke's discussion in chap. 17 of how multimedia materials may contribute to the development of an interactive instead of a linear curriculum).

Taken together, these chapters reflect a more realistic view of technological transformations in educational environments—a view that reaches a balance between the unmitigated optimism of the early 1980s and the pessimism bred by the undelivered promises of the 1990s. Such a balanced view seems appropriate as we move into the next millennium.

There Is a Dearth of Research and Scholarship Available to Understand and Guide Technological Transformations of Literacy

This conclusion is supported most directly in this volume by Kamil and Lane (chap. 19), who report that their survey of four leading research journals revealed that fewer than 1% of the published articles during a recent 3-year period addressed issues related to technology. That finding is especially remarkable when placed in the context of the other chapters in this book. Collectively, the rich and varied empirical questions offered or suggested by the authors whose chapters follow far exceed current efforts to collect data that might address those questions. Although many of the authors here are in the vanguard of literacy researchers interested in technology, their efforts pale in comparison to the scope of questions they raise about technological transformations of literacy. In that sense, this volume is a testimony to the research and scholarship that needs to be done.

Several factors may explain the dearth of research, and acknowledging these factors may be the first step in encouraging needed research. Foremost, the pace at which the literacy landscape is changing, especially in regard to technological developments, makes conducting meaningful research equivalent to hitting a moving target (Kamil & Lane, chap. 19, this volume). Similarly, the fact that an interest in technological dimensions of literacy is relatively new and in the 1980s focused on using computers to enhance conventional curricular goals has slowed the development of theoretical orientations that might be drawn on to guide research. Several of the chapters in this book (e.g., Beach & Lundell, chap. 6; Labbo & Kuhn, chap. 5; Lemke, chap. 17; Tierney & Damarin, chap. 15) and other publications (e.g., Reinking, 1992, 1995; Salomon, Globerson, & Guterman, 1989) indicate that such theoretical orientations are now available. A subtle factor that may limit research is that as technology transforms literacy it can threaten the validity or relevance of existing bases of research (Reinking, 1995). For example, researchers who have much invested in particular approaches to early reading instruction may resist considering the implications of technological alternatives such as those described by McKenna (chap. 3, this volume) because those alternatives might make moot some of the hotly debated questions and issues associated with instruction based solely on printed materials. In addition, as illustrated by Miller and Olson (chap. 20, this volume), a broad variety of research methods may be needed to guide educators about how to integrate new technologies into literacy instruction, a need that is becoming increasingly pressing as indicated in the subsequent chapters by Kamil and Lane (chap. 19) and by Fawcett and Snyder (chap. 7).

It is worth noting that more than half of the chapters in this volume add substantively to our research base by reporting work currently not published or by extending research published elsewhere. However, much more empirical work using the full range of research methodologies and theoretical orientations needs to be done. It was clear during discussions at the NRRC conference associated with this volume that the contributors and the other conference attendees recognized that need and hoped that this volume would stimulate such research.

FINAL THOUGHTS

There is a pervasive fascination today with the awareness that we are on the threshold of a new millennium. Even those reading this book immediately after its publication would find it almost impossible to reserve a hotel room on Times Square in New York City for the evening of December 31, 1999. That fascination reflects to some degree, I believe, a deep-seated need to contemplate one's existence in the stream of time and perhaps to acknowledge that we are all to a certain degree prisoners of the era through which we live. The beginning of a new century, especially one that ushers in a new millennium, is a special invitation to engage in such contemplation. Doing so is especially poignant today because of the unprecedented rate of change experienced by those living during the late 20th and early 21st centuries. Unlike those who lived in early times, people traversing the current millennium have come to expect that rapid and consequential change will occur in less than the span of a single generation. For most of the 20th century, the chronological milestones on the time line of human history have come increasingly close together and consequently their attendant influence on daily life has become more widely recognized and readily acknowledged.

Indisputably, more than ever before in history, these milestones are linked directly or indirectly to technological developments. The development of technologies that have produced the automobile, the airplane, television, nuclear power, and the computer are landmark historical events primarily because they play such a major and often overlapping role in understanding an array of historical trends and events such as urbanization, the election or defeat of political leaders, sending humans into space, and a host of geopolitical conflicts from Vietnam to the Persian Gulf. Indeed, it is almost inconceivable for people living today to contemplate the future of humankind and their own personal future in the new millennium without speculating about how technological advances may effect changes in diverse sociocultural domains such as medicine, law, government and international relations, economics, education, and communication.

Literacy in the modern era has always been recognized as playing a key role in promoting and shaping technological development, for example in the area of science and academics (Kaufer & Carley, 1993). Technology and its relation to literacy have also been commonly viewed as components interacting with a broad range of sociocultural and historical trends (e.g., Eisenstein, 1983). However, what we are coming to know and appreciate more consciously now is that literacy and technology cannot be divorced from one another (Bruce, 1997). Or further, as Ong (1982) argued, literacy can essentially be viewed as a technology; that is, the psychosocial dimensions of literacy cannot be fully separated from the materials and processes for creating texts (see also Bolter, 1991). That more integrated view of literacy and technology as essentially inseparable clearly underlies the contents of this book and the word *transformations* in its title. The appearance of distinctly new technologies that transform the tangible means by which people read and write implies at least the potential for producing a cascade of sociocultural transformations. Although this volume cannot offer definitive predictions about what the ultimate results of such transformations might be, it does heighten awareness about the intimate relation between literacy and technology, and it hopefully will serve as a guidepost in the evolution of whatever literacy will become in the first century of the new millennium.

REFERENCES

Atkinson, R. C., & Hansen, D. N. (1966). Computer-assisted instruction in initial reading: The Stanford project. *Reading Research Quarterly, 2,* 5–26.

Birkerts, S. (1994). *The Gutenberg elegies: The fate of reading in an electronic age.* Boston: Faber & Faber.

Bolter, J. D. (1991). *Writing space: The computer, hypertext, and the history of writing.* Hillsdale, NJ: Lawrence Erlbaum Associates.

Bruce, B. C. (1997). Literacy technologies: What stance should we take? *Journal of Literacy Research.*

Bruce, B. C., & Rubin, A. (1993). *Electronic quills: A situated evaluation of using computers for writing in classrooms.* Hillsdale, NJ: Lawrence Erlbaum Associates.

Burbules, N. C., & Bruce, B. C. (1995). This is not a paper. *Educational Researcher, 24*(8), 12–17.

Burke, J. (1978). *Connections.* Boston: Little, Brown.

Clark, R. E. (1983). Reconsidering research on learning from media. *Review of Educational Research, 53*, 445–459.

"Cloudy days in tomorrowland." (1997, January 27). *Newsweek,* 86.

Cognition and Technology Group at Vanderbilt University. (1994). Multimedia environments for developing literacy in at-risk students. In B. Means (Ed.), *Technology and education reform: The reality behind the promise* (pp. 23–56). San Francisco: Jossey-Bass.

Commeyras, M., & Alvermann, D. E. (1996). Reading about women in world history textbooks from one feminist perspective. *Gender and Education, 8*, 31–48.

Cunningham, J. W., & Fitzgerald, J. (1996). Epistemology and reading. *Reading Research Quarterly, 31*, 36–60.

Daniel, D. B., & Reinking, D. (1987). The construct of legibility in electronic reading environments. In D. Reinking (Ed.), *Reading and computers: Issues for theory and practice* (pp. 24–39). New York: Teachers College Press.

Eisenstein, E. L. (1983). *The printing revolution in early modern Europe.* Cambridge, England: Cambridge University Press.

Flood, J., & Lapp, D. (1995). Broadening the lens: Toward an expanded conceptualization of literacy. In K. A. Hinchman, D. J. Leu, & C. K. Kinzer (Eds.), *Perspectives on literacy research and practice: The 44th Yearbook of the National Reading Conference* (pp. 1–16). Chicago: National Reading Conference.

Frase, L. T. (1987). Computer analysis of written materials. In D. Reinking (Ed.), *Reading and computers: Issues for theory and practice* (pp. 76–96). New York: Teachers College Press.

Freire, P. (1983). *The politics of education: Culture, power and liberation.* New York: Bergin & Garvey.

Kaufer, D. S., & Carley, K. M. (1993). *Communication at a distance: The influence of print on sociocultural organization and change.* Hillsdale, NJ: Lawrence Erlbaum Associates.

Labbo, L. D. (1996). A semiotic analysis of young children's symbol making in a classroom computer center. *Reading Research Quarterly, 31*(4), 356–385.

L'Allier, J. J. (1980). *An evaluation study of a computer-based lesson that adjusts reading level by monitoring on task reader characteristics.* Unpublished doctoral dissertation, University of Minnesota, Minneapolis.

Landow, G. (1992). *Hypertext: The convergence of contemporary critical theory and technology.* Baltimore: Johns Hopkins University Press.

Lanham, R. A. (1989). The electronic word: Literary study and the digital revolution. *New Literary History, 20*(2), 265–290.

Lanham, R. A. (1993). *The electronic word: Democracy, technology, and the arts.* Chicago: University of Chicago Press.

Lynch, C. (1997). Searching the internet. *Scientific American, 276*(3), 52–56.

McLuhan, M. (1962). *The Gutenberg galaxy: The making of typographic man.* Toronto: University of Toronto Press.

McConkie, G. W., & Zola, D. (1987). Two examples of computer-based research on reading: Eye movement monitoring and computer-aided reading. In D. Reinking (Ed.), *Reading and computers: Issues for theory and practice* (pp. 97–108). New York: Teachers College Press.

Means, B. (Ed.). (1994). *Technology and education reform: The reality behind the promise.* San Francisco: Jossey-Bass.

Means, B., Blando, J., Olson, K., Morocco, C. C., Remz, A. R., & Zorfass, J. (1993). *Using technology to support educational reform.* Washington, DC: U.S. Department of Education.

Moore, D. W., Monaghan, E. J., & Hartman, D. K. (1997). Conversations: Values of literacy history. *Reading Research Quarterly, 32*, 90–102.

Moulthrop, S. (1991). Reading from the map: Metonymy and metaphor in the fiction of forking paths. In P. Delany & G. P. Landow (Eds.), *Hypermedia and literary studies* (pp. 119–132). Cambridge, MA: MIT Press.

Moulthrop, S., & Kaplan, N. (1994). They became what they beheld: The futility of resistance in the space of electronic writing. In C. L. Selfe & S. Hilligoss (Eds.), *Literacy and computers: The complications of teaching and learning with technology* (pp. 220–237). New York: Modern Language Association.

Murphy, J. W. (1988). Computerization, postmodern epistemology, and reading in the postmodern era. *Educational Theory, 38*(2), 175–182.

Negroponte, N. (1995). *Being digital.* New York: Knopf.

Newman, D., Griffin, P., & Cole, M. (1989). *The construction zone: Working for cognitive change in school.* Cambridge, England: Cambridge University Press.

Okerson, A. (1991). With feathers: Effects of copyright and ownership on scholarly publishing. *College and Research Libraries, 52*(5), 425–438.

Olson, D. R. (1994). *The world on paper.* New York: Cambridge University Press.

Ong, W. (1982). *Orality and literacy: The technologizing of the word.* New York: Methuen.

Papert, S. (1993). *The children's machine: Rethinking school in the age of the computer.* New York: Basic Books.

Reinking, D. (1987). Computers, reading, and a new technology of print. In D. Reinking (Ed.), *Reading and computers: Issues for theory and practice* (pp. 3–23). New York: Teachers College Press.

Reinking, D. (1992). Differences between electronic and printed texts: An agenda for research. *Journal of Educational Multimedia and Hypermedia, 1*(1), 11–24.

Reinking, D. (1994). *Electronic literacy* (Perspectives in Reading Research No. 4). Athens, GA: National Reading Research Center.

Reinking, D. (1995). Reading and writing with computers: Literacy research in a post-typographic world. In K. A. Hinchman, D. J. Leu, & C. K. Kinzer (Eds.), *Perspectives on literacy research and practice: The 44th yearbook of the National Reading Conference* (pp. 17–33). Chicago: National Reading Conference.

Reinking, D. (1996). Reclaiming a scholarly ethic: Deconstructing "intellectual property" in a post-typographic world. In D. J. Leu, C. K. Kinzer, & K. A. Hinchman (Eds.), *Literacies for the 21st century: Research and practice: Forty-fifth yearbook of the National Reading Conference* (pp. 461–470). Chicago: National Reading Conference.

Reinking, D. (1997). Me and my hypertext:) A multiple digression analysis of technology and literacy (sic). *The Reading Teacher, 50*, 626–643.

Reinking, D., & Bridwell-Bowles, L. (1991). Computers in reading and writing. In R. Barr, M. L. Kamil, P. B. Mosenthal, & P. D. Pearson (Eds.), *Handbook of reading research* (Vol. 2, pp. 310–340). New York: Longman.

Reinking, D., & Schreiner, R. (1985). The effects of computer-mediated text on measures of reading comprehension and reading behavior. *Reading Research Quarterly, 20*, 536–552.

Rheingold, H. (1993). *The virtual community: Homesteading on the electronic frontier.* Reading, MA: Addison-Wesley.

Salomon, G. (1979). *Interaction of media, cognition, and learning.* San Francisco: Jossey-Bass.

Salomon, G., Globerson, T., & Guterman, E. (1989). The computer as a zone of proximal development: Internalizing reading-related metacognitions from a reading partner. *Journal of Educational Psychology, 81*, 620–627.

Scribner, S., & Cole, M. (1978). Literacy without schooling: Testing for intellectual effects. *Harvard Educational Review, 48*, 448–461.

Stix, G. (1994). The speed of write. *Scientific American, 272*(6), 106–111.

Tufte, E. R. (1983). *The visual display of quantitative information.* Cheshire, CT: GR.

Tuman, M. C. (Ed.) (1992a). *Literacy online: The promise (and peril) of reading and writing with computers.* Pittsburgh, PA: University of Pittsburgh Press.

Tuman, M. (1992b). *Word perfect: Literacy in the computer age.* London: Falmer.

Venezky, R. L. (1995). Literacy. In T. L. Harris & R. E. Hodges (Eds.), *The literacy dictionary* (p. 142). Newark, DE: International Reading Association.

Vygotsky, L. S. (1978). *Mind and society: The development of higher psychological processes.* Cambridge, MA: Harvard University Press.

TRANSFORMING TEXTS

Digitized text entails much more than the translation of printed documents into binary electronic form. Electronic text possesses important features not shared with its print counterpart: (a) It is interactive in the literal sense, inviting the reader to impose organizations and compose responses; (b) it can accommodate textual supports (electronic scaffolds) for poor or developing readers; (c) it invites and often requires nonlinear strategies; (d) it can incorporate multimedia components; and (e) it is fluid rather than fixed. These characteristics give electronic text a dynamic quality that is changing forever the nature of what it means to be literate. In consequence, this transformation has serious implications for literacy instruction in a post-typographic age. The chapters in this part describe specific ways in which text is being transformed; they also begin to examine classroom applications of electronic text, although this examination continues in subsequent parts of this volume.

For the learner, electronic text entails unprecedented challenges. Bolter (chap. 1) describes the necessity of redefining literacy to account for visual components, the incorporation of which is so readily facilitated by computers. To be sure, these components may provide readers with assistance as they encounter text, but they also complicate the very nature of what it means to read. Some theorists have, he notes, suggested that text and nontext features perform the same basic function and are thus at a certain level indistinguishable. Readers find it increasingly necessary to construct meaning by a coordinated consideration of both elements. Moreover, the complexity inherent in hypertextual systems has clear implications for the nature of strategic reading. Bolter offers a solid introduction to hypertext, then carries it to the next level. The World Wide Web, he argues, can be thought of as a "global hypertext," one that facilitates endless exploration but may challenge a user's powers of navigation and sense of purpose. Given the addition of visual dimensions, the Web has become an evolutionary crucible out of which new literacies are beginning to emerge.

However, electronic text also affords readers powerful advantages not available in print. The incorporation of special features can assist readers when they encounter difficulties and can also facilitate the process of constructing meaning. Anderson-Inman and Horney (chap. 2) use the term *supported text* to refer to any text that has been equipped with these features. Although it is clear that some features can enhance the comprehension of developmental readers, the principal concern of their chapter is with how such resources can come to the aid of the reader at risk. After a thorough introduction to the types of resources that can now be included in supported text, they examine the implications of such support for readers experiencing difficulties. McKenna (chap. 3) then focuses on a particular type of supportive resource, the digitized pronunciation. His concern is with beginning readers, who, en route to comprehension, face a major bottleneck in the form of limited word recognition skill. Digitized pronunciations are accessible on demand whenever the child encounters an unfamiliar word, and they consequently make it possible to read materials that are at or near the listening level. The positive effects of this kind of supported reading on sight word growth are examined together with the instructional implications of this transformation in the way text is prepared for young readers.

Hypertext and the Question of Visual Literacy

Jay David Bolter
Georgia Institute of Technology

The term *text* has not been easy to define since the 1960s. It was first made difficult by the poststructuralist writers, such as Derrida, Barthes, and Foucault, but their notion of the text and their own texts had relatively little impact on the educational community. Now the computer, which is indeed having a great impact on educational theory and practice, has presented further complications. This chapter considers how the computer is complicating the nature of the text and therefore the question of literacy, with some acknowledgment of the related complications introduced by the poststructuralists as well. The computer is reopening for us the problem of the relation of word and image—specifically how images are constituted as part of the texts that we confront in school and in the working world. Are there two literacies (verbal and visual), or is there only one? This question may now be addressed in the light of electronic texts that combine words and images and do not read (or act) like traditional printed texts. Several of the authors in this volume (including Lemke, chap. 17; Myers, Hammett, & McKillop, chap. 4; and Purves, chap. 14) address dimensions of this issue from various points of view, and their work should lead to further research in what may become one of the leading educational questions in the coming years.

THE WORLD WIDE WEB AND NEW DEFINITIONS
OF LITERACY

In the 1980s the desktop computer established itself with relative ease in the business and academic worlds as a tool for communication and calculation. Word processing has now become more or less the standard form of writing in North America: The computer as word processor has almost replaced the typewriter, which remains useful only for filling out preprinted forms and addressing envelopes. Well-known novelists may feel obliged to tell interviewers that they still write out their drafts in pencil on lined yellow sheets or bang them out on a manual typewriter. However, such behavior is now regarded as a charming idiosyncrasy: Almost everyone who cannot afford his or her own secretary uses a word processor. If electronic writing simply meant word processing, students of literacy in the new medium could understand the needed skills by analogy with skills required for producing printed documents. Writing literacy, therefore, seemed to be a more or less settled issue. Reading literacy has not been problematic either, but for a different reason. Word processing produces linear documents that are meant to be read in the conventional way, preferably on paper but if necessary by scrolling through the document on the computer screen. Thus, the introduction of word processing has not challenged traditional reading practices, except in well-defined technical aspects (e.g., the page size, screen resolution, access to passages in the middle of a document, etc.).

The World Wide Web may change this situation radically. One could argue that the Internet had already complicated notions of reading and writing in the 1980s. Electronic mail became widely available to teachers and students at the college level and seemed to foster a conversational style of writing as well as browsing and casual reading. However, e-mail at least had an analogue in the conventional writing of letters and memos. Analogues for the World Wide Web are more eclectic and less clear. The Web in fact poses two distinct challenges to our traditional notions of writing and reading literacy.

The Web is designed to be hypertextual, whereas e-mail is hypertextual almost by accident. As readers respond to portions of other messages, they spin out the threads of a conversation that others may then follow. Word processing is studiously linear, but the Web is a global network of pages and links. Web designers build these links into their pages, and readers are expected to move from page to page by clicking on and activating links. Both writing and reading on the Web are defined by the expectation of interaction. To design a website, the writer must conceive of the pages as a structure that might be explored in a variety of orders by different readers with different needs. Reading or browsing the Web requires skills in deciphering the possibly complex relations among pages, as well as conventional skills required by the linear prose on each page. Electronic hypertexts were created in the 1980s and early 1990s, but these were generally small documents delivered to an individual computer on a disk or a CD-ROM. Today, the Web is itself one gigantic, interconnected text: In theory (although not in practice) a reader might be able to travel to any page on the Web from any other by following a suitable number of links. Because of its collective and eclectic character, the Web can offer something of intellectual or commercial interest to any literate person in the developed world. This enormous system also raises questions for our culture's notion of writing. How do we teach a student how to "collaborate" with 500,000 unknown fellow writers to produce a written document that millions of people may browse through each day?

In addition to its hypertextual character, there is another reason for the explosive popularity of the Web: It is a graphic as well a verbal medium. Static images appear on Web pages, and animation and video can be delivered in close association with these pages. The Web itself was established by Tim Berners-Lee and his associates at CERN in 1989, ostensibly for distributing physics and other scientific information. This technology was of interest principally to scientists and computer specialists until 1993, when the first graphical browser, Mosaic, appeared. The fact that Mosaic could display graphics together with styled text in a window made the technology compelling to large new audiences. This capacity also means that creating Web pages now requires skills in graphics design as well as hypertextual writing. At the same time, reading Web pages requires an appreciation of the graphics themselves and of the relation between graphics and text. As animation and video (as well as digitized sound) become more widely and easily available, even more skills will be required for Web literacy.

Two decades ago, before word processing and the Web, good academic writing practice could be defined as the ability to frame convincing arguments in an effective prose style. An author could expect his or her readers to proceed through the sentences and paragraphs of a document in a single, logical order. Furthermore, except in certain kinds of scientific writing, the prose could be expected to stand on its own: Illustrations were of secondary importance, and typography was an afterthought, an art left entirely to printers. Today, hypertext and digital graphics call these assumptions into question, and we need, therefore, to examine both the hypertextual and the graphic character of electronic literacy in greater detail.

Characterizing Hypertextual Literacy

By the standards of our rapidly changing culture, hypertext is not especially new. The conventional history dates the idea back to Vannevar Bush, a government science advisor during World War II, who proposed the *memex*, a kind of interactive encyclopedia on microfilm. Ted Nelson coined the term *hypertext* in the 1960s and various experiments went on for a couple of decades. The personal computer made stand-alone hypertext possible in the 1980s, and there developed a body of theoretical literature (Bolter, 1991; Joyce, 1995; Landow, 1992; Lanham, 1994; Moulthrop, 1991a) as well as regular conferences sponsored by the Association for Computing Machinery (ACM), the chief American professional organization for computer science (*Hypertext* '87, '89, '91, etc.), and a European counterpart (*Echt* '92, '94). Drawing on this literature, we can review relatively briefly the theory of hypertext.

The key feature of hypertext is fluid text. Each hypertext is a set of different potential texts awaiting realization (Bolter, 1991; Landow, 1992). The elements of hypertext are verbal or graphic units (the World Wide Web calls them pages) and the links that join these units. When the reader comes to a page, he or she can read that page as a conventional text or graphic design. When the reader finishes, movement to another page is accomplished by activating one of the links. In a rich hypertext, there will be many pages and several links to and from each page. The reader's decisions in following links determine the order of presentation for those pages. The reader's particular experience of the text is determined in part by the decisions that have been made. A rich hypertext can and probably will be different for each reader and with each act of reading. In print technology, the text is obviously fixed by the act of printing. A hypertext is radically unstable and unpredictable in a way that the printed text is not.

It is often said that a printed text is linear, whereas a hypertext is nonlinear, but this is not quite accurate. Our experience of reading takes place in time, and in that sense any particular instantiation of a hypertext, like any particular reading of a printed work, is linear. Hypertexts are not nonlinear, but rather multilinear. The author constructs the text so that it can be read in a variety of orders, and the reader approaches the text with that assumption. The reader believes that specific choices will make a difference. Some printed texts are multilinear, too: For example, newspapers, magazines, and dictionaries are not meant to be read straight through from the first column of the first page to last column of the last page. Nevertheless, a printed book appears to have a "natural" reading order— the order in which the pages are bound—and that natural order determines what seems appropriate in print. Multilinear printed texts must work against this order. It is even possible to realize hypertext in a printed book, as is the case with "make your own adventure" books for children. It is also possible to create an electronic hypertext that is wholly linear, with one link at the end of each unit leading to the next unit. Still, with electronic hypertext, the assumption that the text will be multiple governs our relationship to the text as writers and readers. If a hypertextual writer chooses to create a linear hypertext, the text will be read as a violation of our expectations.

The instability and multiplicity of hypertext defines a new relationship among author, text, and reader—a relationship different from the one that exists with printed technology. A printed text (and by extension its author) lays claim to a special authority. Printed words are typically reproduced in hundreds or thousands of copies and distributed widely to an audience of relatively passive readers. These readers can examine the author's text and approve or disapprove, but they cannot intervene in the text in any significant way. They can make notes and changes in their own copy, but their changes are not available to other readers. The asymmetry of this relationship lends to authors in print a high cultural status. It is remarkable how inclined we still are as readers to give credence to printed words and to their authors. The mere fact that someone has written a successful book on a subject makes him or her an authority to be consulted by the other print and electronic media. As academics and as laypersons, we still quote and cite texts and authors incessantly and seek to borrow their authority for our own words. This authority effect has obvious significance for education, which is still based on texts and in particular on textbooks.

Hypertext and electronic communication in general tend to erode the authority of the text and its author (Bolter, 1991; Landow, 1992). The relationship between author and reader is more egalitarian. The reader can more easily intervene in electronic texts and even become an author. If the author gives the reader a document in word processing format, the reader can open the text and actually change its contents. If the author's text arrives as a posting to the Internet, the reader cannot change the text itself, which has already been received by many other subscribers, but can nevertheless post a reply as part of the same thread. Such a reply can reach all of the same readers and therefore make a claim to the same level of credence and authority. The reader can even include parts of the original message in the reply and so provide a direct and immediate challenge to the original. With a hypertext on a CD-ROM or on the World Wide Web, the reader is not able to intervene in the same way. Even in these cases, however, the act of hypertextual reading works to undermine the authority of the text.

The predominant theory among education researchers today is that reading any printed or electronic text is an active process of meaning construction. Readers must relate the textual elements to their cultural environment and personal history in order to make sense of what they see (see, e.g., Myers et al., chap. 4, this volume). If, in reading print, this process of meaning construction is invisible as the reader's eyes move over the page, the technology of hypertext makes the process partly (although certainly not wholly) visible. What becomes visible are the choices that the reader makes in following links, as each link followed indicates part of the reader's construction of the meaning of the text. The reader seems to be collaborating with the author in the creation of the text, in the sense that the choice of links determines what the reader will next see on the screen. This sense of collaboration enhances the reader's status at the expense of the author's, or of the text itself in the case of apparently anonymous Web pages—an enhancement that contemporary educators would probably applaud. The reader is also perhaps inclined to be more critical and more aware that a text could be other than it is. This critical awareness is certainly in evidence among browsers on the Web. For example, the cynical opinion among obsessive Web browsers seems to be that there are no good websites: They are all flawed either in content or design.

These, then, are the qualities that theorists have identified in hypertext. There have so far been two main classes of hypertexts that illustrate these qualities. A relatively small number of stand-alone hypertexts appeared in the late 1980s and early 1990s, including some highly original works of fiction. For example, Joyce's (1987) *afternoon* shows how hypertext can experiment with shifting points of view to create effects rather different from the effects of printed fiction. Moulthrop's (1991b) *Victory Garden* is another compelling experiment with multiple narrative lines as well as multiple narrators. These and other hypertextual fictions invite, and in fact demand, rereading, and each reading is almost certain to be unique. However, the experience of reading these hyperfictions is not widely shared. The audience for "serious" printed fiction in our culture is relatively small; the audience for hypertextual experimentation is much smaller.

The other important example of hypertext (the World Wide Web) lies at the other end of the scale in terms of popularity. As we have remarked, the whole Web could be considered one vast hypertext with tens of millions of readers. Within this global hypertext, there are many different kinds of websites: academic and research sites, business sites with varied purposes (including public relations, marketing, and sales), entertainment and game sites, sites for personal expression, and even sites for hypertextual fiction. Many of the sites, especially those sponsored by businesses and organizations, do not make much use of the associative possibilities of hypertext; they are instead hierarchical, a set of nested menus, and require a literacy that is close to the traditional techniques of reading, say, the printed yellow pages. Furthermore, most current websites contain materials that have no obvious place in the school curriculum, although this may change as the Web itself begins to define parts of the curriculum. In any case, very little on the Web resembles the written work that we currently expect students to produce.

In the current world of electronic communication, therefore, we have some examples of hypertextual fiction and millions of examples Web-based graphic design. We do not have hypertextual models for the kind of text that still forms the basis of traditional, literary education: the persuasive essay. For many educators, this may be a relief. Perhaps the explanation is that the essay is a dying form. We could argue that it is a product of the age of print, especially if we accept Montaigne as its inventor (see, e.g., Eisenstein, 1979). It may no longer be a genre appropriate to electronic communication, whose defining form is now the website, but in that case, the modern definition of rhetoric is also threatened. Many, perhaps most, educators still teach expository writing as the art of establishing a consistent point of view and delivering a coherent conclusion. Reading nonfiction is taught as the art of discovering the point of view, identifying the conclusion, and then adopting one's own point of view in agreement or dissent. Hypertext challenges those goals and requires new procedures for both reading and writing. For example, a hypertextual "essay" might be one in which the writer (or writers in collaboration) lays out a set of possible points of view without attempting to adjudicate among them. It might lead to a set of conflicting conclusions (depending on the reading order) with no attempt to indicate the relative merit of each. How does one teach students to write or to read such an essay?

Hypertext and hypermedia may work against the very idea of a discursive presentation of an argument. (Alternatives to traditional essays are in fact explored by Myers et al., chap. 4, and by Lemke, chap. 17, both this volume.) Perhaps the essay cannot be severed from its attachment to print technology. There is also another, more radical possibility: that verbal argument itself is no longer compelling in an age of digital graphics. Hypertextual rhetoric may not be much more successful in the electronic medium than traditional print rhetoric, because verbal hypertext itself may only constitute a transition to a different form of communication. The most popular and successful websites are not necessarily elaborately linked hypertexts, but they are visually interesting. Literacy in electronic environments may have more to do with the production and consumption of images than the reading and writing of either hypertextual or linear prose.

Characterizing Graphic Rhetoric

The World Wide Web and popular CD-ROM products have demonstrated that graphic presentation is the most compelling aspect of electronic communication. If our definition of text expands to include electronic communication, then we will have to give graphics a prominent place in that definition. We will have to reconsider the relation between words and images in communication and in education. Words and images have coexisted for hundreds of years in printed texts; however, it was a coexistence based on the presumed superiority of the word. Movable type was designed for the reproduction of alphabetic writing, whereas images, woodcuts, and later copper engravings were confined to specific areas on the printed page. Images were important to certain genres of printed books, such as atlases, anatomies, encyclopedias, and handbooks. Eisenstein (1979) emphasized how the ability to fix and reproduce illustrations and maps in books contributed significantly to the emergence of modern science. However, in general the printed word contained and constrained the image quite effectively, even after the advent of photolithography in the 19th century.

In the 20th century, film and television have challenged the dominance of the printed word, and at least in the popular imagination the two have thoroughly supplanted print as a medium of cultural expression. Although they may agree on little else, a whole range of art historians and media theorists from Gombrich (1982) to Mitchell (1994) to Jameson (1995) agree that we are living in a visual culture. The question now is whether electronic communication will be construed by our culture as an extension of the medium of print or as a new visual medium. Even 5 years ago the answer to that question seemed fairly clear: The computer was a new writing technology in the tradition of the printed book. However, that answer did not foresee the growing importance of static graphics, animation, digital video, and digital audio. In the space of electronic communication, these perceptual media can operate in two distinct ways.

The digital image can enter into a cooperative relation with verbal text. Consider how graphics function on a World Wide Web page. An image can be placed "inline," surrounded by words on the page, where it functions more or less as images have functioned in traditional graphic design for printed publication. However, on the Web page, the whole image or parts of it can also function as anchors that link that page to other pages. A thumbnail image of a work of art can be linked to a more detailed image stored in a separate file. Each region of a map of the United States can be linked to a different page that provides more detailed maps or other, verbal information. In these cases, the graphics are functioning as hypertextual references, just as anchored words and phrases do. The graphics become part of the network of associations that constitute the hypertext and so acquire the qualities that belong to all hypertexts: The graphics become unstable, arbitrary symbols and fit easily into an expanded notion of text. For decades, semiologists and poststructuralists have been working to claim graphics for an expanded definition of text, and they have done so without reference to computer graphics (see Blonsky, 1985). In their view, pictures and words simply become two versions of the same symbolic process. Mitchell (1994), for example, can make the remarkable claim that "[o]ne lesson of a general semiotics, then, is that there is, *semantically* speaking (that is, in the pragmatics of com-munication, symbolic behavior, expression, signification) no *essential* difference between texts and images" (p. 161). Applied to electronic media, this view could be called the hypertextualization of the image. Traditional writers, literary critics, and educators may object to this formulation, as they object even to purely verbal hypertext, but it is really the less radical of the two alternatives.

The other possibility is that the graphics will not enter into a hypertextual relation with words, but will instead simply displace both hypertextual and linear writing. There is a strong Western tradition that images can present reality to us transparently, without the need for words or other arbitrary symbols. The Renaissance invention of linear perspective has led to repeated claims that artists can now show the world as if the viewer were looking through a window onto a real scene (Alberti, 1972). The invention of photography strengthened that claim: Photography, it was argued, was a technology that "automatically" recorded the light that was really there, without the interpretive intervention of the artist (Bazin, 1980). Documentary film seemed to provide even greater realism, and television news now makes the claim that its "live" coverage can "give the viewer the world." This powerful tradition could now influence our construction of the Internet and other forms of electronic communication and lead to the attempt to replace words with digital graphics. Even in CD-ROM multimedia, we can see how images and particularly video are featured at the expense of words. As the Internet increases its bandwidth, recorded video and videoconferencing will become more popular and may well replace verbal e-mail as well as static Web pages that combine words and images. Many have predicted—some happily, others with trepidation—that the Internet will evolve into a system for interactive television.

Two Versions of Visual Literacy

Here, then, are two possible relations between word and image in electronic media: hypermedia or interactive television. (For a different taxonomy, a distinction between the "typological" and the "typographical," see Lemke, chap. 17, this volume.) It is not really a question of the total victory of one or the other, for the heterogeneous character of electronic media suggests that there will be room for both hypertext and interactive television. There will continue to be sophisticated websites or other applications in which images are woven into hypertextual relations with words, and there will be applications in which viewers will interact almost exclusively with streams of digital video. One question worth asking is whether one of these constructions will dominate the other in electronic culture. However, that question is too contentious to answer here. For the purposes of this discussion, we need to keep in mind that both constructions give us a culture different from the print-based verbal culture to which our educational institutions are still adapted. In either case, the image takes on a new importance, and we must ask whether notions of literacy based solely on verbal text can survive. For that reason, it is worth reviewing the debate over visual literacy: Does it in fact constitute a different form of literacy to which our educational institutions must then respond?

Over the past few decades, theorists, art historians, and psychologists have debated whether techniques of visual representation have the same status as the alphabetic representation of language. A closely related question is whether photographs or perspective drawings are artificial or in some sense natural. In *The Languages of Art*, Goodman (1968) argued that all pictures are just as conventional as words, and this radical position has been more or less accepted by poststructuralist and postmodern writers, and probably by educational theorists who subscribe to the social construction of meaning. They could appeal to the (relatively few) studies that have been done indicating that people (often Africans) have difficulty interpreting photographs and perspective drawings, when they are shown them for the first time. On the other hand, there are visual realists who claim that the photographs and perspective drawings are not mere conventions: They have a natural correspondence to reality. Gombrich (1982) made this claim. Jones and Hagen (1980) reviewed the experimental evidence that photographs and perspective drawings are conventional, and they are not on balance convinced. Messaris (1984) argued that even if photographs and film follow conventions, these conventions are themselves easy to learn because they correspond to natural human traits. For example, some film cuts correspond to the natural, saccadic movements of the human eye. Messaris concluded that visual literacy is not comparable to the complex conventions of written literacy. Such writers suggest or imply that we understand pictures and films by using our natural (inherited) visual abilities. If they are right, it is unlikely that we need to educate children to learn to read a new visual syntax, because they can read it with "natural" skills.

There is a correspondence between the two constructions of visual communication (hypermedia or interactive television) and the two views of visual literacy (conventional or natural). Like verbal hypertext and indeed all symbolic writing, graphical hypertexts must be conventional. To read and write graphical hypertexts, students would have to learn a set of rhetorical conventions. On the other hand, interactive television is more likely to be regarded as a perceptual experience, which would then require no conventions and no special learning.

TEACHING AND LEARNING IN A VISUAL CULTURE

Computer technology thus challenges our notions of literacy on several levels. The first challenge is to traditional definitions of good and effective writing and reading. As I have noted, hypertext undermines the rhetorical foundation for the teaching of writing—that is, the need for a unified point of view and a coherent thesis. To include hypertextual writing and reading in the curriculum, we would need a rhetoric appropriate to the associative character of hypertext, as Landow (1992) argued. To comprehend the structure of a given hypertext, the reader must grasp how its links function, which requires, Landow believed, a rhetoric of departures and arrivals. A rhetoric of *departures* prepares readers to understand where a particular link may take them. A rhetoric of *arrivals* orients readers after they have chosen a link and arrived at a new textual location. Joyce (1995) made a similar call for understanding the "contours" of a hypertext. There is certainly room for more research in such hypertextual reading strategies (see Kamil & Lane, chap. 19, this volume).

In some ways, however, the pedagogy of hypertext would not necessarily constitute a break with current educational theory. As I have already remarked, electronic hypertext seems to embody a model of reading as the active construction and critique of meaning. Social constructivists agree that students ought to be critical readers who understand their own role in the process of meaning construction. (Myers et al. make this argument explicit in chap. 4, this volume. Related arguments about the social construction of meaning are offered by Labbo & Kuhn, chap. 5; Kieffer, Hale, & Templeton, chap. 9; Leu et al., chap. 12; and Lemke, chap. 17, all this volume.) Hypertextual writing means creating links as well as text, and the capacity to create intertextual relations among existing materials would seem to be the archetype of the constructivist view of knowledge production. Furthermore, most educational theorists stress the importance of collaboration for effective learning. Hypertext can convince students that reading is an act of collaborating with the author to produce the text, and hypertext can facilitate student collaboration in research and writing (see Beach & Lundell, chap. 6, and Garner & Gillingham, chap. 13, both this volume).

It may be that hypertext fits well with contemporary educational theory, but not necessarily with contemporary practice, which lags behind theory in any case. If so, then introducing hypertextual reading and writing into the classroom could help to stimulate change in the direction now sanctioned by educational theorists. The change could be felt across the curriculum, not just in specific areas of writing and reading practice, for the obvious reason that all the other disciplines (from history and social science to literature to science) are still taught principally from linear textbooks or other printed works. Traditional educational practice is still founded not only on verbal literacy, but on the specific qualities of literacy in print. Hypertextual reading practices would challenge the conventions of narrative history and the scientific concept of cause and effect.

On the other hand, the redefinition of literacy to account for verbal hypertext may be superseded by the more radical task of accounting for graphic representation. Even graphics on the World Wide Web must bring a significant change. As it is, our educational system still regards graphic representation as something to be left behind as the child moves into higher grades. However, high school teachers may soon be assigning Web projects in lieu of traditional essays. If they allow and even encourage students to write with images on their Web pages, then they should teach students how to create and deploy these images (as well as animation and digital video). Such topics are now regarded as a superficial part of the curriculum—nice to have, but easily dispensed with when budgets are tight. In fact, classes in art and video production can be seen as a nuisance by conservative critics of schools, who argue we need to get "back to basics." It seems unlikely that such critics would list the basics as reading, writing, arithmetic, and digital graphic design. Yet Reinking and ChanLin (1994) and Reinking and Watkins (1996) argued that the use of graphics is important in making effective pedagogical use of electronic texts. In addition to the authors in this volume already cited, the case for expanding literacy to include visual and multiple media is made by Flood and Lapp (1995).

The other construction of graphics (as the transparent presentation of reality) obviously constitutes a greater educational challenge, for Western education since the time of the Greeks has taken symbolic representation as its method and principal subject matter. However, there are powerful forces, perhaps even within the educational community, that can push us toward this other construction. Electronic technology is sometimes (oddly enough) offered as a means of promoting authenticity in education (Petraglia, in press). The idea is that the computer can serve as a transparent vehicle for real-world situations as well as for interpersonal communication. That is, computers can be used to simulate the real world and to provide real-time interaction among students separated by great distances. Such applications depend heavily on graphics and digital video; they also depend on the assumption of transparency. If our educational system as a whole followed this line, what would students be taught? They would be taught to use graphics and video not for their hypertextual possibilities, but to bring the authentic into the schools.

With either construction of the visual, mastering digital graphics may become part of the definition of literacy. Lemke (chap. 17) suggests boldly in this volume that multimedia authoring and reading skills will be "generic literacies in the Information Age." However, it is worth recalling that such a suggestion was made early in this century for another visual technology, photography. The art critic Roh (1980) predicted that, just as writing had moved over the centuries from being an elite practice to something expected of every adult and taught to every child in school, so now photography would follow the same trajectory: "[T]he statement is right," he wrote, "that not to be able to handle a camera will soon be looked upon as equal to illiteracy" (p. 156). He was of course quite wrong. It is interesting to consider that photography, film, and television have all had an enormous impact on our society and yet a relatively small impact on our educational practice. It is true that these visual media are used to provide educational materials (photographs in textbooks, instructional films and videos). However, we still do not seem to regard understanding these media as necessary for literacy. Although some media specialists may recommend it (e.g., Messaris, 1984), our educational system as a whole does not see a need to teach students how to view still and moving images, nor do we find it necessary to teach students how to produce these media. It is at least conceivable that the electronic graphics revolution will wash over society and yet leave the school relatively untouched.

However, there is reason to think that the impact of electronic technology on education will be more profound. National, state, and local leaders (and parents) now routinely measure schools by the number of computers and by their connectivity to the Internet. Who ever suggested a national initiative to put cameras, radio, or film facilities into every classroom? Educational leaders may believe that by placing computers in the schools they are promoting traditional scientific and technical education, but they may actually be preparing the way for a revolutionary expansion of the notion of literacy to include graphics. Once the computer and the Internet connections are in the schools, students will want to create as well as view these graphic products. Scanners, digitizing cameras and graphic software make it relatively easy to move from being a passive reader of digital graphics to an active creator. (It was harder to create and develop one's own analog photographs, and harder still to master analog film and video production.)

In short, as I suggested at the outset, the status of graphics and visual literacy may well be the great open question facing education in the coming years. Other trends seem inevitable: an emphasis on a constructivist pedagogy of collaboration and communal knowledge making and a corresponding deemphasis on the old "Cartesian" virtues. But how our educational system will accommodate the changing cultural relation between words and images is less predictable and perhaps even more important.

REFERENCES

Alberti, L. B. (1972). *On painting and on sculpture: The Latin texts of De Pictura and De Statua* (C. Grayson, Trans., with introduction and notes). London: Phaidon.

Bazin, A. (1980). The ontology of the photographic image. In A. Trachtenberg (Ed.), *Classic essays on photography* (pp. 217–237). New Haven, CT: Leete's Island Books.

Blonsky, M. (Ed.). (1985). *On signs*. Baltimore: John Hopkins University Press.

Bolter, J. D. (1991). *Writing space: The computer, hypertext, and the history of writing*. Hillsdale, NJ: Lawrence Erlbaum Associates.

Eisenstein, E. (1979). *The print press as an agent of change: Communication and cultural transformation in early-modern Europe* (Vols. 1–2). Cambridge, UK: Cambridge University Press.

Flood, J., & Lapp, D. (1995). Broadening the lens: Toward an expanded conceptualization of literacy. In K. A. Hinchman, D. J. Leu, & C. K. Kinzer (Eds.), *Perspectives on literacy research and practice* (pp. 1–16). Chicago: National Reading Conference.

Gombrich, E. H. (1982). *The image and the eye*. Oxford, UK: Phaidon Press.

Goodman, N. (1968). *Languages of art: An approach to a theory of symbols*. Indianapolis, IN: Bobbs-Merrill.

Jameson, F. (1995). *Postmodernism, or the cultural logic of late capitalism*. Durham, NC: Duke University Press.

Jones, R. K., & Hagen, M. A. (1980). A perspective on cross-cultural picture perception. In M. A. Hagen (Ed.), *The perception of pictures: Vol. 2. Dürer's devices: Beyond the projective model of pictures* (pp. 193–226). New York: Academic Press.

Joyce, M. (1987). Afternoon, a story. [Computer program]. Cambridge, MA: Eastgate Press.

Joyce, M. (1995). A feel for prose: Interstitial links and the contours of hypertext. In *Of two minds: Hypertext, pedagogy, and poetics* (pp. 227–245). Ann Arbor: University of Michigan Press.

Landow, G. P. (1992). *Hypertext: The convergence of contemporary critical theory and technology.* Baltimore: Johns Hopkins University Press.

Lanham, R. (1994). *The electronic word: Democracy, technology, and the arts.* Chicago: University of Chicago Press.

Messaris, P. (1984). *Visual literacy: Image, mind, and reality.* Boulder, CO: Westview Press.

Mitchell, W. J. T. (1994). *Picture theory.* Chicago: University of Chicago Press.

Moulthrop, S. (1991a). Reading from the map: Metonymy and metaphor in the fiction of "Forking Paths." In P. Delany & G. P. Landow (Eds.), *Hypermedia and literary studies* (pp. 119–132). Cambridge, MA: MIT Press.

Moulthrop, S. (1991b). *Victory garden.* [Computer program]. Cambridge, MA: Eastgate Press.

Petraglia, J. (in press). *Constraining constructivism.* Mahwah, NJ: Lawrence Erlbaum Associates.

Reinking, D., & ChanLin, L. (1994). Graphics aids in electronic texts. *Reading Research and Instruction, 33,* 207–232.

Reinking, D., & Watkins, J. (1996). *A formative experiment investigating the use of multimedia book reviews to increase elementary students' independent reading* (Research Rep. No. 55). Athens, GA, & College Park, MD: National Reading Research Center.

Roh, F. (1980). Mechanism and expression. In A. Trachtenberg (Ed.), *Classic essays on photography* (pp. 154–163). New Haven, CT: Leete's Island Books.

2

▼▼▼▼▼▼▼

Transforming Text
for At-Risk Readers

Lynne Anderson-Inman
Mark A. Horney
University of Oregon

What we know as a culture and who we are as a people is written into text. Without access to the world of text, one's knowledge is limited to what can be communicated orally, illustrated in pictures, or shared by demonstration. Without access to the world of text, one is thrown back in time to an era when books belonged only to the elite and learning was restricted to what was known locally (Burke, 1985). Text is a great leveling agent. It can serve as a personal vehicle for enormous growth in knowledge, with or without the support of society's educational institutions (L'Amour, 1989).

Unfortunately, a large percentage of students in our country are not effective in their attempts to acquire and use information from text due to significant deficiencies in reading. It has been estimated that 10% to 12% of the students in English-speaking countries have reading problems of sufficient severity to inhibit successful acquisition of content-area information and that this percentage increases to more than 50% in many of the more disadvantaged areas of our nation (Miller, 1993). The 1994 National Assessment of Educational Progress (NAEP) in the area of reading (Williams, Reese, Campbell, Mazzeo, & Phillips, 1995) found that only 30% of 4th- and 8th-grade students and 36% of 12th-grade students achieved a "proficient" level of reading for their grade level. Furthermore, between 25% (12th grade) and 40% (4th grade) of the students were not able to achieve even a "basic" level of proficiency, defined as partial mastery of the prerequisite knowledge and skills necessary for work at that grade level. Unfortunately, the problem does not disappear when students graduate from high school. Nationwide, it is estimated that 90 million Americans (or 47% of the adult population) have only rudimentary literacy skills (Kirsch, Jungeblut, Jenkins, & Kolstad, 1993).

For the purposes of this chapter, we use the term *at-risk reader* to refer to all students who, for whatever reason, read below grade level and who, because of this, struggle to comprehend the textbooks and other content materials assigned in school. The term *at-risk* is used by educators to mean different things. For many, the term is used to describe students from a range of social, economic, or environmental conditions frequently associated with school failure (Marchiarola, 1988; Pallas, 1989). For others, the term is used to describe students whose instructional or social interactions in school are not successful

(Hodgkinson, 1991). We have chosen to use at-risk reader instead of at-risk student because it puts our focus on a behavior that is amenable to school intervention, rather than a cultural profile over which schools have little control.

We have also adopted a broadly inclusive definition for the term at-risk reader. Students can be at risk of school failure due to reading problems that arise from any one of a range of factors or from a combination of them (Algozzine & Wood, 1994; Vacca & Padak, 1990). These factors include, but are not limited to: (a) inadequate linguistic experience with English, as may be the case for students from non-English-speaking homes or students who have hearing impairments; (b) poor prereading preparation or academic support from parents, as may be the case for students from environmentally or economically disadvantaged homes; (c) inadequate or inappropriate reading instruction in school; and (d) cognitive or physical disabilities that interfere with learning to read and reading to learn. The adoption of such a broad, functional definition for the term at-risk reader is in keeping with movement in the field of education toward inclusive instructional programs for students with diverse learning needs and it highlights their similarities rather than their differences (Algozzine & Wood, 1994).

The fact that at-risk readers can be students experiencing a wide variety of physical, cognitive, and environmental problems is well documented. For example, most children with learning disabilities are classified as such on the basis of the problems they have with reading (Spear-Swerling & Sternberg, 1994) and many seem to plateau at a fourth- or fifth-grade reading level (Snider & Tarver, 1987). Reading is also a major deficit area for students with hearing impairments (Conrad, 1977; Gallaudet Research Institute, 1985; Holt, 1993; King & Quigley, 1985; LaSasso, 1993; Lowenbraun & Thompson, 1986; Paul & Quigley, 1990), with most deaf students failing to develop reading skills beyond the fifth-grade level. The literature suggests a similar pattern of reading failure and significant reading deficiencies for:

- Students with limited English proficiency (Allen, 1991; Dolson, 1985; Minami & Ovando, 1995; Rigg & Allen, 1992; Wong Fillmore & Valadez, 1986).
- Students from environmentally or economically disadvantaged backgrounds (Chall, Jacobs, & Baldwin, 1990; Juel, 1988; National Assessment of Educational Progress, 1985).
- Students with behavior disorders (Graubard, 1971).
- Students with vision impairments (Miller, 1993).
- Students with motor impairments (Bigge, 1991; Center & Ward, 1984).
- Students who score below average in intelligence (Macmillan & Forness, 1992; Stanovich, 1985).
- Students at risk of school failure for any number of other reasons (Allington & McGill-Franzen, 1989; Richardson, Cassanova, Placier, & Guilfoyle, 1988).

Adding to these populations are a large number of students who struggle with reading for unknown or unidentifiable medical or educational reasons (Algozzine & Wood, 1994).

In short, at-risk readers display a wide variety of literacy deficits that impinge on their ability to succeed in school. Improved literacy for these students, however, is not a simple matter of learning new skills in reading and writing. Instead, literacy must be viewed in the context of the academic expectations and overall mission of education. As students proceed through school, the emphasis comes to be placed less on developing the basic skills of reading and writing and more on using these skills to learn new information.

Recognition of this shift in emphasis led to calls in the 1980s for content-area reading instruction (Vacca & Vacca, 1989), writing across the curriculum (Applebee, 1984; Myers, 1984), and increased attention to study skills (Armbruster & Anderson, 1981b; Askov & Kamm, 1982). Because improved literacy cannot be separated from the learning of content, the term *content literacy* is used to refer to all of these concepts in combination. Content literacy is "the ability to use reading and writing for the acquisition of new content in a given discipline" (McKenna & Robinson, 1990, p. 184).

At-risk readers often find themselves completely unprepared to learn new information in school due to poor content literacy skills. For example, to acquire information from text, at-risk readers are faced with an enormous number of challenges. They must: (a) decode a text that may include a high percentage of unfamiliar words and difficult technical terms, (b) construct meaning from sentences that may be complex in structure as well as novel in content, (c) recognize and interpret language that is intended to be understood figuratively rather than literally, (d) integrate poorly understood new information with inadequate databases of prior knowledge, (e) identify and separate important information from supportive detail, (f) synthesize information by forming a mental image of the "big picture," and (g) question themselves on how well they are understanding what they are reading so they can invoke corrective procedures when comprehension is low.

These challenges are not easy to meet, especially when both skills and motivation may be low. At-risk readers tend to avoid reading activities in school as well as outside school, starting a downward spiral that results in significantly less experience with text than students who do not have reading difficulties. Stanovich (1986) attributed many of the problems evidenced by at-risk readers to the secondary effects of not practicing reading. He used the term *Matthew effects* to describe the phenomenon whereby good readers get better because they take advantage of opportunities to read, whereas poor readers fall farther and farther behind because they avoid such opportunities. The presence of reading difficulties leads to decreased interest in reading on the part of the student and decreased expectation for reading on the part of the teacher. The net result is an educational experience that is less demanding from a cognitive perspective, less rich from a linguistic perspective, and less beneficial as preparation for the next stage in students' educational or vocational careers (Allington, 1977; Mikulecky, 1982; Vacca & Padak, 1990).

In this chapter we propose a technology-based approach for helping at-risk readers face the challenges imposed by their reading difficulties. In the following sections we provide an overview of *supported text*, describe and illustrate its components, share detailed examples of software containing supported text, summarize research we have conducted on what students do when reading supported text, and suggest how supported text might influence future educational opportunities and experiences of at-risk readers.

SUPPORTED TEXT

One approach to helping at-risk readers is the selection or creation of reading environments that support students' efforts to comprehend what they read. Not all texts are equally supportive of the reader and inconsiderate text (Armbruster, 1984) makes reading to learn considerably more difficult. Armbruster and Anderson (1981a) proposed four dimensions along which text should be evaluated to determine its degree of considerateness (structure, coherence, audience appropriateness, and unity) and there is a growing research base to suggest the benefits of modifying text materials to be more considerate of the reader.

Britton, Gulgoz, and Glynn (1993), for example, reviewed 62 empirical studies investigating the effects of providing students with modified text materials to read. They concluded that (a) textbook materials could be rewritten in ways that improved learning, and (b) inserting adjunct aids into text (e.g., headings, preview sentences, summaries, etc.) also had a positive impact on reading to learn.

Building on this research base, there have been a number of experimental attempts to improve reading comprehension by modifying text electronically. In other words, researchers have developed electronic versions of traditional text materials and transformed them in ways that are designed to promote improved comprehension, usually by inserting a variety of text enhancements or electronic resources. We call this *supported text,* text that has been electronically altered in an attempt to be more supportive of the reader. The basic model for providing electronically supported text is simple. Text is displayed on a computer screen for the reader, who proceeds through the document until coming across a word or phrase that, for one reason or another, is problematic. Built into the reading environment is a way for the reader to access auxiliary information (e.g., more text, sound, graphics, etc.) designed to provide assistance and promote comprehension. If the supportive resource (or resources) is helpful, the difficulties are resolved and the reader can continue through the material.

The effects of transforming text to be supportive as well as interactive have been investigated in a wide variety of ways. Early research on using the interactive capabilities of computers to provide students with feedback helpful to them during the reading process began in the 1980s. For example, Reinking and Schreiner (1985) found that text enhancements such as electronic vocabulary support improved the reading comprehension of fifth-grade students. The use of digitized or synthesized speech to provide readers with pronunciations of problematic words and phrases has been widely investigated for more than a decade (e.g., Farmer, Klein, & Bryson, 1992; McConkie & Zola, 1985; Olson, Foltz, & Wise, 1986; Reitsma, 1988; Torgesen, Water, Cohen, & Torgesen, 1988; see also McKenna, chap. 3, this volume). The advent of videodisc and QuickTime® video technologies has enabled these computer-supported reading environments to go beyond the use of text and sound as resources. For example, there have been several recent explorations into using videotaped sign language in combination with English text to enhance the literacy skills and reading comprehension of students with hearing impairments (Hansen, Mounty, & Baird, 1994; Hanson & Padden, 1990; Prinz, 1991).

Most of the research on supported text has explored the use of a single type of media (e.g., synthesized speech) designed to support comprehension in one specific way (e.g., by providing pronunciations of problematic words). During the last few years, however, educators and researchers have begun to investigate the effects of packaging an array of supportive resources into the equivalent of an electronic book. Most of these electronic books present the user with a hypermedia interface (see Bolter, chap. 1, this volume), enabling various types of navigation through the document and access to various types of support. MacArthur and Haynes (1995), for example, described a software system for developing hypermedia versions of students' textbooks called Student Assistant for Learning from Text (SALT). Designed to help students with learning disabilities and other types of at-risk readers, the documents created using SALT provide students with three types of support: (a) compensatory support to improve reading fluency (e.g., glossary for definitions, speech synthesis for pronunciations, etc.), (b) strategic support to guide students' use of cognitive and metacognitive reading strategies, and (c) substantive support to enable modifications that enhance comprehension of content. An evaluation of the system with 10 learning-disabled adolescents revealed significantly higher comprehension scores when the enhanced electronic text was used.

At the Center for Electronic Studying at the University of Oregon, we have also been investigating the use of hypermedia versions of students' reading materials with various types of at-risk readers. In the ElectroText Project (Anderson-Inman, Horney, Chen, & Lewin, 1994; Horney & Anderson-Inman, 1994) we provided a middle school literature class of at-risk students with electronically enhanced versions of the short stories they were reading. Students had hypermedia access to various types of vocabulary support (definitions, pictures, and digitized pronunciations), as well as different types of comprehension questions designed to support specific metacognitive reading skills. Although students established different patterns for using the electronic materials (Horney & Anderson-Inman, 1994), results indicated that those students who made systematic and purposeful use of the available supportive resources rated highest in their comprehension of the material (Anderson-Inman & Horney, 1993).

More recently, we have been investigating the use of supportive text for hearing-impaired students with severe reading deficiencies (Horney & Anderson-Inman, 1995). Under the auspices of a federally funded grant from the U.S. Department of Education, Project LITERACY-HI[1] was a 3-year endeavor to develop hypermedia versions of students' content-area reading materials and evaluate the effects of providing various types of supportive resources designed to motivate reading and increase comprehension. Participating students were provided with electronically enhanced versions of selected textbook chapters on notebook-size computers and taught to use a suite of hypermedia resources embedded into the text for the purposes of improving reading comprehension and promoting content-area literacy.

Various types of media were used to provide the supportive resources: text (definitions and explanations), graphics (pictures and animations), video (American Sign Language [ASL] translations), and digitized sound (pronunciations). Resources in one or more of these media were keyed to unfamiliar vocabulary and technical terms, complex sentences and paragraphs, and abstract and figurative language. In addition, supportive resources were developed to bolster inadequate background knowledge, promote comprehension monitoring, and help students get a conceptual overview of what they were reading. The ultimate goal of the project was to create electronic reading materials with the type of textual supports students with hearing impairments needed to be able to read and understand the same materials assigned to their nondisabled peers. To this end, we worked toward providing the materials to students as needed within the curriculum and on laptop computers that could be carried into mainstream classrooms for use during general education instruction.

During the conduct of the two research projects just described, we came to numerous conclusions about (a) what aspects of content-area text need supportive resources, (b) which types of resources can be constructed to ensure appropriate supports for the maximum number of readers, (c) how those resources can be presented effectively within an electronic medium, and (d) what role each type of resource plays in promoting comprehension of content-area material. Of critical importance was shifting our attention from the types of media available for constructing resources to the differing functions of resources within the process of reading to learn. Many of the conclusions we reached are summarized in the following section, which describes and illustrates what we feel are the essential components of supported text.

[1]Awarded to the Cascade Regional Program for the Hearing Impaired and the Center for Electronic Studying at the University of Oregon from the U.S. Office of Special Education for Project LITERACY-HI: Literacy Improvement via Text Enhancements and Reading Assistance for Children and Youth with Hearing Impairments (Award # H180G30027).

COMPONENTS OF SUPPORTED TEXT

Electronic documents with supported text have three major components: the *presentation* of the text, *keys* that link problematic sections of the text, and *resources* that provide assistance designed to enhance reading comprehension.[2]

Presentation

By *presentation* we mean the main body of text expressing the author's message and the system that presents it. This system consists of one or more physical artifacts and the interface that enables readers to operate them. A simple example of such a system is the printed book. The artifact is the collection of folded, bound, ink-pressed sheets of differing sorts of paper. The interface of the book is the way these objects are organized to present the text. For example, in Western cultures the text is arranged to be read from top to bottom and from left to right. The pages are usually printed on both sides and are numbered sequentially. Text about the text is found among the first and last pages; the text is annotated by notes found at the bottom of the page. Sometimes illustrations are inserted amidst the text and others (possibly in color) are printed on special paper and placed together without reference to their relation to the text, and so on.

It is important to keep this distinction between the text and the presentation system in mind because the presentation system impacts both the immediate comprehension of the text and also the long-term impact of the text on culture. The reason that color images are bound separately in a book is purely economic; the color images require a different and more expensive paper that cannot be easily, and therefore cheaply, bound in individual sheets. Thus, the comprehension enhancement provided by these images is reduced by the economic need to separate them from their textual referents. Such economic considerations are not to be ignored. Gutenberg, after all, did not invent the book; he invented the cheap and standardized book.

A computer-based text presentation reproduces, transforms, or expands all of the functions of print-based text. Figure 2.1 presents an example taken from an electronic version of a fifth-grade social studies book (Beyer, Craven, McFarland, & Parker, 1991) produced with the ElectroText Authoring System (Anderson-Inman, Horney, Chen, & Corrigan, 1994). The basic text has been paginated into a series of displays such as page 4 shown here. On each, a section of the text is displayed in a scrolling field. Readers move among the pages using a variety of navigational tools provided on a pallet (lower right), or as functions from the menu bar. Readers can move through the pages sequentially, jump directly from any page to any other, return to pages listed as previously visited, jump to marked pages, or move by conducting searches for specific words or phrases found in the text. Other tools allow readers to change the text font and font size as well as insert notes into the text.

The system for presenting computer-based text is considerably more complicated than for print-based text and requires a substantial investment in time, money, and effort on the part of the author. This investment can lead to enormous benefits, however, in that the flexibility of the computer allows important changes in the functionality of the document. These include the ability to:

---

[2]Although this discussion is about supported text, much of it is directly applicable to other media. For example, captions incorporated into a film are resources linked to verbal keys in the sound track.

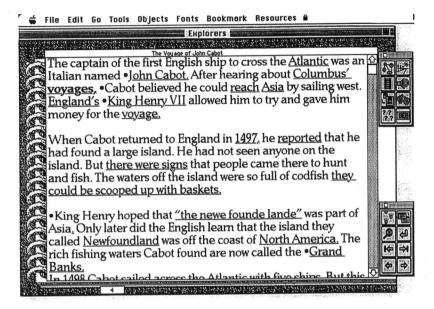

FIG. 2.1.   Computer-based text presentation.

- Repaginate the text and display it in different sizes and fonts.
- Simultaneously display many parts of many different texts in juxtaposition.
- Embed displays from different media within the text.
- Index and search the text on any word or phrase with multilayered Boolean expressions.
- Add an unlimited number of notations to the text.
- Manipulate the text and other displays with other computer applications.

Note that when working with electronic text it is natural to think of the computer as the artifact. This will soon not be the case. The advent of distributed computing via networks such as the Internet forces us to abandon the notion that a document must be a single object. There need not be any single artifact constituting a computer-based text; there can be many and they can be located anywhere.

Keys

Keys are those parts of the text that readers might find problematic. Keys may be individual words, phrases, sentences, paragraphs, or whole sections of the text. Keys may be embedded within other keys. By marking the text as a key, the author is signaling readers that supportive resources are provided in an attempt to assist and expand their comprehension. Students with different reading difficulties will find different parts of the same text problematic and so require different sets of keys. Our work in the development of supported text has led to the identification of nine different types of text that warrant identification as keys. These include:

- General vocabulary: Words and phrases from the general vocabulary that may be unfamiliar for any number of reasons (level of abstraction, antiquity, ambiguity, etc.).

- Difficult constructions: Phrases and sentences that may be problematic for semantic reasons (e.g., figurative language), or because their construction is syntactically complex.
- Definitions: Phrases and sentences that define vocabulary words.
- Proper nouns: Names of people, places, events, and dates.
- Scalar numbers: Numbers providing information about map scales, durations, elapsed and intervening time, sizes, and so on.
- Quotations: Quotations from other sources.
- References: References to earlier chapters, figures, and other materials.
- Rhetorical questions: Questions within the text serving rhetorical rather than study purposes.
- Content vocabulary: Technical terms and phrases crucial to understanding the content of the text—usually key concepts.

Resources

The third part of a supported text document are the *resources* that readers use to assist their comprehension of the keys. Resources can come in an indefinite range of varieties, but we have organized them into eight broad categories: (a) translational, (b) illustrative, (c) supplementary, (d) summarizing, (e) instructional, (f) collaborative, (g) notational, and (h) general purpose.

Translational Resources. Translational resources translate keys into some other form of expression. Examples include rewriting the key into different or simpler language (this includes defining the key), voicing or sounding the key, or translating the key into another language such as Spanish or ASL. In general, translational resources substitute for the key, but they might also explain it. This would be the case when a paraphrase using simpler language is provided to help clarify a complex sentence or paragraph.

Translational resources come in two types: *vocabulary slides* and *language shifts*. In slides, the resource changes the vocabulary of the key, but stays within the same language. It is sometimes possible, especially with short keys, for a slide to be written in such a way that it can be substituted for the original key in the source text. This is generally not the case for language shifts, which translate the key into a different language, where there is seldom, if ever, a one-to-one correspondence between the words of the key and the words of the translation.

We allow for an especially broad definition of what constitutes a separate language. For example, readers who are blind can use devices called screen readers to translate written text into spoken text. However, these devices cannot be used with illustrations. One way to work around this problem is to supply written descriptions of illustrations for blind readers to access in place of the actual graphic. An example of this is shown in Fig. 2.2, a Web page from WGBH Public Broadcasting Station (WGBH, 1996). For each graphic embedded in their Web site, WGBH also inserts the letter D as text. Clicking on the text transfers the reader to a Web page of graphic descriptions. We categorize this as a translational shift resource from a "graphic" language to spoken language.

Illustrative Resources. Illustrative resources include all resources providing examples, comparisons, illustrations, and visualizations. Illustrative resources are often, but not exclusively, multimedia objects. A set of examples of illustrative resources is shown in Fig. 2.3.

FIG. 2.2. Translational resources for readers who are blind.

Supplementary Resources. Information directly related to, but not strictly necessary for comprehension of, the source text is categorized as a supplementary resource. This will include explanations, sidebars, enrichment material, historical references, and references to other parts of the text. An example of an electronic text with supplementary resources is shown in Fig. 2.4, taken from the commercially available CD-ROM *Who Built America?* (American Social History Productions, Inc., 1993). This is a multimedia adaptation of a printed book intended to "integrate the history of community, family, gender roles, race, and ethnicity into the more familiar history of the nation's political and economic development" (American Social History Productions, 1989, p. 2). Text pages such as the one shown on the left of the figure are supported with "excursions" such as the one shown on the right. The excursion in this example, "Memories of the Atlanta Race Riot," is itself supported by three archival audio clips and another section of text.

Summarizing Resources. Summarizing resources provide readers with overviews, summaries, outlines, or abbreviations of the basic text. These can be used to illustrate the global structures of the text, to allow readers to easily distinguish between basic concepts and supporting details, or to illustrate relationships. An example of this last function is shown in Fig. 2.5, a concept map for a chapter on vertebrate evolution designed to illustrate the impact of evolutionary change on each of the major vertebrate body systems.

Instructional Resources. Instructional resources are activities or guidance for readers designed to engage them in actively manipulating the words, concepts, and information from the text. These resources can range from simple reminders to sophisticated tutoring

A set of examples for the key "mushrooms" in a biology textbook.

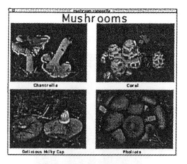

A comparison for the key "The rotation of Mars is 24 hours and 36 minutes" in an astronomy text.

An illustration for the key "Temperature" from an astronomy text.

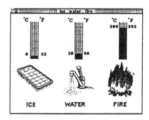

A visualization for the key "Obey the four second rule when following another car" from a driver's manual.

FIG. 2.3.   Different types of illustrative resources.

systems. The phonics "minilessons" described by McKenna (chap. 3, this volume) are a type of instructional resource designed to promote more fluent decoding skills. Other examples include:

- Directions and reminders to readers drawing their attention to features of the text, or presenting advice on how to proceed through the text (e.g., "Remember to survey the entire chapter before beginning to read for details.")
- Questions that allow readers to monitor their understanding of the text. These questions can be in open-ended or closed form and evaluation of the answers can be left to the reader or, to some degree, undertaken by the computer.
- Activities that provide readers with opportunities to practice skills presented in the text, apply concepts in different contexts, and represent concepts, vocabulary, and facts in personally meaningful informational structures.

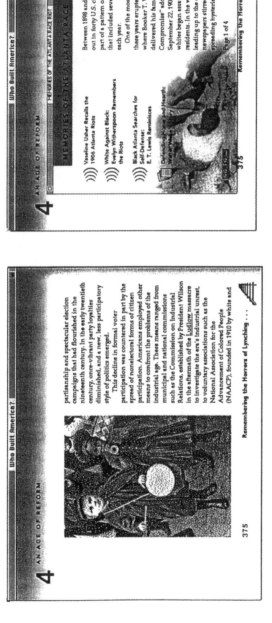

FIG. 2.4. Supplementary resources for Chapter 4: An Age of Reform.

25

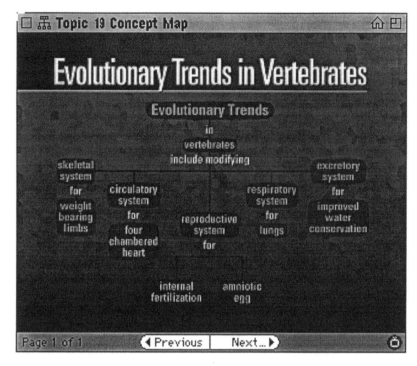

FIG. 2.5.   Concept map summarizing chapter content.

- Instructional presentations to guide readers' understanding of the text, usually via computer-assisted instruction on specific concepts, vocabulary, and facts.
- Mentors and subject-matter experts linked to the text and accessed via telecommunications to provide online assistance. Examples include extensions of the "homework hotlines" operated by some school districts, "telementoring" services (National School Network, 1997), and the Electronic Emissary Project, which links students with subject-matter experts via e-mail (Harris, 1997). Supported text materials provided to readers over the Internet are easily embedded with e-mail links to authors or other content experts ready to provide instructional assistance.
- Intelligent tutoring systems designed to construct and maintain a model of the reader's comprehension of the text, usually by asking questions and evaluating the answers. This information is then used by the system to make recommendations to the reader, invoke other resources judged to be appropriate, force the reader into certain actions, or even restructure the entire text.

Collaborative Resources.   Computer networks can provide powerful tools to support collaboration among readers, enabling them to read the same document simultaneously and communicate with each other about their reading. This process is illustrated in Fig. 2.6 using an electronic version of the Oregon Driver's Manual. One part of the screen presents the text being read and the other part operates a synchronous word processing program called Aspects (Group Logic, 1994). Aspects allows up to 32 individuals, connected via a network, to write and draw simultaneously on a single document, thus enabling readers to collaborative via online discussions with students located anywhere accessible to the network.

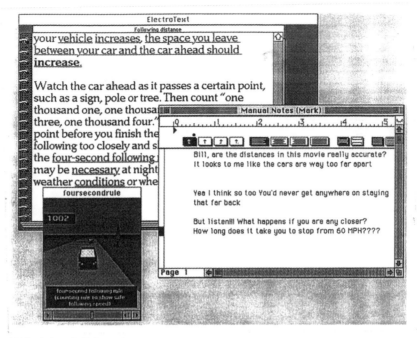

FIG. 2.6. Collaborative resource using synchronous writing program Aspects.

Notational Resources. Notational resources provide readers with writing or drawing tools so that they can take notes as they read and study the text. These can be used to create the electronic version of margin notes or for extensive note taking and information synthesis. Such tools move students to be more active during the reading process and help them to monitor their understanding of the text, both of which are key characteristics of successful learners (Anderson-Inman & Tenny, 1989). Figure 2.7 shows the use of an outlining program linked to the text for the purposes of taking notes from an electronic biology textbook.

General Purpose Resources. Most of the resources already described are designed to be context specific; that is, they are linked directly to the words and concepts of a specific body of text. General purpose resources are not. They comprise the generalized information sources such as databases, encyclopedias, dictionaries, reference lists, and so on, that might support any number of documents. Readers access these resources via links provided in their supported text documents or by functions provided in the computer system. An example of this is the American Heritage online dictionary (Houghton Mifflin, 1990) shown in Fig. 2.8. Such dictionaries are distinguished from the translational resources in the same way that a dictionary differs from a glossary. Glossaries cover only the germane vocabulary and the definitions are context specific. Dictionaries are generalized because of their much larger vocabulary and the definitions cover many possible meanings.

EXAMPLES OF SUPPORTED TEXT

Aesop in ASL

Aesop in ASL: Four Fables Told in American Sign Language (Texas School for the Deaf, 1996) is an example of a supported text document designed to provide resources for students

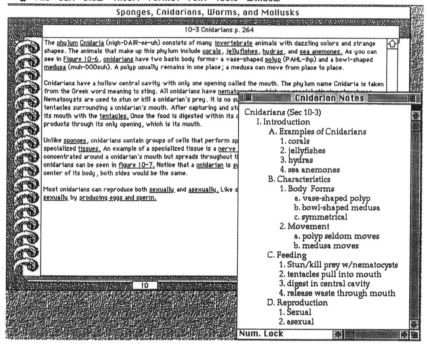

FIG. 2.7.   Notational resource using electronic outliner.

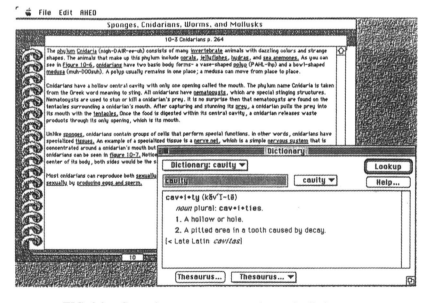

FIG. 2.8.   General purpose resource, electronic dictionary.

FIG. 2.9. "Fox and the Grapes" from *Aesop in ASL*.

with hearing impairments. The CD-ROM presents four of Aesop's fables, each told in a multimedia format combining text, animation, sound, and video. A page from "Fox and the Grapes" is shown in Fig. 2.9. As each page is turned, a short animation depicts the action described in the text. If readers click the lips icon (lower left), the text is voiced phrase by phrase. The ASL icon opens a video window and the text is both signed and voiced. In this way the text is supported by an illustrative resource (the animation) and two sets of translational resources (spoken text and ASL).

Each story also anchors a set of instructional resources with activities on pronouns, sequencing, vocabulary, synonyms, and comprehension. Figure 2.10 shows the synonym activity where students match an English word with an ASL synonym. In most of these activities students are asked to directly translate between English and ASL, or the activity is supported by ASL or spoken translations. Thus, *Aesop in ASL* is an example of supported text emphasizing the use of translational and instructional resources.

Edgar Allan Poe: Selected Works

There are a large number of CD-ROMs on the commercial market containing supported text versions of popular literary works. *Edgar Allan Poe: Selected Works* by Bookworm Software (Poe, 1996) is a good example. This CD-ROM contains electronic versions of six poems and stories by Poe, each of which is infused with a large set of resources keyed directly to words and phrases in the basic text. Figure 2.11 presents the second page from "The Tell-Tale Heart." Although it is not obvious in the figure, some of the text is black and some is red. The red words are linked to resources, many of which provide some sort of commentary on the text (a supplementary resource), like the annotation on this page calling attention to the theme of sanity or insanity that pervades the author's words. The resources can also be reached via an index (see Fig. 12.2) that allows readers to conduct searches for resources matching particular themes, media types, and sources. In addition,

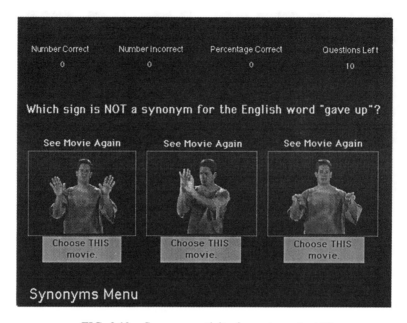

FIG. 2.10.   Synonym activity from *Aesop in ASL*.

the tool pallet in the upper left of the screen provides several notational tools including bookmarks, margin notes, text highlighting, and an electronic notebook. These notations are kept in individual student files, and the teacher can maintain a file of similar notations to be inserted into the text as instructional resources.

In contrast to *Aesop in ASL*, these electronic versions of Poe's works provide a broad range of translational, illustrative, notational, and supplementary supports for the basic

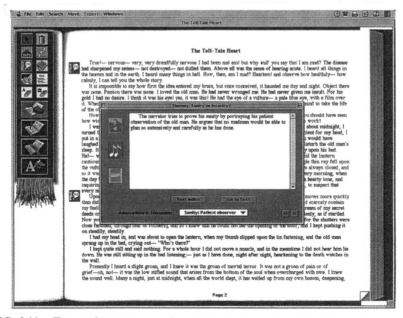

FIG. 2.11.   Text and commentary from "The Telltale Heart" in *Edgar Allan Poe: Selected Works*.

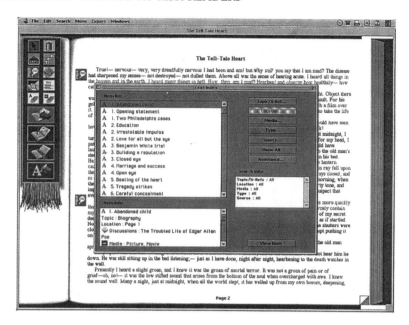

FIG. 2.12.   Index for "The Tell-Tale Heart" in *Edgar Allan Poe: Selected Works.*

text. The emphasis, however, is clearly on supplementary resources designed to present readers with a wide range of literary commentary and notational resources designed to support students' active processing of text.

The Planets

The document shown in Fig. 2.13 is an electronic version of a chapter entitled "Motion in Space" from a third-grade science book (Barman et al., 1989). It was created with the ElectroText Authoring System (Anderson-Inman et al., 1994) as part of Project LITERACY-HI. This document was designed to be read from a laptop computer by mainstreamed students with hearing impairments. The basic text from the chapter has been paginated according to the topic structure provided in the textbook and is presented in a series of screen displays such as shown in Fig. 2.13. Readers navigate among the pages using commands either from the menu bar or from one of the tool pallets on the right.

Underlined words are keys that, when selected, open a window containing icons representing the resources available for that word or phrase. The resources are accessed by selecting the icon that represents the desired resource. Figure 2.14 shows some of the resources available for three different keys: "every 24 hours and 36 minutes," "100 times less," and "craters." Every key is supported with at least two translational resources, a pronunciation, and a text-based definition. Some keys have translations into ASL as well. Other keys are supported with illustrative or supplementary resources such as the picture of a crater and an animation that compares the rotation times of Earth and Mars.

Two forms of notational resources are available from the menu bar. Readers can insert annotations into the text in the form of electronic "post-its." They can also type notes into an electronic notebook. Teachers can use these same tools to provide instructional resources. Instructional and summarizing resources supporting each page of text are also available from the resources pallet in the upper right of the screen. Like the Bookworm

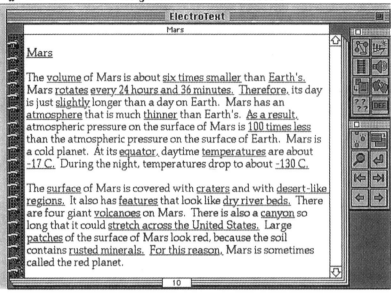

FIG. 2.13. Text and keys on planets from *Addison-Wesley Science*.

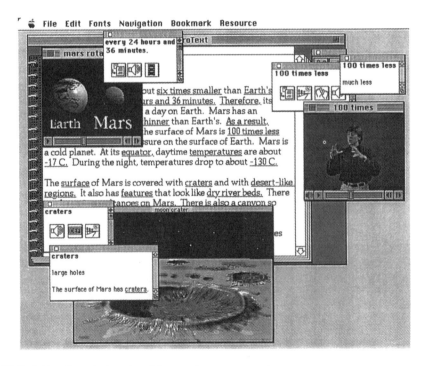

FIG. 2.14. Translational and illustrative resources for a chapter on planets from *Addison-Wesley Science*.

documents described earlier, ElectroText documents such as this one on planets present the reader with a wide range of supportive resources. The concentration here, however, is more on translational and illustrative resources than supplementary resources.

READING SUPPORTED TEXT

The electronic reading environments described in the previous section vary on a wide range of dimensions. Most obvious is the presentation system used to present the text to the reader. For some, the presentation system mimics that of a book, at least superficially. For others, the book metaphor has been abandoned in favor of a more multimedialike appearance. Also obvious is that developers have chosen to support the reader with different types of embedded resources tied to different types of keys. As one might expect, the reading experiences of students using these very different hypermedia documents will vary enormously.

The same is true for different students reading the same document. Different students will approach any given document with different types of preparation, different expectations, and different levels of expertise in the skills required for comprehending what they are reading. Students also vary on their levels of motivation, their persistence, and their interest in the topic. With all these differences, is there anything we can conclude about the experience of reading supported text and its effects on at-risk readers? Over the last 5 years we have been exploring the reading patterns and strategies of students as they interact with various types of supported text. Key to our understanding of what students are doing when they engage the text presented to them in electronic reading environments has been an electronic monitor that records all user interactions with the presentation system, its keys, and its resources. Transcripts of these interactions are then analyzed in order to describe, and eventually draw conclusions about, what students do when they read electronically supported text. The following three sections share some of the conclusions that we have reached during these investigations.

Patterns and Profiles

The ElectroText Project was a 3-year descriptive study exploring the use of supported text with at-risk readers in a local middle school (Anderson-Inman, Horney, Chen, & Lewin, 1994). Using an early version of the ElectroText Authoring System, we created hypermedia documents for several short stories targeted for study in a literature class designed for students with low reading levels. The electronic documents contained four major types of supportive resources: (a) translational resources in the form of definitions and pronunciations for words likely to be unfamiliar, (b) illustrative resources in the form of pictures, (c) summarizing resources in the form of time lines and graphic overviews, and (d) instructional resources in the form of questions designed to help students understand the author's craft and monitor their comprehension of the text. Students read the hypermedia versions of the targeted short stories instead of reading them in print, accessing the embedded, supportive resources as they felt the desire or need to do so. An electronic monitor recorded their interactions with the documents and was analyzed to determine the patterns and profiles of at-risk readers within this specific presentation system.

A review of the monitor transcripts revealed at least six distinctly different patterns for interacting with the text (Horney & Anderson-Inman, 1994). These are:

- Skimming: Moving through the text at a pace too fast for reading or studying.

- Checking: Moving through the text and/or resources systematically, checking things out, but apparently not reading or responding.
- Reading: Moving through the text systematically, visiting pages long enough to read the text but with little or no use of supporting resources.
- Responding: Accessing one or more of the interactive resources and writing responses.
- Studying: Moving through the text systematically, visiting pages long enough to read the text, and using resources in an integrated manner.
- Reviewing: Moving systematically through text that has previously been read, re-reading pages, and/or revisiting resources.

A detailed analysis of when and to what extent students adopted the various reading patterns described led to the following conclusions: (a) students with access to supported text used the studying pattern more frequently than any other pattern, (b) students with access to supported text adopted different patterns at different times, (c) students with access to supported text differed on when in the reading process they employed the various patterns, and (d) reading patterns seemed to vary as a function of the resources available and students' experience with the electronic reading environment.

During the following year, we used more sophisticated versions of the electronic short stories in an attempt to define specific reader "profiles" and compare these profiles with students' levels of comprehension and satisfaction with electronic reading (Anderson-Inman & Horney, 1993). Using results from the electronic monitor, combined with comprehension information obtained from verbal story retells, we concluded that the class contained at least three different types of supported-text readers: book lovers, studiers, and resource junkies.

Book lovers used the electronic reading environment fairly superficially, often interacting with the embedded resources on the first few pages and then abandoning them for a more sequential, linear reading of the document. During the verbal story retells, it was clear that book lovers understood the general plot of the stories but missed many smaller, and more subtle, details. When asked what they thought about reading on the computer, they said they preferred books, often giving reasons that included some mention of books' physical nature. *Studiers* used the electronic reading environment in depth and accessed many types of supportive resources throughout their reading of stories. When asked, studiers were able to provide extremely detailed and accurate story retells and they indicated a high degree of enjoyment concerning the experience of reading on computer. *Resource junkies*, on the other hand, did not take the experience of electronic reading seriously. They were enamored with some of the resources (particularly the digitized pronunciations) and spent much of their time searching for the types of resources they liked. Story retells for this group were weak to nonexistent. Although these students expressed a favorable attitude toward electronic reading, their explanations usually focused on the novelty of the resources, not their utility. In short, we concluded that students approached the task of reading supported text in different ways and with different expectations. Those who took it seriously and used the resources provided to assist their understanding demonstrated superior comprehension of the stories they read.

Strategies for Resource Use

The previous section described our experiences using supported text with at-risk students found to have low reading levels. Some of these students had learning disabilities, but the majority did not. In the following two sections, we describe our experiences working with students who have hearing impairments. Project LITERACY-HI, as described earlier in this chapter, was a 3-year federally funded project designed to explore the efficacy of supported text within hypermedia versions of students' content-area reading materials. Unlike the ElectroText Project, where resources were embedded into examples of narrative writing, most of the documents produced in Project LITERACY-HI were examples of expository text. Although documents varied in the number and type of resources available, most documents included resources representing all of the general types described earlier in this chapter.

Analysis of pilot data (Horney & Anderson-Inman, 1995) revealed that students with hearing impairments could successfully use the electronic reading environments but needed significant instruction and support during the process in order to do so. For example, an eighth-grade student named Maria (whose interactions with supported text are described in detail in Horney & Anderson-Inman, 1995) was provided with three sessions of instruction on how to navigate within an ElectroText document. Following this, she was provided with guided assistance as she read her first document, with the intent of demonstrating how the resources could be used to enhance her understanding of the material being read. When left to read independently, she continued through the text with apparent purpose, but did not access any of the supportive resources. From questions asked by her teacher, a specialist for students with hearing impairments, it was clear that Maria did not understand what she was reading. Renewed guidance on how and when to access the resources prompted her to use the supported-text features of the document, resulting in an apparent recognition of their value. This led to frequent independent use of the resources and a solid understanding of the document's content. With this one student we were able to observe at least three different strategies for resource use: (a) resource avoidance, (b) reading with prompted resource use, and (c) reading with independent resource use (Horney, Anderson-Inman, & Chen, 1995).

Examination of resource use data across the six students who participated in the pilot studies of Project LITERACY-HI also led to preliminary conclusions about when and in what sequence these students tended to use the resources made available to them (Horney & Anderson-Inman, 1995). For example, students tended to use graphic resources (pictures, animations, video) more often than text resources, and they chose graphic resources first if they were available. However, if students knew sign language, the first resource selected was the ASL translation. Students also made good use of the digitized pronunciations, often repeating them frequently in an effort to establish the word in their vocabulary.

Real-Time Readers

The last phase of Project LITERACY-HI was devoted to examining how well students could make use of computer-based versions of textbooks in their actual classes. To investigate this we selected two students, prepared ElectroText documents based on chapters from their textbooks, provided these documents to the students on laptop computers, provided the students with technical support in their classrooms to ensure the proper functioning of the electronic textbooks, and collected data from a variety of sources about the students' experiences. We are now engaged in the analysis of these data.

Students. The earlier phases of the project involved a total of 13 students. From this pool we selected two, Sean and Craig, to serve as real-time readers. The selection process was driven by the characteristics of the students and also by the classes the students were scheduled to take. We looked for students in classes where the teachers planned to use a strong textbook, expected students to read regularly from these books, and had lesson plans sufficiently well established to predict in advance what parts of the textbook would be used and when. This last requirement was driven by the long lead time necessary to create the necessary ElectroText resources for the supported documents.

Sean attended a small, K–12 rural school and we targeted his social studies class for ElectroText documents. This was a combination sixth- and seventh-grade class taught by Mr. Hughes, who also was to be Sean's science teacher. Mr. Hughes taught with a secondary school orientation using regular lectures, reading assignments, and tests. He was a strict disciplinarian and Sean had some difficulty in adjusting to his new grade level, to Mr. Hughes' expectations and teaching style, and to the course content. Sean received a variety of supplementary support services from the school. Once a week he was visited by a teacher of the hearing impaired, who provided tutoring, language development activities, and general assistance for succeeding in school. At midyear, Sean also began receiving assistance from a special education teacher.

Craig attended a moderate-sized middle school in a small city, and we created ElectroText documents for his science class. His science teacher, Mr. Daniels, taught Craig's health class during the fall term and biological science in the spring term. Like Sean, Craig received support from an itinerant teacher for the hearing impaired. Additionally, he was assigned a sign language interpreter. Craig's general reading and academic skills were higher than Sean's and he was considered a successful student.

Documents.   The course curriculum for Sean's social studies class was based on a 1991 textbook, *Eastern Hemisphere* (Beyer et al., 1991). From this book we selected four chapters for ElectroText conversion incorporating a wide variety of resources. The bulk of these resources were in the form of text-based translational definitions and rewordings of words and phrases judged to be problematic by Sean's support teachers. In addition, all of the keys were supported by digital pronunciations. There was also a strong selection of illustrative maps, pictures of historic sites, individuals and artifacts, and a summarizing time line.

Three chapters from Craig's biology book, *Exploring Life Science* (Maton et al., 1995), were transformed into ElectroText documents for him to read. As with Sean, the bulk of the resources provided for Craig were in the form of text and auditory translations. In addition, there were many illustrations taken from the original text and from an accompanying laserdisc. We did not include any sign language translations for Craig despite his use of that communication channel. This was decided after consultations with the supervisor of ASL interpreters who designed the sign language resource in other ElectroText documents. She decided that the general lack of broadly accepted signs for technical terms in science made it unlikely that Craig would benefit from the ASL translational resources we might construct.

Data Sources.   We collected data from several sources about the progress Sean and Craig made with their electronic textbooks. We had field notes kept by project staff and teachers who worked with the students, copies of the notes added to the electronic documents by the students, tests and assignments completed by the students for Mr. Hughes and Mr. Daniels, an additional set of comprehension tests for all chapters read by the students over the course of the year, and transcripts from a keystroke monitor that recorded the date and time of each student interaction with the documents. This last source provided our best data about what Sean and Craig actually did when they used the supported text documents in their content-area classes.

Observations. Although our analysis of these data is incomplete at this writing, we can make the following preliminary observations about the ability of these two students to make use of an electronically supported textbook in a general education classroom:

1. The students learned to use the ElectroText System relatively easily.
2. The students were able to reliably transport the computer to and from school.
3. The students were able to operate the computer within class satisfactorily, without disruption to or from their classmates.
4. During unsupervised reading, students made less use of supportive resources than their teachers thought necessary.
5. The students faced some difficulties coping with differences in pagination between their version of the text and the paper-based versions used by classmates.
6. The students' reading comprehension using electronic documents was equal to or better than their reading comprehension using regular textbooks.

THE FUTURE OF SUPPORTED TEXT

Our work in the area of supported text for at-risk readers leads us to propose a preliminary theory of electronic reading. Our belief is that if the following five statements are true, then electronic reading environments that provide readers with access to embedded resources in the form of supported text are beneficial to students and, therefore, their production and distribution should be encouraged. Our theory of electronic reading includes the following statements. Research on the truth of these statements is still in its infancy. Consequently, we have many more questions concerning the future of supported text and its potential effects on learners than we have answers.

1. Readers face cognitive challenges as they construct meaning from text and these challenges intensify when readers move from learning to read to reading to learn. It will be important to understand more fully the types of cognitive challenges faced by different types of at-risk readers during their attempts to read different types of material. Sample research questions might include: In what ways are the cognitive challenges the same or different for readers who are deaf and readers who come from a non-English-speaking background? To what extent are the cognitive challenges the same or different when students are asked to read a social studies text as compared to a science text? To what extent are the cognitive challenges inherent in expository text more difficult for students than those inherent in basal readers?

2. Electronic text can be transformed to include embedded resources that support readers as they face these cognitive challenges. It will be important to identify usable interfaces for bringing supported text to students, as well as the types of resources most likely to assist students facing various types of cognitive challenges. Sample research questions might include: What are the advantages and disadvantages of maintaining a book metaphor for electronic reading environments with supported text? How is supported text best distributed to students? What design rules should be followed in constructing the types

of resources that constitute supported text? For a given chunk of problematic text, is an array of alternative resources more or less effective than a single resource? How do different distribution mechanisms (e.g., the World Wide Web as opposed to CD-ROM) affect the design specifications of supported text?

3. Readers who have access to electronically supported text can read and study materials more effectively than would otherwise be possible, providing access to text that would normally be beyond their ability. It will be important to determine what types of training are required for students to use supported text and the effects of having access to supported text on students' patterns of reading and studying. Sample research questions might include: To what extent and in what ways do students need to be trained to use supported text for the purposes of reading and studying? Do certain types of students need instructional cuing in order to benefit from supported text. What are the benefits of having access to supported text on students' reading and study behavior? What types of supported text have the greatest impact on increasing student access to content-area reading materials?

4. Readers who use electronically supported text in a purposeful effort to comprehend what they are reading will demonstrate increased comprehension. It will be important to identify what constitutes purposeful and effective use of supported text and how this can be facilitated. Sample research questions might include: To what extent and in what ways is reading within a supported text environment motivating to students? What instructional contexts encourage purposeful use of supported text? How can students' reading behavior in a supported text environment be monitored? What are the effects of accessing supportive resources on students' reading comprehension?

5. The general reading and literacy skills of students who use supported text will improve. It will be important to determine the possible long-term benefits of reading supported text on students' overall reading skills and content literacy. Sample research questions might include: Are students able to transfer information found in supportive resources (e.g., vocabulary definitions) to nonelectronic reading environments? Does long-term access to supported text promote increased levels of independent reading? Does access to supported text documents improve students' abilities to read nonsupported text? What strategies should be employed to encourage students to apply the reading skills developed in a supported text environment to other situations?

Providing at-risk readers with supported text is a beginning step toward understanding how we can construct documents that are accessible and comprehensible to the broadest possible audience. At present, most investigations into the use of supported text have targeted one specific population and provided a few well-chosen resources designed to support their reading comprehension. We envision an era in which all electronic documents are constructed in such a way that they are accessible and supportive to a broad range of readers worldwide.

In this we are encouraged by the ongoing development of the Internet in general and especially the World Wide Web. We feel the Web provides distinctive advantages for the creation and distribution of all kinds of supported text discussed in this chapter. In particular the Web allows:

- Distribution to anyone with Internet services (admittedly this is still far from universal distribution, but given the problems in distributing computer software in any form, the difficulties seem no worse and the potential far greater).

- Easy maintenance and updating (because there is only one copy, changes are instantly available to everyone, everywhere).

- Platform independence (no more problems finding the Mac version or the Windows version or the UNIX version, etc.).
- Interconnectivity with all the myriad of other resources available on the Internet (no more reinventing the wheel).

If research shows that supported text provides at-risk readers with real advantages, and if the Web proves a realistic distribution mechanism, what changes might there be in the roles that teachers and students play and how might instructional environments change? We foresee four major developments. First, well-designed and easily accessible electronic text materials might well free teachers from having to spend large amounts of instructional time teaching the text. In many of today's classrooms, teachers cannot assume that students have read their textbooks or, if they have, that they understood what they read. Uncertainty over student understanding of texts leads to teachers' summarizing the important concepts in class, and even walking students through the text, highlighting main ideas. If teachers can rely on supportive electronic text materials to better assist students with basic comprehension of key concepts, they would be free to devote more of their instructional time to going beyond the text. In short, there would be less class time spent on literal comprehension of the text and more time to devote to higher level thinking and reflection.

Second, well-designed, electronically enhanced text materials have the potential to provide teachers with tools for meeting the learning needs of classrooms with a diverse student body. Universally accessible and universally supportive textbooks would allow a broader range of students to participate in the mainstream of instructional activities. Students who might otherwise have required special materials, and so a special curriculum, and so a special teacher, and so a special schedule, can be integrated with their peers in more instructionally meaningful ways. In addition, the same authoring system that enables developers to embed supportive resources for different types of at-risk readers can be used to embed enrichment resources for high-achieving students. The Web is already being used to develop and distribute large-scale study environments containing multiple interlinked documents and thousands of resources designed to extend as well as support student learning (Anderson-Inman & Horney, 1997). In short, electronically enhanced text materials can be both sufficiently challenging for top students and sufficiently supportive for those struggling with basic concepts.

Third, a new range of original source documents might penetrate the regular curriculum. Such materials are often too difficult for most students, but if properly supported they might become generally accessible to a broader audience. As suggested by McKenna (chap. 3, this volume), supported text materials may force us to abandon our notion of readability in favor of a more functional and environmentally dependent assessment of the materials that are accessible to students. If the texts are well supported, science classes might read and discuss Einstein's original paper on relativity, or Watson and Crick's first description of the double helix. Social studies classes might read the original *Magna Carta*. And English classes might read the *Canterbury Tales* in Middle English or Edmund Spenser imitating Old English in *The Faerie Queen* (Spenser, 1596/1995). Imagine, for example, how much more comprehensible this excerpt from *The Faerie Queen* would be if enhanced with translational resources for the vocabulary and supplementary resources for the allusions:

Lo I the man, whose Muse whilome did maske,
As time her taught, in lowly Shepheards weeds,
Am now enforst a far vnfitter taske,
For trumpets sterne to chaunge mine Oaten reeds,

And sing of Knights and Ladies gentle deeds;
Whose prayses hauing slept in silence long,
Me, all too meane, the sacred Muse areeds
To blazon broad emongst her learned throng:
Fierce warres and faithfull loues shall moralize my song. (Book I, 11. xx–xx)

Fourth, the availability of an electronic library of considerate and dynamically supportive text materials might provide the alternative learning experiences necessary to support students' efforts to achieve the high academic standards embedded in this nation's reform initiatives. A standards-based curriculum places a new level of accountability on both teachers and students. Unfortunately, the educational system is ill equipped to handle the reteaching implied as necessary when students fail to achieve the standards set by their state and local school districts. Easily accessible and highly supportive text materials, distributed to schools via the Web, could play an important role in providing at-risk readers with alternative avenues to learning. The end result may be a significantly higher percentage of students going through school with the support they need to successfully reach the performance goals predictive of success in postsecondary educational and vocational environments.

In short, we believe that far from being the death of text, computers will help us to transform text in ways that address an objection put forward by Socrates at the very dawn of reading and writing:

I cannot help feeling that writing is unfortunately like painting; for the creations of the painter have the attitude of life, and yet if you ask them a question they preserve a solemn silence. And the same may be said of speeches. You would imagine that they had intelligence, but if you want to know anything and put a question to one of them, the speaker always gives one unvarying answer. . . .

Is there not another kind of word or speech far better than this? I mean an intelligent word graven in the soul of the learner, which can defend itself and knows when to speak and when to be silent. (Socrates in *Phaedrus*, cited in Jowett, 1952, p. 139)

Perhaps electronically enhanced text, embedded with a range of thoughtfully produced supportive resources, is a step closer to the more intelligent and dynamic writing desired by Socrates. Because of the many unique features of electronic text (Anderson-Inman & Reinking, in press), reading materials designed to be supportive of students' diverse needs may, in fact, give readers a learning environment that "knows when to speak and when to be silent."

REFERENCES

Algozzine, B., & Wood, K. (1994). *Teaching reading to high-risk learners: A unified perspective.* Boston: Allyn & Bacon.
Allen, V. G. (1991). Teaching bilingual and ESL children. In J. Flood, J. M. Jensen, D. Lapp, & J. R. Squire (Eds.), *Handbook of research on teaching the English language arts* (pp. 356–364). New York: Macmillan.
Allington, R. L. (1977). If they don't read much, how they ever gonna get good? *Journal of Reading, 21*, 57–61.
Allington, R. C., & McGill-Franzen, A. (1989). School responses to reading failure: Chapter one and special education students in grades 2, 4, and 8. *Elementary School Journal, 89*, 529–542.
American Social History Productions, Inc. (1993). *Who built America?: From the centennial celebration of 1876 to the great war of 1914.* [CD-ROM]. The Voyager Company.

Anderson-Inman, L., & Horney, M. A. (1993, April). *Profiles of hypertext readers: Case studies from the ElectroText project.* Paper presented at the annual conference of the American Educational Research Association, Atlanta, GA.

Anderson-Inman, L., & Horney, M. A. (1997). *Anza multimedia project: Designing and distributing a web-based study environment* (Grant proposal funded by the National Endowment for the Humanities). Eugene, OR: Center for Advanced Technology in Education, University of Oregon.

Anderson-Inman, L., Horney, M. A., Chen, D., & Corrigan, W. (1994). ElectroText authoring system [Computer software]. Eugene, OR: Center for Electronic Studying.

Anderson-Inman, L., Horney, M. A., Chen, D. T., & Lewin, L. (1994). Hypertext literacy: Observations from the ElectroText project. *Language Arts, 71*(4), 279–287.

Anderson-Inman, L., & Reinking, D. (in press). Learning from text in a post-typographic world. In C. Hynd, S. Stahl, B. Britton, M. Carr, & S. Glynn (Eds.), *Learning from text across conceptual domains in secondary schools.* Mahwah, NJ: Lawrence Erlbaum Associates.

Anderson-Inman, L., & Tenny, J. (1989). Electronic studying: Information organizers to help students study "better" not "harder"—Part I. *The Computing Teacher, 16*(8), 33–36.

Applebee, A. N. (1984). *Contexts for learning to write: Studies of secondary school instruction.* Norwood, NJ: Ablex.

Armbruster, B. B. (1984). The problem of "inconsiderate text." In G. Duffy, L. Roehler, & J. Mason (Eds.), *Comprehension instruction: Perspectives and suggestions* (pp. 202–217). New York: Longman.

Armbruster, B. B., & Anderson, T. H. (1981a). *Content area textbooks* (Reading Education Rep. No. 23). Urbana, IL: Center for the Study of Reading.

Armbruster, B. B., & Anderson, T. H. (1981b, November). Research synthesis on study skills. *Educational Leadership, 39*, 154–156.

Askov, E. N., & Kamm, K. (1982). *Study skills in the content areas.* Boston: Allyn & Bacon.

Barman, C., DiSpezio, M., Guthrie, V., Leyden, M. B., Mercier, S., & Ostlund, K. (1989). *Addison-Wesley Science.* Menlo Park, CA: Addison-Wesley.

Beyer, B. K., Craven, J., McFarland, M. A., & Parker, W. C. (1991). *United States and its neighbors.* New York: Macmillan/McGraw-Hill School.

Bigge, J. L. (1991). *Teaching individuals with physical and multiple disabilities* (3rd ed.). Columbus, OH: Merrill.

Britton, B. K., Gulgoz, S., & Glynn, S. (1993). Impact of good and poor writing on learners: Research and theory. In B. K. Britton, A. Woodward, & M. Brinkley (Eds.), *Learning from textbooks: Theory and practice* (pp. 1–46). Hillsdale, NJ: Lawrence Erlbaum Associates.

Burke, J. (1985). *The day the universe changed.* Boston: Little, Brown.

Center, Y., & Ward, J. (1984). Integration of mildly handicapped cerebral palsied children into regular schools. *The Exceptional Child, 31*(2), 104–113.

Chall, J. S., Jacobs, V. A., & Baldwin, L. E. (1990). *The reading crisis: Why poor children fall behind.* Cambridge, MA: Harvard University Press.

Conrad, R. (1977). The reading ability of deaf school-leavers. *British Journal of Educational Psychology, 47*, 138–148.

Dolson, D. P. (1985). The effects of Spanish home language use on the scholastic performance of Hispanic pupils. *Journal of Multilingual Multicultural Development, 6*, 135–155.

Farmer, M. E., Klein, R., & Bryson, S. E. (1992). Computer-assisted reading: Effects of whole-word feedback on fluency and comprehension in readers with severe disabilities. *Remedial and Special Education, 13*, 50–60.

Gallaudet Research Institute. (1985). *Gallaudet Research Institute Newsletter.* Washington, DC: Gallaudet College.

Graubard, P. S. (1971). Relationship between academic achievement and behavior dimensions. *Exceptional Children, 37*, 755–756.

Group Logic. (1994). *Aspects* [Computer software]. Arlington, VA: Author.

Hansen, E., Mounty, J., & Baird, A. (1994). Interactive video and sign language for improving literacy skills of deaf students. In T. Ottman & I. Tomek (Eds.), *Educational multimedia and hypermedia* (pp. 241–245). Charlottesville, VA: Association for the Advancement of Computing in Education.

Hanson, V. L., & Padden, C. A. (1990). Computers and videodisc technology for bilingual ASL/English instruction of deaf children. In D. Nix & R. Spiro (Eds.), *Cognition, education and multimedia: Exploring ideas in high technology* (pp. 49–63). Hillsdale, NJ: Lawrence Erlbaum Associates.

Harris, J. (1997). *Electronic emissary project* [Online]. Available: http://www.tapr.org/emissary/.

Hodgkinson, H. (1991). Reform versus reality. *Phi Delta Kappan, 73*(1), 334–339.

Holt, J. A. (1993). Standard achievement test–8th edition: Reading comprehension subgroup results. *American Annals of the Deaf, 138*, 172–175.

Horney, M. A., & Anderson-Inman, L. (1994). The ElectroText project: Hypertext reading patterns of middle school students. *Journal of Educational Multimedia and Hypermedia, 3*(1), 71–91.

Horney, M. A., & Anderson-Inman, L. (1995). Hypermedia for readers with hearing impairments: Promoting literacy with electronic text enhancements. In C. Kinzer, K. Hinchman, & D. Leu (Eds.), *The forty-third yearbook of the National Reading Conference* (pp. 448–458). Chicago: National Reading Conference.

Horney, M. A., Anderson-Inman, L., & Chen, D. T. (1995, April). *Analysis of interactive reading strategies in a hypertext reading environment*. Paper presented at the annual meeting of the American Educational Research Association, San Francisco, CA.

Houghton Mifflin. (1990). American heritage electronic dictionary (Vers. 1.0) [Computer software]. Cambridge, MA: Author.

Jowett, B. (Trans.). (1952). *The dialogues of Plato*. Chicago: Encyclopedia Britannica.

Juel, C. (1988). Learning to read and write: A longitudinal study of 54 children from first through fourth grades. *Journal of Educational Psychology, 80*, 437–447.

King, C. M., & Quigley, S. P. (1985). *Reading and deafness*. San Diego, CA: College-Hill.

Kirsch, I. S., Jungeblut, A., Jenkins, L., & Kolstad, A. (1993, September). *Adult literacy in America: A first look at the results of the national adult literacy survey* (Vol. 17). Washington, DC: U.S. Department of Education, National Center for Education Statistics.

L'Amour, L. (1989). *Education of a wandering man*. New York: Bantam.

LaSasso, C. J. (1993). Reading comprehension of deaf readers: The impact of too many or too few questions. *American Annals of the Deaf, 138*, 435–441.

Lowenbraun, S., & Thompson, M. D. (1986). Hearing impairments. In N. G. Haring & L. McCormick (Eds.), *Exceptional children and youth: An introduction to special education* (4th ed., pp. 357–395). Columbus, OH: Merrill.

MacArthur, C. A., & Haynes, J. B. (1995). Student assistant for learning from text (SALT): A hypermedia reading aid. *Journal of Learning Disabilities, 28*(3), 150–159.

Macmillan, D. L., & Forness, S. R. (1992). Mental retardation. In M. C. Alkin (Ed.), *Encyclopedia of educational research* (Vol. 3, pp. 825–830). New York: Macmillan.

Marchiarola, F. (1988). Values, standards and climate in schools serving children at risk. In D. W. Hornbeck (Ed.), *Schools success for students at risk: Analysis and recommendations of the council of chief state school officers* (pp. 13–24). Orlando, FL: Harcourt, Brace, Jovanovich.

Maton, A., Hopkins, J., Johnson, S., LaHart, D., Warner, M. Q., & Wright, J. D. (1995). *Exploring life science*. Englewood Cliffs, NJ: Prentice-Hall.

McConkie, G. W., & Zola, D. (1985, April). *Computer-aided reading: An environment for developmental research*. Paper presented at the meeting of the Society for Research in Child Development, Toronto.

McKenna, M. C., & Robinson, R. D. (1990). Content literacy: A definition and implications. *Journal of Reading, 34*(3), 184–186.

Mikulecky, L. (1982). Job literacy: The relationship between school preparation and workplace actuality. *Reading Research Quarterly, 17*, 400–419.

Miller, W. H. (1993). *What are learning disabilities? The complete reading disabilities* (The Emerging Worldwide Electronic University Handbook, pp. 1–31). West Nyack, NY: The Center for Applied Research in Education.

Minami, M., & Ovando, C. J. (1995). Language issues in multicultural contexts. In J. A. Banks & C. A. M. Banks (Eds.), *Handbook of research on multicultural education* (pp. 427–444). New York: Macmillan.

Myers, J. W. (1984). *Writing to learn across the curriculum*. Bloomington, IN: Phi Delta Kappa.

National Assessment of Educational Progress. (1985). *The reading report card: Progress toward excellence in our schools. Trends in reading over four national assessments, 1971–1984* (Report No. 15-R-01). Princeton, NJ: NAEP.

National School Network. (1997). National school network exchange [Online]. Available: http://nsn.bbn.com/.

Olson, R., Foltz, G., & Wise, B. (1986). Reading instruction and remediation with the aid of computer speech. *Behavior Research Methods, Instruments, and Computers, 18*, 93–99.

Pallas, A. M. (1989). The changing nature of the disadvantaged population: Current dimensions and future trends. *Educational Researcher, 18*(5), 16–22.

Paul, P. V., & Quigley, S. P. (1990). *Education and deafness*. White Plains, NY: Longman.

Poe, E. A. (1996). *Edgar Allan Poe: Selected works* [Computer software]. Lothian, MD: BIT/Bookworm.

Prinz, P. M. (1991). Literacy and language development within microcomputer-videodisc-assisted contexts. *Journal of Childhood Communication Disorders, 14*(1), 67–80.

Reinking, D., & Schreiner, R. (1985). The effects of computer-mediated text on measures of reading comprehension and reading behavior. *Reading Research Quarterly, 20*(5), 536–552.

Reitsma, P. (1988). Reading practice for beginners: Effects of guided reading, reading-while-listening, and independent reading with computer-based speech feedback. *Reading Research Quarterly, 23*(5), 219–235.

Richardson, V., Cassanova, U., Placier, M., & Guilfoyle, K. (1988). *School children at-risk*. Bristol, PA: Falmer.

Rigg, P., & Allen, V. (1992). *When they don't all speak English*. Urbana, IL: National Councils of Teachers of English.

Snider, V. E., & Tarver, S. G. (1987). The effect of early reading failure on acquisition of knowledge among students with learning disabilities. *Journal of Learning Disabilities, 20*(6), 351–356, 373.

Spear-Swerling, L., & Sternberg, R. J. (1994). The road not taken: An integrative theoretical model of reading disability. *Journal of Learning Disabilities, 27*(2), 91–103, 122.

Spenser, E. (1892). *The complete works in verse and prose of Edmund Spenser*. London: Grosart. HTML markup by Bear, R. (1995). Eugene: University of Oregon. Available at http://darkwing.uoregon.edu/~rbear/fqintro.html. (Original work published 1596)

Stanovich, K. E. (1985). Cognitive determinants of reading in mentally retarded individuals. In N. R. Ellis & N. W. Wray (Eds.), *International review of research in mental retardation* (pp. 181–214). New York: Academic Press.

Stanovich, K. E. (1986). Matthew effects in reading: Some consequences of individual differences in the acquisition of literacy. *Reading Research Quarterly, 21*, 360–406.

Texas School for the Deaf. (1996). *Aesop in ASL: Four fables told in American sign language* [Computer software]. Austin, TX: Author.

Torgesen, J. K., Water, M. D., Cohen, A. L., & Torgesen, J. L. (1988). Improving sight-word recognition skills in LD children: An evaluation of three computer program variations. *Learning Disabled Quarterly, 11*, 125–132.

Vacca, R. T., & Padak, N. D. (1990, April). Who's at risk in reading? *Journal of Reading, 34*, 486–488.

Vacca, R. T., & Vacca, J. A. (1989). *Content area reading* (3rd ed.). Glenview, IL: Scott, Foresman.

Webster, A. (1988). Deafness and learning to read 2: Teaching strategies. *Journal of the British Association of Teachers of the Deaf, 12*, 93–101.

WGBH. (1996). WGBH Educational Foundation [Online]. Available: http://www.boston.com/wgbh/.

Williams, P. L., Reese, C. M., Campbell, J. R., Mazzeo, J., & Phillips, G. W. (1995). *NAEP 1994 reading: A first look* (rev. ed., Vol. 1995 O-402-235). Washington, DC: U.S. Government Printing Office.

Wong Fillmore, L., & Valadez, C. (1986). Teaching bilingual learners. In M. C. Wittrock (Ed.), *Handbook of research on teaching* (3rd ed., pp. 648–685). New York: Macmillan.

3

▼▼▼▼▼▼▼

Electronic Texts and the Transformation of Beginning Reading

Michael C. McKenna
Georgia Southern University

Some of the more provocative distinctions between electronic and printed text that have been discussed in this section, such as the availability of multiple text segments linked in hypertext networks, may have only limited relevance to the circumstances of the beginning reader. It is in the area of electronic resources, designed to support the novice, that textual transformations have their greatest significance in primary classrooms. Anderson-Inman and Horney (chap. 2, this volume) have described how such resources can support the attempts of students experiencing reading problems to negotiate text in the absence of teacher assistance. A more limited set of such resources, including digitized pronunciations of words and oral renderings of larger language units, present educators with a host of issues that will grow in significance as the availability of electronic trade books continues to expand. In this chapter, I examine these issues, clarify central questions, and offer preliminary suggestions.

DEVELOPMENTAL CONTEXT OF THE BEGINNING READER

By the time children reach first grade, the emergence of literate behavior is already evident in most. Children exposed to print in literate homes and nurturing kindergartens will have developed familiarity with many of the conventions of print, such as reading from left to right and from top to bottom and the use of spacing to denote word boundaries. These children typically will have developed the ability to identify letters reliably, and they will possess some awareness of phonemes and possibly a rudimentary knowledge of letter–sound relations. They will also have acquired a speaking and listening vocabulary of several thousand words and a working knowledge of various syntactic structures, making them accomplished at communicating orally (Adams, 1990; Sulzby & Teale, 1991).

Typically, however, they are unable to recognize printed words, with the exception of a limited set of environmentally dependent words (e.g., *McDonald's*). Such readers are poised at the threshhold of the initial stage of reading development proposed by Chall

(1983), the stage at which basic decoding knowledge is acquired. Eventually, this knowledge will become second nature, so much so that its application will in most cases be both unconscious and automatic, freeing attention and conscious mental effort for the task of comprehension (e.g., Adams, 1990; Rayner & Pollatsek, 1989; Stanovich, 1991). Until this point of automatic decoding and fluency is reached, word recognition will constitute a major bottleneck in the child's efforts to negotiate text. At this stage, in order to proceed through unfamiliar material, the child must rely on the assistance of more accomplished readers, such as a teacher, a parent, an older sibling, or an abler peer. In short, attempts to read must be heavily supported if they are to be successful. In the conventional classroom, this necessity can create serious logistical problems because teachers are limited in the number of students they can assist individually, inevitably limiting the amount of actual reading undertaken by each child.

A helpful means of conceptualizing the plight of the beginning reader is the perspective known as the *simple view* of reading (Gough & Tunmer, 1986; Juel, Griffith, & Gough, 1985). According to this perspective, effective reading comprises two principal components: word recognition and listening comprehension. Although this view is by definition a simplification of the reading process, Gough and his colleagues acknowledge that each of these components is complex. The simple view is aligned with present-day conceptualizations of reading as a bottom-up process, one in which decoding is essentially modular (e.g., see Stanovich, 1991). That is, word recognition is performed by a *module*, a mental processing unit that in fluent reading uses letter knowledge to identify words and locate them in the reader's lexicon (that portion of long-term memory devoted to the storage of words and their meanings). Thus, when word recognition becomes automatic, the module can operate with little or no conscious control on the part of the reader. It supplies word meanings automatically, after rapid letter recognition leads to lexical access. For the beginning reader, however, not only does the subprocess of word recognition require conscious attention, but it frequently is unsuccessful in allowing the child to identify a word.

THEORETICAL PERSPECTIVES ON TALKING BOOKS

Talking books—electronic books equipped with digitized pronunciations of words and oral renderings of larger textual units—have the potential to remove the decoding bottle-neck facing beginning readers. By accessing pronunciations of words that are unfamiliar in print, beginning readers should be able to negotiate text at or near their listening comprehension level. This benefit can only be realized, of course, when the process of accessing pronunciations is sufficiently unobtrusive, the children having become accustomed to the process of clicking on troublesome words when reading. Whether youngsters can learn to access pronunciations without a significant impairment of comprehension is one of several important questions involving the utility of talking books. Equally important is whether the type of wide, independent reading made possible by an abundance of electronic books will lead to the incidental learning of words by sight and, beyond that, to increased facility at decoding unfamiliar words when assistance is unavailable.

The potential of talking books lies in the fact that the support they offer can make independent reading a reality long before decoding reaches the point of automaticity. This potential is supported by several theoretical perspectives that relate to how learning is nurtured in environments that are both supportive and challenging. The concept of scaf-folded instruction (Bruner, 1978), originally associated with the assistance provided by a teacher, can be extended to the support offered in electronic environments (see also Askov & Bixler, chap. 10, this volume). Child-accessed pronunciations are in fact one form of what might be called electronic scaffolding.

By facilitating the kind of interaction customarily associated with the teacher–student relationship, such scaffolding may also allow students to operate in their zone of proximal development (Vygotsky, 1978). Salomon, Globerson, and Guterman (1989), in making this case for computers used in literacy acquisition, suggested three qualities software must have in order to simulate the human interaction inherent in Vygotsky's idea. These include (a) modeling, (b) the activation of relevant cognitive operations, and (c) guidance. Their combined effect is the internalization of learning so that it can be applied in new settings independently. Although Salomon and his colleagues suggested that the third of these requirements has proven especially elusive in the design of software, talking books appear to offer at least one form of the humanlike guidance they envisioned. Although such books cannot, of course, substitute for very much of the human interaction needed to develop literacy, they do offer support similar to that a child might expect from a teacher during the process of reading aloud.

With respect to such support, talking books make possible a form of cognitive apprenticeship by permitting children to engage in a complex, authentic, and situated activity (reading) in which the support available to the child eventually fades (Brown, Collins, & Duguid, 1989). The fading, however, is controlled by the child: As proficiency increases, there will be less reliance on the pronunciations.

Talking books appear to be aligned with Vygotskian theory in other ways as well. By permitting children to access pronunciations at will, the power to read (or not) shifts to them and they are positioned to explore books on their own because of the mediation of technology. This shift of control to the child is central to Vygotsky's view of learning, and it is a feature inherent in talking books. Moreover, the likelihood of eventual networks of such books will permit exploration at a higher level—across as well as within books. Networks of this kind will have the potential of expanding the zone of proximal development (see Peters, 1996).

Last, the use of talking books seems conducive to the promotion of positive attitudes toward reading. When early reading experiences are associated with high levels of support and a high likelihood of success, children's beliefs about the outcomes of reading should be positive. Because such beliefs have a formative effect on attitudes toward reading (McKenna, 1994), the decoding bottleneck I have described can cause children to believe that reading is an inevitable source of frustration and failure. Long-term trends in reading attitude development indicate just such a widening gap between the best and poorest readers (McKenna, Kear, & Ellsworth, 1995), which is one manifestation of what Stanovich (1986) called a Matthew effect. Talking books may have the potential to bridge this gap before it widens appreciably and to preempt the effect before attitudes toward reading become substantially negative.

STUDIES OF THE USE OF TALKING BOOKS

Talking books are relatively new and have not been the focus of much research. The majority of existing investigations have examined their effectiveness with children 8 years old and older and who have experienced difficulties in learning to read. The results of these few studies have been uniformly positive. For example, Olson, Foltz, and Wise (1986) conducted an early study into the effects of talking books on both the comprehension and word recognition of disabled readers between 8 and 12 years of age. They reported clear advantages for children using such books. Lewin (1995) obtained comparable results for children 8 to 12 years old in England. Wise et al. (1989) reported similar decoding advantages for U.S. children 8 to 11 years old. Olofsson (1992) also reported advantages for a reading-disabled sample but observed greater benefits for children in Grade 4 and higher than for younger children. Miller, Blackstock, and Miller (1994) observed that with repeated readings of electronic trade books, 8-year-old children accessed pronunciations less frequently with each repeated reading. Their finding indirectly suggests growth in decoding, at least when electronic books are combined with repeated readings of text.

These results, although limited and not addressing directly the issues of sight word acquisition and decoding, were encouraging as a basis for planning a study of talking books with beginning readers funded through the National Reading Research Center (NRRC). The dearth of results obtained with children in kindergarten and first grade meant that such a study would be exploratory. A study by Reitsma (1988) was more directly related to the question. He found that Dutch first-grade students using electronic passages tended to learn targeted words more readily than students in comparison groups. Little was known, however, about the effects of extensive reading of electronic books by beginning readers.

In a series of three studies (McKenna & Watkins, 1994, 1995, 1996), children in ungraded K–1 classrooms read electronic books of first- and second-grade difficulty. In the initial study, the pronunciations that children accessed were linked to brief instructional feedback in the form of analogous words. For example, a child who clicked on the word *hat* would see the word *cat* momentarily appear just above it while a digitized voice said, "Hat—like cat." An analogy was provided for each syllable in multisyllabic words. Although such compare–contrast methods have been shown to be useful in decoding development (e.g., see Cunningham, 1995; Gaskins, Ehri, Cress, O'Hara, & Donnelly, 1996–1997), the phonics analogies proved to be far too intrusive. We found that many of the children were distracted to the point that they could not follow a story, and as a group they failed to outperform classroom controls on decoding measures.

A subsequent study limited the number of analogies by making them available only for regular one-syllable words. In addition, the analogies were rephrased so that the pronunciation of the word on which a child clicked came after the analogy to encourage children to attend to the analogy and not just to the pronunciations they were seeking. For example, a child clicking on the word *hat* would now hear, "Let's see, if c-a-t is cat, then h-a-t must be [pause] hat." Figure 3.1 presents a page from *Sheep in a Jeep* by Shaw (1988). It shows how the analogous word appeared over the textual word on which the child clicked. We found that under these conditions children using the electronic books significantly outperformed control-group children on two sight word measures. It is important to note that control children had experienced rather conventional classroom activities, such as self-selected reading, center time, and teacher-directed word study.

Another important finding also emerged from this second study. Because the children came from ungraded K–1 classrooms, some of the children were understandably limited in their knowledge of print conventions, the alphabet, and sight words. These children, although they reportedly enjoyed their experiences with the electronic books, made virtually no gains in terms of sight vocabulary. This finding suggested that a minimal level of literacy development must be attained before decoding benefits can reasonably be expected to accrue. Alphabet knowledge and a rudimentary sight vocabulary seem to be prerequisites for the reading of electronic books to result in incidental increases in sight vocabulary.

Uh-oh! The jeep won't go.

FIG. 3.1. Page from *Sheep in a Jeep* by Shaw (1988), copyright © 1988, showing a phonics analogy that was provided along with the pronunciation of the word *go*. Reprinted with permission.

In the third study, three electronic versions of 20 popular children's books were employed. The first was a listening version, in which text displayed on the screen was accompanied by a complete digitized oral reading of the text from beginning to end. The second version made available pronunciations of individual words on demand. None of the words, however, was accompanied by a phonics analogy. The third version added such analogies to regularly spelled, one-syllable words. We staggered the introduction of the electronic books to the children, beginning with the listening version to ensure familiarity with the story line, proceeding next to the pronunciation-only version, and finally to the analogy version. A tracking system was added to the computer program to allow us to monitor the number of times children accessed the pronunciations of specific words and the frequency with which they were exposed to phonics analogies.

This third study served as a modified replication of the second in examining the effects of electronic books on the sight word growth of beginning readers. The results were comparable to those of the second study in that those children beginning the study with at least a small sight vocabulary significantly outgained classroom controls. Two findings, however, were unexpected. First, we observed no relation between a child's tendency to learn a specific word and the number of times its pronunciation was accessed. Some children tended to access pronunciations even for words they had successfully identified during a preassessment, a phenomenon we refer to as *overaccessing*. Moreover, some children tended to identify words incorrectly as they read aloud the text on the screen, thus failing to access words even though they seemed to need the pronunciations. This happened frequently when semantically acceptable miscues were made. We refer to this phenomenon as *under-accessing*. It appeared that gains in students' ability to identify words by sight were due to the extensive reading these children did of the electronic books but not necessarily to the words accessed. Under- and overaccessing might well have contributed to this finding by masking a real effect.

The second unexpected finding was that the phonics analogies embedded in the text, introduced only after several exposures to a given book in order to reduce their intrusiveness into the comprehension process, did not lead children to generalize the analogy to an unfamiliar word. Exactly what kind of feedback to provide to children using talking books is an important consideration for software designers (Lewin, 1996), and the results of the third study in this series suggest that pronunciations alone—without hints, analogies, and other embedded instructional information—may be the best approach. Our attempt to contextualize phonics instruction and to associate it with teachable moments (identified, in effect, by the child reading the talking book) proved ineffective. It may well be that direct, systematic instruction in decoding, provided outside the context of talking books, will lead to better results, with the books themselves serving to provide the kind of extensive, scaffolded practice necessary for the attainment of fluency. We plan to investigate that possibility in future studies.

ISSUES AND IMPLICATIONS

Using talking books to assist beginning readers seems consistent with the idea that we are experiencing an irreversible transformation of written texts. Their popularity, marketability, and increasing abundance compel educators to face the instructional and conceptual issues such transformations raise. In the remainder of this chapter, I identify and discuss some of what I see to be the more obvious of these issues, but it is likely that other, unforeseen issues will become evident as talking books become more widely available and more frequently used.

Instructional Level and Readability

The successful use of decoding assistance such as digitized pronunciations to support beginning reading raises important issues involving established concepts like instructional level and readability. In fact these qualities are reciprocal expressions of one another. For example, the following passage (Johns, 1997) has been judged to be of second-grade readability by several well-established readability formulas:

> It was the first time Bill went to camp. He was very happy to be there. Soon he went for a walk in the woods to look for many kinds of leaves. He found leaves from some maple and oak trees. As Bill walked in the woods, he saw some animal tracks. At that moment, a mouse ran into a small hole by a tree. Bill wondered if the tracks were made by the mouse. He looked around for other animals. He did not see any. The only thing Bill saw was an old bird nest in a pine tree. (p. 11)

Conventionally, this has meant that children who can answer from 75% to 90% of comprehension questions over the passage have an instructional reading level of approximately second grade (Betts, 1946). Both readability measures applied to reading materials and performance criteria applied to readers have long research traditions involving samples of children at a range of grade levels. In other words, both have been calibrated in terms of what children can be expected to do at various points in their development as readers.

But how are these categories conceptualized when a passage such as the preceding one is presented electronically, with decoding support in the form of digitized pronunciations? Under such circumstances, a kindergarten student might well be able to comprehend the passage at a higher level than when limited word recognition creates a bottleneck in the reading process. Thus, a text that is of second-grade difficulty in its unsupported print version may be successfully read and comprehended by a child whose instructional level, established using conventional assessments with printed texts, is considerably less. Although from a conventional view this issue may seem no more than a curiosity of electronic text, the probability that talking books will become substantially more prevalent, perhaps even the norm, in primary classrooms will demand our attention. Certainly our conceptualization of the instructional level and its counterpart, readability, must be transformed to account for such developments. The difference between a child's listening level and instructional reading level as defined conventionally relative to print materials is greatest for beginning readers, and the importance of achieving a suitable match between materials and children is also greatest at this point. In this view, teachers of beginning readers might be advised in the near future to consider the listening levels of their students as they recommend electronic books. When inefficient decoding can be disregarded as a potential stumbling block to reading, age appropriateness is a better indicator of suitability than the more traditional notion of readability (Grindler, Stratton, & McKenna, 1997).

Accelerated Reading Growth

According to Chall's (1983) six-stage developmental model of reading, children pass through a distinct decoding stage en route to fluency. The extensive reading needed to achieve fluency has conventionally followed the decoding stage because of the need to first establish a foundation of word recognition ability. However, the support offered by electronic scaffolding makes such reading possible before that foundation can support independent reading. In other words, electronic trade books may hold the potential of blurring the boundary between the decoding and fluency stages by permitting contextualized practice while decoding instruction occurs elsewhere. Such practice has always been possible, of course, whenever an adult or fluent child is available to provide assistance as needed. This kind of assistance must be given on a one-to-one basis by someone who must necessarily attend to the entire reading episode. The logistics of rendering this sort of help, together with the potential for self-consciousness on the part of the beginning reader, sometimes make such an arrangement unfeasible. Electronic books can circumvent these limitations by scaffolding the beginning reader at all times. Thus, the decoding and fluency stages might progress virtually in parallel rather than in sequence, with the ultimate effect of accelerating the development of reading ability and enabling fluency to be attained at an earlier age.

The Role of Context

The availability of digitized pronunciations is likely to discourage children from using context to help them identify unfamiliar words. Although this issue remains contentious, it is now clear that the role of context changes as readers mature. For the novice reader, it is primarily a tool for the identification of words—that is, for locating them in the lexicon once their visual forms are encountered in print. For the fluent reader, it is a means of deciding among multiple meanings after lexical access occurs (Rayner & Pollatsek, 1989; Stanovich, 1991). Consequently, talking books encourage developing readers to behave like fluent ones, an outcome that may be desirable but will necessitate careful inquiry. It essentially sidesteps the interactive compensatory model (Stanovich, 1980), which contends that children use context for the purpose of lexical access only to the extent that decoding fails and that this role naturally diminishes as their decoding ability improves. With talking books, decoding never fails and resorting to context as a fallback position for contending with unfamiliar words is never necessary. In future classrooms, extended reading of a multitude of talking books may mean not only that children do not use contextual strategies but that they do not acquire them to begin with. As long as decoding advances to the point of automaticity, however, this outcome may not be especially dire.

Tracking and Feedback

In the NRRC-sponsored study described in the previous section, we employed a tracking system to monitor the pronunciations accessed by students. Tracking such data can be useful in prescribing and even customizing subsequent instruction. For example, under some conditions those words on which a child frequently clicks for assistance could be listed for a teacher to guide subsequent instruction. Our study and others (e.g., Horney & Anderson-Inman, 1996), however, have raised troublesome questions about talking books designed for this purpose. The underaccessing and overaccessing of words suggest that the tracking data may imperfectly represent a child's true instructional needs.

A more promising alternative perhaps lies in the eventual perfection of voice recognition. A beginning reader's miscues while reading an electronic book aloud could be tracked and analyzed by comparing expected words (those of the printed text) with words actually uttered. Consistent types of miscues might lead the program to identify particular words or categories of words for additional study. For example, a child who says *horse* for *house*, *bucket* for *pocket*, and *Tom* for *Tim* might be encouraged to ask whether words make sense within a story. Because beginning readers customarily read aloud, and sometimes even resist reading silently, voice recognition as a means of monitoring seems a natural adjunct to talking books as software becomes more sophisticated and hardware more powerful. Mostow developed prototypes of electronic books designed with these features through Project Listen at Carnegie Mellon University. He referred to them as *listening books*. (For further information, visit the following website: http://www.cs.cmu.edu/.)

Method of Providing Pronunciations

The results of our studies suggest that there may be little relation between the words accessed by a child and those actually added to the child's sight vocabulary. This finding has preliminary implications for software design because commercial products tend to provide oral renderings of entire phrases when a child selects one word within a given phrase. An example of a phrase that is temporarily highlighted while its digitized oral equivalent is read aloud to the child appears in Fig. 3.2. Although our results suggest that little may be gained by digitizing each word individually, studies designed to test the relative effects of providing pronunciations of single words versus entire phrases are needed to resolve this issue. Providing pronunciations in the context of phrases reflects fluent reading, to be sure, but it may also prevent children from fixating at the right time on the words being pronounced for them. If that is true, then children may not be able to give unfamiliar words sufficient attention to learn them.

Contextualized Instruction

The notion of situating decoding instruction wherever possible within the context of meaningful reading is intuitively appealing. Such instruction takes advantage of teachable moments, thereby illustrating for children the relevance of learning about word recognition

FIG. 3.2. Page from GT Interactive Software's *Just Me and My Dad*, by Mayer (1992), copyright © 1992, showing the last line highlighted as it is read aloud. Reprinted with permission.

(Holdaway, 1979). It also avoids fragmenting language and proceeds from whole to part rather than from part to whole (Goodman, 1986). Further, it is precisely tailored to the needs of an individual reader, which is particularly relevant to reading in electronic environments in which only one child is interacting with the software.

Notwithstanding these presumed advantages, our experience with talking books argues against incorporating explicit instruction, aimed at word study, within the context of assisted reading. Our use of phonics analogies did not translate into generalized orthographic knowledge useful to students in decoding novel words. It is possible, of course, that other formats would have produced better results, but our findings are not encouraging. Moreover, the intrusiveness of embedded instruction, so much in evidence during our initial study, remains an important factor. Children do not, after all, read talking books in order to receive decoding instruction but rather to comprehend and enjoy the books. Embedded instruction may threaten this goal and reduce the willingness to read widely. As noted earlier, attitude theory suggests that beliefs about the outcomes of reading are central to the formation of positive attitudes. If children come to believe that reading is a process filled with hidden lessons, the effect may well be negative.

Present and Potential Features of Talking Books

What features might best complement the basic word recognition support afforded by talking books? A list of possibilities includes some features that have already been implemented and others that might eventually become feasible.

"Play" Options. Special audiovisual effects, associated with illustrations, can be displayed by clicking meaningful parts of these illustrations. Thus, by clicking on a starfish in Broderbund's *Just Grandma and Me* (Mayer, 1992), a child may be delighted to see it

dance to digitized music before settling into its original position on the beach. Some educators may complain about the distraction created by such devices, but adherents argue that they add appeal that the printed versions of the same books can never match. Moreover, the play option can be suppressed, if desired, or used prior to any serious reading of the book (McKenna, Reinking, Labbo, & Watkins, 1996).

Response Options.   Talking books, and their electronic environment, seem well suited to providing children with unique opportunities to respond to literature. Labbo and her associates (Labbo & Kuhn, chap. 5, this volume; Labbo, Reinking, McKenna, Kuhn, & Phillips, 1996) have, for example, used the computer to provide kindergarten children with the means of creating pictorial responses to their reading of a children's book. Labbo's work has been guided by the need to provide a developmentally appropriate means of responding to literature. Except in the sense of emergent writing, characterized by pictures, scribbling, and naive spellings, this necessity precludes more sophisticated written responses even though a child's oral language development might be sufficient to produce such a response. Voice recognition could help children produce written responses well beyond their ability to produce them independently. Such a format would make possible language experience activities with an element of unprecedented immediacy. Rather than following the typical pattern of dictating their stories to the teacher, children could see their own words appear as soon as they were uttered.

Networked Titles.   Beginning readers may soon have hundreds of high-quality titles available to them over networks so that wide independent reading will be facilitated and browsing encouraged. Consequently, they may find themselves faced with navigational problems similar to those confronting older readers in hypertext environments. Intellectual agents may be developed to assist them in locating titles of high interest. For example, at the conclusion of a book the computer may ask the child to rate it, and this rating may be used by the software to suggest comparable titles if the rating is high or to suppress similar books if the rating is low.

Embedded Tasks.   A feature common to hypertexts designed for older readers entails confronting them with occasional comprehension checks in the form of tasks to be completed. Leu and his associates (Leu & Hillinger, 1994), for example, experimented successfully with a variety of interactive tasks within the context of geography texts. For example, at some points students are required to drag place names from a list to appropriate points on a map. If they are correct, the place name remains where they put it; if they are wrong, it jumps back to the list. It is easy to envision comparable tasks built into talking books designed for beginning readers. For example, before allowing a child to proceed to the next page, the computer might ask that the child "Show me _____," with the expectation that the child will then click at an appropriate point in the illustration. Embedded tasks of this nature would encourage, at an early age, reading for comprehension while reading for pleasure. Connecting them to the play option discussed earlier might be an especially motivating means of accomplishing this goal.

More Sophisticated Resources.   Electronic texts designed to support the reading of older students are replete with resources that go well beyond the digitized pronunciations of words (see Anderson-Inman & Horney, chap. 2, this volume). Devices such as glossary entries, explanatory notes, and simplified rewordings may prove useful to some beginning readers as well. That potential is worth exploring in research and development projects.

One resource that might serve a beginning reader is simplified paraphrases of text that is beyond a child's listening level. With such a resource, beginners would be able to derive from relatively advanced text an understanding more commensurate with their current knowledge. The limitation of inadequate prior knowledge suggests that another kind of resource would be aimed at building prior knowledge in order to facilitate comprehension. Informal measures of comprehension now routinely assess prior knowledge in order to judge the extent to which it may be a limiting factor, but complex hypertext networks often serve in effect to supply prior knowledge on demand as readers strategically make their way through the network. An electronic encyclopedia, for example, facilitates cross-referencing to locate articles that may help one better understand the entry with which one begins. A multimedia network might serve the same purpose for beginning readers without recourse to print. Using a graphic interface system, developers could facilitate exploration of concepts by emergent literates. Clicking on various components of illustrations, for example, could lead to oral explanations and descriptions. Such a system might constitute an appropriate precursor of similar systems, involving text, that children will later encounter.

With respect to a specific reading selection, introductory material presented orally could set the stage for reading by activating relevant schemata and building new ones. The second-grade example presented in a previous section of this chapter could have been introduced in such a way that the probability of adequate comprehension was substantially increased. A digitized voice might have informed beginning readers about the concept of summer camp along the following lines:

> Lots of children go to camp in the summer. Camp is a place far from town, a place where there might be trees and lakes and ponds. There are animals to see, and you can sleep in a tent or a cabin. You can walk in the woods and look for interesting leaves and rocks. This story is about what one boy saw when he went for a walk at camp. Read it to find out what he saw.

Providing background information of this nature has the potential to address cultural diversity and to alleviate differences in experience attributable to economic disadvantage.

Visual Transformations of Text.   Preschoolers and even kindergartners often lack prerequisite print concepts that enable them to access the pronunciations they need. Electronic texts could be formatted to introduce and reinforce concepts, such as word boundaries and the left-to-right and top-to-bottom directionality of print. Thin-lined boxes might be used to to encase words, for example, a feature that could be suppressed for certain readers. Likewise, arrows could be used to indicate where to start and in what direction to proceed. These resources are forms of electronic scaffolds that would fade long before digitized pronunciations.

Voice-Activated Feedback.   Voice recognition has the potential to produce more reliable data about the word recognition development of children using talking books. For example, it could be used to provide pronunciations in lieu of the more cumbersome locate-and-click option. A child reading orally typically hesitates on encountering unfamiliar words. Such hesitations, together with the ability of the computer to monitor the point a child has reached in the text segment displayed, could be used to provide the pronunciation of the next word after a predesignated lapse of time.

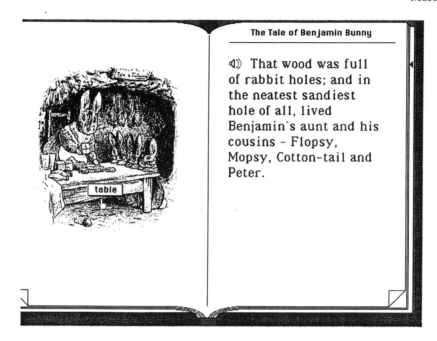

FIG. 3.3.   Page from Discis' *The Tale of Benjamin Bunny* (Potter, 1994), copyright
© 1994, showing an object label that appears when the child clicks on an appropriate
place within the illustration. Reprinted with permission.

Labeled Illustrations.   Some commercial software companies use one-word labels for
objects depicted in illustrations. Such labels appear as a child explores an illustration by
clicking. The oral equivalent of a label is simultaneously provided. The labeling feature
probably adds to the incidental acquisition of sight words facilitated by talking books. An
example of a talking book in which a hidden object label has been revealed after clicking
on the object appears in Fig. 3.3, where a page from *The Tale of Benjamin Bunny* (Potter,
1994) appears.

Animation.   Illustrations that move and change in various ways have already been
introduced in commercial software, and their advent represents one of the ways in which
children's books as a genre may eventually be transformed as authors begin to consider
electronic versions as original rather than as derived media. Animation essentially blurs the
distinction between printed books, which talking books typically seek to simulate, and movies
(or, more precisely, cartoons). Whether animation potentially reduces attention to and reliance
on print is a research question of some importance. As Bolter has suggested (chap. 1, this
volume), the interaction of text and visual features may lead to qualitative differences in
how literacy is viewed and taught. The emerging view may well need to accommodate the
presence of visual components not as distractions from, but as complements of, text.

IMPLICATIONS FOR CHILDREN'S LITERATURE

Most of the electronic features discussed previously proceed from the assumption that it
is desirable for talking books to electronically simulate printed books. However, the nature
of the digital environment makes possible so many modifications that we must inspect this

assumption carefully. Is it really desirable to maintain the appearance of printed books? Several reasons for doing so seem defensible. First, providing children with a format that recreates virtual pages that can be "turned" and that faithfully reproduces illustrations so that electronic versions are readily associated with their print counterparts may give children, at least temporarily, a familiar point of reference and permit smooth segues from electronic to print versions of the same books. Second, making available a limited range of interactions with a text may serve to focus a child's attention, thereby maximizing engagement and instructional impact. Finally, the principal benefit of any simulation is transfer to real settings. Despite the arguments presented by many of the contributors to this volume, teachers still view the goal of reading instruction as preparing children to participate effectively in a world of print. Consequently, talking books are likely to be perceived as temporary substitutes for, and not established alternatives to, printed books. Given the hundreds if not thousands of high-quality children's titles now available in printed form, this perception makes sense.

Judging from their products, software producers have correctly anticipated this view. We find faithful re-creations of the codex book, complete with the animated appearance of turning pages. However, electronic environments invite modifications, and commercial producers can be expected to introduce novel features that they believe will have market appeal. Because the market (those in a position to purchase these products) consists of educators, producers can also be expected to seek a balance between perceived pedagogical soundness and attractiveness to children. The quest for such a balance has led to products that simulate printed books while making them the anchor of numerous features not found in print versions.

The growing convenience and accessibility of technology will eventually lead to an inventory of talking books that rivals their printed counterparts. As the balance shifts, the rationale for maintaining the format of printed books will diminish. I suspect that producers and authors will then begin to exercise the freedom that electronic environments afford. In consequence, they may provide answers to important questions that are now beginning to emerge. For example, how important is it for text and graphics to be presented in pagelike frames? Can alternative formats be more engaging, more informative, and more comprehensible? Most importantly, has the traditional design of printed books shaped and limited the nature of early literacy in ways that are less than optimal and that can eventually be changed?

REFERENCES

Adams, M. J. (1990). *Beginning to read: Thinking and learning about print.* Cambridge, MA: MIT Press.

Betts, E. A. (1946). *Foundations of reading instruction.* New York: American Book.

Brown, J. S., Collins, A., & Duguid, P. (1989). Situated cognition and the culture of learning. *Educational Research, 18*(1), 32–42.

Bruner, J. S. (1978). The role of dialogue in language acquisition. In A. Sinclair, R. J. Jarvelle, & W. J. M. Leveet (Eds.), *The child's conception of language* (pp. 241–255). New York: Springer.

Chall, J. S. (1983). *Stages of reading development.* New York: McGraw-Hill.

Cunningham, P. M. (1995). *Phonics they use: Words for reading and writing* (2nd ed.). New York: HarperCollins.

Gaskins, I. W., Ehri, L. C., Cress, C., O'Hara, C., & Donnelly, K. (1996–1997). Procedures for word learning: Making discoveries about words. *The Reading Teacher, 50*, 312–327.

Goodman, K. S. (1986). *What's whole in whole language?* Portsmouth, NH: Heinemann.

Gough, P. B., & Tunmer, W. E. (1986). Decoding, reading, and reading disability. *Remedial and Special Education, 7*(1), 6–10.

Grindler, M. C., Stratton, B. D., & McKenna, M. C. (1997). *The right book, the right time: Helping children cope with issues.* Needham Heights, MA: Allyn & Bacon.

Holdaway, D. (1979). *The foundations of literacy.* New York: Ashton Scholastic.

Horney, M., & Anderson-Inman, L. (1996, April). *Plugged-in books: Practical advice on using electronic books with disabled readers.* Paper presented at the meeting of the International Reading Association, New Orleans, LA.

Johns, J. L. (1997). *Basic reading inventory* (7th ed.). Dubuque, IA: Kendall/Hunt.

Juel, C., Griffith, P. L., & Gough, P. B. (1985). Reading and spelling strategies of first grade children. In J. A. Niles & R. Lalik (Eds.), *Issues in literacy: A research perspective* (pp. 306–309). Rochester, NY: National Reading Conference.

Labbo, L. D., Reinking, D., McKenna, M. C., Kuhn, M., & Phillips, M. (1996). *Computers real and make-believe: Providing opportunities for literacy development in an early childhood sociodramatic play center* (Instructional Resource No. 26). Athens, GA, and College Park, MD: National Reading Research Center.

Leu, D., & Hillinger, M. (1994, December). *Reading comprehension in hypermedia: Supporting changes to children's conceptions of a scientific principle.* Paper presented at the meeting of the National Reading Conference, San Diego, CA.

Lewin, C. (1995). *The evaluation of talking book software: A pilot study* (Tech. Rep. No. 220). London: Centre for Information Technology in Education, The Open University.

Lewin, C. (1996). *Improving talking book software design: Emulating the supportive tutor* (Tech. Rep. No. 222). London: Centre for Information Technology in Education, The Open University.

Mayer, M. (1992). *Just grandma and me.* [Computer software]. Novato, CA: Broderbund.

McKenna, M. C. (1994). Toward a model of reading attitude acquisition. In E. H. Cramer & M. Castle (Eds.), *Fostering the life-long love of reading: The affective domain in reading education* (pp. 18–40). Newark, DE: International Reading Association.

McKenna, M. C., Kear, D. J., & Ellsworth, R. A. (1995). Children's attitudes toward reading: A national survey. *Reading Research Quarterly, 30,* 934–956.

McKenna, M. C., Reinking, D., Labbo, L. D., & Watkins, J. H. (1996). *Using electronic storybooks with beginning readers* (Instructional Resource No. 39). Athens, GA, and College Park, MD: National Reading Research Center.

McKenna, M. C., & Watkins, J. H. (1994, December). *Computer-mediated books for beginning readers.* Paper presented at the meeting of the National Reading Conference, San Diego, CA.

McKenna, M. C., & Watkins, J. H. (1995, November). *Effects of computer-mediated books on the development of beginning readers.* Paper presented at the meeting of the National Reading Conference, New Orleans, LA.

McKenna, M. C., & Watkins, J. H. (1996, December). *The effects of computer-mediated trade books on sight word acquisition and the development of phonics ability.* Paper presented at the meeting of the National Reading Conference, Charleston, SC.

Miller, L., Blackstock, J., & Miller, R. (1994). An exploratory study into the use of CD-ROM storybooks. *Computers in Education, 22,* 187–204.

Olofsson, A. (1992). Synthetic speech and computer aided reading for reading disabled children. *Reading and Writing: An Interdisciplinary Journal, 4,* 165–178.

Olson, R., Foltz, G., & Wise, B. (1986). Reading instruction and remediation with the aid of computer speech. *Behavior Research Methods, Instruments, and Computers, 18*(2), 93–99.

Peters, J. M. (1996). Vygotsky in the future: Technology as a mediation tool for literacy instruction. In L. Dixon-Krauss (Ed.), *Vygotsky in the classroom: Mediated literacy instruction and assessment* (pp. 175–189). White Plains, NY: Longman.

Potter, B. (1994). *The tale of Benjamin Bunny.* [Computer software]. Buffalo, NY: Discis.

Rayner, K., & Pollatsek, A. (1989). *The psychology of reading.* Englewood Cliffs, NJ: Prentice-Hall.

Reitsma, P. (1988). Reading practice for beginners: Effects of guided reading, reading-while-listening, and independent reading with computer-based speech feedback. *Reading Research Quarterly, 23,* 219–235.

Salomon, G., Globerson, T., & Guterman, E. (1989). The computer as a zone of proximal development: Internalizing reading-related metacognitions from a reading partner. *Journal of Educational Psychology, 81,* 620–627.

Shaw, N. (1988). *Sheep in a jeep.* Solana Beach, CA: Sandpiper Press.

Stanovich, K. E. (1980). Toward an interactive-compensatory model of individual differences in the development of reading fluency. *Reading Research Quarterly, 16,* 32–71.

Stanovich, K. E. (1986). Matthew effects in reading: Some consequences of individual differences in the acquisition of literacy. *Reading Research Quarterly, 21,* 360–407.

Stanovich, K. E. (1991). Word recognition: Changing perspectives. In R. Barr, M. L. Kamil, P. B. Mosenthal, & P. D. Pearson (Eds.), *Handbook of reading research* (Vol. 2, pp. 418–452). White Plains, NY: Longman.

Sulzby, E., & Teale, W. (1991). Emergent literacy. In R. Barr, M. L. Kamil, P. B. Mosenthal, & P. D. Pearson (Eds.), *Handbook of reading research* (Vol. 2, pp. 727–757). White Plains, NY: Longman.

Vygotsky, L. S. (1978). *Mind in society: The development of higher psychological processes* (M. Cole, V. John-Steiner, S. Scribner, & E. Souberman, Eds. & Trans.). Cambridge, MA: Harvard University Press.

Wise, B., Olson, R., Ansett, M., Andrews, L., Terjak, M., Schneider, V., Kostuch, J., & Kriho, L. (1989). Implementing a long-term computerized remedial reading program with synthetic speech feedback: Hardware, software, and real-world issues. *Behavior Research Methods, Instruments, and Computers, 21,* 163–180.

II

TRANSFORMING READERS AND WRITERS

The goal of the chapters in this section is to judiciously examine the idea that computer technology is transforming our traditional notions about the acquisition and development of literacy. Because each chapter offers a unique perspective on particular aspects of the transformation of readers and writers in the digital realm, the first part of this introduction highlights several key assumptions, approaches, and challenges which implicitly underlie all of the chapters. The second part provides brief summaries of the unique topics covered within chapters.

ASPECTS IN COMMON ACROSS CHAPTERS

The intention of these authors is not to provide an extensive review of related research and literature in the field. Rather, the authors of these chapters selectively draw on research that has been instrumental in informing their own bodies of work. This type of selective review allows readers to understand the evolution of thinking that has guided the authors' most recent research as it is reported in the chapters.

The authors also challenge traditional perceptions about the characteristics of texts. All refer to ways in which definitions of text must be broadened when text occurs in an electronic medium. Each considers implications of such definitions when print is no longer static, linear, or permanently affixed to a single page. For example, Myers, Hammett, and McKillop (chap. 4) reflect on a nontraditional conceptualization of text that includes attributes of particular computer programs that offer QuickTime® videos, clip art, and digitized sound, as well as print. Labbo and Kuhn (chap. 5) suggest that the multimedia properties of some software programs are so unique that young children's concepts about the digital print that they encounter on the computer screen are different from their concepts about the print they encounter in books. Beach and Lundell (chap. 6) challenge traditional views of conversational "texts" when dialogue occurs in written form within a computer environment, instead of conversation that occurs face to face.

The authors reconceptualize the processes involved in reader–text interaction or author–text composition. For example, Myers et al. (chap. 4) suggest that hypermedia provides a unique environment that creates opportunities for readers to take a critical stance toward texts. Furthermore, they suggest that writers in a hypermedia medium may juxtapose images, music, and text in ways that expose underlying issues of power, equity, or cultural bias. Labbo and Kuhn (chap. 5) suggest that young children who compose messages with multimedia software often make decisions about how they will graphically represent ideas based on the accessibility of a variety of symbol-making tools.

Research questions asked by the authors have required qualitative methods and qualitative answers. This approach has allowed the authors to understand how readers and writers are being transformed as they make meaning with digital text. Insights and categories reported in the chapters have been drawn from data collected through interviews, field notes, transcripts of talk, printouts of computer-generated work, and participant observations.

ASPECTS THAT ARE UNIQUE WITHIN CHAPTERS

Labbo and Kuhn (chap. 5) focus on the ways in which young children's literacy development is influenced by computers in a classroom context. Writing about their growing body of work in this area, they focus on sociocultural and sociocognitive aspects of literacy development as young children interact with specific artistic and typographic software tools. Noteworthy in the chapter is a consideration of the conceptual insights kindergarten children who work in classroom computer centers gain about literacy and technology.

Beach and Lundell (chap. 6) report on work they have done with seventh graders who engage in computer-mediated communication (CMC) exchanges in computer labs. They argue that such an environment is transforming literacy development and literacy instruction by providing unique opportunities for students to engage in active writing and reading. They provide detailed characteristics of CMC formats, explain the process of how participants construct meaning while accomplishing social agendas, and suggest implications for teaching using CMC in the classroom.

Myers et al. (chap. 4) examine opportunities for students to experience moments of critical literacy when they construct hypermedia texts within a critical pedagogy context. These authors report on research they conducted in classrooms with undergraduate teacher education students in a university setting and with seventh graders in a middle school setting. Based on semiotic theory, the authors discuss critical literacy aspects of hypermedia texts that include critiquing aspects, power aspects, transformative aspects, and emancipatory aspects. Because the authors decided that static figures could not adequately represent their key ideas, they decided not to include figures in the chapter. Instead, they include a World Wide Web address that provides access to electronic versions of the hypermedia projects.

4

▼▼▼▼▼▼▼

Opportunities for Critical Literacy and Pedagogy in Student-Authored Hypermedia

Jamie Myers
Roberta Hammett
Ann Margaret McKillop
Pennsylvania State University

In this chapter we describe moments of critical literacy as students author hypermedia within the context of a critical pedagogy. We use the expression *hypermedia* to refer to electronic hypertexts that require the author to create, and the reader to follow, linked pathways through a whole collection of electronic "texts" presented as computer windows. Each window can present a multimedia experience of combined graphics, photo images, music, voice recordings, and video, as well as words. Highlighted words or images provide links in multiple directions to other windows, allowing the author to express ideas by the nature of the juxtapositions of media in a window and by the connections across windows. Thus we clip and combine the words *hypertext* and *multimedia* to refer to the whole collection and possible pathways through it as a hypermedia project.

The student-authored hypermedia presented in this chapter originated in our own work as teacher-researchers in classrooms in which we sought to contextualize the representation of ideas in hypermedia as critical literacy. We define *critical literacy* as the intentional subversion of meanings in order to critique the underlying ideologies and relations of power that support particular interpretations of a text (we use *text* to refer broadly to all forms of representing meaning such as images, music, and video, as well as words). This subversion happens when authors juxtapose other texts to the critiqued text in order to generate different meanings and thus expose the underlying assumptions or beliefs supporting each meaning. All texts position the reader/viewer as an object of text meaning—as a member of an audience with particular social relationships with other members and with other audiences. When engaged in critical literacy, the author/reader pays particular attention to how texts represent meanings about the self and others, or meanings on the basis of a particular kind of self. By connecting other texts, in which the self is represented or assumed differently, the self as an object of text meaning is dislodged or multiplied in possible meanings. Text meanings become problematic when juxtaposed texts generate new meanings and thus expose different possible underlying ideologies. The reader/viewer becomes transformed from the object of a single text meaning to a subject who, by bringing to bear on one text the potentials of many other connected texts, has multiple possibilities for future being and action. Hypermedia is a particularly powerful environment for this critical literacy practice because it enables the reader/viewer to juxtapose, link, and sequence multiple representations in computer windows that appear rapidly in succession, or simultaneously, as a consequence of the speed and proximity of text and graphic display in electronic space. Thus, hypermedia authoring can support the emancipation of one's self and others through the authoring and publication of critical texts that by questioning representations of the self, expand the possibilities for the self in future actions as a member of a community.

The examples of hypermedia authoring presented in this chapter are drawn from several different classroom experiences with five different groups of English teacher education students, who authored hypermedia projects as part of their university preparation, and one group of seventh graders who authored hypermedia as part of a collaborative technology project. The undergraduates' hypermedia projects explored interpretations of literature framed by larger personally important cultural issues, and the seventh graders' projects taught poetic devices or presented biographies of famous people. Detailed descriptions of these classroom research studies can be found elsewhere (McKillop, 1996; McKillop & Myers, 1998; Myers, Hammett, & McKillop, in press). Our purpose here is to focus on the possibilities of critical literacy realized across our ongoing work with hypermedia authoring, and not a full examination of each unique study.

In all of these studies, students used the Macintosh-based software StorySpace (1994) as the hypermedia authoring tool, and a collection of software to digitize sound, image, and create original Quicktime videos. In StorySpace, authors create spaces that have two functions: (a) to provide a window for displaying text, image, video, and/or simultaneous sound when the window opens; and (b) to hold additional spaces of hierarchically subjugated text windows. Authors make links between the "texts" in the display window by highlighting words or parts of an image that turn into hot buttons linking to highlighted text in other display windows. As the reader travels from window to window, or space to space, following these links, the windows can be set to remain open or to close. The Quicktime videos students created and included in their StorySpace windows usually combined a music sound track and/or voice-over with the visual presentation of several images transitioning one into the next. The examples we describe in this chapter can be experienced in an electronic version at the following World Wide Web site: http://www.ed.psu.edu/k-12/hypermedia/hypermedia.html.

A SEMIOTIC ANALYSIS OF HYPERMEDIA AUTHORING

Pierce's semiotic theory provides the analytic frame for our identification of critical literacy in hypermedia. Meaning within a semiotic framework is always a triadic event in which "a sign is something which stands to somebody for something in some respect or capacity" (quoted in Eco, 1979, p. 180). This definition is the basis for the triad of sign–object–interpretant, in which the sign is something that stands for another something—the object, in the respect or capacity of the interpretant. It is often said that the the meaning of a word, image, or gesture for example, is mediated by the interpretant. The interpretant brings to the surface, so to speak, one particular meaning from many in a sign's potential, and thus contextualizes the moment's particular object. The interpretant represents the intertextual relations of one sign with others. In everyday communication, through constant social interaction using signs to mean one particular object, the intertextual relations that contextualize meaning become conventionalized, assumed, and taken for granted. This everyday experience results in a dyadic sense of meaning by which objects, or words, possess a fixed meaning that can be taught, learned, and always intended in communication. This dyadic sense of meaning underlies the common assumption that a text can contain a meaning put there by the author.

Certainly an author can intend a meaning and build an intertext through redundancy and reference to make one meaning more potential than other possible meanings, but ultimately, the text remains a collection of signs that readers must contextualize through their own set of interpretants. A triadic semiotic meaning explains this possibility for a sign to mean many things, or to be imbued with possibility, because each interpretant, or network of other ideas (signs), when brought to bear on the first sign, mediates its meaning and brings to light a different aspect or layer of the sign's meaning.

In our everyday communication, the interpretant remains largely invisible as we accept a definitional correspondence of our signs to our object meanings, particularly with those with whom we communicate most. However, significations are always grounded in, or mediated by, interpretants. When different meanings arise in a moment of communication, they can be traced to different interpretants that are not equally shared by all participants, that are cultural and ideological, that accumulate through experiences with all types of texts, and that may or may not be made explicit in an attempt to negotiate a shared meaning for the contested sign. The critical literacy practices we have identified in hypermedia find authors seeking to make explict the underlying ideological interpretants of a sign by juxtaposing or linking other signs to create new meanings that force attention toward the recognition of multiple interpretants that are ideological choices that can be negotiated and valued by community members.

Additional aspects of semiotic theory provided us with a basis for deciding which moments of hypermedia authoring were examples of critical literacy and which were not. Semiotic theory explains how a sign functions as an icon, index, or symbol (Eco & Sebeok, 1983). Iconic signs resemble another sign, such as a sketch of a tree representing the life experience of a tree. An indexical sign is a trace of another sign; a puddle of water on the floor is a sign that points toward some meaning and can only be fully interpreted when the relevant interpretants are put into place—no water mark on the ceiling, an empty ice cube tray by the sink, a glass with almost-melted ice cubes in the bottom. A symbolic sign arbitrarily stands for another sign, as is the case in language when an utterance in one language rarely means the same thing in another language.

Iconic and Indexical Representations

The student-authored hypermedia we analyzed represented meanings through the use of all three sign functions. However, we did not define as critical literacy those meanings generated through iconic and indexical signs. Iconic and indexical signs reinforced the dyadic definitional meanings of the texts that were juxtaposed or linked, thereby leaving invisible the underlying ideologies that mediated these meanings. There was no attempt by the authors to make the meaning of either text problematic, or to force the examination of the readers' underlying assumptions that would support the conventional meaning shared by the signs.

For example, authors of an undergraduate project quoted the novel *Ceremony* (Silko, 1977), breaking the prose at the word "he" to insert an image of a Native American smoking what appears to be a peace pipe. The image does not make the sentence or passage problematic: "Josiah had been there, in the jungle; he (image) had come. Tayo had watched him die, and he had done nothing to save him" (p. 19). Likewise the passage does not attempt to make conscious the underlying ideology the reader may use to interpret the image. As an iconic sign, juxtaposed or linked texts like this one function to mirror or reproduce isomorphically the meaning of an already presented sign; thus icons do not offer much potential to embellish, extend, or shift critically the meanings of the original sign. Another example in a seventh-grade project finds a poem about a bird hyperlinked to a realistic watercolor drawing of a bird. In following the link the reader merely sees a picture of a bird while reading a poem about a bird. We do not consider these iconic uses of texts, which most often were used to illustrate physical objects or beings, as moments in which authors intend to construct a critical literacy.

Likewise, indexical signs juxtaposed or linked two texts that pointed toward an obvious, conventional meaning that would be interpreted with either text alone. An indexical sign presented another example of an idea, but did not attempt to make the idea problematic. In one undergraduate project, the image of a woman in a long dress with an apron sitting at a butter churn is juxtaposed with a quote from *The Dollmaker* (Arnow, 1954):

> "You eat it," she said, and with a last glance at Amos took the coffee and hurried out the back door. She walked slowly along the cement walk that led to the front porch, lifting her face to feel the rain, for after the bright whiteness of the hot little room, the cold rain and the dark were like old friends. She tried an instant to look into the sky to find the north star and so find herself, but the lights were bright and the clouds an even gray so that as she sat on the top porch step and drank her coffee she knew not where she was. (p. 38)

The butter churn image is not iconic because it does not illustrate the events of the quote. The image represents Gertie at a different moment in her life, and thus together, the image and the quote point toward a shared meaning about Gertie's life condition. Most likely that shared meaning involves a close relation to nature for life to be meaningful. However, indexical signs in pointing toward a shared meaning that is highly likely with each sign independently do not intend to make either text problematic. The butter churn image does not make the events of the visit to the doctor problematic, nor does the doctor's office, rain, lack of stars, or coffee on the porch step make the butter churn problematic. Although we recognize the possibilities of hypermedia authoring to broaden the concepts of students by connecting ideas across various texts, especially texts from the personal lives of the students, we do not consider as moments of critical literacy these indexical intentions where meanings shared between two different (noniconic) texts are highlighted and reinforced by the juxtaposition. This is a reproduction of the underlying ideologies without making either text problematic.

Symbolic Representations

Symbolic signs generated multiple meanings for texts when seemingly unrelated texts were juxtaposed or linked to create or layer new meanings not usually represented by either text. When this new layer of meaning involved oppositional readings of the texts juxtaposed, we defined an intention to critique, or enact a critical literacy. For example, in one undergraduate project, an image of a torn half stick of gum with a thread over the top is juxtaposed with a few lines from the song "Hello in There" by Prine (1971). This juxta-position brings a new meaning to both texts that would have been highly impossible if the texts were experienced separately. The loneliness of the song layers the half stick of gum with the potential meaning of Boo Radley from the novel *To Kill a Mockingbird* (Lee, 1960). In this novel, which is a central focus of the hypermedia project, Scout continually stuffs gum in the knot of an old tree in the Radleys' front yard, finding it gone each day. If you listen to Prine's song you are more likely to picture an old person walking down the street and not the mysterious Boo Radley who is never seen.

Creating juxtapositions in which the sign functions symbolically is the basis for a critical literacy, even if the new layered meanings do not intend to make either of the juxtaposed texts problematic. As in the example just described, the new meaning of Boo Radley layered on the gum and on the song does not attempt to make visible and question the underlying ideology of loneliness that is symbolized: Why is Boo alone? Why do people become outcasts or recluses? What is the source of loneliness? The gum and song work as sign and interpretant for each other to produce a new object meaning of Boo Radley within the context of this hypermedia project in this particular classroom. Boo Radley is the focus of the juxtaposition, not the underlying ideologies of the half stick of gum or the song.

We believe the examination of the ideologies that ground meanings for texts requires moving beyond producing new layers of meaning for the juxtaposed texts, to moments when the intention for the new meanings is to expose potential underlying ideological interpretants so they can be questioned and critiqued. In a different window from the same undergraduate project, a quotation from the novel *Ceremony* (Silko, 1977) is juxtaposed with a song. In the quote, Tayo speaks of the prejudice he experiences as a half-breed Indian after World War II:

I'm half-breed. I'll be the first to say it. I'll speak for both sides. First time you walked down the street in Gallup or Albuquerque, you knew. Don't lie. You knew right away the war was over, the uniform was gone. All of a sudden that man at the store waits on you last, makes you wait until all the white people bought what they wanted. And the white lady at the bus depot, she's real careful now not to touch your hand when she counts out your change. You watch it slide across the counter at you, and you know. Goddamn it! You stupid sonofabitches! You know! (p. 42)

When the window titled "half-breed" opens to display this quote, the following song lyrics are juxtaposed:

The perception that divides you from him
Is a lie
For some reason you never ask why
This is not a black and white world
You can't afford to believe in your side

This is not a black and white world
To be alive
I say that the colors must swirl
And I believe
that maybe today
We will all get to appreciate

The Beauty of Gray

(Live, 1991)

The juxtaposed song makes problematic Tayo's definition of himself as an inferior half-breed by suggesting that the perception is a lie and life is composed of all the swirling colors. The power of the prejudicial experiences Tayo describes also makes problematic the belief of the song that we will all get to appreciate the beauty of gray. In layering new meanings on both the quote and the song, the juxtaposition highlights the underlying ideological interpretants: On what ground do you accept or reject prejudice? The song seems to suggest that the state of purity suggested by race is a lie; that we are all half-breeds, if not in blood then in experience together. The quote highlights Tayo's perception of prejudice as an inescapable damning part of the half-breed's existence. Together, the hypermedia authors intend to focus the reader on an examination of the ideologies that might support or eliminate prejudice. Semiotically, the juxtaposition generates a critique of prejudice, giving the reader contested texts that must be resolved through an examination of one's own cultural beliefs—Is Tayo wrong? Is the song wrong? Am I wrong? How can Tayo be right? How can the song be right? How can I be right? Then again, as the song suggests, "It's not a black and white world."

Given this theoretical frame for understanding critical literacy, the electronic capabilities of hypermedia allowed the student authors to juxtapose texts through simultaneous presentation or by instantaneous linking. In their hypermedia authoring, these juxtapositions illustrated the sign (iconic), provided new examples of the object meaning (indexical), layered the object with multiple new meanings (symbolic), or through those new meanings made problematic the underlying ideological interpretants (critiquing) of the juxtaposed texts. When authors sought to illustrate the sign or provide another example of an evident text meaning, they remained within a definitional, dyadic, noncritical practice of interpretation by only reinforcing or reproducing conventionally shared meanings for signs. When they layered the object with new meanings, making the original meanings problematic, and sought to make underlying interpretants visible to critique the underlying ideologies and social relations supporting the meanings, they enacted a relational, semiotic, critical practice of interpretation. This critical practice makes possible the transformative and emancipatory aspects of a critical literacy and pedagogy that focus our work as literacy educators and researchers.

ASPECTS OF CRITICAL LITERACY IN HYPERMEDIA TEXTS

Critical literacy, as we have defined it, incorporates a number of interrelated nonhierarchical aspects that we have separated in Table 4.1 for the purposes of our discussion. These divisions encompass resisting representations and exclusions, questioning power and privilege, transforming subjectivities, and empowering or emancipating oneself within a community. In hypermedia, authors can realize these aspects through the construction of projects that push at the meanings of the texts that provide the basis of their project. As teachers, we have framed hypermedia authoring for our students as an opportunity to

TABLE 4.1
Critical Literacy Aspects of Hypermedia Texts

Critiquing aspects	
Readers	• Create oppositional and resistant readings
	• Challenge the perceived erroneous/harmful statements, views, or representations
	• Fill in exclusions and omissions
Power aspects	
Readers	• Question where power lies, who has it, who does not, who gains, who loses in situations and events
	• Analyze and deconstruct representations of power and how it is made acceptable, natural, and the norm
	• Examine and question dominant representations and encodings of power
Transformative aspects	
Readers	• Intervene in and interpret and reinterpret texts
	• Assume and create subject positions for themselves to contest object positions created by texts
Emancipatory aspects	
Readers	• Become "conscientized"
	• Assume subject rather than object positions in their authoring
	• Read their own world critically
	• Create critical texts and exercise authority and knowledge over text
	• Incorporate goals of social change and action

make problematic the ideas and issues that cut across our lives by organizing an examination of the texts that represent those lives.

The contestatory aspect of critical literacy involves the creation of oppositional or resistant readings (Trend, 1994). As a reading activity, this may mean that readers will think about contradictory worldviews, texts, and experiences. StorySpace positions the reader differently so that it is "easy to resist accepting the preferred meaning" (Janks & Ivanic, 1992, p. 307). More important, from our point of view, it allows readers to become writers or composers of new texts that juxtapose contradictory texts with the original texts; thus critical literacy becomes an act of creation in which learners are empowered to challenge and correct representations they perceive as erroneous, harmful, and incomplete in texts or to "offer opposing content, other language and alternative emphases" (Janks & Ivanic, 1992, p. 307).

Critiquing Aspects

In an effort to illustrate how media representations can be contested in hypermedia, the Summer 1995 teacher education student group "indecisive" composed a hypermedia project that included a section on identity. The students created a Quicktime movie that sequenced three images of Pocahantas, then ended with a real photo of a Native American child sitting on a couch in a log home. Above the child on the wall was a painting of two Native American women wearing headbands with a single feather. The four images transition one into the next with background music of Peter Gabriel's song "Shaking the Tree." Initially the group thought of the third image in the sequence, an early-17th-century portrait of Pocahantas (despite the Elizabethan garb), as the "real" Pocahantas in contrast to the Disney image from the recent animated movie; teacher questioning helped the students realize it, too, is a representation reflective of its culture. Between the Disney image and the Elizabethan image is a painting of Pocahantas in a low-cut blue dress with white trim, casually holding the stem of a drooping rose. In the hypermedia window, the movie frame is positioned next to the following text commentary:

> Representations are often assigned to us by the media and long held belief systems. These representations are sometimes accurate; often they're not. Dominant, mainstream representations are believed to be accurate. We want to juxtapose these long-standing portrayals with more truthful representations and explore their effects on identity.

The authors presented the reader with this series of representations of Native American women with the specific purpose of challenging the Disney representation of Pocahantas, which they had found problematic.

In another instance of authoring oppositional readings in hypermedia, students created a Quicktime movie consisting of a series of "spiritual" or religious images— Native American and Christian. They placed the following introduction to their movie in the space:

> As we began our class sessions by talking about *Ceremony* we found that Tayo, a young Native American man, felt that he had caused a drought for his people on their reservation by praying against the rain in the jungles of Vietnam. Tayo begins a spiritual journey through pain, confusion and finally peace. Many people seem to be on spiritual journeys these days as they search for peace and meaning in a hectic and troubled world. Native Americans, like Tayo, are exploring the spiritual roots and ways of their tribal culture, Wondering if what they have lost will help them find their identity.

The students continued with an extended discussion of spirituality in its various forms. By juxtaposing various images and discussions of a variety of kinds of spirituality, including Native American, new age, Christian, Jewish, and so on, and by relating these to humans' relationship with nature, the group contested dominant (traditional) religious views. These new forms of spirituality, they say, share the "aim of transforming individuals and society through spiritual awareness." In their critique of the underlying ideological values of religion, the authors created oppositional readings and challenged what they understood as limited representations of spirituality.

In one of the seventh-grade poetry projects, Cynthia also created an oppositional reading by placing a video clip of a bear catching fish in a stream between the title of her poem "The Crying Fish" and the first line of the poem.

> The Springs are roaring like a lion,
> splashing, thrashing everywhere.
> They flow and flow never dying,
> with the foamy water in the air.
> The fish are hurt so they start crying
> and they do not think that's fair.
> Everyone else is always sighing,
> napping and snacking 'cause they don't care.
>   by Cynthia

Cynthia had originally titled this poem "The Springs" and illustrated it with her own iconic drawing of a mountain stream full of fish. This fulfilled the teacher's assignment to create an illustrated poem. When she began working with her authoring group on the hypermedia project, the teacher showed her a nature film of bears playfully catching fish in a stream. Someone watching this movie outside of the context of Cynthia's poem would most likely be captivated by the natural beauty of the bears playing in the stream full of delicious fish. Cynthia saw something different. She saw the plight of the fish, which she had already represented in the second part of her poem. She decided to juxtapose the poem with the video clip, eliminate her original drawing, and rename the poem "The Crying Fish." She explained her authoring decision in an interview:

> The bear . . . I mean the springs are there pushing them and they have no control over it and then the bears are picking them up and eating them or picking them up and then throwing them back in so they really can't tell them no don't do it. . . . It connected pretty well.

Cynthia's poem became a resistant reading of the video clip of the bear in the stream. Although she did not go into any depth of analysis in her text about the underlying ideologies of control in nature and humankind, which lead her to feel the fish have no control, her juxtaposition intentionally reveals her underlying beliefs and feelings. She shifted the focal meaning of the video clip from the lumbering bear to the plight of the flip-flopping fish. We believe that this moment of critical literacy would not have been possible without the capabilities of hypermedia to connect the ideas of the poem and the video in the same visual space.

Power Aspects

Critical literacy often involves examinations of power: who has it, who does not, and who gains and who loses in existing situations. When reading critically, students deconstruct texts to analyze representations of power, determining how power is made natural, acceptable, or the norm. By juxtaposing different texts, composers of hypermedia can examine and question dominant representations and encodings of the world. The "das grup" undergraduate authoring group created links between four spaces (*roosevelt, cassie, War,* and *different ways*) to question the encoding of privilege by President Roosevelt, the motivations of Clovis and Gertie in the novel *The Dollmaker* (Arnow, 1954), and the construction of class in society as experienced by Scout in the novel *To Kill a Mockingbird* (Lee, 1960). Hyperlinks to other spaces are underlined in the spaces presented here. As the *roosevelt* space opens, the reader hears a recording of Roosevelt saying:

> Not all of us have the privilege of fighting our enemies in distant parts of the world. Not all of us can have the privilege of working in a munitions factory or a shipyard or on the farm or in a mine or in an oil field, producing the weapons or raw materials needed by the armed forces. But there is one front, one where everyone in the United States, every man, woman and child is in action and will be privileged to remain in action throughout the war. That front is right here at home, in our everyday lives, in our everyday tasks. Here at home everyone will have the privilege of making whatever self-denial is necessary not only to supply our fighting men, but to keep the economic structure fortified and secure, during the war and after the war.

Juxtaposed with this speech by Roosevelt is the group's commentary, which begins to deconstruct how the sacrifice of everyday needs can be made into a privilege. As the reader follows the two hyperlinks to the *cassie* space from the word <u>Roosevelt</u>, and to the *War* space from the word <u>privilege</u>, the authors continue to question the acceptability of this privilege mentality.

> *roosevelt*
> It struck me as strange in these books why the characters, at least originally thought that going to war and fighting was a "privilege." But these words from <u>Roosevelt</u> really showed me how there was a different mentality then, how people were convinced that self-sacrifice, was not only their responsibility, but their <u>privilege</u>.
> *<u>Roosevelt</u> links to:*
> *cassie*
> [An image of a poor child who looks hungry, ill-fed, and unclean. Beneath this image is the question:]
> <u>does this look like 'privilege'?</u>

The image of the poor boy in *cassie* and the question, "does this look like 'privilege'?" resignify Roosevelt's words and generate an examination of how power is made normal and honorable. Is it possible to still hold sacrifice as a privilege when it produces conditions of life in which children like the pictured one must live? The *cassie* space has two links, one of which returns to the *roosevelt* space with the word <u>privilege</u>, and the other one which goes to the *different ways* space with the linked words <u>does this look like 'privilege'?</u>

> *different ways*
>   When she squinted down at me the tiny lines around her eyes deepened. "There's some folks who don't eat like us," she whispered fiercely, "but you ain't called on to contradict 'em at the table when they don't. That boy's yo' comp'ny and if he wants to eat up the table cloth you let him, you hear?"
>   "He ain't company, Cal, <u>he's just a Cunningham</u>—"
>   "Hush you mouth! Don't matter who they are, anybody sets foot in this house's yo' comp'ny, and don't you let me catch you remarkin' on their ways like you was so high and mighty! Yo' folks might be better'n the Cunninghams but it don't count for nothin' the way you're disgracin' 'em—if you can't act fit to eat at the table you can just set here and eat in the kitchen!" (pp. 24–25)
> *<u>he's just a Cunningham</u> links back to cassie*

The authors do not provide a commentary to explain how this quote from *To Kill a Mockingbird* layers the meaning of the idea of privilege; however, it is fairly easy to interpret the situation in which Scout is disgracing the Cunningham boy who is invited to eat dinner. Scout is privileged in comparison to the Cunningham boy, and especially in comparison to Cal, the Black housekeeper. Yet privilege does not include acting superior or refusing to act justly toward all others. In connection to the previous linked spaces, the Cunningham boy might be similar in appearance to the image of the poor child, and those in privileged positions must sacrifice in ways similar to those requested by Roosevelt in his speech. The *roosevelt* space had a second link on the word <u>privilege</u> that takes the reader to the *War* space.

> *War*
> Clovis and Gertie, and others around them see the war as a salvation. It is their chance for economic stability. Even at the cost of their family, their lives, and their hope, they

choose to <u>support the war</u>.
<u>*support the war*</u> *links back to roosevelt*

The juxtapositions in these four spaces explore various underlying ideologies that might make privilege normal. In the space *War*, the students' comments investigate how Clovis and Gertie participate in their own oppression by seeing the war as their salvation and chance for economic stability by moving to Detroit to make a lot of money in the factory. This group of spaces does not just question the validity of a war, it forces the reader to reflect on one's own beliefs about patriotism, and how such a positive belief can possibly oppress people. It examines the encodings of privilege during peace and war, and it asks us to consider who wins and loses and why. The possible meanings of the texts in these four linked spaces work back and forth on each other to create an important critique of the underlying ideological interpretants that support privilege in our class society.

In another hypermedia project, the group "indecisive" introduced two juxtaposed video clips (the arrival scene and song "Colors of the Wind" from the Disney animated movie *Pocahontas*, and the buffalo massacre scene from the movie *Dances With Wolves*) with the following commentary:

> The minority culture includes various groups. Some groups are merely excluded from being represented and others are badly distorted in their representations. One group that has been represented in various ways is the Native American culture. Movies such as *Dances With Wolves* and *Pocahontas* develop a certain stereotypical Native American image. This culture is no longer a group with many individual personalities. It has become a group with spiritual and environmental connections, etc. It has been said that a Native American film can not be called thus unless it has eagles, buffalo, and flute music.

This section of the hypertext then continues with:

> *The Indian in the Cupboard* is another movie portraying Native Americans. Native American consultant Jean Shenandoah was brought in during the production of the movie to assure accurate portrayal of the Iroquois nation. I am sure that other consultants were available for the other movies. Shenandoah consulted the elders of her tribe before making any decisions. Are these opinions breaking through dominant culture?
>
> These people have also been represented in television. A recent movie portraying the life of General Custer dealt largely with the repression of the Native American people. Are these movies presenting an accurate picture of the Native Americans?

Having posed this question, the group digitized a section of the Custer movie that included a dream or vision sequence. Bringing all of these different media representations together in one visual space, being able to edit and select key scenes and juxtapose them with other scenes and commentary, provided the authors with a new tool to illustrate questions about power and privilege, and its representation in and influence on the media and popular culture. Without the hypermedia tools, similar resistant readings and examinations of power in dominant representations could be accomplished with a VCR, television, and books, but we believe the process of bringing these various texts together in the electronic space helps students generate the connections as a basis for critical literacy.

Transformative Aspects

As students author resistant readings by juxtaposing multimedia texts, and begin to examine the underlying ideologies of power that support dominant and alternative representations, they initiate the potential transformation of identity through the process of reinterpreting textual meaning. Texts assign object positions or "interpellations" (Althusser, 1984, p. 48) to readers, constructing the identity of the reader simultaneously with the intended meaning of the text. When readers can intervene in or reinterpret a text, they become "subjects" (Freire & Macedo, 1987, p. 53) rather than "objects" of the intended text. When they refuse, expose, or react to the interpellation, in acts of resistance and opposition, they construct a subject position that reflects their own premises and ground rules, that represents thinking differently, and that does not accommodate preferred meanings (Giroux, 1983). They transform the potential of the text, the potentials of a representation, and their potential identity.

The "indecisive" authoring group demonstrated this power to transform personal identity in a space in their hypermedia project titled *representation*:

> The dominant culture, although we [sic] consider ourselves superior, is also affected by the representations of the media. White females have been portrayed in a negative way. Sex, violence, and superiority have been common themes among representations of women. It is difficult for women to detangle themselves from these representations and to form their own identity.

The students accompanied this commentary on how texts define possible representations of female identity with a Quicktime movie that offers a wide variety of images of women juxtaposed with a sound track from a Madonna song that repeats over and over, "Express yourself, don't repress yourself." The first image in the series pictures a woman as the center of attention at a fine restaurant. As she stands with a distressed look on her face, all eyes focus on her. Her hands are positioned on her thighs and her dress is slightly pulled up. At the top of this image, the words "This woman . . ." lead into the multiple-choice options along the bottom of the image: "a) is showing her date her tatoo; b) has an odd way of getting waiters' attention; c) clearly doesn't use Bounce." Transitions morphing several more images of female identity, including the classic Barbie doll in the black-and-white one-piece bathing suit, a young 18- to 21-year-old Asian American woman with her head turned back to look over her shoulder, a 70-year-old woman with a thoughtful hand to her chin, a blond model, and pictures of Belle, Jasmine, and the Little Mermaid who loses her voice to gain her legs, ending with four smiling young girls in casual clothes.

By presenting a variety of representations of what it means to be female, the hypermedia authors challenge popular media and present their own subjective position that expresses their belief that women do not need to conform to the stereotyped images assigned by advertisements and Disney. The students begin to "transform the world by naming it" (Freire, 1970/1992, p. 77). We would argue they do indeed "detangle themselves from these representations . . . to form [and publish] their own identity" in the production of this hypermedia text; they come to interpret their world differently and position themselves differently, for as Davies (1993) stated, students need to:

> Discover themselves in the act of sense making, of importing their own knowledges into the text . . . in order to examine the complex relations between lived experience and the text. They need to discover the ways in which their category memberships (as male or female, as white or black) lead them to interpret differently and to be positioned differently in the text. (p. 158)

Our pedagogical encouragement to students to connect the images and music relevant in their own lives to the issues and lives of those in literature supports the rewriting of their own subjectivities, and the potential meanings of those lives represented in all texts.

The seventh graders' hypermedia projects supported a transformation in their own sense of power over knowledge about poetry. The creation of the hypermedia project followed a series of poetry lessons in which they were taught several poetic devices (onomatopoeia, metaphor, simile, alliteration, rhyme, etc.), one device at a time, then directed to write a poem with that device. They came to see the individual poems as "a metaphor poem," or "an onomatopoeia poem." Each poetic device had its own poem. This consequence of isolated instruction resulted in an unfortunate narrow reading of poetry as one type of poem, and knowledge about how poetry works as belonging to the teacher who checked each poetry assignment. However, through the process of creating the hypermedia project, the students discovered this erroneous representation. Beth commented that, "it [the linking process] showed me even though that we had to know onomatopoeia and stuff like that it showed us like how you can just have it in a poem. It can have all the special languages and that. And it helped you learn." Cynthia remarked, "I think [what helped me to make connections] was to see the connections . . . you read and write but you don't see the connection. We had to link so you had to read . . . first and then you saw those." In their hypermedia project, the students used hypertext linking to illustrate various poetic devices in their poems. The combined text-linking capabilities of StorySpace and the researcher-built-in task of pasting all the poems on a wall chart, then reading them together in the authoring group to discuss and draw hyperlinks to the illustrations of each poetic device, supported the generation of new meanings for the poems. We consider this event an instance of critical literacy and pedagogy because the students reinterpreted their original readings of the poems and set their new meanings up in opposition to those designated by the teacher. The teacher welcomed their new meanings as a fuller understanding of the poetic devices, but from the perspective of the student, they transformed their role as meaning makers from the reception of the teacher's meaning to the production of their own knowledge about all poetry. This is an important shift from the object position of the classroom lessons to the subject position in the hypermedia authoring. Again, the power of the electronic space to bring multiple texts together in one single display, and to link instantaneously from one word to another visual space generates connections, leads to text reinterpretation, and therefore leads to new subjective positions of knowing and being.

Emancipatory Aspects

These transformative (from object to subject position) aspects of critical literacy can be empowering and emancipatory. As Janks and Ivanic (1992) asserted, "Discourse which resists disempowerment means using language in a way that is true to ourselves and true to the group(s) we identify with" (p. 315). The "indecisive" group embraces the potential emancipation of the self: "Representations are a part of our culture. We cannot escape them. We can only examine them in order to better understand ourselves." In becoming conscientized (Freire, 1970/1992), students may "feel empowered to think and act on the larger conditions around [them], and relate those conditions to the larger contexts of power in society" (Shor, 1993, p. 32). As authors of hypermedia they will have the opportunity in the future to bring their questions and critical readings to other readers, which is itself a form of critical action.

Because "consciousness raising . . . is part of the process in which we learn how to emancipate ourselves and others" (Janks & Ivanic, 1992, p. 307), we believe students, like the Fall 1995 group "culture," who created a hypermedia project about the Spiegelman

(1973) text *Maus: A Survivor's Tale*, will continue to be empowered learners and teachers. In their discussion of *Maus*, the group created several spaces about Hitler and the Holocaust. In the space *maus*, they wrote:

> I think the overriding question raised by the study of the Holocaust is whether or not we would have participated in the destruction of the Jews if we had been there. I am reminded of the quote, "for evil to triumph, all that is necessary is for good men to do nothing." I have always enjoyed viewing the Second World War from the American perspective. We were the grand liberators of the death camps. A closer inspection of history leaves me with a less black and white interpretation of the United States' role in this war. There are many indications that our government knew about the death camps long before we entered the war. Is this an example of "good men" doing nothing? To take this a step further, I can imagine myself in Nazi Germany. If I were a German, would I have believed the propaganda? Our media class has shown me that we are willing to believe the propaganda of the consumer culture.

LINKING CRITICAL LITERACY PRACTICES IN HYPERMEDIA TO CRITICAL PEDAGOGY IN THE CLASSROOM

Critical literacy is inherently linked with critical pedagogy. In the social milieu of the critical classroom, students are challenged to read the world critically, to become conscientized, and to adopt goals of social change as an integral part of literacy activities. This conscientization leads to the transformation of both text and reader in a way that is empowering and emancipatory. Readers who assume subject rather than object positions in relation to text need no longer be passive, and hypermedia authoring provides the opportunity to create critical texts that generate this transformation. Because we believe literacy practices are culturally constructed practices with underlying ideologies (Street, 1984), we disagree with claims that hypertext can by its inherent electronic nature transform the author–reader relationship and the experience of literacy in a new age (Bolter, 1991; Landow, 1992; Lanham, 1989). A teacher who wants to coconstruct with students a critical literacy in hypermedia authoring will have to frame the experience of texts and the representation of meaning in hypermedia in critical ways. The following excerpt from one class came at the conclusion of an hour-long discussion about three novels that formed the basis for the students' hypermedia projects:

> Jamie: Having you locate these significant events while you read and then even respond to those in terms of why you find them to be significant, I think is a very basic and important way to get into the interpretation of novels through the collective group rather than through an expert authority in terms of what a novel means. And then really critical is to try to examine why you find those incidents significant. What is it about your own life and your own beliefs that you're bringing into these books, and because those beliefs that you hold are really shaping the interpretations that you're making. So it's important to try to focus not just on the events in the text, but the events that you have experienced that are shaping your interpretations of the text. And, I think that today came out real clear that there are differences of opinion, or there's different meanings for family, and for what change might mean, and for strength, especially when you start talking about gender [pause] so there's a whole lot of, what's the word [pause] well, difference, but maybe even debate, or ahum [pause] challenging, I guess, of what ideas or of what things mean to us. And what I would like to challenge you to do in the next classes in which you're going to work just with your small group—your storyspace group, and whatever it is you need to do to try to create that representation of an idea in these novels, is I'd like to challenge you in terms of whether

or not your representation also questions the meaning of that idea that might be held differently across the culture [pause] whether or not you can bring in different beliefs on those ideas through the images and music and video clips and text, excerpts from other books you've read, from plays, poetry, etc., and read those in as well.

In our recent work, the hypermedia-authoring project has been framed more and more as an examination of cultural issues and ideas that includes links to adolescent novels as well as the media that surround our minds and work to position our identities and values. Whether the hypermedia project is aimed more at literary interpretation or cultural study, a critical literacy practice depends on a pedagogy in which the teacher seizes opportunities to juxtapose students' ideas and class materials as texts to make explicit the underlying values that mediate our meanings for texts. It is important to work to avoid what Giroux (1993) called the appropriation of Freire's work "in ways that denude it of some of its most important political insights" (p. 177). Emancipation is not achieved without a deliberate context for political action in literate acts.

Critical literacy necessarily incorporates both critical thought and critical action. As Shor (1993) stated, "the individual sees herself or himself making the changes needed. A critically transitive thinker feels empowered to think and act on the larger conditions around her or him, and relates those conditions to the larger contexts of power in society" (p. 32). Although our students have been introduced to critical pedagogy, in their largely unsupervised small group work on their multimedia hypertexts, they do not always challenge themselves or each other to become conscientized and to identify their own oppression (McLaren & Leonard, 1993), and they rarely formulate critical projects for work beyond the classroom. Because students do not on their own intervene politically in the larger culture, "turn awareness into action" (Janks & Ivanic, 1992, p. 319), or adopt a political agenda that they articulate in the hypermedia, it may be necessary for the teacher as critical pedagogue to challenge students to consider and incorporate more often their own (personal) experiences in the hypermedia and to reconsider or reread critically their own hypermedia products. McLaren and Da Silva (1993) wrote: "Individuals can gain a greater purchase on social agency through a critical narratization of their desire, through the naming of their own history and through the necessary power to resist their imposed subalternity and the deforming effects of social power" (p. 52). Transforming themselves and naming their worlds in their hypermedia by including the artifacts—songs, movies, and images—of their own lives is a form of political action, and we hope the authors who are education students will pursue further action in their own future classrooms as they practice a critical literacy.

The hypermedia literacy we have presented in this chapter is not radically political, but it is a start. It is an introduction to a political approach that challenges texts, that critiques meaning and authority, and that recognizes texts as political projects and reading and writing as political acts. Hypermedia provides a unique opportunity for students to become "critical and selective viewers, able to reflect critically on media messages, and to use those skills in the production of their own . . . texts" (Luke & Bishop, 1994, p. 109). As Lankshear (1994) wrote, "there is no ultimate *paradigm*—no final orthodoxy—of critical literacy waiting to be uncovered. Rather, there are many ways in which coherent meanings for critical literacy might be—and have been—constructed" (p. 4). Although we have admitted that the electronic space alone will not prompt a critical literacy, we do believe that the form of critical literacy experienced by the hypermedia authors in our classrooms would not have been as powerful and as transformative without the ability to juxtapose and link multimedia texts in a manipulated time and space. This power over the experience of texts awakened the creative genius in the authors, who found in each text new potential meanings realized in connection to other texts. As they juxtaposed selected images, sounds, and print, oppositional representations became ideologically framed identities, knowledge came from within the activity of authoring and socially negotiating interpretations, and personal subjectivity became an act of choosing from various valued possibilities. In the electronic literacy of hypermedia authoring in our classroom communities, we continue to seek pedagogical ways to construct such an emancipatory critical literacy practice.

REFERENCES

Althusser, L. (1984). Ideology and the ideological state apparatuses. In *Essays on ideology* (pp. 1–60). London: Verso.
Arnow, H. (1954). *The dollmaker.* New York: Avon.
Bolter, J. D. (1991). *Writing space: The computer, hypertext, and the history of writing.* Hillsdale, NJ: Lawrence Erlbaum Associates.
Davies, B. (1993). *Shards of glass: Children reading beyond gendered identities.* Cresskill, NJ: Hampton Press.
Eco, U. (1979). *The role of the reader.* Bloomington: Indiana University Press.
Eco, U., & Sebeok, T. (Eds.). (1983). *The sign of three: Dupin, Holmes, Pierce.* Bloomington: Indiana University Press.
Freire, P. (1992). *Pedagogy of the oppressed.* New York: Continuum. (Original work published 1970)
Freire, P., & Macedo, D. (1987). *Literacy: Reading the word and the world.* South Hadley, MA: Bergin & Garvey.
Giroux, H. (1983). *Theory and resistance in education: A pedagogy for the opposition.* South Hadley, MA: Bergin & Garvey.
Giroux, H. (1993). Paulo Freire and the politics of postcolonialism. In P. McLaren & P. Leonard (Eds.), *Paulo Freire: A critical encounter* (pp. 177–188). New York: Routledge.
Janks, H., & Ivanic, R. (1992). Critical language awareness and emancipatory discourse. In N. Fairclough (Ed.), *Critical language awareness* (pp. 295–325). New York: Longman.
Landow, G. (1992). *Hypertext: The convergence of contemporary critical theory and technology.* Baltimore: Johns Hopkins University Press.
Lanham, R. (1989). The electronic word: Literary study and the digital revolution. *New Literary History, 20*(2), 265–290.
Lankshear, C. (1994). *Critical literacy.* Belconnen, Australia: Australian Curriculum Studies Association.
Lee, H. (1960). *To kill a mockingbird.* New York: Warner Books.
Live, X. (1991). The beauty of gray. On *Mental Jewelry* [CD]. Location: Radioactive Records.
Luke, C., & Bishop, G. (1994). Selling and reading gender and culture. *Australian Journal of Language and Literacy, 17*(2), 109–119.
McKillop, A. M. (1996). *The pedagogical implications of student-constructed hypermedia.* Unpublished doctoral dissertation, Pennsylvania State University, University Park.
McKillop, A. M., & Myers, J. (1998). The pedagogical and electronic contexts of composing in hypermedia. In S. L. DeWitt & K. Strasma (Eds.), *Contexts, intertexts & hypertexts.* Cresskill, NJ: Hampton Press.
McLaren, P., & Leonard, P. (1993). Absent discourses: Paulo Freire and the dangerous memories of liberation. In P. McLaren & P. Leonard (Eds.), *Paulo Freire: A critical encounter* (pp. 1–7). New York: Routledge.
McLaren, P., & Da Silva, T. (1993). Decentering pedagogy: Critical literacy, resistance, and the politics of memory. In P. McLaren & P. Leonard (Eds.), *Paulo Freire: A critical encounter* (pp. 47–89). New York: Routledge.
Myers, J., Hammett, R., & McKillop, A. M. (in press). Connecting, exploring, and exposing the self in hypermedia projects. In M. Gallego & S. Hollingsworth (Eds.), *Challenging a single strand: Perspectives on multiple literacies.*
Prine, J. (1971). Hello in there. On *John Prine* [CD]. New York: Atlantic Recording Corporation.
Shor, I. (1993). Education is politics: Paulo Freire's critical pedagogy. In P. McLaren & P. Leonard (Eds.), *Paulo Freire: A critical encounter* (pp. 25–35). New York: Routledge.
Silko, L. M. (1977). *Ceremony.* New York: Penguin.
Spiegelman, A. (1973). *Maus: A survivor's tale.* New York: Pantheon.
StorySpace [Computer software]. (1994). Watertown, MA: Eastgate Systems.
Street, B. (1984). *Literacy in theory and practice.* New York: Cambridge University Press.
Trend, D. (1994). Nationalities, pedagogies, and media. In H. Giroux & P. McLaren (Eds.), *Between borders: Pedagogy and the politics of cultural studies* (pp. 225–241). New York: Routledge.

Electronic Symbol Making: Young Children's Computer-Related Emerging Concepts About Literacy

Linda D. Labbo
Melanie Kuhn
University of Georgia

Kindergarten classrooms at the close of the 20th century are places where young children eagerly splash dripping lines of bright red and yellow tempera paint with thick brushes on easel paper in art centers, pencil in crooked lines of random letters intended to represent their names on sign-up sheets for a turn in sociodramatic play centers, and fill computer screens with a jumble of letters, numbers, squiggles, images, animation clips, and sound effects in computer centers. In each instance, children are using informal tools of expression and available symbol systems to make meaning for various purposes. From a semiotic perspective, symbol systems may include various collections or sets of related communicative and cultural expressions (Eco, 1976, 1990; Gillan, 1982; Goodman, 1976; Lemke, 1993). Thus, sets of symbols employed by children in today's classrooms might consist of oral language, print, icons, scanned images, music, graphs, or numbers. From the perspective of emergent literacy, young children in schools are engaged in learning about the functions and forms of various symbol systems within a classroom culture that values and supports both their independent and socially constructed explorations. Sociolinguists (such as Wells, 1986) propose that young children are viewed as meaning makers who are "learning how to mean" (Halliday, 1975) with oral language as well as with a variety of media and methods.

The purpose of this chapter is to explore the nature of young children's electronic symbol making. We use the phrase *electronic symbol making* to designate the conceptual processes, strategies, and knowledge young children have the opportunity to develop when they use classroom computers equipped with the expressive tools of multimedia and word processing programs. We narrow our focus to the role of a single computer in a classroom center, because we recognize that even though computers over the last 10 years have become more pervasive in elementary and kindergarten classrooms (Becker, 1991; Market Data Retrieval, 1987; Morsund, 1994; Office of Technology and Assessment, 1988), the kindergarten teachers we survey during inservice workshops, presentations at national conferences, and in graduate classes overwhelmingly state that children they teach typically have access to a single computer in a classroom center. Therefore, the first step in looking ahead is to examine what is occurring presently. We also focus on the use of multimedia and word processing opportunities because we are interested in how young children learn about literacy through expressing their ideas with various types of symbols.

Our intent in discussing kindergarten children's opportunities for computer-related literacy development is to consider how the process of emerging literacy may be transformed by the reciprocal interactions among cognitive, social, and linguistic processes involved in computer-related communicative symbol making (i.e., the features of media tools children use in their symbol-making efforts, the attributes of emergent literacy classroom cultures that support children's computer-related symbol making). In the first part of the chapter, we relate broad principles of an emergent literacy approach to understanding literacy development undergirded by a semiotic perspective on symbol making. These principles provide a foundation for the remainder of the chapter, a discussion of insights we have drawn from pertinent research related to kindergarten children's opportunities for development of literacy concepts and learning with computers.

SELECTED PRINCIPLES OF EMERGENT LITERACY DEVELOPMENT

Emergent literacy is an approach to understanding young children's reading and writing development in that particular time period before formal schooling in literacy begins (Sulzby & Teale, 1991). As such, it is a time in the literacy development of a child that typically precedes conventional literacy and conventional literacy instruction (Sulzby, 1989). However, it is important to note that although the focus is on preschool- and kindergarten-aged children for the most part, many children continue to exhibit emergent literacy behaviors well into first grade.

Semiotics, the study of signs and communicative symbols, takes into consideration the evolution of meaningful sign systems within cultural contexts, such as kindergarten classrooms (Labbo, 1996). We believe that the following principles of emergent literacy learning, drawn from Labbo and Teale's (1996) guidelines for conceptualizing appropriate emergent literacy instruction, are relevant to understanding young children's computer-related literacy development.

Children Are Active Constructors of Literacy Knowledge

Several researchers (Ferreiro, 1986; Ferreiro & Teberosky, 1982; Read, 1975) who have taken a constructivist perspective (Piaget, 1962) in investigating how children independently construct knowledge about how print operates have shed light on important cognitive processes involved in literacy development. From a constructivist and semiotic point of view, the child acts on meaningful symbols that are present in a literate environment. Through purposeful, independent endeavors and efforts at problem solving, children are believed to build a knowledge base or schema about symbols and symbol systems. Indeed Pierce (1966) suggested that the hypotheses about symbols and symbol making that children generate when problem solving are crucial to their cognitive development.

Thus, children are viewed as creators of hypotheses about written language that include their concepts about print (Clay, 1975, 1991), the organization of the system of writing (Sulzby, 1986), spelling (Read, 1975), and the purposes of print (Downing, 1970). This perspective is crucial because it raises the possibility that children's solitary ventures on the computer might provide particular opportunities to learn concepts about literacy. What do children learn during such independent explorations? What are features of multimedia and word processing programs that might be instrumental to children's hypothesis making about the processes of communicative symbol making?

Children Learn About Literacy as They Interact With Literate Others

Researchers and theorists who espouse a sociocultural view (Green, Kantor, & Rogers, 1990; Kantor, Miller, & Fernie, 1992; Teale, 1984; Vygotsky, 1978; Wertsch, 1985) of literacy learning suggest that children do so through social interactions with adults and peers who are literate. Thus, routine, socially interactive events that utilize communicative symbols are incorporated, internalized, and ultimately put to use by the child. It has been suggested that the adult role in these interactions is that of a mediator who assesses the child's needs and abilities and offers the appropriate guidance and support to help the child participate in literacy events (Sulzby & Teale, 1991). An apt example of this sort of mediation is provided by Bruner (1986), who described how parents support and slowly withdraw, or scaffold, their support of children's emergent reading of books. This type of qualitative research usually involves a microlevel perspective that closely examines the action and talk that occurs among individuals in routine or daily learning and teaching situations.

Researchers who have looked closely at microlevel child-to-child interactions (Dyson, 1989; Labbo, 1996; Rowe, 1994) submit that when young children are given time to collaborate with peers as they write for an assortment of purposes, they will regularly share and coconstruct literacy knowledge. Chapman (1994), examining first-graders' writing workshop texts over time, reported the crucial role that social interaction played in the development of children as writers who were able to produce a variety of genres. Questions remain about the characteristics of social interactions that occur around electronic symbol making in computer centers. What forms of social interactions occur at the microlevel among children and adults in a classroom computer center? What are children's topics of discussion? Are there opportunities for children to coconstruct knowledge about symbol making and about literacy?

Children Learn About Literacy Through Integrated Language Arts Experiences

Although we agree with Sulzby (1986) that as communication systems oral and written language have distinctive characteristics, research conducted over the last 15 years suggests that all of the language arts (i.e., listening, speaking, reading, and writing) are learned in mutually supportive ways (Teale & Sulzby, 1986). For example, Purcell-Gates (1988) noted that children's early strategies for reading and writing are frequently supported by oral language. Various forms of writing that include invented spelling are related to developing knowledge about decoding and phonemic awareness (Clarke, 1988; Ehri, 1986). The structure and content of literature from stories children have heard is often evident in their attempts to write stories (Cullinan & Galda, 1994; DeFord, 1981).

In a similar vein, Mardell (1995) reported that stories preschool children observed their teacher share influenced their own attempts to tell stories in terms of themes, characters, storytelling techniques, and plot. Thus there appears to be a symbiotic relation among various communicative modes that reside in language processing. Do similar relations exist among the language arts, the fine arts (e.g., color, line, perspective, balance), and the multimedia arts (e.g., sound, animation, icons, scanned images) during the process of electronic symbol making?

Children's Symbolic Expressions Employ Nonconventional but Meaningful Forms

Several researchers have noted that young children may manipulate several sign systems when attempting to make meaning with graphic symbols that are both conventional and nonconventional (Dyson, 1984, 1988; Harste, Woodward, & Burke, 1984; Rowe, 1994). Others have noted that young children often use nonconventional forms of emergent writing in their attempts to express meaning (e.g., scribble, drawing, letter strings; Clay, 1975; Sulzby, 1983; Sulzby, Barnhart, & Hieshima, 1989). Ernst (1994) noted that for many young children writing and "picturing" are complementary and legitimate thinking and symbol systems.

Harste et al. (1984) observed that preschool children are able to move fluidly across sign systems involved with writing and drawing in an effort to communicate meanings publicly. Although these forms of writing are often nonconventional scribbles or strings of letters, the conceptual understanding children have constructed becomes evident as they assign meaning to the marks on the page (either before, during, or after writing). In some of these instances, children have demonstrated that they understand the concept that print carries meaning. The way children employ compositional language as they construct graphic marks, reread them attending to left-to-right directionality as they point to "words," or make statements about their writing, also shed light on their developing literacy concepts. Does electronic symbol making offer the possibility of yet another vehicle for children's development of concepts about both conventional and nonconventional usage of symbol systems?

Children Follow Various Developmental Paths Into Literacy Learning

Emergent literacy research does not support a stage theory, or hierarchy of milestones to be reached in the development from nonconventional to conventional literacy; nor does this body of work suggest that there is a single progression of development that all children go through in becoming literate (Kantor et al., 1992; Sulzby, 1989). On the contrary, although there are general patterns of literate behavior that are observable across many children, the order of each child's literacy development is often fluid, recursive, and somewhat idiosyncratic.

Anthroethnographers who study macrolevel cultural contexts of literacy development suggest that differences in children's academic success and literacy learning in school often have origins in forces outside of schooling. For example, Heath (1983) posited that it is crucial to take into account the alignment or nonalignment between the characteristics of classroom instructional practices and children's ethnic and cultural contexts related to language and literacy learning preferences. Taylor and Dorsey-Gaines (1988) suggested that differences in literacy development may be traced to individual family experiences, rather than socioeconomic status, gender, or ethnicity.

These insights raise the possibility that children who have consistent access to electronic symbol making might chart a unique path to literacy, or might follow multiple electronic paths to conventional literacy. Are there connections among literacy practices in children's homes, literacy-related cultural experiences, and their electronic literacy development in classroom computer centers at school?

CHILDREN'S CONCEPTUAL KNOWLEDGE ABOUT ELECTRONIC SYMBOL MAKING

As we have shown in our brief discussion of selected principles of emergent literacy, much of children's critical learning about literacy before formal schooling in literacy is conceptual in nature. To recap a few of these notions, as children interact with symbols in their environment, with literate others, and with symbol-making tools, they learn that written language has various forms and functions, print carries meaning, narrative stories follow a story structure, and ideas can be expressed with nonconventional and conventional writing. In this section we discuss children's computer-related emergent literacy concepts drawn from selected qualitative research we, our colleagues, and others in the field have conducted in kindergarten classrooms over the last several years.

We recognize that the concepts we note do not provide an exhaustive handling of the topic. Therefore, we view the list as an emerging one and hope that others will continue to add insights as those insights emerge from ongoing research. We group the concepts into two categories that give equal consideration to what children learn about: (a) computers as symbol-making tools; and (b) the process, forms, and products of electronic symbol making. Table 5.1 provides an overview of the concepts we discuss in this section.

Concepts About the Computer as a Symbol-Making Tool

Young children go to classroom centers and expect to engage in activities directly related to the media tools available in that center. For example, when children see paints and paintbrushes they expect to use those tools to create a painting. When they see scissors, paste, and construction paper on a table they expect to create a collage. When they see paper and pencils at a writing center, they expect to write (although the form of writing might range from scribbles and drawing to invented spelling). Because multimedia and word processing programs now contain a hodgepodge of multimedia expressive tools, it is important to understand what children expect to do when they sit down before a com-

TABLE 5.1
Children's Conceptual Knowledge About Electronic Symbol Making

---

Computer as a symbol-making tool
- Computers are used to accomplish personal and public communicative goals
- Computers are places to store and retrieve my own and others' work
- Computers are repositories of symbols and symbol-making tools
- Computer devices are instruments for composing, printing, and publishing
- Computers are used to conduct business
- Computers are used for playing and creating art

Processes, forms, and products of electronic symbol making
- Meaning making may take a variety of multimedia and symbolic forms
- Symbol making is a recursive process
- Symbols are an aid to memory
- Procedures for meaning making rely on dependable action schemes
- Selection of an appropriate symbol system is guided by communicative purpose

---

puter. In other words, what can research tell us about the concepts children gain about the computer as a symbol-making tool?

Recent qualitative research strongly suggests that young children who work in a classroom computer center frequently develop an understanding and expectation that the computer is a communicative tool (Jones, 1994; Labbo, 1996; Labbo & Kuhn, 1996; Labbo, Reinking, & McKenna, 1995; Labbo, Reinking, McKenna, Kuhn, & Phillips, 1996; Labbo, Watkins, & Kuhn, 1995; Olson, 1994). For example, Labbo (1996) studied children of various literacy abilities over the course of an academic year as they used Kid Pix 2 (Hickman, 1994), a program that allows fairly easy movement between artistic tools (e.g., paintbrush, drawing pencil, clip art icons, patterned designs) and word processing tools (e.g., keyboard typing, letter stamps, pencil writing, cutting, pasting, erasing). Findings reveal that they used the computer for a variety of symbol-making purposes and that they adopted various stances toward their computer work. Children in this study focused on the screen as the primary computer locale in which both action and thought occurred. Thus, a metaphor of "screenland" was adopted to describe the types of stances children took toward their work (see Labbo, 1996, for a complete account of the study).

From this perspective of screenland, the children studied approached the screen as a place to play, to create art, or to write. Each of these stances allowed children to construct concepts about the computer as a symbol-making tool. For example, when playing in screenland children learned that they could use the computer to accomplish personal goals (i.e., pursuing the desire to enact a story with computer icons), or social goals (i.e., sharing a visual joke created with drawing tools and icons with a classmate). When taking the stance of an author, they learned they could use the computer to compose and publish narratives as well as expository text. And, as an artist, they realized that they could use the computer to create and print works of art for a class exhibition. Furthermore, these children indicated in interviews that they had grasped the notion that computers were storehouses of a variety of symbols and symbol-making tools. They also understood that they could use a computer to store and retrieve their own and others' work, as evidenced by their actions to save work, open and close work in progress, and reopen files during ongoing computer episodes.

Other research conducted in both preschool and kindergarten classrooms (Labbo & Kuhn, 1996; Labbo et al., 1996; Labbo, Watkins, & Kuhn, 1995) posits that young children understand that computers are instrumental in conducting class-related and business-related work. For example, preschoolers who had the opportunity to participate in field trips to local businesses (i.e., flower shops, bookstores, post offices), or to visit the school office and interview the principal and staff, discovered the functional uses of computers in work associated with running schools and businesses. Children then reflected on those functions when they published classroom books about their findings and when they helped to design, set up, and play in sociodramatic play centers equipped with a classroom computer. During these occasions when the sociodramatic play center was set up as a florist shop, a bookstore, or a post office, children reinforced their schema that computers can (a) keep a record of sales by scanning in a bar code, (b) update the inventory on a database, (c) order necessary supplies through an Internet connection, (d) search digital and Internet information sources related to businesses, and (e) help map neighborhood zip code areas for mail sorting and delivery.

Labbo, Reinking, and McKenna (1995) noted the sociocultural aspects of young children's opportunities to develop concepts related to how computers figure in managing the classroom and supporting instruction and learning. When young children see their teacher model use of the classroom computer to create a calendar of activities, write notes to parents, record classroom observations, create signs for classroom centers, or compose letters, they come to understand managerial and functional uses of the computer as a communicative tool. When young children dictate messages to the teacher and watch their words captured on the screen as the teacher keyboards in the message, they have the opportunity to become aware of the graphophonemic aspects of print.

Forms, Processes, and Products of Electronic Symbol Making

Findings from current research also suggest that children who use programs such as Kid Pix 2 (Hickman, 1994) construct conceptual knowledge about the forms, processes, and products of electronic symbol making. In many of these cases, the type of insights gained seemed to be reflective of particular features of the technology. For example, Labbo (1995, 1996) noted that children who used Kid Pix 2 discovered that electronic meaning making may take a variety of multimedia and symbolic forms that include depictive, transformative, and typographic.

- Depictive symbolism involves using graphic images and icons to represent ideas (e.g., a child pastes a stamp of a shoe on the screen and says, "This is a shoe people wear to work.").
- Transformative symbolism involves using a graphic symbol as a placeholder for another graphic symbol or a symbol from another symbol system (e.g., a child pastes a stamp of a shoe and says "This is a spaceship.").
- Typographic symbolism involves using letters or special effects from the keyboard, the stamp pad, or the pencil function to represent ideas linguistically or as an extension of speech (e.g., a child types a string of keyboard letters and symbols EODLS:$E__) and says, "I liked the visit to the flower shop.").

What is interesting about these observations for the focus of this chapter is the nexus of children's talk, the type of symbols created, and computer features and operations employed in the process of electronic symbol making. A microlevel analysis of the juncture of these elements is important when viewed as an insight into children's orchestration of meaning making. For most of the children studied, oral language and symbol choices suggest that many were influenced by the availability of symbols and tools on the computer. As they sought out, used, and discussed the use of these symbols over time, they learned that symbols are stable placeholders for expressions of meaning. Many children used symbols as a memory aid, as evidenced by the fact that when they revisited work they had previously done they would verbally recall what the symbol had been intended to mean. They also came to depend on particular computer operations and procedures for mean-ing-making schemes. These established procedures became reliable action schemes they could employ in problem solving. As an illustrative example of these factors we offer the following discussion of transformative symbolism.

Transformative symbolism, using a graphic symbol as a placeholder for another graphic symbol or a symbol from another symbol system, occurred across all of the children's stances toward their work on the computer. However, it was most evident when the screen was viewed as a place to play. These playful experiences were important because children simultaneously experienced two levels of exploration that led to conceptual insights. As they were figuring out how the computer hardware worked, they were also examining the various symbol systems they saw on the screen. As a result, many children discovered that there were particular operations to employ in gaining access to symbols (i.e., move the cursor on the screen up to the menu by moving the mouse, press down on the mouse and pull down the desired menu, drag the cursor down to the stamp pad picture, release the mouse to open up a window of stamp pad options, etc.). This access to graphic symbols (i.e., icons or clip art) led to the insight that computers hold a storehouse of graphic images, tools, and symbols that the students could access, manipulate, paste, cut, erase, and repaste on the screen. These observations feature heavily in children's symbol making and accompanying talk described in the following subcategories of transformative symbolism:

1. *Transfigurative symbolism*—Child uses one symbol as a substitute for an object (e.g., a child selects a stamp of a house and says, "Here's a spaceship.").
2. *Graphically abstract symbolism*—Child uses special computer drawing effects to graphically represent sounds or actions (e.g., a child draws a special drawing effect of concentric circles and says, "The spaceship goes 'wooooooossshhh'.").
3. *Dramatic symbolism*—Child creates a make-believe world for role playing, generating and directing dialogue, and manipulating characters' movements (e.g., a child selects a stamp of a boy, moves it across a front yard scene and says, "It's the little boy coming home from school. He says 'Mommy, I'm home!' ").

When children used these three categories of transformative symbolism in composing play episodes, they appeared to be inspired and influenced in their selection of topics, characters, and events by the availability of icons and special effects. Because these types of experiences were often ephemeral and playful, most children adopting this stance did not create a product to be printed out. In these instances, the products of their work at the computer were the lived experiences. In other words, although their intent was not communication but experience, in having the experience, their ability to communicate was enhanced.

During the process of electronic symbol making, many young children learn that composing on a computer is a recursive process (Daiute, 1985) that involves a sense of discovery and figuring out what they want to say as well as figuring out how they want to say it (Labbo, 1996). This appears to be the case for many children because the computer screen offers a surface that is easily changeable. Features of programs such as cutting, pasting, or totally erasing the screen with "explosive" effects seem to invite children to tinker with symbols and with their composing efforts. Some of this tinkering results in substantial revisions of art work, stories, or multimedia compositions. Children who discover tools that can aid in revision often form the concepts that print is malleable and that composing is a process involving manipulation of typographic symbols and ideas.

Findings by some researchers suggest that young writers using word processing programs are released from the sometimes tedious or laborious work of using pencils or markers to form typographic symbols, erasing and reerasing multiple attempts at invented spellings, or even starting a work over several times (Chang & Osguthorpe, 1990). Cochran-Smith (1991) also noted the advantages of the impermanent writing surface of the computer screen. Children learn that their endeavors to collaborate about stories they compose are supported (Hoot & Kimler, 1987; Phenix & Hannan, 1984) because the computer screen is public and offers a more public forum for interaction than a small sheet of paper.

Children who use more conventional or typographic forms in their writing have also been studied when working with a computer word processor. Jones (1994) conducted a study recently that examined the talk and social interactions of friend and nonfriend dyads during a first-grade students' computer-supported writing workshop. Findings suggest that stories generated on word processors were more cohesive structurally and lexically denser than stories composed with paper and pencil. Also noted was children's inclination to engage in metacognitive talk when working at the computer.

Other studies have raised questions about the benefits of computer composing for young children. For example, Newman (1984, cited in Miller & Burnett, 1987) cautioned that software available over a decade ago actually restricted editing or revision options available to students. Olson (1994) conducted case studies of seven first-grade children's writing with traditional versus electronic tools, and reported that composing at the computer resulted in more revisions. However, he cautioned that the revisions tended to be at the surface level and frequently arose from difficulties children encountered with using the computer. Although children tended to spend more time writing with the computer than they did in using traditional tools, there was little difference in the quality and length of texts produced with either pencil and paper or with the computer.

REVISITING SELECTED PRINCIPLES OF EMERGENT LITERACY DEVELOPMENT

At this point we revisit the principles introduced in the introduction of this chapter. We do so to situate the discussion thus far within the framework provided by selected principles of emergent literacy and to reinforce our belief that electronic literacy supports and is supported by the framework.

Thus far, our discussion strongly supports the notion that children have the opportunity to learn about electronic literacy through engaging in both independent explorations and social collaborations. Children's independent explorations of computer functions resulted in generative action schemes. In these instances, the computer interface seemed to serve as a scaffold. On a very simple or easily observable level, the keyboard served as a scaffold for some children who were helped in recognizing letters. On a more sophisticated or complex level, action schemes employed to access stamp pad options were facilitated by both social interactions and independent explorations. Thus, children's opportunities to acquire symbol vocabularies and action schemes came about from a combination of their independent explorations and their social interactions.

Children who we and others have studied also appear to learn about symbol making through integrated language arts and multimedia arts. For example, symbol vocabularies describing action schemes, computer operations, symbols, or typographic terms provided metalanguage that children frequently employed as a type of supportive oral language that accompanied their actions. Children also have opportunities to make decisions about the appropriateness of varying symbol systems for different communicative purposes. This is an important insight given Gee's (1990) position that to be adequately equipped to participate in a literate culture, participants must be able to use appropriate forms of oral or written discourse for various contexts and audiences.

Findings of children's production of electronic nonconventional forms of literacy support earlier findings reported by Sulzby (1986). For example, like the children in her study, those we studied also created various nonconventional forms of symbol making that ranged from scribbling on the screen to keyboarding strings of letters, numbers, and punctuation to copying environmental text and using invented spelling. The ways these nonconventional forms were generated and the talk that surrounded their production suggest that children were gaining conceptual insights related to the communicative purposes of written text. The presence or absence of spaces between keyboard strings also suggest that some children were aware of the spatial separations between-words.

Preliminary findings reported in this chapter also support Kantor et al.'s (1992) position that children follow different developmental paths into literacy. For example, the stances of children toward screenland that Labbo (1996) observed do not represent a hierarchy of skills attainment. Children did not accomplish one stance or level (e.g., playing), then move on to another level (e.g., writing). On the contrary, children shifted among the stances and the symbolic modes according to their own individual intentions. On several occasions, children combined multiple symbolic modes in order to create an effect they found meaningful.

EDUCATED GUESSES AND DIRECTIONS FOR RESEARCH

Before we draw some general conclusions to this chapter, we offer five educated guesses about electronic symbol making that might guide future research efforts. In doing so, we try to address areas where there are gaps in our understanding of emergent electronic symbol making and literacy development.

1. Young children who previously have suffered from low self-esteem and who become proficient enough at using computer multimedia programs to meet their personal and public communicative goals might experience an increase in self-esteem, a factor that has been suggested to be important in academic success. Research is needed in this area.

2. We have suggested in this chapter that young children can gain conceptual insights about symbol making and literacy as they generate and test out hypotheses with computer programs that offer a variety of multimedia resources and easy interface tools. However, as technology develops, more research needs to be done about the relation between particular features of the design of software and children's hypothesis making that accompanies multimedia-based communicative work.

3. Young children's computer-related experiences need to consist of both open-ended activities and tasks that are specifically guided by the teacher. How might the design of these different types of tasks figure into children's opportunities to learn about literacy?

4. Computer multimedia programs can be designed in specific ways to support the literacy development or first language needs of young children of diverse ethnicities in a multicultural classroom. We wonder if there are possible connections among literacy practices in children's homes, literacy-related cultural experiences, and their opportunities for electronic literacy development in classroom computer centers at school.

5. Current notions of what it means to be and become literate will expand to include multiple literacies. Our emerging notions of electronic symbol making are just one aspect related to the conceptual knowledge and forms of literacy that are possible. For example, what roles will visual literacy (Glasgow, 1994), use of sound clips, incorporation of animation or video clips, and critical viewing play in new definitions of literacy? What impact will such notions have on the education of the youngest members of an electronic culture that embraces a new definition of literacy?

CONCLUDING COMMENTS

Almost 30 years ago, the classroom we described in the introduction to this chapter could not have existed in the same form as it does today. The 1960s were an educational era when notions of how children learn were guided by behaviorist theories of skills mastery and reading readiness. Even so, Papert (1996) decided to ask a "what would happen if" question. He wondered what would happen if educators could create a place called "Mathland," a fictitious virtual reality math kingdom where a child could roam around. As they roamed around would they discover numeracy and learn mathematics concepts? What would such a land look like? How could children interface with this virtual environment?

Negroponte noted (in Brand, 1987) that this innovative idea was ahead of its time for two reasons. First, the idea was proposed before the requisite technology (i.e., the personal microcomputer) was available, and second, it required a user-friendly interface that would allow young children to be in control of the technology. Additionally, behaviorist theories of how children learn were not adequate to accommodate Papert's vision or his question. New learning theories and educational approaches were needed before educators could be equipped to understand children's learning experiences in such a technological or virtual learning environment. Papert was able to explore many of his ideas by investigating children's interactions with Logo by focusing on what happens when children act as computer programmers, not as users of computers programs.

Researchers at the close of the 20th century and at the dawn of the 21st century are in the enviable position to be able to explore issues related to Papert's initial question because necessary technologies, child-friendly computer software interfaces, and relevant learning theories that we have reported in this chapter have been developed. We have noted that computer programs now offer young children the use of a range of symbol systems and tools that include sound effects, clip art, Quicktime animation, music, keyboard typing, special effects, and color effects that may be used alone or in combination for expressing their ideas. We have also noted that children have opportunities to develop concepts about traditional and electronic literacy as they interact independently or socially with the computer. Furthermore, we have demonstrated that the computer provides a unique window (or screen) from which to view young children's developing literacy concepts and applications of those concepts.

However, having given recognition to the progress begun in these areas, we are also right to heed cautions such as the one raised by Minsky: "Anything you hear about computers . . . should be ignored, because we're in the Dark Ages. We're in the thousand years between no technology and all technology. You can read what your contemporaries think, but you should remember they are ignorant savages" (cited in Brand, 1987, p. 104).

There is little doubt that we have much to learn. This chapter pauses at a point somewhere between no technology and all technology. We are in the beginning stages of a technological and educational enterprise that has the potential to profoundly impact teaching and learning. We are on the cusp of being able to create richer electronic learning environments because technologies and concepts about what it means to be literate continue to emerge. One might ask, what would happen if we could create a virutal reality kingdom called Literacyland? How would it be different from current visits to screenland? What would such a kingdom look like? How could young children easily interface with such an environment? Unlike Papert's notion of Mathland, where children are plunked down in the middle of a virtual math kingdom, allowed to roam around and and randomly discover numeracy, we believe that rich electronic learning environments will continue to occur best in classrooms where technology is an integral part of how things are done within the classroom culture (Labbo, Reinking, & McKenna, 1995).

REFERENCES

Becker, H. (1991). How computers are used in United States schools: Basic data from the I.E.A. computers in education survey. *Journal of Educational Computing Research, 7,* 385–406.

Brand, S. (1987). *The media lab.* New York: Viking.

Bruner, J. (1986). *Actual minds, possible worlds.* Cambridge, MA: Harvard University Press.

Chang, L., & Osguthorpe, R. (1990). The effects of computerized picture-word processing on kindergartner's language development. *Journal of Research in Childhood Education, 5*, 73–84.

Chapman, M. L. (1994). The emergence of genres: Some findings from an examination of first-grade writing. *Written Communication, 11*, 348–380.

Clarke, L. (1988). Encouraging invented spelling in first graders' writing: Effects of learning to spell and read. *Research in the Teaching of English, 22*, 281–309.

Clay, M. (1975). *What did I write?* Auckland, New Zealand: Heinemann.

Clay, M. (1991). *Becoming literate: The construction of inner control.* Portsmouth, NH: Heinemann.

Cochran-Smith, M. (1991). Word processing and writing in elementary classrooms: A critical review of related literature. *Review of Educational Research, 61*(1), 107–155.

Cullinan, B., & Galda, L. (1994). *Literature and the child.* Orlando, FL: Harcourt Brace.

Daiute, C. (1985). *Computers and writing.* Reading, MA: Addison-Wesley.

DeFord, D. (1981). Literacy: Reading, writing and other essentials. *Language Arts, 58*, 652–658.

Downing, J. (1970). Children's developing concepts of language in learning to read. *Educational Research, 12*, 106–112.

Dyson, A. (1984). Learning to write/ learning to do school: Emergent writer's interpretations of school literacy tasks. *Research in the Teaching of English, 18*, 233–264.

Dyson, A. (1988). Negotiating among multiple worlds: The space/time dimensions of young children's composing. *Research in the Teaching of English, 22*, 355–380.

Dyson, A. H. (1989). *Multiple worlds of child writers: Friends learning to write.* New York: Teachers College Press.

Eco, U. (1976). *A theory of semiotics.* Bloomington: Indiana University Press.

Eco, U. (1990). *The limits of interpretation.* Bloomington: Indiana University Press.

Ehri, L. (1986). Sources of difficulty in learning to spell and read. In M. L. Wolraich & D. Routh (Eds.), *Advances in development and behavioral pediatrics* (Vol. 7, pp. 121–195). Greenwich, CT: JAI.

Ernst, K. (1994). *Picturing learning: Artists & writers in the classroom.* Portsmouth, NH: Heinemann.

Ferreiro, E. (1986). The interplay between information and assimilation in beginning literacy. In W. H. Teale & E. Sulzby (Eds.), *Emergent literacy: Writing and reading* (pp. 15–49). Norwood, NJ: Ablex.

Ferreiro, E., & Teberosky, A. (1982). *Literacy before schooling.* Exeter, NH: Heinemann.

Gee, J. (1996). *Social linguistics and literacies: Ideology and discourses* (2nd ed.). London: Taylor & Francis.

Gillan, G. (1982). *From sign to symbol.* Atlantic Highlands, NJ: Humanities Press.

Glasgow, J. (1994). Teaching visual literacy for the 21st century. *Journal of Reading, 37*, 494–500.

Goodman, N. (1976). *Languages of art.* Indianapolis, IN: Hackett.

Green, J., Kantor, R., & Rogers, T. (1990). Exploring the complexity of language and learning in classroom contexts. In L. Idol & B. F. Jones (Eds.), *Educational values and cognitive instruction: Implications for reform* (pp. 333–364). Hillsdale, NJ: Lawrence Erlbaum Associates.

Halliday, M. A. K. (1975). *Learning how to mean: Explorations in the development of language.* London: Edward Arnold.

Harste, J., Woodward, V., & Burke, C. (1984). *Language stories and literacy lessons.* Portsmouth, NH: Heinemann.

Heath, S. (1983). *Ways with words: Language, life, and work in communities and classrooms.* Cambridge, MA: Harvard University Press.

Hickman, C. (1994). *Kid Pix 2* (Version 2). Novato, CA: Broderbund Software.

Hoot, J., & Kimler, M. (1987). *Early childhood classrooms and computers: Programs with promise.* Urbana: University of Illinois. (ERIC Document Reproduction Service No. ED 201 515)

Jones, I. (1994). First-grade students' computer supported writing: Metacognitive and linguistic effects. *Dissertation Abstracts International, 56*, 453. (University Microfilms No. 95-20, 830)

Kantor, R., Miller, S., & Fernie, D. (1992). Diverse paths to literacy in a preschool classroom: A sociocultural perspective. *Reading Research Quarterly, 27*(3), 185–201.

Labbo, L. D. (1995, April). *Classroom, computer lab, and living room: Case studies of kindergartners' home and school computer-related literacy experiences* (A report of findings related to NRRC funded research). Paper presented at the 40th International Reading Association Conference, Anaheim, CA.

Labbo, L. D. (1996). A semiotic analysis of young children's symbol making in a classroom computer center. *Reading Research Quarterly, 31*(4), 356–385.

Labbo, L. D., & Kuhn, M. (1996, March). *Sociodramatic play and computers in kindergarten.* Paper presented to the Georgia Council of the International Reading Association, Atlanta, GA.

Labbo, L. D., Reinking, D., & McKenna, M. (1995). Incorporating the computer into kindergarten: A case study. In A. Hinchman, D. Leu, & C. K. Kinzer (Eds.), *Perspectives on literacy research and practice: 44th yearbook of the National Reading Conference* (pp. 459–465). Chicago: National Reading Conference.

Labbo, L. D., Reinking, D., McKenna, M., Kuhn, M., & Phillips, M. (1996). *Computers real and make believe: Opportunities for literacy development in an early childhood sociodramatic play center* (Instructional Resource 26). Athens, GA: The National Reading Research Center.

Labbo, L., & Teale, W. (1996). Emergent literacy as a model of reading instruction. In S. Stahl & D. Hayes (Eds.), *Models of reading instruction* (pp. 249–281). Mahwah, NJ: Lawrence Erlbaum Associates.

Labbo, L. D., Watkins, J., & Kuhn, M. (1995, March). *Young children's computer-related literacy development in thematic sociodramatic play centers.* Paper presented at the 45th National Reading Conference, New Orleans, LA.

Lemke, J. (1993, December). *Multiplying meaning: Literacy in a multimedia world.* Paper presented at the 43rd Annual Meeting of the National Reading Conference, Charleston, SC.

Mardell, B. (1995). Apprenticeship in storytelling: Facilitating narrative development in a preschool classroom. *Dissertation Abstracts International, 56,* 1654. (University Microfilms No. 95-31, 437)

Market Data Retrieval (1987, November–December). Computer use still growing among all schools in the U.S. *Electronic Learning, 6,* 12.

Miller, L., & Burnett, J. D. (1987). Using computers as an integral aspect of elementary language arts instruction: Paradoxes, problems, and promise. In D. Reinking (Ed.), *Reading and computers: Issues for theory and practice* (pp. 178–191). New York: Teachers College Press.

Morsund, D. (1994). Editors' message: Technology education in the home. *The Computing Teacher, 21*(5), 4.

Newman, J. (1984, May). *What are we trying to teach?* Paper presented at the Colloquium for Canadian Research in Reading and Language Arts, Lethbridge, Alberta, Canada.

Office of Technology Assessment, Congress of the United States. (1988). *Power on! New tools for teaching and learning.* Washington, DC: Author.

Olson, K. A. (1994). Writing and revising with pencils and computers: An analysis of the processes and products of seven-first grade children. *Dissertation Abstracts International, 56,* 22. (University Microfilms No. 95-13, 449)

Papert, S. (1996). *The connected family: Bridging the digital generation gap.* Marietta, GA: Longstreet Press, Inc.

Phenix, J., & Hannan, E. (1984). Word processing in the grade one classroom. *Language Arts, 61,* 804–812.

Piaget, J. (1962). *Play, dreams, and imitation in childhood.* New York: Norton.

Pierce, C. (1966). *Collected papers of Charles Sanders Pierce.* Cambridge, MA: Harvard University Press.

Purcell-Gates, V. (1988). Lexical and syntactic knowledge of written narrative held by well-read-to kindergartners and second graders. *Research in the Teaching of English, 22,* 128–160.

Read, C. (1975). *Children's categorizations of speech sounds in English* (Research Rep. No. 17). Urbana, IL: National Council of Teachers of English.

Rowe, D. W. (1994). *Preschoolers as authors: Literacy learning in the social world of the classroom.* Cresskill, NJ: Hampton Press.

Sulzby, E. (1983). *Beginning readers' developing knowledges about written language* (Final report to the National Institute of Education, NIE-g-80-0176). Evanston, IL: Northwestern University.

Sulzby, E. (1986). Writing and reading: Signs of oral and written language organization in the young child. In W. H. Teale & E. Sulzby (Eds.), *Emergent literacy: Writing and reading* (pp. 50–87). Norwood, NJ: Ablex.

Sulzby, E. (1989). Assessment of writing and children's language while writing. In L. Morrow & J. Smith (Eds.), *The role of assessment and measurement in early literacy instruction* (pp. 83–109). Englewood Cliffs, NJ: Prentice-Hall.

Sulzby, E., Barnhart, J., & Hieshima, J. (1989). Forms of writing and rereading from writing: A preliminary report. In J. Mason (Ed.), *Reading and writing connections* (pp. 31–63). Needham Heights, MA: Allyn & Bacon.

Sulzby, E., & Teale, W. H. (1991). Emergent literacy. In R. Barr, M. Kamil, P. Mosenthal, & P. Pearson (Eds.), *Handbook of reading research* (Vol. 2, pp. 727–757). New York: Longman.

Taylor, D., & Dorsey-Gaines, C. (1988). *Growing up literate: Learning from inner-city families.* Portsmouth, NH: Heinemann.

Teale, W. (1984). Reading to young children: Its significance for literacy development. In H. Goelman, A. Oberg, & F. Smith (Eds.), *Awakening to literacy* (pp. 110–121). Exeter, NH: Heinemann.

Teale, W. H., & Sulzby, E. (Eds.). (1986). *Emergent literacy: Writing and reading.* Norwood, NJ: Ablex.

Vygotsky, L. (1978). *Mind in society: The development of higher psychological processes.* Cambridge, MA: Harvard University Press.

Wells, G. (1986). *The meaning makers. Children learning language and using language to mean.* Portsmouth, NH: Heinemann.

Wertsch, J. (1985). *Vygotsky and the social formation of the mind.* Cambridge, MA: Harvard University Press.

Early Adolescents' Use of Computer-Mediated Communication in Writing and Reading

Richard Beach
Dana Lundell
University of Minnesota

A group of four seventh-grade girls, each sitting in front of a computer in different corners of a computer lab, are feverishly writing messages to each other. When one student posts a message, all of the others immediately receive it. Then they respond to each other's messages. Other than an occasional shriek across the room, these students are relying solely on writing to engage in an animated conversation. In their messages, they are deftly questioning, challenging, and teasing each other. They also advance some opinions about a range of topics—movies, teachers, peers, and each other's misspellings. They are attentively peering at their screens to read each other's messages in order to infer the emerging ebb and flow of the conversation, inferences that guide their decisions about how to craft their conversations.

Unlike a lot of isolated writing and reading classroom activities, these students are collaboratively engaged in communicating with each other. They are learning writing and reading as social strategies through joint participation in a computer-mediated communication (CMC) exchange. In this chapter, we argue that CMC is transforming literacy instruction by providing environments for active engagement in writing and reading activities. We describe how participation in CMC environments serves to transform readers and writers.

SYCHRONOUS VERSUS ASYNCHRONOUS FORMATS

CMC typically occurs in one of two different formats: synchronous or asynchronous. In a *synchronous* format, participants exchange messages in a spontaneous chat mode in which postings simultaneously appear on the screen, one after the other, mimicking the interactions of oral conversation. Students participate in these online chat exchanges within a networked computer lab employing software that allows them to engage in what is often referred to as an electronic networks for interaction (ENFI) approach. Commonly used software packages includes Aspects (Macintosh), Classwriter (Macintosh), CommonSpace (Macintosh), Conference Writer (Macintosh), Daedalus Integrated Writing Environment (for Macintosh or DOS), Forum (Macintosh), OpenForum (Macintosh), Real-time Writer, and TeamFocus (Day & Batson, 1995). This software typically includes a format for sharing messages by adding one's own message to subsequent messages as a continually scrolling window.

The software can also be used for more *asynchronous* exchanges, in which participants post messages that are read and responded to by others at their leisure without the pressure of engaging in an online, synchronous chat mode. Asynchronous exchanges can also occur through e-mail, listserv, or newsgroup interactions. In contrast to online chat exchanges occurring in a networked computer lab, participants in these more asynchronous formats post messages read by other members of a listserv or newsgroup.

One disadvantage of synchronous chat-mode exchanges is that they may not allow time for students to reflect on the messages they receive or the messages they send (although programs contain options for receiving and entering single messages). In our own courses, we use class listservs that serve as an E-mail journal for students to share comments, reactions to readings, questions, announcements, and sections of previous writings. The listervs also provide us with the ability to download files from websites, sharing that fosters a sense of classroom community. In some cases, we set up specific prompts designed to encourage students to participate. For example, students are assigned certain readings and asked to summarize those readings and to provide their own reactions—reactions that prompt other students' reactions. Students also may set up E-mail exchanges with students in other classes, schools, or different parts of the world (Bruce & Rubin, 1993; Madden, 1993). From our experience, as in any conversation, students are most likely to participate when participants express opinions or ideas that spark controversy or debate. Within this context, when we sense that students are not using the listserv, we assume the role of provocateurs who post messages that may stimulate some controversy or debate.

CHARACTERISTICS OF CMC FORMATS

In this chapter, we focus more on the characteristics of synchronous CMC exchanges, although much of what we talk about applies to asynchronous exchanges. As written conversations, these chat exchanges draw on the processes involved in reading, writing, and oral conversation (Anson & Beach, 1995). They are also similar to other forms of written exchanges—note passing (Jackson, 1992), teacher–student dialogue journals (Staton, Shuy, Peyton, & Reed, 1988), or peer dialogue journals (Beach & Anson, 1992). In discussing the various characteristics of CMC exchanges, we refer to the results of a study of seventh-grade students who participated in a series of CMC exchanges for a period of 3 months using the Macintosh Aspects groupware program. These participants, who were part of an ongoing study of their literacy practices (Beach, 1996), consisted of 12 seventh-grade students (eight girls and four boys) in a largely White, middle-class, suburban junior high school located outside a large Midwestern city. Most of these students had computers in their homes, had used computers in their schools, and were proficient typists. As part of the larger study, these students had previously participated in oral discussions in same-sex groups of four—two groups of girls and one group of boys, for a period of 8 months, in most cases, discussing their responses to literary texts. In contrast to other research studies on CMC exchanges, the students in these groups were accustomed to working together prior to beginning their CMC exchanges. Furthermore, the use of same-sex groups partially mitigated some of the problems associated with mixed-sex groups in which males tend to dominate (Blair, 1996; Eldred & Hawisher, 1995; Kramarae & Taylor, 1993).

As described in the introduction, each of the four students sat in a corner of the lab and exchanged messages. The students were interviewed individually and in groups regarding their beliefs, attitudes, interests, and schoolwork, as well as their perceptions of their oral and computer group discussions. As part of their interview about their chat-line discussion, students were given a transcript of their own discussion and asked to give some "think-aloud" reactions to their postings and to describe the social dynamics at work in a particular discussion. We then analyzed tapes of their interviews, as well as transcripts of their CMC exchanges, to discern certain patterns in their use of and attitudes toward CMC exchanges.

TRANSFORMING READING AND WRITING PRACTICES

We believe that participation in CMC chat exchanges serves to transform reading and writing practices. This assumes that reading and writing in CMC exchanges differs from reading and writing of nonelectronic texts. In reflecting on the differences in the nature of CMC writing, Spooner and Yancey (1996) argued that CMC writing is not necessarily different

> from what writers do off line. In some cases, it looks like a business letter. Sometimes it's a bulletin, sometimes a broadside, sometimes a joke, a memo, a grafitto, a book. . . . We have to think of genres of writing as logically larger than the technologies through which we convey them. . . . Rhetorical situations are not defined by the mechanical process through which they travel, so much as by the social purposes of the rhetors. (pp. 259, 262, 270–271)

This suggests that the primary difference lies in the social or rhetorical context created by the CMC technology, a technology that is continually evolving. As Bolter (1991) noted, anyone on a listserv can "become an author and send his [or her] merest thoughts to hundreds of unwilling readers" (Spooner & Yancey, 1996, p. 101), a phenomenon that was unheard of only a decade ago.

The CMC technology therefore creates a distinctly unique social context in which participants are actively employing reading and writing strategies required for participation in the exchange. They must infer the underlying point of a string of different messages they receive in order to formulate messages relevant to that point. Inferring the point of a conversation is a social process that involves more than simply inferring the gist of messages. It also requires the ability to "read" the social situation. For example, a student who asserts an outrageous opinion quickly infers that the other three students in her group are avoiding reacting to her opinion, the "point" being that she is opening up a hot topic that the others are uncomfortable discussing. Based on their reading of the social situation, students must then formulate a written response in a matter of seconds that meshes with the emerging train of thought.

What is unique to a CMC chat exchange is that, unlike oral conversation or solo writing, participants are receiving immediate written reactions to their messages that they can read and reflect on. They know that because they are more than likely to receive a response or reaction to a message, they need to anticipate potential reactions in formulating their message. This anticipation is consistent with Bakhtin's (1981) notion of answerability—that every utterance contains the potential of future reactions or answers. As Bakhtin noted, "the word in living conversation is directly, blatantly, oriented toward a future answer word. It provokes an answer, anticipates it and structures itself in the answer's direction" (Bakhtin, 1981, p. 280). Because there are only, for example, three other participants in their group, in contrast to a large group discussion, they have some sense of the social boundaries or parameters within which they are operating. Furthermore, each student can contribute at any time to the discussion without having to be concerned with breaking into the conversation. Reticent students are therefore more likely to participate, because they are not waiting their turn to jump into the fray. Moreover, given a range of different topics simultaneously included in the discussion, it is more likely that students will find at least one topic that interests them as opposed to an oral discussion focused on only one topic.

These unique features of CMC exchanges seemed to appeal to the seventh graders in our study. They generally regarded the CMC exchange as enjoyable and actively participated in the various sessions. Some students pointed to the novelty of the CMC exchanges as enjoyable: "It's more fun because you don't do it a lot." They indicated that in face-to-face (FTF) discussions, participants can readily interrupt each other, whereas with CMC exchanges, each participant could contribute their posting without fear of being interrupted. Students could also engage in relatively long turns, because there were no constraints on how long they could hold the floor—constraints found in oral conversation. As one student noted, "If you have something important to say, then you don't get interrupted."

Some students also noted that whereas they were reticent to talk in classroom discussions, they were less so in the CMC exchanges. Several students in one of the female groups mentioned that one of their members, who was normally quite shy and reserved in FTF discussions, was much more likely to participate in CMC exchanges. The reduced sense of intimidation and verbal insecurity created a group camaraderie in which "everyone talks," allowing for a greater degree of equity. Group members would generally all attempt to comment on most of the different topics presented, reflecting an assumption that they all shared an equal voice on different topics. A case study of one student's participation in a CMC exchange in a class of adult students found that although the student had a speech handicap, the relationships he developed with members of his CMC group bolstered his confidence in participating in the large group FTF discussions (Fey, 1993). His speech handicap was less evident in the CMC exchanges than would have been the case in FTF exchanges. Thus, CMC may be particularly helpful for students who, for various reasons, are reticent about participating in FTF conversations.

Constructing Shared Perspectives

In participating in a CMC exchange as a joint, collaborative activity, students mutually construct a shared intersubjective perspective that transcends each of their own individual perspectives. Defining this shared agreement involves what Matusov (1996) described as a "coordination of individual contributions to the joint activity" (p. 29). This entails sharing disagreements, misunderstanding, conflicts, and divergent understandings that then create the need for defining some sense of common ground. As Matusov argued, "At the bottom of any agreement, there is a momentary disagreement that promotes communication (otherwise people would not need to communicate) and it is the dynamic for change in the activity" (p. 29).

The students in our study noted that the more they participated in exchanges, the more confident they became in expressing differences of opinions or disagreements. They also felt more comfortable disagreeing with others in the CMC exchange than in FTF exchanges. This finding is consistent with Knox-Quinn's (1995) analysis of college students' writing using the Aspects program on the topic of multicultural differences. She found that students demonstrated a relatively high level of participation when compared to participation in the typical classroom discussion. Students were able to express controversial opinions in their CMC exchanges, posing 31 questions to each other during a 30-minute session. For the purpose of data analysis, one pair of comments, the initiating comment and the response directed to that comment, was called a *response exchange.* The longest number of successive response exchanges around a single concept was 16 exchanges, exchanges that contained a high number of disagreements, something that rarely occurred in a noncomputer classroom discussion. These results suggest that CMC exchanges can foster disagreements within a relatively safe context. Students may feel less intimidated about challenging others when they are not also confronted with nonverbal reactions found in FTF discussions. In a CMC exchange, students may also have more time to reflect on others' written positions than in FTF conversations, reflections that lead them to formulate counterpositions.

Study participants also noted that, given this sense of safety, they were more likely to formulate provocative, outrageous positions than in FTF conversations, which, in turn, were more likely to evoke reactions and disagreements. One student noted that she was most likely to focus on messages that "hit you in a way that you want to write back—it's got to say something to you; it's got to affect you; it's something you want to write about, something you want to argue with."

Students also expressed concern with instances in which no one reacted to or acknowledged their messages, leading some to feel excluded from the group. As a result, students deliberately posted messages containing unusual, deviant ideas or positions they assumed would evoke reactions or that would stand out from the others, a rhetorical strategy for asserting their status and attracting attention. As Spooner and Yancey (1996) noted, "On less formal lists, power moves toward the most verbal and assertive users—whether they're witty and erudite or not" (p. 271).

Through their participation, students also learned to adapt to the rapid pace of the exchange by resorting to shorter comments in order to maintain their place in the conversational flow. As one student noted, "While you're typing a long message, everyone else is still in the conversation, but by the time yours comes up on the screen, they've already moved on to something else." And another student: "When you want to respond to a comment, you want to get in before anyone else, so you try to make it short. I just type it really fast and get it up there." This poses a problem for students who are slow typists who may not be able to contribute their posting with enough speed.

In this informal exchange, students were willing to explore tentative, or even contradictory, notions or ideas. Halliday (1979) noted that "writing creates a world of things; talking creates a world of happening" (p. 93). Conversational exchanges in an interactive mode, according to Halliday (1979), reveal an unfolding process, whereas formal essay writing in schools is often more preoccupied with finished products. This reflects the extent to which writing in a CMC exchange therefore tends to be more exploratory and tentative whereas formal essay writing tends to be more definitive and finalized.

In entertaining tentative opinions or hypotheses, participants were testing out ideas or "passing theories" (Dasenbrock, 1991) that are presumed open to exploration. As hunches or guesses, they may not have a lot of supporting evidence for their ideas but are curious if other group members would concur or disagree. They employ what Pradl (1996) defined as a "discourse of possibility" rather than a "discourse of certainty." "By seeing our talk in terms of *possibilities,* rather than *certainties,* we come to understand that the way we speak, as much as what we say, has real consequences for participants, who are constantly weighing and choosing among alternative linguistic representations of reality" (p. 104). This contributed to the students' perspective of the CMC exchange as a forum for mutual inquiry in which they did not need to appear to be definitive or authoritative, and could even admit their ignorance about a topic.

THE PROCESS OF CONTEXTUALIZING TEXTS

Understanding how participants construct the meaning of CMC messages requires a conception of reading comprehension as a process of contextualizing. In contextualizing texts, readers construct a context that defines the social meaning of that text. They go beyond simply inferring the gist or content of a text to defining the social agendas and implications constituting their responses. They apply their purpose for reading the text, a purpose often related to a social agenda, for example, to assist others with the information from the text or to share the text with others in order to build a social relationship with them. They are also defining their own stance toward the text that reflects their allegiance to certain beliefs or their membership in a group. By sharing responses that reflect this stance, they signal their beliefs and their group allegiance. In many cases, they enhance their group loyalty by adopting stances in opposition to the stances of other groups.

Prior to participating in the CMC exchanges, the students in our study responded in a series of oral discussions of short stories. One of those stories, written by a high school student, portrays the destruction of a Native American tribe by humanlike wolves who are former members of the tribe. The group of boys responded very positively to the story, focusing on the fact that the story had a lot of action and gory details, a macho stance in opposition to what these boys associated with the more disapproving stances of girls and teachers. The first of two groups of girls also responded positively to the story because they viewed it as an intellectual puzzle, particularly the ending in which it is difficult to distinguish between dream and reality, formulating a composite stance around their shared aesthetic experience with texts. The second group of girls objected more to the violence in the story, noting differences between their own responses and those of the group of boys.

Each of these groups is adopting a stance in opposition to another group's stance, stances that reflect gender attitudes. The boys respond in opposition to what they assume is the girls' stance, and the girls respond in opposition to the boys' stance. For girls, these stances reflect a tension between selflessness and selfishness, between assuming a stance of dutiful concern for others, as consistent with an idealized "good girl" or "good student" role and a sense of independence resistant to this "good girl or student" role, leading to a more authentic role (Brown, 1991; Gilligan, 1990). In one study, girls who resisted academic or parental demands to conform to the dutiful "good student" image defined themselves in opposition to girls who were less socially involved in the school but strived to succeed in school (Finders, 1997). In contextualizing texts such as teen magazines, members of the first group adopted stances in resistance to the second group. One member of the first group asked, "What do they [the second group] read? They probably just read books. They have nothing better to do." Another member concurs, "They probably don't even read these [holds up a copy of *Sassy*]" (Finders, 1997, p. 94). Similarly, members of the second group of girls in our study commented on the pressure to conform to the idealized "good girl" role:

Sarah: I think that boys have the pressure to goof off in class, show off, and be the class clown—stuff like that. The girls are supposed to be the really good students.

Kristine: The housewife.

Sarah: And if a boy is perfect, and he doesn't get into trouble or anything, then he's classified as a dork or something.

In their CMC exchanges, the female groups' conversations were consistently longer and more elaborated than the boys'. Consistent with a "good student" stance, they were more likely to employ task-continuative than task-divergent practices (Bergvall & Remlinger, 1996). *Task-continuative practices* include questions and answers, validation, backchannel comments, repetition, extension, supportive laughter, extended development, or talk. These practices were typically content directed, focused, cooperative, aimed at the group, acquiescent to authority, and accommodating. *Task-divergent practices* include making asides to nearby peers, derisive comments and laughter, and belittling of peers.

At the same time, within the groups of girls, some of the girls were concerned with being on-task and responding to a text, whereas others adopted task-divergent stances. These task-divergent stances are constituted by what Daiute (1993) described as a "youth genre" discourse that involves resisting or parodying adult norms and expectations or the formal "school discourse" (Gee, 1996).

For example, in the printout of the transcript, Beth, Kelly, Molly, and Libby are discussing the story, "Craig the Cat," about an adolescent girl, Wendy, who is obsessed with meeting a rock star, Craig the Cat, when he is in town for a concert, and her girlfriend narrator, Rosalind, who is less obsessed. In responding to each other's messages, they frequently disagreed, a finding consistent with research with college students that found a higher level of disagreement in CMC exchanges than in oral classroom discussion (Knox-Quinn, 1995). When the girls are discussing the question from the book, "Who seems a more typical teenager, Wendy or the other girl?" the following discussion occurs:

Molly: I don't know. It depends, some are like Wendy, some like the other girl!

Beth: Most are like the other girl though.

Libby: Some need a life, like Wendy!

Kelly: Not all teenagers are the same! There is no "typical teenager."

Libby: Right on Kelly!

Molly: I agree Beth!

In this exchange, Kelly adopts "double-voiced" (Bakhtin, 1981) mimicry of the school and textbook discourse inherent in the notion of the typical teenager. Then, on the next page, in response to an activity prompt to "list some habits and quirks of your fave rock star," the girls begin to ridicule the task, simultaneously referring to the fact that their screens keep changing colors:

Molly: Do you have a fav. rock star beth?

Kelly: Mine turns pink now and then!

Beth: Nope!

Libby: Kelly and Beth, do yall have fave stars?

Molly: It keeps gettin blurry and changin colors!

Libby: Sorry Molly hadn't written that when I wro%ote!

Kelly: Too many to count! j/k

In this exchange, the students are mimicking the procedural display, question-and-answer routines associated with school discourse, an expression of resistance inherent in what Finders (1997) described as the "literate underlife." In all of this, these students were contextualizing these messages in terms of their social stances and agendas operating in the conversation. In reading their messages from the point of view of a writer, they had to decide on whether or not to reply, what they would say, and how they wanted to present themselves through their response, and whether their messages were sufficient, relevant, or appropriate. For Witte and Flach (1994), effective writers learn to employ a range of different contextualizing strategies: sizing up and defining a context, detecting signs of honesty and deception in a context, defining relevancy and significance in a context, discerning appropriate behavior, including and excluding others in events, managing conflict, constructing social identity or roles, establishing one's position of authority or status, and determining one's own and others' beliefs and values. The students in our study noted that they were actively engaged in reading others' messages in order to define the flow of ideas and determine their social role in the conversation. One student described her reading process as follows:

> If you're writing a lot, I don't go through and read all of them. I just respond to the last thing. It also depends on what the last thing is; if it's just a word, then you have to go back through and see if there's any questions or if they are asking me something in particular. Usually I go back through to see what they are talking about.

"To see what they are talking about" required students to infer the larger points emerging in the exchange through contextualization of messages. They were therefore aware of the importance of attending to what others were saying as opposed to simply formulating their own messages.

In contextualizing CMC exchanges, students had to learn to attend to those contextualization cues that mark or frame the meaning of their exchanges and anticipate the next steps in the conversation (Auer & di Luzio, 1992; Duranti & Goodwin, 1992). As Erickson (1996) noted, these cues enable participants to " 'read' the ongoing course of the conversational roller coaster as they are riding along in it. This makes it possible for interlocutors to act on their anticipations by 'going for' crucial functional places that are turning points in the reciprocal (syntagmatic) order" (p. 35). Students focused on those cues that "actively signal how the interaction is to be framed" (Gumperz, 1992, p. 42). These cues convey "metamessages" that frame the event by letting "you know how to interpret what someone is saying by identifying the activity that is going on" (Tannen, 1993, p. 33). Students therefore used these cues to infer whether members were requesting, persuading, challenging, arguing, teasing, mimicking, seeking advice, facilitating discussion, establishing social relationships, switching topics, or resisting participation.

The students also had to learn to contextualize messages that are not in a chronological, logical order as is the case with oral conversation. Because students were reacting to different topics at different times, messages appeared to have no logical relations to previous messages. Out of messages A, B, C, D, E, F, and G, only messages C, F, and G may refer to the same topic. As one student described the process:

> You're typing and then you look up and a lot of people have said things and you haven't been reading it and you don't understand things. I always look at the bottom one and you

have to go back through and figure out what they've been talking about. By the time you figure it out, they're on to a new subject.

This leap-frogging of messages required students to contextualize messages by ignoring some messages and highlighting other messages and then linking them together in a logical order. Moreover, other students' reactions to these messages often reflected totally different, conflicting perspectives (Wasser & Bresler, 1996). This forced students to define the relations between seemingly unrelated topics that were being introduced at a relatively rapid pace. As one student noted, "When you're writing, one person can just throw in a question that has nothing to do about anything and then you would answer it and then other people start asking their own questions." And, as another student noted, "You may answer a question after someone else has already answered it."

Students also noted that within their groups, subgroups created their own separate conversations, each with their own topic focus. One pair of students would discuss topics that did not interest other members: "There are four of us and two people are talking to each other; it's boring; you're just sitting there and you want somebody to talk to you."

In contextualizing these messages into a coherent, logical order, students are acquiring invaluable inference strategies. Unlike a lot of decontextualized reading activities in the classroom, the students were motivated to learn these strategies because they were socially engaged in this activity.

Role Anonymity

Another characteristic of CMC exchanges, particularly with large group chat exchanges or listserv exchanges between strangers, is that participants may adopt anonymous roles. Some research on CMC exchanges found that this anonymity was linked to hostile, antisocial behavior most frequently characterized as *flaming* (Dubrovsky, Kiesler, & Sethna, 1991; Lea, O'Shea, Fung, & Spears, 1992; Spears & Lea, 1994). For example, Faigley (1992) found that his college students, who were employing pseudonyms, would often include sexist or racist messages designed to deliberately provoke or even offend other participants. Many of these messages were definitive assertions or generalizations that reflected little sensitivity to complexity. Protected by their anonymity, these participants, Faigley argued, were not concerned with the social consequences of their messages.

Much of the early research comparing the quality of CMC communication with FTF groups painted a relatively negative picture of CMC exchanges. It found that because social cues are filtered out of CMC communication, CMC participants did not achieve the social bonding and interpersonal relationships found in FTF groups (Garton & Wellman, 1995). This research was driven by social context cues theory (Sproull & Keisler, 1991) or social presence theory (Rice & Love, 1987) that assumes that FTF communications provides a richer array of verbal and nonverbal social cues not available in CMC communication. However, as CMC research shifted toward use of field or ethnographic analysis of CMC exchanges, a more positive portrayal of social CMC exchanges emerged (Parks & Floyd, 1996; Reid, 1995; Walther, Anderson, & Park, 1994). Some of this research was driven by an alternative theoretical perspective characterized as social information-processing theory (Walther, 1992, 1996). This theory posits that given the basic need to develop social relationships, participants form impressions of others based on the information conveyed through others' texts. They then test out their assumptions about others over time to generate conceptions of others, further refining or revising those conceptions as they acquire more information.

From this social information-processing perspective, the need to track the evolution of group interaction over time emerged as an important consideration for researchers of CMC. As researchers moved beyond single-shot studies to track the evolution of groups, they recognized that participants need time to develop social relationships, or may take more time to do so through CMC exchanges than through FTF exchanges. The research focus then shifted from "the amount of social information exchanged [to] the rate of social information exchange" (Walther, 1996, p. 10). Because the rate of social information is limited to one single channel in CMC exchanges as opposed to multiple channels in FTF exchanges, it takes more time to convey and acquire social information. It may have been the case that, given a short time span, participants in CMC studies may have adopted a more impersonal, task-oriented stance because they sensed that they only had so much time to complete their task and did not have time for socializing (Walther, 1996). In studies in which time was not restricted, the quality of social relationships improved (Walther et al., 1994). For example, during a relatively extended period of CMC exchanges, 60% of a random sample of newsgroup participants developed personal relationships (Parks & Floyd, 1996). Those participants who made more frequent postings were more likely to develop relationships; females were more likely to develop relationships than males. Many participants turned to other channels—phone calls, letters, and so forth—to bolster their relationships. Thus, rather than create a false distinction between CMC and other forms of communication, it may be more productive to view CMC as complementing rather than competing with alternative modes of communication. This research also suggests that CMC groups need time to learn to adapt to a different communication context. Students therefore need more than one or two initial sessions before they become comfortable using CMC. Then, over time, they learn to employ particular CMC features for social and rhetorical purposes.

CMC as Hyperpersonal Communication

Researchers have also found that the very impersonality of CMC exchanges enhances the quality of communication by focusing participants' attention on the presentation of verbal content as opposed to a lot of distracting nonverbal cues. Walther and Tidwell (1996) identified three features that contribute to CMC as what they described as "hyperpersonal communication" (p. 304): idealized audience conceptions, selective self-presentation, and self-introspection. Given a limited number of cues, participants often create stereotypical, idealized conceptions of their audiences, often leading to positive perceptions of their audiences. Fewer cues also mean that participants can focus more on their own selective self-presentation (Walther & Tidwell, 1996) to portray themselves in a positive light to others. As authors of their own social identities, they can carefully select and reflect on the language they use to convey their ideas and roles. In one study, CMC participants exhibited a greater degree of "private self-awareness" or introspective reflection on feelings and beliefs than did participants in FTF exchanges (Matheson & Zanna, 1988, p. 222). They also have more time to reflect on cues inherent others' messages in order to construct impressions of others. These positive benefits were evident in a study that found that the exchanges of clinically disturbed adolescents over the period of 11 months contained less stress, more positive self-perceptions, and more references to interpersonal relationships (Zimmerman, 1987). Although features of appearance, gender, race, and so forth may always be influencing communication, in a CMC exchange, participants can reveal or hide these features through how they formulate their message.

Creating Social Relationships and Roles

Rather than assume that CMC groups are inherently nonhierarchical, democratic "linguistic utopias" (Pratt, 1987) that mitigate differences associated with gender, class, race, or disabilities (Regan, 1993), recent research indicates hierarchical structures still persist in CMC exchanges (Bruce, Peyton, & Batson, 1993; Hawisher & Sullivan, 1998). For example, although students may participate in a chat exchange free from the imposition of teacher questions, this does not mean that these exchanges will be free of domineering members or controlling questioners. Although previous research on electronic conferences found that males tended to dominate, more recent research with high- and low-level males and females indicates that high-level members of both genders are more likely to dominate (Blair, 1996; Eldred & Hawisher, 1995; Kramarae & Taylor, 1993).

As previously noted in our own study, the group of boys was less likely to engage in extended exchanges than the groups of girls. The girls' conversations were consistently longer than the boys', reflecting differences in how the girls were using their conversations to establish roles and relationships through their talk. The girls expressed more concern about not receiving a reply to a posting than the boys, reflecting their perception of the conversation as a means of maintaining their relationships. They were also more likely than boys to remark on the challenge of being physically separated in CMC exchanges, noting that "it's different from talking because you're separated from the others." Their concern with separation reflects Tannen's (1990) findings that females are more likely to physically relate to each other while engaged in conversation than males. For the boys, not receiving reactions "didn't really matter because it happens to everyone else in the group." The girls may be bringing a different attitude toward the function of conversation as essential to building social relationships, and the boys may have perceived the conversation as functioning more to exchange information (Tannen, 1990).

The students also adopted different social roles related to power relationships that transcend gender differences (Day, Crump, & Rickly, 1996). Some of these roles were based on establishing their social status or "footing" in a context—whether they can assume the role of a leader or that of a follower (Goffman, 1974). Students frequently referred to the fact that certain students did not have the same social status in the group as other students. They were therefore highly attentive to the emerging social framework that defined members' status, rights, and responsibilities as embodied in a range of multiple, competing voices (Burns, 1992; Taylor, 1992). Defining this participant framework, another form of contextualizing, allowed them to determine their power alignments with and against each other, as well as their positions relative to the conversation (O'Connor & Michaels, 1996).

The CMC exchange also provided a relatively safe environment free of the usual physical constraints that inhibit experimentation of social roles. As Feenberg (1989) noted, "the 'I' who presents you with the 'me-as-text' is not exactly the same 'I' who appears in face-to-face encounters" (p. 272). For example, in one newsgroup, a male posing as a female established a number of romantic relationships with other males; once the male's true identity was exposed, other newsgroup members were shocked (Van Gelder, 1991). Because they are participating in anonymous situations, participants may be more apt to exaggerate or accentuate features implying their own identities because those features are not present in a writing exchange. Turkle (1995) argued that current notions of identity as fixed or rather singular or static have given way in a postmodern era to identities or roles as continually being negotiated within virtual communities of Multi-User Dungeons or Dimensions (MUDs) or MUDs-Object-Oriented (MOOs). A MUD or MOO may comprise a virtual institution or site with separate units in which members adopt a range of different roles. In these virtual worlds, participants' perceptions of their talk and "selves" online relies heavily on vocabulary and positioning in the statements that serve to represent roles, requiring new ways of defining the construction of self. This requires them to be skilled performers who create and sustain roles that will be perceived as contributing to a CMC community (Lyman, 1996). For example, within a soap opera newsgroup, certain members assume the role of scribes who take responsibility for retelling episodes other participants may have missed (Baym, 1995). Those who are able to embellish their retellings with wit and humor achieve a reputation within the group as entertainers. In an analysis of group interaction on the alt.tv.x-files computer newsgroup (Ward, 1996), members gained status in the group by making frequent postings, by having some official affiliation with the program as a writer or fan-club leader, or by making intertextual links between the program and other television programs. Insiders also made explicit the conventions and norms constituting appropriate behavior within the newsgroup community. Making irrelevant, off-topic statements (considered as "dreck" or "drivel"), bashing or spreading false rumors about the two celebrity stars of the show, posting sexually explicitly or violent messages, or misusing the newsgroup was considered inappropriate (Ward, 1996). Certain members of the group assumed responsibility for monitoring compliance to the group's norms. When a newsgroup member began spreading false rumors about the female star of the show, she was immediately castigated and told " 'either get with it and get some netiquette or please keep your computer turned off' " (Ward, 1996, p. 8). Learning to participate in a CMC group therefore involves the ability to read or contextualize group members' attitudes and stances—contextualizing that is often driven by assuming such roles as scribe or monitor. The monitor would be attending to instances of inappropriate behavior relative to their own notion of what constitutes appropriate behavior.

In adopting these roles, participants experiment with using different language styles or discourses—religion, psychology, management, science, merchandising, and so forth— that represent certain ways of knowing or ideological stances (Fairclough, 1989; Gee, 1990; Lemke, 1995). For example, newsgroups based on sports are constituted by a discourse of sports talk. Participants share technical expertise about players, rules, and the history of a sport; celebrate the value of competitiveness and hard work; and generally avoid topics related to emotional, interpersonal matters associated with the "feminine" television talk shows. Children and adolescents often adopt a "youth genre" discourse to resist or parody adult norms and expectations (Daiute, 1993). For example, students in this study frequently used the CMC exchanges to parody their roles as students by mimicking the formal school discourse (Gee, 1996) of their classes, which, as they indicated in interviews, were not particularly engaging.

Students would also ridicule and tease each other for adopting certain roles in the discussion, particularly if they were assuming a "good student" role. For example, in one group of three girls, two of the girls who were good friends were continually teasing or ridiculing each other. A third member, who was more of a social "outsider," frequently attempted to mediate their teasing in order to focus the group more on what she perceived to be the discussion topic. She adopted the role of peer mediator based on her beliefs about effective communication: "I don't like it when kids pick on each other. It doesn't make any sense." This same student noted in an oral conversation that she would be less likely to adopt the role of mediator because she is "intimidated easily in classroom discussions [whereas] when you type, people don't take it that seriously." In contrast to the flaming found in more anonymous exchanges, the students noted that their ridicule and repartee was more of a verbal sparring game in which serious consequences were mitigated. One reason for the mitigation was that the students knew each other well and were accustomed to teasing each other in other contexts. As one student noted, "we can make fun of each other and not take it seriously." This suggests that the CMC exchange creates a safety zone in which participants are less likely to be affected by nonverbal, emotional factors, and can experiment with different social roles and uses of language (Hawisher & Selfe, 1992). Students in the study would frequently mimic or parody the language of the initial posting, triggering other participants' word play, thereby extending a string of postings around a word-play genre. For example, in an exchange on the topic of movies, one student mentioned a movie with the title *Dying Young.* The other students then picked up on the word play: "I live dying young."/"I can see why you fell asleep."/"Great! I love dying young."/"I live dying young." They also attended to unusual misspellings that frequently occur due to the rapid pace of the exchange, using them in subsequent postings. This attention to word play and "double-voiced" meanings (Bakhtin, 1981) certainly occurs in oral conversation. However, when reading their own words, students may be more likely to attend to graphic displays, deliberate typos, use of all capital letters, and emoticons.

IMPLICATIONS FOR TEACHING: USING CMC IN THE CLASSROOM

The results of our own research and other studies have a number of implications for using online CMC to transform literacy instruction in the classroom.

Creating Contexts for Learning Through Participation

In thinking about using CMC exchanges, the teacher's role becomes one of creating CMC environments in which students are actively engaged in their own learning through their participation in a collaborative activity of exchanging messages. From the perspective of activity theory of learning (Lave, 1996; Leontiev, 1981; Nardi, 1996; Rogoff, 1995; Wells, 1996) learning occurs through what Rogoff (1995) described as "participatory appropriation" (p. 12) of various social practices. As Hunt (1995) noted, learning is a "byproduct of an activity, not what the activity was focused on . . . we normally don't learn ahead of an activity, but during it, and we engage in the activity before we can possibly understand what the activity is" (p. 1). Similarly, Batson (1994) argued that although students may not be learning formal instructional skills, "they are always learning through participation: how to be students, how to survive in the particular school environment, how to be a child of a particular race and sex in that era" (p. 150). Through participating in the activity, participants internalize these structures. As Batson (1994) noted, "Most people are unaware of the intricate structure of what they have learned from participation, of the intellectual complexity of common sense or the unstated pattern of courtesies that make Emily Post and Amy Vanderbilt sound like primers" (p. 150).

Clarifying Purposes for Using CMC Exchanges

At the same time, both teachers and students need to have a clear sense of purpose for using CMC in the classroom. These purposes may include establishing social relationships, sharing different ideas about a topic, responding to a text, debating an issue, brainstorming about paper topics, collaborating on a joint writing project, or sharing common experiences.

Students can also use CMC as a forum for large group peer conferences. In contrast to paired or small group conferences, they can receive feedback from a large number of different perspectives (Neuwirth, 1996; Santoro, 1996). Writers in one study were more likely to use comments suggested by e-mail than comments given to them orally because they retained more of the information from reading than from listening (Mabrito, 1991). Many CMC programs contain features that serve to encourage peer conferencing. For example, using the Daedalus program, Scenters-Zapico (1995) provided students with a list of peer review prompts in the Daedalus "Current/Assignment" windows that remain on the top of the screen. These prompts included ideas for reacting to initial free writing, the writer's points or claims, confusing sentences, and suggestions for revisions. He then created "InterChange" sessions for groups of three students, in which two students type in reactions to the writer's draft.

As in any collaborative effort, the extent to which students mutually share a common sense of purpose will influence their participation. If students do not have a clear sense of purpose, they are more likely to resort to activities such as flaming. External evaluations of a number of college programs using CMC found that students who had a clear sense of academic purpose for using CMC were more likely to benefit from the use of CMC writing than students who lacked this sense of purpose (Bartholomae, 1993).

Phases of Familiarity in Using CMC

The students in our study indicated that when they began to use the Aspects program, they had difficulty adjusting to the novelty of the CMC exchanges. Teachers need to recognize that students do go through an initial "gee-whiz" phase of adjustment to the novelty of the exchange, resulting in a lot of verbal play (Medwin & O'Donovan, 1995). As one student noted, "The first time we did the chat thing we were so excited that we went hyper." Rather than prematurely dismiss these playful exchanges as simply a frivolous diversion, teachers need to allow students some opportunity to experiment with what one student described as "a different way of talking to someone." When students engage in word play and mimicry, rather than dismissing these exchanges as simply off-task or goofing off, teachers need to perceive this word play as part of experimenting with alternative roles or identities outside of the usual teacher–student academic roles and discourse. As a student noted, "Kids our age—we do that [ridicule] all the time—we do it for fun." Once they became accustomed to the CMC exchange, students in the study then assumed a more serious stance, although not entirely abandoning their playful interactions. As students became more comfortable using CMC, they expressed higher levels of satisfaction, even though some may still prefer FTF exchanges (Olaniran, 1996).

Organizing Chat Groups

In organizing chat groups in the computer lab, we have found that the smaller the group, the easier it is for members to manage the number of different messages from different group members. For example, in a basic writing course for college students, one of us, using a Daedalus Interchange program, organizes group discussions by giving students an activity sheet that may include a list of topic areas, scenarios, or focus questions related to course readings (Lundell, 1996). Students enter the conference screens in groups of three (preferably sitting apart from each other), signing into a topic area that interests them most, or into one about which they may be intending to write a paper. They then select a role in their group, something they negotiate on the screen as they enter the chat screens. These "roles" include a captain or leader who types in a question or prompt from the activity sheet and moves the group along to new questions when relevant, a "know-it-all" or speaker who agrees to speak to the whole class after the activity to sum up the group's discussion, and a "book worm" or scribe who will type in quotes or ideas from the readings to link discussion to relevant passages in their readings. These discussions typically shift from a fairly structured, initial conversation around some of the activity-sheet questions to a more freestyle response branching into other interesting or related issues the students wish to discuss.

We also use the Daedalus program in an asynchronous format to provide prompts or questions for writing as in a case conference. When students were writing about experiences in schools, we provided them with prompts for free writing, reviewing their free writing, and defining the purpose for their writing. We also prompted them to infer their own and their readers' interest in the topic and to compare their own with others' school experiences. As they become accustomed to using this program, the students ideally internalize these prompts and questions for use in subsequent writing.

Responding to Messages

In their interviews, students consistently expressed difficulty in responding to others' messages—the process of contextualizing. In some cases, they were overwhelmed by multiple messages on a range of different topics. In other cases, by the time they had responded, particularly with longer messages, students had moved on to other topics. Students often felt left out when they did not receive reactions to or acknowledgments of their messages. Although some of this may be due to the fact that they are seventh graders, these difficulties also suggest the need for some instruction on strategies for reacting to messages, including discussing the need for acknowledgment of and sensitivity to others' perspectives. Based on their sense of students' zones of proximal development (Vygotsky, 1978), teachers could model perspective-taking strategies for empathizing with others' points of view. This could include restating others' messages in order to establish a clear point of reference for their reactions, questions, or comments. For example, "In your message, Mike, you stated that Holden has no ties to anything. I'm not sure if I agree with that." Students could also pair up in front of screens and mutually respond to messages in an asynchronous mode, engaging in think-aloud responses to the messages by describing the processes they employ in reading and reacting to the messages.

Use of Transcripts

One pedagogical advantage of CMC technology is that participants can simply print out transcripts at the end of a session in order to reflect back on a written record of their exchange. If students were discussing topics relevant for writing papers or conferencing about a draft, they can then use these transcripts as records of their prewriting brainstorming or of recommendations for revisions (Kolko, 1993). For example, Mayers (1996) posted the transcripts of group exchanges to his class bulletin board for future access by students who used them to recall discussion of essay topics. He also incorporated the transcripts into specific assignments. For one assignment, students had to analyze the use of clichés in both their own writing and in the transcripts. In the interviews in our study, students engaged in a think-aloud review of the transcripts, noting instances of turn-taking processes, social facilitation versus domination, topic development, intertextual linking, social roles, and language games. Having an immediately available record of their talk helped them perceive certain conversational patterns that could best be determined from analyzing transcripts.

Collaborative Writing

Students can also use CMC to engage in collaborative writing projects because CMC allows students to physically share the same evolving texts. In an analysis of two groups of four sixth graders collaboratively writing a magazine on the topic of prejudice using the Aspects program over a 12-week period, Mitchell, Posner, and Baecker (1995) analyzed the group interactions to determine how students learned to use the shared workspace of the Aspects program as a tool for collaboration. They found that students initially worked independently, each writing their own text for peer review. As they became more accustomed to using the software, they began to capitalize on the program's synchronous editing capabilities. One student would assume the role of scribe, garnering and collating ideas from the other students who were working at different computers. Because the Aspects program provides sidebars that someone has control of in a text region, students can use that information to then physically identify who is working on a section. The students also found that having computers next to each other facilitated their visual observation of each other's writing. The students also used the program's paragraph locking mode to gain control over revising specific paragraphs without other students' interference. In the end, both groups generated a 32-page magazine that was displayed in a science center. All of this meant that, as a group, they were using CMC to collaboratively conduct inquiry as a classroom community. Similarly, in an 18th-century British literature college class, Hunt's (1994) students shared their e-mail responses. Hunt described this sharing as "inkshedding," whereby students used CMC to exchange responses to the literature read in the course. From their shared messages, participants generated questions. Study groups then wrote reports addressing those questions and shared drafts of those reports via e-mail for further comments. Further sharing of drafts led to further comments and revisions. As participants received comments and questions about their reports, they continually made revisions addressing the comments and questions, and then shared their revised reports. They challenged each other's ideas and incorporated those ideas into their revisions. Through their participation in this ongoing forum, students shifted their writing style from one of formal, academic prose appropriate for essay papers to more informal styles appropriate for social exchanges. For Hunt (1994), this entailed learning a new genre of academic exchange characterized by a dialogic, tentative, exploratory, and critical stance.

EVALUATING GROWTH IN USE OF CMC EXCHANGES

Through participation in CMC exchanges, students are being transformed as readers and writers. They can evaluate those transformations as part of a portfolio self-reflection by reviewing transcripts from the beginning, middle, and end of a course. They may note changes in their ability to contextualize or "read" the social agendas implied by messages in order to formulate responses to those agendas. They may also note changes in their style of social interaction, and their ability to participate in a relevant, appropriate, effective manner. They may also discern changes in their use of language. Students in Hunt's (1994) "inkshedding" class noted that their language became less formal and more playful.

In addition to these social strategies, students are also learning how to mutually construct knowledge. They are learning how to talk and think within the discourse of a particular disciplinary orientation. A group of students in a high school literature class learns how to critically respond to literature texts (Medwin & O'Donovan, 1995). In reflecting on changes in their responses, they may note that they elaborate on their responses in more detail as they develop confidence in discussing texts. They may also note that they employ a wider range of different kinds of responses—whereas they simply summarized story lines in the beginning of a course, they are now making connections to other texts or analyzing a text's cultural assumptions. As they become more comfortable in constructing knowledge, they acquire a sense of power in their own abilities to generate new knowledge (Shallert et al., 1996). Other members of their group appreciate their contribution to the group, enhancing their status as contributing members. Students could reflect on changes in their development of knowledge within the context of a CMC group exchange. They could also reflect on the ways in which their mutual construction of knowledge through participation serves to transform them as readers and writers.

REFERENCES

Anson, C., & Beach, R. (1995). *Journals in the classroom: Writing to learn.* Norwood, MA: Christopher Gordon.

Auer, P., & di Luzio, A. (1992). *The contextualization of language.* Amsterdam: Benjamins.

Bakhtin, M. M. (1981). *The dialogic imagination* (C. Emerson & M. Holquist, Trans.). Austin: University of Texas Press.

Bartholomae, D. (1993). "I'm talking about Allen Bloom": Writing on the network. In B. Bruce, J. Peyton, & T. Batson (Eds.), *Network-based classrooms: Promises and realities* (pp. 237–262). New York: Cambridge University Press.

Batson, M. C. (1994). *Peripheral visions: Learning along the way.* New York: HarperCollins.

Baym, N. (1995). The emergence of community in computer-mediated interaction. In S. Jones (Ed.), *Cybersociety: Computer-mediated communication and community* (pp. 138–163). Thousand Oaks, CA: Sage.

Beach, R. (1996, December). *Early-adolescents' use of social intertextuality.* Paper presented at the annual meeting of the National Reading Conference, Charleston, SC.

Beach, R., & Anson, C. M. (1992). Using peer-dialogue journals to foster response. In R. Durst & G. Newell (Eds.), *Exploring texts* (pp. 191–210). Norwood, MA: Christopher Gordon.

Bergvall, V., & Remlinger, K. (1996). Reproduction, resistance and gender in educational discourse: The role of critical discourse analysis. *Discourse & Society, 7*(4), 453–479.

Blair, K. (1996). Microethnographic study of electronic discourse communities: Establishing exigency for e-mail in the professional writing classroom. *Computers & Composition, 13,* 85–91.

Bolter, J. (1991). *Writing space: The computer, hypertext, and the history of writing.* Hillsdale, NJ: Lawrence Erlbaum Associates.

Brown, L. (1991). A problem of vision: The development of voice and relational knowledge in girls age seven to sixteen. *Women's Studies Quarterly, 19,* 52–71.

Bruce, B., Peyton, J., & Batson, T. (Eds.). (1993). *Network-based classrooms: Promises and realities.* New York: Cambridge University Press.

Bruce, B., & Rubin, A. (1993). *Electronic quills.* Hillsdale, NJ: Lawrence Erlbaum Associates.

Burns, E. (1992). Teaching composition in tomorrow's multimedia, multinetworked classrooms. In G. Hawisher & P. LeBlanc (Eds.), *Re-imagining computers and composition* (pp. 115–130). Portsmouth, NH: Boynton/Cook.

Daiute, C. (1993). Youth genres and literacy: Links between sociocultural and developmental theories. *Language Arts, 70,* 402–416.

Dasenbrock, R. W. (1991). Do we write the text we read? *College English, 53,* 7–18.

Day, M., & Batson, T. (1995). The network-based writing classroom: The ENFI idea. In Z. Berge & M. Collins (Eds.), *Computer mediated communication and the online classroom* (pp. 25–46). Cresskill, NJ: Hampton Press.

Day, M., Crump, E., & Rickly, R. (1996). Creating a virtual academic community: Scholarship and community in wide-area multiple-user synchronous discussions. In T. Harrison & T. Stephen (Eds.), *Computer networking and scholarly communication in the twenty-first-century university* (pp. 291–314). Albany: State University of New York Press.

Dubrovsky, V., Kiesler, S., & Sethna, B. (1991). The equalization phenomenon: Status effects in computer-mediated and face-to-face decision-making groups. *Human–Computer Interaction, 6,* 119–146.

Duranti, A., & Goodwin, C. (Eds.). (1992). *Rethinking context: Language as an interactive phenomenon.* New York: Cambridge University Press.

Eldred, J., & Hawisher, G. E. (1995). Researching electronic networks. *Written Communication, 12,* 330–359.

Erickson, F. (1996). Going for the zone: The social and cognitive ecology of teacher–student interactions in classroom conversations. In D. Hicks (Ed.), *Discourse, learning, and schooling* (pp. 29–62). New York: Cambridge University Press.

Faigley, L. (1992). *Fragments of rationality: Postmodernity and the subject of composition.* Pittsburgh, PA: University of Pittsburgh Press.

Fairclough, N. (1989). *Language and power.* New York: Longman.

Feenberg, A. (1989). The written world: On the theory and practice of computer conferencing. In R. Mason & A. Kaye (Eds.), *Mindweave: Communication, computers and distance education* (pp. 22–39). Oxford, UK: Pergamon.

Fey, M. H. (1993). *Reader response, collaborative writing, and computer networking.* (ERIC Document Reproduction Service No. ED 364 875)

Finders, M. (1997). *Just girls: Underground literacies and life in junior high.* New York: Teachers College Press.

Garton, L., & Wellman, A. (1995). Social impacts of electronic mail in organizations: A review of the research literature. In B. R. Burleson (Ed.), *Communication yearbook 18* (pp. 434–453). Thousand Oaks, CA: Sage.

Gee, J. (1996). *Social linguistics and literacies.* New York: Falmer.

Gilligan, C. (1990). Teaching Shakespeare's sister: Notes from the underground of female adolescence. In C. Gilligan, N. Lyons, & T. Hanmer (Eds.), *Making connections: The relational worlds of adolescent girls at Emma Willard School* (pp. 6–29). Cambridge, MA: Harvard University Press.

Goffman, I. (1974). *Frame analysis.* Cambridge, MA: Harvard University Press.

Gumperz, J. (1992). Contextualization revisited. In P. Auer & A. Di Luzio (Eds.), *The contextualization of language* (pp. 39–54). Amsterdam: Benjamins.

Halliday, M. A. K. (1979). *Spoken and written language.* New York: Oxford University Press.

Hawisher, G. E., & Selfe, C. L. (1992). Voices in college classrooms: The dynamics of electronic discussion. *The Quarterly of the National Writing Project and the Center for the Study of Writing and Literacy, 14,* 24–28.

Hawisher, G. E., & Sullivan, P. (1998). Women on the networks: Searching for e-spaces of their own. In S. Jarratt & L. Worsham (Eds.), *Feminism and composition studies: In other words.* New York: Modern Language Association.

Hunt, R. (1994). Traffic in genres, in classrooms and out. In A. Freedman & P. Medway (Eds.), *Genre and the new rhetoric* (pp. 211–230). Bristol, PA: Taylor & Francis.

Hunt, R. (1995, December 13). *Re: How do you read?* XMCA listserv [Online]. Available: http://communication.ucsd.edu/LCHC/

Jackson, R. M. (1992). The untapped power of student note writing. *Educational Leadership, 49,* 54–58.

Knox-Quinn, C. (1995). Authentic classroom experiences: Anonymity, mystery, and improvisation in synchronous writing environments. *Computers, Writing, Rhetoric and Literature, 1*(2). Available: http://www.cwrl.utexas.edu/~cwrl/V1N2/article2/aspect1.html

Kolko, B. (1993). Using InterChange transcripts recursively in the computer classroom. *Wings, 1*(14). Available: http://www.daedalus.com/wings/kolkoI.I.html

Kramarae, C., & Taylor, H. J. (1993). Women and men on electronic networks: A conversation or a monologue. In H. J. Taylor, C. Kramarae, & M. Ebben (Eds.), *Women, information technology, scholarship* (pp. 52–61). Urbana: University of Illinois, Center for Advanced Study.

Lave, J. (1996). Teaching as learning in practice. *Mind, Culture, and Activity, 3,* 149–164.

Lea, M., O'Shea, T., Fung, P., & Spears, R. (1992). "Flaming" in computer-mediated communication: Observations, explanations and implications. In M. Lea (Ed.), *Contexts of computer-mediated communication* (pp. 89–112). London: Harvester Wheatsheaf.

Lemke, J. (1995). *Textual politics.* Bristol, PA: Taylor & Francis.

Leontiev, A. N. (1981). The problem of activity in psychology. In J. Wertsch (Ed.), *The concept of activity in Soviet psychology* (pp. 37–71). Armonk, NY: Sharpe.

Lundell, D. (1996). Instructional notes. *Teaching English in the Two-Year College, 23*(4), 313–314.

Lyman, P. (1996). How is the medium the message? Notes on the design of networked communication. In T. Harrison & T. Stephen (Eds.), *Computer networking and scholarly communication in the twenty-first-century university* (pp. 39–52). Albany: State University of New York Press.

Mabrito, M. (1991). Electronic mail as a vehicle for peer response. *Written Communication, 8,* 509–532.

Madden, E. (1993). Conferences across classes: Using Daedalus Mail to set up inter-class conferences. *Wings 1*(2). Available: http://www.daedalus.com/wings/madden.1.2.html

Matheson, K., & Zanna, M. (1988). The impact of computer-mediated communication on self-awareness. *Computers in Human Behavior, 4,* 221–233.

Matusov, E. (1996). Intersubjectivity without agreement. *Mind, Culture, and Activity, 3,* 25–45.

Mayers, T. (1996). From page to screen (and back): Portfolios, Daedalus, and the "transitional classroom." *Computers and Composition, 13,* 147–154.

Medwin, S., & O'Donovan, M. (1995, November). *Computer-mediated discussion of literature.* Paper presented at the annual meeting of the National Council of Teachers of English, San Diego, CA.

Mitchell, A., Posner, I., & Baecker, R. (1995). *Learning to write together using groupware.* Toronto: Dynamic Graphics Project. Available: http://www.dgp.toronto.publications/CHI95.html.

Nardi, B. (Ed.). (1996). *Context and consciousness: Activity theory and human–computer interaction.* Cambridge, MA: MIT Press.

Neuwirth, C. (1996, April). *The online writing lab: Computer-mediated tutoring via electronic networks.* Paper presented at the annual meeting of the American Educational Research Association, New York.

O'Connor, M. C., & Michaels, S. (1996). Shifting participant frameworks: Orchestrating thinking practices in group discussion. In D. Hicks (Ed.), *Discourse, learning, and schooling* (pp. 63–103). New York: Cambridge University Press.

Olaniran, B. (1996). A model of group satisfaction in computer-mediated communication and face-to-face meetings. *Behaviour & Information Technology, 15,* 24–36.

Parks, M., & Floyd, K. (1996). Making friends in cyberspace. *Journal of Communication, 46,* 80–97.

Pradl, G. (1996). *Literature for democracy: Reading as a social act.* Portsmouth, NH: Boynton/Cook.

Pratt, M. L. (1987). Linguistic utopias. In N. Fabb, D. Attridge, A. Durant, & C. MacCabe (Eds.), *The linguistics of writing* (pp. 48–66). New York: Methuen.

Regan, A. (1993). "Type normal like the rest of us": Writing, power, and homophobia in the networked composition classroom. *Computers and Composition, 10,* 11–23.

Reid, E. (1995). Virtual worlds: Culture and imagination. In S. Jones (Ed.), *Cybersociety: Computer-mediated communication and community* (pp. 164–183). Thousand Oaks, CA: Sage.

Rice, R., & Love, G. (1987). Electronic emotion: Socioemotional content in a computer-mediated network. *Communication Research, 14,* 85–108.

Rogoff, B. (1995). Observing sociocultural activity on three places: Participatory appropriation, guided participation, and apprenticeship. In J. Wertsch, P. Del Rio, & A. Alvarez (Eds.), *Sociocultural studies of mind* (pp. 139–164). New York: Cambridge University Press.

Santoro, G. (1996). What is computer-mediated communication. In Z. Berge & M. Collins (Eds.), *Computer mediated communication and the online classroom* (pp. 11–27). Cresskill, NJ: Hampton Press.

Scenters-Zapico, P. (1995). Peer review workshops on DIWE: The logistics of pedagogy (or trying out a new terministic screen). *Wings, 3*(1). Available: http://www.daedalus.com/wings/scenters-zapico.3.1.html

Shallert, D., Benton, R., Dodson, M., Lissi, M., Amador, N., & Reed, J. (1996, December). *Conversational indicators of the social construction of knowledge in oral and written classroom discussions of reading assignments.* Paper presented at the annual meeting of the National Reading Conference, Charleston, SC.

Spears, R., & Lea., M. (1994). Panacea or panopticon? The hidden power in computer-mediated communication. *Communication Research, 21,* 427–459.

Spooner, M., & Yancey, K. (1996). Postings on a genre of email. *College Composition and Communication, 47,* 252–278.

Sproull, L., & Keisler, S. (1991). *Connections: New ways of working in the networked organization.* Cambridge, MA: MIT Press.

Staton, J., Shuy, R., Peyton, J., & Reed, L. (Eds.). (1988). *Dialogue journal communication: Classroom, linguistic, social and cognitive views.* Norwood, NJ: Ablex.

Tannen, D. (1990). *You just don't understand: Women and men in conversation.* New York: Ballantine.

Tannen, D. (Ed.). (1993). *Framing in discourse.* New York: Cambridge University Press.

Taylor, P. (1992). Social epistemic rhetoric and chaotic discourse. In G. Hawisher & P. LeBlanc (Eds.), *Re-imagining computers and composition* (pp. 131–148). Boynton/Cook.

Turkle, S. (1995). *Life on the screen: Identity in the age of the Internet.* New York: Simon & Schuster.

Van Gelder, L. (1991). The strange case of the electronic lover. In C. Dunlop & R. Kling (Eds.), *Computerization and controversy: Value conflicts and social choices* (pp. 364–375). New York: Academic Press.

Vygotsky, L. (1978). *Mind in society.* Cambridge, MA: Harvard University Press.

Walther, J. (1992). Interpersonal effects in computer-mediated interaction: A relational perspective. *Communication Research, 19,* 52–90.

Walther, J. (1996). Computer-mediated communication: Impersonal, interpersonal, and hyperpersonal interaction. *Communication Research, 23,* 3–43.

Walther, J., Anderson, J., & Park, D. (1994). Interpersonal effects in computer-mediated interaction: A meta-analysis of social and anti-social communication. *Communication Research, 21,* 460–487.

Walther, J., & Tidwell, L. (1996). When is mediated communication not interpersonal? In K. Galvin & P. Cooper (Eds.), *Making connections: Readings in relational communication* (pp. 300–307). Los Angeles: Roxbury.

Ward, J. (1996). *Don't watch it alone! An ethnography of the alt.tv.x-files newsgroup.* Unpublished paper, University of Minnesota, Minneapolis.

Wasser, J., & Bresler, L. (1996). Working in the interpretive zone: Conceptualizing collaboration in qualitative research teams. *Educational Researcher, 25,* 5–15.

Wells, G. (1996). Using the tool-kit of discourse in the activity of learning and teaching. *Mind, Culture, and Activity, 3,* 74–101.

Witte, S., & Flach, J. (1994). Notes toward an assessment of advanced ability to communicate. *Assessing Writing, 1,* 207–246.

Zimmerman, D. (1987). Effects of computer conferencing on the language use of emotionally disturbed adolescents. *Behavior Research Methods, Instruments, & Computers, 19,* 224–230.

TRANSFORMING SCHOOLS AND CLASSROOMS

Rapid changes in computer-based technology have provided classrooms and schools with the potential to transform students' literacy learning. Long-distance collaborative research projects, communication via e-mail to experts, and the ability to scan databases and create multimedia class projects are a few examples of the variety of engaging opportunities that classroom teachers offer students in schools. In general, computers provide a means for student expression, communication, connection to information, and information processing. They reinforce collaboration, thinking, and learning, and help students make connections outside of the normal school day to the home, workplace, and community.

In the three chapters that follow, we examine some of the conditions that permit such transformations to occur. School systems, such as Summit County Schools in Ohio (see Fawcett & Snyder, chap. 7) are implementing initiatives based on long-term goals and a clear vision for staff and student growth and development. Individual schools, like a school in rural Nova Scotia (see Neilsen, chap. 8), are confronting issues associated with gender and empowerment and seeking ways to increase access to resources outside of their school. Single classroom teachers, such as first-grade teacher Ashley Templeton in rural Georgia (see Kieffer, Hale, & Templeton, chap. 9), are exploring new ways of teaching, learning, and organizing classrooms with technology.

In the first chapter of this section, Fawcett and Snyder (chap. 7) describe how they have worked to understand schools as systems. Their chapter supports the idea that change by systems needs long-term support to take root. They suggest that there is new work to be done—work that focuses on inquiry-based learning with students at the center. The authors invite readers to listen and learn from children who actively create new ways for learning and thinking about technology.

Neilsen (chap. 8) shows how one school utilizes telecommunications as a tool to transform students' feelings about power and authority. These students use the technology to create their own "webs of control." They take learning in directions that no one anticipates, and the result is a clash of authority. Neilsen shows that children in classrooms and schools, where change is going on, are often developing different agendas than teachers and school officials.

Kieffer, Hale, and Templeton (chap. 9) use the case study methodology to describe patterns in Templeton's classroom transformation. Templeton, a novice computer user, changes throughout the school year by first focusing on learning the technology, then developing technology uses in her classroom, and finally, reflecting on her teaching and students' learning. Templeton commits large amounts of her time toward learning the technology. As she becomes a competent technology user, she undergoes a dramatic transformation in her thinking about student learning and technology use in her classroom.

These three chapters only begin to show the capabilities of computer use and barriers to transformation in classrooms and schools. Many teachers work in schools with antiquated wiring systems, limited knowledge of computer skills, and minimal access to technology. Some school systems lack a clearly articulated vision about the role of technology in schools. By describing the efforts of individual teachers who are integrating technology into their existing classrooms, schools involved in exploring telecommunications, and large-scale projects supporting systemwide reorganization and change, we hope to highlight some of the transformative possibilities, but also to challenge readers to continue thinking about issues related to schools and classrooms in need of transformation.

Transforming Schools Through Systemic Change: New Work, New Knowledge, New Technology

Gay Fawcett
Steve Snyder
Summit County, Ohio, Educational Service Center

An education major at a nearby university told us about an ongoing assignment she has for one of her classes: Students must bring a newspaper article about education to be discussed at the beginning of each class. "It's depressing," she said. "I'm starting to think about changing my major. Articles are easy to find, but they nearly all say the same thing—what a horrible job our schools are doing."

In recent years, numerous task force reports and calls for school reform have been issued. According to Hairston (1982), teachers have been "plagued by embarrassing stories about college graduates who can't pass teacher competency tests, and by angry complaints about employees who can't write reports" (p. 81). There is a feeling in the general public that schools are failing in their mission to educate responsible and productive citizens. Our responses to date have generally been reactionary. We have tried to change teacher behavior, tinkered with the organizational structures of schools, overlaid instructional strategies ranging from new math to discovery learning, fattened the curriculum with the agendas of special interest groups, and mandated everything from phonics to busing.

What has remained constant through all school reform efforts is the traditional focus on what is important to be learned in school and how it should be learned. However, modern technology has let the "genie out of the bottle. It is no longer necessary to learn about the American War of Independence by sitting in Mrs. Smith's classroom and hearing her version of it. There are more powerful and efficient ways to learn about the Revolutionary War. And they are all potentially under the control of the learner" (Mehlinger, 1996, p. 403).

The traditional school purpose of transmitting the culture has become extremely complex in the last few years. The information of learning no longer resides in a cultural castle guarded by parents, teachers, and clergy. Knowledge is increasing at such an astounding rate that we can no longer teach students everything they need to know; and the World Wide Web, cable television, pagers, and cellular phones connect teachers and learners in ways we are just beginning to understand.

CULTURAL TRANSMISSION

In her studies of the way in which culture is transmitted, Mead (1978) made a distinction between those cultures that change so slowly that the future is merely a repetition of the past and those in which change is more rapid. She proposed that in bygone days (and in some primitive cultures today) the future was simply a repetition of the past. The same problems needed to be solved, and it worked well to solve them in the same ways. In such cultures, even a change was dealt with in familiar ways. For example, immigrants from the old country tended to build houses of the same architectural style and planted grapes in similar soil. The key conditions for maintenance of such a culture were (a) a lack of questioning, and (b) adults as keepers of the knowledge. In these cultures, which Mead labeled *postfigurative*, people continued to do old work in old ways.

As cultures are forced to make more change, they continue doing the old work, but they do it in new ways. Such work would be exemplified by the transition from kerosene lanterns to electric lights or moving from a typewriter to a word processor. The prevailing model of behavior for members of such societies is their contemporaries. The elders tend to draw on the resources of their peers, whereas the young look to other youth for models of behavior and problem solving (thus generation gaps tend to exist in such societies). Regardless of the source of knowledge, however, the culture continues to do old work, but it does so in new ways. Mead (1978) called these cultures *cofigurative*.

In cultures facing rapid change, which Mead (1978) called *prefigurative* cultures, new problems emerge and the young people help to solve them in new ways because they are not bound up by old solutions. In such cultures, Mead (1978) stated, the elders could say, "I have been young and I know . . . Now, however, children can reply, 'You have never been young in the world I am young in and you never can be' " (p. 63). We are at such a time in history because of the explosion of knowledge and the new technologies that allow us to access and produce such knowledge. Mead suggested that in prefigurative cultures survival may depend on the ability to learn from children. We need new work done in new ways.

This chapter is about looking at learning in new ways. It is about NEW WORK, new knowledge, and new technology. As we have visited dozens of classrooms in the past 2 years where technology is used in new ways, it has been virtually impossible to know whether we are observing a social studies lesson or a reading lesson, an English class or a math class, high achievers or low achievers. In these classrooms, Scribner and Cole's (1981) broader definition of literacy, derived from cross-cultural studies, applies:

> We approach literacy as a set of socially organized practices which make use of a symbol system and a technology for producing and disseminating it. Literacy is not simply knowing how to read and write a particular script but applying this knowledge for specific purposes in specific contexts of use. The nature of these practices, including, of course, their technological aspects, will determine the kinds of skills (consequences) associated with literacy. (p. 236)

We encourage readers to take this sociocultural perspective of literacy and learning when reading this chapter. More importantly, we encourage readers to consider this prefigurative and post-typographic world through the eyes of children.

SCHOOL THROUGH THE EYES OF CHILDREN

As Mead (1978) stated, if we are to learn from our children, "enough trust must be re-established so that the elders will be permitted to work with the young on the answers" (p. 89). We will not be able to use new technology effectively until we are able to view new work and its defining characteristics through the eyes of children. Trust requires that we listen carefully to what students have to say about school.

Recently we interviewed groups of students from Grades 2 through 12 (Fawcett, 1996). The students had all experienced excellent and not-so-excellent teaching, and so they understood the need for systemic change in schools. Amy, a high school sophomore, used a metaphor that aptly describes schools as seen through the eyes of the students we talked with: "I feel like a ping pong ball in school," she said. "Up and down, up and down. Good teacher, bad teacher; interesting teacher, boring teacher; stupid work, fun work. It changes from class to class. So in some classes I learn a lot and I like it, but in other classes I just do what I have to do to get a good grade, and then I forget it."

The students we talked to told similar stories. They described good teachers as those who cared for their students as people, who tapped into their students' interests, and who provided for choice and voice. They talked about working in groups with other students, learning from activities that required them to find answers to their questions in the real world, and completing projects of which they were proud. They praised teachers who did not rely too heavily on tests, textbooks, or videos, and they expressed appreciation for teachers who pushed them to be the best they could be.

On the other hand, the students were quite critical of teachers who seemed to care more about their subjects than about the students they worked with. They said they hated lectures, meaningless assignments (in particular, they cited end-of-chapter questions and study guides), trivial rewards, and teachers who embarrassed students publicly. They were confounded by work that did not seem to have relevance for their lives, such as memorizing dates in history and completing traditional grammar assignments. They also had little patience for teachers who could not maintain class control.

Some of the students had computers in their classrooms, and others did not. They expressed a need for fairness. "All kids should have computers, not just rich kids. If you can't have it at home, then you should at least have it at school," Marnika said. For those who did have access, we again found there was great diversity in how the technology was used, and the students were quite perceptive about effective and ineffective uses. One student told us that there was one computer in each classroom and the students were not permitted to use it: "The teachers make up study guides and stuff on them. My own personal (yet very intelligent) opinion is that they call them 'personal computers' for a reason. If it's personal, then you should be using it for your own learning, not for making work for someone else. I don't think the teachers should use them that way, but, oh well."

Some students told about going to their school's computer lab. They were critical of keyboarding exercises and skill-and-drill software. They praised technology when it provided the opportunity to explore questions they had formulated as a result of a class discussion. Some students enthusiastically described electronic portfolios, home pages, and e-mail to students in other parts of the world. One eighth grader told about exchanging e-mail with Finnish students regarding the prejudice in their country toward Lapps and Gypsies. "I learned more about civil rights that way than I ever did in my social studies classes," he said.

If we are to "work with the young" (Mead, 1978, p. 89) on the answers to their questions, we must trust them as they tell us how schools need to change. After listening to a panel of students talk about school, one principal in the NEW[3] consortium said, "It took a group of 9–12-year-olds to help me see what I had been missing for 22 years. It was right there all the time." Technology has the potential to change schools in profound ways, but, for the most part, "Computers in the schools have soaked up huge capital expenditures without providing any appreciable return on investment" (Reinhardt, 1995,

p. 50). If, however, we listen to students, they will help us to design new work that will help them use new technology to explore new knowledge.

A PRESIDENTIAL CHALLENGE
FOR TECHNOLOGICAL LITERACY

In 1995, President Clinton challenged the nation's businesses, parents, educators, government, and community leaders to work together to ensure that all children in the United States are technologically literate by the dawn of the 21st century, equipped with communication, math, science, and critical thinking skills essential to prepare them for the Information Age. Clinton identified four pillars of technological literacy as follows (*Technological Literacy*, 1997): (a) provide all teachers the training and support they need to help students learn through computers and the information superhighway, (b) develop effective and engaging software and online learning resources as an integral part of the school curriculum, (c) provide access to modern computers for all teachers and students, and (d) connect every school and classroom in the United States to the information superhighway.

The response to the challenge was immediate. Some of the nation's most innovative technology businesses committed resources to work with schools; communities mobilized large numbers of volunteers to lay millions of feet of cable to connect schools with the information superhighway; the Federal Communications Commission began working on a plan to offer discounts on telecommunications services to schools and libraries; and Congress funded grants for school districts to develop new, technology-supported ways for children to learn.

On October 10, 1995, Clinton held a press conference at the White House to announce recipients of the first federally funded Challenge Grants for Technology in Education. The 19 grants were awarded to schools and communities who had a vision for doing things differently. One such grant was a 5-year, $6.8-million project called NEW[3]: NEW WORK, New Knowledge, New Technology. NEW[3] is a collaborative of 18 school districts enrolling 88,000 students, two vocational schools, three universities, foundations, nonprofit entities, and businesses. The initiative is coordinated by the Summit County Educational Service Center in Ohio, but it belongs to every person and organization in the community that cares about the future of children. The vision of the grant is that *every* day *every* child will be so engaged in learning that he or she will learn what is supposed to be learned as he or she becomes a good human being and *every* day *every* adult in the school will passionately model a love of learning. We believe technology can help this vision become a reality.

NEW WORK

The centerpiece of the NEW[3] initiative is the schoolwork of a prefigurative culture. Such work is so dramatically different from schoolwork of the past that we call it NEW WORK. NEW WORK is defined as inquiry-based learning and focuses on the following results: (a) students engage the work, (b) students persist at the work, (c) students experience delight and satisfaction in the products of their efforts, (d) students learn what they are supposed to learn, (e) parents have confidence in the school program, and (e) the community values the learning of the students (Schlechty, 1990).

The term *new work* has generated some controversy in the consortium. Administrators worry that teachers will assume they are being asked to jump on yet another bandwagon; teachers ask, "Does that mean what I've been doing is all wrong?"; and parents and community question, "Does that mean you're throwing out the basics?" The fact that the term has generated so much discussion causes us to cling to it. It has irritated some, frightened some, and caused others just to ponder, but it has been a catalyst for rich discussions about curriculum. Educators outside the consortium who also recognize the need for work that is new have picked up on the term, and we have heard it used in a U.S. Department of Education technology conference (Linking for Learning, Washington, DC, October 6–10, 1996), in another county in our state, and in a manuscript written by Phillip Schlechty of the Center for Leadership in School Reform (1996).

NEW WORK CURRICULUM

The "old work" model of schooling dictated a curriculum of "objective" facts and discrete skills taught in a carefully sequenced hierarchy. In a post-typographic world, however, we repeatedly find that what was "objective" today is a matter for conjecture tomorrow as we explore the world in ways that were impossible a decade ago. Recently, for example, a high school advanced placement physics student told us about watching a television news special about the Hubble telescope. The student was fascinated by the photographic data that seemed to indicate that the big bang theory of how the universe was formed was not correct and that theoretical and anatomical physics were entering a period from which a new theory would emerge. The student, however, reported that the teacher had insisted that he continue to regard the big bang theory as the prevalent paradigm because that was how the course was designed. The student volunteered that he had no further use for the class. The physics instruction was better on CNN than in his advanced placement high school class.

NEW WORK requires that instead of textbook-driven instruction we provide the opportunity for students to explore the world and their place in it. The International Reading Association and the National Council of Teachers of English recently defined curriculum in a manner that reflects this new view: "Curriculum [is] the actual opportunity for learning provided at a particular place and time" (Standards for the English Language Arts, 1996, p. 71). NEW WORK is a curriculum of opportunity, not a curriculum of carefully prescribed scope and sequence. Curriculum in a post-typographic world cannot define an ever-changing content, but must define, instead, the "basic conditions necessary for students to be able to achieve" (Standards for the English Language Arts, 1996, p. 71).

Burke and Short (1994) described three levels of curriculum that can guide such opportunity: (a) curriculum as fact, (b) curriculum as activities, and (c) curriculum as inquiry. Even though "facts" increase and change at an alarming rate in a post-typographic world, content-free learning is obviously impossible. Curriculum in a post-typographic world, therefore, requires that "facts" be viewed as a means to an end, not an end in themselves. Such a curriculum recognizes the need for students to use the facts in activity-based learning. In the past, however, teachers typically decided what facts and what activities students needed. Learning in a post-typographic world requires that students use the facts of curriculum as they are actively involved in answering their own questions—what Burke and Short (1994) called curriculum as inquiry. In all aspects of such a curriculum, the goal is to "judge the quality of the mental trip taken, not the arrival point" (Harste, Woodward, & Burke, 1984, p. 18).

Within such a curriculum, it is impossible to divide curriculum into disciplines to be addressed separately, and a carefully sequenced hierarchy of skills becomes nearly impossible as students delve, on their own, into rich information sources available to them through technology. In the post-typographic world of student inquiry, there is a dynamic interplay of disciplines that cannot be broken into subject areas or time periods in the school day. In the past, integrated curriculum often meant stacking one subject atop another. In a new work classroom, it is impossible to even discern where one subject ends and another begins.

Postman (1995), in *The End of Education: Redefining the Value of School*, drew a compelling contrast between curriculum designed to transmit a traditional culture and curriculum designed to allow students to explore new knowledge through new technology. Postman suggested powerful curricular themes that could allow children to use the facts of curriculum as they are actively involved in answering their own questions. He suggested, for example, that children investigate "spaceship earth"; explore the narrative of the "fallen angel" who continually learns from the mistakes made in encounters with the world; inquire into the grand American experiment in democratic idealism; explore the world of diversity, not to seek and validate differences, but to find common ground; and, finally, learn language, not as a word-making tool, but as the defining quality of one's worldview.

Such themes would resonate with children, inviting them to inquire into what it means to be better human beings and to investigate their place in the world. This kind of curriculum repurposes schools as valuable institutions in a prefigurative culture where the future depends on the ability to learn from children.

NEW WORK IN THE CLASSROOM

The students in Karen's classroom know what a NEW WORK curriculum is. The students are mostly African American and they come from socioeconomically depressed homes. Most of their parents were high school dropouts, and Karen wanted to instill in them a desire for education. Early in the year, the students discussed careers and each decided on a professional from whom they would like to learn. Through friends and with some searching on the Internet, Karen arranged for each student to have an e-mail pal. Dushawn communicated with Jonathan, a young engineer, who designed toys on a 3-D computer system. Dushawn learned how Jonathan used technology in real life and how he needed math as well as artistic talent to make a product. Dushawn recently communicated electronically with Jonathan about a toy airplane he was designing:

Dushawn: Is the airplane hard to design?

Jonathan: It has six parts. That isn't very many, but this is a hard product to design.

Dushawn: Why?

Jonathan: The parts have to fit together just right. The company wants a little man to fit in the cockpit, and I am having trouble getting an angle right.

Dushawn: What is an angle?

Jonathan: It's when two lines come together. This one is a right angle. Look at where the wall and the floor come together. If you run your finger down the wall till you hit the floor and then move along the floor, you have just drawn a right angle.

Dushawn: It looks like an "L."

Dushawn learned that plastic is made from petroleum, that plastic pellets are melted and poured into a mold shaped like the toy, and that there are safety regulations on toys. He knew the difference between a mechanical engineer and an electrical engineer, and he knew that civil engineers design roads and bridges. He said he wants to be a mechanical engineer like Jonathan, and he knew he would have to go to college and be good at math. Dushawn was actively engaged (through communicating on the computer) with the curriculum as fact (reading, writing, and mathematics) as he pursued the questions he had. Karen, his teacher, knew a scope and sequence might be outdated tomorrow, and so she learned to be comfortable with the ambiguity that often pervades NEW WORK.

A group of high school students in the consortium also knows what NEW WORK looks like. One day a student asked Mrs. Connelly why alcohol and cigarettes are so readily available to minors in their community. Mrs. Connelly challenged the class to establish that the assertion was true and, if it was, to develop a community understanding of the problem and to propose solutions. The students worked cooperatively with local law enforcement agencies to gather evidence on businesses selling to minors, statistics on alcohol-related driving, property offenses, and attitudes of fellow students toward substance abuse. Students studied scientific data on the effects of alcohol and tobacco on the body and mathematical data on the effects of substance abuse on health care costs. Much of their research was done over the Internet, and graphing calculators assisted with plotting the data.

Schooling based on traditional cultural transmission would suggest that laws prohibiting the acquisition of dangerous substances would restrict their use, but the reality proved very different. Resolving the complexity of the problem led students to a systems analysis in which the interactions of economic realities, the limited reach of law enforcement, and the behavior of children interact to put tobacco and alcohol within easy reach. Students were engaged in a living laboratory of democratic politics as they took their story to the larger community as well as to the city's legislative body. Proposed solutions were presented in an 8-minute video to community groups.

Curriculum in a post-typographic world will demand that students be trusted to make decisions about their own learning—to "ask questions about and then hypothesize answers to explain the world around them" (Edelsky, Altwerger, & Flores, 1991, p. 26). Obviously, in such an environment, the role of teachers, parents, and the community must reflect "support of, rather than intervention in, the learning" (Harste et al., 1984, p. 206).

NEW WORK THROUGH SYSTEMIC CHANGE

A high priority of the NEW[3] project is to garner such support through systemic reform. Senge (1990) defined systems thinking as "a discipline for seeing wholes . . . a framework for seeing interrelationships rather than things, for seeing patterns of change rather than static 'snapshots' " (p. 68). During the last three decades, systems thinking, spurred by technology, has been applied in such diverse fields as health care, business, economics, politics, and ecology. However, education, for the most part, has continued to ignore this cornerstone of change.

When our nation's governors gathered in the spring of 1996 for their Education Summit, they touted the power of technology to teach and transform U.S. schools. Following the pattern of policymakers from local school boards to the White House, they ignored the glaring reality that few of the successful pilot educational technology initiatives have survived the cultural collision with the harsh realities of life in classrooms (Cuban, 1986; Ladewskii,

Krajcik, & Harvey, 1994). Technology cannot succeed if we ignore the fact that "in a school, everything important touches everything else of importance. Change one consequential aspect of that school and all others will be affected" (Sizer, 1991, p. 32).

Early in the NEW[3] project, a metaphor emerged that captures the systems thinking underlying the grant. We cannot even recall how it began, but it seems to grow by the day. We have come to speak of education as a river. Shortly after the announcement of the Federal Challenge Grant for Technology in Education, someone said, "Our goal is to get all of the river flowing in the same direction." Flowing in the same direction means working toward a common vision of excellent schools with high standards of academic achievement and student conduct. It means, in Goodlad's (1994) words, preparing students for the "privileges and responsibilities inherent in a democratic society, and development of the ability to participate in that society" (p. 636). All of the river means all of the classrooms in all of the schools, all community members, all organizations, all businesses, and all universities—virtually anyone who cares about the future of our children and our country.

The beauty of the river is that we can all be at different points as long as we are flowing in the same direction. There will be rapids, some debris in the river, and even some dangerous waterfalls. However, success will come from the "water's need to flow. Water answers to gravity, to downhill, to the call of ocean. The forms change, but the mission remains clear" (Wheatley, 1992, pp. 15–16). The mission for education must be understood in the context of NEW WORK that allows students to explore new knowledge through the use of new technology. However, the mission cannot succeed unless everyone in the system—educators, parents, students, business people, and the community understand NEW WORK.

NEW WORK AND EDUCATORS

Sometimes superintendents in the NEW[3] consortium point with pride to their "pockets of excellence." Although we would not deny recognition to those excellent teachers working in isolation, we also know that pockets of excellence may not be all that excellent from a student's point of view, as the young lady who talked about the ping-pong effect of schools pointed out. Elmore (1996) proposed that current models of staff development affect only about 20% of teachers. Such small numbers do not result in systemic reform, and the new learnings are often compromised in attempts to scale up, and usually end up looking more like the old practices than the new. Staff development, if framed in a systems perspective, has the potential to engage the other 80% of teachers.

A systemic staff development plan for a post-typographic era is a challenge. The overwhelming temptation is to develop a new curriculum, a new set of workshops to train teachers in the use of technology, and an evaluation scheme that will ensure compliance. That replication of the old model will lead to the same results. Instead, "we must create new models for adults who can teach their children not what to learn but how to learn and not what they should be committed to, but the value of commitment" (Mead, 1978, p. 72). What is needed is staff development that focuses on capacity building, where capacity is defined as the ability to continuously learn (Senge, 1990). In other words, our systems must become learning systems where everyone—teachers and children alike—is committed to continuous improvement.

The NEW[3] project entails an ambitious staff development program designed to build learning systems as NEW WORK supported by technology becomes the norm rather than the "pockets." Each year approximately 500 educators take part in the Academy of Learning and Technology, a year-long program of staff development that takes place in after-school and Saturday workshops, site visits to schools and businesses that use technology effectively, seminars with nationally known technology experts, and in their own settings as they self-organize around classrooms, buildings, and districts.

The Summit County Consortium spent many years prior to the awarding of the Federal Grant for Technology in Education building the capacity for this change. The staff development practices moved over a 6-year period from make-it/take-it, to expert-directed workshops on topics such as constructivism, to a facilitated process of group inquiry and learning. Because teachers were accustomed to sitting passively in workshops and classes, inquiry was very difficult at first. Often it became confused with advocacy, and defensiveness sometimes overwhelmed dialogue. However, over time we began to see subtle shifts. Spontaneous, collaborative networks began emerging, and people seemed more interested in learning from others than in promoting their own practices.

In such a climate, pockets of excellence have begun to inform rather than disrupt schools. An example took place recently. One of the Consortium districts decided to explore alternatives to their traditional teacher evaluation checklist. They asked the Educational Service Center assessment consultant for help. Having worked with student electronic portfolios, she suggested they try electronic professional portfolios as a means of assessing professional growth. For several months, administrators (including the superintendent and treasurer) and teachers began developing their own home pages to illustrate their growth. The process was guided by inquiry as they posed questions about their practice, went about searching for answers, and then shared evidence of their learning. A second district called seeking help with teacher evaluation, not knowing about what the first district was doing. In a traditional staff development model, the consultant would have traveled to the second district and repeated the process. Instead, she connected the two, and the first district is now coaching the second district as they both engage in a new form of technology-supported staff development.

As another example, Carol and Susie are eighth-grade language arts teachers who have taken part in nontraditional staff development that is focused on building the capacity of systems to learn. As a part of the NEW[3] Project, they were invited to become an Invitation to Invention team; there are five such teams in the consortium. Other members of their team include Betsy, a language arts consultant, and Linda, a software consultant. There are no workshops for the Invitation to Invention teams, there is no program to follow, and the only experts are the students who inform their decisions. The team meets weekly to design NEW WORK with and for students. The state language arts curriculum provides the framework for their studies, but within that framework, students explore their own questions about the world and their place in it. When they study a piece of literature, for example, some students choose to research the setting of the story. Others explore the emotions of the characters and write poetry conveying their own feelings. Still others choose to write letters to the author asking how the story evolved. Many times, the inquiries are carried out through electronic research and communication and multimedia becomes the means for showing what they have learned. In the Invitation to Invention model, teachers, consultants, and students interact in a dynamic experience that connects the learning of everyone. The next phase of Invitation to Invention will take place as the consultants move on to other buildings and Susie and Carol form teams with other teachers in their building.

Invitations to Invention have not been limited to classroom teachers and Educational Service Center consultants. The three university partners in the NEW[3] Project have been invited to reinvent teacher education so that professors as well as new teachers entering the profession understand the concept of NEW WORK. Twelve professors, four from each university, devoted the equivalent of one 3-hour semester course working together to identify examples of NEW WORK in their colleges, to share examples of NEW WORK in K–12 classrooms with their colleagues and their students, and to make plans for inviting their colleagues into the process. They compiled a list of standards, based on the Foundation Standards developed by the International Society for Technology in Education (Widmer & Amburgey, 1993) that identify competencies needed by all professional educators to be effective users of information technology both inside and outside the classroom environment. In order to prevent these competencies from becoming an easy checklist of skills, the professors illustrated each standard with a vignette. A listserv has been established to involve other university professors as well as classroom teachers in the dialogue. Additional stories illustrating the standards are shared through the listserv. The following is one of the standards (*Technology Standards*, 1997):

> Standard: Personal Technological Competence through the recognition of TERMINOL-OGY used in the field of technology.
>
> In a multidisciplinary unit on environmental issues, seventh graders developed a curiosity about air purity in their own school building. Working with community volunteers from environmental action organizations, groups of students and their teachers, using borrowed instruments and software, performed scientific tests. The scientific method (developing a hypothesis, collecting and synthesizing data, etc.) was followed. Information from electronic databases and e-mail correspondence combined with local data was compiled. Early drafts were critiqued on the basis of clearly articulated criteria, then improved and redrafted, and then evaluated by teachers and presented to the community via a multimedia display. Throughout, teachers communicated—easily and well—with students, each other, and off-site experts with regard to the technological aspects of the project because of their knowledge of—and comfort with—the terminology of technology.

The 18 school districts have assured the universities that education majors competent in NEW WORK will receive first consideration when hiring takes place.

NEW WORK AND SCHOOL–COMMUNITY RELATIONS

A recent opinion research project (Johnson & Immerwahr, 1994) found that the priorities of many educators were out of sync with the views of the U.S. public. Public Agenda, a nonpartisan, nonprofit research and education organization, conducted a telephone survey of more than 1,100 Americans and found the following (Johnson, Farkas, Friedman, Immerwahr, & Bers, 1995):

> Americans want safe schools that create an orderly learning environment. They want schools that concentrate on teaching basic skills, which their real-world experience tells them is not happening today. They want rigorous standards. And they want an end to what they consider wrongheaded, experimental teaching techniques. (p. 35)

The authors concluded, "Until the schools put 'first things first', broad public support will be scarce" (p. 35).

Although educators, parents, and community members speak with sincerity about the best possible education for children, mistrust and disrespect often obstruct that goal. Teachers and parents often play a blaming game. Teachers blame parents for not being actively involved in their child's schooling; parents blame teachers for not involving them. Ironically, each group accuses the other of the same sins. Teachers often say that parents and community "just don't give a damn" (Walde & Baker, 1990). In a written survey (Fawcett, Rasinski, & Linek, 1997) a majority of teachers reported that parents lack interest in their child's education. Teachers also admitted that they often feel threatened by parental involvement. They fear criticism and said they do not want someone "looking over my shoulder." Parents, in like manner, reported that they were fearful of teachers because they perceive them to be very powerful. They also indicated that teachers often seem so tired and stressed that they appear not to care about their children (D. Younas, personal communication, May 15, 1995).

Too often the schoolhouse door only swings one way, but finding what could make the door swing both ways is a confounding problem. The issue is not so simple as giving the community what it wants. As the Public Agenda Foundation (Johnson & Immerwahr, 1994) pointed out, when the community and schools find themselves at odds, schools can take one of three approaches: (a) decide that the public's concerns require genuine change, (b) determine that the public misunderstands and respond with better communication, or (c) decide that the public's point of view is mistaken and respond by building a constituency for ideas that are not popular but that are worthwhile. In any case, in the post-typographic world this means the democratic process must be fully engaged to lift public schooling above the narrow visions of special interest groups, including educators themselves, and to return ownership and pride in the work our students do to the students in partnership with the community.

One of the goals of the NEW³ Project is to establish a common community vision of excellent schools. The fact that such a goal would form the foundation of a large technology grant is hopeful. Throughout the project, various groups have met to discuss their visions. When we first extended the invitation, we were not surprised to hear from those segments of the community that have traditionally responded: PTA moms, Rotary Clubs, professionals, middle-class parents, and educators. We have had to actively seek other voices—voices that are often ignored or stifled in our democracy. We went into a government-subsidized housing development and sat with parents and children who talked about their dreams for a better life. We went to clergy who were surprised that we recognized the need for their moral authority in our endeavor. We visited an adult literacy lab and asked the clients how the schools had let them down. We met with home-schoolers who are suspicious of any government-funded project. We talked to many students of all ages who clearly articulated what is wrong and what is right about our schools.

We also met with representatives of conservative, Christian organizations such as Eagle Forum and Citizens for Excellence in Education (CEE). The local president of one such organization questioned how we could ever find a common vision. "There are too many opposing agendas," he argued. Yet, as we listened to our community, we found that there were common issues across groups whether we were listening to second graders or clergy, teacher union leaders or African American mothers, CEOs or members of CEE. Everyone talked about the need for basic skills. Adults used that term; students said things like, "I know I need to know how to spell." However, no one stopped there. All agreed that students need to use those skills for solving problems and reasoning. Many people were concerned with equity. We expected the low-income community to plead for modern technology, quality teachers, and safe schools. We were encouraged that affluent parents also asked how the grant would meet the needs of our inner-city children. People described ideal schools as places where students were engaged with their work, where their individual needs and interests were met, and where they learned to get along with others and contribute to society. In short, everyone had a vision of school as a place of dignity and hope for students and teachers. The process will now be continued in the individual districts as educators, parents, and the community dialogue about schools at the local level.

Not only has the grant provided the opportunity for community members to deliberate on what they desire for children, it has provided resources for them to learn about technology and its impact on modern life. The Technology Lab at the Summit County Educational Service Center is open to the community on Saturdays and Sundays, and on weeknights when it is not being used for the Academy of Learning and Technology. An instructor teaches classes of parents and their children, senior citizens, and other community members about the Internet and e-mail for a small registration fee. Scholarships and public transportation are provided for needy families. As these groups experience NEW WORK for themselves, they become increasingly supportive of President Clinton's Challenge for Technological Literacy.

THE UNCERTAIN FUTURE OF NEW[3]

Transforming schools through NEW WORK is a daunting task with no guarantee of success. We believe any prospect for success is tied to our own ability to do NEW WORK, that is, to regard school transformation as a matter of inquiry rather than a matter of fact. NEW WORK for us will require that we listen carefully to our children who will help us learn to ask the right kinds of questions. Learning in a post-typographic world will depend on "freeing the human imagination from the past" (Mead, 1978):

> So the freeing of the human imagination from the past depends, I believe, on the development of a new kind of communication with those who are most deeply involved with the future—the young who were born in the new world. The children, the young, must ask the questions that we would never think to ask, but enough trust must be re-established so that the elders will be permitted to work with the young on the answers. (p. 73)

Our answers will "depend on the existence of a continuing dialogue in which the young, free to act on their own initiative, can lead their elders in the direction of the unknown" (Mead, 1978, p. 73). It will be NEW WORK done in new ways.

REFERENCES

Burke, C., & Short, K. (1994, July). *Curriculum as inquiry.* Paper presented at the Fifth Annual Whole Language Umbrella Conference, San Diego, CA.

Cuban, L. (1986). *Teachers and machines: The classroom use of technology since 1920.* New York: Teachers College Press.

Edelsky, C., Altwerger, B., & Flores, B. (1991). *Whole language: What's the difference?.* Portsmouth, NH: Heinemann.

Elmore, R. F. (1996). Getting to scale with good educational practice. *Harvard Educational Review, 66,* 1–26.

Fawcett, G. (1996, Fall). School through the eyes of children. *The NEW[3] News, 2*(1), 6.

Fawcett, G., Rasinski, T., & Linek, W. (1997). Family literacy: A new concept. *Principal, 76*(4), 34–37.

Goodlad, J. (1994). The National Network for Educational Renewal. *Phi Delta Kappan, 75,* 632–638.

Hairston, M. (1982). The winds of change: Thomas Kuhn and the revolution in the teaching of writing. *College Composition and Communication, 33,* 76–89.

Harste, J., Woodward, V. A., & Burke, C. L. (1984). *Language stories and literacy lessons.* Portsmouth, NH: Heinemann.

Johnson, J., Farkas, S., Friedman, W., Immerwahr, J., & Bers, A. (1995). *Assignment incomplete.* New York: Public Agenda.

Johnson, J., & Immerwahr, J. (1994). *First things first: What Americans expect from the public schools.* New York: Public Agenda.

Ladewskii, B. G., Krajcik, J. S., & Harvey, C. L. (1994). A middle grade science teacher's emerging understanding of project-based instruction. *Elementary School Journal, 94,* 499–515.

Mead, M. (1978). *Culture and commitment: A study of the generation gap.* New York: Doubleday.

Mehlinger, H. D. (1996). School reform in the information age. *Phi Delta Kappan, 77,* 400–407.

Postman, N. (1995). *The end of education: Redefining the value of school.* New York: Knopf.

Reinhardt, A. (1995). New ways to learn. *Byte, 20*(3), 50–52, 62, 66–71.

Schlechty, P. (1990). *Schools for the 21st century: Leadership imperatives for educational reform.* San Francisco: Jossey-Bass.

Schlechty, P. (1996). *Standard-bearer school districts: Organized for results.* (Available from the Center for Leadership in School Reform, 950 Breckenridge Lane Suite 200, Louisville, KY 40207)

Scribner, S., & Cole, M. (1981). *The psychology of literacy.* Cambridge, MA: Harvard University Press.

Senge, P. M. (1990). *The fifth discipline.* New York: Doubleday.

Sizer, T. (1991). No pain, no gain. *Educational Leadership, 48*(8), 32–34.

Standards for the English language arts. (1996). Newark, DE: International Reading Association & National Council of Teachers of English.

Technological literacy. (1997, February 27). [Online]. Available: http://www.ed.gov/updates/PresEDPlan/part1.html.

Technology standards for pre-service/in-service teachers: Goal 7 of the NEW³ Project. (1997). (Available from Summit County Educational Service Center, 420 Washington Avenue, Cuyahoga Falls, OH 44221)

Walde, A., & Baker, K. (1990). How teachers view the parents' role in education. *Phi Delta Kappan, 72,* 319–321.

Wheatley, M. J. (1992). *Leadership and the new science: Learning about organization from an orderly universe.* San Francisco: Berrett-Koehler.

Widmer, C. C., & Amburgey, V. (1993). Meeting technology guidelines for teacher preparation. *Journal of Computing in Teacher Education, 10*(2), 12–17.

8

▼▼▼▼▼▼▼

Coding the Light: Rethinking Generational Authority in a Rural High School Telecommunications Project

Lorri Neilsen
Mount Saint Vincent University, Halifax, Nova Scotia

Illegitimate offspring are often exceedingly unfaithful to their origins. Their fathers, after all, are inessential.

—Haraway (1991, p. 151)

Beyond the blinking cursor is a new frontier, an etherworld posing challenges to the dimensions of our thinking and the boundaries of language. It is a world we access through our fingers even as it defies our definition. Electronic literacy, reading and writing texts through telecommunications, stretches our conventional notions of time, space, and identity. And yet, like all discourse, electronic text is coded according to social and political context and subject to the ideological forces that interpellate all human interaction.

What happens when electronic communication is introduced in a traditional educational setting? What erupts when adolescents, for example, are given a keyboard and a modem in a school culture marked by segmentation of a Balkanized curriculum, hierarchical and authoritarian decision making, and institutionalized ability grouping?

This is the story of the impact of the Learning Connections project, a 3-year study that introduced telecommunications as a medium to research literacy practices in a rural school in the early 1990s. The rapid pace of change in technology over the last several years renders this account, in some respects, a historical one. In technoyears, this is an old story: In calendar time, the events are relatively recent. Yet, in educational terms, these distinctions may be irrelevant; the themes that emerged in this project remain difficult, intransigent problems in introducing telecommunications in schools. In educational terms, Papert's (1993) observation that "schooling" can get in the way of learning is useful: The Learning Connections project demonstrated clearly what happens when the traditional institution of "school" is assailed by the transformations, tensions, and passions of eager students and teachers whose learning chafes institutional assumptions and practices.

In the early 1990s, John Willinsky of the University of British Columbia and I became determined to investigate the role of telecommunications on literacy practices in schools and work settings. What follows is a brief account of the issues and challenges facing the larger, cross-Canadian project and a more detailed analysis of the particular challenges at the Nova Scotia site where I was the project director and principal researcher. Although John and I worked to achieve connections between the activities and agenda of both school settings, one in Vancouver, and one in a rural Nova Scotia community, each of the sites was unique in ways that rendered cross-site comparisons more difficult than illuminating. Further, although we reported findings together about the project as a whole (Neilsen & Willinsky, 1993), the labor-intensive nature of the implementation caused each of us, finally, to focus our research efforts largely on the site at which we worked.

Our original plan was ambitious, and we think, in retrospect, somewhat naive. We aimed to "wire" two high schools from different settings, and create opportunities for teachers in the two settings to integrate cross-country e-mail communication into their curriculum. We also aimed to approach a number of worksites in which e-mail was used. Pairing students with worksite mentors, we wanted to examine the nature of the communication that resulted. What did literacy look like in such diverse communication environments?

CODING THE LIGHT

One of the legacies of the Kuhnian notion of paradigms is the cliched analogy of the drunk looking for lost keys under the street lamp: Like the epistemologically locked researcher, the drunk looks under the lamp because the light is better there. In one sense, I believe that the limitations of our (still largely) modernist view of literacy and curriculum prevent us from seeing electronic communications in new ways. We think of e-mail, for example, as another tool for writing, simply another implement that perhaps increases the speed and facility of communication, but does not, in fact, change the context out of which the communication occurs. In other words, we continue to think of literacy and the tools we associate with literacy as mechanistic skills (Neilsen, 1996). As others have noted (see Beach & Lundell, chap. 6, this volume), the range and variation in electronic discourse forces us to rethink literacy and literacy learning in radically different ways.

In another sense, we can go beyond the street lamp metaphor and look more closely at our understanding of the nature of light itself: how it plays with shadow, breaks apart in different ways, resists boundaries, permeates, changes appearance, color, and form. So, although it is true we only see in the light, it is also true we must look closer at how that light—that focused spotlight—is itself created and how it is constituted.

Writing on computers is playing with light. No longer limited to the visible and tangible marks of carbon or ink on paper, students create their literacy in a microelectronic sphere that not only changes the nature of their communications, but changes the students and the cultures as well. As Haraway (1991) noted, the cyborg consciousness, formed in the fusion of human and machine, is a particularly powerful consciousness for populations thought of as "other": Writing in cyberspace can allow women, people of color, those populations out of the center, to "seize the tools to mark the world that marked them as other" (Haraway, 1991, p. 175). Cyborg politics, as she claimed, is the struggle against phallogocentrism, against the male-centered "code that translates all meaning perfectly" (p. 176). It is a frontier in which coding practices about meanings and contexts are continually challenged, a space where dualisms become problematic. Coding the light, reshaping the semiotics of communicating in an electronic environment, reminds us we are cyborgs, hybrids of machine and organism, and that we can reinvent ourselves constantly.

Light, once only of the sun and the sky, belongs now in a microelectronic sphere of our own creation, responding and shifting to our cybernetic control, and yet slouching still against the shadow of our ignorance. Who holds the light, who shapes it, controls it, and allows it? What happens when such light is introduced into a setting where clear boundaries and definitions of authority and of organizational structures prevail? Electronic literacy prompts sober reflection on these "givens," these assumptions. Education is a field, after all, in in which resistance to change is as strong a force as the appeal of the quick fix, bandwagon, the trendy panacea of the week: In our enthusiastic and "gosh-wow" proselytizing about the transformative potential of telecommunications for schools, have we thought clearly about the dark behind the light, the more fundamental ways in which technology challenges what we have learned to value?

Our thoughts about technology and transformation typically are underwritten by a metamorphosis metaphor such as the change that occurs from caterpillar to butterfly. It is a quintessentially organic image, the natural world unfolding as it should, comfortably bounded by a genetic script. No postmodern simulacra here, no copies of copies; the butterfly takes wing carrying DNA of the original green crawler, playing out the life cycle to its earthbound conclusion. Our constructivist notions of literacy and curriculum, as well as the legacy of our modernist beliefs about linearity and cause and effect in the world make this metaphor appealing. We are especially drawn to it in the Deweyan sense of growth as a natural unfolding or embracing through action, children transforming through their societal experiences into winged adults, presumably able to transform society in the process. We, as adults, are the ones to oversee this transformation, to guide it: As the older generation, we consider this part of our responsibility in life.

The caterpillar moves from the dark to the light. It is easy to assume such a process is linear and predictable, especially where telecommunications and students are concerned: Give them a modem and a password, and they have the key to a new world. They are drawn to the light, and transformed in the process. As adults, we can help shape the experience.

Rarely do we talk of the dark silence between, the chaos, ugliness, and struggle that can mark the change from one form to another. Rarely, too, do we talk of the mutations that can appear. We assume, as the saying goes, that life (or learning, or growth) will unfold as it should. But sometimes, for reasons we never know, something goes wrong: Something dies, or monstrous and unexpected changes take place. In a postmodern conception of the world, such inexplicable and unpredictable occurrences are simply the forms lives may take: Abnormal is part of the mix. For those of us cherishing our modernist assumptions about literacy and learning, mutations and monsters (the aberrant and the abnormal) can teach us if we are prepared to learn that they require response more than control. Placed in the context of schools and technologies, the unexpected, as Bruce and Hogan (chap. 16, this volume) remind us, causes us to come face to face with the limits of our physical and conceptual worlds. What is abnormal: that which does not follow convention and expectation? Or is it the context itself, hostile to difference and resistant to accommodating all the variations the world may offer?

Such questions became most pressing at the Nova Scotia site of the Learning Connections project. As much as teaching us, as educators and researchers about the power of technology to transform students' literacy, the effects of the project taught us much about the power of the contexts in which we implemented the work. Telecommunications made visible the once-invisible systemic values of hierarchy and authority.

TESTING SYSTEMS

As part of a 3-year federally funded telecommunications project, John Willinsky and I connected students from two high schools across Canada with workplace partners and with grade-level counterparts. It seemed simple at the time: We would create electronic communications environments in which students could expand their literacy and chart their horizons through access to writers in work settings and student keypals across the country, and perhaps the world. But e-mail was new to public schools in Canada at that time; it was still confined largely to university settings. Further, business–education partnerships were not common in those years (at least in Canada): Business groups were reluctant to invest in schools, believing that education was a provincial responsibility, and educators seemed wary of corporate money that might turn classrooms into corporate training grounds.

Such systemic beliefs made the challenge of launching a major research project especially difficult. We underestimated the investment of time spent lobbying and selling our idea to school boards, corporate sponsors, individual schools, and network providers. After 2 labor-intensive years of planning, writing, and presenting proposals to schools, systems groups, hardware and software providers, network providers, and district administrators, we had secured enough funding to purchase preliminary equipment. The British Columbia site had received tentative approval from the school board to begin, and we had met with teachers in the respective schools who were eager to work with e-mail in their classrooms.

In technological terms, the West Coast school was at least a generation ahead of the East Coast school when we started, and the gap never closed by the end of the project. Yet the Vancouver school—where the ratio was two students to one computer, and where word processing, graphics, and statistical software were in common use by both students and teachers—was still faced with the challenge of connecting the school computers on a local area network and securing an outside line to the Internet. With all site participants enthusiastic about learning to use e-mail, it seemed a simple hurdle, and yet it was a challenge that would take almost a year to overcome.

In Nova Scotia (where computer use was confined to computer studies courses and the ratio of students to computers was approximately 50 to one at that time) the problems of resolving technical limitations were still on the horizon. We were still seeking Department of Education approval. Although I had secured a major grant from a federal–provincial grant agency outside education with which I could purchase new equipment for the school and hire research assistants, the funds would only be released when I had received the required approval from the Department of Education. Teachers at the school, ecstatic about the news of the award, were not as sanguine about the chances for department approval as I was: They talked of bureaucratic foot-dragging, power politics, and petty control issues, and warned me the approval process might be lengthy.

It is important to explain here that education is a provincial responsibility in Canada. All projects of this magnitude, regardless of the source of their funding, must be vetted by the government department, as well as receive approval from the local school district and the school itself. Although the mandate of the provincial education department is to serve the interests of the public school system in the province, the teaching profession and the public have an uneasy relationship with the Department of Education, seeing it as the driver of often outdated curriculum, the benevolent protector and the meddling arbiter, the last word. In a culture marginalized by the mainstream Canadian political system, such a department tends to value the traditional and suspect the innovative. Typically, teachers have little respect for the department's knowledge of schools, and great resentment about the glacial pace at which its bureaucracy works.

Up to this point, I had never had the experience of shepherding an entrepreneurial project (outside the bounds of educational funding) through the departmental approval channels. Telephone tag, postponed meetings, and what seemed to me like an endless series of stalling tactics finally resulted in a meeting with the curriculum director, a woman trained in statistics and mathematics, and her colleague, the computer consultant. "This proposal is unreadable; the pages aren't numbered," were the director's first words as we began the meeting. Subsequent comments and questions were equally perplexing and irrelevant. All funding partners to date, as well as the Social Sciences and Research Council of Canada, had approved not only the concept, but the research questions and methods. The questions from the director and the computer consultant came in a flood: "Where did this idea come from? Who told you you could do this? You're not a computer teacher. Where is your proof that this will benefit students? What is the specific content these students will be learning? How will you measure it? What will they know? What does this have to do with curriculum?" And, with regard to the section that focused on the use of e-mail to increase reading and writing for non-university-bound students: "How can you expect general students to learn from this? They don't have the intellectual ability to use computers."

Armed with the teachers' enthusiasm and emboldened by the prospect of significant funding from the province, I was not prepared for such resistance. Was this response simply bureaucratic panic at an innovation not created from within the system, not unlike the wolf's discovering the pig has gone to market and returned before sunrise? Was the resistance typical of the patriarchal nature of hierarchies, a threat to the integrity of the master's house? Or were these responses typical of what McNeil (1988) described as the contradictions of control, in which policymakers impose controls and constraints that ultimately diminish the very educational opportunities they are charged with supporting? My reaction was knee jerk: This was paternalism, a clear failure, once again, of adults to let go, to allow young people the opportunity to create their own curriculum. It was also an unwillingess, I was to realize later, of an institutional body to recognize and to welcome a new generation of approaches to education. My field notes documented my frustration.

> I awake at 5 a.m., furious. At eight, I call Ray at the network office (Internet provider), only to learn that he met yesterday with X (the computer consultant for the province's Education Department). It seems he went there after the meeting with me. Ray thinks this fellow didn't even know what the Internet is, let alone what resources it offers. When I call the school, (the English teacher) hopes I'm calling to say "It's a go!" but instead I must ask him to gather again the interested teachers and do another brainstorming of how they see themselves using the network to meet the department's curricular guidelines. They must write more justification for the department, even though the department is not throwing a cent into this project. I log on to Kidsnet, asking "advice-urgent—anyone out there facing similar hurdles to introducing email into schools, and how are you handling them?"

After receiving grudging approval to begin (with the provision that statistically described benefits would be reported to the Department of Education), the Nova Scotia side of the project was now, like the British Columbia side, ready to explore what happens when electronic literacy is introduced into the curriculum. The reaction of the Nova Scotia Education Department to the project confirmed our sense as educators that curriculum had indeed lost the sense of agency the word itself denotes. The focus on content acquisition, accountability, and standardization has created a closed system of possibilities for knowledge, creating subjects of the students and teachers who serve it. Where curriculum is compartmentalized, hierarchies form; where curriculum is static, there is no transformation. Locked in a mechanistic framework in which knowledge is transmitted and acquired, not a fluid process of construction, the province's most influential gate-keeping institution prevailed. To extend the metaphor of the street lamp and the lost keys, the department wanted the lost keys, whereas the project leaders and the school teachers wanted to move the lamppost.

ONLY CONNECT

From the outset, the project was plagued with technical problems. The primitive technology on the East Coast added to the more sophisticated, yet equally frustrating, problems of putting the West Coast computers on a local area network (LAN). For the first year of the project, good ideas and best intentions were the only connection we shared. Retrofitting computers with telecommunications technology, reconciling Macintosh technology with IBM-compatible equipment, providing maximum access through school (not dedicated) phone lines: It seemed as though we were always "one part, cable, clue, short of connecting" (J. Willinsky, personal communication, January, 1990). Vancouver students were skilled in computer use for word processing and graphics; the challenge became connecting their LAN to a dedicated line that would allow them uninterrupted Internet access.

Compared with the British Columbia site, where computer use was in some respects already so common as to be invisible, the technology-impoverished Nova Scotia site saw a marked impact on students and school culture. When students went online to the world, the visibility of this newly introduced tool pushed comfortable educational boundaries and assumptions. Telecommunications represented a new generation in technology, a generation bringing with it conflicts and complications.

The school principal agreed to the installation of new equipment and to the use of telecommunications in the curriculum, but intimated the project was a risky one. As a result, the research team independently oversaw the installation of all computer equipment and coordination of Internet access and use in the classrooms. On site, we worked with school and technical personnel to arrange for cable installers and electricians, for example; we developed and organized training sessions for students and teachers; we created newsletters to inform parents and the community of the goings-on; and we were called on to resolve ongoing technical difficulties and make quick decisions about issues only an influx of new technology could make pressing. The Nova Scotia research team, comprising two on-site researchers and myself, became "jills of all trades": Working with the teachers and the students, we created guidelines and limits for student use, wrote user agreements, handled requests for censorship of Internet offerings, and supervised the computer room while students were online. Four classroom teachers and the librarian worked alongside us to integrate e-mail into their work as teachers of geography, English, computer-related studies, and global history: Together we focused on the "generals," those classes of students not headed for university study. It seemed as though the first year and a half of the project was spent in meetings and technical wrangles, coordinating and planning for connections we hoped would become possible. Occasionally, the school principal would patrol the computer room; otherwise he offered no comment or assistance.

The Vancouver school was already "wired" by this time, with ample on-site systems and administrative resources and support to handle the few technical difficulties they experienced. They forged connections with Createch, a worksite partner in systems development, to track the nature of literacy in the two environments. Compared with the Vancouver site, the Nova Scotia group often felt we were struggling to reach warp speed with Model T technology.

However, the schools differed in more than geography, and once students and teachers began the complicated process of communicating regularly with cross-Canada partners over a 4-hour time difference, the differences became glaring. On the West Coast, the school was located in an upper middle-class district, populated by computer-wise professionals whose children were bright, scholarly, and diverse in background. Many students were first- or second-generation Asians. The majority were headed for professional careers themselves and took their studies seriously. The teaching staff was well versed in word processing and graphics technology and eager to learn about innovations. Although e-mail was new to the school, technology had been an integral part of teaching and learning at the Vancouver site for many years. Fear of the technology was low.

The Nova Scotia school was a sharp contrast. It was a large rural high school whose students were sons and daughters of largely low- to middle-income indigenous fishing families and small-business owners. Students were bused in from far-reaching parts of the region, a ride that took 2 hours for some. The majority of the students were "generals," and, in the school academic hierarchy, were placed near the bottom, just above "special education" students. These generals shared among themselves the 10 rudimentary machines available to them in a frequently locked computer room: ten Commodore PCs with no ethernet cards and no storage memory.

Later, issues of class, race, and gender would surface variously within the bicoastal populations and between them: level of discourse, class assignments, out-of-school activities and opportunities, literate behavior, and expectations for the correspondence seemed often to disrupt the possibilities more than expand them (Neilsen & Willinsky, 1993). In our zeal to foster cross-Canadian conversations, the project directors, assistants, and teachers may not have seen what was obvious to the students themselves: It is asking almost the impossible to bring together someone like Jason, a self-described "party animal" who lives to fix cars and to make the school wrestling team, with Mariko, a poetry writer in the same grade but 2 years younger, who wishes to discuss identity issues in Asian novels. Fascination with the technology was not a strong enough force to sustain an ongoing connection between school sites. Nonetheless, we persevered, believing the cultural bifurcations grounding the study and framing the implementation created essential tensions we were certain would spark enthusiastic inquiry.

The phrase "only connect," familiar to readers of E. M. Forster's *Howard's End*, marked our resolve to bridge gaps between worlds. If we "only connect" adults in the workplace with students in schools to learn more about the communication environments of each, we might make intergenerational ties. If we "only connect" rural students with urban, East with West, college-bound with ready-to-work, we might build a global town hall and improve literacy in the process. If we put together technology-wise teachers in graphics-rich Macintosh labs and rural teachers with little technology experience (and who see computer knowledge and access as the domain of a male computer teacher and vice-principal), we might spark new professional conversations. If we connect schools with each other within the province, the school boards might see the light: They might recognize the possibilities of telecommunications for learning across the curriculum.

As we faced the challenges of only connecting, we focused on the rich potential of the technology and ignored the vast differences in the respective contexts. We hoped against hope that telecommunications might transcend the marked and rooted lives of participants. We worked at systematic inquiry, encouraging teachers and their entire classes to communicate cross-country with the same facility that they would communicate across the hall. When, later in the project, John and I in our respective sites turned our research efforts to our own contexts, largely to meet the reporting requirements for our respective funding agencies, we reflected on the enormity of the challenges we had created for ourselves, the students, and the teachers. We learned, after the fact, the value of situated evaluation (see

Bruce & Hogan, chap. 16, this volume), and realized, too keenly, the systemic forces of resistance to educational change. For my part, I noted several critical incidents that shaped my understanding of the effects of the project, and that informed my understanding of generational and authority differences, not only between people, but also between schools of thought in educational practice.

SEEING THE LIGHT

Once enough money was released to buy initial equipment for the Nova Scotia site, 10 computers using individually coded boot disks enabled a small group of students to begin to connect with the world beyond the school walls (Doran, 1992). By the following year, when the school connected through a LAN, it was apparent the project was to challenge the routine and the structure of the high school in many ways.

> I spoke with the principal who says that if we open up the lab during exam time we will have to take complete responsibility for use, supervision, and activity. He says he fears it could become a real social centre. He wants to know why we issue individual passwords and accounts to students and how we will monitor their mail. He says he will meet with you tomorrow. (Field notes, Research Assistant, 1991)

The general students were the first to find keypals. As they sat in teacher Jeff Doran's classroom, clustered around a single machine with a successful line to the world beyond, they rushed to find a map to locate where their e-mail was coming from: Hawaii, Pennsylvania, Alaska. As they composed questions for their keypals and wrote introductions of themselves, their literacy enabled them to extend their reach beyond the school and the curriculum as they knew it. Soon worksheets on vocabulary were abandoned for a chance to write to a real person they did not know and might never know, but who would write them back. Authentic purposes for their work drew them to the screen.

Once other students became aware of this technological opportunity, the "wildfire-like" enthusiasm that grew in the school soon made the computer room a place to gather for students from all academic streams and social groups. Where once the computer room had been filled during noon hours and after school with male computer-related studies students only, it was now crowded with mixed groups and single-sex clans, button-down shirts alongside leather jackets. The project opportunities, which started as planned with general (nonacademic, academic low-achieving) students, and which succeeded in increasing their reading and writing skills as well as their interest in school (their absenteeism decreased markedly after the introduction of e-mail), were now eagerly sought by other students. Further, we were gathering statistical evidence to show that when a female research assistant or teacher was on duty, the proportion of girls in the room increased.

Within months, the popularity of the medium became too much of a good thing. Teachers were hounded by students who wanted to gain access to the lab to check their mail. Students from the regular academic program who had skipped classes in a required course were often found at a computer terminal using e-mail, contributing to a listserv, or telnetting to exotic sites. Although all students had signed a user agreement to ensure "responsible" use, they tested their boundaries repeatedly, eagerly comparing notes about newsgroups such as alt.bestiality and alt.sex. Many learned quickly to telnet to sites carrying games, chat stations, and otherwise censored material. The map on the wall of the computer room was soon pocked with pushpins indicating exotic keypal destinations; it was an explicitly visible reminder of the successful travels these telecommunicators had made.

But underneath the quiet humming intensity, another tenuously drawn web seemed to be forming, one marking places never before imagined on maps, dangerous, on-the-edge places up to now unreachable in the high school. Each extended stroke in cyberspace cut away the structural fiber of school policy and routine. Teachers and research team members were soon required to meet regularly to discuss issues of censorship, supervision, access, privileges, priorities of use, times, and terms.

> Dear User:
> Please note that when you signed the Learning Connections user policy you agreed to the following conditions: no "sending obscene . . . messages" and no "activity that is considered to be a violation of responsible use of the services."
> Under no circumstances are you to use the telnet access numbers which supervisors have asked you not to use.
> Supervisor

At every turn, the opportunities the project unfolded pushed the edges of school control, and tested the patience of the school administration. At one point, when it seemed there was too much stress on the structure itself, the principal threatened to turn off the switch. By then, however, the network use had proven its curricular value—at least in the conventional sense, and to the satisfaction of the Department of Education—and a critical mass of students had taken the technology and created their own webs of control. In an ironic twist, the Department of Education, the paternalistic force in the original drama, was now accepting kudos for its foresight in agreeing to give such a project its approval. The school became a destination for visitors from other high schools across the province, for educators interested in forging school–work connections, and for the media, interested in covering this "innovative program." The principal was delighted to field these requests and to talk with reporters, other administrators, and teachers who called.

INESSENTIAL FATHERS

It would be too easy to paint the struggles in implementing the Nova Scotia side of the Learning Connections Project as yet another example of valiant innovators tilting at bureaucratic windmills. That interpretation would suggest the project team knew exactly what we were doing before we began, and certainly we did not. We could never have anticipated the nature of the challenges to institutional authority before we began; our responses as researchers were constructed as each new problem arose.

Rather, what was happening in the space around the project needs a language beyond the organic and the antagonistic. At some level, when we conceived the project, we expected to discover within the boundaries of our making; we may have even believed we were contributing to a growing movement of collaborative research, working with both teachers and students toward curricular change. It was action research, tinged with activism in the collective willingness to challenge the status quo, to use computers to resist the hierarchical relations and segmented curriculum in contemporary high schools.

To understand what happened, we required a cyborg sensibility, ironic and lacking in essences. Such a sensibility looks, as Haraway (1991) said, for "a way out of the maze of dualisms in which we have explained our bodies and our tools to ourselves" (p. 181). It goes beyond creating an other, an endless progression of bipolarities that structure our thought and our lives. The way to hear and to see what was happening in the students' learning connections was not to appropriate data for the ongoing instantiation and production of theoretical essences, but to cock our heads, to read it slant, to see it out of time, away from the knowable sons and daughters we produce in the name of theory. When what is happening can no longer be fixed by difference—other and not other—we come close to Trinh's (1991) notion of the Inappropriate/d Other, coded dynamic conditions in relationality deconstructing and unraveling the known and even the wonder/full unknown. Haraway (1991) likened this to diffraction: "Diffraction is a mapping of interference, not of replication, reflection, or reproduction, (mapping) not where differences appear, but . . . where the effects of difference appear" (p. 300). A generation of students, familiar and knowable in the ways they walked the catacombs of the school or worked the alphabet at the keyboard, was in effect becoming unknowable: Our ways of categorizing them were becoming inadequate.

Several incidents highlighted the difficult authority issues that emerged between adults and students, and between girls and boys.

"How Arrogant, How Sad"

> O.K. now for that amusing anecdote. When I was communicating with (Mr. Jones) he began his reply with "Dear Mr? (?) Comeau. He was unsure if Dean was my title or my actual name. Whatever the case, he must have believed I was a high ranking official on our school board as he was ready to send me over 50 pages of material in response to my sociological study of math in the curriculum! And to charge our school board for the photocopies!. I quickly cleared things up and made sure he understood I was just a grade 12 student. (Dean, e-mail correspondence)

Dean was one of the most active users of the network and one who frequented the computer lab to explore the Internet possibilities and to train students on Internet use. Having written an eloquent critique of the way mathematics are taught in high school, he posted a message on a listserv asking for a response to the draft. A math teacher in Colorado was one of the first to respond and was willing to offer further information. The correspondence was collegial until Mr. Jones read Dean's paper and learned he was a high school student.

> Dear Dean:
> After 13 years in this profession, I am still amazed that high school students still make blazing decisions on the basis of so little data. . . . Your lack of willingness to learn whatever will be communicated to your students.
> How unfortunate.
> How arrogant.
> How sad.
> David

Dean was stunned. After overcoming his initial hurt, he decided to reply:

> Dear Mr. Jones:
> I'm sorry I'm such a narrow-minded teenager. I'm still trying to decide if your last message was a response to my not wanting to be a math teacher or if it was concerning my view of math curriculum. If it was in reference to the math teacher, you shouldn't take everything you read so seriously. If it was to the latter, then it isn't me who's being so narrow-minded. . . . Whatever the reason for your last reply, I'm terribly sorry I offended you.
> Dean

Dean included in his response further support for the thesis in his paper and the names of other online correspondents whose work he had compiled to write his critique.

> Dear Dean:
> Sorry I blew up. The thing that got me was when you implied that I had compromised my goals by not becoming a history teacher and "settling" for mathematics. . . . If your work is for a term paper, I would be happy to help you construct a proper survey so you can do some real analysis on the data.
> David

Dean's communicative competence had enabled him to represent himself like an adult on the screen. When he was "found out," revealed as a teenager who dared to speak to an adult like an adult, he was "burned," to use his words. Like all neophytes in telecommunications, Dean learned firsthand that the power of telecommunications to render some cultural markers invisible can be ultimately a dangerous one. Dean transgressed generational boundaries even as he hoped he was transcending them.

"Forget It"

Krista was one of the computer-related studies students who chose to write to a workplace correspondent as an assignment. She attempted to open the conversation by asking a general question: "What do you do in your business?" The correspondent she chose was a senior bureaucrat in the provincial government who responded: "In the first place, this is the government you are writing to, not a business. Don't you know the difference?" The e-mail note was terse, and ended with: "Perhaps next time you write you ought to have your teacher read it beforehand." Not knowing how to continue the conversation (and not wanting to reveal the fact the teacher had, in fact, read and approved her letter before it was sent), Krista dropped the correspondence altogether.

When asked what she thought of the response she had received, she shrugged: "I thought the guy was a jerk." Asked if she wanted to do anything about the situation, she said "Are you kidding? Forget it." Krista learned that not all adults in the world beyond the school were as supportive or interested in fostering her learning as her teachers were. Although she was left without a correspondent to complete her assignment for her course, she refused to write this "jerk": Here e-mail offered her an opportunity for resistance she could use to make her point and to preserve her dignity. Had the comments been made on site in person, she might have chosen otherwise.

"Guess Who's Online"

During the peak of project activity, we enlisted a group of young women and men who wanted to serve as network assistants, conducting research on network use and providing online help to students and teachers. Known as the Network Team, their help was indispensible, as they knew the technology better than anyone in the project except the network installers who worked off site. In an attempt to solve the problem of overcrowding during peak times on the network, two of the young men chose to research a dial-in connection to the school LAN. They worked through the technical details, received the network provider's approval to ensure the connection would not violate a subscriber contract, and prepared a detailed proposal to present to the principal of the school for his approval.

Their innovative solution and their technical skill outshone anyone in the school, including the teachers and administration.

The principal, himself an avid computer user, reviewed the proposal and rejected it out of hand: No out-of-school access would be tolerated. All access to the school Internet connection had to originate in the school, he insisted. Otherwise, it would be impossible to control who was using the system. Although the network provider had given the school a flat rate for access, and although the system was rarely used in the evening, he insisted on on-site use by students only.

A week or so later, one of the young men was approached in class by his friend, who, coincidentally, is the daughter of the principal. "Guess what?" she announced. "Dad can get us on the network from home. We can dial in anytime." The Network Team approached me, as project coordinator. They felt used, betrayed, and victimized by the principal's unjust use of authority.

"Guy Friends Don't Even Notice It"

Three young women, interviewed in their graduating year, a year after the project and the researchers left the school, offered their observations about technology and gender. All three young women—Lorenna, Janis, and Naomi—had been involved in the project from the beginning. Not only were they highly skilled in the use of the technology, they were advocates and proselytizers for computer use among other girls in the school. They credited their continuing interest in technology, in part, to the fact that the project had brought in female research assistants who, although they were not technicians, were skilled in e-mail and Internet use.

Computer use in the school before the project had been dominated by boys and men. One of the female teachers, Susan, eagerly supported network use for young women and for the nonacademic students in her geography classes in particular. At the peak of enthusiasm for the project in the school, Susan had sent me this note:

> Hi Lorri
> The inservice was absolutely thrilling to me. Not only did it give me the confidence to come in here on my own and access my messages, gather info, plan for next year, etc., but it made me realize just how excited the students are. For instance, Pauline French is a very bright student who sometimes (nay, always) needs to be motivated, reminded, prodded, encouraged to reach her potential. She was in here teaching me how to access information through telnet and was actually itching to resume a disussion with a woman in the States who had put her in touch with all sorts of free access networks. I've never seen her so keen. The potential benefits are mind-boggling.
> Susan A.

Susan was unlike the teachers Lorenna, Janis, and Naomi talked about, teachers who, as Janis noted "avoid situations where they don't know the answer, and let their students suffer for lack of opportunity. [These teachers] always have to be the figure of authority and usually can't handle new things."

The young women were not only concerned about teachers who are unwilling to learn; they voiced concerns about the curriculum, in particular the fact that their computer course focused on the history and the parts of the computer, ignoring Internet access and its potential for communication altogether. They saw this as an irony, given that the school was, at that time, perhaps the only high school in the province on the Internet.

Their strongest critique was the way in which the postproject computer culture seemed to revert to the way it was before Learning Connections began. The computer users were again primarily boys and usually of one social group, not the mixed-gender groups and mixed social strata of 2 years before (Alloway, 1995; Beer, 1994). Lorenna noted:

> The guys now hit the computers at noon in hoards. They all attack . . . They hog all the good computers . . . it becomes territorial and they they give off this presence like "get away." They look like neanderthals . . . the look of them would discourage anyone . . . it's negative energy . . . the girls have just stopped trying to get in.

Lorenna added:

> I'm aggressive, but a lot of girls aren't. I feel for the girls who hide away, who don't fight it. I'd really like to see them get an education using computers, but I've heard teachers encourage them to learn wordperfect so they can be secretaries. What about all the other things they can learn?

Lorenna summed up the frustration the three felt about being ignored, trivialized, and intimidated by the boys, even though they were considered leaders among technology users in the school:

> What's so frustrating is that your guy friends don't notice it. Or they don't acknowledge it, because if they did acknowledge it, then they'd have to do something about it. And when you're in a position of power you really don't want to lose it that easily.

Monstrous Transformations

A group of three young men who repeated their graduating year in order to increase their grade point average for entrance to university spent their many spare hours in school at a computer terminal. Resistant to authority in almost every way, they were silent, sullen, and ever-present. Two of them had fathers who were influential in the community. Appeals by the research assistants and the teachers to these students to make themselves useful by teaching other students or sharing their computer time were regularly ignored. Their technological wizardry baffled even the network provider; they were a formidable force (Cohn, 1987). Never overt in their resistance, they instead chose to use the technology quietly and relentlessly to make things happen, to unravel threads, create blockages, and subvert system procedures. After a series of pranks attributed to them, they were restricted to 1 hour a day on the network.

However, their skill was immense and they managed, even to the end of the project, never to get caught. Self-described hackers, they would sit for hours, muscles tensed and eyes dilated and darting, hammering at the keyboard. We watched their jerking elbows and dropped jaws, amazed at the fantasy that gripped their bodies and concerned about how monstrously clear their commitment was. They did not swim in the bitstream, they became it, and no reprimand, punishment, appeal to reason, or human contact could bring them back.

One day, a letter appeared in the supervisors' account:

> Hey there, you stupid son of a bitch. How's your fucking ego doing? You know, you really fucking disgust me with your goddamn attitude. I'd like to see you log on for only an hour a day. You'd probably look for other ways to get your faggit rocks off.
> Oh, by the way, in case you haven't noticed, I can program in any computer language

to date, and if you continue to fuck around, being an asshole, I'm going to crash your fucking system with so many goddamn viruses that you'll have bugs crawling up your ass!

So, you can tell all those fucking supervisors bitches too, that if your goddamn attitude continues, I'll see to it that a group of people who are very against all you faggits will pick their favorite baseball bats and come all the way down their (sic) to beat your fucking skulls in!!

The letter had arrived via a telnet site and under another user name. The network operations manager pieced together information from activity at the nearby university to implicate a computer science friend of one of the students. Because of the student's coyotelike skill in transmutating the message, the evidence, finally, was only circumstantial. No one involved in working with these students, however, ever doubted the message was from them.

CODING THE FUTURE

Learning Connections was a transformative technology, but not in the way we might have imagined it to be. These students and the processes in which they engaged were no longer separate objects of scrutiny under a lamp of our choosing. As a generation, the students embodied the luminescence itself. Whatever we, as irrelevant adults saw happening, we located in the old hallways of our minds: modernist concerns and old agenda items with nods to the postmodern.

Although it might seem as though the adults and their institutional structures—loosely defined here as those who see themselves as gatekeepers, stewards, or authority figures— were the ones who held the reins, they did not. They may have held the power of approval, grades, and privileges, but the students, nimble and generative in front of a keyboard, knew that their technological facility would be the prevailing force.

From the outset, this project made visible the systemic resistance to change in education at the policy and administrative level. If change can be transformative, it requires a recognition that new generations of approaches and practices will challenge, and perhaps supplant, the old. Although the lessons of this project do not support change for change's sake, they do remind us as educators of the vast discrepancy between the speed of change in technological growth and the speed of change in educational institutions, relations, and procedures. The Learning Connections Project also made visible the difference in approaches to change between generations: Students' ease in learning technology soon outstripped that of people who would be their gatekeepers, their teachers, and their authority figures. In a post-typographic world, the cursor and the mouse bring new notions of authority and challenge intergenerational dynamics. This technology is forcing a reinvention of learning from all perpectives, from the individual to the systemic (Franklin, 1990). Teachers, parents, and administrators, humbled by the technological wizardry of youth, are forced to reinvent themselves as well: as guides, as colleagues, and as coexplorers in a new world. Like other changes in educational practice, such as shifts in writing pedagogy or mathematics and science education, the intergenerational tensions that telecommunications can highlight do not merely shift authority from teacher centered to student centered: They force a sea change in our understanding. Who is in charge, and what does that mean? Who has answers, and to what ends are they used?

Telecommunications offers a medium fast enough for the students' semiotically attuned and accelerated minds, malleable enough for play and domination, large enough for their imagination and sexual longing, and as yet, still open to be codified. The heavy hand of authority that reached out to reprimand Krista was swept aside. Young men, in the eyes of astute young women such as Lorenna, looked like dupes. Traditional figures of authority, threatened by the insouciant imagination of men half their age, had to cower at home using skills limp in the face of a new power. The violent pornotechnical force emerging from the monstrous "Lost Boys" brings us to the edge, or perhaps it is the next dimension, of the dark side of Neverland. Telecommunications disrupt as much as they connect: The generation that guards the status quo may have more to learn about the role of school and technology than do the students.

Learning Connections began as a rather conventional project using an exciting new technology to bridge worlds and to work among different discourse communities. The light from the circuitry would shine, we assumed, on transformative notions of curriculum. But as adults we may have other roles to play, for our notions of what problems exist in making curricular connections and fostering literacy learning may be irrelevant for this generation. The problems this generation will face, at least as far as we are capable of imagining them, will be ones of coding cyberspace in ways beyond the imagination of their mothers and fathers, ways that cause tilt.

ACKNOWLEDGMENTS

Permission has been granted from all participants in the study to use their names, a description of these incidents, and the circumstances of the research in academic publication. All names in this article are real names, with participants' permission. I wish to thank the Social Studies and Humanities Research Council of Canada for funding that contributed to the Learning Connections Project.

REFERENCES

Alloway, N. (1995). *The construction of gender in early childhood.* Carlton, Victoria, Australia: Curriculum Corporation.
Beer, A. (1994). Writing, computers and gender. *English Quarterly, 26*(2), 21–29.
Cohn, C. (1987). Sex and death in the rational world of defense intellectuals. *Signs, 12*(4), 687–718.
Doran, J. (1992). *Learning connections: One teacher's story.* Unpublished manuscript, Halifax, Nova Scotia.
Franklin, U. (1990). *The real world of technology.* Toronto: CBC Enterprises.
Haraway, D. (1991). *Simians, cyborgs, and women: The reinvention of nature.* New York: Routledge.
McNeil, L. (1988). *Contradictions of control.* New York: Routledge.
Neilsen, L. (1996). Reclaiming the sign, re-making sense: Feminist metaphors for a literacy of the possible. In J. Flood, D. Lapp, & S. B. Heath (Eds.), *A handbook for literacy educators: Research on teaching the communicative and visual arts* (pp. 203–214). New York: Macmillan.
Neilsen, L., & Willinsky, J. (1993). *Networked learning connections: Literacy, knowledge and power beyond the curriculum.* Paper presented at the annual meeting of the American Educational Research Association, Atlanta, GA.
Papert, S. (1993). *The children's machine: Rethinking school in the age of the computer.*
Trinh, M. (1991). *When the moon waxes red: Representation, gender and cultural politics.* New York: Routledge.

9

▼▼▼▼▼▼▼

Electronic Literacy Portfolios: Technology Transformations in a First-Grade Classroom

Ronald D. Kieffer
University of Georgia

Michael E. Hale
Oconee County Schools, Watkinsville, Georgia

Ashley Templeton
Benton Elementary School, Jackson County, Georgia

Literacy professionals across the United States have transformed their classrooms into more dynamic social environments through innovations with computer-based technology, collaborative learning, and portfolio assessment. New technologies have revolutionized the ways students work and think, making classroom activities more interactive, collaborative, and learner centered. Knowledge construction in classrooms has become more aligned with expression, communication, and information access (Cochran-Smith, 1991; Daiute & Dalton, 1988; Dickinson, 1986; Dwyer, 1994; Kinnamon, 1990). Concurrently, the concept of a portfolio, that is, creating systematic collections of work that represent individuals as learners, has become a way to make evaluation more authentic and meaningful (Graves & Sunstein, 1992; Rief, 1992; Tierney, Carter, & Desai, 1991; Valencia, 1990).

Portfolios vary in design, serving multiple purposes (Callahan, 1995; Kieffer & Faust, 1994; Murphy, 1994) such as providing documentation of learning and progress (Au, Scheu, Kawakami, & Herman, 1990; Simmons, 1991; Valencia, 1990; Wolf, 1989), creating contexts that promote students' growth (Cambourne & Turbill, 1990; Henning-Stout, 1994; Milliken, 1992; Voss, 1992), showcasing exemplary pieces of work (Farr, 1992; Tierney et al., 1991), and encouraging narratives that tell stories of students as literate persons (Graves, 1992; Hansen, 1992a; Kieffer & Morrison, 1994; Rief, 1990). Portfolios can look like scrapbooks, folders, diaries, photo albums, or file cabinets. On a computer, they can fit into preprogrammed systems such as the Grady Profile (Grady, 1991) or they can be created by the learners themselves using word processing tools and multimedia software (e.g. HyperCard, HyperStudio). The process of constructing a portfolio depends on concepts such as ownership and audience, and are influenced by teachers' philosophical views of learning and evaluation (Kieffer, Faust, Morrison, & Hilderbrand, 1996).

In addition to using portfolios primarily for assessment, literacy professionals are recognizing the potential of portfolios to reflect classroom curriculum, teaching, and learning (Arter & Spandel, 1992; Johnston, 1989; Kieffer & Faust, 1996; Kieffer & Morrison, 1994; Murphy, 1994; Valencia & Calfee, 1991). Many teachers are searching for ways to improve their teaching practices. Some examine their theoretical beliefs by valuing reactions and questions from parents and students, observations and critiques from peers, and time to write, reflect, and self-evaluate their work (Graves, 1992; Hansen, 1992b; Paris & Ayres, 1994; Schon, 1987). Portfolios can serve as catalysts for teacher change when literacy professionals listen to multiple voices and gather evidence from diverse sources (Kieffer & Faust, 1994).

Listening to teachers talk about their approaches to assessment and observing their implementation of portfolio assessment in their classrooms can add to our knowledge of the relation between evaluation and instruction. Furthermore, digital technology, an impetus behind electronic portfolios, has the potential to change the way individuals generate, update, recover, link, and process information. Access to extensive amounts of information provided by new technologies has become a prime resource, one that can assist teachers as they strive to evaluate their students' growth and progress toward curricular goals. Moving portfolios from printed to digital media has promise as a way for teachers and learners to negotiate their way through a large volume and variety of information that might be included in a portfolio (Milone, 1995; Moersch & Fisher, 1995; Reilly, Hull, & Greenleaf, 1993).

Unfortunately, most classrooms do not have access to state-of-the-art technology, and many simply fit the technology that they do have into traditional models of teaching and learning (Miller & Olson, 1995; O'Neil, 1995). How can classroom teachers capture a vision of technology and assessment that can potentially change their ways of conceptualizing learning and evaluation? What are the characteristics of electronic portfolios and how might these characteristics support teachers' professional growth, self-awareness, and change? How might electronic portfolios contain authentic and process-oriented information that will help teachers learn about their students and their own teaching practices? How do literacy professionals gain knowledge about their instructional practices from examining students' portfolios and from maintaining and presenting their own portfolios to students and colleagues?

For the past 2 years, we have collaboratively explored the use of electronic portfolios to assess student growth and teacher change. Kieffer and Hale, university researchers, and Ashley, a first-grade teacher, worked together, using qualitative methods such as journal writing, interactive discussion, classroom visits, and a collection of documents to examine how Ashley gained knowledge about her classroom curriculum and instructional practices from a portfolio that she created using software such as Microsoft Word, HyperCard, and HyperStudio. By capturing stories about her growth as a professional, we developed themes concerning how she learned about her students and her teaching through the use of electronic portfolios, and how the classroom was transformed through this approach to assessment. As she reflected on and created her ongoing collection of portfolio material to represent her growth as an educator, she also examined portfolio assessment as it gradually became a dominant feature of her classroom practice. She looked closely at the relation among her portfolio development, her students' portfolios, and her changing teacher practices.

In this chapter, we offer ways that electronic portfolios can support professional growth, self-awareness, and change. We describe how this technology has become an integral aspect of Ashley's classroom, resulting in her changing views toward student literacy, access to technology, classroom decision making, integration of technology into her teaching, and purposes for learning and evaluation. Finally, we outline her evolving vision of the electronic portfolio process and how it has helped transform her classroom into a more coherent and supportive learning environment. We conclude by suggesting implications for future classrooms and schools.

ASHLEY'S EVOLVING PROFESSIONAL PORTFOLIO

Three major themes emerged from our work in Ashley's classroom that frame our discussion:

1. Teacher electronic portfolios supported Ashley's professional growth, self-awareness, and change. The professional portfolio that she created enriched her views about technology, strengthened her evolving vision of literacy learning, and fortified her understanding of the portfolio process.
2. Student electronic portfolios informed Ashley's teaching. She recognized patterns of student learning, became more understanding of student needs, varied teaching strategies, and created new learning experiences.
3. Electronic portfolios contributed to the transformation of Ashley's classroom. Her views changed in thinking about students' literacy, the role of technology in a classroom, purposes for learning and evaluation, and decision-making practices, transforming her classroom into a more nurturing learning context.

Background

In June 1994, Ashley volunteered to be a member of a multimedia workshop conducted by Ron Kieffer and Mike Hale. Nine teachers from three elementary schools and five student teachers were given access to Macintosh Quadra AV computers in exchange for their participation in the study. Their tasks were to learn about multimedia, to develop a teacher portfolio representing themselves as learners, and to write weekly journal entries documenting their reflections about the ongoing work. Although we initially collected data with all participants, Ashley showed an interest in collaborative research and a commitment to a long-term, in-depth case study by volunteering to participate in data collection, analysis, and research report writing.

On the first day of the multimedia workshop, the group talked about their past histories as teachers and brainstormed on computers their current stance on teaching. Ashley's pedagogical beliefs about literacy learning were aligned with the emergent literacy perspective (Teale & Sulzby, 1989). In her first-grade classroom, the language arts were interrelated. The students had many opportunities to read, write, and speak beginning on the first day of school and continuing throughout the year. These language processes mutually supported each other because they were embedded in a variety of learning situations. Reading aloud, singing, dramatic play, storytelling, and exploration of print were all part of the daily routine. Literacy was a purposeful, wholistic, and goal-directed activity, rather than taught as a sequence of isolated skills. Literacy learners in Ashley's classroom learned through active engagement by solving problems, asking questions, and responding to each other's work. Ashley looked for influences of oral language in her students' reading and writing and supported her students' attempts to use language through demonstrations, collaboration, discussion, and response.

The teachers and student teachers also discussed chapters by Graves and Hansen from *Portfolio Portraits*, edited by Graves and Sunstein (1992). During the discussion, Ashley questioned, "Why has it taken so long for teachers to realize the importance of portfolios?" In her journal, she immediately made connections to her students.

> I am excited to think of my students using the computer as a reflection tool themselves. The students will be able to put their work in their computerized portfolio as well as take it home with them. Hopefully they will be able to see their own growth and change throughout the entire year. (June 20, 1994)

Ashley's prior experience with portfolios was minimal. She had created a portfolio in one of her education classes for teacher certification, but admitted that this was more like a scrapbook compiled only to complete an assignment instead of a "type of forced reflection you place upon yourself . . . a great running record of all the things that were important that happened during the year." The fact that she had changed in her thinking about portfolios was represented in her excitement about the concept, her anticipation for doing her own professional portfolio, and her brainstorming of potential portfolio items for the students in her classroom. Ashley envisioned opportunities to share student portfolios with parents, documenting successes, planning units and projects, and creating a tool for reflection to track her own growth and change.

Similarly, her knowledge of computers at that time was limited to word processing, and she had not used computers in her classroom prior to the workshop. In fact, she removed the Apple II that was assigned to her classroom because she felt that is was not contributing to her classroom curriculum. Her opinions changed dramatically as she became genuinely excited about the value of technology with her next group of students.

On the second day of the workshop, the participants discussed future goals in pairs and then with the entire group. Ashley's goals for 1994–1995 later became a part of her professional portfolio:

1. Create a teacher portfolio for various purposes: (a) employer, and (b) yearly class portfolio.
2. Create a student portfolio on the computer: (a) teacher input, (b) student input, and (c) parental view on the computer.
3. Put grade book on the computer.
4. Create a bibliography.
5. Put valuable units into computer for easy accessibility.
6. Create a holiday unit file.
7. Create a teacher theme library including all personal books grouped into appropriate categories.

Ashley had already begun expanding her thinking about uses for technology. She looked forward to using computers to document grades. Her purposes for becoming involved in using portfolios included her students, even though the requirements of the workshop task only asked for a teacher portfolio. For the remainder of the first week, there were opportunities for further conversations about the concept of portfolios as teachers brought in and discussed items for their portfolios. Ashley's journal entry showed her thinking about purposes for portfolios as she continued to envision the possibilities:

> I spent time discussing with others how this "portfolio" will be developed from a collection of many items. I like the idea of having a "SUPER PORTFOLIO" with everything I have

in this folder. Then I want to create specific portfolios designed for specific audiences. I really liked the idea of creating a portfolio in the form of a photo album or something similar. This would help for a smooth viewing of the portfolio. The idea of having a class picture and being able to click on a student's picture and finding the student's portfolio sounds just perfect to me. I can't wait to see all that I am going to be able to do!!! (June 23, 1994)

At that point in time, Ashley saw her portfolio as being a large collection of cards, similar to index cards, linked together using buttons. In HyperCard, a variety of informational formats (text, graphics, still photos, digitized video and sound) can be organized in a nonlinear fashion, allowing viewers to randomly access information, raise questions, and see relations between ideas based on their experience, interest, need, or relevance (Ambrose, 1991). She was excited about using HyperCard to run her portfolio.

Ashley took her computer home at the end of the week. She proudly detached, moved, and reassembled her classroom computer workstation, a risky proposition for a novice computer user. She wrote, "I was really nervous about pulling all the plugs necessary to disassemble the hardware. . . . I was extremely impressed with myself at how quickly and correctly I had reassembled the computer. I turned it on and it worked."

She used her time wisely during the break from the workshop. While packing to move into a new home, she collected portfolio items and conceptualized a picture of her professional portfolio. Materials that she gathered included pictures from past classes, reflections of herself as a writer, exemplary units she developed, and her wedding picture "to show who I am outside the classroom." She planned to scan these items into the computer the next time the workshop class met.

Today I spent time rereading work I had saved in the past. To make my old disks usable on this new computer I had to update the program in which the material was saved in. . . . This took me some time to accomplish seeing that I reread all my old files on my old disks. I really found some interesting material. Some of the material I think I might like to put in my "general" portfolio. I even found pieces of writings that I had forgotten even existed. (July 10, 1994)

Ashley laid out her materials on the floor in the order and arrangement that appealed to her. This beginning collection of portfolio items stimulated thoughts about organization, audience, and reflections of value and worth.

After 2 weeks at home, teachers attending the workshop met for a second week to learn more about the software, help each other solve problems, and work through issues related to learning the technology. Ashley was quite anxious to use HyperCard as a base for her portfolio, so she spent time at home going through the tutorial. She became enthusiastic about using HyperCard as a way to organize her information. In her journal, she wrote, "I really feel like HyperCard is going to be the tool to help me produce the type and kind of portfolio that I have envisioned in my head. I can't wait until tomorrow's class."

She worked through frustrations with buttons and background cards and continued to take risks and to engage in trial and error to learn HyperCard. She showed intuition in solving problems and creating multimedia connections. She also revealed her growing ability to self-evaluate:

Wow!! What a wonderful day!!! I finally feel like I am beginning to know what I am doing. I am really starting to understand HyperCard. Today I spent all my time working with HyperCard. I created 21 cards in my portfolio. After many tries I was finally able to name each card corresponding with the card number given by the computer. The feeling of success was tremendous!!!!! (July 14, 1994)

The workshop was successful for Ashley. She was exposed to the current state-of-the-art Macintosh Quadra AV computer attached to a VCR with word processing and multimedia software. The tasks that were assigned, the development of a teacher portfolio and a reflective journal, each contributed to her belief that this project was relevant to her ongoing growth as a teacher. The format and contents of the portfolio were, of course, her decision. Collaboration and sharing with other participants was built into the workshop and encouraged during the school year, and Ashley had direct access to Ron and Mike throughout the year to support risk taking, solve problems, and celebrate accomplishments. Finally, the use of the computer at home in between workshop sessions allowed exploration and play, practice and discovery, and as the group came back together for interactive sessions, there were opportunities to address important issues and questions that emerged through participants' active involvement.

School began for Ashley before Labor Day. On the first day of school, she took snapshots of each of her students and made each picture into a button. She then began organizing a stack of cards linked to these pictures with students' assessment information. By using the mouse to click on a picture of Jordan, one of her students, a viewer of the portfolio could move quickly to the next card, showing a menu of his assessment information (see Fig. 9.1). She then created buttons under each subject that linked to more cards.

Ashley shared the beginnings of her student portfolios with the students in her first-grade class. During the next several months, her portfolio grew to five sections (students, parents, myself, school, and our class). She created a grade book on the computer and located parent volunteers to take videos of children reading and sharing their writings. She organized video for input into the computer and streamlined her HyperCard stack when she made the second card in her stack the "home" stack so that she could link other cards back to it. However, things did not always work smoothly. Hard disk storage became a problem because of the extensive size of the project, especially the digitized video. This led to the accidental loss of some of her work, and she became frustrated because she had scheduled parent conferences for the next week.

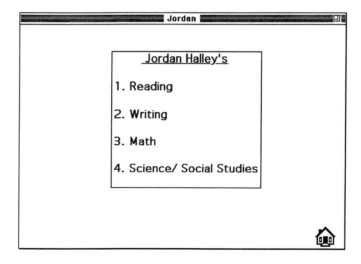

FIG. 9.1.   Jordan's portfolio menu.

Ashley sought help from Ron by phone and eventually worked through these complications, rescanning the lost information and conducting the parent conferences by rescheduling them to a later date. She was confident enough in her abilities to seek help when problems arose. She was not afraid to explore unfamiliar software, and she used her resources and eventually worked through problems on her own.

It is important to note that many teachers who are exploring the use of technology in their classrooms do not have such ongoing technical support from colleagues and university personnel. Ashley's frustrations would have been much greater and might have led to her giving up completely if it had not been for the help of her fellow teachers during interactive sessions and individuals to call when major problems interrupted her work. The social networks developed in this collaborative community were directly linked to her successful development of the electronic portfolio.

Ashley's Professional Portfolio

Ashley presented her portfolio in progress at a Georgia Department of Education Conference in November, and from the positive audience reaction, realized the significance of her work. She shared her ongoing portfolio many other times during the year of its construction using an overhead projection panel. Most notable were her presentations to parents at an open house in September, a second conference for the Georgia Department of Education (toward the end of January), sessions in her graduate classes, and portfolio sharing with the workshop participants in May.

Ashley's professional portfolio was arranged in the form of a family tree (see Fig. 9.2). The use of this metaphor showed the complexity of her professional growth over time, made visible her increased competency in using technology, and indicated that the computer was becoming fully integrated into her professional life. There were nine areas: resources, professional growth and development, book list, teaching philosophy, professional writings, thematic units, parents, reading logs, journals, and student portfolios. Each area contained a button that connected to more information. For example, by clicking on Resources, a reader could quickly pull up references that Ashley had used in her classroom and school such as community, in-school, and in-state resources. Under in-school resources, she listed

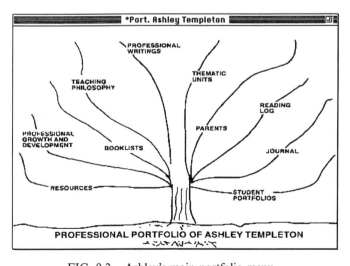

FIG. 9.2. Ashley's main portfolio menu.

some of the people in the school, and by clicking on their name, information appeared with the individual's picture.

Professional Growth and Development was where Ashley put her college transcripts, external evaluations, awards that she had received, her teaching certificate, résumé, goals, and vita. Under external evaluations, she scanned two of her annual reviews with the date, the evaluator, and comments. She noted, "I can look at what this person had to say about my teaching throughout the year and reflect on it." She also scanned in her different conference presentations with a summary of copresenters and conference locations.

In the Teaching Philosophy section, readers could get to know Ashley personally and professionally (see Fig. 9.3). She had a "Why teach?" statement, a self-portrait with biographical information, and teaching videos.

She downloaded articles and papers in the Professional Writings section. It contained experiences, journals, a portfolio from college, and writings from before she started teaching. During a portfolio sharing, Ashley made these comments about her writing:

> By re-reading these pieces, I can compare and see how much I've grown over the years. I can see how my philosophy has changed and how my experiences in teaching have changed the way I believe. I just started my Masters this month, so I want to keep up with all my writing. I also participated in action research last year [see Fig. 9.4]. This writing gives another side of me professionally. I'm writing more research this summer, so I'll also put that in the portfolio as a quick reference.

The Reading Log was an inventory of books Ashley had read personally and professionally:

> It's a great way to keep up with the things that you're reading, and show your kids that their teacher is a reader and a writer outside of class. I think, most importantly, modeling is the best thing a teacher can do for her kids. When they see me as a writer and see what I'm reading, they have more interest in their reading and writing.

The most extensive area was the Student Portfolios. Ashley used the video camera to take snapshots of her kids. By clicking on each child's picture, the viewer could link to

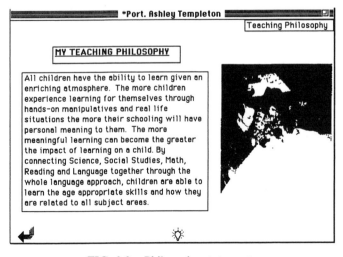

FIG. 9.3.   Philosophy statement.

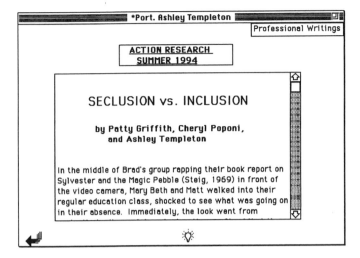

FIG. 9.4. Action research report.

their portfolio. Under each student, there were four areas (reading, writing, math, science/social studies; see Fig. 9.1). Within the reading section, there were five additional areas (book logs, reading orally, book talks, reading journal, and a checklist). Book logs (see Fig. 9.5) were where each child entered in the author, date, and books that they had been reading. They continually updated this section. Even with software as challenging as HyperCard, the students were able to take ownership of many of the tasks involved in constructing the student portfolios.

With help from parent volunteers, Ashley recorded several video clips of children reading throughout the year to document the skills they had accomplished. For example, in one video clip of Jordan and another student, Jordan was reading aloud and the student in the background was helping him read. When Jordan came across a word, he hesitated and tried to sound out. The other student helped him sound out the word and told him that he was doing a good job. Together they were working through reading aloud. Ashley could observe the interaction between the two children, hear the reading, see the other

Jordan		
BOOK LOG		
Book	**Author**	**Date**
We Can Go	J. L. Carbonali	09/07/94
Clifford's Manners	Norman Bridwell	09/07/94
In The Small Pond	Denise Fleming	09/12/94
It Will Not Go	J. Marshall	09/13/94
Tiny	Nellie F. Rider	09/13/94
Amy's Name Is Alice	V. Holt	09/13/94
The Happy Rabbit	Patricia Barton	09/19/94
Come In Boo Bear	David McPhail	09/20/94
Things That Go		09/21/94
Think Big	J. L. Carbonali	09/22/94
Train Song	Diane Siebert	09/22/94
Boo Bear and The Kite	David McPhail	09/24/94
Fox Gets Lunch	James Marshall	09/26/94
The Hat	James Marshall	09/26/94

FIG. 9.5.   Jordan's book log.

child helping him, and hear Jordan asking for reassurance. By viewing a series of sample readings, she could detect changes in reading ability over time.

The reading checklist contained statewide objectives and report cards. The purpose was to keep track of specific skills throughout the year and help parents see their child's progress. The students also selected entries for their reading journals. Ashley described the power behind three journal entries in sequence:

> Here I have three excerpts from the reading journal and I always put the date, what the child actually wrote, and then my response. The children respond in their journals after they have read a book, and many kids use their reading journals to help them keep up with the book log. This particular piece of writing [see Fig. 9.6] says "Insects, geese, crab and how they lived." So it's exactly what the child wrote, and then I responded to it by saying, "Good Job!"

> The second example [see Fig. 9.7] says, "Giant man and he helped people." And my response was, "He was nice to help the people." So it's just a continual communication twice a week between the child and me or the parent if the parent's involved.

> In the third example [see Fig. 9.8], the child is responding, I can see his writing, his response, and I notice that my responses have become richer: "They sure did a lot with apples. This sounds like fun!" By the end of the year, I want to go back and compare with the beginning of the year.

The writing section holds published samples of students' writing, video sharing, peer response, and a checklist. Ashley documented video sharing and peer responses so that she could observe the interaction between the person who was sharing and classmates who asked questions and provided comments from the audience. Samples of Jordan's writing were scanned in showing a piece that Jordan wrote in August (see Fig. 9.9). He wrote, "I like my house." Ashley provided a detailed description of her conference with Jordan.

> When we sit down together, I always ask, "Why do you want to put this in your portfolio?" It has to have a reason to go in there. In this particular case, he said, "Well, because I like my house, it's pretty, and I just like it." So that was his perception of why he put it in and that shows a lot about him as a learner and why it's there. This is a great way to keep up

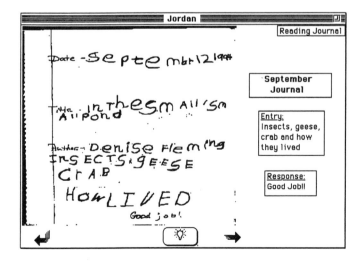

FIG. 9.6.   Jordan's September journal example.

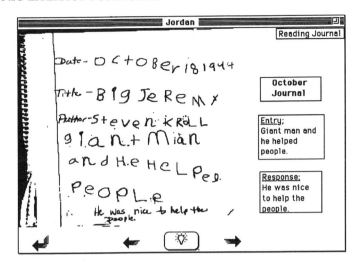

FIG. 9.7.   Jordan's October journal example.

with the kids' writings and get a picture of their work. I can see their writing, their illustrations, and their responses. I can see the growth in use of capitalization, the words not running together, and I can note the growth.

Ashley's professional portfolio transcended the boundaries of traditional paper-based portfolios. She used the electronic media to learn about herself and her teaching. She was able to compile a large volume of information such as her units of study, book lists, student evaluations, and professional writing. A traditional paper-and-pencil portfolio could also contain such information, but hypertext assessment information can be accessed immediately through nonlinear links. Additional buttons continue the flow of information to the viewer of the portfolio. The electronic portfolio also presented to Ashley, her students, and parents a rich multimedia context for comparing work completed over time, updating work in progress, and thinking about relations and connections between and among classroom experiences.

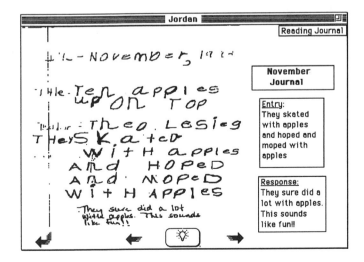

FIG. 9.8.   Jordan's November journal example.

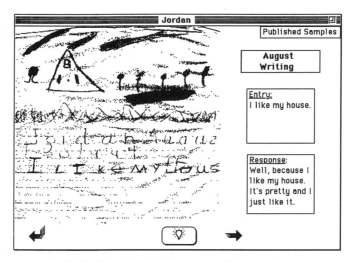

FIG. 9.9.   Jordan's August writing sample.

Ashley Changes Views About Technology and Assessment

In January, following her second Georgia Department of Education presentation, Ashley shifted in her thinking about electronic portfolios. She had heard about a piece of software called HyperStudio, a version of HyperCard that was more user friendly, and at the same time, she discovered a class at the University of Georgia that focused strictly on creating hypertext. Even though there were prerequisites to the class, Ashley received permission to take the course during the spring quarter because she demonstrated her growing expertise in HyperCard. Her goals for her first-grade student portfolios were also changing:

> HyperCard is an excellent program but it is not very user friendly. Because of the computer class I am taking in April I hope to get to know HyperStudio, which is more user friendly. If this is true I will move the student portfolio aspect over to HyperStudio. We will just have to wait and see what all I learn. If nothing else I MUST learn how to do video that is of good quality and not so time consuming. It will be interesting to see what all takes place. I am very pleased with my professional aspect of my portfolio. I will keep it the same adding to it as needed and desired. (March 10, 1995)

Ashley found herself setting new goals and figuring out ways to use this new software as a tool for her students to run their electronic portfolios. She found that HyperStudio was easier for her children to use, but more importantly, student ownership emerged as a critical issue:

> The children are always involved. They help me scan in material, they sit down at the computer and type in things, I'll type in my responses, and they'll type in their reflections and their interests. This is their portfolio. It's their work. It's their portfolio with their interests and their reflections. They are very active, and they are constantly reflecting on why things are added and their importance. (May 20, 1995)

With HyperStudio, prompts come up on the screen in simple language using a dog cartoon character to warn users about problems, ask questions about next moves, and suggest options and choices. Her students chose from the wide selection of colors in the toolbox, used the mouse to physically write and draw, and typed text both as a caption and in a word processing field. They experimented with shapes, illustrated their writing, wrote their names, and typed in their own responses. The students also imported scanned work into their portfolios (see Fig. 9.10).

The student work shown in Fig. 9.10 is very similar to the writing presented in Ashley's professional portfolio. The main difference is in student access and participation in the process. In this electronic portfolio example, Austin imported the writing into his portfolio by himself. He selected the color background and added music tied to the clicking of the arrow (Austin chose a sound called *stair.bonk,* an up scale ending in a loud bonk, to accompany the link). Austin also typed in the response using his choice of the Helvetica font. Ashley's only contribution was typing in the entry field.

By the end of the school year, she was already thinking about technology and portfolios for her next year's classroom. She suggested these changes:

1. Students are going to use HyperStudio for the class portfolio instead of HyperCard.
2. I am going to integrate the computer even more into my everyday activities.

She then set new goals for 1995–1996:

1. Have the students construct a class portfolio.
2. Share the class portfolio with parents at all meetings possible.
3. Continue adding to the professional portfolio as deemed necessary.

In her final journal entry, Ashley reflected on the entire year.

Wow! Another year is over. I can't believe all the things I have learned over the past year. I went from a very limited computer user (i.e. word processing only) to a very computer literate person. I feel I know HyperCard fairly well. Most of my knowledge has come thorough trial and error. I seem to remember more when I learn this way.

Because of this project a lot of neat things have happened to me. First of all I have gotten really excited about computers and all the things I can do with them personally and

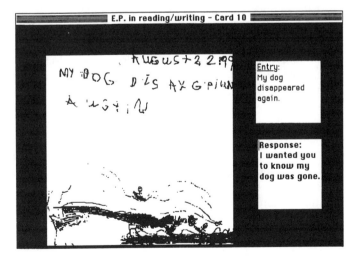

FIG. 9.10.   Austin's HyperStudio portfolio piece.

in the classroom. Next, I have taken a HyperCard class at the University. This has helped me to pick up on other aspects of HyperCard as well as introduce me to HyperStudio. Finally, I am changing my Masters' program to Computer Based Education. Wow!!! This is all so neat for me. (June 6, 1995)

Ashley attributed much of her change to the work associated with the electronic portfolio project. At the same time, technology became important to her professionally and personally. Her vision of the electronic portfolio process evolved and informed her classroom teaching and students' learning. Overall, she continued to be committed to the idea of alternative electronic portfolio assessment.

CHANGING VIEWS TOWARD STUDENT LITERACY AND TECHNOLOGY

Ashley's evolving vision of the electronic portfolio process helped transform her classroom into a more responsive and collaborative environment. For her, the process of creating her portfolio began with reflections on what she had learned over the years. She naturally connected to what was happening in her classroom, asking questions of herself: What have I experienced in the past that represents me as a teacher and learner? How valuable were these learning experiences? What will I do in the coming year with my own students? How can I reflect on the changes in my classroom? How can I get my first graders involved in reflection on change?

As the year progressed, she closely examined her teaching with more questions: Why am I including this activity? Where am I now? Why am I using technology in this way? Her reasons for evaluating students moved beyond providing a grade on a report card as she became involved in documenting progress, growth, and students' reactions. Her favorite question of her students was a simple "Why?" That is, "Why have you chosen this for your portfolio? Why do you like this?

Ashley became more interested in gaining a picture or portrait of her students' abilities rather than judging performance according to existing evidence at a particular point in time. She wanted her portfolios to serve multiple purposes—a historical record of the year, documenting students' progress, showcasing teacher and students' accomplishments, providing a visual representation of growth over time, supporting peer response, and stimulating reflection. She collected portfolio items from her past, but also created items as a way to inform her teaching, and she wanted her portfolios to address multiple audiences (e.g., students, parents, peers). Ashley set expectations and developed the structure of the portfolio, but she struggled to get students more actively involved in the process. Most importantly, she learned, through the process of creating her portfolio and through observing her students' involvement in their own portfolio process, that portfolio creators learn more about themselves through portfolio development than others learn by simply viewing the product. The act of creating the portfolio is similar to the concept of "writing to learn." There is a level of metacognition and self-awareness associated with constructing a portfolio. For Ashley and her students, portfolios have the potential for connecting learning and evaluation in important and profound ways.

Through the development of her professional portfolio, Ashley reconsidered her role as an educator and learner, recognizing how she might change as a result of exploring technology and portfolio assessment. Consequently, portfolios supported her "ways of knowing" about herself and her students. By collecting, selecting, and reflecting on worthwhile learning experiences, she became self-aware of her own learning. At the same time, she recognized the potential in her students' learning:

> I definitely feel like I'm doing a better job. I feel like I'm more aware of what's out there and can help prepare the kids for what it's going to be like when they get out of school, I mean they need to know how to use a computer and to use the materials there. And one of the programs lets them make their own movie so they already know how to, in a first grade sense, make a movie and things like that. It's helped me to view myself teaching. You can't watch yourself while you're teaching. (November 28, 1994)

By placing portfolios electronically onto computers and creating a portfolio of her own along with her students, Ashley took on two major risks, but, for her, the results were satisfying. She gained information about her instructional practices and the students became more actively involved in constructing their own knowledge. In an interview in March, she realized her accomplishments and recognized the value of examining classroom practices.

> I feel that my professional portfolio is very useful. I will forever keep it and just keep adding to it. When I started out, the purpose of that portfolio was for an employer to get a job and then I decided there were so many other things I wanted to include. I wanted it to be useful to me and not just sit on the shelf. . . . It's helped me to reflect on myself as a teacher and to keep up with the things that I've done, the accomplishments I've made where you just kind of forget or file away in your memory, where here you can actually put it on the computer in a neat, creative way and you have a record of what you've done over the year. (March 24, 1995)

Her views concerning the portfolio product shifted during the year. The paper-based scrapbook type portfolio that she developed as a university student evolved to an electronic version run by HyperCard, and then changed, at the end of the school year, giving her students the opportunity to build their own HyperStudio portfolios on the computer. Next year, her thinking about the portfolio process should undergo further change as she develops the idea of first graders creating collaborative and ongoing class portfolios linked with reflection and response.

Ashley's Professional Portfolio Informed Her Teaching

By examining her own portfolio content and reflecting on students' portfolios, Ashley recognized patterns of student learning, student needs, and teaching strategies. She used this information to create new learning experiences.

> You can see, easily see, through my portfolio how I teach, and the order I teach things in, and, at least this year how we did it. . . . I definitely use it as an assessment tool, especially their writing. And listening to them share, you can pick up things that they need to work on, that maybe you missed the first time. Because when they're reading to you, your mind may be focused on words where you might miss something that they really need to work on. So it's kind of a second way to go back over what happened, and look at the things they need to work on, or the things they're doing well. (November 28, 1994)

Portfolios provided Ashley with opportunities to plan for teaching and learning in her classroom. Placing the information on a computer made it more accessible, more interactive, and more efficient. During the process of creating her portfolio, she made complex decisions from her past experience, consulting with colleagues including her students, reading professionally, and reflecting on her electronic portfolio pieces. By making personal connections, thinking about beliefs, recognizing teaching practices, and exposing herself as a learner, she was also noticing patterns, watching students, looking at the big picture, and finding out about students' learning.

Ashley also used her portfolio to help her students recount experiences and make connections through journal writing, conferences, reflection, self-evaluation, and active participation in generating their own knowledge about their growth over time. She helped students select their best work, responded in ways that helped her students set and pursue goals, and supported the gathering of artifacts that provided essential information. She was actively involved in fostering ownership and self-evaluation and set specific goals to move even further in that direction by giving her students more control over their portfolios.

Ashley Changed in Her Philosophy About Technology

Prior to this year, Ashley had removed the Apple II computer from her classroom. When she gained access to the Macintosh, at first, she used it primarily during center time. She later changed to collaborative group access and publishing using word processing during writing workshop. She increased student ownership in the portfolio process and gave her first-grade students continual access to programs on Kid Desk, a system to protect access to personal information, but allow access to predetermined programs.

> At the beginning of the year, we just had two application programs on there that the kids could access. One was Sammy Science House, and they used the computer basically for free center time. I did start my student portfolios at the beginning of the year. But at the very beginning, I was doing most of the work. They had access to them and they could help do things. I was doing all the input. I was afraid to hand it to them. And now we have two computers in the room. During center time, one computer is used for application programs [Kid Works II] and one computer is used for the student portfolios for kids that want to put things onto their portfolio [HyperStudio]. So that time is for them to do the things that they choose. (March 24, 1995)

Ashley gradually integrated technology into her existing classroom. She was active in the learning of her students, serving as a demonstrator, model, and supporter, and she evolved in her beliefs about ownership—that students should create their own stacks, stories, graphics, buttons, and pictures. She began teaching technology to her students in a collaborative, supportive way, and she taught content with it (e.g., reading and writing strategies, information access). Toward the end of the year, she used a HyperCard stack on Germany that she created to go along with her Olympic unit. Technology moved away from being an add-on in her teaching to being a connected element that meshed well with her philosophy of teaching and learning and connected naturally to her ongoing classroom activity.

As Ashley created her portfolio electronically, she also became comfortable with the computer, evolving from having a cursory knowledge of word processing to becoming a computer user professionally as a teacher. She learned multimedia tools that helped her to organize information, digitize video, and scan documents. She became comfortable sharing her learning with other colleagues and reflecting on her teaching. She emerged as an expert in the eyes of fellow teachers, sharing at conferences, sharing in her graduate-level classes, being asked to conduct inservice for colleagues, and changing her master's degree major to instructional technology.

IMPLICATIONS FOR FUTURE CLASSROOMS AND SCHOOLS

Hypertext applications support different ways of learning. When interacting with the hypertext, the user views a variety of informational formats (text, graphics, still photos, digitized video and sound, speech) linked together or presented on the same card. The media show movement and demonstrate interaction providing a rich context for thinking about the information (Ambrose, 1991). For some hypertext viewers, components reinforce one another. Viewers can listen to conversation, reading the transcription and observing action simultaneously on the same card.

Perhaps a more powerful learning situation occurs when the author of the hypertext visualizes its organization and works through various linking mechanisms to make sure that viewers do not get lost in hyperspace. The creator's ways of thinking and learning are reflected in the hypertext. Hypertext authors randomly access information based on their experience, interest, need, and relevance. The nonlinear organization allows learners to process information, raise questions, and see relations between ideas. As learners create their own meaning, hypertext becomes a tool where they collect, organize, and analyze information, constantly making decisions and evaluating progress.

The strength of hypertext is its use of buttons to move through a series of cards. The process of creating a connected stack and the repetition of moving through the stack allows young children the chance to examine past creations and develop stimulating responses and reflection. Most important, and for Ashley this was especially true, teachers can ask very young children for responses to their work (Why have you chosen this piece for your portfolio? Why is this piece important to you?) and help them enter these oral reflections into the computer.

Parents and peers can also be included in this process of reflection and evaluation. When students share their portfolios with friends and with their parents, they can gather reactions to their work. Likewise, teachers can compile parental responses and evaluations made during parent–teacher conferences and, as Ashley did in her portfolio, teachers can record peer response during in-class activities. In these ways, teachers, parents, and the children themselves can see growth over time by moving through stacks of text. They negotiate portfolio partnerships and build a multivoiced collaborative community of readers, writers, and learners.

Based on these observations about hypertext, we suggest the following principles as guides to teachers who wish to consider electronic portfolios as ways to inform teaching and student learning and plan to utilize electronic portfolios to reach that goal.

1. Teachers need to be willing to create their own electronic portfolios along with their students and find their own ways to implement the portfolio process.
2. Involve young students in the portfolio process by increasing their ownership of the process and trusting them as computer users.
3. Nurture a multivoiced community of collaborators by developing dynamic social networks among students, parents, and colleagues.
4. Use the computer as a tool where learners are responsible for collecting, organizing, analyzing information, constantly making decisions, and evaluating progress.

5. Support reflection and self-evaluation as ways to improve teaching and student learning.

Through the course of 1 year, Ashley became more confident about what she knows about her teaching, her students, alternative assessment, and technology. Exploring electronic portfolio assessment supported her knowledge about herself and her teaching practices. She now recognizes that the portfolio creators are the ultimate learners. She is relinquishing ownership of the portfolio construction process and letting her students make complex decisions on the way to self-evaluating their work. By examining her growth and change during the year, it is clear that her classroom next year and in the years to follow will reflect the principles of ownership, access, integration, active exploration, and reflection that gradually became hallmarks of this year's enterprise.

REFERENCES

Ambrose, D. W. (1991). The effects of hypermedia on learning: A literature review. *Educational Technology, 31*(12), 51–55.

Arter, J. A., & Spandel, V. (1992). Using portfolios of student work in instruction and assessment. *Educational Measurement: Issues and Practice, 12*(1), 36–44.

Au, K. H., Scheu, J. A., Kawakami, A. J., & Herman, P. A. (1990). Assessment and accountability in a whole literacy curriculum. *The Reading Teacher, 43*(8), 574–578.

Callahan, S. (1995). Portfolio expectations: Possibilities and limits. *Assessing Writing, 2*(2), 117–152.

Cambourne, B., & Turbill, J. (1990). Assessment in whole language classrooms: Theory into practice. *The Elementary School Journal, 90*(3), 337–349.

Cochran-Smith, M. (1991). Word processing and writing in elementary classrooms: A critical review of related literature. *Review of Educational Research, 61*(1), 107–155.

Daiute, C., & Dalton, B. (1988). "Let's brighten it up a bit": Collaboration and cognition in writing. In B. A. Rafoth & D. L. Rubin (Eds.), *The social construction of written communication* (pp. 249–269). Norwood, NJ: Ablex.

Dickinson, D. K. (1986). Cooperation, collaboration, and the computer: Integrating a computer into a first-second grade writing program. *Research in the Teaching of English, 20*, 357–377.

Dwyer, D. (1994). Apple Classrooms of Tomorrow: What we've learned. *Educational Leadership, 51*(7), 4–10.

Farr, R. (1992). Putting it all together: Solving the reading assessment puzzle. *Reading Teacher, 46*, 26–37.

Grady, E. L. (1991). *Grady profile portfolio assessment: A performance-based assessment tool for teachers.* St. Louis, MO: Aurbach & Associates.

Graves, D. H. (1992). Portfolios: Keep a good idea growing. In D. H. Graves & B. S. Sunstein (Eds.), *Portfolio portraits* (pp. 1–12). Portsmouth, NH: Heinemann.

Graves, D. H., & Sunstein, B. S. (Eds.). (1992). *Portfolio portraits.* Portsmouth, NH: Heinemann.

Hansen, J. (1992a). Literacy portfolios: Helping students know themselves. *Educational Leadership, 49*, 66–68.

Hansen, J. (1992b). Teachers evaluate their own literacy. In D. H. Graves & B. S. Sunstein (Eds.), *Portfolio portraits* (pp. 73–81). Portsmouth, NH: Heinemann.

Henning-Stout, M. (1994). *Responsive assessment: A new way of thinking about learning.* San Francisco: Jossey-Bass.

Johnston, P. (1989). Constructive evaluation and the improvement of teaching and learning. *Teachers College Record, 90*, 509–528.

Kieffer, R. D., & Faust, M. A. (1994). Portfolio process and teacher change: Elementary, middle, and secondary teachers reflect upon their initial experiences with portfolio evaluation. In C. K. Kinzer & D. J. Leu (Eds.), *Multidimensional aspects of literacy research, theory, and practice: Forty-third yearbook of the National Reading Conference* (pp. 82–88). Chicago: National Reading Conference.

Kieffer, R. D., & Faust, M. A. (1996). Portfolios purposes: Teachers exploring the relationship between evaluation and learning. *Assessing Writing, 3*(2).

Kieffer, R. D., Faust, M. A., Morrison, L., & Hilderbrand, C. (1996). *Questions about portfolio processes* (Instructional Resource). Athens, GA: National Reading Research Center.

Kieffer, R. D., & Morrison, L. S. (1994). Changing portfolio process: One journey toward authentic assessment. *Language Arts, 71*(6), 411–418.

Kinnamon, D. L. (1990). What's the research telling us? *Classroom Computer Learning, 10*(6), 31–39.

Miller, L., & Olson, J. (1995). How computers live in schools. *Educational Leadership, 53*(2), 74–77.

Milliken, M. (1992). A fifth-grade class uses portfolios. In D. H. Graves & B. S. Sunstein (Eds.), *Portfolio portraits* (pp. 34–44). Portsmouth, NH: Heinemann.

Milone, M. N., Jr. (1995). Electronic portfolios: Who's doing them and how? *Technology & Learning, 16*(2), 28–36.

Moersch, C., & Fisher, L. M., III. (1995). Electronic portfolios—Some pivotal questions. *Learning and Leading With Technology, 23*(2), 10–14.

Murphy, S. (1994). Portfolios and curriculum reform: Patterns in practice. *Assessing Writing, 1*(2), 175–206.

O'Neil, J. (1995). Technology schools: A conversation with Chris Dede. *Educational Leadership, 53*(2), 6–12.

Paris, S. G., & Ayres, L. R. (1994). *Becoming reflective students and teachers: With portfolios and authentic assessment*. Washington, DC: American Psychological Association.

Reilly, B., Hull, G., & Greenleaf, C. (1993). Collaborative reading of hypermedia cases: A report on the development and testing of electronic portfolios to encourage inquiry in teacher education. *Journal of Technology and Teacher Education, 1*(1), 81–102.

Rief, L. (1992). *Seeking diversity: Language arts with adolescents*. Portsmouth, NH: Heinemann.

Rief, L. (1990). Finding the value in evaluation: Self-assessment in a middle school classroom. *Educational Leadership, 47*(6), 24–29.

Schon, D. A. (1987). *Educating the reflective practitioner*. San Francisco: Jossey-Bass.

Simmons, J. (1991). Portfolios as large scale assessment. *Language Arts, 67*, 262–268.

Teale, W. H., & Sulzby, E. (1989). Emergent literacy: New perspectives. In D. S. Strickland & L. M. Morrow (Eds.), *Emerging literacy: Young children learn to read and write* (pp. 1–15). Newark, DE: International Reading Association.

Tierney, R. J., Carter, M. A., & Desai, L. E. (1991). *Portfolio assessment in the reading–writing classroom*. Norwood, MA: Christopher Gordon.

Valencia, S. (1990). A portfolio approach to classroom reading assessment: The whys, whats, and hows. *The Reading Teacher, 43*, 338–340.

Valencia, S. W., & Calfee, R. C. (1991). The development and use of literacy portfolios for students, classes, and teachers. *Applied Measurement in Education, 4*, 333–345.

Voss, M. M. (1992). Portfolios in first grade: A teacher's discoveries. In D. H. Graves & B. S. Sunstein (Eds.), *Portfolio portraits* (pp. 17–33). Portsmouth, NH: Heinemann.

Wolf, D. P. (1989). Portfolio assessment: Sampling student work. *Educational Leadership, 46*(7), 4–10.

TRANSFORMING INSTRUCTION

The issue of how technology is transforming literacy instruction is possibly the broadest to be addressed in this volume, and it is broached in some manner by every contributor. The chapters in this section have been deliberately juxtaposed to illustrate the wide range of instructional implications. The narrow view—typical a decade ago, when microcomputers first became commonplace in public schools—has been that instructional issues generally revolve about the question of whether to provide children with access to computers in a laboratory setting or to make them available in classrooms. Once this is decided, a related issue is how then to integrate their use into the course of relatively conventional instruction. As the chapters in this part of the volume illustrate, however, the narrow view, although embracing issues that remain important, must be broadened to include a spectrum of related questions. Several of these questions are addressed in the chapters that follow and include adult education, effective software design, and Internet access in the classroom.

Two of the chapters deal with the transformation of instruction in adult settings, although their orientations are extremely different. In fact, it is this difference that underscores the variety of ways in which the transformation is occurring. Askov and Bixler (chap. 10) begin with an overview of effective software design for workplace literacy programs, but they demonstrate how such programs are evolving toward the development of "microworlds"—industry-specific simulations. They also discuss how the extended breadth of these programs is transforming the role of the adult literacy instructor in a direction that leads away from explicit instruction and toward student facilitation. Kinzer and Risko (chap. 11) describe the use of technology not in industrial settings but in the context of undergraduate reading methods classes. Their work with preservice teachers has involved the development of authentic, multimedia case studies in which preservice teachers and their instructors can explore any number of issues involved in literacy education. The teachers consequently see how instructional concepts that have been newly introduced can be applied in the context of real children and real classrooms—a luxury generally not available to undergraduates. These cases, like the microworlds described by Askov and Bixler (chap. 10), make possible a type of anchored instruction in which students use an elaborated case or situation to examine important concepts and their application.

Although Askov and Bixler (chap. 10) explore the question of effective software design, Leu and his colleagues (chap. 12) take a different tack by describing how the direct involvement of classroom teachers can lead not only to extraordinarily engaging programs with solid potential for student growth, but to general principles of design that seem applicable to a range of instructional contexts. Their conclusions are likely to provide the basis for more effective commercially developed software and better informed software review and selection on the part of practitioners.

Like the topic of multimedia case studies, explored by Kinzer and Risko (chap. 11), the subject of Garner and Gillingham's chapter 13 has little if any historical precedent. They examine a variety of ways in which classroom teachers have incorporated the Internet into their literacy instruction. The diversity of their examples enables them to address a host of critical issues ranging from constructivist implications of Internet use to problems of cultural dissimilarity (when, e.g., children in Illinois are suddenly put in contact with a group of Eskimo children). Finally, they address the possibility that Internet access might transform and possibly even eliminate instruction based on conventional textbooks. Like Bolter (chap. 1), Garner and Gillingham (chap. 13) see the Internet as a massive, dynamic text. In their chapter, they examine how this perspective poses a challenge to conventional textbooks, which are likely to be less current, to offer only a single interpretation of facts, and to compel linear, start-to-finish reading.

The true breadth of the issues that now confront us is undeniably revealed in the range of topics addressed by these authors. Consideration of their chapters in toto should apprise any reader of the multidimensional nature of the instructional transformation now underway.

10

▼▼▼▼▼▼▼

Transforming Adult
Literacy Instruction Through
Computer-Assisted Instruction

Eunice N. Askov
Brett Bixler
The Pennsylvania State University

Although many adult literacy educators recognize the value of computer-assisted instruction (CAI), some think of it as only drill and practice because that is the type of software that is most prevalent in classrooms. In fact, many other options for CAI exist—options that can transform instruction. This chapter focuses on designing CAI for adult literacy instruction using research-based methodologies. We recognize the importance of the argument of Leu et al. (chap. 12, this volume) for teacher involvement in multimedia design; we accordingly urge that adult literacy instructors be key members of the multidisciplinary team developing CAI. We also hope that this chapter will assist instructors not only in designing their own software, but also in selecting high-quality commercial software for their adult literacy programs.

First, we consider types of CAI, characteristics of effective adult literacy instruction that CAI can enhance, and the benefits of CAI as background to developing CAI for adult literacy instruction. Next, we discuss the learning theories that should be considered in developing CAI as well as design guidelines. We conclude with a discussion of using CAI in adult education programs.

TYPES OF CAI

Most CAI uses one or a combination of the following techniques:

- Tutorial.
- Drill and practice.
- Training games.
- Simulation and microworld.
- Problem solving.
- Assessment.
- Demonstration and presentation.

The most common of all techniques is the *tutorial*. It is used to introduce new information when objectives must be taught in a sequential manner. Another commonly used technique is known as *drill and practice*. It provides opportunities for practice when mastery of a new skill or information is desired. It should be used after initial instruction by the teacher or by a CAI tutorial.

Training games supplement other instruction and are used to provide motivating and engaging opportunities for practice after a skill or new information is taught. The technique of *simulation* is most often used when practicing a skill in its real context is too costly or dangerous to undertake. It provides an opportunity for experimentation and allows students to test assumptions in a realistic context. Simulations are also used to model real-world situations that are not physically dangerous or costly in order to build realism and relevance into the training situation. When complex environments are created, the simulation may be referred to as a *microworld*.

One of the most challenging techniques used in CAI is *problem solving*. It helps students develop skills in logic, solving problems, and following directions and is generally used to augment higher order thinking skills. *Assessment* is a valid part of any training. Computer-based assessment can be used to initially place and then monitor students' progress within a curriculum. *Demonstration* or *presentation* is best used to support the introduction of new information. It can also be used as a review tool.

Most CAI incorporates one or more of these techniques. A game, for example, might have some of the elements of drill and practice; a tutorial might use problem-solving questions. Before considering the benefits of CAI, characteristics of effective adult literacy instruction need to be considered.

EFFECTIVE ADULT LITERACY INSTRUCTION

Sometimes called *learner-centered instruction,* good literacy instruction focuses on what students want and need to learn rather than on a predetermined, generic curriculum usually delivered by a commercial set of materials. Also called the "functional context" approach to instruction (Sticht, 1987), where the context of basic skills instruction is relevant and meaningful to learners, good literacy instruction in adult contexts has these characteristics:

• Good literacy instruction is meaningful and relevant to the adult student's goals and needs because adults are goal oriented. Skills are more easily transferred and applied outside the classroom if instructional activities are as close as possible to actual job or life tasks. Harman (1985) suggested that "hard-to-reach" adults are best reached in programs where literacy is not the main goal but a tool to reach other goals. Functional context instruction has more intrinsic value to the learner than learning basic skills without a relevant context (Sticht, 1987).

• Effective literacy instruction builds on adults' prior knowledge and life experience. For example, workers can read and interpret job-related materials at higher levels than they can read non-job-related materials (Diehl & Mikulecky, 1980). Similarly, adults, using their background knowledge and experience, can read more difficult materials that are relevant to their families, culture, neighborhoods, and other aspects of their lives. The terminology is familiar and the concepts are those used daily. Thus, if a program aims to improve work-related literacy skills, for example, it would be counterproductive for learners to work with generic materials when they could be working at a higher level with job-related (or other relevant) materials.

Effective literacy instruction that is relevant to adults' background knowledge and experience provides a framework for discussing use of CAI. The next consideration is the benefits of CAI in meeting the learning needs of adults who are engaged in adult literacy instruction.

BENEFITS OF CAI

Properly designed CAI has special benefits for adult students that may also be true for school-age individuals. Learners not only feel in control—they are in control of their learning. The computer actively engages the learner in the instructional process, providing increased student satisfaction (U.S. Congress, Office of Technology Assessment, 1993). As Kearsley (1983) stated:

> Computer-based training is an inherently active mode of learning. The learner must continually do something—answer a question, select a topic, ask for a review, and so on. This contrasts with the inherently passive instructional approach involved in classroom lectures, videotapes, or textbooks. (p. 28)

The computer is nonjudgmental and nonthreatening. CAI is self-paced, flexible, and individualized. Students work at their own pace in a sequence that matches their needs. It provides a "privacy" factor, reducing embarrassment (Turner, 1993). Learners can also work in pairs or groups of three to encourage discussion, group problem solving, and communication skills. CAI provides immediate feedback to trainees on their progress (Turner, 1993). The computer can always match the student's schedule and reach those outside the traditional classroom, providing instruction on the job or at home (U.S. Congress, Office of Technology Assessment, 1993).

CAI also gives instructors increased knowledge of students' mastery of instructional objectives. Management systems for tracking students' progress also inform the instructor of each student's progress. Online assessments ensure that the learner is engaged in appropriate instructional activities. CAI provides consistent instruction that does not vary with a particular instructor's capabilities. In a workplace it can provide a standardization of basic skills training that may be important to the industry.

In addition to the obvious benefits to students, CAI is cost effective. After the initial development costs, CAI is available 24 hours per day. For example, in the Wisconsin Technical College System Board grant from the National Workplace Literacy Program (funded by the U.S. Department of Education), a computer lab is open all the time to employees of Oscar Mayer who want to improve their literacy skills. An instructor, who is in the plant only during daytime hours, monitors students' instructional progress, even those who come in during the night shift. Special arrangements are made for instructional intervention by the teacher.

More students can be served here than in a classroom that does not incorporate CAI. The instructor can focus on those students most in need of individual or small group instruction while the others work individually or in pairs on CAI software programs. Instructional time and costs can be reduced if students learn only what they need. In a workplace setting, CAI does not have to be delivered to all employees at the same time, thus allowing the company to maintain coverage of critical positions. It can also provide computer literacy skills as well as teach literacy to individuals.

Next, we consider the benefits of teaching thinking skills. Although most of the CAI examples in the next section are drawn from workplace literacy (see also Mikulecky &

Kirkley, chap. 18, this volume), they are also applicable in understanding instruction in other adult education contexts.

Higher Order Thinking Skills

Well-designed CAI software helps adult learners think critically, solve problems, and draw inferences (Hornbeck, 1990; U.S. Congress, Office of Technology Assessment, 1988). Software that contains realistic and complex problems to solve is an ideal medium for fostering development of higher order thinking skills (Means & Knapp, 1991). In some software—particularly simulations—the learner is typically required to utilize several aspects of higher order thinking. Although a definition of higher order thinking is often dependent on the background of the person defining it (Resnick, 1987), most people agree that higher order thinking skills are complex and interrelated. Three aspects of higher order thinking—critical thinking, creative thinking, and metacognition—are important to consider when designing software for adult education.

With *critical thinking*, people move from automatic responses to well-reasoned responses, including better processing of available information for decision making (Carman, 1994). Critical thinking affects the way people process incoming information and also the way they express their own thoughts and beliefs. With critical thinking, incoming information is analyzed and evaluated to determine if it is appropriate for one's purpose. CAI can be designed to enhance critical thinking. For example, if a CAI simulation about customer service involves an employee receiving a telephone call from a customer with a problem, the employee must use critical thinking skills to analyze the problem and find a solution. Figure 10.1 (*S.C.O.R.E.*, 1994) illustrates a customer service worker applying problem-solving skills in a difficult situation. In this example, the student (employee) must determine the correct course of action. If the learner is unsure of the correct action, he or she must utilize available resources (in this case a customer service manual) to solve the problem.

People also use critical thinking to clarify their own thoughts and ideas so they can discuss them in an organized way rather than saying the first thing that comes to mind

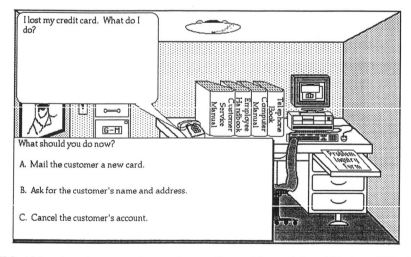

FIG. 10.1.   A customer service worker applies problem-solving skills in a difficult situation.

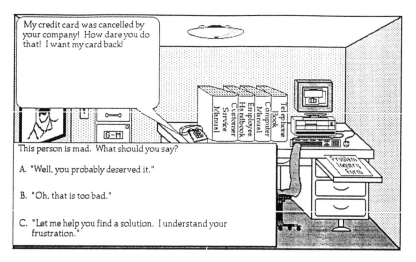

FIG. 10.2. The need for mental clarification before action.

(Brookfield, 1988). Figure 10.2 (*S.C.O.R.E.,* 1994) illustrates the need for this type of mental clarification before action.

Creative thinking allows people to be flexible, to adapt to changing situations (Carman, 1994). With creative thinking, people make connections from the outside world to their own knowledge and skills and vice versa. They see patterns and relations among situations and information. These connections allow people to put skills, knowledge, information, and resources together in different ways for different purposes (Mayer, 1989). Sometimes the information is available through those inferences that require creative thinking. For example, the insurance form represented in Fig. 10.3 contains a question about the sex of the patient. The learner has access to a form with some information on it. Although there is a space on the form for information about the sex of the patient, it was deliberately left blank. However, other relevant information is available, from which the learner must think creatively to reach a correct conclusion. Good CAI allows students to flex their creative muscles.

Metacognition means "thinking about thinking" (Baker & Brown, 1984). When one knows what to do when one does not understand something, one is invoking metacognitive principles. It includes both the knowledge about and the control of thinking behaviors and processes (Carman, 1994). For example, experienced readers know and use strategies, such as using text structure, to better understand and remember information from complex selections (Paris, Wasik, & Turner, 1991). Well-constructed CAI will enhance the metacognitive abilities of the student, such as in the example that appears in Fig. 10.4, from a lesson on using manuals (*S.C.O.R.E.,* 1994). Throughout this lesson, these prompts appear at the appropriate times, enhancing and guiding the learner's metacognitive capabilities.

All higher order thinking demands that individuals be active and purposeful as they react and respond to the world around them (Carman, 1994). Critical thinking, creative thinking, and metacognition are all essential components of successful problem solving. Creative thinking enables one to imagine possibilities for solving a problem. Critical thinking evaluates and tests the pros and cons of those possibilities for strengths and weaknesses. Metacognitive skills direct and control the whole problem-solving process through reflection and prediction, and help people decide when and how to use both creative and critical thinking (Carman, 1994). Software designed for adult education can and should provide a learning environment in which higher order thinking is fostered and

Insurance Claim Form			
Part 1: Insured and Patient Information			
Insured's Name:	Last First Lopez Marie	Social Security # 343-13-5234	
Insured's Address:	Number and Street 4744 Juniper Street	**Group Number:**	
	City State Zip Carptown OH 20921	SE498S	
Patient's Name:	Last First Schmit George	**Sex:** ☐ M ☐ F	
Birthdate:	Mo. Day Yr. 7/23/52	**Relationship to Insured:**	☐ Self ☒ Spouse ☐ Child

Part 2: Prescription Drugs			
Pharmacy Name	**Drug Name**	**Date**	**Cost**

Part 3: Medical Services (Doctor visits and laboratory tests.)			
Dr./Provider Name	**Procedure**	**Date**	**Cost**
Dr. Li	Physical	2/26/97	$35.00
Dr. Li	EEG	2/26/97	$55.00

Insured's Signature: *Marie Lopez*   Date: 3/4/97

[Lesson] [Done]

FIG. 10.3.   A sample insurance form.

Before you read:
  • Did you think about what you already know about credit cards and services like the ones described in the manual?

While you read:
  • Did you notice the way the information was organized?
  • Did you understand the words in the text? Did you try to figure out words you did not know? Did you use a dictionary or ask someone if you could not figure out a word?
  • Did you understand the ideas? Did the information make sense to you, or was it confusing? Why was it confusing? Which parts were confusing?

After you read:
  • Did you try to put the information into your own words?
  • Did you do the math correctly? Did you check your work?
  • Did you have trouble remembering the information when you did not have it in front of you? What did you do to help yourself remember?

This lesson will help you to better understand the manual. It will show you things to do before, during, and after reading.

FIG. 10.4.   Well-constructed CAI.

encouraged. In order to design effective CAI, certain learning theories should be kept in mind.

LEARNING THEORIES TO CONSIDER IN DEVELOPING CAI

Schank and Cleary (1995) stated that all learning is by doing, by constantly having new experiences and attempting to integrate the memory of those experiences into existing memory structures. Effective CAI is interactive, encouraging learning by doing. The reason learning by doing works is that it strikes at the heart of people's basic memory processes. Schank and Cleary believed that people learn how to do things by making mistakes and then correcting those mistakes. By doing this, people learn when rules apply, when to modify or generalize them, and when to make note of exceptions.

Similarly, Rogers and Freiberg's (1994) theory of *experiential learning* states that significant learning occurs when the learner initiates the learning and evaluates it. Learning that is threatening to the self (e.g., new attitudes or perspectives) is more easily assimilated when external threats are at a minimum. Learning proceeds faster when the threat to the self is low. Software for adult education can incorporate all these features, providing an environment that is personally relevant and challenging, yet also safe.

With software for adult education, adult learners should no longer have to worry about making mistakes or feeling evaluated by teachers or peers (U.S. Congress, Office of Technology Assessment, 1993). For people who feel ashamed (unsafe) when making mistakes and are thus afraid of learning-by-doing situations, synthetic environments can provide an opportunity to safely risk mistakes in the process of learning (Dede, 1995). These environments are important for adult learners who may be extremely sensitive to the stigma that often accompanies low literacy.

Effective CAI is also based on the theory of *constructivism,* according to which knowledge is constructed by individuals as they interact with their environment or culture (Rieber, 1992). Constructivist philosophy claims that although a real world exists, we each experience that world differently and thus impose different meaning on the world (Duffy & Jonassen, 1991). The experience in which an idea is embedded is critical to the individual's understanding of and ability to use that idea. Lebow (1993) claimed that constructivist learning environments should contain elements of collaboration so learners can discuss issues and see multiple viewpoints, personal autonomy so learners can become self-sufficient, generativity so learners can construct their own knowledge from experience, metacognitive reflectivity so learners can think about what they did, active rather than passive engagement in the learning process, personal relevance so the learning makes sense, and pluralism so learners can see multiple viewpoints.

Functional context methods of instruction are especially effective and valuable because, like on-the-job training, instruction centered around work- or life-related basic skills is clearly relevant to the adult learner's needs. Thus, functional context instruction is motivating because it has more intrinsic value to the learner (Sticht, 1987). Relatedly, because skills and knowledge are dependent on the activity and context in which they are used (Brown, Collins, & Duguid, 1989; Zondlo, 1995), contextual learning will assist in retention and transfer. Properly designed software for adult education can provide this contextual learning.

An excellent example of how software for adult education can provide contextual learning is the cognitive apprenticeship model (Collins, Brown, & Newman, 1987). Cognitive apprenticeship methods try to enculturate learners into authentic practices through activity and social interaction similar to a craft apprenticeship (Brown et al., 1989). A simulated apprenticeship learning environment can act as a bridge between the theoretical learning of conventional learning and the actual practice of the work environment (Resnick, 1987). For software to provide this bridging, it must have mentoring aspects built into it. These mentoring aspects can take the form of prompts that guide the learner when the learner is having difficulty, just as an expert guides a novice through a difficult task. Hedberg and Alexander (1994) claimed that when virtual reality is used for educational purposes, it offers the possibility of allowing learners to move from novice to expert by participation in communities of practice, for it enables learners to focus on the authentic activities of the community of practice.

The related theory of *situated learning* states that both the learner and the learner's environment are critical elements in any learning situation (Young, 1993). Knowledge and intelligence are viewed as the relationship between the learner and the environment. Thus, in situated learning the environment is just as important as the learner. From this, one can derive that carefully constructed software optimized to simulate the actual work environment will actually lead to a more dynamic learning situation. Streibel (1989) stated, "The best an instructional designer can do is create an environment where the learner's processes of situational sense-making are enhanced" (p. 12).

Knowles' (1984) theory of *andragogy* for adult learning emphasizes that adults are self-directed and expected to take responsibility for decisions. Adult learning programs must accommodate this fact by making the following assumptions about the design of learning: (a) adults need to know why they need to learn something, (b) adults need to learn experientially, (c) adults approach learning as problem solving, and (d) adults learn best when the topic is of immediate value (Knowles, 1984). Because of these assumptions, instruction should be task oriented instead of memorization—learning activities should be in the context of common tasks to be performed, and instruction should allow learners to discover things for themselves, providing guidance and help when mistakes are made. Andragogy is conceptually tied not only to the constructivist values of active engagement and personal relevance (Lebow, 1993), but also to Sticht's (1987) functional context theory via meaningful instruction, and to Schank and Cleary's (1995) notion of learning by doing.

Thus, software designed for the adult learner should be clearly relevant to the learner's needs, provide hands-on experiential activities, provide contextual learning by corresponding to the actual environment where the knowledge and skills the learner constructs will be used, and provide for collaborative activities.

It is difficult to deny that most adults engage in collaborative activities daily in the workplace, but it is only recently that technology has become powerful enough to allow designers to integrate educational collaborative activities into educational software. Much theorizing on this concept exists, however. For group learning environments, Schon (1983) suggested using practice fields in a virtual world that is a constructed representation of the real world. The practice fields can be used for learning teams to allow them to practice together and develop their collective learning skills. Software for adult education used in collaborative learning processes allows learners to see implications of a "bad" decision (Zondlo, 1995). It provides an opportunity to develop insight together, step back and reflect on the expected versus actual results, and learn from the experience in a "safe" (nonthreatening) environment. Collaborative activities can be built into educational software in a variety of ways. The easiest methods to implement are links to e-mail and online chat groups. More difficult to construct are simulations where groups of adult learners work together in a learning environment. Next we discuss considerations in designing CAI for adult education programs.

CAI DESIGN GUIDELINES
FOR ADULT LITERACY INSTRUCTION

The following discussion focuses on research-based design guidelines (see also Bixler & Bergman, 1996) and strategies for creating effective CAI.

Anchored Instruction

In its Jasper Series, the Cognition and Technology Group at Vanderbilt (1990, 1992) coined the term *anchored instruction*. Anchors can provide a common set of experiences for students from which they can draw in their learning (see Kinzer & Risko, chap. 11, this volume). Anchored instruction is a set of situations sequenced in such a way that they give learners an opportunity to detect the parts of their solutions that remain the same across an entire class of problems. The student can then see the parts of the problem-solving process that will work in other situations and the parts that are unique to a particular problem. For example, if the lesson involves instruction in calculating area, the learner could be asked to calculate the area of a wall of a specific height and width in the context of painting a room. In subsequent exercises the learner could calculate the area using walls of different heights and widths. The learner would see that the formula and procedure for determining area remain constant, even though the problems were all slightly different.

Adaptation to Learner Needs

One criterion of good educational software is that it must match the cognitive level of the learner, thereby offering an entry point into the area of knowledge (Rieber, 1993). The software should present simple tasks for the novice learner. As the novice learner becomes an expert, the tasks should become progressively more difficult. Van Joolingen and De Jong (1992) labeled this procedure *progressive implementation*. In progressive implementation, one starts with a view that is a simplification of a domain and then moves via one or more steps to a view that contains all important concepts of the domain.

Scaffolding is another technique that can be used to match the cognitive level of the learner to the learning situation. Scaffolding means supporting learners as they learn new skills, then taking the support away gradually (Bruner, 1978; Guzdial, 1996). Young (1993) claimed that scaffolding is one of the basic tasks a designer should consider when constructing situated learning situations so that eventually the learner is autonomously performing the task; the support to perform the task is no longer needed. (See Anderson-Inman & Horney, chap. 2, and McKenna, chap. 3, both this volume, for more information on electronic scaffolding.)

Learner Control

Learner controls help learners operate and maneuver through a piece of software. Some researchers (Clark, 1982; Steinberg, 1977, 1989) argue that learner control is not desirable because learners usually do not think about what they do not know and are thus poor judges of what they need. Therefore, it is important to make sure the learner controls in a piece of software designed for adult education cannot be used by the learner to proceed on a "learning tangent," taking the learner away from the desired learning paths. Equally important is the need for learners to understand what control they have and to know how and when to use it.

Typical learner controls might include:

- A *Help* button that gives navigational help.

- A *Panic* button that helps learners who are "totally lost" to better understand the nature of their problem so they can choose the appropriate learner control.
- A *Job* button that gives hints about completing the particular activity learners are working on.
- A *Check Work* button that allows learners to ascertain their progress at any time.
- A *Notebook* button that allows learners to write online notes and messages for later reference.
- A *Menu* button that allows learners to exit the scenario and return to the most recent menu.
- A *Stop* button that allows learners to exit the courseware.
- A *Previous Screen* button (if appropriate) that learners can use to back up in an instructional sequence.
- A *Next Screen* button (if appropriate) that learners can use to move forward in an instructional sequence.
- A *Collaborate* button that learners can use to communicate with other learners or instructors.

It should be clear from these examples that learner control does not entail a prescriptive, lockstep sequence but merely sets up desirable parameters and makes assistance readily available. Learner control in this sense actually facilitates a constructivist view of learning.

Information Tracking

Young (1993) stated that information tracking is one of four critical tasks involved in instructional design for situated learning. Van Joolingen and De Jong (1992) also stressed the importance of providing diagnosis. The learning environment should monitor the achievements of the learner and diagnose possible misconceptions. Ideally, the software should diagnose the learner's progress, prescribe additional learning opportunities accordingly, and correct misconceptions. If a learner is floundering, the software should alert the learner to seek the assistance of the teacher or facilitator. The teacher or facilitator should be able to monitor a learner's progress and provide a customized learning prescription.

Interface Design

If the software is divided into different modules or lessons, these lessons should begin with title screens that notify the learner that a new section is being presented. According to Murray (1989), this is a desirable feature. The title screens should also serve as an advanced organizer, a brief, general statement related to what is to follow stated in a highly abstract form (Ausubel, 1968).

In a lesson, screens should be "sparse" in terms of content density wherever possible. A segment of instruction should be broken into small, discreet steps presented sequentially (Baker & Bixler, 1990). This results in screens with a great deal of white space (an area free of information). Instead of diverting the learner's attention, the screens will be clutter free, allowing the learners to concentrate on the concept intended. Unnecessary distractors (such as extra graphics or unimportant backgrounds) should be removed from the screen (Baker & Bixler, 1990).

Large text sizes for print should be used wherever possible (Baker & Bixler, 1990). Most text in books and magazines is 10 or 12 point. Ideally, an 18- or 24-point size should be used because adult learners may have visual difficulties. The use of large text sizes also limits the amount of information placed on one screen, encouraging low content density.

Directions and help should be constantly provided (Baker & Bixler, 1990). One element many adult learners—particularly low-literate adults—share is a difficulty in following directions. Directions should be visible or easily accessible at all times. Learners should be prompted step by step through difficult exercises. *Mirrored prompts* should be used whenever possible. An example of mirrored prompts is having a set of directions at the top of the screen with an additional "What do I do next?" prompt at the bottom of the screen.

Placement of directions and graphics on the screen should be consistent wherever possible. Common phrases for all directions should be used. Graphics should appear in the same general area on the screen in sequential exercises where new graphics may replace old graphics. All menus and interactions that a learner must use in the program should be standardized. Most people have difficulty with an inconsistent interface. Providing an explicit organization increases the memorability of new material (Bower, 1970). Carman (1994) stated that visual organizers are external visualization tools that help learners organize their knowledge and also aid memory.

Summary screens should occur after completion of a section of instruction. They inform the learner that a lesson is finished and also organize and provide a synopsis of the material presented. Summary screens often mirror a title screen, but are augmented with the key concepts the lesson covered. Summary screens embody the metacognitive self-monitoring skill of looking back on what has been learned to determine what should come next (Rigney, 1980).

Desktop computer technology has only recently become powerful enough to support a complex microworld environment. As the power of computer technology increases, it is likely that more microworlds for adult education will be developed.

Authentic Situations in Microworlds

Young (1993) claimed that in situated learning environments, situations must be authentic, having some of the important characteristics of real-life problem solving. Sticht (1987) also stressed the importance of bringing relevance to the learning situation. Adult learners are goal oriented and need to see how what they are learning fits their needs, whether it be for a job, their family, or personal enrichment.

One way to bring relevance to a learning situation via software is through the use of microworlds. The use of computer-based microworlds for adult education is increasing. *A Day in the Life . . .* (1993), published by Curriculum Associates but developed by Penn State's Institute for the Study of Adult Literacy, and *Choosing Success* (1995) by Computer Curriculum Corporation are but a few examples of microworlds currently available for adult educators. The term *microworld* was suggested by Papert (1980) in his description of Logo, a computer-based learning environment that he created for children. He defined a microworld as an incubator, a place where thinking could "hatch and grow with particular ease" (p. 125). Papert's microworld followed several important rules. First, students should work within a constrained environment. For example, students should be given only one instance of a law of physics to work with, rather than many laws. Second, there should be some sort of activity to engage the learner with the subject matter, such as a game.

Third, the microworld should contain all the necessary concepts needed to learn the subject matter. An updated definition of microworlds comes from Zondlo (1995):

> The term [microworlds] has evolved and has now come to mean any simulation (often, but not always, created with a computer) in which people can "live" in the simulation; running experiments, testing different strategies and building a better understanding of the aspects of the real world which the microworld depicts.

The exact definition of what a microworld is is open to scholarly debate. Many people use the terms *simulations* and *microworlds* interchangeably. Rieber (1992) claimed there are two basic differences between a simulation and a microworld. First, microworlds contain the most basic and appropriate elements of a domain as defined by an expert in that domain. Simulations, however, usually strive to completely re-create the environment they mimic and are judged on how well they do so (Alessi, 1988). Second, a microworld allows the user to enter the program at a level appropriate to the user's cognitive level, thus matching the user's needs (Rieber, 1992). Traditional simulations usually do not adapt to the user's needs; the user is instead expected to adapt to the demands of the simulation.

A Day in the Life . . . Instruction is a good example of a microworld. In *A Day in the Life . . . Instruction*, the learner becomes a worker on his or her first day of work in maintenance, retail, heath care, clerical, food service, or customer service. In order to do the job tasks, the learner must use certain basic skills identified through task analyses of the target occupations. For example, the learner has to read the memo from the supervisor, follow the instructions, and do the required job tasks as shown in Fig. 10.5.

In order to do the "paint the room" scenario of the maintenance occupation, for example, the learner has to measure the room, calculate its area, and read the paint can label to know how much paint is needed. The learner is able to navigate among the various rooms at the simulated workplace by clicking on a "go to" button. He or she is able to read the memo and paint can label by the "look at" button. The learner removes the supplies that are necessary for painting the room by the "take" button (which makes the item disappear from the computer screen) and drops them off at the appropriate room by the "drop off" button. If at any point the learner needs assistance, he or she can leave the simulation and enter a tutorial for instruction—for example, on how to read a memo or paint can label. At the completion of the job, such as painting a room, the "supervisor" evaluates the learner's accomplishment of the job tasks, such as taking the correct number

---

Memo

Date: 3/5/97
To:
From: Susan Brown, Maintenance Supervisor
Re: Painting request
I was informed that the walls in room 115 are very dirty. The maintenance records show that the room was painted three years ago. The records also show that the wall color is now off-white.

I would like you to repaint this room the same color some time soon. Check your work schedule on the wall in the Maintenance Department office to find out what day you can do this. On the work schedule, write "painting room 115" in the space for that day. You may also want to see who else is on duty in case you need help moving the furnishings. A copy of the diagram for room 115 is in my out box in case you want to know the room dimensions. Or, you can measure the room yourself.

When you are done, please fill out a Work Completion Form
and put it in my "In" box. Thank you.

FIG. 10.5.   Memo from the supervisor.

of cans of paint. A learning plan is designed for those basic skills that were not used correctly in carrying out the job tasks.

The example from *A Day in the Life . . .* shows how microworlds can embody many of the learning theories and methodologies described here. Desktop computer technology has only recently become powerful enough to support a complex microworld environment. As the power of computer technology increases, it is likely that more microworlds for adult education will be developed.

USING CAI IN ADULT EDUCATION

CAI use should lead to changes in the way instruction is conceptualized and delivered because eventually students must take charge of their own learning. In fact, CAI can be a change agent, becoming the catalyst for a paradigm shift to new instructional approaches within an educational organization (Kearsley, 1983). It changes the role of the instructor from the direct deliverer of instruction to the facilitator of learning. Although this might be threatening to some teachers and tutors, instructors still play an important role in instruction. They must monitor the students' progress, diagnose learning problems, and provide instruction to individuals and/or small groups. The difference is that learners' needs drive the system, not a generic curriculum delivered by an instructor.

Of course, CAI can deliver poor literacy instruction; it is only the vehicle for delivering instruction. When CAI offers effective literacy instruction, as defined earlier, it empowers adult learners; they become responsible for their learning progress. They develop positive attitudes toward learning, not only for instruction through technology, but for all forms of learning. They feel affirmed not only as learners but also as individuals. As Mr. White, an inmate—and a beginning reader—at a state correctional institution, said, as he picked up and literally hugged the computer he had been working on, "I'm right! I know I'm right!" It was, perhaps, the first time he had been successful in a learning situation. Technology that affirms the learners empowers them.

Transforming the Role of the Instructor

Instead of feeling threatened or replaced by technology, instructors—teachers and tutors— need to consider their new roles. The instructor is still essential to mediate between the technology and the learners. Learners need assistance and additional practice even with the best technologically delivered instruction. Teachers and tutors become facilitators more than direct deliverers of instruction.

Learners need help in transferring the instruction delivered by CAI into their daily lives. Instructors can provide the linkage and transfer from the CAI to application in learners' lives. For example, if students learn how to calculate with fractions, they can be given recipes with fractional units or drill bits of different sizes. (Which is larger—$3/8$ or $7/16$?) Instructors who assist learners in bridging the gap between theory and practice provide an essential element in any learning situation.

Instructors can also help learners develop their metacognitive (learning how to learn) skills while using CAI. In fact, effective CAI is ideal for learning and practicing higher level skills, as described earlier. Research (see Baker & Brown, 1984) reveals that learners who have developed their metacognitive skills are more successful in reading. For example, tutors and teachers using CAI can ask learners what they already know about the subject they are about to study and what they need to learn. They can query learners about whether or not they have enough information to answer questions and solve problems delivered by the CAI. They can encourage students to think about what they need to know to learn new information from their reading. They can encourage students to become problem solvers in their literacy studies, using reading and writing as reciprocal processes. They can discuss what they are learning and learn to listen to others' points of view.

Types of Learning Environments

The environment in which CAI is used affects the ease of transition from a traditionally organized classroom or tutoring situation to one that uses CAI. Perhaps more important than the physical setting is the staff's attitude toward learners' use of technology. The willingness to be flexible in designing instruction is crucial. Putting everyone through the same technologically delivered instruction is not a solution that will encourage effective instruction. Three settings are considered here.

Technology Lab. A drop-in learning lab setting may be the most conducive to optimal use of CAI. Beginning readers may be tutored in the lab setting; the tutor offers a combination of print-based and CAI instruction. Similarly, in classroom instruction the teacher gradually moves students into appropriate CAI in addition to small-group instruction. As learners progress, they gradually take more responsibility for their learning. They keep track of their own progress, and they learn how to operate the instructional programs they are using. The role of the instructor gradually changes from the deliverer of instruction to facilitator of learning. Individual and small group instruction is still offered but only as needed. Students assume more control over their learning.

A good example of this model is the Technology for Literacy Center; although part of the St. Paul (MN) School District, it is located in a shopping mall (Turner, 1993). This setting has the additional advantage of maximum flexibility of scheduling for students; many types of technologies are available to the learners in addition to CAI.

The Center for Literacy, the largest community-based literacy organization in Pennsylvania and located in Philadelphia, has a computer lab in a centrally located school. Learners from any program, including tutorials and classes, can drop into the lab and work on the various software programs. Tutors can also come with their students to the lab for supplemental work. The lab is staffed by former students who know the software from personal experience.

On a smaller scale, the Women's Program at the Lutheran Settlement House in Philadelphia has a computer lab in one of its classrooms. The lab is staffed by a Volunteers in Service to America (VISTA) volunteer who works with classes of students. The difficulty of this model, as in the case of the other Philadelphia program, is that close coordination is required between the instructor or tutor and the lab instructor, who should know what the students need. Most of the instructors are part-time employees who do not have the opportunity to use the software so that they know what the various programs teach. The VISTA volunteer, however, has been able to communicate with the instructors to overcome some of these problems. The students assume responsibility for their own record keeping and progress, which encourages independence and empowerment of the learners.

Small Groups. Although the usual model for computer use is one learner per computer, two or three learners can use a single computer, an arrangement that offers an obvious economy because more learners can be served at one time. The real advantage, however, is that weaker students can be helped by more advanced learners. Peer instruction is effective not only for the less advanced student but also for the one who is assisting. The small groups can also work offline in teacher-delivered instruction and group practice activities. The Tri-County OIC in Harrisburg, Pennsylvania, uses this collaborative learning model in delivering instruction both at its instructional site and in the workplaces it serves.

Integrated Learning Systems (ILS). An ILS is a big system that may include software, print, and other media integrated by a management system. The capability of an ILS to offer instruction, usually by CAI, for all learners regardless of level is appealing. Although big systems offer opportunities for learners at all levels, they usually do not use a functional context approach to instruction. It is very difficult to customize these learning systems to a unique group of learners. However, they may be used as a basis for literacy skill development with supplementary instruction focusing on the needs of local learners.

It is possible to create ILS-like packages of software, using a variety of commercial software programs as well as record-keeping software. As long as an assessment and record-keeping system is in place, various types of technologies can be included in the simulated ILS.

Both Mansoor (1993) and Turner (1993) offered excellent discussions of the commercial ILS. Their major drawbacks are their expense, generic instruction, and lack of customization. Their major appeal is their ease of use, not requiring a highly trained staff, although research has shown that a more highly trained staff obtained better results with an ILS (Nurss, 1989).

ESL Learners. Although the Southport Institute report by Mansoor (1993) recommends technology for ESL learners, some learners reject technology in instruction because it does not fit the traditional model of instruction. A common observation is that students from certain cultures view the teacher as the authority; the students' role is to sit quietly and listen. Technology may be considered frivolous, more appropriate as a game than a learning tool. Good language learning, however, is interactive; students must use their English language skills. Multimedia, including CAI, can be used to break out of the traditional mold of instruction. Videos can present common situations that require certain language responses. CAI can present options for responding to the situations presented. Then learners can role-play the situations, such as calling a supervisor to report the need for a sick day.

The interactive videodisc created in South Australia entitled *The Aussie Barbie* (Anderson, 1991) uses the context of an Australian barbecue to demonstrate the appropriate language for a social event. Learners select appropriate responses to situations from various choices shown on the videodisc; branching occurs depending on their responses. Other modules model correct language patterns. The learner is asked to imitate the phrase that is recorded for both learner and instructor evaluation.

Instead of technology being a cultural barrier, it can help nonnative speakers improve their English literacy skills. It can be used in mixed language groups so that English must be spoken in order to communicate about the lesson presented by technology. The group use of the technology provides the support needed for those who are beginning to learn English as a second language. The senior author of this chapter used this model in developing and field testing software in Australia with nonnative speakers (Askov & Cole, 1985).

A FINAL NOTE

If CAI, and technology in general, is to be exploited for its many capabilities in helping adults learn, funding from the federal and state governments needs to be addressed at the policy level. Volunteer literacy programs do not have the resources for technology purchases in spite of the fact that instruction, assessment, and record keeping could be much more effective and efficient with technology. Along with funding for technology must come staff development to upgrade the capabilities of personnel in all types of programs to capitalize on the power that technology has to offer.

In this chapter we have looked at the power of CAI to transform instruction—to make instruction as meaningful to learners as it can be. Unfortunately, most adult literacy programs are not engaged in this transformation. As the prices for computers come down, one must ask why more programs have not taken advantage of the capabilities of CAI. One answer is still the lack of access to appropriate hardware and software for all programs. That problem should eventually be solved with more funding. Another answer may be more difficult to solve—that instructors have not yet been transformed from their traditional roles. Their vision of instruction is still teacher centered. This vision is difficult to change when most instructors are part time and inservice is usually not systematic and long term. Systemic change is necessary for instruction to be transformed into learner-centered instruction that incorporates the best that CAI has to offer. We have offered guidance for those who are ready for transformation.

REFERENCES

Alessi, S. M. (1988). Fidelity in the design of instructional simulations. *Journal of Computer Based Instruction, 15*(2), 40–47.

Anderson, J. (1991). *Technology and adult literacy.* New York: Routledge.

Askov, E. N., & Cole, P. G. (1985). Computer assisted instruction for teaching adults beginning reading. *Adult Literacy and Basic Education, 9*(2), 57–67.

Ausubel, D. P. (1968). *Educational psychology: A cognitive view.* New York: Holt, Rinehart, & Winston.

Baker, G., & Bixler, B. (1990). Computer-assisted design techniques for low-literate adults. *Computers in Adult Education and Training, 2*(1), 18–27.

Baker, L., & Brown, A. L. (1984). Metacognitive skills of reading. In P. D. Pearson (Ed.), *Handbook of reading research* (pp. 353–394). New York: Longman.

Bower, G. H. (1970). Organizational factors in memory. *Cognitive Psychology, 1*, 18–46.

Bixler, B., & Bergman, T. (1996). *Selecting and implementing computer-based training.* Washington, DC: National Alliance of Business.

Brookfield, S. D. (1988). *Developing critical thinkers: Challenging adults to explore alternative ways of thinking and acting.* San Francisco: Jossey-Bass.

Brown, J. S., Collins, A., & Duguid, P. (1989). Situated cognition and the culture of learning. *Educational Researcher, 18*, 32–42.

Bruner, J. S. (1978). The role of dialogue in language acquisition. In A. Sinclair, R. J. Jarvelle, & W. J. M. Levelt (Eds.), *The child's conception of language* (pp. 241–255). New York: Springer-Verlag.

Carman, P. S. (1994). *Helping adult learners develop their higher order thinking skills: A handbook for adult literacy practitioners, staff trainers, and curriculum developers.* University Park: Institute for the Study of Adult Literacy, Pennsylvania State University.

Choosing Success. (1995). [Computer software]. Sunnyvale, CA: Computer Curriculum Corporation.

Clark, R. (1982). Antagonism between achievement and enjoyment in ATI studies. *Educational Psychologist, 17*, 92–101.

Cognition and Technology Group at Vanderbilt. (1990). Anchored instruction and its relationship to situated cognition. *Educational Researcher, 19*(6), 2–10.

Cognition and Technology Group at Vanderbilt. (1992). The Jasper experiment: An exploration of issues in learning and instructional design. *Education Technology Research and Development, 40*(1), 65–80.

Collins, A., Brown, J. S., & Newman, S. E. (1987). Cognitive apprenticeship: Teaching the craft of reading, writing, and mathematics. In L. Resnick (Ed.), *Cognition and instruction: Issues and agendas* (pp. 1–27). Hillsdale, NJ: Lawrence Erlbaum Associates.

Day in the Life . . . (1993). [Computer software]. Billerica, MA: Curriculum Associates.

Dede, C. (1995). The evolution of constructivist learning environments: Immersion in distributed, virtual worlds. *Educational Technology, 35*(5), 46–52.

Diehl, W. A., & Mikulecky, L. (1980). The nature of reading at work. *Journal of Reading, 24,* 221–227.

Duffy, T. M., & Jonassen, D. J. (1991). Constructivism: New implications for instructional technology? *Educational Technology, 5,* 7–12.

Guzdial, M. (1996). *Components of software-realized scaffolding* [Online]. Available http://www.cc.gatech.edu/gvu/edtech/SRS.html.

Harman, D. (1985). *Turning illiteracy around: An agenda for national action.* New York: Business Council for Effective Literacy.

Hedberg, J., & Alexander, S. (1994). Virtual reality in education: Defining researchable issues. *Educational Media International, 31*(4), 214–220.

Hornbeck, D. W. (1990). *Technology and learners at risk of school failure.* Elmhurst, IL: North Central Regional Educational Laboratory.

Kearsley, G. (1983). *Computer based training, a guide to selection and implementation.* Reading, MA: Addison-Wesley.

Knowles, M. (1984). *The adult learner: A neglected species* (3rd ed.). Houston, TX: Gulf Publishing.

Lebow, D. (1993). Constructivist values for instructional systems design: Five principles toward a new mindset. *Educational Technology Research and Development, 41*(3), 4–16.

Mansoor, I. (1993). *The use of technology in adult ESL programs: Current practice–future promise.* Washington, DC: Southport Institute for Policy Analysis.

Mayer, R. E. (1989). Models for understanding. *Review of Educational Research, 59*(1), 43–64.

Means, B., & Knapp, M. S. (1991). Cognitive approaches to teaching advanced skills to educationally disadvantaged learners. *Phi Delta Kappan, 73*(4), 282–289.

Murray, W. R. (1989). Control for intelligent tutoring systems: A comparison of blackboard architectures and discourse management networks. *Machine-Mediated Learning, 3*(1), 107–124.

Nurss, J. R. (1989). *PALS evaluation project.* Atlanta, GA: Center for the Study of Adult Literacy, Georgia State University.

Papert, S. (1980). *Mind-storms: Children, computers, and powerful ideas.* Brighton, UK: Harvester Press.

Paris, S. G., Wasik, B. A., & Turner, J. C. (1991). The development of strategic readers. In R. Barr, M. L. Kamil, P. B. Mosenthal, & P. D. Pearson (Eds.), *Handbook of reading research* (Vol. 2, pp. 609–640). New York: Longman.

Resnick, L. B. (1987). Learning in school and out. *Educational Researcher, 16,* 13–20.

Rieber, L. P. (1992). Computer-based microworlds: A bridge between constructivism and direct instruction. *Educational Technology Research and Development, 40*(1), 93–106.

Rieber, L. P. (1993). A pragmatic view of instructional technology. In K. Tobin (Ed.), *The practice of constructivism in science education* (pp. 193–212). Washington, DC: AAAS Press.

Rigney, J. W. (1980). Cognitive learning strategies and qualities in information processing. In R. Snow, P. Federico, & W. Montague (Eds.), *Aptitude, learning, and instruction* (Vol. 1, pp. 315–340). Hillsdale, NJ: Lawrence Erlbaum Associates.

Rogers, C. R., & Freiberg, H. J. (1994). *Freedom to learn* (3rd ed). Columbus, OH: Merrill/Macmillan.

Schank, R. C., & Cleary, C. (1995). *Engines for education.* Mahwah, NJ: Lawrence Erlbaum Associates.

Schon, D. (1983). *The reflective practitioner: How professionals think in action.* New York: Basic Books.

S.C.O.R.E. (Sales and Customer Service Occupational Readiness Education). (1994). [Computer software]. University Park: Institute for the Study of Adult Literacy, Pennsylvania State University.

Steinberg, E. R. (1977). Review of learner control in computer-assisted instruction. *Journal of Computer-Based Instruction, 3,* 84–90.

Steinberg, E. R. (1989). Cognition and learner control: A literature review, 1977–1988. *Journal of Computer-Based Instruction, 16,* 117–121.

Sticht, T. G. (1987). *Functional context literacy: Workshop resource notebook.* San Diego, CA: Applied Behavioral & Cognitive Sciences.

Streibel, M. J. (1989, February). *Instructional plans and situated learning: The challenge of Suchman's theory of situated action for instructional designers and instructional systems.* Paper presented at the annual meeting of the Association for Educational Communications and Technology, Dallas, TX.

Turner, T. C. (1993). *Literacy and machines: An overview of the use of technology in adult literacy programs* (Tech. Rep. TR93-3). Philadelphia: National Center on Adult Literacy, University of Pennsylvania.

U.S. Congress, Office of Technology Assessment. (1988). *Power on! New tools for teaching and learning.* Washington, DC: U.S. Government Printing Office.

U.S. Congress, Office of Technology Assessment. (1993). *Adult literacy and new technologies: Tools for a lifetime* (OTA-SET-550). Washington, DC: U.S. Government Printing Office.

van Joolingen, W. R., & De Jong, T. (1992). Modelling domain knowledge for intelligent simulation learning environments. *Computer Educator, 18*(1–3), 29–37.

Young, M. F. (1993). Instructional design for situated learning. *Educational Technology Research and Development, 41*(1), 43–58.

Zondlo, J. A. (1995). *Team learning through microworlds: An effective (and fun!) alternative* [Online]. Available http://www.zondlo.com/access/microwld.html.

Multimedia and Enhanced Learning: Transforming Preservice Education

Charles K. Kinzer
Victoria J. Risko
Vanderbilt University

As we look around today's college classrooms, little appears different from two decades ago. Although some classrooms may have a computer and television monitor for the instructor's use, most do not—and surveys indicate that these items remain largely unused even when they are available. When used, computers in college classrooms often take the place of overhead projectors—with instructors being able to show "transparencies" in color and in random order, but without using many of the technological capabilities to enhance instruction. Yet technology in college classrooms offers new tools and benefits for positively influencing preservice education and must, we feel, be integrally woven into preservice curricula in ways that makes college instruction more effective. The use of technology in college classrooms should not only enhance teaching and learning for preservice teachers, but should serve as models for our future teachers who, if research is to be believed, will teach in the manner in which they themselves have been taught. If we want our future teachers to effectively use technology in their future classrooms, they should experience effective uses of technology integrated into their preservice curriculum.

In attempting to find optimal uses of technology in our own preservice classes, we have merged case-based instruction (Merseth, 1991; J. H. Shulman, 1995; L. S. Shulman, 1995; Silverman & Welty, 1995) with features of technology that enhance the case-based approach. We feel that there are many benefits to case-based instruction, but that technology can add to more traditionally used print-based cases in ways that allow preservice students to examine more fully the rich potential of cases. Whereas print-based cases can describe (and thus "filter" what is described through the narrator's lens), multimedia cases under microcomputer control can show the case directly, thus allowing the learner a relatively unfiltered interaction with the substance of the case. We say "relatively unfiltered" because no case can provide all of the contextual background and interactions that are part of a classroom, and editing videotape and determining camera angles also impose a bias, no matter how unintended. However, as we argue later, multimedia cases come much closer to showing reality than do print-based cases, and this reality provides both the instructor and the learner with advantages that show themselves in richer class discussions and more student-centered instruction.

Our original work (Risko & Kinzer, 1991, 1994) was funded by the Fund for the Improvement of Secondary Education, which allowed us to create eight multimedia cases for use in preservice literacy education classes. Four of these cases are targeted toward remedial reading and four toward developmental reading (also known as traditional elementary reading methods). This chapter describes the decisions that we made as we developed the multimedia cases, as well as our vision for transforming preservice literacy education classes more generally through the use of technology and case-based instruction.

WHERE WE CAME FROM: PRESERVICE CLASSES AS WE KNEW THEM

Preservice classes traditionally rely on an instructor's lectures, a textbook, supplementary readings, and a field experience component. The use of such transmission delivery systems for instruction may be conceptualized within traditional-craft and competency-based reading teacher education models, as discussed by Alvermann (1990). Textbooks contain good and relevant information, but this information (no matter how well it is linked to descriptions of classrooms and children) often remains abstract. Procedures in textbooks are typically well presented (and the procedural steps are usually well memorized by students), but they are learned as a series of steps rather than as flexible guidelines that are modified depending on a given instructional situation. Lectures and textbooks have similar advantages and drawbacks. In both instances, the advantages stem from providing much relevant information that is clearly presented and structured in a single source. Good textbooks and lectures not only present procedures (e.g., the Language Experience Approach [LEA], Directed Reading–Thinking Activity [DR–TA], etc.) but also bridge these, explaining how and when each is used, how the various procedures differ from one another, and so on. The disadvantages of lectures and textbooks stem from students not seeing procedures used in contextually grounded situations, where opportunities for analysis of the procedure in use, as well as opportunities for analysis of the decision making that leads up to choosing and appropriately modifying a given procedure are provided for the student. Opportunities for analysis, reflection, and decision making are a central component of multimedia, case-based instruction, and might be thought of as inquiry-oriented reading teacher education (Alvermann, 1990).

We felt that three things needed to be addressed in our courses. First, as discussed already, we felt that our students learned instructional procedures well, but did not feel comfortable in modifying these procedures to meet specific instructional situations or specific students' needs. This was confirmed in informal conversations and through anecdotal data collected by following a subset of our graduates into their first and second years of teaching. Second, we felt (also confirmed informally) that the field experience and practicum components of our courses were often the most valuable. Third, we knew that our preservice teachers were placed in already functioning classrooms in field experiences as undergraduates (as student teachers or as practicum teachers within specific methods courses). Thus, they had little or no experience in making the "up-front" decisions that are critical to successful classroom instruction, because classrooms were already set up. We felt that our students did not have enough experience in making decisions to get ready for the first day of school, which would be required after they were hired for their first teaching assignment. Although our courses, like most others of which we are aware, contain readings, lectures, and simulations that target classroom organization and preparation for "the first day," the time between graduates' getting their first job and preparing for their first class of students is nerve wracking. Preservice students rarely receive experiences relating to the initial preparation of structuring classrooms or planning for incoming students in ways that (as several of our students stated) are "truly meaningful."

PROPOSED RESTRUCTURING: A THEORETICAL BASIS

As we examined our assumptions with regard to our preservice courses, and as we considered carefully the comments from our students, we searched for ways that would enhance our students' learning, retention, and transfer of knowledge to relevant, related situations. We wanted our students to have learned procedures, as well as ways to appropriately modify procedures for given instructional situations, and to do so in ways that approached fluency. We wanted our students to have resources and valuable references available to them through a textbook and readings, but to ground the textbook and readings in relevant and meaningful contexts. Our work to create and use multimedia cases in our preservice classes finds some support in the literature about experts and novices, as well as work in anchored instruction. In what follows, we briefly discuss both of these areas in an attempt to show how findings from these bodies of research were incorporated into our multimedia cases.

Information From Research on Anchored Instruction

Our previous work with anchored instruction (e.g., Cognition and Technology Group at Vanderbilt [CTGV], 1990; Bransford, Kinzer, Risko, Rowe, & Vye, 1989; Schmidt, Meltzer, Kinzer, Bransford, & Hasselbring, 1990) demonstrated that anchors can provide a common experience from which instructors can draw examples. Using videodiscs to show a video-based anchor provides a shared experience for all participants in a class. The videodisc-based anchor mitigates differences in background knowledge, and instructional examples become more relevant because they are linked to a common knowledge base. Also, because the anchor is experienced both by the teacher and the students in a class, shared knowledge develops as part of the classroom community. Our previous work, and work by others (CTGV, 1994; see also Bransford, Sherwood, Kinzer, & Hasselbring, 1985; Brown, Collins, & Duguid, 1989) also implies that contextualized learning facilitates and bridges knowledge and its use, thereby mitigating the inert knowledge factor.[1] In brief, anchored instruction situates learning within a context that is rich and authentic.

Anchored instruction begins with the sharing of a common experience and includes embedded problems along with embedded data that allow the problems to be solved. The structure of the anchor and the instruction that results have been discussed elsewhere for use in various subject areas (e.g., McLarty et al., 1990; Pichert et al., 1994; Askov & Bixler, chap. 10, this volume, also describe anchored instruction as used in an adult literacy application). Within the anchor, as in life, problem situations arise that need to be solved, and the data for solving these are embedded in the anchor. As in life, learners must decide on strategies for solving the problem, appropriate alternative strategies must be considered,

---

[1]As we have discussed elsewhere, anchors that are presented on videodisc or CD-ROM are quite different from anchors based on experiences that are more transient or less accessible when compared to almost instant access to any portion of the anchor provided by these media. The random access nature of videodiscs and CD-ROMs make them more powerful delivery systems for "on-the-fly" instructional uses than a videotape or a book.

appropriate data needed to address the problem must be found, skills needed to use the data need to be learned, and, ultimately, a solution must be provided. Early work at Vanderbilt's Learning Technology Center (see Bransford et al., 1985) showed that White-head's (1929) notion of inert knowledge held true in a variety of situations, that isolated problems (e.g., word problems in mathematics textbooks) do not facilitate transfer to other tasks, and that anchored instruction aided retention and transfer.

Anchored instruction attempts to address three common issues that all teachers must deal with, whether in PreK-12 or preservice classrooms. These issues may be summarized as follows:

1. Teachers face students with a wide range of backgrounds. Research in literacy education has for several decades examined the effect of background knowledge on comprehension and on learning from text (Alexander, Kulikowich, & Jetton, 1994; Bransford & Johnson, 1973; Tyler & Voss, 1982). This research has shown that differences in experiences, expectations, knowledge, cultures, values and other linguistic and nonlinguistic factors play a role in understanding text and in linking new information to existing knowledge.

Although it is more intuitive to see how background knowledge might apply to comprehension of text—for example, to see that a student who comes from a country that might not celebrate Thanksgiving may lack experiential background that would mitigate against comprehension of a novel based on a Thanksgiving dinner—students' background knowledge and experiences play a clear role in preservice literacy education classes as well. Consider, for example, that some students might have come from classrooms where they were taught using a skills-based approach (perhaps a synthetic phonics or linguistic approach), whereas others might have come from classrooms where they were taught in a more holistic manner. An instructor who simply says "think of how you were taught to read" would elicit widely different mental images in his or her students, and the method under discussion would resonate more or less strongly with each individual depending on his or her respective recollections and experiences about being taught to read as a child.

Thus, the diversity of backgrounds in a preservice class means that an instructor's examples will be differentially perceived, and be differentially effective (certainly, they will be differentially linked to respective students' existing knowledge), depending on students' differing backgrounds. In short, differences in our preservice students' background knowledge and experience make teaching more difficult and less effective.[2]

2. There is often little shared knowledge among teacher and students. In ideal situations, the teacher and learner know what each other knows with regard to already-known information and new, to-be-learned information. This can be related to Vygotsky's notion of the zone of proximal development (Vygotsky, 1978, 1986).

In the zone of proximal development, mediators can help learners solve problems that are slightly beyond their ability. However, this requires that the teacher and learner share knowledge about what each other knows. Yet, because of the range of background knowledge in a class, it is difficult for teachers to link new to existing knowledge. It is difficult for teachers to have a high level of shared knowledge with the large number of students in the typical preservice education classroom.

---

[2]We do not mean to imply that diversity in backgrounds and experiences is to be ignored or is unfortunate. It is necessary to celebrate diversity, realizing, however, that it can cause difficulties in understanding examples that may be unrelated to some students' knowledge or cultural base. Diversity can and should be used to extend and expand all students' knowledge.

3. Knowledge often remains inert; it is not accessed and used in appropriate situations. Whitehead (1929) and others (Bereiter, 1984; Sherwood, Kinzer, Bransford, & Franks, 1987; Spiro & Jeng, 1990) pointed out that facts and procedures can be memorized or used in one context, but are not always accessed when needed—especially when the information is required in transfer tasks.

Students often learn procedures in preservice classes and can state the appropriate procedure in class discussions and on examinations. Yet, when in a field experience situation, students often do not use the "known" procedure when needed. In effect, their knowledge is inert. Similar examples can be drawn from vocabulary teaching and learning, where students can demonstrate on paper-and-pencil tests definitions when prompted, but do not do well in unprompted tasks or use the "new" words in appropriate, everyday conversations. Yet instruction that is closely linked to a variety of situations, and that requires decision making and analysis, can facilitate the use of learned knowledge (CTGV, 1992; Sherwood et al., 1987). To complete the vocabulary example just noted, we had previously shown that two groups of students (one experimental and one control) could provide equally well definitions for words, but that the experimental group (taught the definitions embedded in an anchor) used the words in spontaneous conversations significantly more often (Kinzer, McLarty, & Martin, 1989). Thus, we felt that addressing the inert knowledge issue in preservice education was important and feasible through the use of anchored instruction and videodisc-based cases.

Information From Research on Experts and Novices

Research about experts and novices has been done in many domains, and it is not our purpose to review this extensive literature here. However, consistent findings, across domains, indicate that experts and novices differ on at least three dimensions: their knowledge base, their pattern recognition, and their fluency. Interested readers are referred to Alvermann's (1990) discussion of studies regarding experts and novice teachers in reading education, as well as discussions by Berliner (1986, 1987). However, although differences between experienced and less experienced teachers appear to exist, there are at least two difficulties with *expert* and *novice* as global labels when discussing teachers. First, all of us exhibit expertlike behavior in certain areas, but not in others. That is, in a large category such as reading instruction, we might see expert behavior when observing informal assessment, but not when observing management of instruction. This can lead to designating teachers as novices overall, when only a certain aspect of instructional behaviors have been observed.

Second, as Berliner (1986) and Alvermann (1990) noted, it is easy to confound the difference between expertise and experience. A large amount of experience may not result in expertlike behavior in the sense discussed by Berliner (1987), although there are certainly differences in teachers' teaching behaviors and in their application of teaching knowledge and strategies, and these differences might place teachers at different points on a continuum of expertlike behavior. Thus, we do not use expert and novice to differentiate preservice and inservice teachers because attempting to delineate expert behavior based on experience or on observations of one (or even a small subset) of instructional aspects is inappropriate in our view. We use expert and novice as labels to differentiate pattern recognition and fluent access and use of knowledge. In the following, we provide a brief example about how these differences might play themselves out with regard to two teachers.

Consider two teachers, both of whom enter a classroom and scan the room. Based on what they notice, one teacher might exhibit expert behavior by deciding to move or separate some students, thus eliminating the potential of a later problem. The other teacher does not do so and has a behavior management problem to deal with later. In this example, the expert scanned the room and, with pattern recognition skills and an appropriate knowledge base, anticipated a potential problem. The novice might have lacked the pattern recognition skills to recognize the set of factors or circumstances that would cause a later problem, may not have had the appropriate knowledge base, or may not have accessed appropriate knowledge (the knowledge was inert). To conclude this example, expertlike behavior includes rapid and appropriate decision making—patterns are recognized and appropriate knowledge applied with fluency. Even if a novice, on reflection, recognizes the reasons for a problem after it occurs, fluent pattern recognition and appropriate action did not occur (although this reflection and recognition would likely facilitate the development of this process).

What we have presented here is similar to the fluent selection of strategies as appropriate to teaching conditions as discussed in terms of conditional knowledge by Reinking, Mealey, and Ridgeway (1993; see also Paris, Lipson, & Wixson, 1983). They argued that developing conditional knowledge should be the focus of teaching, with declarative and procedural knowledge (respectively, the ability to define a strategy and to carry out a strategy) becoming important "only as they relate to developing students' conditional knowledge" (p. 459). Reinking et al. (1993) provided a four-part model with analysis of strategies and decisions related to variables in a teaching context as the central component to developing conditional knowledge. The other three parts of their model (modeling for students, providing practice, and informing students about strategies and procedures) are acknowledged as important functions and as being related to the development of conditional knowledge, but it is the analysis function that is critical.

As we looked for optimal ways to implement instructional approaches that would facilitate students' developing conditional knowledge and for ways to address students' differences in background knowledge that would result in our preservice teachers' learning becoming accessible rather than inert, it became apparent that anchored instruction and a case-based approach had advantages that would directly address the issues discussed in the previous two sections. As discussed, anchored instruction addressed issues of shared, background knowledge and had been shown to mitigate the inert knowledge problem, and case-based instruction has long been recognized as a way to provide data and decision-making scenarios that lead to reflection and analysis in ways that lectures do not. In the following, we present our view of multimedia, case-based instruction and the advantages that this provides our preservice education students.

OUR TRANSITION TO CASE-BASED, MULTIMEDIA ANCHORS IN PRESERVICE EDUCATION

Our preservice classes look quite different now than they did 6 years ago.[3] As we have reported elsewhere, there is increased class discussion (and, correspondingly, less instructor talk), increased participation by a greater number of students, increased higher level questioning, and increased student-initiated questions and discussions (Risko, Yount, & McAllister, 1992). Although a textbook and readings are still used, examination of videodisc-based

---

[3]Our cases have been in use for 6 years, in both remedial reading and developmental reading preservice classes. Three different instructors have used or are using the cases at our home institution. They are also in use in at least five other universities.

cases forms the core of our courses, together with a student book that contains print-based artifacts pertaining to the case.

Initial Decisions: The Boundaries of a Case

Our initial decision on the way to transforming our preservice classes dealt with what to include in our cases. Cases can focus on an individual lesson, one or more students, a given instructional procedure, or many other facets of instruction. Our decision, however, was to make the classroom a case—to include in our cases as many factors as possible that impact and influence children's learning in classroom situations. Given a sociocultural view of learning that recognizes that many factors interact to influence classroom instruction, this implied that we needed to include at minimum:[4]

- Teachers, who are shown in classrooms "doing instruction" as well in interviews discussing their students, their work, and the instructional decisions they make.
- Teacher colleagues, who teach in the same school in classes above and below the central, target classroom and who provide insight about children's learning as a continuum across classrooms in a school.
- Parents, who, in interviews, comment on their views about the teacher's instructional program, support for homework, their child's learning, and the like.
- Students, who are interviewed about their learning, talk about their work, and are shown in classroom instructional situations.
- Administrators, who discuss their school's demographics, place the target classroom in a larger context, and discuss instructional philosophy on a schoolwide basis.
- Discussants, who are professional educators and researchers representing different content domains, including literacy, and who provide their perspectives on case issues and dilemmas.
- Students' work that is collected over time and that can form the basis for analysis of possible needs as well as show growth over time in a "portfolio" sense.*
- Teachers' lesson plans, where one can analyze plans in the context of the classroom situation and examine changes that occurred.*
- Students' test scores, where summary lists of standardized scores as well as more informal measures are provided for analysis of multiple sources of information that can be compared to students' actual learning and demonstrated ability in the classroom.*
- Much classroom video to document instruction and show instructional procedures as well as teacher–student and student–student interactions.

In examining this list, the advantages of providing case-based instruction through technology as opposed to using print-based cases become more evident. In addition to the benefits of computer-controlled multimedia allowing an instructor and learner to quickly and accurately revisit appropriate scenes, computer-controlled multimedia cases have two additional advantages over print-based cases. First, print-based cases do not allow one to

---

[4]Asterisked items appear in a paper copy student book, with only sample pages scanned into the software. This allows original work to appear more authentic, allows it to be more easily accessed, and allows our students to more easily compare students' work, test scores, or teachers' lesson plans independently as a homework assignment.

experience authentic classroom situations in ways that closely approximate a "real-time" basis. That is, print-based cases are usually narratives that are written by an observer (either with or without reference to a videotape) or by the classroom teacher who reflects on, presents, or discusses what occurred in the classroom.

Regardless of whether the print-based case is a narrative description of a general teaching segment (perhaps an entire language experience lesson) or a specific issue (perhaps one instance of a disruptive student's behavior), the fact that the case is written after the fact means that it is influenced by the perceptions, recollective nature, and subconscious biases of the writer. In effect, the readers of a print-based case are not interacting with what is, but with what is stated. A video case, however, allows the student the chance to become the observer rather than the third-party listener or reader. The "raw data" of a video-based case are preserved and presented, allowing for a more powerful, real-time analysis of embedded data rather than consideration of recalled data.

Second, readers of print-based cases are reading only one aspect of an instructional segment. For example, a description of what is happening in one part of the classroom might describe in detail what is happening with one student, but not take into account another student's behavior, attention, or difficulty. Reading the description again does not move one beyond what is written (although a different perspective can be brought to bear on how to interpret what is being read). Random access video, however, allows not only a reinterpretation and reconsideration of what is happening from a different perspective, but also allows one to attend to a different aspect of what is viewed again—perhaps the students in the background, the quiet student in the group, "body language," teacher wait time, or any number of other things that are inherently a part of any classroom video. In short, the viewer is not limited by having his or her focus drawn to a specific aspect of a situation as determined by the writer of a written case. This refocusing, revisiting, and looking at a video segment in new ways for new purposes is one advantage of using computer-controlled video-based cases in preservice instruction and also mitigates a potential problem that arises from the use of videotape.

In any video of a classroom much is occurring at the same time, as alluded to already, and there is a danger that students will not focus on the desired aspect of the segment on initial viewing. Simply stated, because there is much to notice, there is a possibility that a student will notice something peripheral to the central issue under class discussion. The random access, accurate revisiting of scenes (available to users of videodisc and CD-ROM technology) allows instructors to refocus students' attention on aspects of the video segment that may have been missed.

Without rapid random access capabilities, revisiting segments of the case is difficult. It takes a significant amount of time to move from one part of a videotape to another (time that seems interminable when waiting for a tape to wind in front of a class of students), and accurate search for a beginning point of a desired scene is also not possible. Thus, the use of microcomputer control of a videodisc or CD-ROM tends to encourage revisiting the case—an important aspect of this instructional procedure—and argues against videotape as the medium of choice for case-based instruction in preservice classes if the cases are a substantial length.[5] The ability to revisit case segments quickly and accurately also resolves the problem of students having missed something, or having focused initially on something that is less pertinent to the instructor's goals at a given time.

---

[5]Our cases are 1 hour in length. In addition to control by computer, random access control of a videodisc player can be achieved through a bar code reader or the hand-held remote control unit that is available for this technology.

Additional Decisions: Options for Using Multimedia Cases to Enhance Instruction

Multimedia cases can be used in two general ways. One involves a presentation system used by the instructor in a whole-class situation. The other involves the use of cases that are explored as out-of-class assignments by students in a computer lab or at home. The former implementation uses cases on videodiscs; the latter on CD-ROMs. Each has its benefits and its drawbacks. The CD-ROM version allows students to work independently on the cases in a computer laboratory or at their own home computer. However, the CD-ROM image is not as large or as clear as a videodisc image presented on a television monitor. We feel that a television monitor used with videodiscs is optimal for presenting images to groups of 25 students or less in a classroom situation because they can be used in full light and have much higher video fidelity when compared to LCD projection panels.

In our preservice classes, the instructor uses a presentation system consisting of a microcomputer, videodisc player, and large-screen television or projection system. With the presentation system under instructor control through software on the microcomputer (see Fig. 11.1) the instructor, before class, programs the videodisc to play segments that can be used to enhance discussion and contextualize target concepts. The icons at the top of Fig. 11.1 show instructor choices. Choosing the "video segments" icon allows the instructor to play preprogrammed segments that appear at the bottom of the screen. Clicking one of the preidentified segments plays the respective segment. Clicking the "edit video" button at the lower right-hand corner of the screen allows the instructor to change or add new segments, and this is how segments are initially entered into the software.

Entering video segments into the software for use in class is a prerequisite for multimedia case-based instruction and is important for reasons beyond simply getting the

FIG. 11.1. Control software with video segments that have been entered by an instructor prior to class.

segments ready for class. It is critically important that the instructor know the case well before using it in class. This requires multiple viewings of the case, which is accomplished as one parses the case into segments for use in class. This "up-front" time is similar to what conscientious instructors put into class preparation when selecting and familiarizing themselves with a new textbook or class reading assignments. As all good software should, the program presented here makes the selection of video segments as user friendly as possible and requires little or no expertise on the part of the user. The "edit video" menu is shown in Fig. 11.2. Using this feature, an instructor can play the video until the desired starting point for a given segment is found and then clicks the "start here" button. The video can then continue playing until the desired ending point is found, at which time the "end here" button is clicked. The software enters the starting and ending point codes for the segment automatically for the instructor. Any desired description for the segment can be entered into the "segment description" box and the selection is then entered into the software. Similar steps are used to edit existing segments, which can also be overwritten by a new segment or can be deleted by using the "edit video" menu.

Selecting the "interviews" icon allows the instructor to choose from a menu of picture icons divided into three areas: principals and teachers, parents, and discussants (see Fig. 11.3). In each instance, when a picture icon is chosen the picture moves to the right-hand box (to indicate which is the activated selection), and preselected video segments are shown in the space at the bottom of the screen (this is a scrolling field—as many segments as desired can be entered). Selecting the "edit video" button allows the instructor to program in new video segments or to edit existing ones, as already described. In this manner, the instructor can provide for a class authentic voices from the school's principal, other teachers in addition to the teacher who is the target of the case, and discussants who comment on the classroom scenes shown to the students.

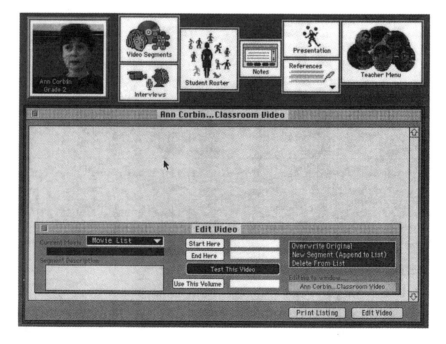

FIG. 11.2.   Video edit menu, allowing users to preview video segments, establish beginning and ending points, enter descriptors, and add segments to the software for use in class.

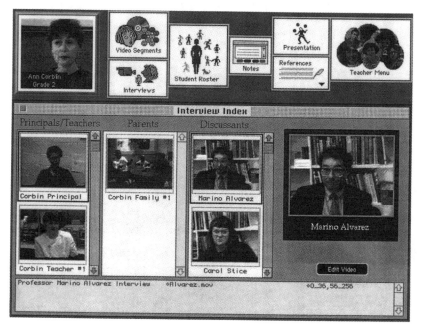

FIG. 11.3. An example of the "interviews" option, where users can choose to hear from teachers, administrators, parents, and discussants.

The student roster icon provides the instructor with a student list from which selected student data (along with selected lesson plans from the students' teacher) can be shown. Selecting a specific student allows the preservice students to examine and to discuss that student's test scores as well as the student's work (see Fig. 11.4). The classroom teacher's lesson plans (Fig. 11.5) can also be presented and the corresponding video segment shown, followed by the teacher's comments about changes and decisions that were made as the lesson progressed. However, not all of the students' work (or all lesson plans) are entered into the software. Only a representative sample for class discussion has been scanned. The bulk of these items are in a student book, which the preservice students bring to class for analysis and discussion, or work on independently or in groups as homework assignments. Selected children's work was collected approximately 1 month apart to allow discussion of their growth and to facilitate analysis of patterns in what approximates a portfolio for target students.

The "notes," "presentation," and "references" icons can also be used by the instructor in whole-class situations, but are perhaps most useful when used in CD-ROM, individual implementations. The "notes" icon allows the user to write notes about what is being viewed. In individual implementations, students write notes in response to their course instructors' questions, or write what they notice about specific scenes. These notes can be stored, compared to others' notes, printed, and handed in. The "presentation" icon is similar to the "video segments" icon shown in Fig. 11.1. However, the "video segments" icon can be locked after an instructor enters segments. Video segments in this location cannot be modified without the use of the instructor's password and students who use the software cannot accidentally erase or change the instructor's input. However, a beneficial use of the technology is to have students find appropriate case segments to illustrate what they have learned about topics under discussion—perhaps topics such as questioning, teacher wait time, assessment or specific instructional procedures.

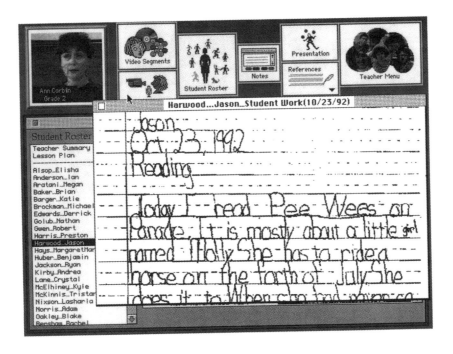

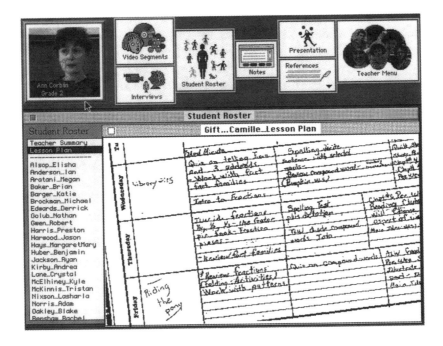

FIG. 11.5. Samples of the teacher's lesson plans, corresponding to classroom video, appear in the software. Additional lesson plans appear in a student book that accompanies the cases.

A benefit of restructuring preservice classes to include multimedia cases is that students can use the software to prepare presentations for their classmates where they present what they have found about a respective topic and use the technology to illustrate their discussion. We feel that this generative aspect of case-based instruction solidifies concepts for our students. Also, the use of the cases by students in their presentations allows them to use technology in appropriate ways, and allows them to frame the class discussion around the anchor using shared knowledge, as discussed earlier in this chapter.

The "references" icon opens a set of references that can be inserted by the course instructor, or by students, to form a database of relevant readings for a given course. The references can be easily modified to reflect readings pertaining to a given instructor's syllabus, and abstracts can be added as desired (see Fig. 11.6). Furthermore, video segments can be linked to readings so that students can read an abstract (or an entire reading, although this must be done outside the software) and then view segments of the case that illustrate the point of the reading(s). The "notes" icon can then be opened for students to write their thoughts about the video and readings, especially if (as often happens) the readings present an idealized version of a concept or procedure, and the classroom case segment shows that this must be modified depending on children's needs or classroom factors.

We feel strongly that the cases that we are describing do not replace textbooks or readings that instructors deem necessary. As Reinking et al. (1993) pointed out, readings, including textbooks, provide a good method for transmitting procedural and declarative knowledge; what is lacking is a system that can provide a vehicle for developing and enhancing preservice teachers' conditional knowledge. Thus, textbooks and class readings are embedded within our case approach as described here. Instructors can assign readings that develop declarative knowledge. Then, the cases extend what students have read so that strategies and procedures are contextualized and made visible, along with teachers' modifications of strategies and procedural steps in authentic environments. This allows

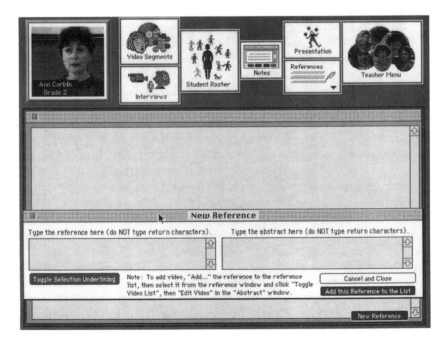

FIG. 11.6. References can be added by the instructor or the students, customized to a course syllabus.

preservice teachers to analyze the application of abstract procedures and reflect on the data and decisions that resulted in the modification of procedural steps. There is an important link, therefore, between readings and multimedia cases; the use of one does not preclude the use of the other.

We believe that providing readings before or after use of the video cases can be equally successful. If readings are done before the video cases, then students can be asked to identify the procedural steps occurring in the case segment, as well as any modifications to the steps that were presented in the readings. If readings come later, then students can abstract and "discover" the procedural steps occurring in the video, then read the idealized version, and go back to the video to examine data that led to modifications of the procedure in classroom use. Both methods have value and are determined by an instructors' personal philosophy, class structure, and goals.

WHERE WE ARE NOW: PRESERVICE
CLASSES AS WE KNOW THEM

Our preservice classes use multimedia cases throughout the semester. The semester begins with a discussion of a case and a presentation of an anchor segment that presents a coherent story of the target classroom. This segment becomes a common reference point for the class members. Students and instructor explore the case together, moving into new areas of the case as questions arise and as knowledge to address issues that are raised becomes important. The class syllabus is structured to reflect important concepts that must be covered throughout the course, but the concepts are listed as goals to be met, rather than as weekly subject headings that must be covered on a given day. Much group work is done to discuss the cases. Often several groups in the class will be required to look at a given part of the case at the same time, with each group given specific, different reasons to look at one or more scenes. For example, one group might watch scenes from a man-agement perspective, another group from a procedural perspective, and yet another group from a teacher–student interaction perspective. Later, the groups come together to discuss their perceptions in a modified "jigsaw" approach to learning. Technology is used through-out the class to support presentations by the instructor or by the student(s), and the benefits of learning as social interaction (as noted by Vygotsky, 1986) are realized through the use of the multimedia cases in our preservice classes.

Currently, we are examining the effect of our multimedia cases on our students' learning and teaching decisions. In one set of studies conducted across several semesters, we analyzed classroom discourse within our methods classes. Patterns generated from this analysis indicate that students who are in the multimedia classes ask more questions and more higher level questions (Risko et al., 1992) than students in similar classes that do not use the multimedia cases. Additionally, we observed that the multimedia students begin to cross-reference multiple sources of information and develop a comprehensive view of teaching issues and problems much earlier than their peers enrolled in classes not using these cases. During case discussions these students assume multiple roles as they question case content, elaborate on each other's contributions, and generate connections between text readings and concepts embedded within the cases. These preservice teachers evaluate different perspectives and explain those that guide their thinking when making decisions about problems associated with literacy learning and instruction. As they weigh options for instruction, we notice that they refer to situational and student factors when suggesting ways to modify procedures they read about in their textbooks. This flexible use of procedural information seems to be an important outcome of their involvement with the multimedia cases.

We also have indicators that show students in these classes refer to the cases to guide their teaching in practicum settings (Risko, 1995; Risko, Peter, & McAllister, 1996) and in other classes, and that they retain case information for a substantial period of time. Prior to our use of multimedia cases, our students had difficulty with problem analysis and resolution. They expected quick solutions to their problems and had difficulty adjusting their plans when their lessons did not develop as they expected. With the introduction of our multimedia cases, we noted carefully how our students responded to problems they were experiencing in the practicum that followed the methods course. First, these students were much more prepared than those observed in previous semesters to frame their problems based on multiple sources of information and to identify specific factors contributing to these problems. They referred frequently to case information to help them think about their own instructional dilemmas. Second, the students generated alternative ways to solve their problems and these solutions were not random but were thoughtful, comprehensive, and appropriate. This ability to modify instructional experiences carried over from their involvement in case analysis, as described earlier. Third, similar to their experience with case-based discussions in the college class, these prospective teachers sought support for the teaching ideas that were still developing. Collaboration and dialogue with the course instructors and their peers served as an important scaffold and appeared to make a difference in the students' ability to reprocess relevant issues and move on with their teaching. Last, these students were not uncomfortable with the difficulties they were experiencing. Their history with the multimedia cases seemed to prepare them to expect problems and dilemmas associated with instruction and as a consequence of this awareness, they were persistent in their problem-solving efforts. This experience with case methodology seemed to boost their confidence in their ability to resolve their problems and feel comfortable with their instructional decisions.

Additionally, students' retention of case-related information across semesters was noted by our student teaching seminar instructor. The seminar is taken by students up to 1 year after they are in the literacy methods courses. Students who have used the cases as part of the methods courses refer back to these cases when sharing their experiences as student teachers. They often contextualize problems and issues they confront in student teaching by relating their current experiences to similar experiences studied in the cases. Interestingly, not all students in the student teaching seminar have come through the reading methods classes that use the multimedia cases, and these students' discussion in the student teaching seminar is relatively compartmentalized. That is, although all students in the student teaching seminar share their individual stories and problems and receive advice and support from the group, the students who were in methods classes that used the cases refer to them specifically. These students and the others who participated in the case-based methodology class immediately share a more meaningful experience—their stories are grounded and contextualized, and richer discussion and problem solving appears to result (D. Granier, personal communication, January 1994).

WHERE WE WOULD LIKE TO BE:
OUR PRESERVICE CLASSES AS WE ENVISION THEM

As we move toward the year 2000 and become increasingly aware of the possibilities that technology continues to provide, we envision numerous changes to our preservice education classes. These changes will, we feel, continue to make use of multimedia, case-based instruction for as long as it is impractical for all of our preservice teachers to participate in a single, meaningful, shared, field experience. Field experiences will continue to be an important part of our preservice methods classes, and will be augmented with multimedia case-based instruction to provide a shared context to which individual field placements can be related. In addition, however, we expect to incorporate many technological enhancements that are now becoming available—enhancements that relate to the Internet and World Wide Web, to extended networking capabilities, and to televideo. These and other tools will all have a role in our futures.

For example, World Wide Web sites will provide our preservice teachers with the capabilities to work closely with elementary school teachers and students, sharing questions and correspondence that will provide additional realism and meaning to our classes and that will provide further grist for analysis and reflection. We envision communities of (preservice) learners moving beyond our classroom walls. The World Wide Web site for our preservice classes (recently completed) will allow shared discussion of cases by preservice students and instructors from around the nation. As ISDN telephone lines become available in our preservice classrooms and computer laboratories, our students will be able to see and hear children, their classrooms, their work, and their teachers on a real-time basis. At present, we are able to link our preservice class with one school using Color QuickCam technology. This technology will continue to improve in quality and in cost, and has conferencing links and capabilities that will enhance university–school relations. Of course, online viewing of a classroom has the drawback that instructors will not know what will be shown and thus class discussions cannot be well planned. Online video will thus need to be captured and pressed to CD-ROMs for later use as it becomes relevant within the curriculum structure of the preservice class (desktop CD-ROM pressers are now available for less than $500 and prices will continue to drop).

We see the growth of multimedia cases in preservice education classes on a trajectory similar to the growth of (now widely used) case-based instruction in schools of law, business, and medicine, where cases took their place as powerful instructional tools and increasingly replaced more traditional lecture methods (see, e.g., Williams', 1992, review of the growth of case-based instruction in law and medicine). As more powerful computers that include CD-ROM capabilities become less expensive and are purchased in increasing quantities by undergraduates (perhaps as a requirement for university admission), more exploration of multimedia cases will take place outside of the preservice classroom, with students coming to class ready to present and discuss case segments that are relevant to a given topic.

The look and capabilities of university classrooms is also changing. As university classrooms are renovated, projection systems with built-in connections for computers are becoming available, and this trend will continue. Instructors will soon be able to come to class with their laptop or external hard disk, plug this into a wall plate (or use an infrared, wireless system) and be ready to use technology in their classes. Projection systems will become better able to show video in a clearer fashion in well-lit rooms. As MPEG video compression becomes more widely used and provides full-screen and full-motion video with greater video fidelity (compared to the relatively poor quality CD-ROM images now available when larger than quarter-screen sizes are used), computer-controlled multimedia in preservice classrooms will be seen increasingly as a feasible and desirable instructional tool. Digital video disc drives, able to read CD-ROMs but with enhanced storage capabilities, will be able to store up to 2 hours of video, making longer video segments commonplace in computer applications. (Digital video disc drives have already been announced and will be standard on all Macintosh computers within the year.)

Because literacy education is our area of expertise, we have chosen this area to explore the possibilities of multimedia, case-based instruction. However, the principles and benefits discussed in this chapter can be used equally well in other domains, and others have done so (see, e.g., Barron & Goldman, 1994, for similar uses in preservice mathematics education). Thus, although we see clear advantages to multimedia case-based instruction in preservice literacy education, we feel that the benefits and possibilities discussed in this chapter are within reach and will transform preservice education more broadly. In summary, these benefits and possibilities include instruction that

- Is authentically contextualized.
- Can serve as an anchor for instruction.
- Is interactive through microcomputer enhancements.
- Allows individual instructors to modify their syllabus, textbook, and desired reading assignments.
- Allows student exploration of authentic settings that contain multiple participants.
- Maximizes social interaction in preservice learning environments.
- Allows students to use multimedia cases and technology to create their own multimedia presentations to explore concepts and present their thoughts.

REFERENCES

Alexander, P. A., Kulikowich, J. M., & Jetton, T. L. (1994). The role of subject matter knowledge and interest in the processing of linear and non-linear texts. *Review of Educational Research, 64*(2), 210–252.

Alvermann, D. E. (1990). Reading teacher education. In W. R. Houston, M. Haberman, & J. Sikula (Eds.), *Handbook of research on teacher education* (pp. 687–704). New York: Macmillan.

Barron, L. C., & Goldman, E. S. (1994). Integrating technology with teacher preparation. In B. Means (Ed.), *Technology and education reform* (pp. 81–110). San Francisco: Jossey-Bass.

Bereiter, C. (1984). How to keep thinking skills from going the way of all frills. *Educational Leadership, 42,* 75–77.

Berliner, D. C. (1986). In pursuit of the expert pedagogue. *Educational Researcher, 15,* 5–13.

Berliner, D. C. (1987). Laboratory settings and the study of teacher education. *Journal of Teacher Education, 36,* 2–8.

Bransford, J. D., & Johnson, M. K. (1973). Consideration of some problems of comprehension. In W. Chase (Ed.), *Visual information processing* (pp. 383–438). New York: Academic Press.

Bransford, J. D., Kinzer, C. K., Risko, V. J., Rowe, D. W., & Vye, N. J. (1989). Designing invitations to thinking: Some initial thoughts. In S. McCormick & J. Zutell (Eds.), *Cognitive and social perspectives for literacy research and instruction: 38th Yearbook of the National Reading Conference* (pp. 35–54). Chicago: National Reading Conference.

Bransford, J. D., Sherwood, R. D., Kinzer, C. K., & Hasselbring, T. S. (1985). *Havens for learning: Toward a framework for developing effective uses of technology* (Tech. Rep. No. 85.1.1). Nashville, TN: Vanderbilt University, Learning Technology Center. (ERIC Document Reproduction Service No. ED 262 752)

Brown, J. S., Collins, A., & Duguid, P. (1989). Situated cognition and the culture of learning. *Educational Researcher, 18,* 32–41.

Cognition and Technology Group at Vanderbilt. (1990). Anchored instruction and its relationship to situated cognition. *Educational Researcher, 19,* 2–10.

Cognition and Technology Group at Vanderbilt. (1992). An anchored instruction approach to cognitive skills acquisition and intelligent tutoring. In J. W. Regian & V. J. Shute (Eds.), *Cognitive approaches to automated instruction* (pp. 135–170). Hillsdale, NJ: Lawrence Erlbaum Associates.

Cognition and Technology Group at Vanderbilt. (1994, October). Anchored instruction and situated cognition revisited: A response to Tripp. *Educational Technology,* 28–31.

Kinzer, C. K., McLarty, K., & Martin, G. (1989, March). *Some effects of macrocontexts on vocabulary learning.* Paper presented at the annual meeting of the American Educational Research Association, San Francisco, CA.

McLarty, K., Goodman, J., Risko, V. J., Kinzer, C. K., Vye, N., Rowe, D. W., & Carson, J. (1990). Implementing anchored instruction: Guiding principles for curriculum development. In J. Zutell & S. McCormick (Eds.), *Literacy theory and research: Analysis from multiple perspectives* (pp. 109–120). Chicago: National Reading Conference.

Merseth, K. (1991). *The case for cases in teacher education.* Washington, DC: American Association of Colleges of Teacher Education and American Association of Higher Education.

Paris, S. G., Lipson, M. Y., & Wixson, K. K. (1983). Becoming a strategic reader. *Contemporary Educational Psychology, 8,* 292–316.

Pichert, J. W., Smeltzer, C., Snyder, G. M., Gregory, R. P., Smeltzer, R., & Kinzer, C. K. (1994). Traditional vs. anchored instruction for diabetes-related nutritional knowledge, skills, and behavior. *The Diabetes Educator, 20*(1), 45–48.

Reinking, D., Mealey, D., & Ridgeway, V. G. (1993). Developing preservice teachers' conditional knowledge of content area strategies. *Journal of Reading, 36*(6), 458–469.

Risko, V. J. (1995). Using videodisc-based cases to promote preservice teachers' problem solving and mental model building. In W. M. Linek & E. G. Sturtevant (Eds.), *Generations of literacy* (pp. 173–187). Pittsburg, KS: College Reading Association.

Risko, V. J., & Kinzer, C. K. (1991). *Improving teacher education with technology and case based instruction.* Fund for the Improvement of Postsecondary Education.

Risko, V. J., & Kinzer, C. K. (1994). *Improving teacher education through dissemination of videodisc-bases case procedures and influencing the teaching of future college professionals.* Fund for the Improvement of Postsecondary Education.

Risko, V. J., Peter, J., & McAllister, D. (1996). Conceptual changes: Preservice teachers' pathways to providing literacy transaction. In E. Sturtevant & W. Linek (Eds.), *Literacy grows* (pp. 103–119). Pittsburg, KS: College Reading Association.

Risko, V. J., Yount, D., & McAllister, D. (1992). Preparing preservice teachers for remedial instruction: Teaching problem solving and use of content and pedagogical knowledge. In N. Padak, T. V. Rasinski, & J. Logan (Eds.), *Inquiries in literacy learning and instruction* (pp. 179–189). Pittsburg, KS: College Reading Association.

Schmidt, C. R., Meltzer, L., Kinzer, C. K., Bransford, J. D., & Hasselbring, T. S. (1990). *The effects of video and oral media on story comprehension and writing.* Paper presented at the Biennial Conference on Human Development, Richmond, VA.

Sherwood, R. D., Kinzer, C. K., Bransford, J. D., & Franks, J. J. (1987). Some benefits of creating macro-contexts for science instruction: Initial findings. *Journal of Research in Science Teaching, 24,* 417–435.

Shulman, J. H. (1995). Tender feelings, hidden thoughts: Confronting bias, innocence, and racism through case discussion. In J. A. Colbert, P. Desberg, & K. Trimble (Eds.), *The case of education* (pp. 137–158). Boston: Allyn & Bacon.

Shulman, L. S. (1995). Just in case: Reflections on learning from experience. In J. A. Colbert, P. Desberg, & K. Trimble (Eds.), *The case of education* (pp. 197–217). Boston: Allyn & Bacon.

Silverman, R., & Welty, W. M. (1995). Teaching without a net: Using cases in teacher education. In J. A. Colbert, P. Desberg, & K. Trimble (Eds.), *The case of education* (pp. 159–171). Boston: Allyn & Bacon.

Spiro, R. J., & Jeng, J. (1990). Cognitive flexibility and hypertext: Theory and technology for the non-linear and multidimensional traversal of complex subject matter. In D. Nix & R. Spiro (Eds.), *Cognition, education and multimedia: Exploring ideas in high technology* (pp. 163–205). Hillsdale, NJ: Lawrence Erlbaum Associates.

Tyler, S., & Voss, J. F. (1982). Attitude and knowledge effects in prose processing. *Journal of Verbal Learning and Verbal Behavior, 4,* 331–351.

Vygotsky, L. S. (1978). *Mind in society: The development of higher psychological processes* (M. Cole, V. John-Steiner, S. Scribner, & E. Souberman, Eds.). Cambridge, MA: Harvard University Press.

Vygotsky, L. S. (1986). *Thought and language* (A. Kozulin, Ed.). Cambridge, MA: MIT Press.

Whitehead, A. N. (1929). *The aims of education.* New York: Macmillan.

Williams, S. M. (1992). Putting case-based instruction into context: Examples from legal and medical education. *The Journal of the Learning Sciences, 2,* 387–407.

12
▼▼▼▼▼▼▼

Grounding the Design of New Technologies for Literacy and Learning in Teachers' Instructional Needs

Donald J. Leu
Syracuse University

Michael Hillinger
LexIcon Systems

Philip H. Loseby
Syracuse University

Mary Lou Balcom
Jonathan Dinkin
Mary Lou Eckels
Jackie Johnson
Kathie Mathews
Ruth Raegler
Syracuse City School District

Chapters in this section explore how new technologies are transforming instruction in classrooms and other learning environments. Clearly this is taking place as preservice teacher education (Kinzer & Risko, chap. 11, this volume) and adult literacy programs (Askov & Bixler, chap. 10, this volume) are being altered by new instructional tools. In addition, one can see this happening as students in distant classrooms communicate with one another over the Internet (Garner & Gillingham, chap. 13, this volume), constructing new meanings for themselves and for others in the world around them.

We wish to provide a counterpoint to this discussion. As important as it is for instruction to accommodate new technologies, it is just as important for the design of these technologies to accommodate the instructional needs of teachers for literacy and learning. In a time of rapid technological change it is easy to forget that new instructional technologies should be designed to serve instruction in the classroom, not the reverse. Unless new technologies are designed to meet teachers' needs, it is unlikely many teachers will use them and, as a result, it is unlikely we will unlock the potential they possess for ultimately transforming instruction. The issue is not solely how instruction should change in the face of new technologies. Rather, an equally important question is: How might new technologies change to meet the instructional needs of classrooms? In this chapter we describe a project that explored this question.

A CENTRAL PARADOX OF TECHNOLOGY
IN SCHOOL CLASSROOMS

Increasingly, a fundamental paradox is becoming apparent to those who study the use of new technologies for instruction: Although new technologies are becoming more widely available, they are not always appropriated by teachers and systematically integrated into the curriculum (Anderson, 1993; Becker, 1993; Miller & Olson, 1994; Papert, 1993; Reinking & Bridwell-Bowles, 1991; U.S. Congress, 1995). This presents a central problem for those who seek to transform literacy and learning through the use of new technologies. As technological change occurs more and more rapidly, redefining potentials for literacy and learning, how do we ensure that teachers fully exploit these potentials during classroom instruction?

Although this problem exists with many technologies, an instructive case may be seen with computer technologies. In the spring of 1995, U.S. schools had 5.8 million computers in use for instruction, approximately one for every nine students or two to three per classroom (U.S. Congress, 1995). Despite the availability of computer technology, however, teachers reported minimal use of computers for instructional purposes. Reports from secondary schools indicated that only 9% of students used computers for English class, 6% to 7% for math class, and only 3% for social studies class (U.S. Congress, 1995). In elementary schools, computers were seldom integrated into central areas of the curriculum; often they were used after assigned work had been completed for games and gamelike experiences (Becker, 1993; U.S. Congress, 1995).

Previously, student access to computer technologies has been seen as a problem of availability; increasingly, it is being viewed as a problem of curricular integration. The failure to integrate computer technologies into the curriculum is a serious concern. We need to begin to engage our students in the electronic literacies of their future. The rewards for our students are as important as the futures we wish to provide them.

Undoubtedly, there are many reasons for the failure to integrate computer technologies more systematically into the literacy and learning curriculum (Kinzer & Leu, 1997; Leu, 1997). Insufficient staff development, lack of software, classrooms overwhelmed by new curricular initiatives, and the perception that technology teachers should be responsible for this area, not classroom teachers, may all be important sources of the problem. In this project, we explored an alternative explanation: Sophisticated software is often designed by technical experts without more systematic consideration of the specific needs of teachers and students for literacy and learning (Anderson, 1993; Becker, 1993; Leu & Reinking, 1996). As a result, teachers often choose not to use computer technologies because they do not see a clear match between available software and what they do in the classroom.

Traditional approaches to software development begin with design principles grounded in theory and research and then software is developed around these principles. If we wish to overcome the limited appropriation of technology by teachers, we must take a different tack and begin by identifying teachers' instructional needs. Design principles for new technologies must be developed inductively out of the nature of teachers' instructional needs, not imposed on teachers by technical experts unfamiliar with the reality of classroom contexts. Only then are we likely to develop electronic environments that will be systematically integrated into classroom learning experiences by teachers who immediately see their potential for instruction. Only then are we likely to transform literacy and learning as teachers use these new technologies to explore the instructional potentials they contain.

To be fair, software publishers are increasingly attending to actual classroom needs as they develop products for this market. More companies are involving teachers in the development process in order to create products that will be purchased by schools. Usually, however, classroom teachers only play an advisory role, testing nearly completed versions of software after basic design decisions have been made.

The project we report on here attempted to determine which features would evolve when teachers controlled design decisions as a complex multimedia program was developed to meet their classroom literacy and learning needs. We also wanted to explore the nature of these features to see what common patterns, if any, they expressed. We expected teachers to identify concerns that were important to their classroom needs through the design features they employed. Such information would be useful in guiding the design of new technologies to support literacy and learning, ensuring a more receptive home in the classroom by teachers who would actually use them. We also hoped that such an approach might result in an alternative model for the design of new technologies by software publishers.

THE SCHOOL CONTEXT

The elementary school (K–6) where this project took place is located in an urban school district. Approximately 650 students attend classes in this building; approximately 40% of students receive free or reduced-price lunches. The school has a diverse student body with about 45% of children from minority ethnic groups. It has a national reputation for the inclusive programming of exceptional students; children with mild, moderate, and severe handicapping conditions are mainstreamed into regular classrooms. The building is an older structure, located near a major university. Computer technologies slowly have been making their way into the school. When we started the project, each of the teachers had a computer, but it represented an older technology (Apple IIe) and these were used largely for games after assigned work had been completed. At least one of the machines had been out for repair for nearly a year and was not available to the teacher. None of the teachers were familiar with multimedia technologies available for faster machines.

The entire sixth-grade team of teachers agreed to participate in this project. All six teachers participated in the design and development of the final software product. Two teachers were identified by the team of teachers to be focal teachers—teachers who would use the software in their classrooms and be observed during the 2-year project. Both focal teachers and all but two of the teachers in the team had more than 10 years of teaching experience. All were permanently certified and all were tenured in this school district. The team met once each week for an hour or more to coordinate instructional plans and activities. Three teachers team-taught social studies, science, and an enrichment class, each taking responsibility for one of the subject areas.

The project also included a university researcher responsible for directing and evaluating the project, a multimedia software developer responsible for turning the teachers' ideas into a multimedia software program, and a graduate assistant responsible for coordinating content development.

Social studies instruction in these classes focused on the civilizations of ancient Egypt, Greece, and Rome. These were specified in district and state curricula as the topic areas to be covered in Grade 6. Each teacher implemented this program in a slightly different fashion as the team comprised a variety of beliefs about best instructional practice. One teacher believed in more teacher-directed instructional practices organized around targeted skills. One teacher believed in more student-directed instructional practices focused around inquiry projects. The beliefs of the other four teachers fell on a continuum between these two perspectives.

Despite the variety of perspectives, there were three features common to social studies instruction in these classrooms: content focus, meaning construction, and communication. First, teachers developed the content of instruction around each of the three ancient civilizations. Each of the three ancient civilizations was explored for approximately one third of the year. Each teacher indicated that the district social studies guidelines determined their content in this area. As one teacher put it, "We all focus our social studies on Egypt, Greece, and Rome. This is a district requirement."

Second, teachers supported children's construction of meaning from multiple information sources through projects the students completed. Students completed assignments that required them to explore a variety of information resources and create their own interpretations and synthesis of that information. None of the classrooms relied on a single textbook for their study of these civilizations. Each used a wide variety of information resources. As one teacher described their work, "We don't use a textbook anymore. We use a lot of different kinds of resources because we want our students to pull together a lot of different information."

Third, teachers developed opportunities for students to communicate the meanings they had created to others in the class. Often this took place through oral presentations of written assignments and visual information displayed on posterboard. Posterboard presentations were common in these classrooms as a vehicle for sharing the meanings students had constructed about each of the ancient civilizations.

Teachers implemented these three patterns in a manner consistent with their individual beliefs about teaching and learning. The most skill-oriented teacher, for example, described her social studies program this way:

> It's important for my students to develop the skills related to critical thinking as we study ancient Egypt, Greece, and Rome . . . I also want them to acquire effective reading, writing, and speaking skills. Listening, too. We do projects and students present what they have found to others. I teach skills as we work on our projects.

The least skill-oriented teacher put it this way:

> We explore the civilizations of Egypt, Greece, and Rome. I want my students to . . . learn about the events, culture, and literature in these civilizations and then share this information with other students. I want them to think critically about these events and how others view them. I don't teach a lot of skills in isolation, except for those who really need it. I think the students learn these through their projects.

Content focus, meaning construction, and communication appeared to be three elements central to the social studies programs in each of these classrooms. These patterns appeared to be relatively independent of a teacher's relative emphasis on specific skill instruction.

THE NATURE OF THE SOFTWARE DESIGN
AND DEVELOPMENT PROCESS

The multimedia software designed by these teachers was developed over a period of 1 year. There were three phases to the development process: an initial software development conference, four revision sessions during the first school year, and a final revision conference at the end of the first year of the study. Throughout this process, we were guided by a central principle: Teachers on our development team should make final decisions about both the content and the design of the multimedia software that emerged from our development process.

Software Development Conference

The initial software development conference took place during the summer preceding the first school year of the study. It lasted for 5 days. During this time, the general design and development process was explained: Teachers would work to design the software they wanted to use in their classroom, the multimedia programmer would develop this software according to their specifications, and then teachers would have the opportunity during the first year to evaluate what had been developed and to make revisions until the software met their instructional needs.

Discussions ensued as to which part of the instructional program the software should focus on. Eventually, it was decided to develop software for social studies and include myths from each of the civilizations as literature selections. The teachers decided that the ancient civilizations of Egypt, Greece, and Rome would be the content focus of the software in a thematically organized software program.

Following this, the project director and the multimedia software developer shared a number of multimedia programs on CD-ROM to demonstrate different design features (video, graphics, games, text patterns, bulletin boards, e-mail, vocabulary support, etc.) that would be possible in a multimedia program. As each was demonstrated, the teachers and the rest of the team discussed whether the feature might be useful in the program they were to develop.

The first 2 days were spent largely on brainstorming ideas and possibilities. Teachers used this time to develop a sense of what was going to be possible. Others used this time to develop a better sense of the instructional program in sixth grade. The final 2 days were spent making preliminary design decisions so that the multimedia software developer would have a place to begin drafting the design of the program. Basic interface decisions were made by the teachers: the use of an interactive time line, the use of e-mail, the use of maps as a basic graphical interface, the use of informational icons that would appear on each of the maps during different time periods, the use of a bulletin board, the use of Post-it Notes or stickies, and a record-keeping system for the teachers. In addition, the focal teachers developed a list of key concepts for each civilization in several categories: art, architecture, and culture; important people; central historical events; and "strange but true" facts. Over 150 items were included in this list. In addition, they identified three myths for each civilization to be included as literature selections. Finally, the focal teachers provided the project director with a large set of resources from their classrooms to be used in developing the content information, the literature, and the graphics for the multimedia program.

Revision Sessions

Four times during the school year, review and revision sessions were held at the school for teachers to review current progress on the software program and make revisions in the interface and content. These were held in an attempt to be certain that the software matched teachers' classroom needs as closely as possible. Each session lasted for 3 to 4 hours and took place during a half-day staff development session scheduled by the district. Typically, the project director would show the teachers the latest iteration of the software, allow teachers time to work with the software, and then discuss changes the teachers would like to see made. This information was shared with the software developer who made the changes requested by teachers.

During the fall, the project director and graduate assistant recruited six graduate students to assist with content development for the key concepts identified by the teachers. Students wrote the text entries, scanned graphics for each item, and identified appropriate segments from videos obtained from the Discovery Channel and the History Channel on the local cable system. In addition, maps of the civilization boundaries and trade routes during each of the time periods were developed. These were reviewed by teachers and sent to the multimedia software developer to be included in the program.

A number of minor modifications were requested by the teacher team during the revision sessions. These included a few minor additions to the student pack (a location for writing, sending, and receiving information) and to the bulletin board. All of these changes were requested to make the software easier for teachers and students to use.

There were two major changes requested by the teacher team during these revision sessions. One major change requested by the teacher team was inclusion of videos of students as important historical or mythical figures. Teachers wanted students to do research on a famous historical or mythical figure, develop a costume for this person, and then be videotaped answering a prepared set of questions. The teacher team wanted to include these videos in a design feature called "interviews." In an interview, users would click on a button containing a question for a historical figure (e.g., "Why are you famous?", "What was a typical day like for you?", or "What type of clothing did you wear?"). After clicking on this button, a video segment would play from the tape of the student portraying this figure who had been recorded.

A second change was inclusion of a monitoring system so that teachers could keep track of what students had visited during their exploration of the multimedia environment, the meanings they had constructed, and the messages they had sent. A monitoring system was developed to enable teachers to quickly obtain this information at the end of each day.

Final Revision Conference

A completed version of the software was used in the focal teachers' classrooms during the last half of the first year of the project. This enabled teachers and students to use it within the classroom and evaluate its use. A final revision conference took place in the summer following the first school year. Only a few minor changes were made by the teachers during this session. Most involved programming bugs that had been discovered during the use of the program. One major addition was made to the program. This was a "treasure hunt" requested by the teachers as a way of taking students through the information structure that had been developed in order to help them learn the interface.

ANALYSIS STRATEGIES

In order to induce software design principles from the design choices made by teachers, we borrowed from formative experiment traditions (Newman, 1990; Reinking & Pickle, 1993) and from qualitative research traditions using constant comparative analysis (Glaser & Strauss, 1967; Lincoln & Guba, 1985). As with a formative experiment, we identified the goal: a multimedia program designed by teachers to support literacy and learning. Then we determined what it took "in terms of materials, organization, or changes in the technology to reach the goal" (Newman, 1990, p. 10). Having developed the multimedia program to the satisfaction of the teacher team, we then looked at the content and the major design elements in their program using constant comparative analytic procedures (Bogdan & Biklen, 1992). In this analysis we employed inductively derived categories in order to develop design principles, or themes, descriptive of the content and function of the major program elements. After the design principles were identified, we then used member checking techniques to evaluate and refine our analysis of the design principles implicit in the work of this teacher team. Each teacher reviewed the principles that were identified and was provided with an opportunity to review, refine, and supplement this analysis.

WHICH SOFTWARE DESIGN PRINCIPLES EMERGED WHEN DECISIONS WERE MADE BY A TEAM OF SIXTH-GRADE TEACHERS ON THE BASIS OF THEIR CLASSROOM NEEDS?

Looking at the final version of the software designed by these teachers, there seemed to be at least three themes, or design principles, that guided many of their decisions and appeared in the final product. First, there was a clear emphasis on content that was already a part of the instructional program in these classrooms. Second, teachers included features that allowed both teachers and students to construct their own interpretations of the information within this program and communicate those meanings to others. Third, teachers wanted the ability to monitor how students explored the information structure and the meanings they were making of the information present there. We describe each of these design principles here.

The Content of Multimedia Software Matched Closely the Content Teachers Included in Their Regular Instructional Program

An important early concern voiced by teachers was that the content in this program reflect the important concepts covered in the classes during their units on the civilizations of ancient Egypt, Greece, and Rome. As one teacher commented during the initial software development conference, "We need to be certain this matches the information we already want our students to learn." This idea was immediately supported by each of the other teachers.

As a result, the teachers in this project developed a master list of key concepts they considered important in their instructional program on the three ancient civilizations. This task was led by the two focal teachers, but all of the teachers had an opportunity to add to the list. Items included in this list included important historical and mythical figures (e.g., Hatshepsut, Zeus, Cleopatra); important items from the art, architecture, and culture of each civilization (e.g., The pyramids of Giza, the Olympics, Roman coins); important events (e.g., The rise of Thutmose, The assassination of Caesar); and three myths from each civilization (e.g., *The Death of Osiris, Romulus and Remus, The Golden Touch*). Added to this list were several items discovered by the content research team, including items for a category identified by the teachers—amazing facts (e.g., Greek medicine, the mummification process).

Software Design Features Allowed Students to Construct
Their Own Interpretations of the Information Within This
Program and Communicate Those Interpretations to Others

Many of the design features selected by teachers and incorporated into the final multimedia software appear to share a common characteristic: They allowed students to construct their own interpretations of the information within the program and communicate those meanings to others. We refer to these elements of the program as constructivist–communicative design features. They appeared important to teachers as they developed the final software product. We describe each of these features in what follows.

The Interactive Time Line. Figure 12.1 illustrates the main window of the program developed in this project and several features important to understanding its use. The main viewing window contains maps of various time periods and geographical regions along with icons containing information about that time and location. Figure 12.1, for example, shows informational icons available for the year 2000 BC in Egypt. Users navigate through time by sliding the box in the interactive time line at the top of the window. They navigate to different geographical regions by selecting one of the buttons at the bottom: World, Mediterranean, Egypt, Greece, and Rome. Each time period and each geographical region contain different informational icons: A microphone icon represented an interview with an important personality; a newspaper icon represented an important historical event; a building icon represented an important aspect of art, architecture, or culture; and an icon with a face looking surprised represented information about an "amazing fact" from that civilization. Clicking on one of the icons opens a graphic or video and a text window

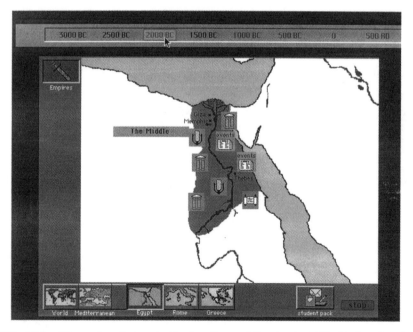

FIG. 12.1.   The main window in Explorations of the Ancient World showing the interactive time line and several other features for accessing communicating information.

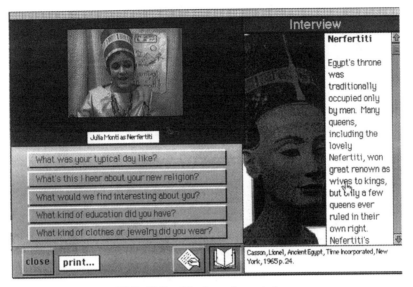

FIG. 12.2.   The interview window.

explaining the significance of that informational item as in Fig. 12.2, for example. In addition, the button for the student pack at the bottom of this window opens up a tool packet for students allowing them to communicate with other users about the information they find.

Teachers developed the interactive time line as a way to navigate through the different time periods in the program and allow students to infer changes to civilizations over time. They hoped students would note the rise and fall of various civilizations (e.g., Old Kingdom, Middle Kingdom, New Kingdom) and think about the reasons for these changes. "We need to have them see how civilizations change over time," was the way one teacher put it during the initial software development conference.

The Interviews.   One of the informational icons was an image of a microphone. This represented an interview with a historical or mythical figure from the time and geographical region displayed on the map window. Figure 12.2 shows an interview window of Nefertiti. Clicking on any of the questions at the bottom would generate the appropriate video response by the student who researched this figure and who had earlier recorded her answer. In addition, a window appears on the right containing textual information and a graphic of this figure.

Interviews allowed students to construct information by using a number of outside resources (the class encyclopedia, books, and other information resources in the school library) and then to communicate this information through the video interviews that were recorded and imported into the program. Users constructed information about this figure by selecting questions they wanted answers to and by reading the information in the text window. The team of teachers developed this design feature during one of the revision conferences.

Dictionary Items.   As with many software products, the program developed by this team of teachers contained a dictionary feature. This provided meanings of challenging vocabulary items. These could also be pronounced by clicking on a speaker icon. A unique aspect of this

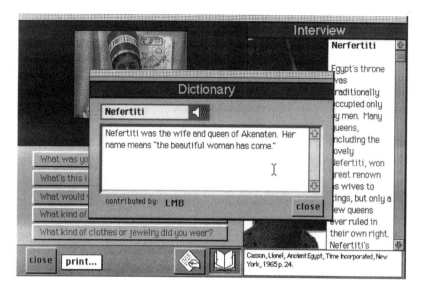

FIG. 12.3.   The dictionary window showing a student-generated entry.

design feature, however, was that students could construct their own meanings for any word in the text window and thus construct new vocabulary items. Figure 12.3 shows the dictionary window with an entry added by a student. Once they closed this window, the vocabulary word would appear in red, indicating that this word now contained a vocabulary definition. Note, also, in Fig. 12.3 that the initials of the person who constructed the meaning for a dictionary entry are placed at the bottom of the dictionary window.

The Notepad.   Clicking on the button for the "student pack" in the main window opens up a feature that teachers found central to this program. The student pack contains a number of design features that allowed students to construct meaning and communicate these meanings to others. One of these design features was the notepad. This is a writing space students used to construct meanings from the information they encountered in the program. This was used to send messages to others about information and locations, to create a guided tour for other students (one of several assignments developed in some classrooms), to write a sticky before posting it, to write an item for the bulletin board, or to write an assignment before submitting it to the teacher. Figure 12.4 shows the notepad window.

Publishing on the Bulletin Board.   Clicking on the button "publish," at the top of the notepad (see Fig. 12.4), would send a student's writing to a bulletin board. The bulletin board was located on the window where students first entered the program. The bulletin board was a feature teachers developed to provide students with a location to publish their work for the entire class to read. Figure 12.5 shows the bulletin board, illustrating the first page of a guided tour developed by a student.

Read.   Clicking on the button "read" at the top of the notepad (see Fig. 12.4) would allow users to read e-mail that had been sent to their mailbox. An example may be seen in Fig. 12.6. Teachers wanted an e-mail system so that students could communicate their developing understanding of the information in this program to other users. To meet this

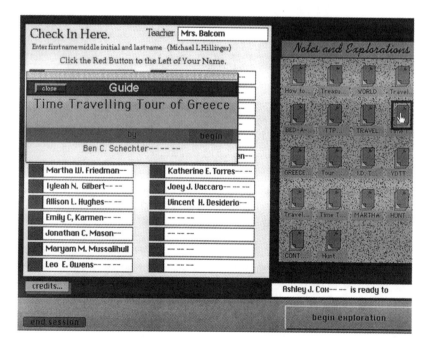

FIG. 12.5. The bulletin board, the destination of the "publish" button.

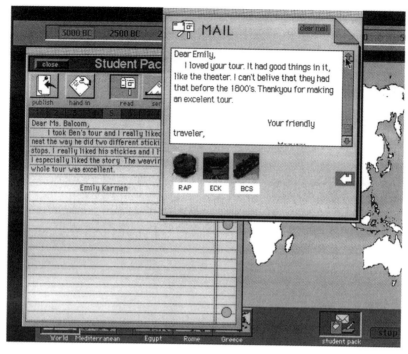

FIG. 12.6.   The mail window.

need, the software developer created an e-mail system that ran on the single computer in each of the focal teachers' classrooms.

Send.   To send an e-mail message to another user, students clicked the "send" button at the top of the notepad (see Fig. 12.4). This sent a copy of the information on a student's notepad to a designated person. This feature was used frequently by students to communicate information about the program. It was also used as a part of several classroom assignments developed by teachers. When students developed a tour of one of the civilizations, for example, students were required to advertise their tour by sending messages to others.

Sticky.   A sticky was the term used to describe an electronic Post-it Note that could be placed on any window in the program. This allowed students to post information throughout the program to communicate with other students. Often this was meaning that students had constructed as a result of their interaction with information in the program. Figure 12.7 illustrates one example of a sticky posted next to a "strange but true" icon with a video of how bodies were mummified in ancient Egypt. You can also see how the initials of the name of the student who posted this information are displayed.

Shoot.   A final feature, "shoot," allowed students to add images to information they communicated to others. If students opened their notepad when an image window was open, clicking on the shoot button would add a copy of that image to the message they sent to someone else. This allowed students to contextualize information they sent to others. Figure 12.8 shows an example of how such a message appeared before being sent.

FIG. 12.7. An example of a sticky posted in a map window.

FIG. 12.8. An example of using the "shoot" button used to append an image to a message.

Software Design Features Allowed Teachers to Monitor the Meanings Students Constructed and the Information They Shared With Others

A final design principle may also be inferred from the design decisions made by this group of teachers. During revision conferences, it became clear that teachers wanted to be able to quickly monitor the meanings students constructed and the information they shared with others. The discussions about which information should be recorded by the system focused on keeping track of the meanings students were generating and the information they shared with others. The teacher record-keeping feature went through several iterations during revision conferences until teachers appeared satisfied with the final structure. An

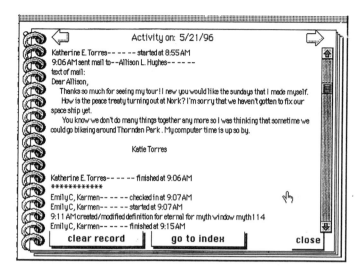

FIG. 12.9. An example of the teacher records folder showing the information recorded for two students.

example can be seen be seen in Fig. 12.9, which displays a message sent by one student to another. It is instructive to note the information on the second student regarding new dictionary meanings this student constructed and added to one of the myths.

As teachers used the program in their classes, this feature proved to be a very popular one. It allowed teachers to quickly check the program at the end of the day and review the meanings students had been constructing and communicating. Often teachers would send students e-mail messages about their work, suggesting ideas or praising them for what they had accomplished. Several times, teachers observed inappropriate types of messages being sent by students and had brief conversations with the students involved to establish appropriate etiquette for computer messages (cf. Neilsen, chap. 8, this volume).

OBSERVATIONS ON MULTIMEDIA DESIGN PRINCIPLES
EMERGING FROM TEACHERS' NEEDS

We have argued that a fundamental paradox exists with respect to computer use in school classrooms today: Although computer technologies are becoming more widely available, they are not becoming fully appropriated by teachers and integrated into classroom learning experiences. This limits the potential of computer technologies to support students' literacy and learning. It also limits the potential of new technologies to ultimately transform instruction. Often, the cause may be that software has been designed by technical experts without fully considering the specific needs of teachers and students. As a result, teachers often have a difficult time seeing how a software product will fit within their curriculum.

If we wish the potential of multimedia software to be fully appropriated by teachers, we must take another course. Design principles must be developed out of the nature of teachers' instructional needs, not imposed on teachers by technical experts unfamiliar with the reality of classroom contexts. Only then are we likely to develop electronic environments that will be systematically integrated into classroom experiences to support literacy and learning. Only then are we likely to transform literacy and learning as teachers appropriate these new technologies and explore the new instructional potentials they contain.

This project explored design principles that emerged as classroom teachers, not technical experts, made final decisions about the design of multimedia software to be used in their classrooms. We wanted to discover the design patterns teachers favored within multimedia technologies by observing the choices they made in developing a program for their classrooms. This information would be useful to guide the design of new technologies, increasing the likelihood they would actually be used by teachers and students to support literacy and learning.

From our observations, three design principles emerged when teachers were supported in developing multimedia software to meet their instructional needs in the classroom. First, the content of multimedia software designed by these teachers matched very closely the content teachers included in their regular instructional program. Second, a number of features allowed students to construct their own interpretations of the information within this program and communicate those meanings to others. Finally, the design of the software allowed teachers to monitor the meanings students constructed and the information they shared with others. Several of these design principles mirrored the reality of life in these classrooms; several reflect instructional opportunities that become available with new information and communication technologies.

One can see the influence of classroom patterns in the concerns teachers had for the content of the multimedia software to match closely the curricular content of their social studies program. Teachers clearly wanted this program to represent the information in the social studies program they covered in class and considered essential to their units. They selected items they knew to be important to their classroom activities and content that was a part of the district's guidelines for social studies. If we expect multimedia software to be integrated into a central location in the school curriculum, software developers will need to pay close attention to the specific content needs of teachers and the curricular guidelines established by schools, districts, and states.

It was surprising to us that the CD-ROM educational software we looked at during this period was so unrelated to the specific content developed in these classrooms, even when much of it focused on the ancient civilizations studied in these classes. As a result, teachers chose not to use it. Content match appears to be critically important for teachers as they select software experiences for their students.

A second design principle also appeared in the choices teachers made: Many features developed by teachers allowed students to construct their own interpretations of the information within this program and communicate those meanings to others. Both patterns were found in these classrooms before the software was developed. Thus, it is likely they were initially prompted by classroom patterns of teaching and learning.

What was different about a number of the features related to this design principle, though, was that they enabled students to simultaneously construct and communicate meaning. As students constructed meanings, they often communicated these meanings to others electronically; as students communicated electronically with others, they often constructed new meanings about the information in the program. The nature of the dictionary, for example, enabled students to simultaneously construct meaning and communicate this meaning to others. The same was true for several elements of the notepad developed by teachers: the publish-on-the-bulletin-board feature, the read-and-send features, the sticky feature, and the shoot feature. Each enabled students to rapidly communicate meanings they were constructing of the information available in this program. This aspect may very well reflect new instructional potentials existing within this technology that teachers discovered and exploited as they developed this software, thereby transforming the nature of literacy and learning in their classrooms.

Before this software entered the classroom, students had constructed meaning over a period of time as they worked on their classroom projects and communication did not take place fully until they made their formal presentation to the class. Within this multimedia program, teachers appeared to exploit the technology to develop meaning construction and communication opportunities that took place simultaneously, or nearly so. This suggests that the design of new technologies for classrooms should take maximum advantage of electronic communication opportunities as these enable students to simultaneously construct and communicate meanings about important information.

Much of the commercial software we evaluated during this period contained more static than dynamic information structures (e.g., Encarta, A Cartoon History of the World, Voyage Down the Nile). That is, students could not construct their own meanings electronically within these programs, nor could they electronically communicate those meanings to others. Yet, that is precisely what these teachers wanted their software to do. Software publishers need to consider ways to more completely exploit the important new opportunities for simultaneously constructing and communicating meanings within multimedia software.

Finally, a third principle emerged from the design features expressed by these teachers: The design of this software allowed teachers to regularly monitor the meanings students constructed and the information they communicated to others. It is interesting to note that this need was not initially expressed by teachers; it evolved from revision conferences after they saw the potential of the multimedia program and as they considered new possibilities for it in their classrooms. The fact that teachers developed this potential only after seeing early drafts of the multimedia program suggests that this design feature is one that emanates more from the technology itself than from traditional instructional patterns.

Students' meaning construction and communication are less visible to teachers within multimedia software; it is not always easy to see the specific information resources students are using while they are on a computer. This may prompt teachers to seek ways to more carefully monitor ongoing interactions with the program and the learning and communication that results from these interactions.

Our observations indicated the focal teachers used the monitoring feature of this software often. At the end of nearly every day, these teachers would go to the computer to see what students had done during the day. We also noticed an important consequence of the daily monitoring by teachers: Teachers frequently provided formative evaluation comments to students through e-mail messages. Thus, electronic literacy and learning environments, because they are less visible to teachers, may lead teachers into monitoring more closely the work that is taking place and, when the software also contains opportunities to communicate with students electronically, may increase opportunities for formative evaluation of students' work.

As we consider the design of new technologies for literacy and learning, it would seem useful to keep this third design principle in mind: Teachers appear to value opportunities to monitor ongoing interactions in electronic environments, especially when this can be done quickly. Monitoring interactions within an electronic context where teachers may communicate with students may lead to increased formative evaluation of students' work.

The design principles we discovered in this project may be useful starting points for software publishers to consider as they design more appropriate electronic environments for literacy and learning. In addition, however, this project suggests that new potentials for instruction may also manifest themselves when teachers are closely involved in the design of new technologies for their classrooms. Providing simultaneous opportunities for meaning construction and communication within electronic environments and monitoring opportunities for teachers appear to have transformed the nature of instruction in these classrooms.

To be certain, however, not all teachers have classrooms where students are encouraged to construct their own meanings and then communicate those meanings to others. Many classrooms are designed around principles of skill mastery, memory of concepts, and demonstration of factual knowledge. Although these teachers may not find the software developed in this project fits their particular needs, it is also important to note that the teacher team in this project represented a wide variety of beliefs, including at least one teacher with a more specific skills point of view.

SPECULATING FORWARD TO NEW TECHNOLOGIES
SUCH AS THE INTERNET

We did not begin this project with the idea that a development team such as ours should be created at each school site in order to develop more appropriate multimedia software for teachers. This is not feasible given the costs and the time involved. Instead, we simply sought to discover design principles for multimedia software that teachers found especially useful for their classrooms. We hope these principles may ultimately find their way into commercial software designed for classrooms so that this software is more systematically integrated into classroom teaching and learning.

It is interesting, however, to speculate from these results forward to new technologies that are beginning to become available such as the Internet. Teachers similar to those in our study may find the software environments of the Internet to be more compatible than most types of multimedia environments currently available on CD-ROM or in integrated learning systems. Resources on the Internet contain several design principles we found to be important to teachers in our project: Content exists to meet central curricular needs and meaning construction and communication may take place simultaneously as students and teachers communicate with others.

Many classrooms, for example, are beginning to participate in Internet projects with other classrooms around the world (see Garner & Gillingham, chap. 13, this volume). During Internet projects, classrooms exchange scientific observations, share literary responses, or develop other collaborative ventures. Each of these projects involves content central to the curriculum as classrooms construct and exchange the meanings they make. A classroom in Japan, for example, has recently used e-mail to invite students from around the world to develop interview questions about the meaning of peace, an important curricular area for this classroom. The Japanese students were traveling to Hiroshima on a field trip and intended to use these questions as they interviewed citizens of Hiroshima about peace. They promised to share the results with other classrooms around the world on their return (Leu & Leu, 1997).

Other projects feature more permanent websites such as the one developed by Brian Maguire, a third-grade teacher in upstate New York, and a parent in New Jersey. They have developed a wonderful site for young children to exchange writing and pictures about monsters at Minds Eye Monster Exchange (http://www.csnet.net/minds-eye/). The location includes a chat room, lesson plans, and many other features to support communication and literacy learning among young children at schools around the world. Over 200 classrooms and 6,000 children have participated in these exchanges.

The rapidly growing interest in Internet projects has resulted in a number of registries for these activities so teachers can connect with other teachers about similar content interests.

Examples include: Global SchoolNet's Internet Project Registry (http://www.gsn.org/gsn/proj/index.html), Classroom Connect's Teacher Contact Database (http://www.classroom.net/contact/), or The Global School House (http://www.gsh.org/class/default.htm).

One might speculate that the growth of Internet projects makes concerns about the failure of commercial, multimedia software to follow grounded design principles somewhat moot. It is possible that teachers and students will simply take these matters into their own hands, ignore commercial multimedia software, and begin to engage in electronic projects on the Internet that meet their needs for relevant content as they construct and communicate meanings important to their classrooms. This possibility would be entirely consistent with results of this project and will be increasingly likely unless commercial software publishers begin to pay closer attention to grounding the design of new technologies for literacy and learning in teachers' instructional needs.

ACKNOWLEDGMENTS

Some of the ideas presented in this chapter resulted from a research grant sponsored by the U.S. Department of Education, Office of Educational Research and Improvement, under Grant R117E40125. The opinions expressed in this document do not necessarily reflect the position or policy of the U.S. Department of Education, and no official endorsement should be inferred. Important assistance was also provided by students in the reading degree programs at Syracuse University.

REFERENCES

Anderson, R. E. (1993). The technology infrastructure of U.S. schools. *Communications of the ACM, 36*(5), 72.

Becker, H. J. (1993). Computer experience, patterns of computer use, and effectiveness—An inevitable sequence or divergent national cultures? *Studies in Educational Evaluation, 19*, 127–148.

Bogdan, R. C., & Biklen, S. K. (1992). *Qualitative research for education: An introduction to theory and methods.* Boston: Allyn & Bacon.

Glaser, B. G., & Strauss, A. L. (1967). *The discovery of grounded theory: Strategies for qualitative research.* New York: Aldine DeGruyter.

Kinzer, C. K., & Leu, D. J., Jr. (1997). The challenge of change: Exploring literacy and learning in electronic environments. *Language Arts, 74*(2), 126–136.

Leu, D. J., Jr. (1997). Caity's question: Literacy as deixis on the Internet. *The Reading Teacher, 51*(1), 62–67.

Leu, D. J., Jr., & Leu, D. D. (1997). *Teaching with the Internet: Lessons from the classroom.* Norwood, MA: Christopher Gordon.

Leu, D. J., Jr., & Reinking, D. (1996). Bringing insights from reading research to research on electronic learning environments. In H. van Oostendorp (Ed.), *Cognitive aspects of electronic text processing* (pp. 43–76). Norwood, NJ: Ablex.

Lincoln, Y. S., & Guba, E. G. (1985). *Naturalistic inquiry.* Beverly Hills, CA: Sage.

Miller, L., & Olson, J. (1994). Putting the computer in its place: A study of teaching with technology. *The Journal of Curriculum Studies, 26*, 121–141.

Newman, D. (1990). Opportunities for research on the organizational impact of school computers. *Educational Researcher, 19*(3), 8–13.

Papert, S. (1993). *The children's machine: Rethinking school in the age of the computer.* New York: Basic Books.

Reinking, D., & Bridwell-Bowles, L. (1991). Computers in reading and writing. In R. Barr, M. L. Kamil, P. B. Mosenthal, & P. D. Pearson (Eds.), *Handbook of reading research* (Vol. 2, pp. 310–340). New York: Longman.

Reinking, D., & Pickle, J. M. (1993). Using a formative experiment to study how computers affect reading and writing in classrooms. In D. J. Leu, Jr. & C. K. Kinzer (Eds.), *Examining central issues in literacy research, theory, and practice* (pp. 263–270). Chicago: National Reading Conference.

U.S. Congress, Office of Congressional Assessment. (1995). *Teachers and technology: Making the connection.* Washington, DC: U.S. Government Printing Office.

13

▼▼▼▼▼▼▼

The Internet in the Classroom:
Is It the End of
Transmission-Oriented Pedagogy?

Ruth Garner
Mark G. Gillingham
University of Illinois at Chicago

The Internet is so popular right now that both isolates, who relate mostly to machines, and intensely social individuals, who relate mostly to people, are enthusiastic about what they can accomplish with Internet access. Predictions for the not-too-distant future are dizzying: "We will socialize in digital neighborhoods in which physical space will be irrelevant and time will play a different role" (Negroponte, 1995, p. 7). "Everyone must be both learner and teacher; and the sheer challenge of learning can be managed only through a globe-girdling network that links all minds and all knowledge" (Perelman, 1992, p. 22). Even schools—highly predictable places where time is almost always divided into periods, space into rows, knowledge into pieces, and students into tiers—are embracing the Internet. Many teachers are eager to move ideas back and forth across time and space, and are enthusiastic about classroom Internet access.

Both the enthusiasm and the access are uneven. First, there is absence of familiarity and accompanying anxiety among some teachers. After all, the median age of the approximately 2.8 million teachers in the United States is 42 (Office of Technology Assessment, 1995), meaning that most of them attended school before computers even appeared in classrooms. As for access, a recent report from the National Center for Education Statistics (Heaviside, Farris, Malitz, & Carpenter, 1995) reported that access to the Internet currently privileges secondary schools over elementary, large schools (with enrollments of 1,000 or more) over small, and—most disturbing of all in a democracy—rich districts (those able to afford electrical work, initial connectivity, and recurring access fees) over poor ones.

Despite this unevenness, many teachers have become quite enthusiastic about classroom use of the Internet, and we became curious about how this enthusiasm plays out inside classrooms. What happens, we wanted to know, to school, one of the most predictable of institutions, when the Internet becomes part of the place?

We set out to study Internet-active classrooms, receiving permission from six adventuresome teachers and their students to "eavesdrop" on their classroom Internet conversations for one academic year. We had located the six teachers in a variety of ways: One was a former student, now a beginning teacher; another is a relative; and all of the others were self-nominated when a teacher who had allowed us access to conversational records reported learning a great deal from our preliminary interpretations and recommended to a distant colleague that he or she participate as well. We were pleased that, among the set of participants, there was considerable diversity. Both men and women participated, teaching experience ranged from 0 to 23 years, two teachers taught in a tiny village whereas another taught in a city of 1.6 million, and grade levels ranged from fourth grade through high school.

Our primary data were of course the very words of the teachers and students. Because the year's conversational records could be forwarded, stored, and retrieved with ease, the data were remarkably rich and inviting, and themes emerged across classrooms (e.g., both students and teachers tell stories, the technology is mostly invisible). We supplemented conversational records with information gleaned from lengthy e-mail exchanges with teachers about classroom context and (at the end of the year) about our interpretations. In some instances, teachers suggested a slight revision of interpretation, based on additional information about classroom events. The result of the year's work was a set of six case studies (Garner & Gillingham, 1996), from which we draw liberally for this chapter.

THE TEACHERS

We labeled the teachers "adventuresome," and they are undeniably that. It is not the case that any one of them is what Tyack and Cuban (1995) described as a compliant recipient of an outside mandate for change in instructional practice. No district or building administrator has pressed technology reforms on them. They have, in every case, initiated classroom use of the Internet because it fits in well enough with their familiar teaching routines (Olson, 1988) and at the same time makes their teaching more efficient or satisfying.

The appeal is somewhat different in each classroom. For instance, Ruth Coleman, a fifth-grade teacher in Joliet, Illinois, values the unpredictable parts of the school day, but she also values the predictable. School days are divided into periods during which specific subjects are studied, and certain activities are sanctioned at certain times of the day (e.g., children are encouraged to speak in whole-class discussions about what they have read, but are encouraged not to do so while the teacher or another child has the floor, or while they sit in the book corner reading silently).

Coleman's purpose in participating in the "Learning Circles" project (Riel, 1994) and in connecting with teacher Chris Meier and his class for the year-long correspondence that we analyzed in one of the case studies was twofold: Her students could acquire a richer understanding of important themes (e.g., local community history) than they could if they only consulted school textbooks, and they could learn how to use language in new ways. They learned, for example, how to repeat topics from message to message, sometimes in exactly the same order, to connect to a distant correspondent. They learned how to use detail to make ideas particular, familiar, and memorable. Many of them came to realize that they needed to reformulate what they had written, tailoring their language to meet the needs of distant readers. Nearly all of them learned how to monitor their written communication for trouble spots, such as unconventional spelling and punctuation, absence of local coherence, and ambiguity. Supported by Internet use, and increasingly on their own, Coleman's students learned to negotiate new rhetorical territory.

In Meier's fifth- and sixth-grade classroom and in Hugh Dyment's high school classroom, the Internet provided something a little different: an opportunity for Yup'ik Eskimo children and adolescents in the tiny, isolated village of Tununak, Alaska, to practice speaking and writing in their second language (English). Meier and Dyment were not engaged in a campaign to rid their students of a first language labeled as undesirable; on the contrary, the teachers wanted them to be able to converse, compose, and comprehend in both Yup'ik and English. Meier and Dyment would agree with the way Delpit (1995) put it: "The point must not be to eliminate students' home languages, but rather to add other voices and discourses to their repertoires" (p. 163).

In a village with a strong hold on its native culture and language, one located 300 miles from the nearest road, the Internet was in fact one of the few places where English could be practiced authentically (in meaningful social contexts) and comfortably (with time to seek assistance and polish messages before sending them off). The tiny village had oil royalties, and was thus rich in the technical tools needed for Internet communication.

The students in Tununak wrote wonderful stories to persons outside the village—some to Coleman's students, others to adults who had lived for a time in Tununak, but now lived in the "Lower 48." Topics were matters of importance in Tununak—family and community (especially for the girls) and hunting (especially for the boys).

Most of the narratives resembled stories told by elders in the village: They were reality-based tales, involving the narrator, adhering to actual order of events, and sometimes including an interpretation of the meaning of the events recounted. The stories conformed to universals of narrative identified recently by Bruner (1996)—including unfolding of crucial events, presence of both action and intention, and centrality of trouble in the accounts. The students' fluency in English improved over the course of the year's storytelling. Their teachers observed more unity of expression, increased grammatical competence, and improvement in the mechanics of spelling, capitalization, and punctuation.

In Kathy Plamondon's seventh-grade classroom, there was still another reason to use the Internet. Plamondon was a first-year teacher in La Center, Washington, a small town in the Pacific Northwest, home to loggers and mill workers who had been laid off recently when federal injunctions against logging the old-growth forests of the area—along with overlogging and automation of the industry—had made jobs scarce. Parents were not highly educated, and only a handful of students cared about being successful at school. Boasting was about stealing "chew" from the only store in town or taking the family car out for a joy ride on nearby country roads—almost never about academic achievement. Few of Plamondon's students aspired to college or even vocational school. Many planned to drop out after ninth grade, and they were loud and disengaged in class.

Feeling frustrated, Plamondon introduced the students to KIDCAFE, an international e-mail list for 10- to 15-year-olds. It is free, something to which kids themselves post messages, and then read and reply—no grades, no coercion to participate. Adults do not interrupt students, change the topics, or comment on the worth of the ideas expressed; they only moderate conversations that take place, rejecting messages that contain personal insults or that disrupt the flow of information through intimidation. On KIDCAFE, during the time that we followed the discussion, students generated powerful arguments, presenting adultlike claims and evidence on topics important to them (e.g., euthanizing unwanted dogs, evolution, gays in the military, and wearing hats in school).

Surely one reason for interest in KIDCAFE was that the students, not teachers, selected the occasion, audience, and topic for discussion. This is absolutely the opposite of how Cazden (1988) described most classroom talk, where teachers, but not students, have the right to speak at any time and to any person, using any volume or tone. Kathy's students not only came to school to write back and forth on KIDCAFE about topics of interest; they came early and stayed late to do so.

We have decided that the Internet appealed to Daniel Wilcox, a high school teacher in Santa Maria, California, because he was a seasoned teacher in search of professional conversation—someone looking for what *New Yorker* writer Seabrook (1995) described as private conversational space within the public space of the Internet. Wilcox and Dyment from Tununak conversed late at night. At first, it was about their adolescent students, Latino for Wilcox and Yup'ik for Dyment. Later, it was about what to teach and how, specifically about teaching *Night*, Elie Wiesel's (1982) account of his life in a Nazi concentration camp. Still later, it was about the unpredictability and uncertainty of teaching.

These two experienced teachers used the Internet to break down the isolation and loneliness of classroom life. Meier (1995) pointed out that few policymakers understand what it means to teach a subject year after year following someone else's design. Teachers do though, and they also understand why they and their colleagues can be prickly and defensive about their work in classrooms: This is work that involves making life-altering decisions every day. It is "difficult, demanding, draining work" (Ayers, 1995, p. 2). Wise teachers engage in conversations about practice, providing something to each other that no one else can give: a set of examples of stunning (and lousy) instructional ideas, a discussion of the joys and woes that accompany everyday work with young people.

The sixth teacher we studied, Kathy Nell, is a veteran of 23 years of teaching 3- and 4-year-olds, then second graders, and most recently fourth and fifth graders in the Philadelphia school system. Nell and her students had a website, complete with text, pictures, moving images, and even audio clips. The resources needed to maintain the site were substantial: The children themselves composed and peer-edited at one of two computers in the room (one belonging to Nell, and one that she received from a grant, just like the two modems in the room that the students use to check their own mail). Nell and a district technical expert actually published the work, and scanning of some of the art work was done by Nell's nephew at his house. Apparently it is not uncommon for teachers to have to dig deeply into their own pockets (and schedules) like this to support classroom Internet work (Schrum, 1995). Nell, like others, was working well in advance of significant support from her district.

The fourth graders had rare opportunities for literature-based learning and for understanding that authorship is not transcribing or paraphrasing someone else's ideas; it is moving the highly individual ideas in one's head to the printed page (or computer screen). The children could read and write about books, expressing their feelings about what they read and about connections between what they read and their own lives. They could publish this work, inviting comment. Nell inserted envelope icons throughout the Web pages as prompts to distant readers ("Class 308 would love to hear from you"), and when a child in another classroom selected the icon near a particular piece of work, an Internet mail window opened up, and the child in, say, North Dakota or California, could write back. (Responses came from all 50 states and many other countries.) Nell even generated "electronic portfolios" for all of the students. If a distant correspondent wanted to see all of a particular fourth-grade author's writing, the person could access the work plus pictures and an audio clip from the student just by clicking on the student's name.

TEACHER LEARNING, INSTRUCTIONAL CHANGE

It was apparent to us, almost from the start of our year-long data collection, that the six teachers had in common an enormous enthusiasm about their classroom Internet work. After all, as each of them told us many times, geographically dispersed teachers and students can use the written word as a conversational medium. They can learn from one another.

What did the teachers learn? How was instruction in the six classrooms transformed by the Internet activity? We found three large changes and many small ones. We discuss the large ones here, two rather briefly and one in more detail.

An obvious change was the expansion of materials and methods in each teacher's repertoire. One teacher told another about successful questioning techniques; three debated about how heavy-handed teacher editing of messages should be; two others had an extended discussion about teaching about rhetorical matters (e.g., figuring out what your conversational partner is likely to know about a particular topic). Many messages touched on old progressive education issues (e.g., how to unleash imagination, how to make learning its own reward). A fairly desperate call came from the first-year teacher for suggestions about how to encourage open, but respectful, conversation in the classroom. A number of requests for engaging book titles and informative websites appeared throughout the year. The teachers came to trust each other enough to share examples of what had worked for them with particular students—and what had not.

A second change was reinvigorated teacher reflection on practice—the sort of thing that teacher educators urge teachers-to-be to do, that student teachers practice doing, and that experienced teachers find almost impossible to do as they end up, instead, doing what Lieberman (1992) described so well: Keep students busy (preferably, but not always, profitably), attempt to follow the curriculum, and try to survive isolation, loneliness, and a fear of losing control. The clearest example of public reflection on practice was of course the extended conversation about day-to-day actions and career-long conceptions that occurred between Wilcox and Dyment, but all of the teachers engaged in considerable reflection—with each other as attachments to their students' exchanges and with us in setting context and in responding to our preliminary and more polished written interpretations. They had the obstacle of nonstop instructional and supervisory responsibilities at school, but the asynchronous nature of the medium allowed them to receive messages all day long and to reply at the end of the school day, often in the evening from home. It was in reading many of the teachers' written reflections that we came to understand how much in advance of significant support from their districts they were operating, how they—not the district or a building administrator—had accepted new technologies and attempted to integrate them with other resources in the classroom. Instructional innovation, in other words, was occurring, as Yocam (1996) noted it usually does, at the level of the individual teacher.

A third change—one with enormous consequences for schooling, in our view—was a movement away from transmission-oriented pedagogy. The clearest instance of this movement probably occurred in Nell's fourth-grade classroom in Philadelphia. As we said earlier, Nell and her students used the Web all year long both as a publication outlet for their poems, stories, and artwork and as a source of information. Nell's Web work is not a curricular add-on, a set of playful activities that she schedules only on Friday afternoon when other curricular objectives have been met and the children are too fidgety to do anything rigorous like mastering the hard skills of composing, calculating, or problem solving.

It is in fact reinvented teaching and learning, with new patterns of work in place: The children's activity is seldom private and competitive, often public and collaborative; there is very little teaching-as-telling from Nell; and because the Web is available to serve as both outlet and source, there is considerable reading and writing in the classroom. With 23 years of teaching experience, Nell is quite clear about the knowledge, skills, and dispositions that she wants the fourth graders to develop, but much of the specificity of each week's work evolves from exchanges on the Web and the interests of the children. Kathy's curriculum is one about which Duckworth (1996) would say, "the unexpected is valued" (p. 8).

One of the best examples that we observed of valuing the unexpected and using materials on the Web to meet curricular goals emerged from a local tragedy—a terrible Christmas Eve fire at the Philadelphia Zoo, which resulted in the destruction of the entire primate collection. The fire was described in the national media as the worst disaster in the history of American zoos. Nell knew that her students would know about the fire, would feel a very personal loss of the animals they had visited, and would want to say and do something. But what?

One thing that she helped them do immediately was to sort out fact from rumor by using the local newspaper website as a source of information. According to the Yahoo indexing service, 43 newspaper organizations publish online papers in Pennsylvania, so Nell's students had no difficulty finding a source. At a single site they found a current *Philadelphia Inquirer*, a current *Philadelphia Daily News*, and archived issues dating as far back as 1981.

They were able to learn how many animals had died (23), how they had died (smoke inhalation), and what had apparently gone wrong (faulty smoke detectors, little supervision of the animals during holiday hours). This was breaking news, updated many times during each day. This current, frequently updated nature of most of the online papers is reason enough to celebrate classroom Web access. (As *New York Times* writer Zuckerman [1997] described newspaper publishing on the Internet, it represents a return to the way print journalism was practiced in an earlier generation when big-city newspapers printed multiple editions throughout the day, and reporters phoned in hourly updates to colleagues in the newsroom who would do rewriting.) All of this is quite different from the way we used to receive news at school—via kiddie papers that presented very dated (and very sanitized) versions of events.

Helping the children to access the online papers was very different from teaching-as-telling. In many cases, an individual student made a discovery about what had happened at the zoo before Nell did. Many educators (e.g., see Sandholtz & Ringstaff, 1996) have commented on a shift in expertise in the classroom, noting that students frequently become more knowledgeable than their teachers in using particular computer applications. Wise teachers accept this shift, Sandholtz and Ringstaff (1996) suggested and capitalize on student knowledge. The shift in Nell's class (who knew what, who told others) was even more dramatic, in our view, in that it was about ideas, not equipment or software. Who, after all, discovered how many animals had died and how? (The students accessing the local newspaper website when breaking news became available were the first to know.) Who told this information? (The students did.) Who listened and learned? (The teacher did.)

Using the local newspaper website as a source of information about the fire made the children better informed. However, it did not make them feel much better. They still needed to express their personal responses to the fire, their sadness about the animals, and their fears that fire might harm them as well. Strong emotions and passions, as is often the case, needed to be addressed (hooks, 1993), and some of this occurred in open classroom discussion, in which students' beliefs about blame and consequences were expressed.

In addition, Nell suggested to the class that they do some persuasive writing (a curricular expectation, in any case) about the death of the primates (the unexpected). They would take positions for or against keeping animals in captivity and would use standard argument structure of claims and evidence. The Web was the outlet for the arguments, which were about evenly divided between for and against. Arguments were published with authors' names, and, as usual, envelope icons were inserted as prompts to distant readers to write back to the authors (which some adults and children did). We include one example here, an argument from Kenneth, who is opposed to keeping animals in zoos. Like all the other quite remarkable texts that we read, Kenneth displays what Newmann (1991) labeled *empathy*—an attempt to incorporate the experiences of others (in this case, the experiences of the zoo animals) into one's own thinking:

> Zoos are a big problem. I think that they should let all wild animals in the zoo go back to the jungles. I believe zoos are very bad for animals. I feel zoos should all be closed down. I think they should let all animals go because some kids throw rocks at the wild animals in the zoo. I think they should not have taken wild animals out of Africa in the first place. I think they should close all zoos because some animals such as monkeys have forgotten some of their natural skills. By 1990 the extinction rate may reach several species an hour around the clock. I think zoos are like jails to animals. They the trainers should not make animals do tricks Dolphins live in a world of sound and their sounds are bouncing back at them in a tank. I think zoos are very cruel. On December 24, 1995, human error and careless construction caused a fire at the Philadelphia Zoo. Twenty-three primates died in that fire. Even though 90% of mammals and 75% of birds in captivity were bred in zoos we still capture animals in the wild. Here are some ideas one: Stop making animals do tricks. Two: Free all the animals. Three: Close zoos.

THE INTERNET, TEXTBOOKS, AND TRANSMISSION MODELS

One might reasonably ask, "What is the place of school textbooks in an Internet-active classroom, a classroom like Nell's?" The answer "in the storeroom, locked up" is too glib, for Nell still uses textbooks alongside Internet resources. However, it is true that the Internet represents a way of offering up ideas that textbooks cannot match: It is current, it invites us to use information selectively, and it presents multiple interpretations of events and phenomena.

Textbooks are not current. When Nell's students experienced a need to know about the local Christmas Eve zoo fire, textbooks were of little use. Students might have learned something from bound volumes with a long shelf life about particular primates or about the general purposes of zoos, but they would find no information on the recent tragedy. When they sought information about the fire, even last week's newspapers were useless. Frequently updated online papers were the best source for the students.

Also, textbooks are seldom read selectively in K–12 classrooms, where a start-to-finish treatment is the norm. Even if teachers subscribe to principles of in-depth examination of a few topics rather than superficial coverage of many, it is difficult, with a fat, familiar textbook in hand, not to fall into the textbook-as-tyrant trap: "I got to the Louisiana Purchase by this time last year. I'm afraid that we won't finish the book at this rate." From this vantage point, digressions linked to student interest—in fact, much of Nell's curriculum, where, as we have said, the unexpected is valued—are seen as an impediment to moving through the book.

The power of the Internet, on the other hand, lies in part in its very scale and design. It is, Negroponte (1995) reminded us, a decentralized network of more than 50,000 separate networks—a network of networks. No user would be silly enough to attempt to access everything on the Internet. Users can select from a mass of information what they need to solve a puzzle at hand (as Nell's students did when they wanted current information about the fire). Or, given a less defined goal, they can browse, savoring the unexpected by entering a topic and clicking on links that take them deeper and deeper into background material. The first example is like a scholar's running into a library 10 minutes before closing needing a single quotation, and running to the library shelf where he or she knows the book in which the material appears is shelved. The second example is like the same scholar, who has 2 hours this time, starting in the part of the library where familiar books are shelved, and then plucking books from nearby shelves and scanning them for material of interest. (Nell is vigilant, we should mention, in monitoring the educational value and absence of vulgarity in websites accessed in her classroom. Just as Leu and Leu [1997] advised, she uses bookmarks to note sites that she particularly wants students to visit. There is still plenty of room for student choice about which sites get extended visits and which ones get only a quick glance.)

What concerns us most about textbooks is that, except in the rarest of cases, they do not present multiple interpretations of events and phenomena. Instead, they are "particular constructions of reality" (Apple & Christian-Smith, 1991, p. 3), someone's selection and organization of all possible knowledge. Luke, de Castell, and Luke (1989) said about textbooks that they have unrivaled status as legitimate school knowledge and that they are protected by institutional rules about who owns them (schools), who selects them (sometimes teachers, never students), and who will be penalized if they are not cared for and venerated (students). They are beyond criticism—textbook as icon, ideal for transmission-oriented pedagogy.

The only remedy until very recently for this sort of thing has been a teacher's deciding to use parts of several texts, each with its own perspectives and insights. Many experienced teachers of our acquaintance (particularly history teachers) have in fact replaced a single, costly textbook with a variety of cheaper paperback texts. However, now, with Internet access, multiple perspectives are also available with just a few clicks. Students and teachers can begin to engage, via new technologies, in what Hawkins (1996) called "grappling with complexity" (p. 38).

In fact, Hawkins (1996) argued that it is no longer necessary to seek out multiple interpretations of events. Competing perspectives and conflicting facts are presented openly and abundantly on the Internet. Students will encounter ambiguity and discrepancy there, Hawkins noted, even if a teacher celebrates fixed facts and received knowledge in his or her classroom.

We recently tested Hawkins' (1996) point about perspectives and facts. Recalling that Nell had suggested to her students that they search a set of websites related to endangered species (she thought that the students might find information on reproduction in captivity that they could use in their persuasive essays), we spent about an hour searching some sites as well. One of the first ones that we located was devoted to rainforests (Rainforest Action Network, 1997). A link to a "Kids' Corner" was provided, and it was there that we located a list of eight steps that children might take to save endangered species in the rainforest. Most of the steps were general, in the sense that they advised somewhat vague actions and did not mention specific boycotts (e.g., tell your family members not to buy items made of ivory, coral, reptile skins, or cat pelts; persuade your parents not to buy tropical hardwoods unless they are from sustainable sources). One step was different in that it advised getting everyone in the family to avoid buying products from Texaco, which is currently being boycotted for rainforest destruction. We checked Texaco's home page (Texaco Online, 1997) and were not surprised to discover that they had posted a "Vision and Values" statement that presented a corporate image of environmental sensitivity and responsibility—one that included a "remediation program" in Ecuador that involves "revegetating" land cleared for previous operations. The action network and the corporate websites do exactly what Hawkins (1996) suggested: They present competing perspectives and conflicting facts.

The competing perspectives and conflicting facts on the Internet present a huge opportunity, of course, for teachers. They prompt teachers to develop among students the truly important understanding that persons and events described in text (in bound volumes or in online versions) are never described without some intrusion from the tellers. Every time a person is characterized or an event is described, the individual doing the characterizing or describing imposes some structure and meaning—at the very least by choosing to tell some things and not others (Garner & Alexander, 1994). Teachers can help students tolerate some uncertainty amidst variant textual accounts, and they can provide them with the tools needed to evaluate accounts—assessing why bias might exist, looking for corroborative detail across accounts.

If Nell, for example, had wanted to teach her students how to respond to the discrepancies in account in the environmental action website and the Texaco corporate site, she might have turned to the much-acclaimed book, *Savages* (Kane, 1996), in which the author provided his "take" on the Texaco presence in the Ecuadorian Amazon. The book provides detail that could be compared to that found at the two websites. Nell and the students might have read Kane's description of a symbiotic relationship between Texaco and a group of North American missionaries who together "lured" the indigenous people, the Huaorani, from their traditional lands to a small protectorate. They could have read about the oil company's penetration of the Amazonian watershed along a 60-mile-long road, the Auca:

A rusty steel pipeline runs alongside the road. In some places the pipeline rests right on the ground, and in others it is raised on stilts. Men tether their horses to it, women spread their washing on it to dry, and children play on it. On a clear day the metal soaks up so much equatorial sun that it's hot to the touch, and when you rest a hand on it you feel the oil pulsing along inside. . . .

Oil and oil-waste spills are common on the Auca. Trucks plow into the pipeline, trees fall on it, and in some places it is nearly rusted through. It has no check valves, and when it ruptures it can spill for days, until someone at a receiving station far down the line notices a drop in production. (pp. 27–28)

To return to Nell's classroom and the year's Internet work that we observed, the consequences of what she did with the Web are, as we said earlier, enormous. Put simply, there was an inevitable equalizing of status in her classroom between teacher and student. After all, both had access to knowledge—to all of the competing perspectives and conflicting facts—in a way they would not have had if their teacher had acted as the sole interpreter for them of a single, particular-perspective textbook, a role that Luke et al. (1989) described as analogous to that of mediator between the biblical text and the common person during the Middle Ages.

Not in Nell's classroom! When she and her students wanted to know more about the fire at the zoo, Nell did not follow a transmission model, reading aloud from yesterday's news accounts or lecturing about the disaster. There were no fixed facts, and there was no received knowledge. Rather, the Web was used, and children who happened to have access to the local newspaper website when the story was updated were able to present to the class the most current information about how many animals had died, how they had died, and so forth. In this situation, as Perelman (1992) put it, "expertise is more in the network, less in the person" (p. 59). This is an inviting shift for adventuresome, bold teachers (surely the six we studied), perhaps not for all.

SO, WHERE DO WE GO FROM HERE?

In general, as we noted earlier in our discussion of competing perspectives and conflicting facts, we are comfortable with some uncertainty. Certainty among educational researchers and policymakers—about which children can learn or which teaching methods work, for example—worries us. When it comes to rapidly changing technologies, only the most foolish among us would claim to know with certainty which technologies will be introduced to schools in the next few years and, more importantly, which ones will actually support reinvented teaching and learning. In the spirit of tolerating some amount of uncertainty, we conclude this chapter by posing two questions about where Internet activity in the classroom will go from here—two questions for which we have no answers:

1. Is the national imperative to "wire the schools," stated and restated from the White House on down, really going to result in a narrowing—rather than widening—of the gap between "have" and "have-not" school districts? (This is a question about equity of access to information and communication opportunities, not about technology alone.)

2. When we describe school change in the next decade—the "from what to what," as Dwyer (1996, p. 16) put it—will we find that most teachers use new technologies for old purposes, such as teacher telling of fixed facts? (Reading recent requests for proposals from various federal agencies, we were struck that invitations to produce electronic textbooklike materials could move us an enormous step backward from use of multisite, multiperspective Internet searches like the ones that Nell's students are conducting right now.)

We should note that we have considerable faith in the wisdom of most teachers. We recognize that they are in fact the arbiters of how children are treated and of how materials are used inside classrooms. Once their classroom doors are closed, it is they, not distant researchers, policymakers, or administrators, who determine what occurs in students' lives for about 6 hours each day. We believe that many teachers, given the opportunity, will discard old models of transmission of knowledge in favor of constructing knowledge via what Perelman (1992) described as the "globe-girdling network that links all minds and all knowledge" (p. 22). We have studied six teachers who have done just that.

REFERENCES

Apple, M. W., & Christian-Smith, L. K. (1991). The politics of the textbook. In M. W. Apple & L. K. Christian-Smith (Eds.), *The politics of the textbook* (pp. 1–21). New York: Routledge.

Ayers, W. (1995). Introduction: Joining the ranks. In W. Ayers (Ed.), *To become a teacher: Making a difference in children's lives* (pp. 1–4). New York: Teachers College Press.

Bruner, J. (1996). *The culture of education.* Cambridge, MA: Harvard University Press.

Cazden, C. B. (1988). *Classroom discourse: The language of teaching and learning.* Portsmouth, NH: Heinemann.

Delpit, L. (1995). *Other people's children: Cultural conflict in the classroom.* New York: New Press.

Duckworth, E. (1996). *"The having of wonderful ideas" and other essays on teaching and learning* (2nd ed.). New York: Teachers College Press.

Dwyer, D. C. (1996). The imperative to change our schools. In C. Fisher, D. C. Dwyer, & K. Yocam (Eds.), *Education and technology: Reflections on computing in classrooms* (pp. 15–33). San Francisco: Jossey-Bass.

Garner, R., & Alexander, P. A. (1994). Preface. In R. Garner & P. A. Alexander (Eds.), *Beliefs about text and instruction with text* (pp. xvii–xxii). Hillsdale, NJ: Lawrence Erlbaum Associates.

Garner, R., & Gillingham, M. G. (1996). *Internet communication in six classrooms: Conversations across time, space, and culture.* Mahwah, NJ: Lawrence Erlbaum Associates.

Hawkins, J. (1996). Dilemmas. In C. Fisher, D. C. Dwyer, & K. Yocam (Eds.), *Education and technology: Reflections on computing in classrooms* (pp. 35–50). San Francisco: Jossey-Bass.

Heaviside, S., Farris, E., Malitz, G., & Carpenter, J. (1995). *Advanced telecommunications in U.S. public schools, K–12* (Publication No. NCES 95-731). Washington, DC: U.S. Government Printing Office.

hooks, b. (1993). Transformative pedagogy and multiculturalism. In T. Perry & J. W. Fraser (Eds.), *Freedom's plow: Teaching in the multicultural classroom* (pp. 91–97). New York: Routledge.

Kane, J. (1996). *Savages.* New York: Vintage Books.

Leu, D. J., Jr., & Leu, D. D. (1997). *Teaching with the Internet: Lessons from the classroom.* Norwood, MA: Christopher Gordon.

Lieberman, A. (1992). The meaning of scholarly activity and the building of community. *Educational Researcher, 21,* 5–12.

Luke, C., de Castell, S., & Luke, A. (1989). Beyond criticism: The authority of the school textbook. In S. de Castell, A. Luke, & C. Luke (Eds.), *Language, authority, and criticism: Readings on the school textbook* (pp. 245–260). London: Falmer.

Meier, D. (1995). *The power of their ideas: Lessons for America from a small school in Harlem.* Boston: Beacon Press.

Negroponte, N. (1995). *Being digital.* New York: Knopf.

Newmann, F. M. (1991). Higher order thinking in the teaching of social studies: Connections between theory and practice. In J. F. Voss, D. N. Perkins, & J. W. Segal (Eds.), *Informal reasoning and education* (pp. 381–400). Hillsdale, NJ: Lawrence Erlbaum Associates.

Office of Technology Assessment. (1995). *Teachers and technology: Making the connection* (Publication No. OTA-EHR-616). Washington, DC: U.S. Government Printing Office.

Olson, J. (1988). *Schoolworlds/microworlds: Computers and the culture of the classroom.* Oxford, UK: Pergamon.

Perelman, L. J. (1992). *School's out: A radical new formula for the revitalization of America's educational system.* New York: Avon.

Rainforest Action Network. (1997, January 6). [Online]. Available http://www.ran.org/ran/.

Riel, M. (1994). Educational change in a technology-rich environment. *Journal of Research on Computing in Education, 26,* 452–474.

Sandholtz, J. H., & Ringstaff, C. (1996). Teacher change in technology-rich classrooms. In C. Fisher, D. C. Dwyer, & K. Yocam (Eds.), *Education and technology: Reflections on computing in classrooms* (pp. 281–299). San Francisco: Jossey-Bass.

Schrum, L. (1995). Educators and the Internet: A case study of professional development. *Computers and Education, 24,* 221–228.

Seabrook, J. (1995, October 16). Home on the net. *New Yorker,* 66, 68, 70, 72, 74, 76.

Texaco Online. (1997, January 6). [Online]. Texaco, Inc. Available http: www.texaco.com/.

Tyack, D., & Cuban, L. (1995). *Tinkering toward utopia: A century of public school reform.* Cambridge, MA: Harvard University Press.

Wiesel, E. (1982). *Night.* New York: Bantam.

Yocam, K. (1996). Conversation: An essential element of teacher development. In C. Fisher, D. C. Dwyer, & K. Yocam (Eds.), *Education and technology: Reflections on computing in classrooms* (pp. 265–279). San Francisco: Jossey-Bass.

Zuckerman, L. (1997, January 6). Don't stop the presses! *The New York Times,* pp. C1, C7.

V

▼▼▼▼▼▼▼▼

TRANSFORMING SOCIETY

Literacy has always been recognized as having sociocultural implications, but the chapters in this part are a reminder of how technology adds poignancy to those implications. Taken together, more than chapters in the other sections, they go beyond an examination of current technological transformations that are effecting changes in specific dimensions of literacy. Although, as in other sections, there are concrete examples of current technological developments and their potential effects on literacy, the authors of chapters here are really concerned with how the dynamics of social and cultural change are firmly grounded in technology and vice versa. The societal transformations they explore extend beyond the classroom but clearly have implications for literacy instruction in schools. A common theme then is that technology, society, culture, and literacy inside and outside of classrooms are not adequately understood separately. When viewed from that perspective, what may appear to be an isolated transformation is really part of a sociocultural tapestry into which individual lives and experiences are woven.

Inevitably, such a perspective leads to historical reflection and analysis provided in this section particularly by Purves (chap. 14). He provides a thoughtful analysis of how there are societal constants pertaining to literacy that are realized in some fashion regardless of what technologies are used for reading and writing. He argues that there have been three revolutionary developments in the history of literacy: the alphabet, the printing press, and digital information. Regardless of the technologies associated with these developments, he maintains that reading and writing have remained iconic; they have always been essentially used for communication aimed at accomplishing human purposes; and they always shape human consciousness. Similarly, he argues that literacy, regardless of technology, must serve humanity's need to establish a center of learning and the performance of rituals. Using hypertext as an example, he then poses the more-than-rhetorical question of how these constants can be met in the world of digital texts. We are the flies, he says, in the web of hypertext who must disentangle ourselves from the revolution of digital information to determine how we will connect with a literacy that transcends the conditions created by any particular technology.

Tierney and Damarin (chap. 15) extend this analysis to show how technology is an integral part of social learning in contexts as diverse as preschool children using conventional media to create an imaginary city, adolescents who become inducted into a community of boogie board surfers, and aboriginal Australian clans whose traditional art forms are influenced by encroaching modernism. The roles of technology and media in these situations are shown to have much in common with their experiences in studying the effects of infusing state-of-the-art computer-based technologies into secondary classrooms over an extended time. They view "media and text as inextricably connected with ongoing interactions [that serve] as cultural tools forming students' identity of themselves and of their individual and collective view of society" (p. 253). They speculate that new media introduce new themes into a culture and the digital forms of writing may encourage more risk taking.

Bruce and Hogan (chap. 16) tackle similar issues and explore similar themes, but they argue against a "technological determinism" that unnaturally isolates technology from social factors, proposing instead an ecological model of literacy. An ecological model, they argue, allows us to see technology as embedded within a matrix of social relations that shape literacy. They point out that technology is often an invisible force operating within that matrix because new technologies tend to disappear as they become fully integrated into people's experiences. The new technologies associated with literacy today allow us to consciously examine how technology shapes literacy, particularly in defining ability and disability.

Again, echoing these themes, Lemke (chap. 17) reminds us that literacy has many meanings and levels of meaning, and is perhaps best conceptualized as "literacies," all of which share the common denominator of being socially determined. Taking a semiotic point of view, he then presents a case for how new technologies not only expand reading and writing into the realm of multimedia, but also how this shift has implications for society and schools. For example, he explains how multimedia may promote an increased emphasis on topological meaning and a decreased emphasis on the more narrow emphasis of typological meaning that has led to more categorical thinking about textual information. Likewise, he sees this shift as promoting what he calls an "interactive" as opposed to a "curricular" learning paradigm in schools where students will have greater freedom to learn what they want, when they want.

Finally, no consideration of societal transformations of literacy would be complete without a consideration of how technology is affecting the workplace. Work and options for employment are fundamental to any consideration of societal changes, and literacy in the modern era has shaped and been shaped by an understanding of the workplace. Such issues are the focus of Mikulecky and Kirkley (chap. 18). They support their observations that "technology and the new literacies associated with it have transformed the workplace arguably more quickly and more deeply than any of our other institutions" (p. 303). They provide several examples of how workers today need high levels of literacy that include the ability to analyze and synthesize information to make quick decisions independently. They discuss how new technologies not only precipitate international trends for new kinds of workers but how those same technologies can be used to assist in the development of such workers. In doing so they parallel one of this book's major themes: Technology acts as both a stimulus for the transformation of literacy and a mechanism for dealing with that transformation.

14

▼▼▼▼▼▼▼

Flies in the Web of Hypertext*

Alan Purves
State University of New York at Albany

The form of the written word has changed over the years since the technology of writing has developed. So, too, have the uses and practices of the scribes who read and write. Today we are in the midst of what I have called the "Third Information Revolution," and we are as flies trying to figure out what has happened to the air through which the webs of text and media have been spun. I would like to say something about the revolution and the consequences for those whose profession is the training of scribes. I use the word *scribes* advisedly, for I do not believe that schools are so much in the business of teaching the populace to read and write as they are in the perpetuation of a scribal class that is concerned with the preservation and transmission of information. If we were confined to teaching reading and writing, we would finish our job in 4 years. We have the other 8—or 10 or 12—to train a variety of scribes.

In making these remarks, I draw heavily on one book that I have recently completed, *The Web of Text and the Web of God*, as well as on one that I am currently engaged in writing entitled *Landmarks in Literacy*. In the latter, I survey 10 key points in the history of man's interaction with the technology of writing, concluding with a look to the future. In both books, I suggest that the written word is affected both by technology and by social forces, and that the two interact in a variety of ways. There have been over the centuries three massive revolutions in the palpable shape of text, in the nature of the reader, and in the center of learning. The first came with the use of alphabetic print and the development of papyrus, the second came with the printing press and paper, and the third was the development of digital information.

---

*This chapter requires an explanation due to Dr. Alan Purves' untimely death during the preparation of this volume. The text of this chapter was originally presented by Dr. Purves as an invited keynote address at the October 1996 conference on technology and literacy organized by the editors of this volume and funded by the National Reading Research Center. Dr. Purves was in the process of revising his talk to conform more closely to the format of a book chapter at the time of his death. We have exercised some cautious editorial discretion in our own revisions to his conference paper published as a chapter here. However, given the circumstances, we consciously chose to minimize deviations from Dr. Purves' original text, and we would like to ask readers to keep this in mind. We believe readers will find much evidence in this chapter of Dr. Purves' strong intellect and keen insights.

Through all of these changes, however, certain key principles about written language and literacy have persisted, although they may become hidden from time to time. They have become increasingly apparent through the development of hypertext and hypermedia, the two manifestations of the third information revolution. The first is that written language is essentially iconic. It is a complex of images that represent ideas and concepts more than it does sounds or even oral language. The second is that written language is not a means of communication involving sender, message, and receiver. It is a medium for the storage and retrieval of information. At times, it has been used as a mass medium, but its persistent use has been as a nonmass medium used particularly for four human purposes: religious, commercial, political, and aesthetic. The religious purpose has tended to affect the other three in part because the spiritual side of people's lives cuts across the other three. The third is that the ways in which written language is perceived and used have become intertwined with and have helped define the history of human consciousness.

I can illustrate these points with two stories, both drawn from earlier times of writing. These appear in the Appendix. They are illustrative of the shift brought about by having a written record and by the shift brought about by having what Olson (1994) called "The World on Paper." I do not dwell on them, but move to a consideration of hypertext itself.

THE LOOK OF HYPERTEXT

The idea of hypertext causes us to look once again at what we have been looking at almost unconsciously all these years. The fact of seeing text on the screen causes us to think about what it means to look at and see the text on a page or on sheets of paper. For me, one of the key aspects of a text is that it must be seen to be read, unless it is in Braille; then it must be felt. This key fact tends to recede from our consciousness when publishers and printers, particularly in the scholarly field, seek to make the text appear invisible and the book or article a bland and boring affair.

In traditional texts, the visible text is read in two-dimensional space that has an invariant sequence according to custom. In one of the oldest written languages in history, Chinese, the written language and its surface features come from a variety of visual and iconographic sources with little connection to the spoken language. It was designed to be read equally well by people who spoke nearly different languages, and it developed a calligraphic style that focuses on the surface, the brush stroke, as well as on the grammar and syntax. The relation to the oral word is virtually nonexistent. The Chinese writing system reminds us who use alphabetic systems based on phonetic relations between squiggles on the page and sounds that we make and out of which we make sense, that our written language need not have been that way and that the visual design of the text is a great part of our understanding its message. Too often we tend to think of writing as if it were devoid of pictures, when in fact it is itself a picture.

One attribute of written language and texts is that their two-dimensional nature may limit conceptual space as well as text space. By limiting conceptual space, I mean that because we begin at the top, we may well be conditioned to think hierarchically out of habit. This habit based on our sense of the page helps set the patterns of lists and classification systems. We may alternate between top-down and bottom-up, and we may reverse the left–right movement as in Hebrew, but these are minor variations. Because we also go left to right, we have tables such as calendars and grids that enable us to look at things in cells. We see things as cross-related even though the horizontal–vertical relation may be one of many. We can simulate cubes, but we cannot easily indicate shifting relations. These limitations brought about by the fact of the text on the page may have rhetorical consequences in what we consider as important in the disposition of ideas on the page or pages. The way in which we arrange texts with "headings" and "footnotes," besides using bodily imagery, provides us with a visual metaphor of hierarchy that sees the bottom as lower in importance than the top. As a result we see the top of the page as containing the important aspects of the text, but we also see the beginning and end of the message as having greater consequence than the middle. These are the parts enclosed to the large blank spaces. This again is a visually based rhetoric, and it is one that in part determines how we arrange our ideas into an order that is commonly understood.

When the text becomes electronic, what happens? We see a part of the writing on a screen, but it is not like looking at the pages of a book or sheets of foolscap. Actually, we see a set of contrasting spaces or pixels shaped by a complex combination of digital commands so as to give one the illusion of seeing letters, words, fonts, and paragraphs. These images can be saved or discarded by a keystroke. They may be moved and manipulated in any one of a number of ways. With my word processing program, I can see them as a scroll, as they might be pages in a book, or as a running outline in which I can hide from view large amounts of text that are (I hope) still in the machine. One feature of the electronic text is that although we see it on the screen, or at least parts of it, we assume it is there even though it is not there as text but as a collection of pluses and minuses, in which we place blind faith. The text is simultaneously visible and invisible.

If I put the text into a desktop publishing program, I can take the separate parts of what I have written and move them around on a mock-up page, I can surround the text with illustrations, or surround a picture with the text. I can put it into a number of columns or rows. However, I cannot do much more than that. What emerges has to be looked at as if it were a virtual set of pages in a book or magazine. I can open a number of different documents at once and move back and forth between them, although with some difficulty.

This difficulty disappears or is lessened if I put the same text into a hypertext program. I can take each paragraph or chunk of text that I want to keep and have it appear as a separate segment encased in a box or "space." These then appear as an array of spaces on a screen, and I can go into any one of the spaces with the click of a mouse. I can also drag the spaces around on the screen, nest them inside each other, or link with any one of a number of devices to other spaces. I can create different pathways between the spaces so that a reader can follow any one from a particular space and go to as many as a dozen other spaces. The relations between parts are multidirectional and instant, not simply up or down or across and sequential. The parts themselves change from segments of words to collections of words, images, moving pictures, sound, or the like, all stored in a binary fashion, all able to be called up as a succession of images on the screen, perhaps never to be printed—for doing so would hold them in a static form, where they are moving, always in a complex network of relations with each other—a web of internal connections that can be linked to ever expanding webs in cyberspace, always and never there at the same time.

The limits of hypertext are also the limits of the screen, but one can have multiple windows and screens and thus appear to move through a third dimension and perhaps even into other dimensions. The largest unit of a hypertext is a web, which could theoretically be arranged as a single visible hypertext were the screen large enough, but which is usually portrayed as a series of windows within windows, each window containing a network of what is contained below or within it. One must usually move through the web sequentially in order to encounter the various weblets, but one may also go back to the larger web. The web exists in a self-contained hypertext, but is at its most potent and far-reaching on the World Wide Web, the electronic master Web accessible through various online services. This web is constantly expanding. In a web, the links are multiple and not necessarily hierarchical or cross-tabbed. The movement from place to place may be in many directions. One is taken out of two-dimensional space, at least metaphorically.

THE VIRTUAL SIMULACRUM

We believe that what we see on the screen is the text, but it is only a simulacrum of the text, just as a copy of the book is only a simulacrum of the text. In the literate world before print, a book was what one copied down from an oral recitation or what one had copied from a manuscript. It was a record of an oral performance and was often used to summon up a subsequent performance. With print, there came multiple copies of a text that were identical. No one of them was any more the "true" text than any other. In the past century, scholars, led, perhaps by Biblical scholars, have sought to identify that true text in critical editions, variorums, and what was known as textual scholarship (this was perhaps a fool's chase, for there was no more a source manuscript of the Bible than there was Homer's original draft of *The Iliad*). All of these searches were for the source or immanent text, which is the one from which all others are either simulacra or debased copies. In many cases, the search has proved fruitless, for if an author revised a manuscript to create a printed version and then corrected the printed version several times for subsequent editions, there is no clear rule for determining which version is the immanent text. Recent editors of writers such as Samuel Taylor Coleridge or Dante Gabriel Rossetti have found it useful to have each of the versions available on disk or as a site on the World Wide Web rather than to decide that one version was the true one. What they have amassed is a compilation of textual images that can be manipulated in multiple ways.

If the immanent text is hard to pin down in the case of printed books, it is even harder to pin down in the electronic world because the electronic text or even the hypertext has less semblance of permanence than the written or printed "hard copy" appeared to have. One can copy disks, true, but the hypertexts change with each reading, and if they are added to or manipulated by readers, then the modified disks prove unwieldy objects through which to retrieve an "original version." Similarly, no two readers move through the web in the same way, and even a single reader is hard put to retrace his or her journey.

COMICS AS A WAY OF UNDERSTANDING HYPERTEXT

When we think of hypertext, we search for an analogy. In some sense, there is no clear analogy, it is all too new and too different a medium, having no text but what one can lose in a power failure. However, many of us who grew up in the world of print find an analogy in the newspaper and particularly in the comic pages or the comic book. Certainly this is true for me, for the comics were central to my education in the world of text. These are clearly the print texts where the visual is most clearly and obviously a major player, as they are based on a combination of printed word and image, and laid out in a manner that requires a particular sort of visual layout and processing. Marshall McLuhan (1994) noted that the newspaper's juxtaposition of article and advertisement meant a curious junction and disjunction. I find a similar point of reference in comics. Comics help me and many others understand what it means to have the spaces and links of hypertext and also to comprehend the nature of printed texts and how they work.

Comics were a staple of the recreational diet of most of those who grew up in the 1930s and 1940s. We could read about sports in comics, follow the war in comics, learn about the forces of good and evil in comics, and even read most of the classics in a comic book version. The military even used them to explain the principles of war machinery and field sanitation. Print comics were supplemented on Saturday by the movies and particularly the serial and the news and cartoon that went with the feature, but the staple diet was the comic. It is still with us, just as it has been with people since the Caves of Lascaux, the tombs of the Pharaohs, the Bayeux Tapestry, or The Book of the Hours. In India, comic book versions of *Ramayana* and *Mahabarata* are popular versions of the texts—or were until the videos appeared. They are popular because they do not pretend to be other than visual, and they combine the graphic system of written language with another graphic system to be a thoroughly visual medium. They are, perhaps, the Western version of Chinese calligraphic writing; certainly they are like scroll paintings. The comic is built on an interplay of picture and text. It is an entirely visual medium in that the eye must be used to make sense of the relation between picture and text. The text must be seen in order to know who is speaking—if indeed it is speech that is in the bubbles.

The comic strip and the comic book form one of the print precursors of hypertext—or perhaps are themselves an early form of hypertext. The major theoretical work on comics has been done by Will Eisner (1990) in *Comics and Sequential Art*, Scott McCloud (1993) in *Understanding Comics: The Invisible Art*, and Harvey (1996) in *The Art of the Comic Book: An Aesthetic History*. I think that it will help to explore them as a way of understanding hypertext, but also as a way of understanding the world of texts and writing.

Comics work by taking text out of the lockstep convention. They do so by adding space to text and most clearly by treating the text as but a part of the iconic complex. Traditional texts are framed in dimensions. They go across and down. Of course the pages add thickness, but how does that figure, when we see only one double-page spread at a time? Generally the thickness of the book is not a factor in its imaging of reality. The reader and the writer are forced into a cross-linear pattern, and the pattern is generally rigid—left to right, top to bottom, and so on to the next page of the codex; recto, verso, recto, verso until we get to the thick cover and are let out.

Comics provide a chance to break and to understand this configuration. The gutters between the panels and the shape of the panels on the page form a hypertext configuration. That is to say that the reader (guided by the artist, of course) connects the panels in many different ways. The connections may be temporal or visual. The resultant pattern on the page may be horizontal–vertical or it may be circular, or (using arrows) a criss-cross or boustrophedon (the form of text that reverses itself at each line like the movement of an ox pulling a plow). In the newspaper, the separate strips form a tapestry of two or three dozen separate patterns that one may read in any order. Some readers tell me that they scan and search for specific strips, others tell me that they read them in a vertical boustrophedon, down one column and up the next, and thus four times on a double-paged spread.

In another way, comics resemble hypertext. In the newer comics, particularly those created by Stan Lee and in some of the serial strips like *Doonesbury* or *Prince Valiant*, the basic narrative conventions have been changed so that there is no story with a beginning, middle, and end. The reader can come into the book with any issue or the strip on any day. The characters come in and out and the relation between volumes or weeks is one of associational links in a web, not a sequenced short story or novella—the preferred form of the earlier comics.

Gutters

In comics, the gutter is where the reader interpolates a connection between frames. According to McCloud (1993), the most frequent types of connections implied by gutters are: moment-to-moment, action–reaction, subject-to-subject, scene-to-scene, aspect-to-aspect, and non sequitur. The reader, of course, can make other connections or break them. The gutter serves some of the function of the rest in music or more particularly the silence between movements. It also serves the function of the space between words in a sentence, sentences in a paragraph, and paragraphs in text, or between the spaces in a hypertext. The connections and links are made by the reader, who then works together with the artist to be a re-creator of the comic, the book, or the hypertext.

Sequence

These connections that are made by the mind in looking at a gutter are such that the reader creates a sequence from the arrangement of spaces on the page. This sequence can be from upper left to bottom right as is the normal sequence in the West, but it need not be. There can be arrows that lead the reader through a serpentine or even an inverse path. The sequence helps us to relate the space of the picture to the idea of time that is contained in the pictures and often between them.

Comics and Hypertext

In their great variety, comics help us to understand the ways in which hypertext and writing on the screen work. They do so by showing us the intimate relation of text and picture and therefore of the pictorial nature of text. They lead us to an appreciation of the icon and the image and its part in our making sense of the relations among objects, and they point to the ways by which the writer and the reader work together to make meaning. However, comics go further than that. They lead us back to an appreciation of the image as a positive and integral part of our use of written language; they reconnect us with the world of the picture and the icon (see Bolter, chap. 1, this volume). Through comics we can see our cultural roots in protowriting (the cave drawing, the pictograph on a stone, the Native American sand painting, the pattern, the calligraphy of the handwriting on the wall). The new form of communication on and off screen is iconic. Because it is iconic, it causes us to rethink the iconic nature of texts as well as hypertext.

THE NATURE OF READERS:
WHAT IS IT WE DO WHEN WE READ A TEXT?

What is it we do when we read a text? The simple and immediate answer is that we see the various marks on the page—letters, groups of letters we call words, groups of words we call sentences and paragraphs, groups of sentences and paragraphs we call chapters and sections. We see them, and we work at making connections across the blank spaces between them. That is reading—filling in the white spaces between words—or reading in and between the lines. After we make those connections, we make others between what we already know and remember and what we see. People who write about reading use the term *response* to describe these connections between the text and the reader's mind and memories. The term implies that readers are like Pavlov's salivating dogs even though the research tends to suggest that such is not the case. The fact of hypertext suggests that the role of the reader is much more like that of the author. I would argue that when we read hypertext we are coauthoring the text. It was so in the world of print even though we tended not to be aware of it.

A Surfeit of Authors

In the world of hypertext there are many authors as well as scribes. There are the authors in the machine, the programmers and keyboarders, and the readers who rewrite the text each time they read it. In this world, there is a surfeit of authors; everyone is an author. There is an originating author, but the originator may simply set forth the pieces of the game or the spaces of the hypertext and create the web. The successive users (readers) can re-create, change, and reorder the spaces. They, too, are authors of their part of the hypertext web by creating weblets within the web. The hypertext is highly mutable. Given the fact that it consists of a set of spaces and links between them that different readers can combine in different ways, the hypertext is not the set production of an author; it is mutable in each reading, which creates a new web. Just as Adam read in order to name, so the reader of a hypertext simultaneously reads and composes. The activity is a tangible version of what authors have been doing for centuries. With hypertext, the operation is patent, not hidden.

That being the case, where is authority over the text? Where is authority in the text? To whom or to what is there to be obedience? Who is the originator of influence? It would seem to be an anarchy. Do authors today have the same sort of authority as they did of old? Has the author disappeared or receded in the world of hypertext? Actually, the author lost authority before the advent of hypertext—at least the literary author lost it. From the time of Aristotle, Western critics have focused their concern and research on the actions of the author or the action of the reader. Modernist critics sought to focus on the text itself, to strip away the perceiving self so as to see the object as in itself as it really is, but their efforts have since been seen as fruitless. The object is hard to isolate from the artist and the viewer. Yeats (1957) asked "How can we know the dancer from the dance?" (p. 446). We might also ask who can tell the reader from the text? In the heyday of modernist criticism, the poem was an autonomous object whose meaning and value could not be authorized by the writer. The author creates a work of art that remains immutable and silent like a statue. Then the author steps aside. The text stands alone and in this modernist view, the immutable text is an object for criticism and remains in a sense, dumb. Archibald MacLeish (1976) summed it up with the expression from *Ars Poetica*, "A poem should not mean but be" (p. 107).

Later, as the modern critics gave way to the postmodern ones, there came to be an emphasis on the reader as the authority for meaning. Who is in control is a perplexing question. Equally perplexing is this question: Who are the authors in and of the word-processed text? Who is the author of this book? Me, the programmers, my colleagues who made comments and suggestions, the spell checker, the editors, the printer? The author can do nothing about it, and perhaps does not want to; for the creative act of coauthoring is finally liberating. However, some authors find it discomfiting and use various tricks and devices to assure the reader that they are in control. There has been a spate of books in which the author (or the assumed author) becomes a character in the book, telling the reader that he or she is really in control over the characters and their lives. This phenomenon occurs in the fiction of Umberto Eco, Michael Ende, Salman Rushdie, and others. They are following the lead of Laurence Sterne and Jorge Luis Borges who developed the idea of the author as master trickster, the person who controlled the whole illusion of the fiction. They tried to claim authority, but in doing so they raised the question as to whether the author had any control or not. The author has not surrendered authority but shared it with the readers.

Author! Author?

The author is displaced and the reason lies in part in the dilemma I cited earlier, but it is also a feature of the ways by which the mass media have tended to treat the author. The author may not be the central figure in a film or a television script. It is usually the actor or the director. The director is often seen as the auteur, but it is often hard to determine the degree of control of a Steven Spielberg or a Jane Campion. In the case of Woody Allen or Spike Lee we seem to have the sense of clear authority. For Allen, it is also because he is the visible person in the film, the star. To a great extent the authority of the media is transferred from the author to the actor. In the world of mass media, authority goes to the visible or the audible, not to the originator, script, writer, director, or camera person, those who most surely determine what we see and hear. The emphasis is on the who, not the what.

In the world of hypertext, there are a number of authors: (a) the program authoring team, (b) the writer of the original text, (c) the writers in the program (e.g., the sorters, spelling checkers, organizers, editors, and converters), (d) the networked coauthors, and (e) the readers who redact the text as they read. The hypertext is in some sense never finished. This does not mean that we cannot identify authors A and B; author C is invisible; author D is somewhat more elusive; author E is the role that most of us inhabit, although we may shift roles among the other four.

Authority and Control of Hypertext

Who controls the reading of the hypertext? The writer clearly established the spaces in the first place and also forged the links. However, each reader can take a variety of different paths and ignore, reorder, change, delete, and supplement spaces and paths. Who is the boss anyhow? Is being the boss the right question? The question? Have we all along avoided the question? Isn't the hypertext question simply bringing into plain sight a series of questions we should have been asking all along about all sorts of texts? If the question of control and authority changes with respect to text, what are the broader implications in society? What are the theological implications?

The Writer Controls the Text, the Text Controls the Reader, Convention Controls the Writer. Invisibly, the text controls how we read. The comic book is a useful example of how this control operates, but also how we maneuver through the apparent and invisible controls. Hypertext changes the form of control as well as the nature of control. In electronic space, where simultaneous text spaces surround the reader and writer or are displayed on the screen, the motion of reading or writing is not determined by the left-to-right, top-to-bottom, front-to-back fixity of the book. One may float through the spaces in a number of different orders and skip from the inside of one space to the outside of another. This skipping occurs for both writer and reader. The number of dimensions of movement expands. It is unlikely that two readings will be precisely the same. The fixity of print controlled writer and reader.

No such control now exists. There are other kinds of control: the memory of the machine, the nature of the program, the size and resolution of the screen.

However, writer and reader can surf on the text just as they can surf on the Internet or cable television. This means that hypertext differs from traditional text in being not nonlinear, but multilinear. Perhaps multidirectional is the better word. It also differs in that the visible text and the conceptual text are not coincident. An interactive hypertext adds the possibility for the readers to take the spaces and make new connections, to add spaces, and to add to the space. In this sense the reader is an author and a group of readers are coauthors. The reader or author creates a new text order. This means that the nature of interpretation is different from that which has often been posited.

The Relation of Interpretation to the Text.   When we think about interpretations, we think about them in relation to the thing we call a text. The text is the common element of a large number of interpretations (or perhaps one of the common elements). But how we think of a text can vary; we can see it in relation to the author, to language, to other texts, to the world, and to the reader. That is, the text can be seen as an expression of an individual whose name we may know; someone wrote a letter or a book, and we can wonder what he or she meant. But we could simply see it as a selection of written language; so we would just examine the vocabulary and the grammar and see what meaning emerges from them. That is what people do when they try to decipher a strange or mysterious text like the Rosetta Stone.

Another way of looking at any one text is to see it in relation to all the other texts that have been written, as if it were a part of a large jigsaw puzzle of texts. Scholars of the Bible do this when they try to determine the relation of one Gospel to another, or to determine where one part of the prophets fits into the larger scheme of prophecy literature. Still another way of viewing the text is as a point of reference to an external world, so that we assume that a set of numbers in a telephone directory are a signal for anyone to punch those numbers on a phone and speak to the person listed. We make the same assumption about history and many textbooks; the events they describe are what actually happened. Finally, we may think of the text as being intended to affect an audience; what happens to us as readers is what is important. Any text can be interpreted with reference to any one or combination of this set of relations. None of them is any better or more correct than any other, but scholarly wars are fought over which should prevail, and which one does prevail at a given time can affect a great number of other aspects of our mental and spiritual lives.

Critics and philosophers have worried and disputed long about the relation of interpretations to the text. There are thousands of interpretive articles and treatises on *Hamlet* and even more on the Book of Job. Many of them attack previous ones in order to build their point. When I was a graduate student working on my dissertation, I had to establish first that no one had ever written on my specific topic and second that I had read all the other critics and either refuted them or used them to support or extend my argument. I remember a philosophy graduate student telling me I was lucky to be working on Coleridge; he was thinking about working on Immanuel Kant and that meant 3 years of reading just to establish his topic.

One question that interpretations raise is that of validity. Is one reader's interpretation of either *Hamlet* or Job closer to the true meaning of the book than the other's? Or is each of them as probable as any of the others? These raise the question as to whether there is a true meaning and how we would know if we found it. The answer to that question depends in part on how we view the text. The argument is whether the appropriate metaphor is that of an onion or that of barnacles. If we see the text as an onion, we see the interpretations as peeling away the protective layers of skin until we arrive at the kernel or essence of the true meaning of the text. This position is expressed by the philosopher Georg Gadamer (cited in Weinsheimer, 1985), who argued that the text has a deep meaning that can be uncovered by the hermeneutic method. If we take up the barnacle position, we are in the camp of the French philosopher of deconstruction, Derrida. This school of thought argues that the text is a surface on which interpretations attach themselves. The result is that a complex of texts on texts has been built. We cannot say that any of them is closer to the center, for the hull of the text is impenetrable.

Or, we may take the position that a text is a space in a hypertextual world. In that case, both Gadamer and Derrida are held in balance. Within the text–reader space there is the hermeneutic approach that seeks to unfold or create or coauthor a deep meaning; simultaneously, the meaning of that coauthorship is necessarily piled onto or related to other hermeneutic attempts in a larger web of meanings that constantly unfold and expand and become interrelated and attenuated. The world of hypertext suggests that as we read, we peel the onion, but a part of the outer peel is encrusted with barnacles, and to the next reader who visits the text space and sees what we have done (provided we left our mark), we too are a barnacle, and so on, ad infinitum. Hypertext therefore sharpens the question of the relationship of a reader with the text by raising and holding as paradox that the reader is both passive and active; the reader both makes meaning of the text and takes meaning from it.

THE DISSOLUTION OF CENTERS OF LEARNING AND THE RESHAPING OF CULTURE

Within a culture or society, there has always been some center of learning, a special time or place whereby the lore of the culture could be passed from generation to generation and where the learning could be added to and modified. It could be seen as the storehouse of information out of which the knowledge of the individual and the learning of the culture could be formed. Jacques Ellul (1985) argued that the center of learning in the oral world is the ceremony. In the written or print world, it is the library. Where is it in the electronic world? This is a political and epistemological question of great moment. It is also a pedagogical question, for it speaks to the future of the whole educational enterprise.

Where do I go to be connected to the past, to gain that sense of wholeness that enables me to see how I am related to such entities as my heritage, my culture, and my roots? One that I have turned to has been the library, the set of books and documents that form the repository of things known: my genealogy, the history of America, the classics, the Bible. But I have also turned at times in my life to a variety of rituals, to the ceremony of the dinner table, to the church service, to the classroom, to the annual professional meeting. These also provide a center of learning and culture.

The Persistence of Ceremony

Ellul (1985) suggested that in the world of print we leave ceremony behind. I do not think so. It is in ceremony that books take on their place. The center of learning may have been the library, but it was also a set of actions in and around the library. When I was a graduate student, there was a time to enter the library, people whom one saw there daily, to whom one spoke. There were set places for different orders of students. There were rituals of leaving books in spaces, of checking out books, and of sharing. The coffee breaks were a part of the library and its use.

Centers of learning may shift in accordance with the technology, but that does not mean that the new center forsakes some of the trappings of the old. In the oral world, the ceremony, be it one of birth, growth, marriage, conquest, or death, provided a means for a culture to express its strongest feelings about those things that mattered most—the things that are related to the cycle of life. The ceremonies, rituals, and lore associated with these issues are the constituents of culture according to Giambattista Vico (1984); they are what distinguish one culture from another. They set the patterns for stories, rituals, and taboos. In the ceremony the elders teach the younger about the past of the culture and about what distinguishes the culture from others.

We can see the vestiges of these ceremonial centers of learning in the variety of rituals that cultures have today. The birth, marriage, and death of a culture may be individual or communal. Thus we can see that the ceremonies surrounding sports events are a part of the learning of the culture of the team and of the sport. The entrance of the team, the playing of the national anthem, the warm-up, the intervals between action, the victory and defeat rituals, all of these are ceremonies in which the elders initiate the youth—whether spectator or player. Such ceremonies may be part of the daily routine of a family; what happens on arising, the service of breakfast or dinner, the devotions before going to bed. Rituals are clearly the center of learning in many religions. What goes on in the service, who speaks, in what tones, what instruments are allowed, where people sit, how they sit or stand: All of these are part of the learning of the group. In an oral society these ceremonies—daily, seasonal, or periodic—were the foci of all the knowledge of that culture. They remain so as the foci of such cultures as that of a family or a community.

The Library

When Ellul (1984) named the library as the center of learning in the print society, I think he was suggesting that the repository of the book, rather than a single book, serves as the center. The library is the place to which one goes to find the book or books that are reputed to contain the important knowledge of the society. The knowledge is not contained in a single book but in a collection. It is a collection that accretes over time just as the ceremony accretes and changes over time. The early libraries were restricted in what they contained, so it was easy to see that learning was in the totality of the library.

Such appears to have been the case of a library like the one at Alexandria or at Pergamum, the home of parchment. Such appears also to have been the case of the library in the Hebrew temple and particularly in the monastery. There, in the scriptorium, the place where books where kept and copied, lay the heart of the learning and the culture of that monastery. However, the monastery library was also the place from which books were taken to be read aloud from at the ceremonies of the monks or nuns. There would be reading at meals and at various services. Most of these readings were from the sacred scripture, but some also were from the church fathers. The library served a function within the world of the monastery, so that the learning came not simply from the reading of the book, but from the book's becoming a part of a ceremonial and scriptural process.

The Secular University

The library, of course, expanded out from the monastery and into the secular world. As the universities were created—Bologna, Paris, Oxford, and Cambridge—they found at their center the library. This building was the repository of what was known in the field.

It was the place that served as a hub of the university. However, the function of the library as a center of learning did not mean that ceremony disappeared. The texts of the library were read by the students and the scholars and teachers. Yet, it was not simply the solitary reading and accumulation of knowledge that has been important in the university; ceremonies around the reading are equally important.

One form of ceremony is the lecture, the large forum in which the professor, the person of learning, talks about a book that is in the library and that the students have presumably read. The lecture serves as a commentary on the book, a set of notes to the codex of the book, and an addition to it. The book sits at the center of a secular liturgy of talk about what is the meaning or what are the meanings of the book. Thus the library becomes a source for talk, not just for reading.

Another form of talk about the book that takes place in the center of learning is the colloquium or the seminar. In this format, the master reader of the book inducts a group of neophytes into ways of talking about the book. The rules of this discourse are carefully rehearsed and practiced by the students so that they, too, can become masters. They are not learning to lecture—not yet—but they are taking part in a communal liturgical reading of the text. In some versions, the seminar is formal; in others it is informal. The end, however, is induction into the ceremonies of learning around the book.

Stephen Leacock (1923), the Canadian humorist, described the peculiarly British version of this seminar, when a small group of students came to the don's study, having read the book, and waited while the don smoked at them and occasionally grunted. This form is also known as the tutorial. Here the ceremony places greater responsibility on the catechumens. In all of this activity of ceremonial talk about the secular scriptures of the university, the object is to increase the size of the library. It is important to learn not only to talk about the books one reads, but to add written commentary on them in the form of notes, treatises, criticisms, and the like. As the process continues, the library swells. It grows beyond its bounds as it becomes increasingly important for the ceremony to include commentaries from outside the walls of a particular university. So, the commentaries from one center of learning are added to others, and the whole swells.

When I was a graduate student in the 1950s, we were told that in order to claim a dissertation topic, we had to read everything else on the topic and prove that our topic was new—"a contribution to scholarship" was the term used. For that reason, my colleagues in philosophy claimed, no one wrote a dissertation on Kant; it was impossible to get through the reading. In literature, this seemed true of Shakespeare. People published handbooks at that time to help students find a topic that had not been pursued. Such a stricture could not be applied today in most areas of the humanities, history, or even the social sciences. The amount of information on a topic grows too fast. The library can no longer be the center of learning. Where in hyperspace is it?

The Heart of the Machine

In an age where libraries are connected electronically, where bibliographies and databases are online and updated daily, it is difficult to locate a center of learning. Many universities are cutting down on their actual book and journal purchases in favor of using other sources of information. It is possible to browse the catalogs of other university libraries and thus create a hyperlibrary.

There is no reason for the university campus to be built around a library. In fact there is no reason for a campus. During the past 20 years there has been a growth in the "open university" or "the university without walls," the campus that has no central lectures or seminars and no library. It is the correspondence school gone high-tech, using televisions, telephones, and computers to connect students to each other and to faculty. There may be sites where groups can congregate, but with the advent of the bulletin board or the wide area network, these are not as important to the smooth functioning of the open university as they once were. Another feature of these campuses without walls is that they do not use a permanent faculty of professors and dons. There may be course designers and lecturers, but they are separated from the mentors or discussion leaders. The faculty, therefore can be a group of independent "wandering scholars," rather than a cozy group of people who meet for lunch at the faculty club.

The university has no center and the library is no longer a physical center. There may still be ceremonies, but they may well differ from the ceremonies of the lecture and seminar. As yet, we do not know what they might be, although it would seem that there must be some means for talk, the learning of rituals, and other means of certifying the induction of the individual.

However, the electronic university is one where the center is the circumference. Or rather, there is no center in that all is outside. Learning exists in a moebius strip or a Klein bottle. All sources of information are available to anyone who has a computer and a modem. These people can connect with any database; bring into their rooms text, pictures, sound, and information on all subjects in virtually all media; and then re-create or combine it in any one of a number of ways. The center of learning is the electric plug or the telephone line. Perhaps it is the screen or the mouse. Perhaps it is the hard drive. But there must be some ways for the individuals to participate in the ceremony of learning. Can they do it physically? Can they do it virtually?

Cyberlearning

The center of learning is the focal point for the individual to connect to the larger human and social world. When the center of learning was in the ceremony, it was because through the various ceremonies and rituals people learned what it was to be social, what knowledge was worth being passed on, and what it was that helped constitute a culture. The learning was transmitted from person to person or group to individual. We learned through sight and hearing and imitation by our bodies.

With the advent of writing, there came to be the possibility that information could exist outside of the minds and mouths and movements of the people who created that information. The repositories of learning became impersonal; they survived the individual and the community. The individual could plug into the communal texts or their repository, the library. The people in charge of the library, of course, determined what knowledge was worth having. In this respect it was no different from those who controlled the ceremonies. However, it is wrong to think that the library replaced the ceremony. It supplemented it at first; then it came to dominate the ceremony as it took on more and more of the responsibility for maintaining itself as the center of learning. But in doing so, the library developed ceremonies about its use. It had initiation rites and sacred dates and times. Ceremony remained.

The library could be relatively small and local for a long time, but as transportation changed the relationships of people and as printing enabled the reproduction of texts and their spread around the world, the information and learning grew too large for there to be all but a few large libraries with their branches. The scholarly world flowed from the

New York Public Library to the Library of Congress to the British Museum, the Bibliothèque Nationale, and the Moscow Library. As the amount of information became too large and unwieldy, the electronic revolution enabled it to manage the vast conglomeration of materials. First there came library networks and complexes of interlibrary loan.

Now the library itself appears to be at risk of being supplanted or supplemented electronically. There need not be a physical repository of objects we call books or journals. There can be tapes or chips or disks with digitized language, sound, or images. The physical center that is the library is dissipated into thousands of nodes. The learning is diffuse and infinitely reorganizable into home collections garnered on the Internet, downloaded onto a hard drive or a Bernoulli disk, and then read or heard.

However, this does not mean that the concept of library is gone, just as ceremony failed to disappear with the advent of the library. Both remain; both are important centers of learning. They have changed and they take their place enfolded into the new cybercenter, but at the same time they enfold it. Just as the library replaced the ceremony as the center, the ceremonies of the library themselves became centers of the centers of learning. So too, the cybercenter replaces the library, but the library is the repository of the cybercenter and the ceremonies of access and use remain paramount. We cannot avoid enfolding the present in the past and holding onto those centers of learning that have worked for us.

IN CONCLUSION

These are but three of the massive changes we are undergoing with the advent of hypertext and hypermedia. They are paralleled by massive changes in transportation, and in the new world of images and sound as hypermedia, a topic that could be another chapter. These are changes that are presaged and marked intellectually by what we have called postmodernism, which I would probably call *post-textualism*. The ethos of the printed text is disappearing.

Books and printed matter will not go away. That is not what I mean; rather, I mean that the ways of thinking about and with and through text are changed utterly by the new technology. The technology is helping to change our very consciousness. The way we viewed things when I was a student is not the way my grandchildren will view them. Today we see the web of text differently, and we read differently. We think of what the center of learning is differently, and this means that education and the training of scribes will change. They will go on, because it is ever more important to have a scribal population, not merely a literate one. For me the process of change is fascinating, and I am enjoying the world I see.

REFERENCES

Eisner, W. (1990). *Comics and sequential art*. Tamarac, FL: Poorhouse Press.
Ellul, J. (1985). *The humiliation of the word* (J. M. Hanks, Trans.). Grand Rapids, MI: Eerdmans.
Harvey, R. C. (1996). *The art of the comic book: An aesthetic history*. Jackson: University of Mississippi Press.
Leacock, S. (1923). *College days*. New York: Dodd Mead.
MacLeish, A. (1976). *New and collected poems*. Boston: Houghton Mifflin.
McCloud, S. (1993). *Understanding comics: The invisible art*. Northampton, MA: Kitchen Sink Press.
McLuhan, M. (1994). *Understanding media*. Cambridge, MA: MIT Press.
Olson, D. R. (1994). *The world on paper*. New York: Cambridge University Press.

Vico, G. (1984). *The new science of Giambattista Vico* (T. G. Bergin & M. H. Fisch, Trans.). Ithaca, NY: Cornell University Press.

Weinsheimer, J. (1985). *Gadamer's hermeneutics: A reading of truth and method.* New Haven, CT: Yale University Press.

Yeats, W. B. (1957). Among school children. In P. Allt & R. K. Alspach (Eds.), *The variorum edition of the poems of W. B. Yeats* (p. 446). New York: Macmillan.

APPENDIX

Sumer 3000 BCE

It was a hot day at the bazaar. But then it was always a hot day at the bazaar. Hot, dusty, and dry. The camels and asses laden with the huge jars lumbered down the track. Calls and cries of drovers echoed off the mud walls. In front of the doorway Martuk sat, cross-legged, his tray on his lap. On the tray were sets of bullae. Each one was about the size of a dropping—and about the same shape, Martuk thought, as he lifted each clay pouch and shook it checking for the rattle.

His master came up behind him. "I hear that the oil caravan is on its way here. Be ready son. I do not want to be cheated."

"Yes, Master. I shall be ready." Alert and tense, he put the tray under a cloth.

The sound of camel bells grew louder as did the cries of the drovers. Martuk sat straight, staring at the tent opposite him until he spotted out of the corner of his eye the short plump figure of the leader of the caravan walking a few paces ahead of the first heavily laden camel. The camels headed on past towards the great warehouse.

"So, young slave, is your master within?" The man asked in a peremptory voice, taking his pack from his shoulders and squatting down in front of Martuk.

"He is within."

"Tell him I have ten jars of the best olive oil to sell him."

"I do not think he will want less than fifteen, sir."

"And I shall sell them, but I shall want to take with me seven jars of dried figs and six jars of sesame seed."

The master came out from his shop where he had been listening to the exchange. "So," he said, "this oil is good? It had better be; the last you brought was rancid."

"Freshly pressed from the trees in the foothills," replied the man.

"Very well, then see to the exchange, Martuk."

The man reached into his pack and counted out fifteen bullae. Martuk tested each one by looking at the symbol on the pouch and shaking it to hear the rattle. Then he uncovered a corner of his tray and counted out seven bullae with a different symbol and six more with still another symbol. The set the man had given him he put on a red cloth; the other on a blue cloth. He looked at the man. The man nodded. Martuk covered his tray, folded the cloths around their precious cargo, and called to the boy who had been playing in the dirt nearby.

"Little brother," he said, and handed him the two cloth parcels. "Take these to the warehouse and give them to Set. Do not lose them and have Set open each carefully and look to the jars for a match."

"Yes, Martuk." The boy scampered off. The man and Martuk's master went in for a ceremonial glass of wine. Martuk thought about what he had done. In the dirt in front of him, he traced the figures he had been examining so carefully. They were clear, he thought.

Why bother with the molded symbols inside? The markings on the pouch are enough for me. He pondered.

Venice, 1503 CE

"I am not sure that I like the idea," the Duke said testily. "This is not the way books should be."

"But father," protested the son, "think of people like me."

"You should simply have to wait, just as I did." The Duke snorted, "Books are meant to be treasures, particularly the books of the ancients. I believe people should pay several gold ducats for an Aristotle, a Virgil, or a Plutarch, not a matter of a few soldi."

"Besides," he added. "Books should be big. Handsome folios bound in the best burnished calf with tooling and fine gold lettering. Messer Aldus is simply ruining the whole idea of the book."

The Duke turned to go out of the shop of the Aldine Press. From out of the back room Master Aldus himself came. He saw the older man's back and the younger man's grimace of disappointment as he turned to follow. "Wait, my Lord Duke," Aldus called. "Things may not be as dire as you think."

Aldus Manutius and his partner Andrea Torresini had recently joined forces. Aldus was the scholar, the man who had studied Greek in Rome as well as in Ferrara before coming to Venice to take advantage of the new methods of printing. Knowledgeable in Latin and particularly Greek, familiar with nearly all the ancient authors, he had determined to present to the world the best copies—the most correct versions of the ancients. The world should have all of the ancient writers available in this new form of printing that would insure that no copy was corrupt. After fifteen years of study and five years mastering the art of printing, he made his move and established his press.

Unhappy with the heavy printing type that had come from Germany, Aldus had admired the Roman straight line type of Nicholas Jenson. He had hired a type founder and setters as he built up his Aldine Press and slowly his reputation and his sales had grown. Now he had a partner and the expansion was beginning. He did not want to lose a customer like the Count—or one like his son. He remembered only too well being like that young man, eager to have the classics that he could hold and read—and yet having no money and being forced to rely on a patron's library where he could look, but not touch or mark.

"My Lord Duke, do not despair," Aldus continued as the older man turned around and glowered at him. "You shall have your fine books. Take a look at this folio copy of the Georgics, Sire. Notice that the type is not the squared off Roman, but a new design we have perfected. The letters slant just like the finest Italian hand. I have called it 'italic.' No, we will continue to produce grand books for libraries, folios and quartos, nothing but the best rag carefully sewn and bound in tooled calf. This will cost several gold ducats."

The Duke beamed, and his son looked dismayed. Noticing this look, Aldus continued, "And for you Messer Antonio, and for the young scholars who want to know the classics, I have designed a new kind of book. The sheets are designed in eight sections, an octavo, which will produce a small volume that you may carry with you in your purse or in a saddlebag. These will be bound in a simple cloth or half leather and will be sold for a few soldi only. These will be the student's editions, the Aldine editions of all the classics, so that the young may grow in full knowledge of the wisdom and beauty of the ancients. What a wonderful world of knowledge we shall have, Messer Antonio."

The younger man was beside himself with joy at the prospect, and the father responded. "Messer Aldus, I must say I admire you. You are going to make learning and beauty come to Venice and all of Italy . . . and I shall still have my treasures."

15

▼▼▼▼▼▼▼

Technology as Enfranchisement and Cultural Development: Crisscrossing Symbol Systems, Paradigm Shifts, and Social-Cultural Considerations

Robert Tierney
Suzanne Damarin
Ohio State University

In our view, technologies have various evocative potentials and invite use toward varied, often contradictory, ends: to liberate or to subjugate; to support reflexivity and transferability or to limit engagements to rote learnings; to support understandings of cultural plurality and multiple epistemologies or to indoctrinate a singular totalizing perspective.

Underlying our perspective is a recognition that through the ages people have developed symbol systems and these symbol systems have afforded new possibilities for engagement with self, others, and the world. Various means of representations open us to new possibilities, including achieving new insights and ways of interacting with others, ourselves, and ideas. When different groups are given the opportunity to use different media or symbol systems to explore their world or to solve problems, they depict similar phenomenon differently. Using various media, they cut and paste drawings, talk, and play to achieve different perspectives on their world, solve problems, make plans, and communicate with others. With advances in technology, the same differences are apparent with electronic media. Electronic communications are apt to involve a mix of transactions and media including speech, faxes, word processing documents, scanning, and video images as different media are being used separately and together to communicate, solve problems, explore ideas, and acquire new understandings.

In this chapter, we explore how the media, the media's role, and one's history with that media define human possibilities. As we explore the possibilities of situational learning experiences, we find ourselves wanting to stretch the sheets of past theories beyond the beds they seem somewhat to cover.

It is as if, in our search for a theory or theories to guide our thinking about making meaning, we find ourselves at a confluence of perspectives that include semiosis and a desire to understand cultural and individual development. We have come to view media and text as inextricably connected with ongoing social interactions and thus serving as cultural tools for forming students' identity of themselves and of their individual and collective view of society. Also important is the status of societies, the status of individuals, and the status of texts themselves. We find it impossible to extract media or a text as a single fixed entity apart from the flow of time and the fabric of verbal and nonverbal exchanges.

As we examine media and texts in different settings, albeit influenced by our sociopolitical biases and by our interest in semiotics and cultural practice, we find ourselves gravitating toward a view of literacy and technology that may diverge from the dominant traditions of the past. In our view, we do not see technology or literacy as single objects of study or single acts of comprehension or conversation, but as ways of knowing the world and ways of building other linkages, which are simultaneously orgasmic and fluid, fabriclike and patterned, individual and social.

Much of our discussion is drawn from the integration of technology as we have observed its use over a period of 5 years in classrooms supported by state-of-the-art technology where high school students engaged in computer-based projects integrated into the curriculum. These classrooms were unique because they represented technology clearly integrated into classroom life for an extended period of time, supported by adequate resources and the continuing professional development of teachers. The classrooms were part of the Apple Classroom of Tomorrow (ACOT) project at West High School in Columbus, Ohio. West High is situated in a lower income area of Columbus. The racial mix within the classrooms includes Appalachians, African Americans, and Asian Americans. Four connected classrooms on the third floor of the high school house ACOT activities and the shared office spaces of the teaching staff. Typical high school subjects were integrated through team teaching, especially for mathematics and science, English, and social studies. There were several workstations set up around each room, together with a rich array of computers and specialized equipment such as laserdisc players, scanners, and desktop publishing facilities. Students had little difficulty finding access to a computer or equipment that afforded video interface capabilities, desktop publishing, and other resources.

One of the goals of ACOT was to examine how technology might be integrated into classrooms as a way of informing Apple Corporation's Advanced Technology Group and its developers about the demands classrooms might place on technology—both software and hardware. ACOT was also intended to serve as a means of clarifying how technologies might serve classrooms if and when state-of-the-art technologies were infused fully into classrooms and were accompanied by supporting resources. The staff and students were engaged in ongoing professional development and their introduction to software and hardware sometimes preceded its availability in the general marketplace.

In order to relate these observations to a fuller discussion of technology, in this chapter we compare situations involving very different technologies. One such situation involved preschool students' use of more conventional technologies—namely paper, cardboard, and various art supplies or "hands-on" resources—used in conjunction with the development of what they came to call Creature City. Comparisons will also be made to what have been referred to as *backyard technologies*—that is, people engaged in recreation or sports. In particular, we describe young children learning boogie boarding in Australia. Finally, we compare technologies that are even more distant from classrooms using computer hardware and software. In hopes of furthering a cultural and historical perspective, our final situation describes the nature and role of bark art that Australian aborigines have produced for centuries.

Our own views of these situations are influenced by our own semiosis and social transactions. The lenses that we have used or the filters we have applied are part of our own sociopolitical history. Tierney is an Australian with some ancestors dating back to the earliest colonialists or postinvasion period and some to more recent Irish and Norwegian immigrants. The description and observations of boogie boarding are tied to Tierney's sustained observations of his sons Shaun and Christopher. The description of the Reggio Emilia preschool project at Campbell Hall is drawn from observations of a project with which Tierney's younger son was involved. The description of ACOT was tied to a collaborative endeavor with Apple Computer, teacher colleagues, and friends at The Ohio State University and West High School. Both of us as coauthors were involved for an extended time with ACOT. Again, our purpose is to explore characteristics of actual uses of media by individuals and groups in different settings and to use these descriptions as a basis for discussing technologies as ways of knowing complex phenomena, particularly from a sociopolitical perspective. The uses we describe range from the use of wood, stone tools, and natural dyes to paper products and to state-of-the-art computer-based multimedia platforms. Some of the settings are in schools and some are not. On first glance, the cases may not appear parallel; on closer examination, they yield some striking, and we think, provocative parallels. We begin with a brief introduction of these situations.

AN OVERVIEW OF THE SITUATIONS

The technology-supported classrooms at West High School associated with the **ACOT project** represented an attempt to provide students with state-of-the-art technology in a constructive learning environment wherein they enlisted media to explore topics, solve problems, and pursue their own projects (see Tierney et al., 1992). Students were able to interact with a community of learners in various subject areas within a context that allows them to explore and learn with a range of multimedia software, databases, and word processing software. Projects and units were carefully selected, planned, and implemented with problem solving in mind. Throughout the projects, the teachers considered ways to facilitate the students' engagement with issues, concepts, and problems as they used media as adjuncts to their learning and simultaneously studied the value of the media for so doing. The students themselves provided one another with help in various forms including expertise, if needed, as well as ongoing critical feedback.

The projects with which the students were engaged represented a wide range of problems, topics, and issues. Typically, the teachers worked together to decide on projects; in many instances, the projects cut across subject areas. Students might be assigned projects such as developing and launching their own rockets, developing video portfolios about themselves, constructing a scaled-down version of the city of Columbus, developing leaflets for community agencies using desktop publishing, and so forth. Often projects involved an extended exploration of a topic. For example, an exploration of China was one such long-term project. In their projects, students were encouraged to explore topics using a range of media and to present an exhibit or demonstration for classmates, teachers, or students in other classes. They might integrate their projects using widely available computer programs such as PageMaker, HyperCard, and SuperCard, using a mix of scanned images, video, and multilevel stacks of ideas. They also had access to computers at home where they could pursue classwork or projects that they might decide to initiate themselves. This level of infusing technology may not be typical, but may be necessary to study the impact of computer media on learning and to develop the culture of the technology classroom to the point to which computer use is universally appropriated.

The **Creature City** project involved the development of a city by a group of children in the Sophie Rogers preschool in Columbus, Ohio. The Sophie Rogers preschool serves as a laboratory for teacher preparation at Ohio State University. The population is an ethnic mix of 4- and 5-year-olds who attend the school 5 days a week. The school is staffed by teachers who also supervise preservice teachers. Over previous years, the teachers have been engaged in a range of professional experiences in which they have explored the role of media in learning as well as community involvement. Stemming from these interests, they have worked closely with the Reggio Emilia preschool staff in Italy and have participated in exchange visits. What began as a simple activity turned into an in-depth project involving the students in designing a miniature city based on their excursions to various buildings as well as what they borrowed from one another and past experiences. The project took several months as they developed their plans, gathered working materials such as cereal boxes and cardboard tubes, constructed their buildings, laid out the city, introduced landscaping as well as miniatures of themselves, and finally invited their families to explore their city with them.

Our inclusion of **boogie boarding** as another situation for analysis is tied to the view that everyday recreational or sports activities employ technologies that afford ways of knowing that parallel electronically based explorations of ideas. Our discussion of boogie boarding is based on Tierney's observation of his two sons in Australia. Boogie boarding occurs at the confluence of surfboard riding, belly boarding, and body surfing and in some ways began as an alternative to or precursor to surfboard riding. Tierney's sons Shaun and Christopher became engaged with boogie boarding in conjunction with their father's stories about surfing and making connections to skateboarding. Although their introduction to the sport had begun on the east coast of the United States, their sustained and in-depth engagement occurred in Australia when they had the opportunity to watch boogie boarders daily and try it themselves once their cousins loaned them boogie boards. They immediately became engaged in conversations about boogie boarding, including cutting, doing spinners, and going for the better waves. They would select waves to try and try again and meanwhile were attentive of what others did, including what they wore and some of their paraphernalia such as flippers, wet suits, gloves, and so forth. Immediately, they became engrossed in conversations about the waves as well as equipment and arranged for their cousins to accompany them as they pursued the purchase of their own boards and eventually wet suits, and so forth. Simultaneously, they watched videos of surfing, pursued magazines about boogie boarding, and displayed posters in their bedroom. Almost daily they would head to the ocean looking for the right waves to try boogie boarding. Conversations with their friends and cousins extended to sandbars, tides, the uniqueness of each wave, each wave set, dangerous conditions, and issues of balance, weight distribution, and the relation of body position to direction and speed. They also helped develop an interest in boogie boarding among their friends back in the United States and began to share their understanding of boogie boarding with others. Over the next several months and years, they became keen boogie boarders, taking their places alongside their friends and their cousins as their understanding and ability to read the ocean expanded.

Finally, our analysis of the **bark art** of the Kunwinjku in western Arnhem Land serves as a historical and cultural comparison. Australian aboriginal clans have used various media such as rock paintings, bark art, dance, facial markings, and music to explore their world and as a means of communication. Viewed objectively, the art employs earth shades in powerful brush strokes representing abstract depictions of animals or other objects. Studying the art, especially its creation and how it is woven into the fabric of life, it is possible to appreciate the art as more than artistic expression and as a way of community building and knowing. We focus on the Kunwinjku's bark art as a feature of their cultural life. To many Westerners, the Kunwinjku art may be perceived as artistic expression with iconic connections to their religion, customs, and environment. It is pursued as souvenirs or artistic artifacts because of visual attraction. To the Kunwinjku, however, the art serves a variety of other functions, especially in its creation. The creation of the art connects clan members to one another and their setting and history.

On one level, these situations can be seen as making different use of separate technologies across unique situations; on another level they suggest that technologies serve similar functions regardless of the situation. We elaborate on this view as we take a closer look at how these diverse technologies all involve ways of knowing and anchor cultural practices.

TECHNOLOGY, LEARNING, AND COMMUNITY BUILDING WITH ELECTRONIC MEDIA AT WEST HIGH

Historically, communication technologies have been used to connect people across distance and time, and around issues, problems, and shared experiences. Undergirding any communication among people is a web of verbal and nonverbal acts that can involve multiple exchanges, multiple participants, and multiple layers of meaning. Teachers and students in schools live their lives amidst many such networks; their lives involve for example, a mix of face-to-face encounters, telephone exchanges, and various print and nonprint media. Over time, these continuous communications and exchanges create the fabric of life, and they define who we are as individuals and how we relate to others in various communities.

By changing the nature of communication, new technologies also change communities within which we live. For example, in some settings e-mail has led to a shift in communication practices that is reshaping the nature of the community itself, including community membership and the nature of participation (see Garner & Gillingham, chap. 13, this volume). At our university, for instance, faculty have become increasingly dependent on e-mail for routine communication; in turn, e-mail appears to have leveraged different expectations as to the conventions and norms of community participation. We come to expect e-mail to take the place of some face-to-face negotiations, to increase accessibility to information, and to permit a wider participation in decision making. E-mail and other new communication technologies may challenge or perpetuate traditional power relationships as well as the manner of negotiation to which individuals and groups are accustomed (see Neilsen, chap. 8, this volume). We also face a host of dilemmas such as addressing the hardware and software demands of new forms of communication and dealing with the shifts in power relationships they may promote.

Even as these new technologies affect the way we communicate, they may also contribute to developing new ways of knowing and new perspectives. These technologies have the potential to offer diverse media that can serve as vehicles for criss-crossing topics or pursuing multilayered compositions. The West High students' China project is a good example. The China project coincided with an exhibition of Chinese artifacts in Columbus dating back to the earliest emperors in China. The students were encouraged to explore various facets of life in China during early imperial dynasties and, toward these ends, were given access to the exhibit and other resources including experts on that period, videos, laserdiscs, photos, and print materials. The students grouped themselves around common interests and in the context of conversations with their peers they began gathering resources in the form of books, pamphlets, photographs, videos, and so forth. With the computer-based technologies and the media they supported, each of the projects became a composite of media involving the development and capturing of conversations, observations, scanned images, video clips, or experiencing firsthand food of the times, different ways of dressing, sporting activities, and so forth. Their explorations of their specific topics involved a mix of these conversations that were tied to reading, viewing films, examining actual artifacts at the exhibit, and firsthand experiences and interviews with experts. Each of the students' explorations took a variety of different turns as their group explored their topic with these media.

The students could be seen discussing what they wanted to do as they directed one another's attention to material they had located in books and other resources stacked on the floor, portions of video they had discovered, as well as scanned images and text they had generated. As they examined the stacks of materials, the explorations of the topic and their projects moved forward. Sometimes the discussions centered on what was relevant, what was irrelevant, and how ideas were related; at other times the discussion focused on how the different media could complement one another or which medium was more effective. As they explored different topics, they generated video screens that combined text, images, and sound, and they discussed how these screens connected to one another should be sequenced. With the electronic media they were using, the students could insert buttons that, if clicked, accessed other layers of information (e.g., a map depicting the Great Wall, additional information on related events, a graphic display of the sequence of events, or a video clip).

Ideas were not treated as unidimensional and sequential; the students embedded ideas within other ideas. The students spent a great deal of time considering how the issues that they were exploring might be explored across an array of still pictures, video segments, text segments, and sound clips. The images, sound tracks, and text connected with each other in complex ways, yielding a multilayered smorgasbord of image, sound, and print. Student presentations included the computer-based mixes of multilayered visual information together with text on various facets of a topic. Supplementing the technology-based presentations were food tastings, posters, verbal presentations, and demonstrations of sports. If outsiders came to this learning situation with traditional views of media and learning, they might not realize what was occurring. Some might see the media as providing ways to make learning more concrete. However, educators attuned to the role of media in transforming ways of knowing would likely recognize that situations such as the China project represent environments in which students are exploring their world with media that afford the use of multiple symbol systems (see Lemke, chap. 17, this volume). They are accessing a range of materials and media connecting them to their environment and providing them with opportunities to study that environment. Indeed, within the class there were ongoing exchanges across group projects to consider how the media are related to the learning that is occurring. As students are exploring ideas, they are integrating their use of media and other resources in a project driven by inquiry. The media appear to complement one another and enrich the students' pursuits. As Siegel (1995) suggested, multimedia explorations afford "a generative power that comes from juxtaposing different ways of knowing, not in an endless play of crossing and crisscrossing, but as a way of positioning students as knowledge makers and reflective inquirers" (p. 473).

However, such learnings do not cloak the sociopolitical positioning that is also transpiring in these situations. Technology contributes to and defines community dynamically by creating a space that is more than a latent social niche. In the classrooms that we observed, the technology contributed to students' sense of who they were individually and collectively. The informal and more formal exchanges served as markers designating team membership and individual enculturation in the shifting practices of the group. This shifting was observable as students pursued their progress and as they learned from one another over time. For example, we observed a wider use of animation and a shift in how students began to view text following the introduction of hypertext. As students became aware of hypertext, they were attracted to its potential to afford a more dramatic presentation of ideas that was more engaging. In developing this awareness some students served as pioneers and some as agents. In turn, increased status was conferred on those who were pioneers or those who were willing to help others. For example, the students, unbeknownst to the teachers, kept tabs on who was willing to help others and who was not. In these ACOT classrooms, the media were intertwined with the emerging fabric of the classroom in a pattern involving the teacher, students, and the possibilities created by new electronic media, but that extended to interactions that did not involve electronic media as well.

In some ways, the students' experience of community building with technologies may foreshadow a future in which electronic or technological expertise and capabilities advantage certain communities over others. There are issues of control within any community. The teachers at West High pursued ways to engage students in collaborative efforts and they also struggled with issues of control and communication; many of the challenges that they faced with the introduction of such technologies emerged at the intersection of new technologies with established modes of classroom operation (see Neilsen, chap. 8, this volume). From our perspective, it appeared that the teachers were concerned that their control of the classroom and their power could be threatened. For example, networked students could open a floodgate of exchanges that might undermine teachers' leadership and their need for a disciplined approach to learning, especially with the students' increased access to resources, means of communication, and expertise. The teachers often struggled with the same issues of control that on a larger scale face governments today. Even in democratic countries such as the United States, government regulation of telecommunication seems to walk a fine line between control and regulation, between the demand for freedom of speech and the desire to maintain control of the media for the public good.

Rules of society and access to diverse media may perpetuate the power of some groups and contribute to the subjugation of others. The changing role of literacy or exclusion from access to becoming literate in using new electronic media is viewed by some as extending a history in which African slaves were prohibited from learning to read. In this context, unequal access to technologies, especially within public schools, is seen as subjugating African Americans (Damarin, in press). Interestingly, Willmot (1988) made a similar point in his history of the settlement or invasion of Australia by the English, which he saw as a well-orchestrated portrayal of aborigines as primitive objects through the omission of any official discussion of their resistance to the British authorities. This analysis is consistent with Niranjana's (1988) extended discussion of the power relationships perpetuated by colonialists through the production of certain texts. To a large extent, their observations fit with a view that technology has to do with the achievement of status where expertise becomes a mode of exchange or currency for achieving status, identity, and a sense of belonging and having a future. It is as if the technologies of communication serve several enculturation functions simultaneously; for example, as the site for a class struggle (Volosinov, 1973) and as the site for belonging and being (Gee, 1990). The thesis that community building is at the core of technological change becomes more apparent in the subsequent examples.

CREATURE CITY: TECHNOLOGIES AND WORLD BUILDERS

In the Creature City project, the use of media meshed with the emerging fabric of community as preschool students were engaged in using more conventional materials in the development of an imaginary city that came to be referred to as Creature City. A description of the project and ways it contributed to building community can be found in the following account written by the children's teacher:

> After the first set of experimental buildings was made (which the group later decided to "trash" because they "weren't very good"), the children focused on constructing a specific building. They chose to take responsibility for a particular building from their list of buildings that they wanted to create for the city. To help the children work more effectively and efficiently, they worked in small groups of 2–3 children collaborating together. At times children from other groups came over to offer suggestions or to aid problem-solving of another group. For example, Christopher and Edith were working on the baseball stadium together while John and William worked on Jurassic Park. When Jurassic Park needed grass and John and William weren't quite sure how to represent it, they checked with Christopher who explained how he represented grass for the baseball field. They spent many months creating buildings of all sorts. The list of buildings they needed to make continued to grow. They also had cottages and several interesting machines.
>
> Work on the buildings sometimes lasted an hour or even longer as the children were so incredibly interested and invested in their building. By March, they had buildings everywhere, all over the school and still more ideas from the children. They ordered two pieces of plywood to serve as the base for the buildings and carefully thought out a map so that the police station was close to the jail and the dinosaurs were away from the rest of the city. Using the map as a guide they anchored the buildings to the plywood, they began organizing, negotiating and implementing the painting of the roads (black), grass (green), water (blue), deep water (purple), lines of the roads (yellow and white/solid and dashed), sidewalks (grayish-white). They created flowers, bushes, trees, animals, snakes, frogs, dinosaurs, etc. An electronic fence was established around Jurassic Park. In addition, work on the bridges and walkways commenced after a research trip to the hospital walkways. Finally, people were introduced. They used photographs of themselves reduced and glued to harder construction paper. Thus, the children became a part of their own city. The last addition to the city was flags and signs which were made with clay, toothpicks, and construction paper. They used the large signs from the block area as models. The children copied the shapes of the signs as well as the letters and then strategically placed them by the roads in the city.
>
> Of course, they needed to have a big party to celebrate all their work. They invited all the families to come to their city party. The children planned out games for the parents to play and got all the materials ready for the games. They made prizes for the winners of the games (which turned out to be everyone so they needed lots of prizes). They planned food to cook for the families and, also, wrote a note to let everyone know about their plans.

As this account suggests, the act of creating the city was inseparable from other social negotiations and positioning. Students learned together and about one another at the same time they negotiated connections with one another as they established norms for group membership in their real and imagined worlds. A sense of belonging to the groups occurred through a commitment to the group's norms, whether that entailed using similar markings, dress or procedural display. Status was achieved by being part of the groups and by developing expertise to be shared.

The technology became both the basis for sharing and a means for sharing. As the students worked together they acted as a community and in so doing adopted different roles and achieved different status within that community. Students alone or with others contributed to different sections of the city at the same time as expertise was differentiated and distributed. This social participation extended beyond negotiated manipulations around the embodiment of an unoccupied city. The city also represented their interests and their worlds. Indeed, their relationship to the city was as both maker and citizen on several occasions, especially as they pasted their own photos on the city, invited their parents to participate in the celebration of the city's completion, and bade their final farewell by disposing of it at the end of the year.

The Creature City project among this group of preschool children has much in common with other simulated worlds that make use of new technologies such as Disney World, and other fantasy and computer-based microworlds. These simulations and the possibilities of virtual reality are increasingly the stuff of both entertainment and education, which begin to overlap and become dynamically integrated. Just as filmmakers rewrite the texts of popular culture into their own versions, Drew, Emily, and the other preschool children of Sophie Rogers rewrote Spielberg's *Jurassic Park* into their own stories and city. The children created a simulacrum, although a small-scale one that was ultimately celebrated and then discarded. Their city was a "copy without an original" and as Baudrillard (1983) argued, such simulations mask the absence of an underlying reality. In making their simulation, the children learned valuable skills and lessons. Interestingly, their city was created first by adding buildings, followed by people, then their symbols and rules of behavior. What is marked in this approach is the prior importance of their own presence in the development of their living and working space. Salient discourses of media and technology are permeated today with such ideas and activities of worlds and world building; we think it is important not only that teachers encourage and support such activity, but also that they help students recognize their own imprints on the worlds they create.

The Creature City project brings to the fore two processes: (a) the process of beginning an evolving classroom project and bringing it to completion some 18 months later, and (b) the process of developing creatures from cylinders and designing and building the city for them. The processes occur simultaneously. The classroom is built and rebuilt from the bottom up in response to human contributions, needs, and activities. The classroom and its activities emerge, guided by the teacher with attention to moment-to-moment contingencies.

In this context, the project emerges not as the implementation of a planned teacher-directed activity, but through the teacher's creative response to children's interest and excitement. The activities allow children to use simple artifacts such as cylinders and yarn, in ways of their own choosing. The children repurposed these simple technologies toward their own conscious or unconscious ends and they investigated the properties of objects in relation to their effects on the senses. Later, and in a more scientific mode, they engaged in research. They became observers of the elements of the world they constructed around themselves, engineers constructing models that embodied properties observed, and ultimately they became scientific planners who mapped out a city. The risk, however, is that, like players of Sim-City and related computer simulations, children can take on roles of city planners with little regard for their forgotten or little-understood inhabitants. Some opportunities for community building are then lost.

Although the Creature City project may be unique among preschool activities, projects to create models of cities or other sociocultural spaces are not uncommon in schools. The West High classrooms involved in ACOT implemented a project in which the students created a working scale model of the Columbus downtown. Kelly (1994) described a virtual reality project in which middle-grade students not only created environments, but also their inhabitants of that environment, using scientific principles and their own creativity. With the proliferation of world-building software, more students will undoubtedly engage in such activities (see Fawcett & Snyder, chap. 7, this volume).

BOOGIE BOARDING: BACKYARD TECHNOLOGIES
AND BECOMING ONE WITH OTHERS

The community building and involvement with technologies is particularly apparent in everyday situations involving "backyard technologies" such as those that enable swinging, volleyball, and boogie boarding. Boogie boarding, which we focus on in this section, represents a real-world learning experience that involves various technologies and media in complex and dynamic ways that are inseparable from the learning experience itself. In our observations of boys learning to boogie board, we saw them use several technologies and media simultaneously as they explored boogie boarding, solved problems, achieved new perspectives, developed expertise, and advanced their knowledge. In learning boogie boarding, the boys enlisted conversations, photos, magazines, videos, firsthand experience, observations, conversations, analysis of themselves and peers, and advice across a range of situations. At the same time they sent letters and e-mail messages from Australia to friends in the United States about surfing, and they used their newfound expertise to have conversations with grandparents and uncles. The media associated with boogie boarding were rarely separate and discrete from these interactions, but were, indeed, embedded within and a part of the social situations of the activity itself. The media provided both a stimulus and a vehicle for learning, prompting questions; arousing interests; and affording comparisons, connections, analysis, evaluation, and goal setting. To be a boogie board rider entailed becoming initiated into the full range of activities associated with the sport.

Boogie boarding has much in common with Hacker's (1987) analysis of the backyard technologies of swings and see-saws. As a feminist sociologist and activist she celebrated the innocent pleasures simple technologies can afford. Although the design of swings varies across cultures, as a childhood activity swinging is nearly universal. The boogie board and the swing represent technologies whose sole purpose is pleasure. Each is simple in its design, and each affords its users the benefits of technological transparency (see Bruce & Hogan, chap. 16, this volume). Technologies work best when they are transparent, that is to say, when we do not notice them but know or experience the world through them (Damarin, 1995; Ihde, 1990). The best swing does not pinch, wobble, or squeak; it becomes transparent as the body and the swing become a single entity allowing the swinger to experience wind in the face and a feeling of flying. Similarly, boogie boarding is most satisfying when the board and boarder become one; when the boogie boarder bends his or her knees or adjusts his or her weight, he or she need not think about the board; it has become an extension of the body.

With the boogie board, Shaun and his brother Christopher were clearly experiencing the pleasure of backyard technologies. However, much of the innocence and simplicity of the swing is gone. A boogie board requires extensive practice and the shaping of complex skills for mastery. Practice entails planning and thus invites and requires investigations of weather and tides, of ideal shapes and materials for the board and so forth. The boogie board brings its devotees into the arenas of capitalism's conspicuous consumption and, relatedly, of the haves and have-nots, and of us and them. Notwithstanding the role of dress and behavior as markers or badges of membership in a boogie boarding community, the commodification of boogie boarding has attracted commercial interests. Paraphernalia can be bought and used to change the experience (e.g., fins) or to extend it beyond its typical season (e.g., wet suit); clothing and other items extend the experience of boogie boarding from the water to land. The search for and the acquisition of additional equipment brings the boogie boarder repeatedly not only into the marketplace of commodities, but also into the sphere of adolescent peer pressure for consumption. The concept of "posing" among adolescents in relation to the boogie boarding culture raises other issues. As Shaun stated: "Posers were those who wear the dress but do not do it; but they also include those who do it, but do not dress as if they do." The young practitioners of boogie boarding are not entirely swept up by this commodification; in discussion and practice they examine the trade-offs between the implicit technological values of simplicity and transparency versus the advertised conspicuous consumption values of added gear and other signifiers.

At least temporarily, boogie boarding is all engaging. For the boys all the media, technology, and knowledge at their disposal and all the means for accessing them are absorbed into their pursuit of boogie boarding. Reading texts and experiencing phenomena through their relation to boogie boarding both expands their relation to them and delimits meanings. They are more attentive to and knowledgeable about what counts as a "great wave," but the foregrounding of this knowledge might entail the moving other ways of knowing the sea to the background. The irregular occurrence of great waves can make invisible the regularities of the ocean, tides, and moon.

Increasingly, cultural theorists are examining the ways in which biology and culture come together in individual lives (e.g., Ormrod, 1995) using the concept of *performativity* to emphasize gender, race, class, and age as performance. In this view, society offers certain ways of behaving that are associated with various ways of being male or Black or young, and so forth. In this view, individuals, whether male or female, are not born masculine, for example, but become so by selecting particular forms of masculinity and performing the behaviors associated with those forms. The collected practices of boogie boarders, predominately although not exclusively practiced by young White males, define a way of being a masculine adolescent in the late 20th century. Thus, this activity offers young people not only recreation and a domain for knowledge construction, but also a peer group and an identity. As the sociological papers collected by Grint and Gill (1995) and other resources indicate, certain ways of interacting with technologies define particular types of gender identity in Western society. In particular, working with systems (M. Tierney, 1995) and hacking (Hapnes & Sorenson, 1995) define some masculine cultures and behaviors; young men reproduce these behaviors in the process of constructing themselves as bearers of particular types of masculinity. Similarly, boogie boarding, complete with cultural practices surrounding it, defines and becomes a way of being a young man in Western society. At the same time, for Shaun and Christopher it was an important way of connecting with a cultural practice that afforded more specific connections with their Australian father and their cousins now living in Australia.

Boogie boarding and its near relation surfboarding have achieved a place in our culture where they are productive of identity and stable enough to have become a metaphorical resource for guiding activities with other technologies, most notably the Internet. "Surfing the net" like boogie boarding involves "getting wet" in the ocean of information, being able to recognize a "great page," and knowing which pages should be allowed to flow by. Good engines for net surfing are transparent in ways analogous to the boogie board—and, as with boogie boarding, there are multiple ancillary gear and gadgets, some of which extend the activities and others of which contribute to the culture tied to it. From a gender perspective, it is important to note that the metaphor of surfing brings to computer technology a youthful and largely masculine set of cultural understandings and practices. In the domain of computing, these biases multiply the focus on youth and masculinity already present within cultures of mathematics and science.

The time-honored sociopolitical functions of text can be seen operating in Western society in ways parallel with the technologies used in the examples described thus far. The discussion of the political character of technological integration in communities is apparent in the aforementioned preschoolers' "hands-on" experiences of the Creature City project, in boogie boarding, and in the nature and role of technology in West High School. We suggest that these sociopolitical functions of technology have deep roots in cultural and societal development. To explore this issue further, we now turn to the bark art produced by the Kunwinjku as a point of comparison in analyzing how viewing technology from a cultural perspective applies to a technology that has been maintained for thousands of years.

KUNWINJKU BARK ART AS A WAY OF KNOWING AND SUSTAINING CULTURE DEVELOPMENT

Kunwinjku bark art mirrors the conventions of social relations within and across Kunwinjku clans. The study of their art, therefore, affords an opportunity to study the clans, their regional identities, and their social and cultural norms. Artistic innovation reflects the process of social change as the artist represents changes in society and in the world outside it. Prestige and power in Kunwinjku society is organized principally in relation to the acquisition and control of ritual knowledge, that is, the knowledge of the actions of ancestral beings and the ceremonies associated with them. Subjectively, artists consider their repertoire of subjects as reflecting their ritual knowledge and related personal knowledge. Taylor (1987) described the learning experiences of one of the Kunwinjka as follows:

> He first learnt to paint from his close kin, his father's brother, mother's brother and elder brother when he was living in Oenpelli and working in the day at the abattoir with them. Later when he was living near Kurrkurrh and Kumarrirnban he was taught by his own father as well as his classificatory father of the Mok clan, who was living with them at the time. Later he and his father moved to Marrkolidan out station where he married a Kardbam clan woman. When his father died, the Kardham father of this woman and another of his mother's brothers who was living at Marrkolidban became responsible for teaching him how to paint. (p. 121)

The Kunwinjka have a system of apprenticeship that involves learning from others, especially members of one's extended family. Indeed, family members carefully monitor progress in the development of skill based on experiences. The art occurs amidst observations, conversations, self and peer analysis, and advice across a range of situations. The media used to produce art are rarely separate from these interactions; indeed, the media are embedded within a part of the social situations.

Kunwinjka use art to explore this relationship to ancestors and to the environment, especially traditions and knowledge about the relation of animals to their day-to-day existence. Also, in some ways each piece of art is akin to a collaborative project for expanding learning and refining a craft. The reproduction of the artistic system does not involve the transmission through time of exactly the same paintings with exactly the same meanings. Rather, young artists acquire conceptual structures that help generate similar types of paintings with similar interpretations. Artistic innovation reflects the process of social change as the artist represents his or her experience of changes in society and in the world outside it.

Interestingly, contemporary Kunwinjku bark painters produce their works for sale, but the proceeds help them live a relatively secluded lifestyle in small communities located on traditional lands. Nonetheless, several questions drawn from analysis of developments related to Western media and technology have emerged. First, in what ways do these recent developments preserve the traditional culture? For example, if the sale of bark art allows the Kunwinjku to maintain their geographical separation from the European-Australian communities, is there a related cost to the culture? In particular, does the assimilation of abstractions and new meanings into the art based on market considerations change the functions of the art within the culture? Second, because bark painting is closely tied to the understanding of sex and gender of the Kunwinjku clan, is the increased demand for bark art affecting gender roles? If males come to understand their relation to the ancestral beings, their setting and history through learning and practicing the production of art, how do women come to know these things? Third, is the introduction of new themes into the art tantamount to introducing these themes into the culture itself?

These and similar questions are analogues to issues that arise in study and analysis of Western media and technology development. Indeed, we find the parallelism between modern-day rituals of learning and the Kunwinjku's deep-rooted traditions, especially the sociopolitical dimensions of how and what is learned, to be quite striking. Just as Kunwinjku bark art might be narrowly perceived as abstract depictions of their religious beliefs and elements within their environment, so the Creature City project can be viewed as simply a representation of a city and boogie boarding or involvement with technologies in West High can be seen as merely learning certain skills. However, each of the activities described is much more than that. Indeed, the experiential worlds that are developed are facades that simply shade the dramas, ways of knowing, and sociopolitical positioning that are occurring. For example, undergirding many of the projects by West High students is an ongoing negotiation of new forms of texts and sociopolitical positioning by the students with one another, with teachers, and other stakeholders, which is not unlike the Kunwinjku or students at Sophie Rogers preschool or the boogie boarder. West High students were quick to showcase their attempts to make their projects more dynamic with graphic interfaces and animation. The students in the technology-supported classrooms saw themselves pushing the edges of one another's engagement and norms for text as they pursued ways to create texts that were more dynamic and engaging. The changing identities, emerging status, and forms of participation that are tied to diverse media and technologies are remarkably similar across each of the four contexts we have described.

DISCUSSION

Kunwinjku bark art might be narrowly perceived as abstract depictions of religious beliefs and elements within a relatively small and circumscribed community. Similarly, the Creature City project can be viewed simply as representative of a city, boogie boarding might be dismissed as trivial play, and the ACOT classroom might seem so far removed from a typical classroom as to be unworthy of much attention. However, close examination of these situations through the lenses of media and technology reveals that these four seemingly disparate situations are parallel along several dimensions. First, in each case technologies involve connections with others (friends, ancestors, collaborators, mentors, advisors) across time and place, which entail the development of conventions and norms of behavior. These connections occur in the process of exploring the world through technologies and media. In each situation learners are involved in community building where technologies or literacies are not inanimate, singular ends unto themselves, but are mechanisms for individuals and groups to make continual linkages with the social and cultural dimensions of their world.

Whether the media are driven by complex hardware and software or by simpler, less complex media and technologies, we posit that educators need to consider the extent to which technology lends itself to ways of knowing and students' engagements in learning. Media can support alternative ways of knowing including ways that are less focused on the written or spoken word as the sole vehicle of expression. It is within the power of all media and technologies to democratize, engage, empower, and enhance the voices and identities of students. Not all uses of media and technology, regardless of their relative sophistication, support these ends, however. We prefer an approach to infusing technology into education for the possibility that multimedia can be generative, open-ended, flexible, and empowering ways as opposed to ways that are narrow, determined, and constrained (see Bruce & Hogan, chap. 16, this volume).

Often when schools consider a shift toward multimedia they focus on the supplies and materials they will need or the hardware and software they can afford. These are important considerations, but they should not be seen as more important than a consideration of how students and teachers view the contribution of technology to their school lives. Sometimes the possibilities associated with software are limited by the orientation of the teacher or predisposition of the students and how the media are integrated. For example, an emphasis on laboratories or other settings where collaborative exchanges may be stymied is antithetical to the community-building activities we have described here. Or, an emphasis on software that limits the extent to which electronic technologies can be used as tools detracts from the generative and integrative potentials afforded by new technologies.

One of the key foci of infusing electronic media into classrooms is finding a meaningful social niche for technology wherein users find technological tools as a means for achieving new possibilities, solving problems, and exploring one's own world and the worlds of others. For example, because it relied on ancient artifacts produced in a non-Western culture, the China project of the West High School classrooms invites contrast and comparison with the Kunwinjku clan situation described earlier. In both projects, non-Western cultural products are commodified and consumed by Western society, but the mechanisms of this commodification are different. In the ACOT experience, Chinese cultural artifacts, together with English language expert accounts of the lives and culture that gave rise to them, are objectified and made available to students as resources for their own knowledge construction and representation. The students interpret and describe these in English, represent them using the norms and practices of Western media and technology, and organize them using Western principles. The result is comprehensive and impressive, but always a Western portrayal of the Eastern life and culture of China. Postcolonial scholars such as Spivak (1990), Mohanty (1984), and Said (1978) elucidated problems implicit in this approach to "first world" knowledge about "third world" cultures. Numerous questions follow from these observations, one being whether the China project included a self-reflexive process in which the U.S. students studying China considered their biases and the limitations of their own understanding of a culture different from their own. Such reflexivity has become a standard part of qualitative educational research, reflecting educators' understanding that our various positionalities contribute to our understanding of the lives and cultures of others. Despite our acceptance of the need to uncover bias in our own knowledge, the importance of uncovering bias is too often neglected in the education of students.

With the advent of user-friendly technologies, users do not need extensive technical skill to access these tools. However, they may need a community within which to explore their use, a community that provides access as well as nurturing support and mentoring. This type of community support demands access beyond the use of technology for only a few hours a week; it demands opportunities to explore the technologies as tools for accessing ideas, communicating with others, exploring multimedia palettes for creative expression, and using databases.

Sometimes the support must be economic as well as sociopolitical because the use of new technologies and media is constrained by a lack of resources. Inequitable access to resources also tends to perpetuate sociocultural inequities, which may diminish the privilege, status, and identity of students. Most states are faced with inequities across schools in terms of access to these new tools. Sometimes the possibilities are constrained by the nature of schooling and the school's vision for how technology might be used. In some situations the technology is viewed only in terms of its support for conventional learning and achievement rather than as a literacy tool that may transform current practice (see chapters in Part III of this volume).

In these conceptions and realizations, the shortsighted assessment of the worth of technology may be determined less by its potential contributions to new ways of learning and community than by how well the technology advances traditional test performance and maintains traditional hierarchies of power and privilege.

We would hope that media and technology are viewed as supporting dialogue and explorations as do other forms of literacy. However, empowerment in the short run of classroom and real-life activity may not produce empowerment over the longer run, and may even curtail it. Uses of media and technology that encourage students to become either smug or fearful regarding the completeness of their knowledge, for example, may preclude their ability to engage in dialogue or other activities that might further or deepen their knowledge.

Especially for young women, it is important to allow discussion and the development of understanding, not only regarding the topic of instruction, but also the facilitating effect of media and technologies. Engaging students in the processes of selection and acquisition of new technology-based material for classroom use can also contribute to their learning and empowerment. Similarly, for at-risk students and others who have had little opportunity to use advanced media and technologies at school or at home, it is critical that they have opportunities to work with media and technology and that they be provided sufficient time to develop skills and support for them as to compete with their more affluent peers.

We hope that by raising the sociopolitical issues related to technology and literacy that we have illustrated their ubiquity and their importance. The examples that we have employed detail technologies woven into the fabric of the lives of communities and of individuals as community members. Interwoven as such, technologies serve as both needle and thread—serving as a tool and contributing to the pattern of life. In this role, technologies appear to spur explorations as well as serve as markers of status and development. A technology may serve culture; it may contribute to cultural continuity, cultural ecology, cultural self-determination, or cultural expansion. A technology may serve as a frame that is gendered or has other leanings. Likewise, technologies may contribute to linkages both within and across cultures, furthering cultural bonding that may contribute to cultural isolationism, cultural imperialism, or cultural cross-fertilization. By scrutinizing technologies as cultural practice we hope at least to obtain our bearings in the evolving communities of technoculture.

REFERENCES

Baudrillard, J. (1983). *Simulations*. New York: Semiotext(e).
Brown, J., Collins, A., & Duguid, P. (1989). Situated cognition and the culture of learning. *Educational Researcher, 18*(1), 32–41.
Damarin, S. K. (1995). Technologies of the individual: Women and subjectivity in the age of information. *Research in Technology and Philosophy, 13*, 185–200.
Damarin, S. K. (in press). Educational technology and equity in education: A search for convergence. *Theory Into Practice*.
Gee, J. (1990). *Social linguistics and literacies*. New York: Falmer.
Grint, K., & Gill, R. (Eds.). (1995). *The gender–technology relation: Contemporary theory and research*. London: Taylor & Francis.
Hacker, S. (1987). *Pleasure, power, and technology: Some tales of gender, engineering, and the cooperative workplace*. Boston: Unwin-Ryman.
Hapnes, T., & Sorenson, K. H. (1995). Competition and collaboration in male shaping of computing. In K. Grint & R. Gill (Eds.), *The gender–technology relation: Contemporary theory and research* (pp. 174–191). London: Taylor & Francis.
Ihde, D. (1990). *Technology and the lifeworld: From garden to earth*. Bloomington: Indiana University Press.
Kelly, R. V., Jr. (1994, Fall). VR and the educational frontier. *Virtual Reality Special Report*, pp. 8–15.
Mohanty, C. (1984). Under western eyes: Feminist scholarship and colonial discourses. *Boundary, 12*(3)–*13*(1), 333–358.
Niranjana, T. (1988). *Bringing the text to legibility: Translation, post-structuralism, and the colonial context*. Unpublished doctoral dissertation, University of California, Los Angeles.
Ormrod, S. (1995). Leaky black boxes in gender/technology relations. In K. Grint & R. Gill (Eds.), *The gender–technology relation: Contemporary theory and research* (pp. 31–47). London: Taylor & Francis.
Said, E. (1978). *Orientalism*. New York: Pantheon.
Siegel, M. (1995). More than words: The generative power of transmediation for learning. *Canadian Journal of Education, 20*(4), 455–475.
Spivak, G. C. (1990). *The post-colonial critic*. New York: Routledge.
Taylor, L. (1987). *The same but different: Social reproduction in innovation in the art of the Kunwinjka of western Arnhem land*. Unpublished doctoral dissertation, The Australian National University.
Tierney, M. (1995). Negotiating a software career: Informal work practices and "the lads" in a software installation. In K. Grint & R. Gill (Eds.), *The gender-technology relation: Contemporary theory and research* (pp. 192–209). London: Taylor & Francis.
Tierney, R. J., Kieffer, R. D., Stowell, L., Desai, L. E., Whalin, K., & Moss, A. G. (1992). *Computer acquisition: A longitudinal study of the influence of high computer access on students' thinking, learning, and interaction* (Apple Classrooms of Tomorrow Report No. 16). Cupertino, CA: Apple Computer.
Volosinov, V. N. (1973). *Marxism and the philosophy of language*. Cambridge, MA: Harvard University Press.
Willmot, E. (1988). *Pemulwuy: The rainbow warrior*. Sydney: Bantam Books.

16

▼▼▼▼▼▼▼

The Disappearance of Technology:
Toward an Ecological Model of Literacy

Bertram C. Bruce
Maureen P. Hogan
University of Illinois at Urbana–Champaign

Diverse voices have outlined the advantages or disadvantages of technology as they have emerged within classrooms, businesses, communities, and families. Enthusiasts vaunt technological changes, which they contend can effect a more equitable distribution of power. They invoke issues such as empowerment, equality, access, speed, efficiency, liberation, and the development of a global community in support of a pro-technology agenda. As an example, Rheingold's (1993) account of the growth of electronic communication in the Bay Area is framed in terms such as *grassroots groupminds* and *new electronic villages,* terms that call forth the potential of new technologies to support a renewal of community. Going further, some proponents promote a form of technological determinism in which new tools or media alone are seen as bringing about a better world.

More cautious observers warn that technologies can be used to reinscribe existing inequitable power relations. They see technology implicated in the loss of jobs, and poor working conditions (see Mikulecky & Kirkley, chap. 18, this volume), surveillance, and regimentation, and caution us about censorship and unequal access. They note that even well-intentioned tools can be used to forward an antidemocratic agenda and that some new technologies support abuses by their very design. Ellul (1980) sees the overall process of technicizing society as "the end of man [humanity]." Technology, he says, "disintegrates and tends to eliminate bit by bit anything that is not technicizable" (p. 203). The result goes far beyond the subordination of humanity to technology.

Thus, we are often faced with a choice between a typically positive, technological determinism and a more negative, social determinism (Bromley, 1997; Bruce, 1993). Rather than conceptualizing the debate via these mutually exclusive and equally deterministic structures, we examine how prevailing ideologies construct the meaning of technologies in different situations. In fact, when technology is used to accomplish specific goals, for certain individuals, in a particular setting, it can be used to liberate or oppress. That is why situated studies of how literacy technologies are used in classrooms, workplaces, or homes and reveal more about these issues than do analyses of technologies or social relations alone (Bowker, Star, Turner, & Gasser, 1997).

We tend to think of technology as a set of tools to perform a specific function. These tools are often portrayed as mechanistic, exterior, autonomous, and concrete devices that accomplish tasks and create products. We do not generally think of them as intimately entwined with social and biological lives. But literacy technologies, such as pen and paper, index cards, computer databases, word processors, networks, e-mail, and hypertext, are also ideological tools; they are designed, accessed, interpreted, and used to further purposes that embody social values. More than mechanistic, they are organic, because they merge with our social, physical, and psychological beings. Thus, we need to look more closely at how technologies are realized in given settings. We may find that technological tools can be so embedded in the living process that their status as technologies disappears.

THE DISAPPEARANCE OF TECHNOLOGY

As technologies embed themselves in everyday discourse and activity, a curious thing happens. The more we look, the more they slip into the background. Despite our attention, we lose sight of the way they give shape to our daily lives. This disappearance effect is evident when we consider whether a technology empowers people to do things that would be difficult, or even impossible otherwise.

Consider for example, the telephone. As it comes into use, it is initially considered a novelty that permits new and interesting, but hardly necessary actions. Later, as it is used more widely, the actions it affords move from novelty to habit, the tool becomes commonplace. Soon it is treated as part of daily activity. We might say, "I talked to my friend today," without feeling any need to mention that the telephone was a necessary tool for that conversation to occur. Through this process, we move from looking at the technology as an addition to life to looking at life through that technology. The embedding of the technology in the matrix of our lives makes it invisible. In fact, the greater its integration into daily practices, the less it is seen as a technology at all.

Thus, writing is no longer viewed as a technology; instead, only its newest manifestations take on that role. Each literacy technique—quills, movable type, ball-point pens, typewriters—passes through phases of technology to tool, from unfamiliar to familiar, and from visible to invisible. Already, word processing, once a new technology, is now considered to be just the way people write. Web page writing conceived as a new technology ability today, will not be so in a few years.

Further, as a tool becomes embedded in social practices, our conception of the ability required for an individual to use that tool changes as well. In the early stages of use, disability is counted as a flaw in the tool: We say that poor design of the technology makes it difficult to use. Later, the disability becomes an attribute of the user, not the tool. We say that the user needs more training, or worse, is incapable of using the tool. Once the status of the tool as technology has fully merged into daily practice, the disability to use it becomes an essential attribute of certain people.

For example, stairs are an architectural technology that empower people to move easily from one floor of a building to another, floors themselves being a technology to increase the ratio of floor space to land and building surface area. But ordinarily, we do not consider floors, or even stairs, as technologies; their ubiquity makes them invisible. Operating invisibly, stairs empower some just as surely as they disempower others.

People who use wheelchairs can move easily within a single floor, but they become disabled by the presence of stairs. The stairs construct wheelchair-ness as a disability. Even if one insists on characterizing wheelchair-ness as a brute fact, a fixed property of the individual, the consequences of that fact are radically altered by the architectural technology. Consider how the addition of elevators to a building reconstructs wheelchair-ness as a minor disability. The important point is that the ambient technologies can alternately able or disable an individual many times in the course of a single day.

This process is one of the crucial ways in which all literacy technologies—slate tablets, typewriters, word processors, networks, computer interfaces, databases, the Web—are ideologically embedded. Effective use of the dominant reading and writing technologies then becomes the defining characteristic for new forms of literacy (Bruce, 1995). Lack of such ability can be conceived as an inherent disability, located in the individual, which might or might not be alleviated through various measures, such as providing more time, easier texts, skill training, tutoring, help features, donations of equipment, and so forth.

But if we recognize that these tools are constructed, we begin to see how design choices create ability and disability. Lack of English fluency, for example, has now been constructed as a literacy disability with respect to the Web, because so much of the Web content and even the Web software tools are in English. Not owning or being able to use a computer is constructed as a disability for attaining a college education. A competent writer may be locked out of an editing job for lack of desktop publishing skills. Thus, new literacy abilities, and consequently, disabilities are continually reconstructed. In this sense, discussion about participation in any literate society must be referenced to that society's current and emerging literacy technologies.

One implication of this is a lack of choice. We cannot simply choose our tools (i.e., to write longhand, use a typewriter, a word processor, or e-mail) in order to be literate participants. Instead, the technology chooses us; it marks us as full, marginal, or nonparticipating. Haas (1996) makes a similar point in her call to consider the materiality of literacy, how its various manifestations over time have always been linked to specific bodily and physical realizations. An obvious implication is that teachers of literacy must consider how new technologies help to reconstruct reading and writing processes for their students.

Students and parents increasingly expect convenient access, explicit instructions, and the use of computer technology in the classroom. Similarly, teachers expect students to have computers at home. Thus, computer use is becoming an integral aspect of academic achievement. The promise of learning more through new technologies is becoming a premise, a requisite for success. A danger is that the mere presence of computers may signal that all is well when little has actually changed in the reading and writing ecology.

The disappearance of technology is more than a metaphor. We cannot see most microprocessors because they are now hidden in artifacts such as telephones, fax machines, cars, dishwashers, and even athletic equipment. Such hidden microprocessors have been called *embedded systems* because they are not obvious in these devices and their function may be invisible to the user. Thus, the infrastructure of the larger world is becoming infused everywhere with software. Soon, General Motors will sell more microprocessors than IBM, because microprocessors will control speed, navigation, braking, suspension, climate, and airbags (Fiddler, 1996).

Embedded systems may entail a loss of control in one sense. Fewer people will be able to fix their own cars or any number of household appliances. They will need to rely more on experts, and they will need to pay for that expertise. On the other hand, these systems can create a more user-friendly world, what some have called "soft technology" (Norman, 1993). Their overall effect will depend on the social conditions and power relations that surround their use.

Similarly, literacy tools are becoming embedded systems. For an increasing number of people, writing means typing on a personal computer, reading means browsing a newspaper on the Internet, and researching means accessing a library database via modem. If a computer hard drive crashes while using today's literacy tools, most people will need to rely on an expert to fix it. Literacy today is becoming dependent on embedded systems that are invisible to the user.

One implication of this embedded technology is that we need to look more carefully at how technology is affecting our lives even when we cannot see it directly. Literacy means not just reading and writing texts, but "reading" the world, and the technological artifacts within it.

AN ECOLOGICAL MODEL FOR LITERACY TECHNOLOGIES

Awareness of how technologies merge with daily practices leads us to view technology and literacy as constituent parts of life, elements of an ecological system (see also Bromley, 1997; Latour, 1988; Law, 1991). This viewpoint gives us a basis for understanding the interpenetration among machines, humans, and the natural world. Lemke (chap. 17, this volume) has a similar conception of literacy, which he describes as part of an ecosocial system:

> Literacies cannot be adequately analyzed just as what individuals do. We must understand them as part of the larger systems of practices that hold a society together . . . if we think the word *society* means only people, then we need another term, one that, like *ecosystem*, includes the total environment: machines, buildings, cables, satellites, bedrock, sewers, farms, insect life, bacteria.

Thus, literacies, and the technologies of literacy, can only be understood in relation to larger systems of practices. Most technologies become so enmeshed in daily experience that they disappear; that is, they are no longer seen as technologies. They become the ordinary; in order to see them, we must make the familiar strange. As T. S. Eliot (1943) in "Little Gidding" expressed it, "And the end of all our exploring/Will be to arrive where we started/And know the place for the first time" (p. 59).

Eliot's words resonate for us as literacy educators because we have the responsibility to make the familiar strange—not only to rethink the uses of technologies, but also to know it again for the first time as we consider where our students may be starting. We must recall what it is like to be a novice or to be less privileged. We need to critically examine what has become commonplace, normalized, and even invisible. In some cases, we may need to depend on our students to navigate the voyage because they may be more expert.

A question often arises in the technology debates: Do we use technology, or does technology use us? Idhe (1990) rejects both alternatives, and instead sees people as living within a technologically textured ecosystem. The relations between humans and technology are both sensory and contextual. Because kinesthetic perception is always part of the process of using technology, we can imagine our bodies as extended through artifacts, forming hybrids. Idhe says a technology is not simply a tool, but an artifact with intentionality. In Latour's (1988) terms, technologies are actors in social systems, as are texts, maps, physical spaces, and artifacts of all kinds.

If we assume that technology is necessarily embedded in cultural practices, it is only one step further to see people as caught within not just specific technologies, but in "technology," a process Heidegger (1977) calls *enframing*. He argues that we must understand technology as an activity that surrounds us, as in his famous assertion, "everywhere we remain unfree and chained to technology, whether we passionately affirm or deny it" (p. 311). The essence of technology lies in the way it "comes forth" or reveals itself in human activity. Heidegger wants us to understand technology as an inescapable part of our social world and ultimately, of our basic values. The crucial question then becomes: What is the essence of technology? He warns us that we may perceive all entities in the life world, in the ecology, as a "standing reserve," simply as resources to serve technology. Technology provides a way to order, and then, more ominously, the way to be ordered.

SOCIAL RELATIONS AND TECHNOLOGIES

People write social relations through the languages of technology, constructing hierarchies and fields of inclusion or exclusion through silicon chips, wires, and video displays. The sentences we write with technologies describe our social life, as surely as the cave paintings of Lascaux or the Mayan calendar tell tales of earlier social worlds. However, technologies also serve to prescribe, to turn social intentions into tangible realities. Latour (1991) encapsulates this point as, "technology is society made durable" (p. 103).

How can this be? How is it that a plastic box full of electronic components can tell the tale of social relations? According to Selfe and Selfe (1994), interface designs are geopolitical borders, a sort of cultural contact zone. They encourage English teachers and students to critique its politics. Such a critique might start with their observation that standard "computer interfaces do not . . . provide direct evidence of different cultures and races that make up the American social complex, nor do they show much evidence of different linguistic groups or groups of differing economic status" (p. 486). They argue that these interfaces, with desktop metaphors, Eurocentric icons, and English language defaults, are markers of capitalism and class privilege. A corporate ideology becomes its primary orientation, which promotes the commodification of information. Information as commodity then translates into big business for commercial networks. Selfe and Selfe also propose that the interface maps the kind of knowledge imbued with hierarchical values characteristic of Western patriarchal cultures rather than knowledge as bricolage—a more intuitive, associative, organic, and perhaps feminine process. The interface, then, is a political, ideological and epistemic borderland where we in fact "write our lives" with technology.

We need to disentangle this complex in order to see how ideology is woven through it. In the sections that follow, we explore how technologies function as ideological tools, focusing on four intertwined themes. First we examine how ideology influences the design of technologies. Second, we examine the distribution of technologies, including questions of access. Third, we consider ideological aspects of using technology. Finally, we look at how we interpret the effects of technologies.

DESIGN OF TECHNOLOGIES

One arena for ideology to operate in is the design of technologies. New information technologies are often designed to forward democratic ideals through interaction, collaboration, and sharing of information. A familiar example is local area networks that allow multiple users to share folders as part of their collaborative work. Shareware and groupware programs (such as the synchronous[1] program InterChange) allow real-time conversations

---

[1]Synchronous programs support real-time conversation in written form, unlike email, which is usually used asynchronously.

among multiple users for collaborative writing (Bruce, Peyton, & Batson, 1993). Such programs can facilitate equal access as they are designed to give voice to many participants. As Beach and Lundell (chap. 6, this volume) show, computer-mediated communication can "create an engaging dialogic forum for social literacy practices."

In a similar spirit, the Internet, what McChesney (1995) calls "society's central nervous system" (p. 14), with its millions of users, can foster new relationships and even build new communities based on shared interests and information (Rheingold, 1993; Spender, 1995). These relationships and communities can be far-reaching, relatively inexpensive, and increasingly multilingual, multicultural, and global (see Garner & Gillingham, chap. 13, this volume). In principle, the weblike design of literacy technologies can offer a more equitable distribution of information than any technology we have previously known.

At the same time, both hardware and software design can disrupt the democratic process and the community-building ideals. For example, InterChange does not erase power hierarchies. Users of these programs still understand who has the authority to initiate, lead, direct, and silence discussions. Furthermore, the texts are controlled by a teacher, administrator, or technologist who can easily monitor students' exchanges without their knowledge or permission. Similarly, within corporations, groupware has become attractive to managers in part because it furthers their ability to monitor and control employees.

Other authors have voiced concern about how epistemology is embedded in the design. Could it be that militaristic ways of knowing and masculine desire are buried in the design of certain technologies? Sofia (in press), drawing on insights from psychoanalysis and semiotics, suggests that the design of the contemporary computer recalls its militaristic male-centered history, a history that has helped further a view of the computer as fetish, which in turn may exclude females' attitudes. As she explains:

> Computers seem to embody the very essence of rationality, working as they do with principles of digital code and processing, and formal logic. Educationalists who believed technologies were neutral . . . were surprised by the rapidity with which patterns of masculine domination and female exclusion emerged with the introduction of computing in schools.

Sofia (in press) claims that computer technology, with its connection to one subgenre of science fiction fantasy, with its attendant notions of control and domination, speaks especially to adolescent males. Militarism, formal logic, and science fiction contribute to what is largely a male computer culture, which some females may find uninviting. The result is that computer culture reproduces negative attitudes toward computer use among women. To offset this trend, Sofia recommends that feminists appropriate computers in their own way, rejecting the "informatics of domination," fetishism of the "androcentric science fiction culture," and fantasies of the computer as "second self."

It is important to be careful here: The notion that interfaces or digital codes enforce any one set of values teeters toward the technocentric view, beyond which the tool determines social practice. Nevertheless, the discussion of gendered technologies points to yet one more way that ideology can be embedded in the design of technology.

DISTRIBUTION OF TECHNOLOGIES

A second arena for ideology to operate through technology is that of distribution and access. Consider the case of people who are blind or visually impaired: With older technologies of text, many individuals accommodate to dominant literacy practices, for example, by using Braille or audiotape. New technologies pose a new array of opportunities but also the need for new accommodations. To a certain extent, the wide availability of Internet resources and technology such as speech generation and recognition promise greater access than ever before. However, reliance on graphical interfaces, the abandonment of support for older technologies, and limitations in access time or training can exclude the same individuals from the global information community. Thus, the deployment of computers and how they are used bears on the degree to which visual impairment functions as literacy disability.

In a similar fashion, people in other groups find their access to literacy limited in new ways. Technology, of course, is not free and it is no surprise that those with the most money have the best technology if they want it; those within the lower socioeconomic brackets, as well as racial minorities and females, have less access than other groups (Sutton, 1991).[2] Access is thus partial, restricted, and stratified. With so much rapid change so quickly, new hardware and software are quickly developing to meet consumers' needs. Even technophiles have difficulty keeping up with the trends. To have access to technology, people have to be aware of it, have the means to purchase it, and have the knowledge to use it. Awareness, means, and knowledge can be restricted and privileged. For many, the promise of technology is still remote; for others it is a premise—something that is a normal and already invisible part of everyday life.

Research by Michaels, Cazden, and Bruce (1985) supports the theory that unequal access to technology operates at many levels: "As is so often the case with new technologies, computer use is more apt to reinforce existing patterns rather than change them" (p. 36). In schools, for example, there are inequalities in the ratios of computers to students in software usage and in classroom use. Even when schools have computers, poorer schools often have less sophisticated software. Use may be limited to drill-and-practice software rather than to the Internet and to the problem solving that is more likely to be emphasized in affluent schools. Even when adequate hardware and software are available, schools may implement the technology in ways that further exacerbate inequality; for example, by limiting access to students who are pulled out of regular classes.

In higher education, access to technology can also accentuate economic difference: Many schools now require students to purchase computers. The University of Illinois Law School now requires new students to have a computer.[3] Associate Dean Colombo explained that "for lawyering in the twenty-first century, law students are just going to have to have computer skills—a wide variety of them" (Wurth, 1996, p. A-1). Besides using computerized databases to do legal research, the students may also use document assembly programs, e-mail, and the Web when they are finally hired by a law firm. Also, the law school is hoping that students will receive more one-on-one attention with their law instructors through e-mail communication and electronic exercises.

For those students who can barely afford law school, the addition of the requirement to purchase a computer can be a burden. Thus, the requirement illustrates the presumption that those without technical expertise and the means to afford technology will probably not succeed as lawyers in the 21st century. Thus, computers now delimit the potential for academic success, even before a student considers applying to law school.

As information technologies merge with communications technologies, what can be done with a computer now depends on the quality of network connections. New computers

---

[2]Based on a review of research on equity and computers in the schools throughout the eighties in K–12 classrooms.

[3]Other law schools such as the University of Richmond, Stanford, Duke, New Mexico, and Oregon have similar requirements.

TABLE 16.1
Network Speed, Media, and Users

Type	Speed	Text in 1 Minute	Other Media in 1 Minute	Typical Users
14.4 modem	14.4 kb/s	25 pages	1 black-and-white diagram	School
28.8 modem	28.8 kb/s	50 pages	1 color picture	Home
56 modem	56 kb/s	130 pages	Audio	
ISDN-64	64 kb/s	1 book (150 pages)	Compressed, small window video	Consultant
ISDN-128	128 kb/s	2 books	10 pictures	Small business, some homes, magnet schools
T1	1.54 mb/s	12 books		Medium-size business
Cable modem	10–30 mb/s	16–48 books		Major corporations
T3	45 mb/s	72 books	Full video	Military, multinational corporations

are quickly linked into local area networks and the Internet within organizations and at least to some extent through the telephone in homes and schools. With an inexpensive connection, a user can transmit and receive ordinary text albeit at a slow rate. Faster connections allow the transmission of audio, pictures, and video. This means that "being on the Internet" varies tremendously depending on the kind of network connection one has. Those with faster connections can gather and transmit more information, and in short, do more with their computers. As information becomes increasingly accessible for some but not all citizens, network speed becomes an index of power in society.

In the 21st century, computer literacy means not only being familiar and comfortable with computers, but also having access to information. Network speed therefore becomes an indicator of literacy practices, just as the possession of a quill pen once was. As Table 16.1 shows, more powerful affiliations have access to more information.[4] The more access they have to information, the more powerful they become within an information-based economy. In this sense, then, power relations are reinforced rather than equalized.

One could think of network access as being analogous to having a membership card for a huge library. The 3,000 times difference in speed means that some members have access to thousands of books, as well as graphics, audio, video, and large data sets; it is as if these members have carte blanche to the Library of Congress. Others, however, are restricted to a limited number of plain text materials; it is as if these members can only go to a community bookmobile. Differences in access become even more significant to the extent that graphics, audio, video, virtual reality, and other media become standard means for representation. Thus, different network speeds differentially construct ability. Again, power relations are shaped both by the technologies and by the existing structures that support social stratification.

An interesting side to the power achieved through network speed is that those privileged social actors, living with an accelerated consciousness (i.e., faster is better) in a product-centered society, may increasingly experience a deteriorating quality of life. Dobrzynski (1996) writes that many American corporate workers are burdened by an excess of e-mail

---

[4]Some of the numbers in the table are approximate. For example, cable modems are shared among users, so the actual transmission rates can be much lower than 30 mb/s. Also, different types of data compression, image size and so on markedly affect how much can be transmitted; there is a clear trade-off between document quality and quantity. Nevertheless, the general pattern shown in these examples still holds: Common transmission rates vary by several orders of magnitude and that has qualitative consequences.

and voice mail messages. Corporate downsizing has meant a loss of support staff, so corporate workers deal directly with communications overflow. Some employees go in early, stay late, or use their weekends to respond to e-mail correspondence. It could also be true that high-technology companies are experiencing more communication, but at a lower level of quality and a higher level of irrelevance. Discussions about retirement surprise parties and theater tickets are flirting for employees' attention, whereas more pressing issues such as market reports and plans for product demonstrations may be overlooked, or at least deferred. Because workers are not talking to each other face to face as much any more, management will need to worry about possible misunderstandings and trivial or recreational material comingling with the important.

Rifkin (1995) thinks that the word *karoshi* will be more than a Japanese cultural phenomenon. The term describes a person's emotional and physical breakdown caused by high-tech stress. In a post-Fordist, state-of-the-art workplace, Rifkin imagines, it will soon be a global, cultural condition. This new kind of stress, which may even change workers' biorhythms as they try to calibrate their biology with computer response time, can lead to chronic fatigue and even a fatal breakdown. *Karoshi* is a clear example of how the technology merges with not only our social, but also our physical beings. Of course, for some employees, the inclusion of more recreational discourse within the workplace and new modes of interaction may mark an improved quality of life. Thus, the same effect may be positive or negative depending on one's perspective, a theme we return to later in this chapter.

Another consideration is that, with respect to access to the Internet which has so much information and so many users, we need to perhaps stop asking what is wrong with texts (a tenet of critical thinking), but rather, what is right with them? Which texts are useful? How do we know? Whose ideas are salvageable? Why? Because much of the information on the Internet is unrefereed, and increasingly commodified, the Internet raises new questions about authority and access to unbiased information. In serious academic journals, for example, the manuscripts are carefully reviewed and the journals themselves are typically free of blatantly commercial advertising, although they may have invitations to subscribe to other journals or professional organizations. The Internet, however, has characteristics of both shopping malls and academic journals (Bruce, 1995; Burbules & Bruce, 1995). Will it evolve into an international coffee shop or a high-tech billboard? Will it foster more global dialogue or more corporate monologue? What do we want it to be? How does it fit in with our democratic ideals? Where do we fit in the process?

McChesney (1995) urges concerned Internet users to fight for the kind of information system that guarantees noncommercial access. If not, he warns, cyberspace could be transformed into a giant marketplace:

> The contours of the emerging communications battle are unclear, but most business ob-
> servers expect a flurry of competition followed by the establishment of a stable oligopoly
> dominated by a handful of enormous firms. What is clear is that the communications
> highway will not be devoted to reducing inequality or misery in our society. In fact, without
> any policies to counteract the market, the new technologies will probably create a world
> of information have's and have-not's, thereby exacerbating our society's already consider-
> able social and economic inequality. (p. 17)

The distribution of high-tech communications information is unequal in a stratified society. Who will guarantee that it will not be constrained by corporate leaders? What kind of policy should ensure that nonprofit, noncommercial, and reliable information has equal access?

USE OF TECHNOLOGIES

Regardless of how a technology is designed and distributed, the use people make of it becomes a third arena in which ideology can operate. In some cases, the use is for democratic ideals, perhaps to invite student collaboration and more equitable participation. Or, teachers may encourage students to expand their horizons through electronic chats with students from other communities (see Garner & Gillingham, chap. 13, this volume). These changes in schools can also encounter stiff resistance as Neilsen (chap. 8, this volume) documents. Moreover, technology used for censorship, surveillance, and control, countering the very ideals it can promote.

Recently the spirit of the global community has taken an inward turn, as more people are recognizing ways in which technology can be used to gather information surreptitiously. There is an increased demand for cryptography software. Those with greater technological control, especially government agencies and big corporations, can be interlopers, controllers, and censors. Large companies now establish firewalls to separate their information from the public. Some countries, notably Singapore and China, have discussed creating firewalls between their entire countries and the rest of the world.

Computer systems cannot guarantee privacy, and the amount of personal information in databases is disturbing. An interested party can all too easily access information about a person's credit history, spending habits, insurance claims, and health history. This information, or misinformation, can make one vulnerable to credit card fraud, restricted health insurance, and bothersome marketing ploys. Using MapQuest, one can find the address of nearly anyone in the United States, including a map and directions to their house. If you carry a mobile phone, your whereabouts are tracked continually and stored in a telephone company database, even when you are not talking on the phone. What do potential abuses of technology say about our right to privacy in a democratic society? The information age has ushered in a redefinition of public and private space which we are only beginning to understand.

And what of the right to free speech? According to Browning (1996), the Internet is learning to censor itself. The Platform for Internet Content Selection (PICS), developed by the WWW Consortium, is trying to resolve the moral issues that lie at the core of regulating information on the Net. As Browning puts it, "PICS promises to create a do-it-yourself censorship that will allow everybody both freedom to speak and freedom not to listen" (p. 38). The goal of the rating system is to allay government responsibility for censorship. Instead, users can access self-rating schemes, such as SafeSurf, which allow them to find out information about a website's violence, nudity, sex, and language content. Thus, PICS would provide users with "a vast interlinked system of reference, recommendation and reputation" (Browning, 1996, p. 38). The rating system would necessarily be ideological: How much, and to what degree, are violence, nudity, sex, and foul language acceptable? To what extent does banning so-called immoral content coincidentally ban sites that promote political issues such as gay and lesbian rights or destruction of landmines? How are the categories defined? The creators of the systems such as SafeSurf will devise algorithms based on their own set of values.

What has been referred to as "Netwars" is another way that ideology penetrates the use of technologies. For example, America Online, a commercial service, does not provide access to most White nationalist news groups. Although the popular service is trying to promote tolerance and equality, a democratic ideal, it also limits freedom of speech, another democratic ideal. Ideological Netwars thus summon a whole set of issues about defining democracy in cyberspace.

INTERPRETATION OF THE EFFECTS OF TECHNOLOGIES

A fourth arena for the operation of ideology through technology is the way we interpret its effects. For example, a company's downsizing that becomes possible by reliance on more technology is frightening if you are a worker who could be displaced by a machine. However, if you are a corporate director seeking greater efficiency, you would welcome the same technology. If you are a literature student who needs to find a Shakespeare quote quickly, you could find it easily on the Web. However, from your instructor's point of view, this easy access could be negative if the use of quotes was supposed to be an indicator of deep reading.

One can interpret the technologically based changes in the economy in similar ways. Automation in the context of corporate restructuring is leading to a decrease in human labor, especially in the manufacturing and service sectors (see Mikulecky & Kirkley, chap. 18, this volume). For large, technologically advanced companies, the profit margin increases as production becomes more efficient. However, two negative aspects accompany this greater efficiency. The first is increased unemployment, with workers displaced by automated systems in both manufacturing (e.g., rubber, mining, electronics, textiles) and service sectors (e.g., bank tellers, secretaries). The second aspect, a corollary of the first, is that unemployed or underemployed people cannot contribute much to the economic growth that these products promise. According to Rifkin (1995), the two problems indicate a growing dual, or cleaving, economy for the 21st century. The cleaving, Rifkin warns, will occur both nationally and globally. The first economy, the utopian one, will be made up of highly trained, well-educated knowledge workers in an information-based economy. The second economy, for the reserve of other workers, will be struggling with unemployment, part-time work, and jobs left in the service sector, such as waitressing, construction, automotive maintenance, painting, and so forth.

Thus we find two economies and a growing chasm between them. As Rifkin (1995) suggests, "Ironically, the closer we seem to come to the technological fruition of the utopian dream, the more dystopian the future seems" (p. 56). Literacy no longer means just reading and writing to secure a decent job, even one that does not require much of either. Literacy means reading the technological world, including the relation of technologies to these dual economies.

CONCLUSION

Despite many differences in conceptions, various scholars (Connell, 1996; Heidegger, 1977; Idhe, 1990; Latour, 1993) have pointed to a consensus regarding the study of technology: The more we examine technology, the less we find it useful to focus on its technical attributes per se, and the more we see the need to understand the ways in which ideology is embedded within it. To understand what a technology means, we must examine how it is designed, interpreted, employed, constructed, and reconstructed through value-laden daily practices. Following this line of argument, the concept of situated evaluation has been proposed to evaluate changes as new technologies are adopted (Bruce, Peyton, & Batson, 1993; Bruce & Rubin, 1993).

A social setting produces an ideological matrix that includes both laudable and deplorable realizations of technology. What does this mean for the transformation of literacy in coming years? The ecological model suggests understanding literacy technologies as embedded throughout social practices, often in invisible ways. There is as much reason to be cautious as to be celebratory. Although it is clear that technology can enhance literacy by providing motivation, access to information, new worlds to students, faster communication, and real-time communication with peers, using technology in educational settings requires continuing critical analysis.

The 21st century occasions new ways of conceiving and teaching about literacy. Because of the increasing generation of information through new recent technology, teachers need to consider, perhaps more than ever, how they will teach students to select and critique texts, especially those on the Web. Additionally, literacy teachers need to be ready to handle a wide range of student familiarity and ability with writing and researching technologies. They need to recognize that a computer is a tool, but also a symbol that indexes privilege (Bromley & Apple, in press; Stuckey, 1991). Teachers will need to assess how technologies relate to students' positions in the dual economies, thus expanding the meaning of critical literacy (Muspratt, Luke, & Freebody, 1997) to encompass new means of representation. They may also need to revise their conception of text, as students learn how to read and write hypertexts, graphs, charts, mathematical equations, pictorial models, and even virtual realities.

An important part of literacy education now is to consider a range of options for learning, including a wide range of technologies. One-on-one conferencing and peer editing are still fine ways to teach college writing. This can be done via e-mail or through office visits and peer editing workshops, and in different settings. Reading exercises that celebrate multiple interpretations can be done with or without computer assistance. An ecological model of literacy helps us to visualize the whole, and to see a range of options as part of the whole, neither dismissing nor naively accepting technology wholesale.

Finally, researchers need to do more situated studies that detail the complexities of literacy within an ecological model, and to see how ideology operates within situations where literacy, technology, and humans interact. We may then approach a more rounded understanding of how technologies can either promote or forestall equality.

REFERENCES

Bowker, G. C., Star, S. L., Turner, W., & Gasser, L. (1997). *Social science, technical systems and cooperative work: Beyond the great divide.* Mahwah, NJ: Lawrence Erlbaum Associates.

Bromley, H. (1997, Winter). The social chicken and the technological egg. *Educational Theory, 47*(1), 51–65.

Bromley, H., & Apple, M. W. (in press). *Education/technology/power: Educational computing as a social practice.* Albany: State University of New York Press.

Browning, J. (1996, September). The Internet is learning to censor itself. *Scientific American, 275,* p. 38.

Bruce, B. C. (1993). Innovation and social change. In B. C. Bruce, J. K. Peyton, & T. W. Batson (Eds.), *Network-based classrooms: Promises and realities* (pp. 9–32). New York: Cambridge University Press.

Bruce, B. C. (1995, November). *Twenty-first century literacy* (Tech. Rep. No. 624). Urbana: University of Illinois, Center for the Study of Reading.

Bruce, B. C., Peyton, J. K., & Batson, T. W. (Eds.). (1993). *Network-based classrooms: Promises and realities.* New York: Cambridge University Press.

Bruce, B. C., & Rubin, A. (1993). *Electronic quills: A situated evaluation of using computers for writing in the classroom.* Hillsdale, NJ: Lawrence Erlbaum Associates.

Burbules, N. C., & Bruce, B. C. (1995, November). This is not a paper. *Educational Researcher, 24*(8), 12–18.

Connell, J. (1996). Exploring some of the educational implications of Idhe's philosophy of education. *Educational Foundations, 10,* 5–12.

Dobrzynski, J. (1996, April 28). @wit's end: Coping with e-mail overload. *The New York Times,* p A2.

Eliot, T. S. (1943). *Four Quartets.* New York: Harcourt Brace.

Ellul, J. (1980). *The technological system* (J. Neugroschel, Trans.). New York: Continuum.

Fiddler, J. (1996, April). *Embedding the information revolution* (Computer Science Colloquium Series). Champaign–Urbana: University of Illinois.

Haas, C. (1996). *Writing technology: Studies on the materiality of literacy.* Mahwah, NJ: Lawrence Erlbaum Associates.

Heidegger, M. (1977). The question concerning technology. In W. Lovitt (Trans.), *The question concerning technology and other essays* (pp. 311–341). New York: Harper & Row.

Ihde, D. (1990). *Technology and the lifeworld.* Bloomington: Indiana University Press.

Latour, B. (1988). Mixing humans and non-humans together: The sociology of a door-closer. *Social Problems, 35,* 298–310.

Latour, B. (1991). Technology is society made durable. In J. Law (Ed.), *A sociology of monsters: Essays on power, technology, and domination* (pp. 103–131). New York: Routledge.

Latour, B. (1993). *We have never been modern* (C. Porter, Trans.). Cambridge, MA: Harvard University Press.

Law, J. (Ed.). (1991). *A sociology of monsters: Essays on power, technology, and domination.* New York: Routledge.

McChesney, R. (1995, July 10). Information superhighway robbery. *In These Times, 19,* 14–17.

Michaels, S., Cazden, C., & Bruce, B. (1985). Whose computer is it anyway? *Science for the People, 17,* 36, 43–44.

Muspratt, S., Luke, A., & Freebody, P. (1997). *Constructing critical literacies.* Cresskill, NJ and Sydney: Hampton Press and Allen & Unwin.

Norman, D. A. (1993). *Things that make us smart: Defending human attributes in the age of the machine.* Reading, MA: Addison-Wesley.

Rheingold, H. (1993). *The virtual community: Homesteading on the electronic frontier.* New York: Addison-Wesley.

Rifkin, J. (1995). *The end of work: The decline of the global labor force and the dawn of the post-market era.* New York: Putnam.

Selfe, C., & Selfe, R. J., Jr. (1994). The politics of the interface: Power and its exercise in electronic contact zones. *College Composition and Communication, 45*(4), 480–504.

Sofia, Z. (in press). Computers, gender and technological irrationality. In H. Bromley & M. Apple (Eds.), *Education/technology/power: Educational computing as a social practice.* Albany: State University of New York Press.

Spender, D. (1995). *Nattering on the nets.* North Melbourne, Australia: Spinifex.

Stuckey, J. E. (1991). *The violence of literacy.* Portsmouth, NH: Boynton/Cook.

Sutton, R. E. (1991). Equity and computers in the schools: A decade of research. *Review of Educational Research, 61*(4), 475–503.

Wurth, J. (1996, June 2). Personal computer on UI school supply list. *The News Gazette,* pp. A1, A10.

17

▼▼▼▼▼▼▼

Metamedia Literacy:
Transforming Meanings and Media

J. L. Lemke
City University of New York
Brooklyn College School of Education

Literacies are legion. Each one consists of a set of interdependent social practices that link people, media objects, and strategies for meaning making (Beach & Lundell, chap. 6, this volume; Gee, 1990; Lemke, 1989b). Each is an integral part of a culture and its subcultures. Each plays a role in maintaining and transforming a society because literacies provide essential links between meanings and doings. Literacies are themselves technologies, and they give us the keys to using broader technologies. They also provide a key link between self and society: the means through which we act on, participate in, and become shaped by larger "ecosocial" systems and networks (see examples in the following and in Lemke, 1993a, 1995c). Literacies are transformed in the dynamics of these larger self-organizing systems, and we—our own human perceptions, identities, and possibilities—are transformed along with them.

That, at least, is the Big Picture as I would sketch it today. Let me try to fill in a few of the details that are particularly relevant to our concerns here. The notion of literacy as such seems to me to be too broad to be useful. I do not think we can define it more precisely than as a set of cultural competences for making socially recognizable meanings by the use of particular material technologies. Such a definition hardly distinguishes literacy from competence at cooking or choosing your wardrobe, except for the particular semiotic resources used to make meaning (language vs. the cuisine or fashion system) and the particular material artifacts that mediate this process (vocal sounds or written signs vs. foods or clothes). There was a time perhaps when we could believe that making meaning with language was somehow fundamentally different, or could be treated in isolation from making meaning with visual resources or patterns of bodily action and social interaction. But today our technologies are moving us from the age of writing to an age of multimedia authoring (see Purves, chap. 14, and Bolter, chap. 1, both this volume) in which voice-annotated documents and images, and written text itself, are now merely components of larger meaning objects. The meanings of words and images, read or heard, seen static or changing, are different because of the contexts in which they appear—contexts that consist significantly of the other media components. Meanings in multimedia are not fixed and additive (the word meaning plus the picture meaning), but multiplicative (word meaning modified by image context, image meaning modified by textual context), making a whole far greater than the simple sum of its parts (see Lemke, 1994b, 1997a). Moreover all literacy is multimedia literacy: You can never make meaning with language alone; there must always be a visual or vocal realization of linguistic signs that also carries nonlinguistic meaning (e.g., tone of voice or style of orthography). Signs must have some material reality in order to function as signs, but every material form potentially carries meanings according to more than one code. All semiotics is multimedia semiotics, and all literacy is multimedia literacy.

The European cultural tradition, among others, has long recognized and made use of these multimedia principles even in ordinary printed texts (cf. Alpers, 1983; Bellone, 1980; Eisenstein, 1979; Olson, 1994), whether in manuscript illustration or the use of diagrams in technical writing. But there has been a certain modern logocentrism (Derrida, 1976) that has identified language alone as a reliable medium for logical thought, and written language as the primary medium of, first, authoritative knowledge, and lately of all higher cognitive capacities (see Olson, 1994, for a reprise of these arguments and Lemke, 1995b, for a critique).

If we are required to specify exactly which semiotic resources and which material technologies define a particular literacy, then we have as many literacies as there are multimedia genres (cf. Gee, 1990). These can perhaps be further subdivided (and so the number of functional literacies further multiplied) by considering whether comptence with both the technologies of production and the technologies of use are to be included. When writing required pen and paper or typewriter, and reading required only the book (and maybe your eyeglasses) these distinctions were simple to maintain. But today whether you wish to read hypertext (see Bolter, chap. 1, this volume) or write it, you still need much the same hardware and software technologies, and you need both new authoring skills and new interpretive skills to use them.

Finally, in the spirit of Latour's (1987, 1993) work on actor networks in the study of technologies in society, we need to count other people as part of the technological ecology of literacy practices. (Latour constructed social networks from both the human and the nonhuman actors, such as technical artifacts in a social ecology of cultural practices). The network of interactions that renders a text or multimedia object meaningful is not limited to those between the author or user and the object, but must also include those with teachers, peers, and communities of people who embody the practices that make a particular sign combination meaningful. Isolated from all social interaction, humans do not learn to talk or write. However appealing the ideology of individualism may make the stereotype of the lone writer or reader, the fact that texts and signs are socially meaningful is what gives them their usefulness and makes them possible. What looks like the same text or multimedia genre on paper or on screen is not functionally the same, follows different meaning conventions, and requires different skills for its successful use, when it functions in different social networks for different purposes, as part of different human activities. A literacy is always a literacy in some genre, and it must be defined with respect to the sign systems deployed, the material technologies involved, and the social contexts of production, circulation, and use of the particular genre. We can be literate in the genre of the scientific research report or the genre of the business presentation; in each case the specific literate skills and the relevant communicative communities are very different.

In the study of written language literacy, there is still considerable debate about how important it is that the material signs of writing are relatively more permanent or more evanescent, how they are organized in space and time, and what counts as writing (Mathematics? Braille? Videotapes of American Sign Language?). Some of these questions remain of interest for particular genres and technologies, but few of them have yet been reconceptualized in the context of the new multimedia technologies (see Harris, 1995, and Lemke, 1997b).

We also need to reconceptualize the relations between literacies and the societies in which they operate, and the role of people in these larger processes (e.g., Lemke, 1995b; Olson, 1994). We need to improve our older ways of talking about these phenomena. It is no longer sufficient to imagine that societies are made up of isolated human individuals, tentatively linked by voluntary social contacts, with individual and autonomous minds somehow dissociated from the material world. We cannot get by anymore thinking that there is just one thing called literacy or that is it simply what individual minds do when confronted with symbols one at a time.

Every time we make meaning by reading a text or interpreting a graph or picture we do so by connecting the symbols at hand to other texts and other images read, heard, seen, or imagined on other occasions (the principle of general *intertextuality*; cf. Lemke, 1985, 1992, 1995a). Which connections we make (what kind and to which other texts and images) is partly individual, but also characteristic of our society and our place in it: our age, gender, economic class, affiliation groups, family traditions, cultures, and subcultures.

Literacies are always social: We learn them by participating in social relationships; their conventional forms evolved historically in particular societies; the meanings we make with them always tie us back into the fabric of meanings made by others.

Literacies are legion. Each different register, genre, or discourse formation (Bazerman, 1988, 1994; Foucault, 1969; Gee, 1990; Halliday, 1977, 1978; Lemke, 1995c; Martin, 1992) is the product of some particular subcommunity going about its special business. Being a native speaker, knowing the grammar, and checking the dictionary, is not enough to understand the texts of these specialized communities as their members understand them, unless we also know their contexts of use. Broadcast accounts of cricket test matches are mostly incomprehensible to me even with a rudimentary knowledge of terms and rules and an hour or two watching, even when watching a match as I hear the commentary. I am not sufficiently a member of this community, do not have enough experience, have not heard enough commentaries, seen enough matches, or understood the strategies of the game and the culture of this community. It is no different if you pick up a research article on quantum cosmology or biotechnology development, or a technical report on needed equipment repairs in an electrical generating station, or a Japanese *manga* comic book. It does not matter if the medium is voice or video, diagram or text. What matters is knowing how to make meaning like the natives do.

Literacies cannot be understood as passive receptivities. Making sense with a printed text is a complex and active process of meaning making not so different from writing the original of that text (say by editing and modifying a previous draft, or cobbling together from sets of notes a final coherent text). Both reading and writing are meaning-making processes of the same kind. They are in no sense inverse to one another (Harris, 1995; Lemke, 1989b). All that is different are the situational affordances: The other human or inanimate players we interact with to make our meanings—be they writing partners or marks scratched on paper.

It has been a long time since the technologies of literacy were as simple as pen, ink, and paper; and in the era of print, as before, literacy has rarely meant verbal text alone. Many of the genres of literacy, from the popular magazine article to the scientific research report, combine visual images and printed text in ways that make cross-reference between them essential to understanding them as their regular readers and writers do. No technology is an island. Every literate meaning-making practice is interdependent with skills from keyboarding to page turning, typesetting to bookbinding, and copyediting to marketing and distribution (in the case of print technologies). As our technologies become more complex they find themselves situated in larger and longer networks of other technologies and other cultural practices (Latour, 1993).

Publishing yourself on the World Wide Web may cut out many of the old print middle men, human and machine, but in addition to simple writing and typing skills, you need to be able to operate the software and hardware to get your work formatted properly in HTML (hypertext markup language), loaded on a server, and connected to the Internet. Someone has to write and update those programs; design, manufacture, sell, and deliver the hardware; configure it; maintain the network; develop the protocols; and offer technical assistance and service. As a universal information processor, the same computer can serve many of these purposes, which makes the process look simpler; but what people have to know to use the computer, and to design and maintain this whole system of practices, becomes far greater, both materially and semiotically. Some people somewhere have to manipulate more different kinds of matter in more different ways. We have to know how to do more different sorts of things (collectively and individually).

Literacies cannot be adequately analyzed just as what individuals do. We must understand them as part of the larger systems of practices that hold a society together, that make it a unit of dynamic self-organization far larger than the individual. In fact, if we think the word *society* means only people, then we need another term, one that, like *ecosystem* includes the total environment: machines, buildings, cables, satellites, bedrock, sewers, farms, insect life, bacteria, and everything with which we are interdependent in order to be the complex community that we are. We could not be the community we are unless we did the things we do, and most of what we do depends not just on the physical and biological properties of all these system partners, but on what they mean to us.

Dynamically, the total system we are talking about, the one within which we need to analyze changes in literacies and technologies, is not of course a system of things at all. It has to be a system of interdependent processes in which these things participate, and which link them, and us, together into a system. Biological and geological processes, human activities, and social practices—regarded as one system of interdependent goings on: an "ecosocial" system (Lemke, 1993a, 1995c). Within this system we have to follow out the links and networks of interdependence: which practices where and when are interdependent with which other practices elsewhere and elsewhen. Critical among these processes, insofar as human action matters to the dynamics of the system, are the meaning making practices by which we humans interpret, evaluate, plan, and cooperate, including our many literacy practices. (The boundary between literacy practices as such and meaning making, or semiotic signifying practices in general is a fuzzy one. Core literacy practices are usually distinguished by code, language, and by medium, spatial, visible, and durable. (For efforts to deal with the limitations of such definitions, see Harris, 1995; Lemke, 1997b.)

We no longer have to separate our material technologies so radically as we once did from our cognitive strategies. People with bodies participate in activities and practices, such as jointly authoring a multimedia Web document, in which we and our appliances are partners in action; in which who we are and how we act is as much a function of what is at hand as of what is in head. This is the powerful new viewpoint on human activity and society that many disciplines today are converging toward, whether they speak of actor networks (Latour, 1987; Lynch & Woolgar, 1990), situated or social cognition (Hutchins, 1995; Lave, 1988; Rogoff, 1990), ecosocial semiotics (Lemke, 1993a, 1995c), mediated activity (Engestrom, 1990; Wertsch, 1991), or cyborg transgressions (Bryson & deCastell, 1996; Haraway, 1991; Sofia, 1995). Instead of theorizing causal relations from one autonomous domain to another (technologies to literacies, literacies to minds, minds to societies), if we unite all these domains as participants in the myriad subnetworks of an ecosocial system, we can give detailed accounts of their interdependencies and the self-organizing dynamics of this complex system. We need to break down the artificial boundaries we have tried to create between the mental and the material, the individual and the social aspects of people and things interacting physically and semiotically with other people and things.

Today new information technologies are mediating the transformation of our meaning-making communities. We can communicate more often and more intimately with more geographically and culturally diverse communities than ever before. Online conferences and listserv groups, the denizens of chat rooms, and the pioneers of MUDs and MOOs (Day, Crump, & Rickly, 1996; Harrison & Stephen, 1996; Unsworth, 1996) are extending old communities and creating new ones (Rheingold, 1993). People who corresponded a few times a year and met once or twice at conferences can now be in regular contact by e-mail, by inexpensive (we hope) voice Internet, and perhaps soon, bandwidth and the regulators willing, by videoconferencing. You can have a more significant dialogue with someone in Australia than with someone across the hall, and sustain it just as easily. You can don a new gender or identity, in masquerade or for exploration of possible selves (Day et al., 1996; Stone, 1991). You can experience new kinds of relationships to people and be treated differently by them. You can lurk and listen in communities you might someday want to join. You can have a first taste without risk or commitment, and you will hear viewpoints expressed that you might not otherwise have come into contact with, or might have discounted prematurely out of prejudice if you identified their source in other ways than what cyberspace makes possible.

Every new community, every transformed community, potentially represents a new literacy. Every new system of conventional practices for meaningful communication already is a new literacy embedded in new technologies. All participation in new communities, in new social practices, potentially makes available to us new identities as individuals and new forms of humanity as members of communities. Insofar as education is initiation into communities, and especially into their generic and specialized literacy practices, new information technologies, new communication practices, and new social networks make possible new paradigms for education and learning, and call into question the assumptions on which the older paradigms rest.

Old practices migrate en masse to new or transformed ecosocial systems: We re-create much that is already familiar. Our Web documents initially look like print documents. Our online communities initially grow out of familiar institutional groupings. But our new online homes come equipped with new appliances, our old practices take on new meanings in these new settings, new opportunities will get taken up, and new serendipities become likely. Change and transformation are at work.

TRANSFORMING LITERACIES

What are the new literacies that new information technologies are making both necessary and possible? The generic literacies of the Information Age will certainly include multimedia authoring skills, multimedia critical analysis, cyberspace exploration strategies, and cyberspace navigation skills (Lemke, 1996b).

But there is also an even more important question to consider. How can we understand what they demand of us, and how can adopting and adapting them transform social relationships and social structures? I discuss in the following some larger themes that go beyond specific literacy skills and that I believe will define the most radical transformations in literacy and literacy education that the new technologies may bring.

Multimedia Literacies

Multimedia authoring skills and multimedia critical analysis correspond closely to traditional skills of text writing and critical reading, but we need to understand how narrowly restrictive our literacy education traditions have been in the past in order to see how much more students will need in the future than we are now giving them. We do not teach students how to integrate even drawings and diagrams into their writing, much less archival photo images, video clips, sound effects, voice audio, music, animation, or more specialized representations (mathematical formulas, graphs and tables, etc.). For such multimedia productions it does not even really make sense any more, if it ever did, to speak of integrating these other media into writing. Text may or may not form the organizing spine of a multimedia work. What we really need to teach, and to understand before we can teach it, is how various literacies and various cultural traditions combine these different semiotic modalities to make meanings that are more than the sum of what each could mean separately. I have called this multiplying meaning (Lemke, 1994b, 1997a) because the options for meanings from each medium cross-multiply in a combinatorial explosion; in multimedia meaning possibilities are not merely additive.

At least this is so in principle. In practice, every multimedia genre and every multimedia literacy tradition restricts the enormous set of possibilities to only some allowed or favored combinations, but there are still always more than what one would get just by adding those of each medium separately. No text exactly duplicates what a picture means to us: text and picture together are not two ways of saying the same thing; the text means more when juxtaposed with the picture, and so does the picture when set beside the text.

We need also to realize that these multimedia skills are not advanced skills that should only follow learning the separate media literacies. Young children's early modes of communication integrate vocal articulations with large-motor gestures; they only gradually learn to differentiate gestures from drawing, and drawing from writing, as independent systems for making meaning. They are perfectly ready to learn integrated multimedia literacies from the start, and of course they do: They learn to read picture books while talking with adults and playing with toys that resemble images in the books. They begin to write and draw while telling stories and leaving traces of their gestures on paper, walls, and refrigerator doors (cf. Dyson, 1991; Hicks & Kanevsky, 1992; Lemke, 1994b). However, our theories and teaching of literacy have long been too logocentric. Whereas children are learning to distinguish different semiotic resources (e.g., drawing from writing), thus opening up larger combinatorial spaces for using them in coordinated ways, we are only teaching them to use one: written language. When we do teach other modes, such as singing, drawing, or mime, we still do not teach students about the traditions and possibilities for combining these with writing and with each other. That needs to change, very quickly and very thoroughly, if we are to help students develop sophisticated multimedia literacies. Their new authoring skills will hopefully enable students to create multimedia portfolios (cf. Kieffer, Hale, & Templeton, chap. 9, this volume) that will help teachers remove the logocentric bias from our evaluations of their understanding and competence, as well as enable them to produce the kinds of meanings they really want to mean.

Likewise, critical interpretive skills must be extended from the analysis of print texts to video and film, to news photos and advertising images, to statistical charts and tables, and mathematical graphs. We must help students understand exactly how to read the text differently and interpret the image differently because of the presence of the other. We even need to understand how it is that we know which text is relevant to the interpretation of which image, and vice versa. All of this requires, at least for teachers and media specialists, a useful understanding of multimedia semiotics.

I am currently trying to develop such a general theory of multimedia based on seeing how three universal semiotic functions—presentation (creating or describing a world), orientation (taking a stance toward the presentation and its audiences), and organization (linking parts into wholes)—draw on the resources of each available semiotic modality (language, typography, images, music, etc.) to produce a meaning effect (Lemke, 1989a, 1995c, 1997a). For instance representational imagery in painting presents the world, but figure perspective orients the view to it, and the composition of masses and vectors of edges and lines organize its parts into a coherent whole. In text, we present with propositional content, orient with mood (command vs. question) and modality (*may* vs. *must*), and organize with genre structure (introduction, body, conclusion) and cohesion (*John . . . becomes . . . he . . .*).

Other related work in social semiotics is also contributing to this understanding (e.g., Kress & van Leeuwen, 1996; O'Toole, 1990, 1994). With such a functionally motivated framework for desribing what is possible in multimedia, it should be possible not only to analyze particular multimedia works, but to compare different approaches and traditions in terms of which possibilities they make use of and which they do not. We may even be able to identify new combinations worth trying out.

Both authoring skills and critical interpretive skills for multimedia potentially transform not just the ways students and teachers communicate information and ideas, but also the ways in which we learn and teach. Kinzer and Risko (chap. 11, this volume) report on ways in which prospective teachers can learn by producing multimedia analyses of their initial teaching experiences. Goldman-Segall (1992) and Tierney and Damarin (chap. 15, this volume) provide analogous case studies of students learning through multimedia production. In both cases the integration of video and pictorial realism, providing context and complexity, with textual analysis, providing focus and conceptualization, help define and transform viewpoints on our own and others' experiences.

Informatic Literacies

The literacies of the Information Age are not just about making and using multimedia. They also include *informatic literacies*: the skills of the library user as well as those of the text user. These are skills for categorizing and locating information and multimedia objects and presentations. Cyberspace will be many things: the world's ultimate shopping mall, humanity's most enticing playground, the university of universities, and, especially from a literacy point of view, the library of all libraries. Search and retrieval strategies will be subsumed in the arts of exploration and navigation; we will replace a metaphor in which texts come to us (e.g., downloading them from a remote server) with one in which we go to them (navigating though virtual 3-D worlds that represent servers and their contents). What strategies are useful for finding out what kinds of knowledge exist in the world? How do you browse the library of cyberspace? Once you pick an area of interest, how do you systematically explore it? Once you decide where you want to go, what do you have to know to get there? Librarians spend years learning how information is classified and sorted according to the conventions of a hundred disciplines and interest areas. What do they know that we all need to know? How can we represent the topography of information in ways that will make it easier for all of us to navigate around in it?

Without all these skills, future citizens will be as disempowered as those who today cannot write, read, or use a library. These are the necessary skills of our future literacies, those we will all need. However, new information technologies also open up possibilities for extending our literacies in other ways, and many of us will choose to develop additional kinds of literacies that perhaps not everyone will need, but that will confer great benefits on those who acquire them. I discuss in the following two potentially important categories of such value-added literacies: quantitative–mathematical literacy and cross-cultural literacy.

Typological and Topological Meaning.   Analyzing multimedia semiotics has led me to ask some old questions in new ways and to begin to see the history of writing, drawing, calculating, and displaying images visually in a different light (Lemke, 1994b, 1997a). I am coming to believe that we make meaning in two fundamentally complementary ways: (a) by classifying things into mutually exclusive categories, and (b) by distinguishing variations of degree (rather than kind) along various continua of difference. Language operates mainly in the first way, which I call *typological.* Visual perception and spatial gesturing (drawing, dancing) operate more in the second, *topological* way. As I have already argued, real meaning making generally involves combinations of different semiotic modalities, and so also combinations of these two rather general modes. The semantics of words in language is mainly categorial or typological in its principles, but the significant visual distinctions in handwriting (e.g., writing more boldly or in slightly larger letters) or calligraphy, or the acoustic effects of speaking a bit more loudly or forcefully, make sense along a continuous spectrum of possibilities, topologically. (In mathematics, topology studies matters of relative nearness, connectedness, continuity, etc.). Even in specialized subject areas like science, mathematics, art, or music, the educational curriculum has followed the logocentric tradition in emphasizing conceptual categories and semantic distinctions and has neglected to educate students about topological principles of making meaning by creating and interpreting differences of degree as well as differences of kind. I believe that the new multimedia technologies will make the salience and importance of topological kinds of meaning far greater, and that an emphasis on these two complementary modes of meaning making may help students grasp kinds of meanings (e.g., those based in quantitative and mathematical reasoning) that have tended to elude many of us in the past.

What is it that pictures, drawings, diagrams, graphs, tables, and equations do for us that verbal text alone cannot? What can we do far better still with combinations of texts and these other media? What is it exactly about a picture that even a thousand words cannot say as well? Or about a diagram and its caption that tell us far more than a drawing or a text alone could do? Why has natural science chosen to speak so often in the language of mathematics? And is mathematics really a language? Should mathematical and quantitative literacies be considered integral parts of a multimedia literacy for today and tomorrow?

To answer these questions it helps to distinguish these two rather different kinds of meaning, or strategies for making meaning, that all human cultures seem to have evolved. We make meaning by contrasting types or categories of things, events, people, and signs. For instance, we distinguish right from left, up from down, male from female, fruit from vegetable, motion from rest, red from blue, x from y, ahh from ohh, buying from selling, live from dead, and writing from drawing. This is the basis of the semantics of natural language, and of the analogous representations of identifiable types, kinds, categories, qualities, and so on, in other media. Most are based on a logic of either–or. Within a category we can often distinguish and contrast many different subcategories, and so on to great delicacy of typological categorization and description. Our verbal sentences construct a small number of semantic relations among categorial processes, participants, and circumstances (cf. Halliday, 1985; Martin, 1992), and from this comes our conceptual reasoning. However, this is not the whole story of human meaning.

Some of these categorical distinctions also allow differences by degree, so that there is now a possibility of intermediate cases that are in some measurable or quantitative sense in between others: higher and lower, nearer and further, faster and slower, or more reddish orange. However, there is nothing that is in between motion and rest, or living and dead, and no mix of the letters x and y. Language does recognize difference by degree, but has very few and quite limited resources for describing such differences. Other forms of meaningful human action, however, are wonderful at indicating shades of intermediate degree: the rise of an eyebrow, the tension in a voice, the breadth of a gesture, the depth of a bow. Space and time, movement, position, and pacing define for us the possibility of meanings that are more topological, matters of degree, of almost-the-same, and just-a-bit-more-or-less, of what is *like* because it is near to or almost equal to, rather than *like* because it does or does not possess certain criterial properties for membership in a category, for being of some type. Typological and topological meaning are complementary in many fundamental ways.

Because language is so heavily biased toward the construction of typologically grounded meanings, it requires complementary partners that are better at constructing topological meaning, especially when what we are trying to make sense about is a phenomenon that changes in important ways by degree. You cannot readily describe in words the shape of a draped bolt of fabric, but you can gesture that shape and you can draw it (if you have learned the necessary skills). If the shape represents data on the pressure at different places inside a nuclear reactor system, it is not good enough to say the pressure is increasing very quickly near the containment dome: You want to measure the rate of increase and extrapolate it graphically or algebraically.

Many cultural phenomena seem to be strictly typological, but topological or quantitative analysis can undermine this illusion (e.g., biology finds no quantitative basis for racial categories). Other phenomena (like the phonemes of our native language) we learn to perceive typologically, even though a topological or quantitative analysis may be hard pressed to see how (e.g., the acoustic spectra of language sounds on an oscilloscope screen do not neatly fit phoneme categories, so you cannot "see" where particular letters or even whole syllables begin or end—and sometimes cannot see them at all). Many natural phenomena, however, yield rather directly to analysis by degree, in space, in time, in movement or change, in mass, in temperature, and in all the other quantitative variables that science has found so useful.

Our concepts tend to depend on the typological semantics of language or other media of representation, but our experience in the world as material bodies in space and time interacting with an environment shows us the importance of topological meaning as well. It is no accident that the most systematic extension of natural language into topological domains of meaning, known to us as mathematics, has arisen historically as a kind of bridge between conceptual language and quantitative measurement and description. Or that mathematics has been built from both sides: from language through arithmetic to algebra and functions, and from continuous variation in the environment to visual depiction to geometric diagrams and Cartesian graphs. The modern unification of algebra and geometry is only one chapter in the long history of the semiotic integration of typological and topological meaning.

Many people experience great difficulty with quantitative and mathematical reasoning, beginning from just those points where, historically, mathematics went beyond what natural language could comfortably deal with, inventing notions like complex ratios and fractions, partially compensating operations and reciprocal inverses, continuously varying functions and equations with multiple factors and operations. Natural language has no problem with integers, with simple fractions or ratios, and with addition and subtraction. It can just barely get around multiplication, and begins to give up with division. Many mathematical concepts that are confusing or resist easy explanation and learning in natural language alone become far clearer with visual representations and manipulatives combined *with* natural language. It is not a matter of substituting one for the other, but of combining them together: conceptual typological reasoning and quantitative topological accounting.

Not every aspect of human cultural life yet requires sophisticated quantitative and mathematical reasoning. It is not yet part of the literacy skills of most nontechnical genres. For many purposes the combination of visual-image representations, including abstract ones like graphs and tables, and verbal ones is sufficient. However, I suspect that extending multimedia literacy to include mathematical representations could become much easier with new information technologies. Expanded use of and familiarity with visual representations will make it easier for students to deal with quantitative relations expressed also in more formal mathematical terms (numerical or algebraic). If the time comes when a new generation's multimedia literacy is as much at home with quantitative reasoning and representation as with depiction and verbal text, then ideological oversimplifications based purely on category names, like White versus Black, straight versus gay, or masculine versus feminine will be vulnerable to quantitative deconstruction for far more people than the few technical specialists who understand these arguments today. The cultures, attitudes, and characteristics of real people have never fit the pigeonhole categories of our typologies and stereotypes. Too many real people have claims, to some degree and in some ways, to fit both sides of these dichotomies, to be members of many categories whose names and definitions make them seem mutually exclusive. Our lived realities cannot be faithfully represented in purely typological ways; too many people have no voice where there are no other ways to make sense. The topological potential of multimedia literacy can help give voice, dignity, and power to real hybrid people. It can undermine an ideological system that limits personal identities to a few available and approved social pigeonholes and let us see and show one another the much larger multidimensional universe of real human possibilities.

Global Cultural Literacies. Information exchange, academic and business collaboration, and even entertainment and shopping, are very soon going to be much more global and cross-cultural than ever before in human history. The dominance of cyberspace by the European American cultural tribes will inevitably be short-lived. Asian societies have the technology and the confidence in their cultural traditions to ensure that global exchange will not take place entirely on our terms, as it has for the past couple of centuries. We may not welcome the loss of our economic hegemony and our impossibly exaggerated standard of living relative to the rest of the world's population, but we should certainly welcome new ways of making meaning. English may or may not survive as the lingua franca of the Internet (a lot depends on whether machine translation ever becomes effective, fast, and cheap), and although it would not hurt Americans particularly to learn a non-Indo-European language with a nonalphabetic script, what seems most likely is that non-European traditions of visual design and aesthetics (e.g., Asian-European hybrids in multimedia) will become extremely important to the evolving genres of cyberspace. In time other cultural traditions will join the mix in substantial ways as well, as African-European cultural hybrids already have in music and visual arts styles.

Increasingly, members of our online communities are going to come from non-European-American cultural backgrounds. We are going to have to learn to communicate effectively with them, and to learn effectively from them. Our economic success, our intellectual opportunities, and perhaps the long-term cause of world peace and harmony depends on our success in this. Because we have been on top for so long, it will be harder for many upper middle-class Americans and Europeans to learn how to listen across cultural differences. Most of the rest of the world has long since had to learn how to listen to us.

As we face the many tasks of communication and design, of combining and integrating text with graphic images both abstract and iconic, not to mention animations, videos, sound, and so forth, we will want to consider all the resources, all the traditions, and all the possibilities in the human repertoire. We will need to do this as the next phase of world cultural evolution speeds up. We will be moving beyond the era of national and ethnic cultures to an era of diverse cultural hybrids, each with a global community of members and aficionados. The new world cultural order will be no less diverse and complex than our present one, but its basis will extend beyond geography and family heritage to encompass shared interests and participation in activity-centered communities (see examples in Tierney & Damarin, chap. 15, this volume).

The global human heritage provides more than just geocultural diversity as a resource for new ways of making meaning: It also provides the historical diversity within each of our cultural traditions. Visual and textual forms and the conventions for combining them have passed through many interesting historical turns, some of them largely lost to present-day awareness. The study of the history of semiotic media is likely to become an increasingly important part of scholarship, and a richer resource in the curriculum. In my own work I have been greatly impressed by what can be learned from the rich resource of a comprehensive, global history of mathematical notations (Cajori, 1928), or from the growing literature on the history of visual representations in many fields (e.g., Alpers, 1983; Bellone, 1980; Eisenstein, 1979; Skelton, 1958; Tufte, 1983, 1990; see also Olson, 1994). Vast as this underappreciated literature is, there is more still on the representational conventions of non-Western cultures. Both Western and non-Western media history are likely, in my opinion, to richly reward study, appreciation, and appropriation for the purposes of constructing and teaching our future multimedia literacies. These then are the key directions for transformation of our contemporary literacies as we enter the Information Age: We certainly need generalized multimedia and informatic literacy skills now, and we will probably also need more quantitative topological and more global historical literacies for the near future.

TRANSFORMING LEARNING PARADIGMS

With so much to be learned, we need to give some thought to how new information technologies may transform our institutional habits of teaching and learning. There are two paradigms of learning and education contending in our society today, and the new technologies will, I believe, shift the balance between them significantly (Lemke, 1994a).

The *curricular learning paradigm* dominates institutions such as schools and universities. The curricular paradigm assumes that someone else will decide what you need to know and will arrange for you to learn it all in a fixed order and on a fixed schedule. It is the educational paradigm of industrial capitalism and factory-based mass production. It developed simultaneously with them, and in close philosophical agreement; it feeds into their wider networks of employment and careers, and resembles them in its authoritarianism, top-down planning, rigidity, economies of scale, and general unsuitability to the new information-based fast capitalist world (discussed later). It is widely refused and resisted by students, and its end results provide little more of demonstrated usefulness in the nonacademic world than a few text literacies and certification as a member of the middle class.

The *interactive learning paradigm* dominates such institutions as libraries and research centers. It assumes that people determine what they need to know based on their participation in activities in which such needs arise, and in consultation with knowledgeable specialists; that they learn in the order that suits them, at a comfortable pace, and just in time to make use of what they learn. This is the learning paradigm of the people who created the Internet and cyberspace. It is the paradigm of access to information, rather than imposition of learning. It is the paradigm of how people with power and resources choose to learn. Its end results are generally satisfying to the learner, and usually useful for business or scholarship. It is perhaps also the paradigm of *fast capitalism* (Gee, 1996; Lemke, 1996a), in which economies based on the production and circulation of information favor rapidly changing work groups of flexible individuals engaged in projects that produce "just-in-time" results for niche-market customers. It may tend to produce less common learning among the members of a society and favor specialization over liberal arts education.

These two educational paradigms are in fundamental conflict, and many disappointments that schools are not more eager to adopt computer-mediated information technologies may perhaps be laid at the door of this largely unrecognized conflict (Hodas, 1994).

The curricular paradigm is failing disastrously in the United States today. Anyone who has spent time in urban schools, even the better ones, can tell you that things are even worse than standardized tests and statistics indicate. Most students really do not see the usefulness of most of what they are being expected to learn. Many know they are unprepared for what they are scheduled to learn this year. The nation is trying to develop a national curriculum at a time when only the most rudimentary elements of school-based learning (say up to Grade 8) are demonstrably of value to most citizens when they leave school. Beyond that, whatever some will use, others will not need at all. We are trying to impose uniform learning at a time when there has never been more radical inequality of every kind among students of a given age. Fortunately, the institutional arrangements for schooling in the United States are so decentralized that a national curriculum in practice (as opposed to agreements in principle) seems unlikely ever to actually happen. I believe that the effort to create a uniform content-centered national curriculum may in fact seriously hamper our transition to more effective and appropriate educational models for the globally competitive future.

What seems to be generally agreed among educators and many citizens and prospective employers is that we want people, of whatever age, who can guide their own learning and who know enough to know how to learn more, including where and to whom they should turn for useful advice and relevant information. We want people who know things that they want to know, and people who know things that are useful in human enterprises outside schools. We want people who are at least a little critical and skeptical about information and points of view, and have some idea how to judge their reliability. Beyond this, however, there is no general social consensus about the content of education beyond what could be learned in the first 8 or 9 years of schooling, and there is no basis in empirical research for deciding what every citizen would actually find it useful to know after leaving school. My personal view is that if such research were done it would not find much of anything universally necessary beyond what could be taught in those basic years. It is perhaps time that we put behind us the U.S. preoccupation with nation building and common culture. We are indissolubly tied together by our interactions with and interdependencies on one another, and it really does not matter, except for ideological purposes, how much alike we are or are taught to pretend we are.

Every effort to construct a common curriculum is an effort by some people to impose their values on others who probably do not agree. Only demonstrated necessity or substantial usefulness to most people can morally justify curricular uniformity, especially in the context of a coercive educational system (i.e., one in which participation is not voluntary and resistance is punished by sanctions that go beyond the inevitable consequences of our own actions). It is particularly morally questionable that curricular education is imposed on the weakest members of our society: those who are forbidden many of the political and legal rights of all other citizens, solely because of their age. Fully empowered adults would not tolerate the faults of many of our schools: their authoritarianism, their educational incompetence, their inadequate resources, and their physical conditions. The very young may have little choice about their helplessness; they cannot yet operate the machinery of our complex society at even the most basic levels. We cannot empower them. But from an age somewhere between 10 and 13 years old, depending on the individual (and governed at least a little by the extent of opportunities afforded), we know that increasing numbers of younger citizens can exercise adult rights and want to, but are not permitted to, and are prevented from doing so by law and by force. It is arguable that the curricular paradigm survives in our schools mainly because of, and perhaps in part in the service of, the political domination of citizens in their second decade by older and more powerful adults.

New information technologies will make it possible for students to learn what they want, when they want, and how they want, without schools. Not all students will have equal or even immediate access to these technologies (cf. Bruce & Hogan, chap. 16, this volume), but those who do will surely see the possibilities. Curricular education will not be able to compete for sheer educational effectiveness or economic efficiency with the learning services that will become available online and in portable media for interactive education. The interactive paradigm need not be one of isolated learning, or even of exclusively computer-mediated learning. Social interaction among peers and between learners and mentors and other experts will take place online, one on one and in groups of various sizes. Some of this interaction will be live in real time, and some will be asynchronous, as with listservs and newsgroups. Face-to-face groups will still play an important role, as will direct interaction with teachers. However, the proportions of time spent in each of these learning modes will change radically, and the diversity of approaches to learning will increase (Garner & Gillingham, chap. 13, this volume).

What will necessarily be radically different, however, is the single issue of control. In the interactive paradigm, students will pursue topics, interests, problems, and agendas of their own and of the groups they participate in. They will encounter the fundamental categories, concepts, and principles of all the basic disciplines, whatever trails they blaze through the forests of knowledge, precisely to the extent that these notions really are fundamental and widely applicable and therefore necessarily to be found wherever we travel. But they will all fashion for themselves essentially different educations, with only that degree of commonality that arises from interaction with others and from the common usefulness of common notions.

The interactive learning paradigm, once its information technology infrastructure is in place, will also very likely be a lot cheaper than the present schools and curricula arrangements. We will not need a separate material infrastructure for education nearly to the extent that we do today; education will be one function of a multipurpose technology. We will not need to buy all the working time of so many teachers, but only to compensate sufficiently the people who make themselves available to students online, and the few specialists who will staff more specialized learning facilities. Those who produce great interactive learning environments will be well paid by the marketplace. A great deal of productive labor potential now tied up in chalking-and-talking curricula to captive class-room audiences will be liberated to enrich the general information economy.

What will the new information technologies be that can best support an interactive learning paradigm and make use of those multimedia and informatic literacies that will genuinely be needed by everyone?

TRANSFORMING TECHNOLOGIES: TOWARD METAMEDIA LITERACIES

The first generation of interactive learning technologies has mostly been, not unexpectedly, simply a transposition of the textbook model of education to a new display medium. Trees may be grateful, but little about the nature of learning changes, perhaps only the increased motivation for some students generated by novelty. But as soon as online text becomes digital (as opposed to bitmapped images of the page), it is easily searched, and if it can be searched, it can be indexed and cross-referenced. Now the text is also simultaneously a database, and hypertext is born (Bolter, 1991, chap. 1, this volume; Landow, 1992; Nelson, 1974). If we can use a word or phrase in the text as an index entry to find other occurrences, and also add cross-references to other specific items in the same text, why not then make links to other texts? In the simplest cases, hypertexts offer us only one link per item, but there is no inherent limitation of this kind in the concept or the technology. If we can jump from one text to another, and to multiple landing points from each jumping-off point, we will need some navigational assistance in order to backtrack and to get a sense of the text space we are mapping out and traversing. Because the topography of these links is nonlinear, a two- or three-dimensional image or map is a useful navigational tool. It can be established by an author and later customized or reconstructed by each reader.

Now learning changes. Instead of being the prisoners of textbook authors and their priorities, scope, and sequence, we are free agents who can find more about a topic they skimped on, or find alternative interpretations they did not mention (or agree with, or even consider moral or scientific). We can shift the topic to match our judgments of relevance to our own interests and agendas, and we can return to a standard, textbooklike development later. We can learn as if we had access to all these texts, and as if we had an expert who could point out to us most of the relevant cross-references among them. We now have to learn to exercise more complex forms of judgment and we get a lot of practice doing so.

The next generation of interactive learning environments adds visual images and then sound and video and animation, all of which became practical when speed and storage capacity can accommodate these information-dense topological forms of meaning. From the typological point of view, text has very low redundancy, it does not code in much more than is needed to make the key distinctions between one word and another, but visual images typically contain all sorts of typologically irrelevant information—which is for that very reason potentially critical to their topological meaning capacity. (Compression strategies need to be careful not to be overly biased toward preserving typological meaning at the expense of potentially valuable topological meaning. If you reduce the number of bytes allotted to Aunt Hilda's voice message as much as you could for her e-mail message, you could probably still make out the words, but it would not sound like Aunt Hilda anymore.) These more topological media cannot be indexed and cross-referenced for their internal content (what the picture shows, say) but must be treated as whole objects. Even so, as objects they can become nodes for hyperlinks, and so hypermedia is born (see Bolter, chap. 1, this volume; Landow & Delany, 1991). The importance of the corresponding multimedia literacies has already been discussed, but it is worth noting that it is not only using hypermedia, but authoring them that the new technologies make easier. Today anyone can edit audio and video at home, produce good-quality animations, shape three-dimensional objects and environments, combine them with text and still images, add music and voice, and produce works far beyond what any publisher or movie studio could have done until a few years ago.

The key to interactive learning paradigms, however, is neither hyperlinks nor multimedia, but interactivity itself. Interactive media present themselves differently to different users depending on the user's own actions. This can be as simple as seeing one image rather than another after clicking on a link, but it becomes educationally useful to the extent that the result of the interactions accumulates intelligently, so that the whole history of my interaction with a program influences what it shows me when I click on that link. This is the basic principle of *intelligent tutoring systems* (ITS; see Wenger, 1987), a parallel development to educational hypermedia, but still mainly within the curricular paradigm. An ITS program constructs a model of the user over time and customizes its responses to lead the user optimally to a fixed learning goal. Each different user potentially follows a different pathway, but all end up in the same place.

What would we get if we combined the dynamic user-customization of an ITS with the learning paradigm of exploring and navigating interactive hypermedia? The purpose of a user model then would not be to create a path to a fixed goal; goals would be emergent for the user as a result of interacting with the media. The user model would catalog where we had been, our learning styles and preferences, our prior background in different subjects, and could offer us a filtered set of choices for each next jump or link that would optimize their potential value for us. The program could be set to offer narrow or wider ranges of choices, index the options by various criteria useful to us in making the ultimate choice ourselves, and include a certain percentage of serendipitous surprises. Like a human tutor, the program would get to know us, and in effect make suggestions to help us make the most of our time in cyberspace. It could tailor the text and images it generated to our needs (cf. Hovy, 1987). It would also need to be able to reconfigure information from one medium to another, to the extent that this is possible, varying the relative emphasis of text, voice, still images, videos, animations, and degrees of abstraction, either by selection from available items, or by conversion from one to another. This would, accordingly, be in fact a *metamedia* system.

With such a technology we could be free to learn in the language and dialect of our choice, with the visual-aesthetic styles of our choice, and the mix of media we learn from best. Just as various document definition languages (such as SGML, HTML, and VRML; Hockey, 1996) allow different browsers to customize how they present the same text and image files, one can imagine our metamedia system's source files to contain data in abstract representations that could be variously displayed as text, chart or table, graph, diagram, visual image, video, and so on (cf. Arens, Hovy, & Vossers, 1992) according to user preference and ITS tutor recommendation.

Original source media are thus going to be relinked and their displays transformed endlessly by different individual and group users who are sharing files. Systems will need to keep track of user annotations and overlays (backing up earlier versions), user-added links, user transformations of medium, user-defined sequencings, and so on so that any original source file or complete metamedia work will exist in many customized versions, each with a traceable history. Some of these versions will conceivably become more popular with new users than the originals, and some may come to be recognized as classics, even as all of them get endlessly modified. Various user communities will determine what constitutes value-added in this process, and what is transient or idiosyncratic. Intelligent metamedia tutoring systems will, of course, have to be able to sort through the many available versions as they seek optimization for their user. Users will inevitably gain some sophistication in this process as well, as they provide the tutor with explicit instructions and responses to queries, as well as statistical patterns of past and continuing choices, to which the tutoring program will be sensitive.

TRANSFORMING HUMANITY

The ultimate display medium is reality itself: what we see and hear, touch and feel; what we manipulate and control; where we feel ourselves to be present and living. Our bodies are integral parts of larger ecosocial systems: We live in those systems materially as sensory signals and motor feedback, heat exchanges and nutrient and waste flows link us into them; and we live in them semiotically as we make culturally and personally meaningful sense of our participation. Reading a text, our verbal and visual imaginations can begin to conjure a second world of meanings in addition to the usual realistic ones. Watching a film on a large screen, the divergence between sense data and fictional illusion diminishes; we can experience terror or a sensation of falling while watching a fabric screen and sitting in a fixed chair. It is possible to intercept many of the signals by which our bodies locate themselves in space, time, and reality and replace them by other signals. To do this we have to monitor our actions and efferent motor signals as well as supply new inputs, because our bodies create reality out of the relation between outgoing efferent and incoming afferent nerve impulses. A fast enough computer can simulate reality well enough to fool a large part of our body's evolved links with its environment. We can create virtual realities, and we can feel as if we are living in them. We can create a sense of full presence (cf. Benedikt, 1991; Rheingold, 1991).

Within a virtual reality (VR) environment, all other media can be presented and coordinated. What VR technologies add is greater interactivity: We can make more things happen in VR worlds, and that is partly why we feel that they are more real. However, they do not have to happen according to the laws of normal physics, or the constraints of our normal ecological environment, provided the timing of action and reaction is precise enough to make them seem equally real. In principle in VR we can learn by doing, without consuming proportional material resources as we would in the normal world, without the attendant risks to life and limb, or the consequences to our life-sustaining ecosystem. And we can do what is simply not normally possible: We can change reality by acts of will or small motor commands, we can be the sorcerers of our dreams and our nightmares.

We can also learn to be a different sort of human being (Lemke, 1993b). We can walk, not through a simulated Martian valley, but by telepresence and a robot sensor system, on the actual surface of Mars. We can sound with whales and soar with eagles. We can observe the earth from space in real time, and zoom in to any place that is visible and monitored. We can observe on our normal human time scale the changes in a rainforest over decades as seen from space. We can burrow with insects. We can grasp biological molecules and do chemistry by hand as the molecules react according to their quantum laws. We can expand the scale of direct human experience in space and time to the limits of our technology. And we can do all these things as children.

What kinds of humanity are possible for us if we can learn in these ways and have these experiences from our childhood? What are the possibilities, and what are the dangers?

The literacies of VR converge with, and indeed go beyond, the literacies and wisdoms of human life itself. What is a literacy when the distinction between reading and living itself is nominal? When a reality becomes our multimedia text, enhanced by the sorcery of hyperlinks that can carry us not just from page to page or text to text, but from place to place, from time to time, and from the cosmological scale to a world of quarks? Is this a dream or a nightmare?

Yes, we could become lost in this cyberspace, not for want of navigational aids, but because we may prefer the worlds of our own imaginations to those within which we evolved. Literacy confers both power and vulnerability: the power to add a second meaning world to the one our bodies are enmeshed in, but also the vulnerability of mistaking the former for the latter. The power comes when we add one to the other; the danger if we substitute VR for ecological reality. The semiotic capacity of human beings makes us infinitely adaptable in terms of the meanings we attach to our experience, but not all of those possible adaptations will allow our species to survive. In the lifetimes of students now in our schools, these issues will have to be faced. Will the literacies we teach today help them choose wisely?

No one can predict the transformations of 21st-century society during the information technology revolution. We certainly cannot afford to continue teaching our students only the literacies of the mid-20th century, or even to simply lay before them the most advanced and diverse literacies of today. We must help this next generation learn to use these literacies wisely, and hope they will succeed better than we have.

REFERENCES

Alpers, S. (1983). *The art of describing*. Chicago: University of Chicago Press.
Arens, Y., Hovy, E., & Vossers, M. (1992). On the knowledge underlying multimedia presentations. In M. Maybury (Ed.), *Intelligent multimedia interfaces* (pp. 280–306). Stanford, CA: AAAI Press.
Bazerman, C. (1988). *Shaping written knowledge*. Madison: University of Wisconsin Press.
Bazerman, C. (1994). Systems of genres and the enactment of social intentions. In A. Freedman & P. Medway (Eds.), *Rethinking genre* (pp. 79–101). London: Falmer.
Bellone, E. (1980). *A world on paper: Studies on the second scientific revolution*. Cambridge, MA: MIT Press.
Benedikt, M. (1991). *Cyberspace: First steps*. Cambridge, MA: MIT Press.
Bolter, J. D. (1991). *Writing space*. Hillsdale, NJ: Lawrence Erlbaum Associates.
Bryson, M., & de Castell, S. (1996). Learning to make a difference: Gender, new technologies and in/equity. *Mind, Culture, and Activity, 3*(2), 119–135.
Cajori, F. (1928). *A history of mathematical notations*. Chicago: Open Court.
Day, M., Crump, E., & Rickly, R. (1996). Creating a virtual academic community. In T. M. Harrison & T. D. Stephen (Eds.), *Computer networking and scholarship in the 21st-century university* (pp. 291–314). Albany: State University of New York Press.
Derrida, J. (1976). *Of grammatology*. Baltimore: Johns Hopkins University Press.
Dyson, A. H. (1991). Toward a reconceptualization of written language development. *Linguistics and Education, 3*, 139–162.
Eisenstein, E. (1979). *The printing press as an agent of change*. Cambridge, UK: Cambridge University Press.
Engestrom, Y. (1990). *Learning, working, and imagining*. Helsinki: Orienta-Konsultit.
Foucault, M. (1969). *The archeology of knowledge*. New York: Random House.

Gee, J. P. (1990). *Social linguistics and literacies*. London: Falmer.

Gee, J. P. (1996). On mobots and classrooms. *Organization, 3*(3), 385–407.

Goldman-Segall, R. (1992). Collaborative virtual communities. In E. Barrett (Ed.), *Sociomedia: Multimedia, hypermedia, and the social construction of knowledge* (pp. 257–296). Cambridge, MA: MIT Press.

Halliday, M. A. K. (1977). Text as semantic choice in social contexts. In T. A. van Dijk & J. Petöfi (Eds.), *Grammars and descriptions* (pp. 176–225). Berlin: de Gruyter.

Halliday, M. A. K. (1978). *Language as social semiotic*. London: Edward Arnold.

Halliday, M. A. K. (1985). *An introduction to functional grammar*. London: Edward Arnold.

Haraway, D. (1991). *Simians, cyborgs, and women*. New York: Routledge.

Harris, R. (1995). *Signs of writing*. London: Routledge.

Harrison, T. M., & Stephen, T. D. (1996). Computer networking, communication, and scholarship. In T. M. Harrison & T. D. Stephen (Eds.), *Computer networking and scholarship in the 21st century university* (pp. 3–38). Albany: State University of New York Press.

Hicks, D., & Kanevsky, R. (1992). Ninja Turtles and other superheroes: A case study of one literacy learner. *Linguistics and Education, 4,* 59–106.

Hockey, S. (1996). Computer networking and textual sources in the humanities. In T. M. Harrison & T. D. Stephen (Eds.), *Computer networking and scholarship in the 21st century university* (pp. 83–94). Albany: State University of New York Press.

Hodas, S. (1994). Technology refusal and the organizational culture of schools. In *Cyberspace superhighways: Access, ethics, and control: Proceedings of the Fourth Conference on Computers, Freedom, and Privacy* (pp. 54–75). Chicago: John Marshall Law School.

Hovy, E. H. (1987). Generating natural language under pragmatic constraints. *Journal of Pragmatics, 11*(6), 689–719.

Hutchins, E. (1995). *Cognition in the wild*. Cambridge, MA: MIT Press.

Kress, G., & van Leeuwen, T. (1996). *Reading images: The grammar of visual design*. London: Routledge.

Landow, G. P. (1992). *Hypertext: The convergence of contemporary literary theory and technology*. Baltimore: Johns Hopkins University Press.

Landow, G. P., & Delany, P. (Eds.). (1991). *Hypermedia and literary studies*. Cambridge, MA: MIT Press.

Latour, B. (1987). *Science in action*. Cambridge, MA: Harvard University Press.

Latour, B. (1993). *We have never been modern*. Cambridge, MA: Harvard University Press.

Lave, J. (1988). *Cognition in practice*. Cambridge, UK: Cambridge University Press.

Lemke, J. L. (1985). Ideology, intertextuality, and the notion of register. In J. D. Benson & W. S. Greaves (Eds.), *Systemic perspectives on discourse* (pp. 275–294). Norwood, NJ: Ablex.

Lemke, J. L. (1989a). Semantics and social values. *WORD, 40*(1–2), 37–50.

Lemke, J. L. (1989b). Social semiotics: A new model for literacy education. In D. Bloome (Ed.), *Classrooms and literacy* (pp. 289–309). Norwood, NJ: Ablex.

Lemke, J. L. (1992). Intertextuality and educational research. *Linguistics and Education, 4*(3–4), 257–268.

Lemke, J. L. (1993a). Discourse, dynamics, and social change. *Cultural Dynamics, 6*(1), 243–275.

Lemke, J. L. (1993b). Education, cyberspace, and change. Information Technology and Education Electronic Salon, Deakin University, Australia. (ERIC Document Reproduction Service, No. ED 356 767)

Lemke, J. L. (1994a). The coming paradigm wars in education: Curriculum vs. information access. In *Cyberspace superhighways: Access, ethics, and control: Proceedings of the Fourth Conference on Computers, Freedom, and Privacy* (pp. 76–85). Chicago: John Marshall Law School.

Lemke, J. L. (1994b). *Multiplying meaning: Literacy in a multimedia world* [Paper presented at the National Reading Conference, Charleston SC]. (ERIC Document Reproduction Service No. ED 365 940)

Lemke, J. L. (1995a). Intertextuality and text semantics. In M. Gregory & P. Fries (Eds.), *Discourse in society: Functional perspectives* (pp. 85–114). Norwood, NJ: Ablex.

Lemke, J. L. (1995b). Literacy, culture, and history: Review of *The World on Paper*. *Communication Review, 1*(2), 241–259.

Lemke, J. L. (1995c). *Textual politics: Discourse and social dynamics*. London: Taylor & Francis.

Lemke, J. L. (1996a). Emptying the center. *Organization, 3*(3), 411–418.

Lemke, J. L. (1996b). Hypermedia and higher education. In T. M. Harrison & T. D. Stephen (Eds.), *Computer networking and scholarship in the 21st century university* (pp. 215–232). Albany: State University of New York Press.

Lemke, J. L. (1997a). Multiplying meaning: Visual and verbal semiotics in scientific text. In J. R. Martin & R. Veel (Eds.), *Reading science* (pp. 87–113). London: Routledge.

Lemke, J. L. (1997b). Review of: *Roy Harris, Signs of writing*. *Functions of Language, 4*(1), 125–129.

Lynch, M., & Woolgar, S. (Eds.). (1990). *Representation in scientific practice*. Cambridge, MA: MIT Press.

Martin, J. R. (1992). *English text*. Philadelphia: John Benjamins.

Nelson, T. H. (1974). *Dream machines/Computer Lib*. Chicago: Nelson/Hugo's Book Service.

Olson, D. R. (1994). *The world on paper*. Cambridge, UK: Cambridge University Press.

O'Toole, M. (1990). A systemic-functional semiotics of art. *Semiotica, 82,* 185–209.

O'Toole, M. (1994). *The language of displayed art*. London: Leicester University Press.

Rheingold, H. (1991). *Virtual reality*. New York: Simon & Schuster.

Rheingold, H. (1993). *The virtual community: Homesteading on the electronic frontier*. Reading, MA: Addison-Wesley.

Rogoff, B. (1990). *Apprenticeship in thinking*. New York: Oxford University Press.

Skelton, R. A. (1958). *Explorers' maps: Chapters in the cartographic record of geographical discovery*. London: Routledge & Kegan Paul.

Sofia, Z. (1995). Of spanners and cyborgs. In B. Caine & R. Pringle (Eds.), *Transitions: New Australian feminisms* (pp. 147–163). New York: St. Martin's.

Stone, A. R. (1991). Will the real body please stand up: Boundary stories about virtual cultures. In M. Benedikt (Ed.), *Cyberspace: First steps* (pp. 81–118). Cambridge, MA: MIT Press.

Tufte, E. R. (1983). *The visual display of quantitative information*. Cheshire, CT: Graphics Press.

Tufte, E. R. (1990). *Envisioning information*. Cheshire, CT: Graphics Press.

Unsworth, J. (1996). Living inside the operating system: Community in virtual reality. In T. M. Harrison & T. D. Stephen (Eds.), *Computer networking and scholarship in the 21st century university* (pp. 137–150). Albany: State University of New York Press.

Wenger, E. (1987). *Artificial intelligence and tutoring systems*. Los Altos, CA: Morgan Kaufmann.

Wertsch, J. (1991). *Voices of the mind*. Cambridge, MA: Harvard University Press.

18

▼▼▼▼▼▼▼

Changing Workplaces, Changing Classes: The New Role of Technology in Workplace Literacy

Larry Mikulecky
Jamie R. Kirkley
Indiana University, Bloomington

Technology and the new literacies associated with it have transformed the workplace arguably more quickly and more deeply than any of our other institutions. The heavy growth in manufacturing jobs during the middle of the 20th century leveled off and then diminished during the final third of the century as white-collar clerical, sales, service, and management jobs increased. Technology has played a key role in bringing about these changes and in shaping the way people spend time as they perform their jobs.

Predictions and speculations about trends—especially in relation to technology and work—are complex, diverse, and often wrong for lack of anticipating the unexpected. For example, futurists at the 1938 World's Fair predicted the next 50 years would bring urban utopias with each person having a personal automobile or helicopter as all shared in the multiplying wealth brought about by technology. Few anticipated that personal vehicles would also create suburbs, smog, abandoned inner cities, and new social class designations. In the middle 1990s, we still do our best to predict the future. Rifkin (1995) saw a future requiring less work with technology, making it possible for fewer workers to produce needed goods and services. He called for us to reap the rewards of the high technology revolution while beginning to plan for those displaced by it. Shannon (1996) noted that for every high-paying computer programming job created, the economy creates nine new cashier jobs. He doubted that increased literacy abilities will make high-paying jobs available to everybody. He stated that at current cashier salaries, only those in two-parent households with both parents fully employed can hope to live comfortably.

This chapter does not speculate several decades ahead, nor does it suggest that literacy training will bring wealth and happiness to all. It instead attempts to present what we know about current workplace literacy demands (even in relatively low-paying cashier jobs) as these jobs are influenced by technology and organizational change. The chapter also examines what we know about how prepared American adults are to meet these new technological literacy demands and what resources we have available to prepare children and adults for the current and near future demands.

We are now in a position to sort out conflicting arguments about what technology has done to skill requirements in the workplace. During the late 1980s and early 1990s, scholars studying the labor market put forth several theories attempting to explain what has transpired in the fluid, mixed, and difficult-to-examine workplace. Early evidence provided support for several conflicting points of view. These ranged from the *deskilling thesis,* which holds that technology has simplified skills required in the workplace, to the *compensatory thesis,* which holds that new skills are simply replacing old skills but the level of skill remains the same, to the *upgrading thesis,* which holds that current employees must retain their old skills while learning new skills associated with technology. In addition, because technology makes it possible for an individual to do several jobs, employees must learn the skills of multiple jobs (Attewell, 1992).

Early limited studies in a few workplaces have provided some support for each of the conflicting viewpoints. It has only been in the 1990s that careful industry-by-industry analyses of two decades of labor data have been possible. Attewell (1992) summarized these analyses for the manufacturing industries: "In sum, the occupational employment data for manufacturing since 1976 show a process of upgrading through occupational redistribution. Higher-skill occupations are growing relative to lower-skill ones in both production and non-production employment" (p. 64). Bishop and Carter (1991) projected job growth from the years 1988 to 2000 across all occupations in the Bureau of Labor Statistics database. They concluded that the "high-skill share of job growth between 1990 and 2000 will be substantially higher than during the 1980s" (p. 227), with low-skill jobs accounting for only 10% of job growth. They further noted that growth is differential, even across occupations. For example, "the sales jobs which grew most rapidly during the 1980's tend to require the greatest amount of education and training" (p. 241).

Associated with higher skilled occupations as well as many more low- and middle-skill occupations are increased requirements in (a) the breadth of literacy expertise, and (b) the complexity of literacy performance. Even students who have mastered traditional school literacy face challenges. Learning to appreciate narrative fiction or to follow logically presented discussions in textbooks is important, but only marginally related to the literacy skills required to gather information from multiple print and technological sources and use such information to solve problems. The complexity of literacy processing in many low- and middle-level jobs has increased to include making critical judgments about the accuracy, current relevance, and unexpressed messages implicit in information.

FORCES INFLUENCING LITERACY DEMANDS

Several forces have brought about and continue to influence transformations of literacy in the workplace. These intertwined economic, organizational, and technological forces have changed the nature of most work. Among these forces are participation in the global marketplace, democratization of workplace decision making, synchronous production, and multiple roles on most jobs. New technology permeates the work activities of nearly half the adult population and creates new literacy demands for communication, gathering information, solving daily work-related problems, and monitoring performance.

Participation in the Global Marketplace

One pressure driving many businesses to use more technology and change the way they operate is participation in the global marketplace. Businesses wishing to function internationally or to subcontract with large corporations doing international business seek certification for high quality control and productivity standards. For example, any commercial firm wishing to do business with a member firm of the European Economic Community must comply with International Standards Organization (ISO) guidelines (Weiss, 1993). The guidelines identify, describe, and measure the degree to which a business has implemented 20 or more elements of quality assurance. To meet certification in these areas, businesses must document procedures, provide training, and demonstrate that all employees are able to inspect, measure, and test for quality. This quality testing usually involves employees participating in quality assurance groups, setting productivity goals, monitoring quality, and communicating with other workers (including those at other locations) so that waste of time and material is cut to a minimum.

Low- and middle-level hourly occupations now require higher than previous levels of literacy, communication, computation skills, and use of technical tools for processing and communicating information. Large corporations give more work to subcontractors who have attained ISO certification and less or none to subcontractors without certification. Such certification means high quality control standards and reduced expenses because waste is reduced. Many uncertified employers have lost work, shrunk in size, or gone out of business. At certified businesses, tasks formerly belonging to middle-level managers have been allocated to work teams. Middle-level managers have been released as companies downsize or rightsize, depending on which euphemism is used in a particular workplace.

Democratization of the Workplace

Increased democratization of the workplace refers to the trend for wider worker involvement in deciding how work will be performed. Demands for high quality and rapid decision making render obsolete the old-style organization of a boss who makes decisions and workers who simply follow orders. More decision making, information processing, and communication responsibilities have been given to small work teams. These teams are often comprised of high school graduates without any postsecondary education, and in some cases, they are high school dropouts. These teams use technology to gather and analyze information as they help set goals, monitor effectiveness, make suggestions for changes, and sometimes help set policy for bonuses.

Synchronous Production and Continuous Improvement

The activities of workers in the new democratized workplace often revolve around a form of synchronous production in which quality is monitored and guidelines adjusted regularly at each stage of production. Adjustments are based on analysis of the monitored information by teams of ordinary workers with a goal of continuous improvement in overall production. Synchronous production embraces a wide range of problem solving, communication, and quality control strategies that are designed to lead to the most efficient, highest quality, most flexible way to produce everything from better automotive parts to better service in an insurance firm or hospital. The vision is for every worker and every manager to monitor and improve the way the entire production or service process operates. Being responsible for merely a small portion of the job is no longer acceptable.

Three elements of synchronous production merit particular attention from educators. These are (a) just-in-time target delivery, (b) statistical process control (sometimes called quality process control), and (c) self-management teams (also called quality assurance groups or employee participation groups).

Manufacturers save money by no longer stocking large inventories that cost storage space and are often pilfered. Instead, they communicate on a daily and sometimes hourly basis with suppliers within and outside the company, letting them know exactly what they need and when. This requires increased record keeping and communication on the part of those actually doing the daily work. Statistical process control and quality process control refer to the process of having workers anticipate defects, problems, or mistakes (e.g., defective parts or overly long answering time on phone calls or processing customer requests) by monitoring, recording, graphing, and interpreting measurements of dozens and sometimes hundreds of points in the production or service process. Employees often write brief reports and suggestions for improvement of the process. In manufacturing, monitoring occurs at each step from delivery of raw materials to finished product. In service industries, this occurs at each step from initial requests to final satisfactory delivery of service.

To hold contracts at developed nation wages, one must produce parts (e.g., electronic switches, motors, door locks, dresser drawers) that have fewer than one mistake for every 20,000 parts manufactured. A mistake can be a drawer slide that is off by less than a hundredth of an inch or an electronic switch whose contact points are off by a few thousandths of an inch. In customer service industries, parallel quality standards exist for wait time, accurate forwarding of requests, cleanliness, customer satisfaction, and so forth. Quality monitoring has become part of even the most menial of jobs.

Many of the decisions about how to respond to quality monitoring information are made by worker self-management teams. Some teams are comprised of workers within a single department who determine from monitored information where mistakes and slow-downs occur. They produce brief reports that suggest changes and set new goals that are then monitored. Some changes involve interactions with other departments, so some teams are made up of representatives from several departments. Representatives present infor-mation, take notes, and report agreed-on changes back to home departments. The levels of communication and literacy skill required for participation on such teams is a good deal greater than that previously required of most hourly workers.

Multiple Roles on the Job

In the past, a person could learn or memorize a fairly limited menu of tasks and perform adequately on most low- and middle-level jobs. In the restructured workplace, this is no longer the case in even relatively low-paying jobs. Technology makes it possible for fewer people to perform complex jobs very quickly, so a single worker can now do a week's worth of work in a few hours. Just-in-time production schedules do away with employees working at memorized tasks to build up inventory. The goal is to now deliver products and services just in time or nearly immediately after they are requested. The end result is that an individual must learn the technology to allow him or her to do his or her old job in a fraction of the previous time. Because the worker has more time available, he or she must also learn the jobs of former workers who have been laid off or downsized. The demands are further increased by the shortened life cycle of products. For example, in 1990 it took 6 years for an automobile to move from concept to production. The time is now 2 years (Pritchard, 1996). New products mean new tasks and job roles. At times when there is newly demanded work to be rapidly performed, workers are expected to read guidelines and flexibly shift from job task to job task as needed. Workers being paid at approximately the same relative rate as 10 to 15 years ago for doing a single task are now expected to perform multiple tasks with the only preparation being the time it takes to review a brief task description in a manual or a printed job aid attached to a workstation.

WHAT LITERACY DEMANDS LOOK LIKE IN THE NEW WORKPLACE

Restructuring and technology have changed the nature of many job descriptions from the factory floor to the corporate office. These changes place new literacy demands on workers and transform the way jobs are done. To demonstrate how new technologies and organizational changes are affecting workplace literacy skills, we offer several vignettes based on current jobs.

New Demands on the Factory Floor: Using Statistical Processes and Quality Control in Manufacturing

Because new technology produces products so rapidly, the costliness of mistakes is greatly multiplied. Hourly workers must monitor the quality of what is produced, make adjustments, and communicate compiled information so that systemwide adjustments can be made. The following example describes an hourly job in a wood products plant:

> Several times an hour, the machine operator takes samples of lengths of planking and measures the length of each unit. This involves using and reading a digital printout. The data are then recorded by keying results into a data management program. This is done each quarter hour, and then data from several trials are tracked. The machine operator uses a computer with menu choices to calculate means and the range of the sample values. This information is graphed, and the worker must interpret the graphs in terms of how much measurements exceed acceptable parameters for quality. The worker needs to decide whether production is sufficiently within preset parameters, and if not, how much to adjust the settings on the machine. Too small an adjustment will not solve the problem, and too great a change will turn underweight into overweight, producing a new production problem. Keep in mind that the machine is still in production while all this is happening, and the worker's speed in dealing with the sample and making the decision will avoid costly wastage of materials and production time. Because of the rapid speed of machinery, a 30-minute delay can mean the waste of several thousand dollars of product. Toward the end of the day, the worker will use a word processing program to type a brief end-of-shift report describing decisions, anticipated problems, downtime, and reaction times if help was requested from another department to perform minor repairs on a machine. These reports are then e-mailed to a central site where patterns of machine problems are examined and decisions made about replacement and major repair.

New Demands: Managing Production in Quality Control Teams

One way in which the workplace has become more democratic is in the way teams of workers make decisions about how to achieve goals of higher quality and more rapid response. This form of workplace democracy calls for greater literacy, communication, and problem-solving skills. Quality monitoring and just-in-time production also figure into most team decisions. The following example describes the work of an ISO-certified subcontractor producing electric motors for the automotive industry.

Six hourly workers representing various stages of production meet once or twice weekly in what are called quality assurance teams. The purposes of these teams are to identify problems, jointly set new productivity goals, and discuss the results of monitoring productivity at various stages of production (i.e., Where are the mistakes or slowdowns happening and what can be done about it?).

A typical team problem is too much inventory on the floor (e.g., skids loaded with parts or finished product). A major productivity goal is just-in-time production so that material is ready exactly when it is needed for the next stage of production or for the customer. This reduces inventory stored on the floor, saving warehouse space and reducing spoilage, breakage, and pilfering.

To solve problems like this, team members call up inventory graphs on the computer and either print them directly or use desktop publishing applications to arrange them in meaningful handouts. These are often line graphs that record the amount of inventory in various locations at various points in time (e.g., by the hour, day, week, or month). Synthesizing information from these graphs enables the team to determine when buildups of excess inventory (e.g., parts or finished product) are occurring. Team members offer problem-solving suggestions on why the buildups are occurring. For example, what would happen if a worker at Stage 3 went to help at Stage 4 every other hour? Additional information is then gathered on suggested possibilities. This can involve computations using simple calculators. In some cases, custom-designed data management applications do calculations and plot graphs. Alternative computations of output might involve computing half-day splits of time or 2-hour splits of time. Speculations about machine breakdowns might involve checking when the machine was last overhauled and recalibrated, looking up projected times between maintenance, and computing time to go. Pulling up machine records of the questionable machine during a comparable time during the last maintenance cycle would provide information to justify a call for early maintenance. New and old work orders would be scanned to see how many parts are called for to complete a special order that took a machine offline. Based on performance so far, computations and estimates would be made for how long it would remain offline.

The culmination of all this brainstorming and quantitative information gathering is a provisional plan that will be typed into the word processor for distribution to workers not at the meeting but involved with various stages of production. This agreed-on plan would identify which workers and machines would do what tasks during which times. It would involve setting goals, counting and making measurements at regular intervals, and recording data to monitor the various stages of production. After 5 days' time, the quality assurance team meets again briefly to determine how well goals were met and how well problems were solved.

New Demands for Solving Problems in Customer Service

Customer service and sales are two of the more rapidly growing occupational areas. Increasingly, competition for business is based on the quality of service provided. This usually means that good decisions must be made by the person who is providing the initial service. Workers without a great deal of training and education are now expected to use technology to gather information, rapidly answer questions, and often make decisions formerly made by managers. In the following example, computer technology and retrieval make accessible to every customer service representative (CSR) the equivalent of thousands of pages of information. Rapidly accessing accurate information, updating the information base, and making good decisions have now become integral parts of many jobs.

A CSR handling billing inquiries receives a telephone request for late payment. After asking for the customer's name, the CSR can examine the whole of that customer's record on a computer screen and check on the payment history. Rapid screen reading of print organized in blocks of information is required. At this point, there is an initial decision to be made: How reliable is this customer? Can any extension of time be given? Written policy guidelines to guide the CSR are accessed via hypertext help screens or performance support systems.

If an extension seems to be in order, the CSR then accesses another hypertext screen to consult a set of rules concerning the length of such an extension and whether some percentage of the bill must be paid immediately. After calculating the effect of the rules (in this case using another function of the computer), the CSR tells the customer the result and generates a discussion on the possibility of the customer paying as required. If the CSR is unable to answer the questions during the brief time the customer is on the phone, a letter will need to be sent. A word processing program with several dozen form letters will be called up on the screen. The CSR will be expected to select an appropriate form letter from menus, modify the address and body of the form letter appropriately, and print a letter and envelope to be mailed to the customer.

Managing Information in the Office of Today

A secretary at a middle-sized corporation begins her workday by turning on her computer. Much of the staff communicates through e-mail rather than by memos or phone calls. After she opens her e-mail account by typing in her name and password, she finds 15 new messages. She first scans the computer screen and determines which messages are most important to read. She skips over less important messages until she has more time. As she reads each message, she makes handwritten notes of actions she needs to take, such as reserving a conference room and ordering word processing software for the new computers. She then composes and sends a message to the work team to which she is assigned, informing them of an upcoming meeting. She saves each message in an appropriate folder on the computer. Her computer folders are similar to folders in filing cabinets; she uses them as a place to save and store information.

Her next task is to prepare charts for a team presentation to be made later today. She reads instructions from an e-mail sent by a team member requesting her to make a chart that shows the fluctuating prices of oil over the past 2 years and then create a graph that will show the patterns of prices over the past 12 years. She opens her computer's spreadsheet software, which consists of small boxes or cells that enable her to create tables and graphs, perform calculations, and store information. This is a complex, multistep process that requires her to use hypertext help screens several times to clarify questions.

The day will continue with requests for information, documents to be designed, meetings to be scheduled, and two or three emergencies arriving via fax, e-mail, and telephone. The secretary's day will be a stream of information to be understood, processed, and communicated.

The jobs highlighted in most of these vignettes are held by individuals with little or no postsecondary education. The pay is above minimum wage, but not by an extraordinary amount. Over the past decade, most of these workers have seen a steady increase in the skills and flexibility demanded of them, and they have also seen fellow workers released as employers downsized to become more competitive. Because there are fewer of them in a given department, they have less social support and must function independently much more often. When they spend time with others, it is often in a scheduled meeting with its own new set of literacy and communication demands. When work demands increase beyond their capacity to function, they face the additional chore of informally training temporary workers. The most competent and highly trained of these temporary workers may be offered full-time positions. On top of all this, newly arriving technologies keep the new demands coming.

NEWER TECHNOLOGIES LIKELY TO INFLUENCE WORKPLACE LITERACY INFORMATION MANAGEMENT

In addition to the literacy demands just highlighted, newer technologies likely to influence workplace literacy demand constantly appear. Because of this, it is a challenge for workers to keep their technology skills current and up to date. To do this, they must have the ability to learn rapidly from short courses delivered at the workplace or from tutorials built into software applications.

Some examples of newer technologies likely to influence workplace literacy demand are the Internet and intranets (i.e., specialized internal versions of Internet sites most commonly used within corporations or large businesses) and electronic performance support systems (EPSSs).

Internet and Intranets

Declining access costs and increased computer power are making the Internet more accessible. This means the Internet can be used to support people in the context of doing their jobs. This support can range from the use of specialized online news services to specialized websites within a company, called *intranets*. Intranet websites are usually not accessible to the general public. They are especially useful in allowing departments to provide up-to-date information to each other and for businesses that operate from different locations to allow everyone to function with comparable, accurate information (Sprout, 1995). In many cases, websites serve as bases for electronic performance support systems designed to teach employees and help them perform their jobs.

EPSSs

The traditional EPSS is a computer application or series of applications that provides integrated information, tools, and methods, electronically, on demand, at the moment of need (Gery, 1991). The purpose of this type of system is to support the performance of a job or task. An EPSS is designed to provide tools, resources, and support systems to fit specific environments. It usually consists of some type of interactive support and guidance. Depending on what is needed in the environment, it might contain a database of resources and information, a coaching and guidance system for help with certain tasks such as making decisions, methods for communicating with colleagues, simulations of job tasks, job aids, or administrative tools such as project management software. EPSSs often contain a built-in set of computer tools such as a word processor, e-mail, database, and spreadsheet applications. Increasingly, these systems focus on enabling one to perform specific tasks, such as learn new information while on the job (Gery, 1995; Hudzina, Rowley, & Wager, 1996).

EPSSs are usually integrated directly into a person's working environment for greater convenience and usability (Barker & Banerji, 1993; Laffey, 1995). Guidance is provided when it is needed and in the context of the working environment. The support offered by an EPSS means that learning is not done outside of a person's work activities but instead in the context of the activities themselves.

As these systems develop, they have the potential to greatly influence not only how jobs are performed, but also how people teach and learn in the workplace. The influence that these technologies will have on job performance and training is not yet clear. In some cases, information and guidance in computer memory may deskill jobs. In other cases, individuals working with EPSSs may find themselves expected to do multiple jobs and make decisions that were never available to them before. Similarly, some of what is taught in training classes is likely to change. People still need knowledge bases to interpret information, but what is in these knowledge bases will change as new information and skills are needed.

Schooling before a job is likely to involve mastering two basic knowledge bases: (a) basic knowledge of key concepts related to an industry, and (b) basic knowledge about the use of information tools like EPSSs. The fine-tuning related to a current job may be learned, just in time, while on the job. In fact, many agencies providing temporary help currently list their employees in just such a fashion (e.g., some knowledge of the insurance industry and mastery of particular word processing and database tools). To this list of mastered tools, we may now add use of the Internet, intranets, and EPSSs. The literacy demands involved in such tool use go beyond reading simple expository and narrative prose to being able to access the Internet, comprehend information presented on screens, and use such information and applications to solve problems.

WHO CAN MEET CURRENT
AND FUTURE WORKPLACE DEMANDS?

Technology and the reorganization of work have transformed and increased the literacy demands in many occupations. This increase in demand is especially apparent in businesses that have downsized and restructured in order to become more competitive in the global economy. These new demands and this new competitive stance give rise to the question of how prepared we are as a people to perform in this transformed workplace.

There is no solid research that directly addresses the degree to which adults can meet the increased and transformed technological literacy demands of the workplace. The most recent adult literacy information available comes from the National Adult Literacy Survey (NALS), which was conducted in the early 1990s (Kirsch, Jungeblut, Jenkins, & Kolstad, 1993). Nearly 27,000 adults participated in this survey that involved responding to sample real-world literacy tasks of graduated difficulty. These tasks are rated on a scale ranging from 0 to 500 for difficulty.

Although few of the NALS items involved technology, many of the NALS items are parallel to tasks that have been reported as common in workplaces and use materials of comparable difficulty to workplace materials. An example of a very basic workplace parallel with NALS is the simple task of being able skim to locate the name of a country in a short newspaper article (rated 149 on the 500-point scale). An individual scoring at 149 on the NALS would have an 80% probability of being able to accurately locate the country name. Individuals with lower scores might also be able to succeed, but probabilities would be lower.

Many very basic workplace tasks are similar to such superficial newspaper reading and involve skimming brief prose descriptions (sometimes on computer screens) to find a detail such as a product number or name. Other NALS items have counterparts in the workplace. For example, being able to accurately total a fairly simple bank deposit entry is rated at 191. This item reflects widespread job tasks involving simple calculations in which consistency and accuracy are crucial. Additional NALS items are listed in Table 18.1 along with the difficulty scores.

Each of the items in Table 18.1 has a common correlate in workplaces. Workers are regularly called on to interpret written instructions, enter information on forms, and calculate totals. NALS scores of employees indicate that most, but not all, can consistently succeed with basic tasks such as those listed here. The success rate drops significantly, however, with slightly more difficult tasks similar to those in the workplace scenarios presented earlier in this chapter. For example, more than half of employed adults had difficulty (a) problem solving to answer a caller's question using a nursing home sign-out sheet (rated 298), (b) summarizing in writing the gist of a newspaper article (rated 328), (c) determining correct change using information in a menu (rated 331), and (d) using a table to compare and summarize in writing the features of two credit cards (rated 387).

In addition, workers in some occupations have quite low average performance scores. For example, employees in laborer, service, farming, forestry, fishing, craft, machine operative, and transportation operative occupations had average performances in the 250 to 270 range with a large fraction of workers scoring below 225. The vast majority of workers in these occupations are likely to have difficulty with accurate, consistent performance on problem-solving literacy tasks similar to items at or above 300 ratings on the NALS. Cleaning and maintenance and nonsupervisory farming and nursery workers demonstrated average proficiencies below 250. Individuals employed in food preparation, child care, construction, and as motor vehicle operators averaged below 275. From half to three quarters of workers in these low- and middle-level occupations had difficulties with several of the tasks similar to those called for in restructured workplaces.

To be categorized in the lowest level of the NALS (i.e., scores below 225) one must fail to accurately and consistently (80% of the time) locate intersections on simple maps, complete addresses on order forms, and calculate postage fees. These are rudimentary basic skills and considerably below those called for in restructured workplaces. In cleaning and maintenance occupations, from 32% to 45% of workers scored below the levels of these rudimentary tasks. From 20% to 35% of workers in food preparation, child care, farming and nursery, construction, and motor vehicle operation also scored below these items on at least one scale. In every occupational area, some individuals performed at this lowest NALS level. The percentages ranged from 1% of teachers and other professionals to a relatively high 13% in health support occupations. Approximately 10% of sales personnel performed at the lowest level, whereas 5% to 6% of clerks and secretaries performed at the lowest level range. Because literacy tasks in high-performance workplaces appear to be at Level 3 (i.e., 275 or higher), it may be more useful to consider percentages of workers scoring below Level 3. Nearly 40%

TABLE 18.1
Additional NALS Items

Prose	250	Locate two features of information from a sports article.
	275	Interpret instructions from an appliance warranty.
Document	230	Locate an intersection on a street map.
	259	Locate and enter background information on an application for a social security card.
Quantitative	238	Calculate postage and fees for certified mail.
	270	Calculate total costs of purchase from an order form.

of health support personnel and sales personnel perform below Level 3, as do approximately 30% of clerks and secretaries. To reiterate, performing below Level 3 does not mean that one cannot read. It does mean, however, that being able to independently and consistently comprehend most high school to college-level difficulty training materials and much current workplace print information is unlikely.

Demands and skills differ workplace by workplace, but it seems apparent that technology and the reorganization of work have transformed and increased the literacy demands in many occupations, especially in businesses intent on paying developed nation wages while competing in the global economy. Increasingly, even lower middle-class wages are associated with performing competently in a transformed workplace such as those portrayed in the vignettes. There are still some low-skilled jobs that have not been moved out of the country or turned over to automation. Indeed, there are some deskilled jobs that require less skill now than previously. In most cases, however, these jobs pay minimum wage, have no future, and keep a full-time worker at the poverty level. The implications of these changed skill and remuneration patterns leading to an increasingly polarized society have been discussed at length by Reich (1992) and others (Osterman, 1993). The challenge for educators is to use every tool available to help more adolescents and adults reach ever higher and transformed levels of workplace literacy competence. This is not a guarantee for avoiding poverty, but for most it is a prerequisite.

PREPARING LEARNERS FOR NEW
WORKPLACE LITERACY DEMANDS

Definitions of literacy have been multifaceted and diverse for most of this decade (Venezky, Wagner, & Ciliberti, 1990). The workplace examples presented earlier expand the definitions to include the use of technological tools to interpret, examine, analyze, and synthesize information. The reorganization of the workplace and new advances in computer technologies have increased as well as transformed the traditional literacy demands in many occupations. For employees using new technologies, literacy demands include being able to access and comprehend information presented on computer screens, to analyze the use and reliability of information, to change information to other structures (e.g., from a chart to a graph), and to apply information to solve problems. This form of active and interactive literacy is quite different from simply reading an announcement or form.

Technology has not only changed the literacy demands of the workplace. It also plays a role in helping adults and adolescents learn to meet these demands. Technological learning tools are present in some educational programs that prepare adolescents and adults for the new literacies of the workplace. In terms of complexity, these technological tools range from a host of tutorials and self-paced drill and study applications to sophisticated simulations. Use of the Internet in some workplace literacy classes provides unparalleled access to custom-designed materials and to specialized collaboration and communication among learners.

As instructors use these technological tools to prepare learners for new workplace literacy demands, several broad goals should frame the use of the new educational technologies. These goals are (a) learning to think critically in solving problems, (b) becoming familiar with the use of technology tools for processing information, (c) expanding the breadth of materials encountered by learners, and (d) developing habits of mind suitable for lifelong learning.

Learning to Think Critically in Solving Problems
With Computer Simulations

Literacy educators will need to focus on providing training in thinking and problem-solving skills. Imel (1990) indicated that each of the three major occupational groups requiring the highest levels of educational attainment is projected to grow more rapidly than average. To function in these occupations, people will need to learn and apply higher order thinking skills such as inquiry, investigation, organization, reflection, reasoning, analysis, and problem solving. To make transfer likely, these skills will need to be learned using ill-structured problems like those found in the real world or on the job. Educational methodologies, such as problem-based learning, are particularly effective for teaching such skills. Problem-based learning involves students in solving problems similar to ones found in the real world. Since the early 1990s, the U.S. Departments of Labor and Education have recommended that elementary and secondary schools increase their use of large-scale projects that involve teams of students in solving real problems in accomplishing real tasks. These projects (e.g., fully planning and taking a trip, operating a recycling drive, or producing a publication) should require teams of students in identifying and allocating resources, processing and communicating information in several forms, working in groups, monitoring performance, and using technologies appropriate to problems (U.S. Department of Labor, 1991, 1992). Such problem-based learning fosters student acquisition of a body of knowledge in the context in which it will be used (Barrows, 1994; Savery & Duffy, 1995). By focusing on broad skills such as these, educators will be more likely to increase the connections between various knowledge bases and later job performance.

To augment problem-based learning, computer simulations are an excellent tool for teaching students to think critically and solve problems. Simulations can place learners in settings beyond the classroom in situations that ask them to read, write, communicate, and solve problems. Computer simulations have been used increasingly in education and training programs. Simulations are increasingly used by businesses, governments, and the military because they are safer and cheaper than real-world training. They provide opportunities to learn skills by using different scenarios, creating virtual people and environments, and creating random or rare circumstances that may not happen in real life but are still important to learn. They are also useful because they familiarize learners with new technologies while providing a safe environment for learning a skill when the real environment is either dangerous or inaccessible. Yet another advantage of electronic simulations is the possibility of linking distant groups so they can interact and train together (Child, 1997).

Simulations using workplace settings have been developed to provide the opportunity for developing skills for problem solving, information processing, critical thinking, and collaboration. Classroom Inc., working together with the New York City Board of Education and over a dozen other partners, has developed several computer simulation series that re-create problem solving in the workplace. These simulations are designed to provide some general knowledge about the workplace, but more importantly to create opportunities for developing general workplace literacy and problem-solving competencies. Current simulations deal with the hospitality industry, heath care, banking at the teller or customer service level, and financial services at the lending, savings, and investment level (Classroom, Inc., 1995).

One example is the Chelsea Bank simulation, which places students in the role of bank teller. Students are confronted with customers who are pressed for time, confused, and sometimes are their friends. They must make decisions about cashing checks, making initial loan recommendations, and providing appropriate bank services. This requires asking questions of customers and trying to discern accurate information from lifelike answers that sometimes wander and are occasionally evasive. Success usually requires using the computer to look up credit records, examining the bank procedure manual, and perhaps asking further questions. Before decisions can be made, students must discuss and evaluate conflicting information with other students in the group. Final decisions about what to do are followed by typing into the computer reflections about impact on the customer, the bank, and the person making the decision. As students successfully resolve problems, they are promoted to handle more complex customer service problems.

The literacies associated with critical thinking and problem solving in a simulated banking environment are similar to those found in real life. Students must work collaboratively to gather and analyze information, identify problems, evaluate solutions, make decisions, and reflect on the consequences of those decisions. There are many types of simulations available on the market to help students better prepare themselves as thinkers and problem solvers. Although the objectives of many simulations do not explicitly include improving literacy and language, each does require the use of reading, listening, speaking, and writing skills.

Teaching Learners to Use Technology Tools in the Context of Work

Raybould (1995) indicated that 85% to 90% of a person's job knowledge is best learned on the job. By integrating technology skills with on-the-job learning or job-specific training, workers can gain valuable job knowledge as well as technological literacies. Rather than focusing specifically on teaching learners how to use computer technologies, educators should focus on teaching students how to use these technologies within the context of specific work environments and within specific work-related problems. Although teaching general technology skills is somewhat valuable in and of itself, it is more effective to combine such instruction with job-related skills. Workplaces often have information tools that are generally used by many to accomplish specific tasks, such as writing form letters, managing inventory, or tracking spending. Therefore, rather than teaching someone simply how to use a spreadsheet, it is more valuable and powerful to teach them bookkeeping skills while using the spreadsheet as a bookkeeping tool. The key is to tie the technology into a specific problem that one might encounter in the workplace.

Not all learners have jobs, but most have some needs to which technological tools can apply. A useful way to prepare such learners for the new technological workplace is to have them use the technology to search for jobs. One example of this was cited in *USA Today*.

> UCLA is teaching low-income job hunters to use the Internet at churches, community centers and libraries. Applicants looking for hotel housekeeping work can get on Marriott's resume database just by calling an 800 number and answering questions by pushing a button. (Jones, 1996, pp. B1–B2)

Many adolescent and adult learners have little or no experience in using copy machines, faxes, word processing, and even telephones for business use. Incorporating such information technologies into group projects can go a long way toward expanding familiarity with some of the new literacies of the workplace.

Expanding the Breadth of Materials

Many learners have experience with only a narrow range of literacy and types of materials. Most reading in schools is in the form of either narrative prose from novels and anthologies or expository prose from textbooks. Few students confront, let alone critically use the vast range of information encountered once a person leaves school.

The prohibitive expense and space needed to purchase and store a wide array of materials is one reason sometimes offered for using a single textbook for all students in a class. The end result, however, is that many students find the breadth and depth of literacy in school is considerably less than that found outside of school—especially in workplaces with a future.

A computer connected to the Internet and a printer can help expand the range of materials and information displays available to learners. Educators have access to a wide variety of reading materials on practically any topic of interest to a learner or instructor. The many online news services representing a variety of viewpoints and even cultures can be used as a basis for critical reading instruction. If a learner wants to learn more about managing money or smart shopping, the learner can access these resources on the Web.

One new form of interactive literacy not available in textbooks is e-mail. By using the Internet, communication tools such as e-mail can be used to "talk" to students in other classes and programs. This experience has direct workplace transfer as electronic communication in the workplace becomes more common. Literacy learners and English as a second language (ESL) students can make use of a wide variety of discussion lists and newsgroups designed to allow students learning ESL to discuss topics with each other via e-mail. These discussion lists cover such topics as business, current events, cinema, music, technology, and sports (Frizler, 1995). A more sophisticated Internet tool is schMOOze University, technically called a multiuser object oriented (MOO) environment. In practical terms, an Internet user can move his or her character into several different rooms in the virtual university where various topics are being discussed by ESL students in written English. In addition, it is possible to play games like Scrabble or Hangman, access an online dictionary, and improve understandings of English grammar through a grammar maze activity (Falsetti, 1995).

Lifelong Learning: Using Programs for Self-Study

Lifelong learning has become a constant in the lives of many workers and will become a constant in the lives of many more. Knowledge investment along with capital investment have become the critical elements for determining the productivity in the workplace (Drucker, 1994). Without knowledge, the usefulness of capital investments such as machines and technologies is greatly reduced. Therefore, people need to continuously gain applied knowledge in specialized areas in order to successfully perform their jobs. The flood of regularly introduced new technology accelerates this process.

The preceding discussion of Internet use is one means for developing in learners a lifelong learning habit of mind. Seeking and finding new information to educate one's self is empowering and can become habit forming. Being in a community that attributes status to an individual who has found or learned something new can go a long way toward supporting such a habit of mind.

Not all learning can occur by simply seeking information on the Internet. Some learning takes a good deal more guided practice, feedback, reflection, and use. With constant changes in the workplace and technological advances, individuals will need to update their education and knowledge bases quite often. Although formal education will still be important, on-the-job and individual training will continue to play an increasingly important role in the lives of adults. Computer-delivered, self-paced study applications, which are available when the learner is available, can help address this aspect of individual lifelong learning.

Self-paced study applications have been used in training and literacy programs for some time now. These computer applications offer learners the opportunity to gain mastery of basic skills or of a certain body of knowledge and then test themselves on the new skills or knowledge. Although sometimes not much different from self-scoring workbooks, tutorial applications have the advantage of providing some form of interaction with learners and can provide models and guidance as to why responses are not accurate (Mikulecky, Clark, & McIntyre, 1989). Tutorial applications often present information that is divided into categories and proceeds from easy to difficult levels. The learner must often master one level before proceeding to the next.

Programmed Logic for Automated Teaching Operations (PLATO) was one of the early computer-based drill and practice applications. It is currently used in some workplace basic education and general equivalency diploma (GED) classes to help learners master basic literacy and computational skills as well as basic knowledge in several content areas related to the GED examination. In addition to workplace programs, PLATO is used by public schools, community colleges, and community-based literacy programs. PLATO is delivered via an online network and contains instruction on many subjects (e.g., Reading 1, Pre-Algebra, and Job Skills for the Real World). Each module contains tutorials, drills, applications, reviews, and mastery tests. Assessment tests for various PLATO courses diagnose and prescribe individualized learning paths. PLATO has grown over the years to provide instruction in a broad range of areas.

Several literacy tutorials and drill applications are available to help learners develop job-specific knowledge. One example is R.O.A.D. (Real Opportunities for Advancement and Development) to Success, developed by the Institute for the Study of Adult Literacy (http://www.psu.edu/institutes/isal/software.html) at Pennsylvania State University. This computer-based tutorial application helps learners prepare to pass the written portion of the Commercial Driver's Examination. It uses the Commercial Driver's License (CDL) study manual to help those who wish to drive commercial vehicles to develop the reading skills and content knowledge needed to pass the federally legislated Commercial Motor Vehicle Driver's License exam. This software provides multiple-choice questions that enable the learner to practice and test knowledge of the CDL manual. It has been used by thousands of low-literate truck drivers who have entered literacy classes with a specific and pressing goal for learning.

Although self-paced study applications may be considered traditional and less innovative than simulations, they have several advantages. Although older drill and practice applications were often limited to text and a few simple illustrations, current software developers are incorporating multimedia features that include images, sound, and video. This makes these applications not only more attractive to use, but multimedia can provide added features to the learning experience, such as visualization and modeling. Because adults in workplace literacy programs often are forced by work schedules to attend programs sporadically, self-paced study applications can be an important tool for helping them achieve their educational goals. Also, adults learn at quite different paces from one another, and computer tutorials are particularly useful in adult learning environments because they are individually paced and provide immediate feedback to the learner.

Because practice and feedback can be time consuming for a teacher to provide, a computer can be an effective tutor for teaching skills through practiced repetition. This can save both time and money. Drill and practice applications are often used as a form of independent study or self-paced study either separate from or supplemental to group instruction. In spite of early instructor concerns about the lack of a human element, program evaluations for over a decade suggest that adult learners enjoy these applications and perform on tests as well or better than average students in noncomputerized classrooms (Haigler, 1990; Mikulecky, Clark, & McIntyre, 1989; Turner, 1993).

SUGGESTIONS FOR HELPING INSTRUCTORS MEET NEW DEMANDS

Literacy instructors also face new workplace demands themselves. They are experiencing many of the same new job and literacy demands as other employees. With downsizing, many companies are cutting back on training and literacy programs and fewer people are often required to do more work and take on multiple responsibilities. Instructors are also being required to keep abreast of new computer technologies and literacies themselves. To prepare learners, they are expected to know how to use many of the computer technologies workers use and must understand many of the new demands they face.

Perhaps the most beneficial technological tool for helping literacy instructors keep their knowledge current is the Internet. It can provide instructors, many of whom are often cut off from educational colleagues, with access to many additional forms of support and information. This support can include membership in a growing number of literacy-related newsgroups and listservs, connections with the most recent research and teaching ideas, and access to EPSSs designed especially for literacy instructors and tutors.

Instructors can use the Internet to keep themselves informed about current research and teaching ideas. One of the more useful resources on teaching and research ideas is through a University of Pennsylvania site (http://litserver.literacy.upenn.edu/Products/prpbt.htm) that allows any visitor to freely download nearly 100 recent research and practitioner publications produced by the National Center on Adult Literacy. A dozen of these publications deal with workplace literacy and eight directly address technology and adult literacy.

Another website developed at Indiana University and entitled Literacy Online (http://www.thinkshop.edu/al) supports adult literacy teachers and tutors (Kirkley & Duffy, 1997). Teachers and tutors can use the website in the context of their teaching. It contains strategies, lesson plans, resource materials, and a newsgroup in which teachers and tutors can communicate with each other on various issues. The system was designed to help teachers and tutors develop effective lesson plans, become more effective teachers by learning about various strategies and frameworks, and provide opportunities for communication and collaboration. This website is an example of a Web-based EPSS system in the sense that it provides communication and idea exchange as well as access to information and resources.

CONCLUSION

Technology and the restructuring of work to compete in the global economy have increased the breadth and depth of workplace literacy demands, although a shrinking percentage of minimum wage, deskilled jobs still exist. Multiple job roles, quality monitoring, team planning, print communication, and regular reeducation are increasingly parts of jobs that have not left the continent or been automated. To maintain the same relative pay status, middle- and low-level workers are expected to do more, using a much higher level of literacy, communication, and problem-solving skills.

Results from the NALS indicate that most adults have mastered rudimentary literacy skills, but large percentages are likely to have difficulty with newer, more complex uses of workplace and technological literacy. A similar problem exists for adolescents in school who tend to encounter only a relatively narrow range of literacy (e.g., narrative prose and expository textbooks) in their classes. For individuals with low literacy skills, there are fewer productive places to find employment. Higher levels of literacy skill do not guarantee protection from poverty, but they do seem to be a prerequisite.

Some of the same computer and Internet technologies that have raised the literacy demands of the workplace can be used to help educate people to meet these demands. For both adolescents and adults, the most likely path to success lies in integrating the new technologies into the activities of everyday learning. Computer simulations, tutorial applications, the Internet, and information processing and electronic communication tools can be used to address several important learning goals. These goals are (a) learning to think critically in solving problems, (b) becoming familiar with the use of technology tools for processing information, (c) expanding the breadth of materials encountered by learners, and (d) developing habits of mind suitable for lifelong learning.

Technology has helped transform the organization of work and literacy in the workplace. This transformation has brought with it concerns and questions about the unequal distribution of resources, the polarization of society, and the role of nationalism in a world of global employers and economies. Improved and expanded literacy is not the solution to all of the problems engendered by these transformations, but it is likely to be of help. It does seem clear that individuals who cannot function in the transformed workplace have considerably fewer choices than those who can. Our intent is not to imply that education should be solely defined by the needs of corporate America. However, as educators we have the dual goals of helping people expand their minds and their productivity as citizens. Indeed, for any long-term success to result with either goal, we must usually succeed with both goals.

REFERENCES

Attewell, P. (1992). Skill and occupational changes in U.S. manufacturing. In P. Adler (Ed.), *Technology and the future of work* (pp. 46–88). New York: Oxford University Press.

Barker, P., & Banerji, A. (1993). *Case studies in electronic performance support.* Paper presented at AI-ED '93: World Conference on Artificial Intelligence in Education, Edinburgh, Scotland.

Barrows, H. (1994). *Practice-based learning: Problem-based learning applied to medical education.* Springfield: Southern Illinois University.

Bishop, J., & Carter, S. (1991). The worsening shortage of college graduate workers. *Educational Evaluation and Policy Analysis, 13*(3), 221–255.

Child, D. (1997). Patterns of simulator use within a military training environment. *International Journal of Instructional Media, 24*(1), 43–53.

Classroom, Inc. (1995). *What are the Classroom Inc. simulations?* (Available from Classroom, Inc., 245 Fifth Avenue, Suite 1901, New York, NY 10016.)

Drucker, P. (1994). The age of social transformation. *Atlantic Monthly, 273*(4), 53–80.

Falsetti, J. (1995, March). *What the heck is a MOO and what's the story with all these cows?* Paper presented at TESOL '95, Long Beach, CA.

Frizler, K. (1995). *The Internet as an educational tool in ESOL writing instruction.* Unpublished master's thesis, San Francisco State University. Available: http://thecity.sfsu.edu/~funweb/thesis.htm.

Gery, G. (1991). *Electronic performance support systems.* Boston: Weingarten.

Gery, G. (1995). Attributes and behaviors of performance-centered systems. *Performance Improvement Quarterly, 8*(1), 47–93.

Haigler, K. (1990, June). *The job skills education program: An experiment in technology transfer for workplace literacy.* Paper prepared for the Work in America Institute, Harvard Club, New York.

Hudzina, M., Rowley, K., & Wager, W. (1996). Electronic performance support technology: Defining the domain. *Performance Improvement Quarterly, 9*(1), 36–48.

Imel, S. (1990). *Locating and selecting information: A guide for adult educators.* Columbus, OH: ERIC Clearinghouse on Adult, Career, and Vocational Education. (ERIC Document Reproduction Service No. ED 325 657)

Jones, D. (1996, August 26). Casting a net for job seekers. *USA Today,* pp. B1–B2.

Kirkley, J., & Duffy, T. (1997). In B. H. Khan (Ed.), *Web-based instruction: Development, application, and evaluation.* Englewood Cliffs, NJ: Educational Technology Publications.

Kirsch, I., Jungeblut, A., Jenkins, L., & Kolstad, A. (1993). *Adult literacy in America: A first look at results of the National Adult Literacy Survey.* Washington, DC: National Center for Educational Statistics.

Laffey, J. (1995). Dynamism and electronic performance support systems. *Performance Improvement Quarterly, 8*(1), 31–46.

Mikulecky, L., Clark, E., & McIntyre, S. (1989). Teaching concept mapping and university level study strategies using computers. *Journal of Reading, 32*(8), 694–702.

Osterman, P. (1993). *How common is workplace transformation and how can we explain who adapts.* Chicago: Spencer Foundation. (ERIC Document Reproduction Service No. ED 362 646)

Pritchard, P. (1996). *MINDShift: The employee handbook for understanding the world of work.* Dallas, TX: Pritchett & Associates.

Raybould, B. (1995). Performance support engineering: An emerging development methodology for enabling organizational learning. *Performance Improvement Quarterly, 8*(1), 7–22.

Reich, R. (1992). *The work of nations.* New York: Vintage Books.

Rifkin, J. (1995). *The end of work: The decline of the global labor force and the dawn of the post-market era.* New York: Putnam's.

Savery, J., & Duffy, T. (1995). Problem based learning: An instructional model and its constructivist framework. *Educational Technology, 35*(5), 31–38.

Shannon, P. (1996). Critical issues: Literacy and educational policy. *Journal of Literacy Research, 28*(3), 442–449.

Sprout, A. (1995). The Internet inside your company. *Fortune, 32,* 161–164.

Turner, T. (1993). *Literacy and machines: An overview of the use of technology in adult literacy programs.* (Tech. Rep. No. TR93-03). Philadelphia: National Center on Adult Literacy, University of Pennsylvania.

U.S. Department of Labor. (1991). *What work requires of schools—A SCANS report for America 2000.* Washington, DC: Author.

U.S. Department of Labor. (1992). *Learning a living: A blueprint for high performance.* Washington, DC: Author.

Venezky, R., Wagner, D., & Ciliberti, B. (1990). *Toward defining literacy.* Newark, DE: International Reading Association.

Weiss, E. (1993). The technical communicator and ISO 9000. *Technical Communication, 40*(2), 234–238.

TRANSFORMING LITERACY RESEARCH

The guiding question for this section was: What are the questions that must be addressed as digital reading and writing become more common, and what approaches to research will be most useful in addressing those questions? The two chapters in this section address respectively the two parts to this question. First, Kamil and Lane (chap. 19) provide a broad overview of the many new and largely unresearched questions that have emerged from the increasing prevalence of electronic forms of literate experience. They provide a plethora of examples that fall into categories ranging from theory, textual design, pedagogy, and curriculum, to instructional management and change. They point out that the types of questions that become most important depend on one's stance on the ultimate contribution of research to practice. Furthermore, they document that, for the most part, mainstream outlets for literacy research have published little research related to technology and literacy.

Addressing the second part of the guiding question, Miller and Olson (chap. 20) point out the inadequacies or at least the incompleteness of available research addressing how computer technology affects classroom instruction. They argue that, although there are notable exceptions, much existing research does not take into account the many interacting features of classrooms and of the hardware and software used in them. Likewise, many studies are conducted from a standpoint of advocacy driven by an all-encompassing positive vision of technology or by atypical infusions of state-of-the-art hardware and software. Not discounting the value of these studies, they argue for a transformation of research through the use of intensive case studies driven by a more detached and neutral stance aimed at examining how teachers appropriate available technologies. They cite several examples of this approach from their own and others' work.

Both chapters reflect a common denominator implied by all of the chapters in this book. The transformations that are occurring or that are likely to occur in texts, in readers and writers, in classrooms and schools, in instruction, and indeed in society imply that a radical restructuring of literacy research may be on the horizon. Conventional research questions and the theoretical perspectives of a typographic world from which they are derived may be moot, irrelevant, or completely transformed in a post-typographic world. The potential scope of such a transformation is exceedingly broad and consequential for those interested in literacy, and much more could be said specifically about the transformation of literacy research in a post-typographic world. However, the two chapters in this section give a clear glimpse of what lies on the horizon.

Researching the Relation Between Technology and Literacy: An Agenda for the 21st Century

Michael L. Kamil
Stanford University

Diane M. Lane
Scioto-Darby School
Hilliard, Ohio

It is always difficult to look at the current state of a field and prescribe the direction that field should take for the future. What we have attempted to do in this chapter is to characterize the directions current research in technology and literacy have taken and, using that as a guide, suggest where future research should go. We have also attempted to be more systematic about laying out some research agendas, uncovering what we see as some of the often hidden assumptions that have been associated with previous attempts to do so. Finally, we describe the implementation of technology in one school as a source for questions that literacy and technology research must address.

There are at least three facets of literacy research on which technology can have an impact. The first of these is what we choose to call the *operational aspects* of research. Operational aspects of research include the tools used to collect and analyze data relating to research. In a review of the various influences of computers on research in reading, Kamil (1987) pointed out the variety of these aspects and noted that reliance on such tools for collection and analysis of data was vital. We believe that the greatest impact of technology thus far has been on collecting and analyzing data, and that impact is likely to increase even further. It is difficult to imagine a contemporary research project that does not entail some form of technology, from video or audio recordings as data, to computerized data storage and analysis. These trends will clearly continue, but it is unlikely that these operational aspects will change in a qualitatively dramatic way over the near term.

The second facet of technology's impact on research is *dissemination*. It is also difficult to conceive of a contemporary research project that does not use some form of technology for either researching published findings, publishing the findings of the study, making use of e-mail to contact other researchers, or using word processing to prepare the manuscript. Reinking (1995) reported the explosive growth in the number of electronic journals, using data from 1994. However, it is even more explosive now. In a current survey (*Association of Research Libraries,* 1995) of electronic publications, the number of journal and newsletter titles was 700. This number has increased by over two thirds since 1994 and sixfold since the first edition (there were 110 listings in 1991, 240 in 1993, and more than 400 in 1995).

Despite the attractiveness of these alternative modes of dissemination, there are cautions. Grzeszkiewicz and Hawbaker (1996) studied 130 online, full-text journals. Although the sample was limited, they concluded that librarians and users should be aware that total reliance on electronic versions of journals are not a satisfactory option because very few of them contain full-text versions of articles.

The third facet of literacy research to be affected by technology is *problem conceptualization or identification*. Some technological developments have begun to affect the way in which we conceive of appropriate problems to study. Some research has been conducted from the standpoint of how new technologies may transform literacy. However, we believe that this is the facet of technology and literacy research most likely to grow and indeed where growth is most needed. In the field of literacy research today, there are several relatively modest research agendas that have arisen without a systematic explanation of how they are related. One of the purposes of this chapter, then, is to look at those research agendas and to look at how they might coalesce into a coherent agenda for the future. To do this effectively we need to examine the current trends in research related to technology and literacy.

A SURVEY OF RESEARCH PUBLICATIONS IN TECHNOLOGY AND LITERACY

Before research agendas can be set, it is important to look at the state of affairs that exist, and will consequently determine the course of future research. Toward that end, we conducted a simple study. We selected four research journals considered to be in the mainstream of literacy research, two in reading and two in writing: *Reading Research Quarterly*, *Journal of Reading Behavior* (recently changed to *Journal of Literacy Research*), *Research in the Teaching of English*, and *Written Communication*. These journals have been determined to have the highest citation rates among literacy journals (Shanahan & Kamil, 1994). The volumes in all of these journals from 1991 to 1995, representing the previous 5-year period prior to our work on this chapter, were examined for research related to computers or other technologies. Any article that examined the effects of literacy and technology (other than conventional print) was included.

We discovered that for the two reading journals, there was a total of three articles dealing with the relationship of technology to reading, and only one that dealt with computer technology. Of a total of 256 articles, 3 is only about 1% of the published articles. The situation is somewhat better for writing journals. There were nine articles dealing with writing and technology, out of a total of 181 articles, or approximately 5%. Combined, the total number of technology articles published in these four journals was 12 out of a total of 437 articles, or 2.7%. In addition, most of the technology articles in this 5-year period were published in 1991 and 1992 when all but two of the technology articles appeared in the four journals reviewed in our study.

By way of comparison, an ERIC search using the descriptor *computer-assisted instruction* produced 18,056 citations. Using *computers and reading* produced 1,022 citations; using *computers and writing* yielded 1,467 citations; and using *computers and literacy* produced 2,071. Although these may not all be research related, they clearly represent a volume of material at least two orders of magnitude greater than that found in the mainstream literacy journals.

Further, in an extensive analysis of National Reading Conference (NRC) publications, Baldwin et al. (1992) looked at all of the NRC publications from 1952 to 1991. They did an analysis by content as well as methodology. In their analysis of key concepts, the terms *computer* or *technology* simply do not appear. However, *television* does occur, as perhaps the only technologically related term. Beyond NRC publications, we do know that in the years between 1960 and 1990, some important, and, perhaps, milestone articles were published on reading and technology. Of particular note is the work of the Stanford Project, one of the original attempts to use computer technology to teach reading (Atkinson & Hansen, 1966–1967). A strong reaction to this work was published by Spache (1968–1969), with a reply by Atkinson (1968–1969).

The *NRC Yearbooks* have contained three reviews of technology and reading (Kamil, 1982; Reinking, 1995; Spache, 1967). It is instructive to note that the emphasis on technology and reading differed among these three reviews. Spache (1967) focused on the use of reading machines to train students to read better and faster. His review was early enough that computer technology did not play a prominent a role except in the analysis of text. In 1982, the computer revolution was in full swing and the focus was on the capabilities of computers and software. Much of Kamil's (1982) emphasis was on the use of the computer as a tool in research and on the use of technology to teach reading. Reinking's (1995) review focused on the notion of text and how it has been, or will be altered by technology. The concern was more with the shape of literacy in the future as it was for any concerns of the present. This review represented a clear disconnection from earlier perspectives as Reinking suggested that new conceptions of literacy were needed. As we approach a similar task today, the emphasis in educational computing seems to be focusing on the issue of connecting individuals to the world via the Internet, disregarding questions of literacy in any form. This review represents a shift in emphasis from an earlier review (Reinking & Bridwell-Bowles, 1991). In the earlier review, the emphasis was on conventional literacy; in the later review it was focused on the nature of literacy in a technological environment. We are certainly close enough in time to Reinking's (1995) review that it remains highly relevant, despite some definite shifts.

What can we conclude from the state of research in technology and literacy? The simple, and we believe, wrong conclusions are that there is little or no research being done on technology and literacy, and that there is more work being done on technology and writing than on technology and reading. This conclusion is simply wrong, first because there are more outlets for technology-related literacy research than these four journals. These data can lead to one of two assumptions about literacy and technology. The first possible assumption is that technology is viewed by the literacy research community as either a relatively unimportant problem or one that cannot be solved easily. The second possible assumption is that all of the difficult problems have been solved. However, any cursory examination of either the extant research or the situations in schools will show this possibility to be untenable.

In addition, a large number of conventional print journals dealing with technology issues have been started during the past 5 years. It is likely that much of the research that might have appeared in the literacy journals has actually appeared in these other outlets. What is important for the purposes of this chapter is that there are important data for the research that will be conducted concerning literacy and technology in the future. One other condition might account partially for the scarcity of mainstream literacy and technology publications. Some of the studies reported in mainstream journals that were not specifically related to technology were conducted in environments where technology was being used in either instructional or applied literacy contexts. The focus on the research was on the nontechnological aspects of the situation (e.g., staff development). Note, however, that such studies did not deal with basic issues of what the effects of technology on literacy were. It also suggests that the relation of technology to literacy has not made a detectable impact on the thinking of literacy researchers in the problem conceptualization stage.

AGENDA SETTING IN READING RESEARCH

An analysis of what this general neglect of interest in technology means can be aided by using Mosenthal's (1993) analysis of agenda setting in reading research. He suggested that we need to consider the question: "Whose problems and goals should be addressed in reading research?" In response to this question, Mosenthal laid out three perspectives for framing problems and goals that might create reading research agendas: the administrative-efficiency perspective, the client-satisfaction perspective, and the emancipatory perspective.

In the *administrative-efficiency* perspective, the goals of education and reading are to socialize students and to provide education that is relevant, to job demands, for example. This perspective maintains that the way in which this goal is accomplished is through centralized decisions about standards, curricula, and assessments. In the second perspective, that of *client satisfaction*, the focus is on the goals and problems of all individuals, so that each person can develop a sense of personal value. To accomplish this, the emphasis is on distributed decision making. Finally, the *emancipatory* perspective assumes that the role of education is to change the educational, social, and political structure. The emphasis is on equally empowering all classes of individuals. Mosenthal (1993) suggested that we need to form an agenda for research that incorporates all of the perspectives, rather than only one. What is important is to look at the way in which current research and practice fits into these perspectives.

For example, at a societal level, computer technology is clearly viewed by many educators and researchers as having the potential for creating a liberating "culture" among its users, including how it offers the potential for greater access to information. The following quotation illustrates one such perspective:

> What we will be able to do with tomorrow's computer systems is a vast step forward from what we were able to do in the past. At the Institute for the Learning Sciences, we are now producing computer systems that interact with people in more engaging ways than before. Our systems allow children to try out things in simulated worlds of our own making, and sometimes of their own making; they allow children to fly their own ship to the moon, design their own animal, or direct their own newscast. This technology will allow us to support what is one of the most important parts of a good educational system: the cultivation of individual initiative in students. (Schank & Cleary, 1994, p. 43)

At the same time, the use of computers for communication carries with it the potential for an anarchistic culture that may work against some agendas. A quick "surf" around the Internet supports the accuracy of this previous point. Government attempts to bring electronic communication under central control suggest the administrative-efficiency perspective at work. The problems of providing equitable access to computer technology relate to the emancipatory perspective and its influence on current research agendas. In addition, the potential of computers and the Internet for providing more access to publishing raises both the client-satisfaction and the emancipatory perspectives. As we lay out the directions for research in technology and literacy in the remainder of this chapter, we return to these three agendas.

These agenda-setting perspectives also offer another possible insight into the current meager state of technology research on literacy in mainstream journals. Because many conventional researchers may be threatened by a loss of power as we turn to a new form of text and delivery, they may have chosen to ignore the issues and problems raised by technology. Some researchers may believe that technology has the potential to lessen the traditional power of teaching and dehumanize the profession. Although these conclusions are purely speculative, they need to be examined as possibilities.

DIRECTIONS FOR LITERACY RESEARCH IN TECHNOLOGY

The development of new technologies has necessitated that research methods used to evaluate learning and performance using those technologies be reevaluated to determine whether the questions and methodologies used to study them are still appropriate. In many cases, technological advances are simply instrumental in making conventional tasks more efficient. This is a useful point to begin considering new directions for literacy research. In this section we discuss some questions and issues for research on technology and its effects on literacy that we believe should be examined systematically. We attempt to create a road map of areas that need considerable investigation. Our purpose is to help direct thought in productive ways as literacy researchers move through a maze of old and new technologies and their impact on literacy.

Research Issues in Learning and Using Technology

One of the critical questions that arises about the relation of technology to literacy is whether or not views of literacy need to be revised in light of new technologies. A host of theorists has argued that technology will clearly require a new or at least expanded definition of literacy (Bolter, 1991; Neuman, 1991; Papert, 1993; Reinking, 1995). This issue presents us with a dilemma. If we accept the notion that a new definition of literacy is required, we will clearly be setting an agenda in a way that is disposed to favor new technology. The converse is also true. That agenda may well require radical rethinking of our research methods and tools.

In either case, we need to proceed with our evaluations of the impact of technology on children, adults, society, and culture. We may need to reexamine our basic assumptions about how we find answers to questions involving technology. Or, we may not have a choice. Often, technology drives applications. If a new technology is developed, it often finds a new application, rather than simply replacing older ones. Our job is to analyze new technologies to see where they have value for literacy. We also must filter these questions through the lenses of the agendas we wish to set.

There are some tentative data supporting the conclusion that using technology in instruction does improve general school performance. The Center for Applied Special Technology (CAST) found that students with online access (to the Internet) showed "significantly higher scores on measurements of information management, communication and presentation of ideas" (CAST, 1996).

Literacy and Using Established Technologies

Although there is much research concerning the use and implementation of established technologies such as film, audio recordings, video recordings, television, and radio, there has been relatively little mainstream literacy research in these areas. Neuman (1991), for example, treated the problem of literacy and television, arguing that television has not replaced or diminished literacy. Neuman went on to argue that there may be multiple paths to literacy, of which television provides one alternative. Clearly, there is a need for continued research in this medium, particularly as it becomes integrated with computer technology.

Returning to Mosenthal's (1993) categories of research agendas introduced earlier in this chapter, the administrative-efficiency perspective favors those learning media such as television that can be easily assessed and that can be controlled in the service of creating a mass culture. Client-satisfaction perspectives, on the other hand, might lead educators to develop agendas whereby the centralization of educational television (broadcast from centralized sources) was viewed as undesirable. The emancipatory perspective might view television as desirable, if television were employed to promote diversity.

Flood and Lapp (1995) made a strong argument for expanding definitions of literacy to include visual literacy. This changes the definition of literacy from what it has been conventionally, but the implication—that a new definition of literacy is a necessity—is in line with many of the other arguments being put forth. We do need to reconsider even the basic definitions of the concepts with which we work in literacy research.

There are far fewer studies of audio and other video technologies related to literacy, but the logic on the conclusions reached in the preceding paragraphs parallels those by Neuman (1991) as she advocated a new or expanded definition of literacy. Once again, continued research is clearly required to piece out the effects of these media as they impact on literacy. However, once again, caution is clearly needed. The computer has become the technology of choice as these other technologies are incorporated into software or come under the control of computer hardware and software combinations. It will be increasingly difficult to separate different technologies into discrete categories (see Lemke, chap. 17, this volume).

When it comes to future research into the effects of conventional technologies, we have not yet answered many of the basic questions. We must continue to attempt to clarify the relation between these conventional technologies and literacy. We must continue to do this even as they merge into a single, multidimensional, computer-centered technology.

Literacy and Learning "New" Technologies

The careful reader will quickly note that this section title is clearly not parallel with that of the previous section. The missing parallelism is deliberate and purposeful. When new technologies are developed, it is often difficult to see how they will ultimately be used. What we have been resistant to do, as a field, is conduct careful and extensive studies of the technologies as they develop and as we learn how to use them. This resistance is not entirely the fault of individual researchers, because technology is often introduced faster than the research that might study it. However, for educational environments, the implementation of technology lags behind other fields (Singer, Dreher, & Kamil, 1982). We clearly need to conduct studies that not only account for the rapid innovation, but also consider the far slower pace of adoption of technology by schools. This may entail rethinking the way in which we researched these problems or the scale with which those research projects are conducted. We will have to focus more on what is delivered rather than on the technology itself.

It will not be possible to maintain the status quo. We simply cannot allow technology to be introduced at an accelerating pace and have the broader literacy research community on the sidelines.

We have clearly not addressed the question of what basic cognitive processes are involved in using present technologies related to literacy. Consequently, we have obviously not dealt with the processes involved in learning and using new technologies related to literacy. Whereas we do substantial research in basic processes of reading and writing, there is only a minimal effort when it comes to the technological aspects of literacy. For example, we know quite a bit about reading conventional text, but we know relatively little about the processes involved in reading hypertext. Are those processes the same? Are they different? Do they overlap? If so, by how much? If not, what processes are unique to each type of text? If the processes are similar, our current research methods may be sufficient. If not, we may need to ask new and different questions and to develop different methods for answering them.

Literacy, Social Interactions and Technology. In recent years, the notion of situated cognition, collaborative learning environments and similar perspectives emphasizing the social dimensions of learning have begun to influence educators and researchers, particularly in mathematics education (Anderson, Reder, & Simon, 1996; Brown, Collins, & Duguid, 1989; Donmoyer, 1997; Greeno, 1997). We have seen relatively less of these perspectives in literacy education, and decidedly less when the relation between computers and literacy is considered. With this in mind, we propose a set of critical research questions that must be answered with respect to the relation of technology, social interactions, and literacy.

The way in which individuals interact with each other in the presence of new technologies may have a profound effect on literacy, literacy instruction, and the ways in which all education is delivered. The current emphases on social interactions are but precursors to an expanded potential to communicate among increasingly larger groups in the course of learning. The communication might be centered on common projects or on searches for information. In any event, these forces are beginning to shape the way in which education is conducted. In turn they are beginning to shape the ways we communicate. Once again, we need a careful research program that monitors and explores these issues, yet is sensitive to the agenda perspectives. The current interest in the Internet as an educational tool is one example. Giving students the freedom to communicate with anyone in the world may be viewed in a positive light, but may have the consequence of confusing the traditional roles of teachers and students. We need to evaluate how well the use of Internet resources meshes with the educational objectives of the classroom.

Equity Issues: Who Gets Technology?

There have been recurrent questions about who gets access to computers (see, e.g., Sayers, 1995; Sutton, 1991). These questions center on both the economics of the implementation and on gender issues. Gender issues include interest in, and propensity toward, using computers. The economic questions are real and need to be addressed (Chipman, 1993). In California an estimate of the necessary funding for integrating technology into classroom instruction over the 4 years from 1996 to 2000 is $10.9 billion. Efforts to solve this problem have involved corporate donations of new, used, or refurbished equipment; volunteers to help staff and maintain the technology; and making the technology the focus of the school. (See, e.g., documents relating to how technology was implemented by the Issaquah School District: http://alphasvr.liberty.issaquah.wednet.edu/info.htm.)

An administrative-efficiency agenda can be seen underlying issues of cost. There is general evidence that the general use of computers can provide greater cost-effectiveness than other interventions (Niemiec & Walberg, 1986). Although Niemiec and Walberg (1986) found this savings for general computer use, the meta-analysis on which the conclusion was based found reading instruction delivered by computer to have relatively high effect sizes (Niemiec, 1987; Niemiec & Walberg, 1985).

Literacy research has simply not addressed the complexity that underlies equity issues related to technology. Issues about access to technology seem only peripherally related to literacy. They are not. If literacy and technology are becoming intimately linked, and we believe they are, the issues of access are of paramount importance. We cannot, for example, afford to create a class of individuals, for whatever reason, that has little or no access to such critical literacy tools.

Gender.   Gender issues have been, to date, addressed by relatively conventional methods. We have assumed that gender is marked by physical characteristics. Computer-mediated communication changes those physical characteristics.

The work of Turkle (1984, 1995) has shown that conventional notions of identity (and, consequently, gender) have been radically altered through some aspects of computer-based activities. For example, role-playing games allow individuals to experiment with a broad range of identities. Role-playing allows individuals to adopt, in an interactive computer environment, any number of different identities including adoption of a different gender. What this suggests is that our conventional ways of looking at the effects of gender on literacy and literacy-related activities may no longer be sufficient to give us the information we need. This set of issues has recently surfaced in a "conversation" about feminist theories and their relation to literacy, education, and research (Commeyras, Orellana, Bruce, & Neilsen, 1996).

In turn, gender and technology becomes a crucial area of research as more of our interpersonal interactions are mediated by the computer screen, without face-to-face interactions with people. Determination of gender may be missing in these computer interactions and, in turn, require that we account for this in our literacy instruction in schools. This analysis may well extend into areas such as voice and register in literacy. There is some question of whether gender equalization (the notion that gender either becomes irrelevant or ceases to favor one gender over the other) always happens when communication is mediated by computers. Selfe and Meyer (1991) found that it did not. This issue is clearly unresolved and, at the very least, research in questions of computer-mediated identity needs to be explored in detail. A review of the research of many of the issues on the use of electronic networks in composition can be found in Eldred and Hawisher (1995).

The mitigating possibilities that video may become a routine part of online communication (e.g., Fetterman, 1996) require that we approach this conclusion cautiously. In any event, we need to conduct careful research in this area. Specifically we need to know what will happen if we move from text-based communications, which provide some degree of gender equalization, to a visual mode, where conventional gender cues again become available.

Language.   Those who speak, read, and write English and surf the Internet will find little or no discomfort due to language; those who do not will find almost immediate discomfort. There are technological and historic reasons for the nearly exclusive use of English on the Internet. However, those reasons do not relieve us as a community of literacy researchers from the responsibility of determining what the effects of a single language are on literacy. This concern is particularly critical as more children come to our public schools without English as a first language. These students, who are often affected by being in lower socioeconomic groups, have the added burden of being denied access to a degree because they do not share the lingua franca of the computer world.

At the same time, current computer technology offers a relatively untapped resource for revolutionizing learning to read in a second language. Inexpensive CD-ROM versions of text with accompanying audio are available worldwide. The addition of oral cues to the language can certainly facilitate learning. However, we have no systematic body of research evaluating these products or methods. We may not be able to rely on our traditional research methodologies and measures as we gather evidence on these problems. The research will, of necessity, be far more interdisciplinary than much past research. We will need the cooperation of specialists in educational curriculum, technology, linguistics, literacy, and many other fields.

Does Technology Make a Difference?

An important research question to be asked is whether it is the medium that is used or the content that is presented that produces the most substantial learning effects. This question has a fairly long history, beginning with Clark's (1983) conclusion that it was the content that determined learning rather than the medium. Kozma (1991) attempted to refute Clark's position in an article published as part of an entire issue devoted to this question. Kozma suggested that because of the interactive nature of much of learning, the media could not be dismissed.

Another aspect of this debate is found at the "No Significant Difference" website (http://tenb.mta.ca/phenom/phenom.html). This site is a compilation of 218 research reports from 1945 to 1995 that compared instruction with and without technology and found no significant differences. These findings span a range of technologies, methodologies, and settings. These conclusions hinge on whether or not technology is used to do something that cannot be done in any other fashion. For example, hypertext cannot be implemented without computer technology. The same content simply cannot be incorporated into a teaching lesson in any practical way using any other technology. Such contemporary examples favor Kozma's (1991) position over Clark's (1983). However, we still need to determine whether the presence or absence of a particular difference matters. Or is it possible that technology can deliver some instruction that will free teachers to do other instruction that is not effectively delivered with technology? In addition, we need to ask whether technology can do things that matter instructionally that a traditional teacher cannot. There may be advantages to the use of technology that go beyond what is typically measured.

A recent addition to the discussion was provided by Mayer (1997). He showed that the answer to the question of whether multimedia learning is effective cannot be answered in a unidimensional way. For example, students who had low prior knowledge and high spatial ability did best in his multimedia learning situations. Although Mayer's work was limited to science learning, the answers should provide a guide for the way in which such questions should be approached in other fields.

How does this relate to literacy? Of critical importance is the issue of whether or not there is an advantage to using technology when it comes to literacy instruction. Clearly, we have answered this question affirmatively for some activities such as word processing (cf. Bangert-Drowns, 1993; however, for a "mild" caveat on this issue, see Cochran-Smith, 1991).

The jury is still out when it comes to reading. For example, hypertext may allow some advantages, but for certain types of conventional reading and searching, it has disadvantages (Gillingham, 1993). We still need to determine how educationally relevant hypertext will be. For a discussion of the effects of a different type of hypertext, see Anderson-Inman and Horney (chap. 2, this volume).

Research in Literacy on the Internet

Because the Internet is such a growing presence in contemporary reading and writing and promises to remain so, it is important to examine literacy demands in using it. Several separate domains of literacy knowledge are involved in using the Internet, and it is important to look at each one in the context of needed research. Three that we examined here are the World Wide Web, hypertext, and e-mail.

World Wide Web.   Being literate on the Web and on the Internet places special demands on the reader. The volume of text one encounters in the course of a brief "surf" is massive, even though much of the content is graphical. However, most of the text encountered is expository. To demonstrate this, we analyzed a small sample of websites. A series of 50 random sites was selected using the Yahoo Random Site Selector (http:\\www.yahoo.com). Each site was classified as primarily narrative or primarily expository. Some sites were completely graphical and were not analyzed. In order to get a sample of 50 sites containing textual information, 70 attempts were made. Twenty sites were either not functional or contained no text. Of the 50 sites that contained text, 48 contained expository text, whereas only 2 sites contained narrative text. We believe that this proportion is probably a reasonable estimate of the type of text on the Web.

However, the instruction students receive in conventional print media is often primarily narrative. Such an awareness suggests a series of research questions that need to be investigated. For example, what demands are placed on the reader by the text that is encountered in the most prevalent forum for computerized text when compared to the abilities students develop as a result of conventional instruction? Such questions might form the core of a systematic program of research that may prove to be critical for literacy instruction.

Failure to answer such questions may have serious consequences for the field of literacy research and points to a major problem in setting a research agenda for technology and literacy. A common attitude among computer developers and engineers is that the time lag between generating research findings and applying them to educational uses of computers is simply too great (Singer et al., 1982). From an engineering perspective, innovations should be implemented and used until they prove to be inappropriate or are supplanted by new technologies. The slow pace of literacy research pertaining to technology works against this perspective. Thus, we need to accelerate the pace of our research in literacy problems before the opportunities to answer the questions are swept away by the quickened pace of technological innovation.

Hypertext.   The predominant form of text on the Internet is not only informational, it is presented and sometimes written as hypertext; that is, certain elements in the text are linked to other texts. The linked text, usually a word or phrase, can lead one to additional information, definitions, or other information related to the word or phrase, or unlike printed texts, to a relevant video.

There is a modest literature about the nature of hypertext, much of it theoretical (Bolter, 1991; Duchastel, 1988; Laurillard, 1993; Lunin & Rada, 1989; Rada, 1989; Rouet,

Levonen, Dillon, & Spiro, 1996). However, what is clearly missing from the literature is a systematic analysis of the relation between reading hypertext and reading conventional text. Clearly, many of the strategies that are useful and necessary in reading a conventional text are not effective and may be even dysfunctional in reading a hypertext. For example, reading to the end of a difficult portion of text in which a hypertext link is available may be counterproductive. It may be better to explore the link to attempt to disambiguate the meaning. On the other hand, it may also interfere with comprehension to stop reading and explore the link. This latter problem is particularly acute because the destinations of many links are unknown to the reader. That is, the reader cannot know in advance what is "linked" to a word, phrase, or graphical representation before following the link. Perfetti (1996) made an interesting attempt to deal with some of these issues about the relation between hypertext and conventional text, but the reasoning is based on very little data. Until we have data about whether or not students can and do utilize hypertext in productive ways, we will have no way of grounding theory.

Clearly, nothing in any of the current literacy curricula prepares students for this sort of reading, which requires navigational strategies not needed in reading conventional printed texts. To guide the development of appropriate curricula, we need research that investigates the metacognitive dimensions of reading hypertexts. Little research has addressed this issue. However, Gillingham's (1993) work is an example of the type of research that is needed. He found that hypertext may interfere with comprehension when the goal is to answer specific questions.

What is particularly troubling about the increasingly widespread discussion and use of hypertext is that we know very little about its efficacy across a range of readers. We need an extended program of research to examine the underlying cognitive processes of reading hypertext among readers of varying abilities. Such research will allow us to determine how best to prepare students for this new form of reading. We also need to examine alternative configurations of hypertext. For example, a line of research might be dedicated to investigating the ways in which hypertext links could be differentiated so that readers could anticipate what sorts of information they might find when they do explore a particular link (see Anderson-Inman & Horney, chap. 2, Lemke, chap. 17, and Purves, chap. 14, all this volume).

E-mail.   Arguably, the single most explosive use of technology has been in e-mail for routine communication, discussion groups, chat rooms, and the distribution of other business and entertainment products, services, and information. The primary literacy demand in e-mail is writing. Writing e-mail messages not only requires clear communication, but typically puts a premium on much shorter lengths of messages. Although reading is certainly a factor, the brevity of most e-mail would seem to mitigate the effects of reading ability.

The style of e-mail is somewhere between a conversation and a letter. It has little of the formal style of hard copy letters, but it is clearly more formal than a face-to-face conversation. Consequently, it may be that researchers have assumed that findings from studies of writing and oral communication provide sufficient information to answer most of the questions about e-mail issues.

However, there is a growing body of literature on e-mail (Tao, 1996). Much of what has been done relates to business communication and to the issues of what happens when communication is mediated by computers. An interesting phenomenon associated with e-mail is the monitoring of e-mail by employers. This seems to be the result of a conflict of agendas (administrative-efficiency and emancipatory). The same sort of conflict may also appear in school as students come to have access to the Internet and e-mail. What will be important in future research will be to partial out the educationally relevant literacy aspects. We need to know whether e-mail can be an essential part of literacy instruction or whether it is simply another interesting but optional form of communication.

In order to study the literacy issues related to the Internet, a careful consideration of the outcomes of education is needed. Research will not be effective unless there is a match between evaluation and the outcomes that are expected within the traditional school curriculum. The questions associated with newer visions of school made possible by technology will be qualitatively different from those that have traditionally been asked. As suggested by Mosenthal (1993), it will be important to assess underlying agendas as well as the research questions they generate. Consequently, new research methodologies may be needed to supplement the traditional ones, although it is not possible to predict precisely what they might be. They will probably rely on a combination of using technology to record more information about situations in which literacy is practiced and new theoretical underpinnings of problem conceptualizations.

Hardware Questions

Once again, hardware questions simply do not seem like conventional problems for literacy research. Although questions of hardware have not become typical mainstream literacy issues, they represent critical aspects of how literacy will be affected by technology.

Reading From a Computer Screen Versus Reading From Paper. Early studies showed that reading from computer screens was more difficult than reading from hard copy (Daniel & Reinking, 1987; Gould & Grischkowsky, 1984; Haas & Hayes, 1985). Although the problem has been partially alleviated by better monitors and better graphics capabilities, this is still a problem that deserves additional study. What many existing studies have not taken into account is the computer's capability for searching text. Search times were one of the measures used to demonstrate that reading at a computer screen was less efficient than reading on printed pages. However, today most word processing programs, Web browsers, and other computer programs have extensive search capabilities. Consequently, the time required to find information in text may be mediated by factors other than visual search. We need, again, to revisit these problems in light of what we know now.

The availability of massive amounts of conventional text translated into electronic representations (cf. Project Gutenberg, 1996) on the Internet suggests that problem of reading from a computer display may have been ignored or that it may not have been so severe in practice. There seem to be no data available on the number of persons who actually read Project Gutenberg texts at their computer screens for recreation rather than to search for specific portions of the text, such as a quotation or a fact. The original Project Gutenberg texts were simply electronic versions of the conventional text. Newer texts have at least some hypertext characteristics. A directory of other electronic sites on the Project Gutenberg home page lists 25 other sources for electronic texts (Project Gutenberg, 1996).

In any event, we need to know how to present text on a computer screen in optimal fashion, from organization of content to its display. These lines of research will clearly be linked with the hypertext research discussed in a previous section.

Keyboards or Voice Input. Another area of needed research in the coming years is the role of different media in defining literacy (see Lemke, chap. 17, this volume). As computers become capable of processing speech for more than simple commands, it will be important to investigate the effects of speech combined with writing. We are moving from computers that are merely visual displays for text to machines that can actually read the text on the screen to the user. As this happens, we need to be aware of the possibilities and the potential problems of conceptualizing literacy across the different modalities. Should we continue to emphasize the need for keyboarding skills? Should we concentrate more of our efforts in preparing students to use dictation as a primary means of composing? Should we spend more time being concerned with handwriting as an input system? Answers to these questions may be crucial as technology permeates classroom environments.

Complexity of Software. One of the difficulties with current software for literacy instruction is that it is difficult to use in the classroom setting. There is such diversity in what is taught in literacy and how it is taught that the role of teachers is fraught with difficulty as they attempt to integrate commercial software packages into conventional print curricula. It is instructive, for example, to compare the issues pertaining to literacy to issues in mathematics instruction. There are relatively specific national standards for the teaching of mathematics (Ball & Schroeder, 1992; National Council of Teachers of Mathematics, 1991). Given that these standards suggest that there are certain skills that should be developed, a mathematics curriculum is more amenable to the incorporation of a piece of software that, for example, teaches students the concept of symmetry. This may require little or no effort on the part of a teacher.

Comparing the situation in mathematics with literacy, we have, as yet, no official literacy standards for which software could be developed such that all teachers would immediately recognize the need and place for a specific piece of software. Current versions of standards for literacy are such that they are probably too general for software developers to instantiate in ways that will satisfy teachers (see, e.g., *Standards for the English Language Arts,* 1996)

This situation is clearly an example of conflicting perspectives that affect setting agendas for reading research. The desire for standards is an area in which Mosenthal's (1993) administrative-efficiency perspective might dominate to the detriment of his client-satisfaction or emancipatory perspectives. Research in literacy and technology always must account for the variant agendas underlying both the research and the ultimate applications of the research.

SOME OBSERVATIONS ON IMPLEMENTATION
OF COMPUTERS IN A SCHOOL SETTING

We fully believe that the future of education and literacy and technology are inexorably linked. As the world becomes more technologically oriented, students will need ever greater degrees of skill with those technologies. In turn, as students become more sophisticated with technology, there will be ever greater demands for technology outside school.

We further believe that literacy and education will also become more important outside of schools, in nontraditional settings such as the home and workplace. However, we believe that educators must carefully consider how those environments as well as technological implementations impact on literacy and literacy instruction. For the present, we believe they need to monitor carefully changes being wrought by technology in our schools. To that end, we present the following observations about the implementation of technology in a school setting.

As always, in these settings, there are competing agendas. Teachers are often concerned about emancipatory or client-satisfaction agendas. Administrators and parents are often interested in the administrative-efficiency agenda of technology. Students may have interests that attract them to emancipatory agendas. We use this brief set of observations to highlight those questions that are and are not being addressed as schools adopt and implement technology solutions.

This set of observations focuses on a single school near a large Midwestern city. It has been the largest growing school district in the state for the last few years. The enrollment currently includes 10,600 students and over 1,000 employees.

Throughout the 1992–1993 and 1993–1994 school years, administrators, teachers, and community members met to develop a technology plan for the future. These meetings resulted in four specific action plans that were recommended to the Board of Education for implementation in May 1995, and accomplished by the end of June 1996.

The initial four plans focused on:

1. Selecting and purchasing hardware and software to bring all schools to locally developed minimum standards.
2. Wiring all buildings to Ohio School Net standards and improving connectivity within the district and beyond.
3. Provide intensive training to selected teachers from each building to provide a core of expertise across the district and across the grade levels.
4. Establish a training and learning resource center at a central location in the district for ongoing staff training and a central repository of selected resources.

It should be made clear that although the technology plan refers to hardware, software, and staff training the focus of the plan is on the students. The district adopted a goal to prepare graduates to thrive in the 21st century. For every graduate to reach this goal, each student must acquire skills in technology, beginning at the primary level.

Financial Issues and Resource Persons

In 1995 a bond issue was passed by the voters to purchase the hardware for the district. Each elementary school received $180,000, each middle school received $240,000, and the high school received $360,000. At present, the bond issue money should last for approximately 2 more years. It is not yet obvious where continuing funding will be found.

Each school within the district had one paid technology assistant (TA; classroom teacher) to deal with hardware and software problems. In addition, a network of teachers from each school was picked to become facilitators for a year. The TA and the facilitators worked as a team. They were required to write a technology plan for their building before they could obtain funds for the individual school. The facilitators were to train the teachers in their building with a set of workshops after school. To encourage teachers to attend, one school required attendance of teachers at a certain number of inservice workshops to receive a new computer for their classroom.

The following observations were made in individual classrooms in a single school. They seem to be representative of experiences across the district, as indicated by discussions among the facilitators at group meetings.

Examples of Problems in Using Technology in the Literacy Curriculum

After a study on whales, a class of first-grade students used the computer to view a CD book on whales, as a follow-up to the conventional reading task. In another context, after a discussion about letter writing, the students made greeting cards, notes, or sent e-mail messages to other students, parents, or pen pals. These represented the primary uses of literacy in the class. The main question that troubled the teacher in this class was: "Where will I find the time to integrate a computer program that will enhance my students' needs?"

Finding time during the day to use the computer was a frequent concern. Teachers in the school adopted different formats to use the computer in the classroom. Computers were used with a class in a laboratory or with a small group of students in the classroom working on projects; they were used by individual students during free time or as supplemental activities; and they were also used to reinforce some of the learning that had taken place in the class. The choices among these formats did not seem to be the result of a systematic plan, either for individual teachers or for the teachers as a group.

Students. "When is it my turn to *play* (emphasis added) on the computer?" a child asked his teacher. The positive motivation that computers provided clearly assisted teachers, with the students spending additional time on the learning tasks. Students were able to explore a topic on the Internet, download relevant information, write about it, and print or e-mail it to a teacher, parent, or friend, all in a single sitting.

Computers were not simply used only for reinforcement and remedial practice. They were used to challenge learners in developing independence in researching new material and facts. Technology provided opportunities to integrate all facets of literacy: reading, writing, speaking, listening, and thinking. Overwhelmingly, the students preferred using a computer to using pencil and paper. When asked, they would reply that using a computer was fun and the latter was work. Many older students felt more confident with a computer than with pencil and paper because they could correct it immediately without erasing and still have a neat printed copy. The spell-check built into the word processors helped students correct their errors more readily. Students spent more time on the content of reports because word processors made the writing and editing easier.

What did not work well revolved around several different concerns. Software that could not be used independently by the student was particularly troublesome. If during teaching time something happened to the computer, it was very difficult for the teacher to leave a group of students and fix the problem. This situation created frustration for the teacher and the students.

Another problem that occurred was software unfamiliar to the teacher. An intermediate-grade teacher often let students read the directions. The burden for primary teachers was different. For software that had little or no reading requirements, students could work independently; if the literacy requirements were above those of the primary students, the computer became a management problem in the class.

Keyboarding was also a major problem. Many elementary students did not have the ability to use a keyboard. Young students became frustrated finding the letters. The keyboard itself was too large for the younger children, making it more difficult to type a word. There was no consistent provision for providing keyboarding instruction.

Perhaps the most striking feature of these observations is that they are focused so much on nonliteracy concerns. Issues of time and training seemed to outweigh many other concerns. Teachers and administrators are still struggling with more basic issues: time, money, and management. It was rare that teachers actually had time, energy, or assistance in adapting literacy or literacy instruction to accommodate to the technology available.

Research and development are clearly needed to find ways to make literacy software more teacher- or curriculum-friendly. We need to find ways to write software that adapts to the curriculum or goals of the teacher rather than vice versa (see Leu et al., chap. 12, this volume). It is simply too much to ask teachers to use a piece of software and adapt their teaching styles to one suited to technology. Until this bottleneck is cleared, the results of technological implementations largely will be less than satisfactory.

Another observation is that it is not higher level issues that caused most of the problems in this implementation. Teachers were not, for example, worried about critical thinking so much as they were worried about keyboarding or finding the time to use computers. Apparently there were conflicting agendas among parents who wanted their children exposed to technology, teachers who had insufficient time or training to use technology appropriately, and administrators who had to coordinate the support of the technology in the curriculum. There was also little evidence of new emphases in literacy that took into account electronic forms of reading and writing. We found few instructors teaching students about visual literacy, hypertext, and so on. Although these new literacies can be found in some implementations (e.g., whenever Internet resources were used for instruction), their presence still does not represent the norm.

The final telling factor is that the district in which these observations were made was able to fund the implementation at reasonable levels. In our experience, we have seen far too many districts that cannot afford to begin implementing the use of technology at even these levels. As this example highlights, coordinated efforts in research are needed to determine how students can gain access to technology in cost-effective ways. Until and unless these problems can be solved, they will continue to weigh even more heavily on financially strapped school districts. The result may easily be even greater disparity in access to technology between students from different socioeconomic levels.

THE FUTURE OF TECHNOLOGY, RESEARCH, AND LITERACY

Our review of the needed changes in the direction of research and technology in relation to literacy is clearly incomplete. We have focused on the agendas that undergird literacy and technology research, the conducting of research on literacy in technology environments, and practical applications of technology in schools. Our point has been that too often the agendas and agenda-setting factors of research in these areas have been ignored. There is relatively little systematic research focusing on well-defined problems related to literacy and technology. The practical applications of technology-related literacy research are often hindered by mundane practical matters that are part and parcel of the daily reality of schools. All of these issues create serious questions that need to be addressed. It is easy to be pessimistic, especially given the relatively small volume of research dedicated to addressing these problems.

Unfortunately, research into the problems and processes of literacy and technology has advanced little beyond what it was 10 years ago. An acceleration in the amount and a focus on specific types of problems such as those we have outlined in this chapter will allow, we hope, the research in these areas to reach a critical mass. Problems related to technology and literacy need to become more a part of mainstream literacy research, instead of being considered secondary to more traditional strands of research. We need to examine literacy through the lens of technology to see special problems and issues that need the attention of researchers. This is certainly not to imply that other lenses, more common in mainstream research, are unimportant. It merely states what should be obvious. If we ignore the technological perspective, we may forfeit the opportunity to shape the future of literacy. Clearly the efforts and perspectives detailed in the chapters of this volume represent a solid start in placing research related to technology and literacy more centrally within the mainstream literacy research.

In addition, several research areas that we have reviewed here are in need of urgent attention, either because we know little about the effects of technology in those areas or because the technology has the potential for dramatically altering some of our mainstream beliefs about literacy. Current conceptions of literacy will not suffice either practically or theoretically when exposed to the light of technological advances. It is likely that several versions of literacy, based both in printed and digital environments, will coexist for the near future. Information will continue to be the ultimate commodity, but it will be available in a variety of forms: text, hypertext, graphic, video, and even as oral language (Negroponte, 1995). Computer technology has the potential for allowing the same information to be generated and presented in any of these forms at the discretion of either the user or the producer. We need careful, comparative research about the effects of combining diverse presentations for a variety of purposes. It is likely that we will find new purposes for these different forms of information and research will be useful to track these different forms of literacy.

All literacy researchers need to be ahead of, or at least synchronized with, the engineering cycle—the time from conception of a piece of hardware to its obsolescence—as we develop ways to incorporate changing technology in education environments. Too often literacy researchers are left in the position of having to react to new technologies rather than anticipating their effects. One critical need is to assess the various agendas that affect the way in which we conduct our research and the implementations of technology we choose to investigate. Only in light of both research findings and research agendas can we make informed decisions about what practices have high probabilities of success in preparing people to be literate for today and for tomorrow.

There is an urgent need for such research in conventional educational settings where traditional conceptions of literacy seem to overwhelm the new, emerging conceptions of literacy. For example, in our analysis of one school district we noted that the concerns over money, training, time, and conventional methods overwhelmed concerns for literacy. We believe that new research methods will have to be adopted to answer questions that cannot be answered by traditional methods alone. Some of them exist, but others will have to be invented. Approaches such as that used by Reinking and Watkins (1996) in which research questions focus on the resources needed to make a specific implementation succeed may be one of the waves of the future. As their work suggests, it is too late to ask questions such as whether we should allow students access to the Internet. Rather, we should be conducting research that asks questions such as, "What does it take to use Internet connections successfully in teaching literacy?" There is a great deal of work to be done. The questions are intriguing and the implications of the knowledge generated are as enormous as is the scope of the work daunting. Research in these areas of literacy and technology has the potential to transform schools and schooling as well as literacy and literacy instruction.

REFERENCES

Association of Research Libraries 5th Edition Of Directory Of Electronic Publications. (1995). Available: Gopher://arl.cni.org:70/11/scomm/edir/edir95.

Atkinson, R. (1968–1969). A reply to a reaction to computer-assisted instruction in initial reading: The Stanford project. *Reading Research Quarterly, 3,* 418–420

Atkinson, R., & Hansen, D. (1966–1967). Computer-assisted instruction in initial reading: The Stanford project. *Reading Research Quarterly, 2*, 5–26.

Baldwin, S., Readence, J., Schumm, J., Konopak, J., Konopak, B., & Klingner, J. (1992). Forty years of NRC publications: 1952–1991. *Journal of Reading Behavior, 24*, 505–532.

Ball, D., & Schroeder, T. (1992). Improving teaching, not standardizing it. *Mathematics Teacher, 85*, 67–72. Available: http://www.enc.org/on-line/ENC2214/2214.html.

Bangert-Drowns, R. (1993). The word processor as an instructional tool: A meta-analysis of word processing in writing instruction. *Review of Educational Research, 63*, 69–93.

Bolter, J. D. (1991). *Writing space: The computer, hypertext, and the history of writing.* Hillsdale, NJ: Lawrence Erlbaum Associates.

Brown, J., Collins, A., & Duguid, P. (1989). Situated cognition and the culture of learning. *Educational Researcher, 18*(1), 34–41.

CAST (Center for Applied Special Technology). (1996). *The role of online communications in schools: A national study.* Available: http://www.cast.org/stsstudy.html.

Chipman, S. (1993). Gazing into the silicon chip. In S. Lajoie & S. Derry (Eds.), *Computers as cognitive tools* (pp. 341–367). Hillsdale, NJ: Lawrence Erlbaum Associates.

Clark, R. E. (1983). Reconsidering research on learning from media. *Review of Educational Research, 53*, 445–459.

Cochran-Smith, M. (1991). Word processing and writing in elementary classrooms: A critical review of related literature. *Review of Educational Research, 61*, 107–155.

Commeyras, M., Orellana, M., Bruce, B., & Neilsen, L. (1996). Conversations: What do feminist theories have to offer to literacy, education, and research? *Reading Research Quarterly, 31*, 458–468.

Daniel, D. B., & Reinking, D. (1987). The construct of legibility in electronic reading environments. In D. Reinking (Ed.), *Reading and computers: Issues for theory and practice* (pp. 24–39). New York: Teachers College Press.

Donmoyer, R. (1997). Introduction: This issue: Refocusing on learning. *Educational Researcher, 26*(1), 4, 34.

Duchastel, P. (1988). ICAI systems: Issues in computer tutoring. *Computer Education, 13*, 95–100.

Eldred, J., & Hawisher, G. (1995). Researching electronic networks. *Written Communication, 12*, 330–359.

Fetterman, D. (1996). Videoconferencing on-line: Enhancing communication over the Internet. *Educational Research, 25*(4), 23–27.

Flood, J., & Lapp, D. (1995). Broadening the lens: Toward an expanded conceptualization of literacy. In K. A. Hinchman, D. J. Leu, & C. K. Kinzer (Eds.), *Perspectives on literacy research and practice: Forty-fourth yearbook of the National Reading Conference* (pp. 1–16). Chicago: National Reading Conference.

Gillingham, M. (1993). Effects of question complexity and reader strategies on adults' hypertext comprehension. *Journal of Research on Computing in Education, 26*, 1–15.

Gould, J., & Grischkowsky, N. (1984). Doing the same work with hardcopy and with CRT terminals. *Human Factors, 26*, 323–337.

Greeno, J. (1997). Response: On claims that answer the wrong questions. *Educational Researcher, 26*, 5–17.

Grzeszkiewicz, A., & Hawbaker, A. (1996). Investigating a full-text journal database: A case of detection. *Database, 19*(6), 59–62.

Haas, C., & Hayes, J. (1985). *Reading on the computer: A comparison of standard and advanced computer display and hardcopy* (CDC Tech. Rep. No. 7). Pittsburgh, PA: Carnegie-Mellon University, Communications Design Center.

Kamil, M. L. (1982). Technology and reading: A review of research and instruction. In J. Niles & L. Harris (Eds.), *New inquiries in reading research and instruction*: Thirty-first yearbook of the National Reading Conference (pp. 251–261). Rochester, NY: National Reading Conference.

Kamil, M. L. (1987). Computers and reading research. In D. Reinking (Ed.), *Computers and reading: Issues for theory and practice* (pp. 57–75). New York: Teachers College Press.

Kozma, R. B. (1991). Learning with media. *Review of Educational Research, 61*, 179–211.

Laurillard, D. (1993). *Rethinking university teaching: A framework for the effective use of educational technology.* London: Routledge.

Lunin, L. R., & Rada, R. (1989). Hypertext: Introduction and overview. *Journal of the American Society for Information Science, 40*, 159–163.

Mayer, R. (1997). Multimedia learning: Are we asking the right questions? *Educational Psychologist, 32*, 1–19.

Mosenthal, P. (1993). Understanding agenda setting in reading research. In A. P. Sweet & I. Anderson (Eds.), *Reading research into the year 2000* (pp. 115–128). Hillsdale, NJ: Lawrence Erlbaum Associates.

National Council of Teachers of Mathematics. (1991). *Commission on Teaching Standards for School Mathematics, Professional Standards for Teaching Mathematics.* Reston, VA: Author.

Negroponte, N. (1995). *Being digital.* New York: Knopf.

Neuman, S. (1991). *Literacy in the television age*. Norwood, NJ: Ablex.

Niemiec, R. P. (1987). Comparative effects of computer-assisted instruction: A synthesis of reviews. *Journal of Educational Computing Research, 3*, 19–37.

Niemiec, R. P., & Walberg, H. J. (1985). Computers and achievement in the elementary schools. *Journal of Educational Computing Research, 1*, 435–440.

Niemiec, R. P., & Walberg, H. J. (1986). CAI can be doubly effective. *Phi Delta Kappan, 67*, 750–751.

Perfetti, C. (1996). Text and hypertext. In J. Rouet, J. Levonen, A. Dillon, & R. Spiro (Eds.), *Hypertext and cognition* (pp. 157–161). Mahwah, NJ: Lawrence Erlbaum Associates.

Project Gutenberg Home Page. (1996). URL: http://www.promo.net/pg/ Available: bit.listserv.gutenberg.

Rada, R. (1989). Writing and reading hypertext: An overview. *Journal of the American Society for Information Science, 40*, 164–171.

Reinking, D. (1995). Reading and writing with computers: Literacy research in a post-typographic world. In K. Hinchman, D. Leu, & C. Kinzer (Eds.), *Perspectives on literacy research and practice* (pp. 17–33). Chicago: National Reading Conference.

Reinking, D., & Bridwell-Bowles, L. (1991). Computers in reading and writing. In R. Barr, M. L. Kamil, P. Mosenthal, & P. D. Pearson (Eds.), *Handbook of reading research* (Vol. 2, pp. 310–340). New York: Longman.

Reinking, D., & Watkins, J. (1996). *A formative experiment investigating the use of multimedia book reviews to increase elementary students' independent reading* (Reading Research Rep. No. 55). Athens, GA: National Reading Research Center.

Rouet, J., Levonen, J., Dillon, A., & Spiro, R. (Eds.). (1996). *Hypertext and cognition*. Mahwah, NJ: Lawrence Erlbaum Associates.

Sayers, D. (1995). Educational equity issues in an information age. *Teachers College Record, 96*(4), 769–773.

Schank, R., & Cleary, C. (1994). *Engines for education*. Hillsdale, NJ: Lawrence Erlbaum Associates.

Selfe, C., & Meyer, P. (1991). Testing claims for on-line conferences. *Written Communication, 8*, 163–198.

Shanahan, T., & Kamil, M. (1994). *Academic libraries and research in the teaching of English*. Champaign, IL: National Conference on Research in English and Center For The Study of Reading.

Singer, H., Dreher, M., & Kamil, M. L. (1982). Computer literacy. In A. Berger & H. A. Robinson (Eds.), *Secondary school reading: What research reveals for classroom practice* (pp. 173–192). Urbana, Illinois: National Council for Research on English, Cosponsored by ERIC and the National Institute of Education.

Spache, G. (1967). Reading technology. In G. Schick & M. May (Eds.), *Junior college and adult reading programs—Expanding fields: The 16th yearbook of the National Reading Conference* (pp. 178–184). Milwaukee, WI: National Reading Conference.

Spache, G. (1968–1969). A reaction to Computer-assisted instruction in initial reading: The Stanford project. *Reading Research Quarterly, 3*, 101–109.

Standards for the English Language Arts. (1996). Newark, DE: IRA/NCTE.

Sutton, R. (1991). Equity and computers in the schools: A decade of research. *Review of Educational Research, 61*, 475–503.

Tao, L. (1996). *What do we know about email—An existing and emerging literacy vehicle?* Unpublished manuscript, Department of Reading Education, University of Georgia, Athens.

Turkle, S. (1984). *The second self: Computers and the human spirit*. New York: Simon & Schuster.

Turkle, S. (1995). *Life on the screen: Identity in the age of the Internet*. New York: Simon & Schuster.

20

▼▼▼▼▼▼▼

Literacy Research Oriented Toward Features of Technology and Classrooms

Larry Miller
John Olson
Queen's University, Kingston, Ontario

This chapter discusses how features of new information technology interact with features of classrooms in the quest to foster children's literacy abilities and their attitudes toward literacy. We believe focusing on these features points to several lessons that may be learned through the intensive study of classroom culture as an orientation toward research. We begin by describing the potential values and problems associated with three major sources of information about how technology may aid educators in their endeavors: visionary theory, lighthouse projects, and large-scale implementation studies. We recognize that there are additional ways to examine the research on literacy and computers (Reinking & Bridwell-Bowles, 1991). Although there are advantages inherent in these formats for conducting research into technology and literacy, there also are deficiencies that leave incomplete pictures of practice. Because of this inadequacy, we argue for a fourth method of study: intensive case studies of closely watched classrooms.

We believe that much research examining the use of technology in classrooms is based on ideas of what technology should exemplify; thus, such inquiries may be founded on a position of advocacy. When a position of advocacy is adopted prior to the initiation of research, computers may become objects of research rather than only one element interacting with diverse factors in a complex learning environment. On a practical level, research driven by an ideal vision may encourage school authorities to allocate resources, especially those related to technology, to facilitate a single conception of computer use.

In this chapter, we present an argument for using intensive case studies as an alternative method of exploring technology's role in learning in general, and literacy learning in particular, acknowledging that the most complete understanding will evolve from multiple sources of inquiry. Based on the idea of closely observed classrooms, we draw on our investigations, as well as on those of other researchers, to describe how insights from this form of exploration may assist educators in understanding the complex interaction among learners, teachers, and new information technology in the context of individual classrooms.

VISIONS, LIGHTHOUSE PROJECTS,
AND LARGE-SCALE STUDIES OF TECHNOLOGY

Visions

Bork's (1981) statement that computers would revolutionize education was accompanied by the assertion that "by the year 2000, the major way of learning at all levels and in almost all subject areas will be through the interactive use of computers" (p. 269). His contention was typical of seers of this era. Moursund (1981), in his role as editor of *The Computing Teacher*, was equally optimistic that computers would serve as change agents in reforming education.[1] These visions, along with competing perspectives by thinkers such as Papert (1980) and Dwyer (1980), represented a valuable service as they alerted educators to the potential technology offered to learners and teachers. Exciting new possibilities for characterizing how children might learn in a technology-rich environment and how teachers might foster this learning stimulated the school transformation movement that continues today. Visions such as that expressed by Bork (1981) endure because many persons continue to think that technology will lead the way in developing innovative, productive ways to educate students.

Early visions of how technology would reform education often were general in nature although some spoke directly to literacy acquisition. Projects such as the Stanford Computer-Assisted Instruction (CAI) Program in Initial Reading, carried out by Atkinson, Fletcher, Chetin, and Stauffer (1970), were based on a desire to ameliorate children's reading problems. Part of the allure of this approach was that computers would individualize instruction, with the concomitant idea that teachers would be free to carry out "more creative, generative forms of instruction" (p. 37). The developers of the Stanford Project pointed out the excitement generated, both among students and teachers, for the endeavor. These types of ideas about how computers would foster literacy persist, and although today's technology is more advanced, there are continuing beliefs in the motivational value of computers along with their ability to individualize instruction because they are patient, nonjudgmental tutors.

Bowers (1988) pointed out that technology is not value free, and some perspectives of how technology would reform education created as much anxiety, especially among teachers, as excitement (see Bruce & Hogan, chap. 16, this volume). It is easy to understand this consternation as some visions appeared to be based on contempt for teachers and schools as much as a view of the positive aspects of technology (e.g., Perelman, 1992). Indeed, the often-used term *technological reform* implied past practice was somehow flawed or inadequate, but literacy teachers did not appreciate being told they would become obsolete or reduced to the status of learning managers (Jobst, 1983; Lickleider, 1983). Moursund's (1981) technological vista of education exposed one aspect of his thinking that permeates the literature on restructuring, even today, by contending that "not all teachers will be able to adjust to the influx of computers into education" (p. 23). This statement is typical of the notion that educational restructuring is best led from the top down by dynamic leaders who understand the ideal of technology's role in this enterprise, a notion that persists (Kearsley & Lynch, 1994; Ray, 1992).

---

[1]We thank our colleague Peter Chin for pointing out that early visionaries frequently spoke of technology as an instrument for reform, but that reforming is different from transforming. Reforming calls for a turning over of the old, with the implication that past practice is valueless. Transforming implies a modification, a change, without the invidious comparison of past and transformed practice (see also Reinking, introduction, this volume).

Despite our concerns with visionary theory, it would be wrong to contend that such thinking has no place in education. Educational ideas are a starting point for a dialectic about the usefulness of a particular viewpoint in practice. Just as Dewey and Schwab posited ideas about the nature of teaching and learning, which were debated vigorously at their conception, a rich dialogue about the potential and appropriateness of technology should be carried out today (Beynon & Mackay, 1992; Mackay, Young, & Beynon, 1991). Visions may offer a foundation for establishing a fertile research agenda, with the caveat that investigators must not engage in research solely as advocates. Unfortunately, discussion about technology often is portrayed as dissent, and those persons who question or produce evidence contrary to the desired perspective are sometimes castigated as Luddites.

Lighthouse Projects

A natural extension of visionary theory was the creation of what might be called a lighthouse or *beacon schools*. Advocates of a particular type of learning as well as commercial hardware and software developers created special centers or cooperated with existing schools to demonstrate the feasibility of their ideas, of computer use in general, or of specific software programs. One of the more interesting and instructive enterprises, even though it did not focus directly on literacy, was the Brookline LOGO Project, carried out by Papert and his colleagues (Papert, Watt, deSessa, & Weir, 1979). Papert's (1980) book, *Mindstorms: Children, Computers, and Powerful Ideas*, created excitement in the educational community, interest that also captured public attention.

The role of the turtle, a tangible component of the LOGO language package developed by Papert, who regretted the public focus on this device, eventually became a focus for criticism. Despite an initial titillation with turtles, critics emerged because researchers could not find support for the learning that was supposedly taking place; they had difficulty documenting transfer of the skills and strategies LOGO was claimed to evoke. Some researchers observed the artificiality of the LOGO learning experience, and went on to decry Papert's misapplication of learning theory (Sloan, 1984). Although the debate continued (Papert, 1987), the use of LOGO diminished to the point where it is seldom found in today's schools.

Notwithstanding the points made by Papert's critics, we think there is another reason why his learning vision was not adopted. As Papert (1980) pointed out, he was not concerned about the turtle; he saw it simply as a vehicle for Piagetian learning, and, as Papert stated, "which to me is learning without a curriculum" (p. 31). Learning without a curriculum is not an idea familiar to the typical teacher, and both the visionary and those carrying out studies based on his vision failed to see this incongruity. Furthermore, studies carried out in classrooms where teachers were kindred spirits in the LOGO movement failed to reveal the anomaly.

Even though some lighthouse projects were developed to make manifest the virtues of technology in general, for example, the Apple Classroom of Tomorrow, or to demonstrate a particular application of technology, some form of evaluation typically was carried out. However, the evaluations often failed to take into account important variables. Teachers working in these projects frequently were selected specifically for their interest in the technology. Important support, such as the presence of technicians, was provided, and participants often received special training. There is certainly nothing wrong with creating lighthouse environments because much can be learned about what is possible to achieve in such ideal settings (Collis & Moonen, 1990), but they cannot be viewed as typical of situations found in most classrooms.

In the area of literacy, numerous first glimpses of technology's promise were demonstrated through lighthouse projects. For example, Owen's (1995) Writers in Electronic Residence project depicted how a writing program, taking advantage of the Internet, may enlist the advice of recognized authors to enhance students' composing through interactive discussions. The creation of *Bubble Dialogue*, one of the programs that emerged from the Language Development and HyperMedia Research Group in Northern Ireland, shows how ongoing beacon projects, supported by research, can result in software refinements as well as how such tools may be used in the classroom as scaffold structures for literacy acquisition (Cunningham, Angeli, Morton, & Cunningham, 1996; O'Neill, McMahon, & Cunningham, 1991).

As mentioned previously, most lighthouse projects are led by champions of computer-based learning, persons, or sometimes corporations, with a stake in ascertaining their success. If the project is school-based, these leaders seek out like-minded persons—teachers who have knowledge about and an interest in technology—to staff the undertaking. Therefore, it is not surprising that the reports emanating from these projects have come under attack (e.g., Freyd & Lytle's [1990] and Slavin's [1990] critiques of IBM's *Writing to Read* program).

The lessons learned through lighthouse projects should not be dismissed just because they are supported strongly with both human and technological resources, or because the software used in them is developed by large corporations. However, the reports associated with beacon projects tend to be overwhelmingly positive, and many describe increased motivation for learning, teacher enthusiasm, pedagogical change, and enhanced teaching and learning opportunities. We do not know if this motivation, teacher enthusiasm, and enhanced teaching and learning opportunity would be found in normal classrooms where teachers may not have the same stake in the project's success. We also do not know from these studies how specific groups of students or individuals might react to the introduction of the technology. Therefore, reports emanating from lighthouse projects should be recognized as a special type of research, and educators need to understand the limitations regarding transfer to normal classrooms.

Large-Scale Technology Studies and Implementation Projects

There are two kinds of large-scale studies related to technology: (a) those that attempt to examine factors such as student access to computers, the nature of the technology, and teacher application use; and (b) those designed to create systemic change. This latter type of project often is based on a particular perspective of how technology should be used; thus, such implementations represent a manifestation of visionary theory (see, e.g., the "new work" described by Fawcett & Snyder, chap. 7, this volume).

Typically, large-scale implementation studies of new information technology are carried out at the district, state, or provincial levels, although others are conducted by countries that have a national curriculum or through international cooperation. Surveys of computer use and practices, referred to as thermometers of what is happening, mirror the scale of implementation studies (e.g., Pelgrum & Plomp, 1991; Watson, 1993). In a survey conducted by Pelgrum and Plomp (1991), the authors wanted to learn about how computers were used internationally; thus, the sample consisted of schools in 21 countries. The study revealed availability of computer hardware and software, general purposes of school computer use, and staff training, to mention some of the issues examined.

Implementation investigations may focus on obtaining evidence of increased learning, where technology-enriched classroom learning is compared to learning in traditional classrooms, but most of these projects are equally interested in drawing from the implementation experience itself in order to understand the pathways schools should take in making technology an integral component of education. In other words, at the onset of the study there is an assumption that technology is valuable, and difficulties encountered normally are portrayed as barriers to be overcome (U.S. Congress, Office of Technology Assessment, 1995). This U.S. report, which presents an overview and summary of numerous large-scale implementation studies, is typical of an advocacy-based interpretation of research.

At the completion of these large-scale studies, conclusions often are drawn about the conditions necessary to foster the effective use of technology, with common themes being the need for strong leadership, a clear statement of intended use, adequate access to technology, sufficient time on task for students, necessary technical support, increased inservice education for teachers, and a standard for measuring learning. Because of their scale, they also have revealed some of the costs in monetary and human resources necessary to implement the use of technology in schools (U.S. Congress, Office of Technology Assessment, 1995), but, as mentioned previously, such problems are seen primarily as temporary problems or obstacles to surmount.

In fairness, there have been large-scale implementation studies that overcame many of the problems associated with advocacy research even though the technology under study clearly was the result of an educational and technological vision. In the case of Quill, a computer-based system developed to support writing, the creators concentrated first on a vision of how best to foster children's writing (Bruce & Rubin, 1993; Rubin & Bruce, 1985). On the basis of this perspective, the program was developed. This approach, thus far, was not unique, as other software developers have created packages based on a particular learning perspective or theoretical orientation (Miller & Burnett, 1987). What is distinct was that the program reflected the lessons from research that pointed toward the viability and value of certain pedagogies that were then embedded into the software.

After extensive field testing, the authors carried out a large-scale implementation study; however, their research techniques were different from similar studies because they used ethnographic methods for data gathering, with a focus on how different classroom teachers in different contexts used the software. Although the investigation was based on a large-scale implementation model, they chose to study the project from a classroom perspective, that is, situated learning. From this study came two important lessons, typically absent when the findings of other types of research are examined: the powerful role prior practice exerts in using technology and the recognition of alternative realizations of an innovation, by both teachers and students.

APPLYING THE LESSONS LEARNED FROM VISIONARIES, LIGHTHOUSE PROJECTS, AND LARGE-SCALE IMPLEMENTATIONS

In addition to advocacy positions, there are other problems with studies based on visions, lighthouse projects, and large-scale implementations, highlighted by findings that despite increased access to technology, actual use is not robust; moreover, teachers continue to use computers in traditional ways such as skill development and reinforcement (U.S. Congress, Office of Technology Assessment, 1995). One reason for the apparent lack of impact on the general use of technology lies in the difficulty in applying the lessons learned to other situations, especially individual classrooms. Consider two frequently mentioned guidelines for successful implementation: Teachers must buy into the use of technology and there must be clearly defined goals for computer use. The two guidelines go together because it is the strong advocate, armed with clear goals, who will persuade teachers to adopt the innovation.

Having teachers "get on board" goes back to the time when computers were first introduced into schools. As Baker (1983, 1985) pointed out, the promulgation of computers appeared to proceed with a missionary zeal seldom seen in education, a trend that continues today as evidenced by Siegel and Holzberg's (1994) statement: "To convert teachers to multimedia, you've got to first get them into the church" (p. 31). Teachers who did not embrace technology were scourged, as seen by Moursund's (1981) statement, quoted previously, and the "problem" of technological refusal continues to be a frequently discussed topic (Hodas, 1993). Baker contended that although some teachers saw technology as an inspiration, others viewed it as an intrusion. Olson (1984, 1988) added to this discussion by pointing out that the views of experts, embedded in technology, might conflict with teachers' normal practices and routines, and thus create dissonance.

Another reason the lessons of most lighthouse and large-scale implementation projects have not filtered down to schools is their neglect of classroom culture, a point that brings us to our discussion of another way to study how computers live in schools. Schofield's (1995) 2-year investigation is representative of studies that look intensely at the social and educational context of classrooms into which technology is introduced, focusing on such issues as the changing role of teachers, changes in peer interaction, modifications of classroom social order, and the interaction of gender and race with computer-based learning.

THE CASE FOR CASES: WHAT DO CLOSELY WATCHED CLASSROOMS REVEAL?

The value of case studies in literacy education has been recognized because of the insights this type of research renders (e.g., Bissex, 1980; Dyson, 1989; Graves, 1975). Case studies have been a part of the literature on technology since its inception, but even this type of research tended to be influenced heavily by advocates who saw value in computer-based learning. Notwithstanding the caveat that case studies in technology can be influenced by advocacy positions, there is much to learn from this approach. Our approach here will be to demonstrate, rather than simply discuss, some of the values of case studies by offering insights gleaned from those investigations we have conducted, supplemented by the work of other researchers using similar methods.

Even when researchers engage in the process of intensive classroom observation, there are different ways to carry out this endeavor. Schofield (1995) used traditional ethnographic data-gathering techniques—field notes and repeated semistructured interviews with teachers and students—during her 2-year study of how computer usage influenced social processes and how the social context of classrooms shaped computer use. Cochran-Smith, Paris, and Kahn (1991), studying beginning writers' interaction with word processing, used some of these same methods but also acted as participant observers.

Reinking and Watkins (1995), adopting the notion of a formative experiment design, extended the manner in which data are gathered in closely observed classrooms by examining the factors that enhanced or inhibited a theoretically supported pedagogical goal, in this instance increasing the amount and diversity of students' independent reading. The tool they selected for this pedagogical intervention was multimedia book reports. These formative design studies are unique in that the researchers balance their roles by designing the pedagogy, assisting with implementation, and observing the teachers carry it out (see also Bruce & Rubin, 1993; Reinking & Pickle, 1993).

Our special interest focuses on teachers who are held in high regard by children, administrators, parents, and colleagues as quality educators. All the teachers in our studies used computers to some extent prior to the inception of our investigations, but they did not describe themselves as technophiles, and none had a particular stake in the software used (Blackstock & Miller, 1989; Burnett, Blackstock, Miller, & Warkentin, 1989; DeJean, Miller, & Olson, 1995; Miller, DeJean, & Olson, 1996; Miller & Olson, 1994). Unlike Reinking and Watkins (1996), we normally make no attempt to intervene in children's and teachers' use of computers, although, as with the Cochran-Smith et al. (1991) study, the realities of the classroom often require more participation than originally planned, especially in terms of serving as technical advisors.

We concur with Mehan (1989) that computers are part of a larger social system, and that one must consider the relation between the classroom and technology as mutually influential rather than unidimensional. With this thought we turn to examples of the types of issues that may be revealed in closely watched classrooms, recognizing that only a small subset of the whole is presented here.

Our case studies are driven by the question: What sense do teachers and children make of the technology being used? Based on this general question, we often focus on specific aspects of literacy learning such as teachers' and children's interaction with word processors, or we examine how a particular type of software such as CD-ROM talking books is integrated into the curriculum. Like Schofield (1995), we are interested in how the classroom culture affects technology as well as how it is affected by it. We try to adopt a neutral position in our research; that is, not to serve as advocates of any particular perspective about the value of technology. Often, as shown in the next section, unforeseen issues arise.

Incidental Learning

The question—What happens when young children engage in using computers in the informal curriculum?—was not one of our original research focuses in any of our case studies. Perhaps one reason for this oversight was because it is not a question addressed in large-scale investigations so the extant literature did not alert us to this issue (see the recent work by Labbo & Kuhn, chap. 5, this volume, for an exception). However, computer free time, as it is sometimes called, seems to take place in many classrooms. In all our studies, teachers provided opportunities for children to self-select software and use it without direction. Some of the teachers built computer choice time into normal classroom routines, although others set up schedules so children could use the computers as they chose during recess, lunchtime, or after school. We first observed what and how children learned in these informal settings during the Schools, Computers, and Learning Project (Blackstock & Miller, 1989–1990), in which the clear choice of the Grade 1 children during computer choice time was *Offshore Fishing*, a simulation of fishing on the Grand Banks in the Atlantic Ocean. The reason most children gave for returning repeatedly to this simulation, which was designed for Grade 5 and 6 students as part of a thematic unit on the maritime provinces, was that it was "neat" or "fun" (cf. Leu, 1996).

Many of our observations revealed the general cognitive processes used by the children in determining such things as the best places to fish, how to use sonar and the depth finder, which nets should be used with certain types of fish and shellfish, and, most important, how to find the elusive shark that lurked in the waters. We observed that these children used their *fuzzy knowledge,* that is, knowledge that might be partly correct from an adult perspective, to formulate what we called *floating hypotheses* about which actions to take. We called the hypotheses floating because the children created and modified them as they interacted with the program.

This program was designed for older students, and the teacher tended to dismiss the children's interest in it; however, as we observed the first-grade children, it became clear that much situated literacy learning was taking place; that is, literacy learning that occurred in a special setting and because of children's needs. Words that normally would not be introduced formally in first grade, such as *depth, sonar, lobster, shrimp,* and *fuel tank,* were recognized by most students. Other words, necessary to manipulate the ship or to select simulation variables (e.g., season choice or difficulty level) also were known by most of the children; for example, *trawl, drag, action, turn,* and *autumn.* We did not measure transfer effects during our study, so caution must be exercised in making claims about the children's vocabulary acquisition; however, so-called environmental print learning is a common element in many primary classrooms, and the use of this medium is advocated by early childhood educators (Morrow, 1989). Much has been written about direct instruction of reading skills with computer-assisted instruction; however, our case study revealed an instance of informal literacy development. What is interesting is the lack of recognition this type of learning received by the teacher who seemed to be interested mainly in the "advertised" values of computer-based learning.

Much of our recent research has centered on how teachers and children use CD-ROM talking books, including fiction and nonfiction sources (DeJean et al., 1995; Miller et al., 1996; see also McKenna, chap. 3, this volume). Both third-grade teachers in these studies used CD-ROM talking books as one formal component of literacy instruction, but they also permitted children to use talking books in whatever manner they desired during recess, lunchtime, and after school. Working in partnership, because that was the format the teachers used normally, children often created activities involving the books. For example, two children decided they would narrate *The Paper Bag Princess,* imitating an inherent feature of CD-ROM talking books by playing the roles of different characters. One student, a girl, assumed the female parts, and the other, a boy, read the male roles, and the expression they used while reading aloud was noticeably similar to the narration contained in the software. A third student, who was watching, offered to become the narrator of the story, a role the students had been sharing. At this point, the three students, collectively, decided to turn the book into a play for classmates.

One of the more popular programs used during free selection time was a CD-ROM disk entitled *DaVinci.* Initially surprised by its acceptance, given its relatively sophisticated content, we discovered the source of its popularity. Embedded in the disk, which gave information in a multimedia format about DaVinci's life, inventions, art, and writing, was a game where the participants could maneuver one of his flying machines across the French countryside, trying to avoid hazards. "Don't hit the Eiffel Tower," one boy cautioned another. The researcher, intrigued, asked the student how he knew the structure in the program was the Eiffel Tower. "Well," he answered. "I read about it, but you know what, that couldn't be the real Eiffel Tower because DaVinci died before it was built." As his partner played the game, the student showered the researcher with a wealth of knowledge about DaVinci. More probing revealed that the student, stimulated by the CD-ROM disk, selected DaVinci as the inventor he would research as part of a thematic unit on how things work. This interest led him not only to use the DaVinci disk, but it also stimulated him to read hardcover books on the man as well as the entry on DaVinci in a CD-ROM encyclopedia. In one way, what was accomplished in this informal learning situation was similar to what was seen in Reinking and Watkins' (1996) formative study, where hypermedia book reports were used as a pathway to increase students' independent reading, although the outcomes in this latter instance were planned.

The situations described in this section offer but two examples of how productive literacy learning may occur when children interact with technology in informal ways. The computer in these situations acted as a stimulant to literacy learning. The lessons of these vignettes might be referred to as unintended, positive results of computer use. Both lighthouse projects and large-scale implementation studies tend to report teachers' appreciation of the motivational power of technology, but by observing children closely, some of the reasons for this finding may be discovered as well as how this motivation may be harnessed to support literacy learning.

Truncated Learning

Features of technology have the power to attract learners and, potentially, to nurture learning in ways unintended by either software developers or teachers, as was seen in the previous section. However, the features embedded in software programs or the configuration of hardware in the classroom also may interfere with learning. Leu (1996), alluding to Birkerts' (1995) contention that multimedia may foster superficial rather than deep reading, believed educators need to think carefully about how this medium is used, and not be seduced into thinking students are acquiring literacy and learning simply because they are engaged with a CD-ROM disk or browsing sites on the World Wide Web.

Our case studies demonstrate how one feature of CD-ROM talking books, animation, may detract from reading rather than enhance it. Animation in CD-ROM talking books is promoted as one of the most enticing features, with the implication that movement will stimulate children to read the books repeatedly. One of the Grade 3 teachers decided on the following routine for engaging the children in reading talking books: (a) listen to the narration of the book; (b) read the book aloud, taking turns and using the reading assistance features if needed; and (c) complete the follow-up activities, referring back to the story—either in hard copy or CD-ROM version—if necessary.

The children quickly adopted their own routine: (a) listen to the story while chatting, looking out the window, or playing with the mouse; (b) play with the animation until all options were exhausted; (c) complete the follow up activities by referring back to the story on the CD-ROM, or, if in use, the hard-copy version.

It is easy to blame the teacher for not ascertaining that the children were engaged in reading the books in the manner prescribed, but if we analyze her expectations for the software, prior experience with CD-ROM talking books, and normal classroom routines, this seeming inattentiveness can be understood. Jacqueline (a pseudonym), the teacher, read the literature on CD-ROM talking books, and not just the producers' brochures but also several articles (e.g., Parham, 1993; Truett, 1993). All sources singled out the positive values of animation without mention of the potential distraction from print. Jacqueline's prior experience with talking books consisted of the orientation our research team presented, where we demonstrated each of the features without comment about its potential value or possible problems it might spawn because we wanted to observe the sense the teacher and children made of the medium. Perhaps most important, Jacqueline's typical classroom routines and observations of children informed her that they worked well in pairs, engaging consistently in productive learning. Finally, Jacqueline knew that an often-cited value of computer-based learning is that it will free teachers to engage in other useful activities while children are involved with software programs, and she practiced this dictum.

Activating the animation became the children's raison d'être, and it appeared this feature was truncating their literacy engagement. It is possible that the tendency to play with talking books occurred because the animation was a novelty; however, activating the animation continued the entire term. Students indeed reread the books repeatedly, if "read" is the correct term, but their pattern of engagement did not vary. One student turned to a researcher during a session with a talking book and exclaimed, "Just wait till you see what is going to happen next!" Thinking the student was going to reveal an exciting part of the story, the researcher watched as he turned the page. "Watch this," he continued. The boy then began to click on every object or person that could be animated, commenting that he knew everything on the page that would move, sing, or speak.

Other studies complement our investigations of classroom culture, providing a fuller account of such phenomena. For example, results from Scoresby's (1996) experimental study, which were unavailable to us when we carried out our investigation, add to the discussion of how the features of CD-ROM talking books may enhance or detract from comprehension. One of Scoresby's findings was that animations hindered recall of textual information. He also discovered that the children who spent the most time on task, that is, engaged in reading talking books, were the ones who were exposed most to animations. However, this additional time on task did not result higher recall scores; indeed, as Scoresby (1996) pointed out, "the animation-available groups were significantly lower than participants who spend much less time within the storybook" (p. 89).

Scoresby's (1996) work does not end the discussion, even though his experimental findings supported our case study observations. Matthew (1996) used both Discis Books and Living Books in her comparative study of the influence of CD-ROM books and traditional books on readers' comprehension. Even though Living Books are highly animated, and Discis Books are not, students who read both types of CD-ROM books demonstrated better story retellings than those reading hardcover version of the same books. Perhaps Matthew's work indicates that it is the classroom context, as much as the multimedia itself, that influences student's reactions to animation. More thought and study are needed, in both experimental and real-world contexts.

These studies and others that speak to issues related to CD-ROM talking books offer different perspectives on different dimensions related to the medium. Together, they may offer a better image of the whole than can be seen through any particular lens. For example, Lewin's (1996) development work and subsequent piloting of talking book features demonstrate the value of considering learning theory as one design dimension. Miller, Blackstock, and Miller's (1994) small-scale investigation showed how repeated readings of talking books—using available assistance features—may result in a decrease in the need to use these options, but it also pointed out the diverse ways children called on the program for help (see McKenna, chap. 3, this volume, for another description of how young children use assistance features).

A second example of truncated learning may be seen when the needs of individual readers conflict with the inherent features built into software. Returning to our classroom observations of children reading CD-ROM talking books, we noted that both third-grade teachers in our study selected two children to read the books together. In the second part of our investigation (Miller et al., 1996) we noticed that Lynda (pseudonym) typically used a variety of grouping patterns in literacy learning, including pairs, so there was no prior indication this pattern would be unproductive when applied to CD-ROM talking books. Lynda did not use talking books that featured animation so the problem observed in the first segment of the study did not reoccur; however, Lynda adopted the same routine as Jacqueline to engage the children in reading. Perhaps because of the lack of distraction due to animation, the children listened intently to the narration of the books, but when it came time for reading the books independently, disharmony arose. The assistance feature, which offered word pronunciation, syllabification, and word definition, was activated by clicking on a word, but only one child controlled the mouse so only that child's needs could be met. What ensued were "mouse wars," where children would race to the computer to gain the opportunity to control the mouse. The unsuccessful student became dependent on the benevolence of the mouse controller to access words, and when this "good will" did not develop, verbal battles, trickery, and minor scuffling ensued.

A glib solution to the mouse wars situation would be to assign individual students to read a talking book; thus, the needs of any particular child would be met by the assistance features. There are two problems with this resolution. First, even though pairing students caused a unique problem, it also offered the opportunity for two students to carry out the follow-up activities collaboratively, a productive aspect of the activity. Second, the logistics of the situation, access to a finite amount of hardware and software, necessitated the grouping pattern. Case studies may reveal complex interactions, but they do not necessarily provide solutions to problems that arise.

Plumbing the Unknown: New Ways of Thinking About Literacy Learning

Because computer programs are relatively new to schooling, there are aspects of their impact on literacy learning about which little is known. Using Dyson's (1986) notion of symbol weaving, which is an umbrella term for the mutually supportive systems of drawing, talk, and writing, we conjectured how new information technology, especially software that incorporated artistic tools with word processing, might affect this process. At the same time we kept in mind that Dyson's observations were made with children using traditional tools such as pencils, paint, and crayons (Blackstock & Miller, 1992). Our speculations were supported with only a modicum of observational evidence, but in the meantime Labbo and her colleagues conducted a series of case studies examining how teachers and children might use such software and how tools that potentially support symbol weaving may interact with this process (e.g., Labbo, Reinking, & McKenna, 1995). Using a semiotic framework for analysis, Labbo (1996) demonstrated and revealed young children's symbol making using Kid Pix 2, a program that provides for drawing and writing. One of Labbo's (1996) categories called "Playing in Screenland," intrigued us as we began our next case.

Currently, our research team is engaged in a study into how Grade 2 children use a particular program, The Castle, as a tool in creating fairy tales. The creation of fairy tales was but one aspect of an integrated unit on the topic, but it was a favorite activity of the children in Lynda's classroom. Because of her unfamiliarity with the program, and the lack of time to learn about it, Lynda asked one of the researchers to introduce the program and work alongside the children as they created their stories in pairs. The program contains a simple word processor that permits insertion and deletion of text, a limited choice of fonts and type, a store of clip art suitable for providing scenes, props, characters for fairy tales, and, most important, the options of animation and sound generation. We treated Lynda's invitation as an opportunity to explore different ways of using the program. For example, with some pairs of children we asked them to keyboard their story, create and animate the scenes, and then narrate the tale. In other words, the children engaged in all aspects of symbol weaving, and the researcher's role was one of an interested interloper. However, with other pairs, the researcher acted as scribe, and assumed a more active role by guiding the children through the activity, much in the way described by Labbo et al. (1995) in their study.

Both patterns of teaching, and children's reactions to them, created problematic situations, or so it seemed. The children who were expected to write their stories on the computer using natural spellings, tended to ignore text, writing only the briefest tales. They spent much time exploring different backdrops, adding music, selecting items from the clip art bank to place in scenes, and, most of all, animating. One team of two boys spent 12 minutes on the opening scene alone, sprinkling gargoyles throughout a castle, expanding and shrinking a dragon, and adding characters that never appeared in the text. Returning to Labbo's case study, it is interesting to consider the children's actions using her category of Playing in Screenland. Labbo's case, and her interpretation of the children's actions, opened our eyes to the possibility that more was taking place than first appeared.

If we examine only text and the pictures sprinkled with gargoyles and other objects, an obvious conclusion would be that the products were meager. The stories tended to be trite, and even though the children spent much time engaged in creating the scenes for categories, they showed little interest in the print copies, which represented only flatland. However, when we listened to their talk, the students wove magical and whimsical stories of evil sorcerers who cast spells and potions. The dialogue they added to the stories through the narration option, which never appeared in text, represented another dimension that often was three times longer than the written tales. As Dyson (1986) contended, young children see the three components of symbol weaving as equal partners, even if adults tend to focus on text. These children seemed to conform to Dyson's description, even though they were engaged in a multimedia production program.

When the researcher acted as scribe, the written stories increased in length. However, the stories had a sameness about them, following a standard pattern. Furthermore, the children readily accepted the suggestions of the scribe for content so their ownership of the stories was usurped. They seemed to tolerate the scribe's effort to focus on the story text because this action took little time, and the children learned quickly that they could begin creating the scenes, animating, and adding music and narration once the text was produced. As with the first group, large blocks of time were spent with animation and adding dialogue, and the talk between the students was imaginative and rich. Often the children created stories parallel to the written one although they resisted efforts to revise the text. Frequently heard comments were "Let's pretend . . ." or "I'll be dragon and you be the gargoyle."

What should be made of our observations of these two ways of inviting children to create fairy tales using the multimedia tool built into The Castle? Is the time spent with the program worth the learning? Some of the pairs took more than an hour to create one story; however, such an observation equates learning with production. Dyson's (1986) work tells us that talk should be valued in conjunction with text, and it appeared that the features inherent in the software were important stimulants to the children's meaning making. These kinds of questions, and the tentative answers they generate, demonstrate that we are plumbing the unknown when children and teachers engage in some forms of computer-based literacy meaning, and, as Labbo (1996) pointed out, children writing, creating art, and playing in screenland may cause us to refine and to expand our definitions of literacy and how one becomes literate.

Persistence of the Pragmatic

Advocacy-based studies often point out that teachers tend to resist technology. Negative assessments of teachers' resistance to change in general (Lortie, 1975; Sarason, 1991), and technological change in particular (Cuban, 1986), are well documented, but this perception of teachers' attitudes frequently is treated in two opposing manners when the issue of how computers might transform education is considered. The first viewpoint acknowledges teachers' reticence toward change but endows the computer with the power to overcome such an attitude or at least act as a powerful lever for change (Fullan, Miles, & Anderson, 1988; Knapp & Glenn, 1996). Others simply contend that teachers' ideas about their role in fostering learning must change if the potential of technology is to be realized (Collins, 1991; Shank, 1994).

The second viewpoint on change recognizes that understanding classroom culture is central to any transformation of schools; however, there are alternative perspectives about how this knowledge should be applied. Tobin and Dawson (1992) used their understanding of classroom culture by embedding features into a software package they believed would influence teachers to adopt a constructivist approach toward learning. This notion of computer program as Trojan horse (cf. Olson's 1984 use of the metaphor) implies that school transformation might best be carried out if it is disguised or implanted within technology.

Schofield and her colleagues (Schofield, 1995; Schofield, Davidson, Stocks, & Futoran, 1997) took a different approach to the issue of transformation by attempting to discern the beliefs and actions of the participants involved in enacting change. One of their investigations focused on how technical staff associated with a major university collaborated with public school educators in an effort to make the Internet a conduit for learning (Davidson, Schofield, & Stocks, 1997). Salient categories affecting the collaboration included the values, routines, norms, beliefs and orientations in the technical and public school worlds. The lessons learned from such studies tend to be somewhat equivocal because they suggest avenues for change, but likewise they recognize that the main value of this type of inquiry lies in generating an awareness of complexity in using technology to carry out transformations in classrooms and schools.

When teachers' classroom routines and practices are studied, especially during the introduction of technology, there is a tendency to analyze their behaviors as either enhancing or inhibiting the use of computers. Our research has taken this dichotomous approach, but we also attempt to understand why prior practice is such a powerful force by examining it on its own merits (Miller & Olson, 1994). When the term persistence of the pragmatic is applied to how teachers use computers, the implication typically is negative. Another way to consider the persistence of the pragmatic is to accept the notion that good teachers do things for good reasons. As indicated earlier, the teachers observed in our studies were experienced, respected educators. Their normal literacy practices included direct instruction of skills, reading aloud to children, and thoughtful discussions of literature. The daily schedule included large blocks of time for independent and collaborative reading and writing. Their rooms were inviting places for literacy learning, and frequent use was made of themes where content was integrated with the arts and the language arts.

When we considered the teachers' literacy practices using computers, some of their actions surprised us, and one interpretation of our observations would be to view the teachers as either resisting technology or using it in narrow, more inhibited ways. However, on other occasions they modified their teaching practices to accommodate the technology.

Lynda, for example, refused to use the set of CD-ROM talking books that featured animation. At the time, we had no knowledge about the reason for her decision; however, given the information that emerged later, her judgment was sound from our perspective. She also adopted the same routines for engaging children in talking books that were used for hardcover books. Critics might point out that she was adapting technology in an incremental manner, or that prior practice was acting as a powerful determinant of how she used this particular type of software. A rejoinder might be "Yes, and what's wrong with that?" Her independent book reading program, into which the CD-ROM books were integrated, was successful as it engaged students in reading for authentic reasons, provided her with rich diagnostic information about their reading needs and interests, and allowed her to build reading skills in context. The result of our observations indicates that teachers' actions in the mutual adaptation of technology must be considered on their own merits, and prior practice should not automatically be viewed as an inhibiting factor.

Real and Contrived Uses of Computers in Literacy Learning

Upitis (1990), a colleague in one of our investigations, examined how teachers in three school projects used e-mail to communicate with distant classrooms. She discovered that teachers tended to design contrived uses of available technology by creating electronic versions of traditional pen-and-paper activities. She described two examples, taken from the Schools, Learning, and Computers Project, to support her contention. The first was a pen pal project, where children in Hennigan School in Boston were paired with children in an elementary school in Kingston, Ontario. Introductory letters were sent and the teachers developed activities where the children would collaborate on various projects; however, interest waned quickly and the formal project was discontinued. Interestingly, once the letters to pen pals were no longer required, several children in both schools began an extended, vibrant correspondence. They reshaped the activity by pretending to be aliens, the Dr. J. group. The Boston children responded by calling themselves the Hotshots from Planet Hennigan.

In another instance, teachers from Kingston, in conjunction with educators in schools from different countries, decided to have children write round-robin stories, where each class would contribute a segment to the whole. As Upitis (1990) pointed out, the project appeared to be sparked by the need to produce a tangible product rather than any real desire to collaborate in story writing. The greatest excitement for the children seemed to be that they could communicate with students as far away as Australia, an interest not followed up by the teacher.

Upitis (1990) made a distinction between really needing a tool and creating a use for a tool, arguing that too many contrived projects rely on the second option. Upitis' assertion is even more relevant today because electronic communication among schools is becoming easier and more prevalent, and as Eurich-Fulcer and Schofield (1995) pointed out, there is no lack of success stories (see also Garner & Gillingham, chap. 13, this volume). Moreover, access to the information available on the World Wide Web is increasing, and browser programs such as Netscape permit students to directly incorporate pictures, graphics, text, and even sound and animation into their reports. Of course the latter two items may be used only if the report remains in disk form, a point that relates to Reinking's (1994a, 1994b) contention that we may have to reformulate our notions of print to accommodate electronic texts.

SUMMARY AND CONCLUSIONS

This chapter focused on different ways of considering both the potential and reality of new information technology in fostering literacy learning. We acknowledged the value of both visionary theory and the lighthouse projects that put these conceptions into practice as well as the large-scale computer implementation studies that offer useful insights into the macrolevel problems and successes that emerge when computers are integrated in the curriculum. In spite of the merit of the aforementioned ways of examining both the potential and reality of computer-based literacy learning, we argued there currently is a neglected component in this endeavor: the lessons that may be gleaned through studies of closely observed classrooms where the culture of the classroom and school is considered.

Fine-grained analyses of how computers live in schools may add to our knowledge in several domains: the role of prior experience in using computers; how existing routines, techniques, and classroom environments influence computer use; how teachers' espoused theories of computer use are tempered by the realities of the classroom; how informal literacy learning transpires in a computer environment; and how unintended consequences that affect learning negatively may emerge because of inherent features in certain types of software.

Important issues that receive attention in macrolevel implementation projects, such as collaborative learning, may be seen through a different lens when students' interactions are scrutinized. Much has been made of the computer's potential to encourage collaborative learning; however, large-scale studies tend to reveal only that children do work together in computer-based learning environments. Intensive case studies may demonstrate more fully the nature of these collaborative experiences (Crook, 1994; Dickinson, 1986). Finally, as Reinking (1994a, 1994b) asserted, the acts of reading and writing will change in the post-typographic era, as will the manner in which literacy is fostered through new communication mediums. Some of our understanding of these transformations will emerge from studying how these mediums inhabit the real world of schools.

As with all types of research, problems are encountered in situated learning studies. By definition, if one wishes to study situated learning, care must be exercised in trying to extend the lessons learned. We believe that the lessons learned by observing the interaction among teachers, children, and technology in the classroom culture may offer signposts to other educators, but unlike large-scale projects, where evaluations frequently lead to implementation guidelines that may be considered models for others to follow, these intensive cases are best seen as highlighting the complex issues involved in using computers to enhance learning, issues that may have to be addressed by educators in unique ways because each educational setting is different. Thus, the lessons learned from closely observed classrooms are best characterized as consciousness raising.

REFERENCES

Atkinson, R. C., Fletcher, J. D., Chetin, H. C., & Stauffer, C. M. (1970). *Instruction in initial reading under computer control: The Stanford Project* (Tech. Rep. No. 158). Stanford, CA: Institute for Mathematical Studies in the Social Sciences.

Baker, C. (1983). The microcomputer and the curriculum. *Journal of Curriculum Studies, 15*, 207–210.

Baker, C. (1985). The microcomputer and the curriculum: A critique. *Journal of Curriculum Studies, 17*, 449–451.

Beynon, J., & Mackay, H. (1992). *Technological literacy and the curriculum*. London: Falmer.

Birkerts, S. (1995). *The Gutenberg elegies: The fate of reading in an electronic age*. New York: Ballantine.

Bissex, G. L. (1980). *Gnys at wrk: A child learns to write and read*. Cambridge, MA: Harvard University Press.

Blackstock, J., & Miller, L. (1989). *Yes, but are they learning anything?: Interim report #3 from the Kingston regional pilot test centre.* Toronto: Queen's Printer for Ontario.

Blackstock, J., & Miller, L. (1989–1990). Floating hypotheses and fuzzy knowledge: Computers and the informal curriculum. *Journal of Computing in Childhood Education, 1*(2), 37–56.

Blackstock, J., & Miller, L. (1992). The impact of new information technology on young children's symbol-weaving efforts. *Computers and Education, 18,* 209–221.

Bork, A. (1981). *Learning with computers.* Bedford, MA: Digital Press.

Bowers, C. A. (1988). *The cultural dimensions of educational computing: Understanding the non-neutrality of technology.* New York: Teachers College Press.

Bruce, B. C., & Rubin, A. (1993). *A situated evaluation of using computers for writing in classrooms.* Hillsdale, NJ: Lawrence Erlbaum Associates.

Burnett, J. D., Blackstock, J., Miller, L., & Warkentin, I. (1989, April). *Teachers' use of technology: Wave upon wave.* Paper presented at Computer Assisted Learning '89, Guilford, England.

Cochran-Smith, M., Paris, C. L., & Kahn, J. L. (1991). *Learning to write differently: Beginning writers and word processing.* Norwood, NJ: Ablex.

Collins, A. (1991). The role of computer technology in restructuring schools. *Phi Delta Kappan, 73*(1), 28–36.

Collis, B., & Moonen, J. (1990, April). *Computers in experimental school settings: A new paradigm in educational research?* Paper presented at the European Conference on Education and Information Technology, Herning, Denmark.

Crook, C. (1994). *Computers and the collaborative experience of learning.* New York: Routledge.

Cuban, L. (1986). *Teachers and machines: The classroom use of technology since 1920.* New York: Teachers College Press.

Cunningham, D. J., Angeli, C., Morton, M. L., & Cunningham, M. L. (1996, April). *Bubble dialogue: Tools for literacy.* Paper presented at the annual meeting of the American Educational Research Association, New York.

Davidson, A. L., Schofield, J. W., & Stocks, J. (1997, June). *Implementing educational technology: Cultures and collaborative efforts.* Paper presented at the Ed-Media/Ed-Telecom Conference, Calgary, Alberta, Canada.

DeJean, J., Miller, L., & Olson, J. (1995, June). *CD-ROM talking books: A case study of promise and practice.* Paper presented at the annual meeting of the Canadian Society for Study of Education, Montreal, Canada.

Dickinson, D. K. (1986). Cooperation, collaboration, and comport: Integrating a computer into a first-second grade writing program. *Research in the Teaching of English, 20,* 357–378.

Dwyer, T. (1980). Heuristic strategies for using computer to enrich education. In R. P. Taylor (Ed.), *The computer in the school: Tutor, tool, tutee* (pp. 87–103). New York: Teachers College Press.

Dyson, A. H. (1986). Transitions and tensions: Interrelationships between the drawing, talking, and dictating of young children. *Research in the Teaching of English, 20,* 379–409.

Dyson, A. H. (1989). *Multiple worlds of child writers: Friends learning to write.* New York: Teachers College Press.

Eurich-Fulcer, R., & Schofield, J. W. (1995). Wide-area networking in K–12 education: Issues shaping implementation and use. *Computers and Education, 24,* 211–220.

Freyd, P., & Lytle, J. H. (1990). *A corporate approach to the 2 R's: A critique of IBM's writing to read program, 47*(6), 83–88.

Fullan, M. G., Miles, M. B., & Anderson, S. E. (1988). *Strategies for implementing microcomputers in schools: The Ontario case.* Toronto: Queen's Printer for Ontario.

Graves, D. (1975). An examination of the writing process of seven year old children. *Research in the Teaching of English, 9,* 227–241.

Hodas, S. (1993). *Technology refusal and the organizational culture of schools.* (ERIC Document Reproduction Service No. ED 366 328)

Jobst, J. (1983). Computers and the obsolete English teacher. *Focus, IX*(3), 89–92.

Kearsley, G., & Lynch, W. (Eds.). (1994). *Educational technology: Leadership perspectives.* Englewood Cliffs, NJ: Educational Technology Publications.

Knapp, L. R., & Glenn, A. D. (1996). *Restructuring schools with technology.* Needham Heights, MA: Allyn & Bacon.

Labbo, L. (1996). A semiotic analysis for young children's symbol making in a classroom computer center. *Reading Research Quarterly, 31,* 356–385.

Labbo, L. D., Reinking, D., & McKenna, M. (1995). Incorporating the computer into kindergarten: A case study. In K. A. Hinchman, D. J. Leu, & C. K. Kinzer (Eds.), *Perspectives on literacy research and practice* (pp. 459–465). Chicago: National Reading Conference.

Leu, D. J. (1996). Sarah's secret: Social aspects of literacy and learning in a digital, information age. *The Computing Teacher, 50,* 162–165.

Lewin, C. (1996). *Improving talking book software design: Emulating the supportive tutor* (CITE Rep. No. 222). Milton Keynes, UK: The Open University.

Lickleider, J. C. R. (1983). The future of electronic learning. In M. A. White (Ed.), *The future of electronic learning* (pp. 71–85). Hillsdale, NJ: Lawrence Erlbaum Associates.

Lortie, D. C. (1975). *School-teacher: A sociological study.* Chicago: University of Chicago Press.

Mackay, H., Young, M., & Beynon, J. (1991). *Understanding technology in education.* London: Falmer.

Matthew, K. (1996, April). *A comparison of the influence of CD-ROM interactive storybooks and traditional print storybooks on children's reading comprehension.* Paper presented at the meeting of the American Educational Research Association, New York.

Mehan, H. (1989). Microcomputers in classrooms: Educational technology and social practice. *Anthropology & Educational Quarterly, 20,* 4–21.

Miller, L., Blackstock, J., & Miller, R. (1994). An exploratory study into the use of CD-ROM storybooks. *Computers in Education, 22,* 187–204.

Miller, L., & Burnett, J. D. (1987). Using computers as an integral aspect of elementary language arts instruction: Paradoxes, problems, and promise. In D. Reinking (Ed.), *Reading and computers: Issues for theory and practice* (pp. 178–191). New York: Teachers College Press.

Miller, L., DeJean, J., & Olson, J. (1996, March). *A case study of one Grade 3 teacher's use of CD-ROM technology.* Paper presented at the annual meeting of the Canadian Society for the Study of Education, St. Catherines, Ontario, Canada.

Miller, L., & Olson, J. (1994). Putting the computer in its place: A study of teaching with technology. *Journal of Curriculum Studies, 26,* 121–141.

Morrow, L. M. (1989). *Literacy development in the early years: Helping children to read and write.* Englewood Cliffs, NJ: Prentice-Hall.

Moursund, D. (1981). Introduction to computers in education for elementary and middle school teachers. *The Computing Teacher, 9*(3), 17–23.

Olson, J. (1984, June). *Microcomputers in the classroom: Trojan horse or teacher's pet?* Paper presented at the annual meeting of the Canadian Society for the Study of Education, Guelph, Ontario, Canada.

Olson, J. (1988). *Schoolworlds/microworlds: Computers and the culture of the classroom.* Oxford, UK: Pergamon.

O'Neill, B., McMahon, H., & Cunningham, D. (1991, April). *Bubble dialogue within a language awareness support system.* Paper presented at the annual meeting of the American Educational Research Association, Chicago.

Owen, T. (1995). Poems that changed the world: Canada's wired writers. *English Journal, 48*(6), 48–52.

Papert, S. (1980). *Mindstorms: Children, computers, and powerful ideas.* New York: Basic Books.

Papert, S. (1987). Computer criticism vs. technocentric thinking. *Educational Researcher, 16*(1), 22–30.

Papert, S., Watt, D., deSessa, A., & Weir, S. (1979). *Final report of the Brookline LOGO project part II: Project summary and data analysis* (AI Memo No. 545 & LOGO Memo No. 53). Cambridge, MA: Massachusetts Institute of Technology.

Parham, C. (1993). CD-ROM storybooks: New ways to enjoy children's literature. *Technology and Learning, 13*(4), 34–44.

Pelgrum, W. J., & Plomp, T. (1991). *The use of computers in education worldwide.* Oxford, UK: Pergamon.

Perelman, L. J. (1992). *School's out: Hyperlearning, the new technology, and the end of education.* New York: Morrow.

Ray, D. (1992). Educational technology leadership for the age of restructuring. *The Computing Teacher, 19*(6), 8–14.

Reinking, D. (1994a). *Electronic literacy* (Perspectives in Reading Research, No. 4.). Athens: University of Georgia, National Reading Research Center.

Reinking, D. (1994b, December). *Reading and writing with computers: Literacy research in a post-typographic world.* Paper presented at the meeting of the National Reading Conference, San Diego, CA.

Reinking, D., & Bridwell-Bowles, L. (1991). Computers in reading and writing. In R. Barr, M. L. Kamil, P. B. Mosenthal, & P. D. Pearson (Eds.), *Handbook of reading research* (Vol. 2, pp. 310–340). New York: Longman.

Reinking, D., & Pickle, M. (1993). Using a formative experiment to study how computers affect reading and writing in classrooms. In D. J. Leu & C. K. Kinzer (Eds.), *Examining central issues in literacy research, theory, and practice* (pp. 263–270). Chicago: National Reading Conference.

Reinking, D., & Watkins, J. (1996). *A formative experiment investigating the use of multimedia book reviews to increase elementary students' independent reading* (Research Rep. No. 55). Athens: University of Georgia, National Reading Research Center.

Rubin, A., & Bruce, A. C. (1985). *Learning with quill: Lessons for students, teachers, and software designers* (Reading Education Rep. No. 60). Champaign: University of Illinois, Center for the Study of Reading.

Sarason, S. B. (1991). *The culture of school and the problem of change.* Boston: Allyn & Bacon.

Schofield, J. W. (1995). *Computers and classroom culture.* New York: Cambridge University Press.

Schofield, J. W., Davidson, A. L., Stocks, J., & Futoran, G. (1997). The interest in school: A case study of educator demand and its precursors. In S. Kiesler (Ed.), *Culture of the Internet* (pp. 361–381). Mahwah, NJ: Lawrence Erlbaum Associates.

Scoresby, K. (1996). *The effects of electronic storybook animations on third graders' story recall.* Unpublished doctoral dissertation, Brigham Young University, Salt Lake City, UT.

Shank, R. (1994). Active learning through multimedia. *Multimedia, 1*(1), 69–78.

Siegel, J., & Holzberg, S. (1994). To convert teachers to multimedia, you've got to first get them to the church. *Electronic Learning, 14*(3), 31.

Slavin, R. E. (1990). IBM's writing to read: Is it right for reading? *Phi Delta Kappan, 72*, 214–216.

Sloan, D. (Ed.). (1984). *The computer in education: A critical perspective.* New York: Teachers College Press.

Tobin, K., & Dawson, G. (1992). Constraints to curriculum reform: Teachers and myths of schooling. *Educational Technology Research and Development, 40*(1), 81–92.

Truett, C. (1993). CD-ROM storybooks bring children's literature to life. *The Computing Teacher, 21*(1), 20–21.

U.S. Congress, Office of Technology Assessment. (1995). *Teachers and technology: Making the connection* (OTA-EHR-616). Washington, DC: U.S. Government Printing Office.

Upitis, R. (1990). Real and contrived uses of electronic mail in elementary schools. *Computers and Education, 15*, 233–243.

Watson, D. (Ed.). (1993). *An evaluation of the impact of information technology on children's achievement in primary and secondary schools.* London: Department of Education.

Author Index

Subject Index

A

Access, technological, 221, 274–277, 328–329
Administrative-efficiency perspective, 326–327
Adult education, *see* Computer-assisted instruction (CAI);
Preservice education
Aesop in ASL: Four Fables Told in American Sign Language, 27, 29, 30f
Anchored instruction
    adult education, 175
    preservice education, 187–189
Andragogy theory, 174
Apple Classroom of Tomorrow (ACOT), 254, 255, 257–259, 266–267
Assessment, 167–168
At-risk readers, *see* Supported text
Authorship, *see* Hypermedia authoring; Hypertext

B

Beginning readers, *see* Talking books

C

Classroom environment, *see* Computer-mediated communication (CMC); Learning Connections Project (Nova Scotia); NEW WORK project (Ohio); Portfolios, electronic; Research, classroom setting for
Client satisfaction perspective, 326–327
Collaboration, *see also* Social interaction
    and computer-mediated communication (CMC), 96–98, 105, 108
    and hypertext, 4, 10
Communication, electronic, *see* Computer-mediated communication (CMC); Learning Connections Project (Nova Scotia)
Community, *see also* Social interaction
    building of, 258–259, 260–261, 265–266
    and school relations, 124–126
    support from, 267
Compensatory theory, 304
Computer-assisted instruction (CAI), *see also* Software design

benefits of, 169–172
    creative thinking, 171, 172f
    critical thinking, 170–171
    metacognition, 171–172
environments for
    and ESL learners, 181, 330–331
    integrated learning systems (ILS), 181
    small groups, 180–181
    technology labs, 180
funding for, 182
guidelines for
    anchored instruction, 175
    information tracking, 176
    interface design, 176–177
    learner control, 175–176
    learner needs adaptation, 175
    mirrored prompts, 177
    progressive implementation, 175
    scaffolding technique, 175
    use of microworlds, 168, 177–179
and instructor transformation, 179–180, 182
learner-centered, 168–169
software design for, 157, 170–174, 175–177, 181
theories of, 172–174
    andragogy, 174
    constructivism, 173
    experiential learning, 173
    functional context, 173
    situated learning, 174
types of, 167–168
Computer-mediated communication (CMC), *see also* Learning
Connections Project (Nova Scotia)
    asynchronous, 93
    contextualizing of, 98–105, 107
        impersonality in, 102
        role anonymity in, 101–102
        role creation in, 103–105
        task-continuative practices in, 99
        task-divergent practices in, 99
    implications for classroom
        chat group organization, 106–107
        collaboration, 96–98, 105, 108
        familiarity of CMC, 106
        message response, 97, 107

About the Authors*

Lynne Anderson-Inman is an Associate Professor of Education in the College of Education at the University of Oregon where she is Director of the Center for Advanced Technology in Education. She is also Director of the Center for Electronic Studying, a research group that explores and evaluates computer-based strategies for enhancing reading, writing, and studying in schools. She has published widely in both literacy and technology journals. She currently serves on the editorial board of *Reading Online,* an electronic journal sponsored by the International Reading Association. She also edits that journal's "Electronic Classroom" section.
lynneai@oregon.uoregon.edu

Eunice N. Askov, Professor of Education, is the Director of the Institute for the Study of Adult Literacy at The Pennsylvania State University. She provides leadership and conducts research in adult literacy through projects involving applications of technology to instruction, workplace literacy, family literacy, special needs populations, and staff development. She is also Department Head in the Department of Adult Education, Instructional Systems, and Workforce Education and Development, and she coordinates the Adult Education graduate program.
ena1@psu.edu

Mary Lou Balcom completed her B.S. in Early Childhood Education at SUNY, Oswego, and has taught at various elementary grades in the Syracuse City School District for 18 years. She is currently Staff Development Facilitator at Edward Smith Elementary School, Syracuse, New York.
mlbalcom@aol.com

Richard Beach is a Professor of English Education at the University of Minnesota, Twin Cities. His research focuses on responses to literature and media, teaching of literature and composition, and teacher education. He is a former President of the National Conference on Research in Language and Literacy.
rbeach@maroon.tc.umn.edu

Brett Bixler has a masters degree in instructional systems and is Senior Instructional Designer with the Jack P. Royer Center for Learning and Academic Technologies at the Pennsylvania State University. He employs educational technologies and learning theories to produce learner-centered, active, and collaborative learning environments.
bxb11@psu.edu

Jay David Bolter is Director of the New Media Center and Professor in the School of Literature, Communications, and Culture at the Georgia Institute of Technology. His work with computers led in 1984 to the publication of *Turing's Man: Western Culture in the Computer Age.* His second book, *Writing Space: The Computer, Hypertext, and the History of Writing,* published in 1991, examines the computer as a new medium for symbolic communication. He is currently collaborating with Professor Richard Grusin on a book about the historical and theoretical significance of digital visual media.
jay bolter@lcc.gatech.edu

* Please note that a few of the authors do not have e-mail addresses.

Bertram C. (Chip) Bruce is a Professor of Curriculum and Instruction, Bioengineering, and Writing Studies at the University of Illinois at Urbana-Champaign. His current research focuses on how communication and information technologies can support inquiry teaching and learning. He has written widely and developed software including *Quill,* an integrated computer-based writing program; *Statistics Workshop,* an interactive system for learning statistical reasoning; and *Discoveries,* a series of CD/ROM-based multimedia environments for supporting student interdisciplinary inquiry.
chip@uiuc.edu

Suzanne Damarin is a Professor in the School of Educational Policy and Leadership at Ohio State University, where she specializes in Cultural Studies of Education, particularly educational technology and mathematics education. Among her current projects is an analysis of the successes and failures of educational technologies through the theories of Deleuze and Guattari.
sdamari@postbox.acs.ohio-state.edu

Jonathan Dinkin completed his M.S. in Elementary Education at SUNY Cortland in 1976 and has taught in the elementary grades for 18 years. He has also worked as a language arts specialist. He currently teaches 6th grade at Edward Smith Elementary School, Syracuse, New York.
aveeya@aol.com

Mary Lou Eckels holds dual certification in Special Education and Elementary Education from Syracuse University. She has held a variety of teaching positions at the elementary school level. She currently teaches 6th grade at Edward Smith Elementary School, Syracuse, New York.

Gay Fawcett is Director of Curriculum and Instruction for the Summit County Educational Service Center in Ohio. A former classroom teacher and language arts consultant, she holds a Ph.D. from Kent State University. She has published articles in journals such as *Educational Leadership, Phi Delta Kappan, Language Arts, Reading Research and Instruction, Reading and Writing Quarterly,* and *Holistic Education Review.* Gay is also associate editor for *The Reading Teacher,* and a co-director of the New 3 Project, a $6.8 million Federal Technology Innovation Challenge Grant.
gayf@summit.k12.oh.us

Ruth Garner is a Professor of Education at the University of Illinois at Chicago. Her scholarly work addresses children's reading, particularly children's use of cognitive and metacognitive strategies to monitor and improve their text comprehension. She recently co-authored a book with Mark Gillingham that presents six classroom cases involving teacher and student communication on the Internet.
rgarner@uic.edu.

Mark G. Gillingham is a specialist in technology in education and teacher preparation at the University of Illinois at Chicago. His scholarly work addresses the place of technology in teaching and learning about teachers and learners. Currently, he is following the development of teachers as they use electronic communications to share their daily experiences with one another.
markgill@uic.edu

Dr. Michael E. Hale is the Instructional Technology Coordinator for the Oconee County School System in Georgia. He has been involved in several projects employing interactive video in classroom observer training and science measurement software. He currently works with teachers to enhance their use of instructional technology in support of student learning.
mehale@negia.net

Dr. Roberta Hammett is currently with the Faculty of Education, Memorial University of Newfoundland, St. John's, Canada, where she teaches secondary English language arts education and graduate courses pertaining to literacy. She is interested in literacy applications of computer technology.
hammett@morgan.ucs.mun.ca

Michael Hillinger is a multimedia developer and founder of LexIcon Systems in Sharon, VT. He holds a Ph.D. in Cognitive Psychology from Rutgers University and was a National Institutes of Health Postdoctoral Fellow at the University of Texas Center for Cognitive Science. He has conducted research and software development for public and private agencies including the National Science Foundation, the Department of the Navy, and General Electric.
mlh@lexiconsys.com

Maureen P. Hogan is a doctoral candidate in the Department of Curriculum and Instruction at the University of Illinois at Champaign-Urbana. Her dissertation project examines institutional and popular discourses surrounding youth and alternative schooling. Other research interests include the implementation of critical and feminist pedagogies, and how technology changes literacy.
m-hogan@students.uiuc.edu

Mark A. Horney is a Research Associate at the Center for Advanced Technology in Education at the University of Oregon. His work falls within the broad rubric of "electronic studying" and involves developing and investigating applications of tool software in educational settings. He has published widely on the theory and use of hypertext.
mhorney@oregon.uoregon.edu

Jackie Johnson has taught various grades throughout her career with the Syracuse City School District. She currently teaches 6th grade at Edward Smith Elementary School, Syracuse, New York.

Michael L. Kamil is Professor of Education and Director of the Learning, Design, and Technology Program in the School of Education at Stanford University. He researches the uses of expository text for reading instruction and the cognitive processes involved in reading hypertext. A co-editor of the *Handbook of Reading Research, Volumes. 1 - 3,* he is also a former editor of *Reading Research Quarterly* and *Journal of Reading Behavior.*
mkamil@leland.stanford.edu

Ronald D. Kieffer is an Assistant Professor of Language Education at the University of Georgia, with more than 20 years of teaching experience at various levels from the elementary school through the university. He currently teaches courses in early childhood language arts and children's literature. His research interests focus on assessment, the composing process, and classroom technology and literacy. He was a co-researcher on the Apple Classroom of Tomorrow (ACOT) Project at West High School, Columbus, Ohio.
rkieffer@coe.uga.edu

Charles K. Kinzer, Associate Professor of Education, is Director of Graduate Studies for the Department of Teaching and Learning, and Research Scientist at the Learning Technology Center at Vanderbilt University's Peabody College. He teaches graduate and undergraduate courses in literacy education. For the previous 6 years, he co-edited the *National Reading Conference Yearbook,* while pursuing research interests in literacy, technology, and teacher education. He has published on those topics in various literacy journals.
charles.k.kinzer@vanderbilt.edu

Jamie R. Kirkley is a doctoral student in Language Education and Instructional Systems Technology at Indiana University. She edits the "Graduate Section" for *Reading Online*, an electronic journal sponsored by the International Reading Association. Her research interests center on workplace literacy and technology, adolescent reading, and computer-mediated communication.
jkirkley@indiana.edu

Melanie Kuhn is a doctoral student at the University of Georgia. A graduate of Harvard University and Cambridge University, she is interested in theoretical and applied issues pertaining to reading difficulties and technology. She is also interested in how social class relates to the development of literacy.
mkuhn@coe.uga.edu

Linda D. Labbo is an Associate Professor of Education in the Department of Reading Education at the University of Georgia. Her primary research interests focus on young children's literacy development related to technology, cultural diversity, and informational text.
llabbo@coe.uga.edu

Diane M. Lane currently teaches second grade at Scioto Darby Elementary School in Hilliard, Ohio. For the previous 3 years, she collaborated with Professor Michael Kamil in investigating the use of non-fiction tests in her classroom. She serves as the technology coordinator for her school, and is training to become her school's literacy coordinator.
diane_lane@fclass.hilliard.k12.oh.us

J. L. Lemke is Professor of Education at the City University of New York and co-editor of the journal, *Linguistics and Education*. His current research focuses on the multimedia semiotics of website design and its role in online education.
jllb@cunyvm.cuny.edu

Donald J. Leu is a Professor of Education in the Reading and Language Arts Center at Syracuse University. He served as co-editor of the *National Reading Conference Yearbook* for six years and has published extensively in the areas of reading, technology, and literacy. His current scholarship explores the new forms of literacy and learning taking place on the Internet and the consequences for teachers and students.
djleu@syr.edu

Philip H. Loseby completed his Ed.M. at Harvard University and is a doctoral student in Reading Education at Syracuse University. He currently teaches in the Juneau School District in Juneau, Alaska.

Dana Lundell, a doctoral candidate in Curriculum and Instruction at the University of Minnesota-Twin Cities, is currently writing her dissertation. She is a writing instructor in the General College and serves as Coordinator for the Center for Research on Developmental Education and Urban Literacy. Her scholarly interests include basic writing, graduate student socialization, service-learning, and academic literacies.
lunde010@maroon.tc.umn.edu

Kathie Mathews is a graduate of Syracuse University holding certification in Elementary Education. A teacher for 20 years, she currently teaches 6th grade at Edward Smith Elementary School, Syracuse, New York.

Michael C. McKenna is Professor of Education at Georgia Southern University in Savannah, Georgia. He has conducted research funded through the National Reading Research Center by the Office of Educational Research and Improvement, US Office of Education. That research has investigated how "talking books" many enhance word recognition in beginning readers. His publications have also addressed other technological applications particularly in the areas of content literacy and assessment.
mmckenna@peachnet.campus.mci.net

Ann Margaret McKillop is Assistant Professor of Education in the Curriculum and Instruction Department at the University of Maryland where she teaches courses in secondary language arts and technology applications in classrooms. Her research interests include students' construction of hypermedia, composition, reader-response theory, media literacy, and interdisciplinary curricula.
am194@umail.umd.edu

Larry Mikulecky is a Professor of Education and Chair of the Language Education Department at Indiana University. He researches a variety of literacies, including workplace literacy. His most recent work addresses the impact of technology on literacy and on preparing students for the demands of new literacies.
mikuleck@indiana.edu

Larry Miller is an Associate Professor of Education at Queen's University, Kingston, Canada. His interests focus on teachers' use of technology in fostering literacy, children's use of multimedia composing tools, and the translation of reading theory to practice.
millerl@educ.queensu.ca

Jamie Myers is an Associate Professor at The Pennsylvania State University, where he has taught English Education and Critical Ethnography since 1989. He holds a Ph.D. from Indiana University, Bloomington, Indiana. His current scholarly interests focus on promoting collaborative generation and critique of multimedia representations of the self, others, and the world. He is also interested in how technology supports the social construction knowledge.
jmm12@psu.edu

Lorri Neilsen, Associate Professor of Education, was the principal researcher in an award-winning study of telecommunications and literacy in Canada in the early 1990s. She is the author of books, articles, and research reports related to writing, literacy, and feminist research methods. Currently, she is studying

the relationships among writing, gender, and the art of qualitative inquiry.
lorri.neilsen@msvu.ca

John Olson is Professor Emeritus at Queen's University, Kingston, Canada. His current interests include the process of curriculum change as seen from the point of view of teachers, teachers' use of technology, and science curriculum.
olsonj@educ.queensu.ca

Alan Purves, before his untimely death during the preparation of this volume, was a Professor Emeritus at the State University of New York at Albany. He had a long and distinguished career as a scholar focusing on literary theory and cross-cultural studies. He was honored in 1982 by being elected as one of only five individual members of the International Association for the Evaluation of Educational Achievement. He served as that organization's chair from 1986 to 1990. During his career, he authored several seminal books that influenced literary theory, pedagogy, and curricula. In the years before his death, he became increasingly interested in how literacy was evolving in relation to new technologies in the information age particularly in his book *The Scribal Society*.

Ruth Raegler holds an M.S. degree in Elementary Education from Syracuse University and is tenured in the Syracuse City School District. She currently teaches 6th grade at Edward Smith Elementary School, Syracuse, New York.

David Reinking is Professor of Education at the University of Georgia where he serves as Head of the Department of Reading Education. From 1992 through 1997 he was a principal investigator for several technology-related research and development projects funded through the National Reading Research Center by the Office of Educational Research and Improvement, U.S. Office of Education. He currently serves as the editor of the *Journal of Literacy Research*. His scholarly interests center on how new technologies affect literacy and its development in schools. He has published extensively on these topics.
dreinkin@coe.uga.edu

Victoria J. Risko is a Professor of Language and Literacy at Peabody College of Vanderbilt University. Her research interests include the uses of multimedia to support literacy development and teacher education, reading comprehension, and instructional strategies for diverse learners.
riskovj@ctrvax.vanderbilt.edu

Steve Snyder is the Director of Instructional Technology for the Summit County Educational Service Center in Ohio. He graduated from Princeton University in 1972, and holds an M.Ed from Kent State University. A strong advocate of technology and staff development activities, he currently serves as a co-director of the New 3 Project, a $6.8 million Federal Technology Innovation Challenge Grant.
steves@summit.k12.oh.us

Ashley Templeton has taught for six years in Georgia's public schools. She holds a bachelor's degree in Early Childhood Education from the University of Georgia, and recently completed her master's degree in Computer-Based Education from the same institution. She currently teaches second grade at Whit Davis Elementary in the Clarke County School District, Athens, Georgia.

Robert Tierney, a native Australian and long-time resident of the United States, is Professor and Director of the School of Teaching and Learning at Ohio State University. In his recent work, he has researched literacy from various perspectives, undertaking projects that explore students' meaning making. His work includes extended studies of students' learning with multimedia in conjunction with the Apple Classroom of Tomorrow project. He is especially interested in social semiotics, cultural studies, and ways of knowing that reflect an understanding of subjectivity and socio-political contexts.
tierney.4@osu.edu